THE ANCIENT EGYPTIAN ECONOMY

This book is the first economic history of ancient Egypt covering the entire pharaonic period, 3000–30 BCE, and employing a New Institutional Economics approach. It argues that the ancient Egyptian state encouraged an increasingly widespread and sophisticated use of writing through time, primarily in order to better document and more efficiently exact taxes for redistribution. The increased use of writing, however, also resulted in increased documentation and enforcement of private property titles and transfers, gradually lowering their transaction costs relative to redistribution. The book also argues that the increasing use of silver as a unified measure of value, medium of exchange, and store of wealth also lowered transaction costs for high value exchanges. The increasing use of silver in turn allowed the state to exact transfer taxes in silver, and provided it with an economic incentive to further document and enforce private property titles and transfers.

Brian Muhs is Associate Professor of Egyptology at the Oriental Institute and the Department of Near Eastern Languages and Civilizations at the University of Chicago. He studies the history of ancient Egyptian social, economic, and legal institutions, particularly during the transition from pharaonic to Ptolemaic and Roman rule, and has published two books on taxation in Ptolemaic Egypt, as well as numerous articles.

THE ANCIENT EGYPTIAN ECONOMY

3000–30 BCE

BRIAN MUHS
The Oriental Institute and the Department of Near Eastern Languages and Civilizations, University of Chicago

CAMBRIDGE
UNIVERSITY PRESS

CAMBRIDGE
UNIVERSITY PRESS

University Printing House, Cambridge CB2 8BS, United Kingdom

One Liberty Plaza, 20th Floor, New York, NY 10006, USA

477 Williamstown Road, Port Melbourne, VIC 3207, Australia

4843/24, 2nd Floor, Ansari Road, Daryaganj, Delhi - 110002, India

79 Anson Road, #06-04/06, Singapore 079906

Cambridge University Press is part of the University of Cambridge.

It furthers the University's mission by disseminating knowledge in the pursuit of education, learning and research at the highest international levels of excellence.

www.cambridge.org
Information on this title: www.cambridge.org/9781107113367

First published 2016

A catalogue record for this publication is available from the British Library

Library of Congress Cataloging in Publication data
Names: Muhs, Brian Paul, author.
Title: The ancient Egyptian economy, 3000-30 BCE / Brian Muhs, The Oriental Institute, University of Chicago.
Description: New York : Cambridge University Press, 2016. | Includes bibliographical references and index.
Identifiers: LCCN 2015039555 | ISBN 9781107113367 (hardback)
Subjects: LCSH: Egypt–Economic conditions–To 332 B.C. | Egypt–Civilization–To 332 B.C.
Classification: LCC HC33.M84 2016 | DDC 330.93201–dc23
LC record available at http://lccn.loc.gov/2015039555

ISBN 978-1-107-11336-7 Hardback

CONTENTS

ACKNOWLEDGMENTS

This book has been a long-term project, and consequently I owe thanks to a great many people for their support and encouragement over the years. I first conceived of the idea for this project while I was at the Papyrological Institute at Leiden University, 1997–2011. I was stimulated by my discussions with the late Pieter Willem Pestman, and with the students in his Ancient Egyptian Law course, which I took over from him and taught between 1998 and 2010. I also learned a great deal from many other colleagues at the Papyrological Institute, and I am grateful to the Gratema Stichting for their financial support between 2005 and 2008, which allowed me to write the first drafts of this book.

Most of the book was written or rewritten after I came to the University of Chicago, where I profited greatly from the lively culture of interdepartmental debate. I would like to thank the participants in the Ancient Societies Workshop in 2011, and the Franke Institute noon lecture series in 2012, where I presented selections from my work in progress. I was also greatly stimulated by the symposia organized by the Working Group on Comparative Economics between 2013 and 2015, with the support of the Neubauer Collegium for Culture and Society. I would particularly like to thank Alain Bresson of Classics and Glen Weyl of Economics, as well as David Schloen, both for organizing the symposia and for their many conversations with me on matters economic and otherwise. I am also indebted to Martha Roth, Dean of the Division of Humanities, Theo van den Hout, Chair of the Department of Near Eastern Languages and Civilizations, and Gil Stein, Director of the Oriental Institute, for granting me a two-quarter research leave, which I used in part to make crucial revisions to the manuscript.

The book also benefitted from numerous discussions with and comments from my colleagues in the Oriental Institute of the University of Chicago. I presented materials from my work at an Oriental Institute volunteers' lecture series in 2011, at an Oriental Institute members' lecture in 2013, and at an Oriental Institute faculty connections seminar in 2014. I am grateful to Gil Stein and David Schloen again for their lively and stimulating conversations in and out of these venues. I would also like to thank my colleagues Jan Johnson, Robert Ritner, and Nadine Moeller, as well as Oriental Institute members

Stephen D. Smith and Judith L. Baxter, for reading versions of the manuscript and commenting on them.

I wish to acknowledge my gratitude to Asya Graf, editor at Cambridge University Press, for being willing to take on and support this project, for facilitating the review process, and for her many helpful suggestions. I would also like to thank the anonymous readers for their willingness to read my manuscript, and for their useful comments on it. I particularly thank Andrew Monson for his extremely detailed commentary, which greatly improved the book.

Most of all, however, I thank my wife Tasha Vorderstrasse, for her countless invaluable suggestions after listening to me talk about the manuscript on innumerable occasions. I could not have written it without her limitless encouragement and support, and thus it is to her that I dedicate this book.

ABBREVIATIONS

ÄA	Ägyptologische Abhandlungen
ÄAT	Ägypten und Altes Testament
AfP	*Archiv für Papyrusforschung*
ASAE	*Annales du Service des antiquités de l'Egypte*
ASP	American Studies in Papyrology
BASOR	*Bulletin of the American Schools of Oriental Research*
BASP	*Bulletin of the American Society of Papyrologists*
BdÉ	Bibliothèque d'Étude
BIFAO	*Bulletin de l'Institut Français d'Archéologie Orientale*
CdÉ	*Chronique d'Égypte*
CNI	Carsten Niebuhr Institute Publications
CRIPEL	*Cahier de recherches de l'Institut de papyrologie et d'égyptologie de Lille*
EES	Egypt Exploration Society
EU	Egyptologische Uitgaven
EVO	*Egitto e Vicino Oriente*
Enchoria	*Enchoria, Zeitschrift für Demotistik und Koptologie*
GM	*Göttinger Miszellen*
HdO	Handbuch der Orientalistik
HÄB	Hildesheimer Ägyptologische Beiträge
IBAES	Internet-Beiträge zur Ägyptologie und Sundanarchäologie
IFAO	Institut français d'archéologie orientale
JARCE	*Journal of the American Research Center in Egypt*
JEA	*Journal of Egyptian Archaeology*
JESHO	*Journal of the Economic and Social History of the Orient*
JJP	*Journal of Juristic Papyrology*
JNES	*Journal of Near Eastern Studies*
MDAIK	*Mitteilungen des Deutschen Archäologischen Instituts, Abteilung Kairo*
MIFAO	Mémoires publiés par les membres de l'Institut français d'archéologie orientale
NINO	Nederlands Instituut voor het Nabije Oosten
OIP	Oriental Institute Publications

OLA	Orientalia Lovaniensia Analecta
PLB	Papyrologica Lugduno-Batava
RdÉ	*Revue d'égyptologie*
SAK	*Studien zur Altägyptischen Kultur*
SAOC	Studies in Ancient Oriental Civilization
SBL	Society of Biblical Literature
WZKM	*Wiener Zeitschrift für die Kunde des Morgenlandes*
ZÄS	*Zeitschrift für Ägyptische Sprache und Altertumskunde*
ZPE	*Zeitschrift für Papyrologie und Epigraphik*

INTRODUCTION

This book examines the history of the ancient Egyptian economy, from the earliest written records at the beginning of the Early Dynastic Period, around 3000 BCE, until the end of the Ptolemaic Period and the Roman conquest of Egypt in 30 BCE. During these three thousand years, the ancient Egyptian economy underwent numerous changes, as did ancient Egyptian society and culture. This book explores the relationship between the changes in the economy on the one hand, and changes in social and legal institutions on the other. In particular, it will correlate economic changes with the development of writing and money.

In the past, many economists have assumed that the human "propensity to truck, barter and exchange one thing for another" is logical, inevitable, and universal,[1] and that economic behavior is the rational and predictable result of this propensity, together with supply, demand, and the available technology. This assumption, sometimes described as formalist, underlies classical, neoclassical, and Keynesian economics, and implies that economic behavior has changed primarily as a result of technological innovation. Formalist assumptions also underlie many discussions of the ancient Egyptian economy,[2] and a few Egyptologists have even argued for the direct applicability of Keynesian economic models to ancient Egypt, suggesting that state redistribution limited market price fluctuations,[3] or that state tax demands stimulated growth.[4]

In contrast, some economic historians and ancient historians have assumed that economic behavior is a learned behavior that is embedded in and therefore unique to each culture, and that modern Western economic behavior is a relatively recent development, which has only achieved the appearance of universality through colonialism and globalization.[5] These assumptions are sometimes characterized as substantivist, in contrast to formalist economic models, and they imply that economic behavior has changed primarily as a result of cultural change. Many Egyptologists have also adopted a substantivist approach to the ancient Egyptian economy, arguing that market exchanges played a limited role in price formation,[6] and that most distribution occurred through institutional redistribution,[7] or through reciprocal gift-giving,[8] even in riverbank marketplaces,[9] and in long-distance river trade.[10]

More recently, however, there is a growing recognition among ancient historians that the formalist–substantivist dichotomy is overly reductionist,[11] and that economic behavior results from a complex and dynamic interaction between biological imperatives and bounded economic rationality, individual experience and social networks, cultural norms and legal and political institutions.[12] Some Egyptologists have similarly questioned whether purely formalist or substantivist models can explain the ancient Egyptian economy.[13] This book will therefore employ a New Institutional economic approach, which examines the relationship between changes in economic behavior on the one hand, and cultural norms, legal and political institutions, and technological innovations on the other. This approach has been used profitably in the Aegean,[14] but has not yet been applied to ancient Egypt. The ancient Egyptians would not have thought in these modern terms, but their behavior would nonetheless have been constrained by the institutions that these terms describe.

NEW INSTITUTIONAL ECONOMICS

Ronald Coase formulated some of the basic principles of New Institutional Economics in 1937, though the name was coined much later to distinguish it from the earlier school of Institutional Economics associated with Thorstein Veblen. Coase noted an apparent paradox in neoclassical economic theory. The market was supposed to be efficient and self-organizing through the price mechanism, and yet firms did not organize themselves through the price mechanism. Firms employed entrepreneurs and managers to allocate resources and labor through redistribution, rather than contracting out every business activity. Coase resolved this paradox by proposing that there were transaction costs involved in using the market, which could be avoided by conducting business within firms. He cited sales taxes as a concrete example, but he argued that other transaction costs arose from uncertainty, such as the cost of discovering the prices for various activities on the market, or the cost of negotiating and writing innumerable short-term contracts instead of a few long-term ones. Of course, firms also had internal transaction costs, many of them inefficiencies arising from not using the market.[15]

Other economists have elaborated the concept of transaction costs, subdividing them into search costs, measurement or information costs, negotiation or bargaining costs, and enforcement or policing costs. Search costs arise from finding opportunities for exchange, from locating potential exchange partners, and from identifying the most appropriate exchange partners. Marketplaces, fairs, bourses, commodity and stock exchanges, and internet lists can lower search costs, because they bring potential exchange partners together and allow them to compare offers for exchange. Measurement or information costs arise from defining and comparing the quantity and quality of goods offered for exchange; they are sometimes treated together with search costs, or with negotiation costs. Physical marketplaces and fairs can lower measurement costs by allowing comparison of goods on offer, as can the use of official weights, measures, and certificates of quality and purity. Negotiation or bargaining costs arise from establishing terms of exchange acceptable to both parties, such as the place, time, and form of payment and delivery. Customary terms of sale, sanctioned by law, can lower negotiation costs. Enforcement costs arise from establishing and enforcing property rights, and from recording and enforcing agreements for the exchange of property rights. Effective legal institutions backed by a centralized state can reduce enforcement costs. On the other hand, new technologies such as the Internet have increased enforcement costs for intellectual properties.[16]

Douglass North championed the use of new institutional economics and transaction costs in economic history. North suggested that transaction costs could be used to understand ancient as well as medieval and modern economic history. He accepted the substantivist assertion that nonmarket allocation systems predominated for most of history, and that market-based neoclassical models can therefore only explain a small fraction of historical economic behaviors. However, North disagreed with the substantivist assertion that markets and economic rationalism did not develop until the early modern era. Instead, he argued that nonmarket and market allocation systems have always coexisted, and that the choice between them is an economically rational one determined by transaction costs. North cited Coase's assertion that modern firms exist because nonmarket firm-internal transactions have lower transaction costs than firm-external transactions in the market. By analogy, ancient nonmarket allocation systems presumably existed because they too had lower transaction costs than the available markets. This could easily occur if the transaction costs of ancient markets were high, as a result of limited numbers of suitable exchange partners, limited information about such partners and their goods and services, and limited enforcement of transaction agreements.[17]

Enforcement

North identified the key institutions that governed economic choices as property rights, the state, and ideology. He argued that property rights were dependent upon effective third party or state enforcement, and the effectiveness of the state was in turn dependent upon ideology. He argued that the interaction between these institutions determined the transaction costs of available economic options, and thus shaped individual economic choices and the economy as a whole.[18] Douglass North and Robert Thomas argued that in medieval Europe, rulers enforced overlapping property rights that maximized their revenues in the short term, but discouraged private individuals from making long-term improvements to property, investments in trade, or technological innovations, because many of the benefits went to other parties or "free riders."[19] In early modern Europe, however, some emerging nation-states began to enforce private property rights that encouraged private individuals to make improvements, investments, or innovations, because the individuals could expect to retain the bulk of the resulting benefits. The nation-states enforced these private property rights, even though they restricted their revenues in the short term, because the resulting long-term economic growth allowed them to capture more revenues, particularly from trade, even though they constituted a smaller proportion of the economy.[20]

North has emphasized the importance of third party or state enforcement of property rights for economic growth in early modern Europe,[21] but he and others recognized that formal or hierarchical organizations could also enforce property transfer agreements, particularly within weak or fragmented states, or between them. In the twelfth and thirteenth centuries CE, merchant courts at the Champagne trade fairs in northern France enforced a private "Merchant Law" on traders between northern and southern Europe, who often did not know one another, and frequently came from regions under different legal authorities. The courts recorded agreements such as those for future delivery, and banned traders who failed to deliver or who delivered inferior goods from future participation.[22] In the thirteenth and fourteenth centuries CE, merchant guilds evolved in late medieval Europe to compel rulers to guarantee the security of foreign merchants and their property. Rulers were loath to provide guarantees unless forced to do so, but individual merchants lacked the leverage to force them. Merchant guilds could compel all of their members not to trade with cities whose rulers did not provide security, creating effective embargoes that could compel rulers to provide security. In Italy, trade was dominated by a few major cities whose governments acted like merchant guilds to compel trading partners to provide security to their merchants. In politically fragmented Germany, however, the Hanseatic League coordinated merchants in numerous cities to the same ends. In early modern Europe, politically integrated states like England took over the functions of merchant guilds.[23]

Avner Greif has argued that informal or nonhierarchical organizations could also enforce property transfer agreements. In the eleventh and twelfth centuries CE, a group of Jewish merchants in the Muslim part of the Mediterranean, known as the Maghribi traders, emigrated throughout North Africa and the Levant, where they served as agents for each other. The members of this coalition operated under a variety of legal authorities, so they could not enforce agreements through a legal system. They, therefore, agreed that if one member accused another of cheating, the remaining members would refuse to deal with the cheater again, effectively depriving him of his livelihood. The long-term cost of cheating, therefore, far outweighed any short-term profit, and thus served as an effective deterrent.[24] Greif argued that the Maghribi traders' collectivist cultural beliefs encouraged sharing of information and collective enforcement, in contrast with contemporary Italian Genoese merchants whose individualist cultural beliefs discouraged the same behavior.[25]

The ancient Egyptian state was primarily interested in enforcing its own property rights for tax collection purposes. It did enforce individual property rights, but only insofar as they increased the efficiency of state revenue extraction. Consequently, responsibility for enforcing individual property rights was frequently shared with a variety of formal and informal organizations, or even private social control. This is most evident in the early first millennium BCE, when the Egyptian state fragmented and the temples took over the responsibility for enforcing property transfer agreements.

Documentation

This study will argue that the ability of states, organizations, and collectives to enforce property rights and property transfer agreements depends in part on documentation. Increasing use of documentation to hold individuals accountable across space and time lowers enforcement costs, and increasing collection and preservation of data to predict future outcomes lowers information costs. This applies to the initial development and subsequent diversification of applications of writing, as well as to the modern advent of digital documentation and the exploitation of big data.

Documentation existed before writing, of course, in the form of witnesses, human memories, and testimonies. Memories of important transactions could be strengthened and reinforced with accompanying public spectacles and rituals. In the ancient Near East, the development of writing did not immediately replace such nonwritten documentation, and indeed even now it has not fully done so. Furthermore, studies of writing in the ancient Near East have shown that it can serve several different documentary roles, which usually coexist, though their relative significance may vary.[26] At one level, written documentation can be used to hold writers accountable and to enforce obligations. Writers retain documentation in case they are audited, so it does not have to be organized for accessibility to others.[27] At another level, written documentation can be used collect data in order to predict future outcomes, and make planning decisions based on these predicted outcomes. Documentation is retained and organized for accessibility to others for easy access and regular consultation.[28]

Egyptian history began with the invention of hieroglyphic writing at the end of the fourth millennium BCE. In the earliest periods of Egyptian history, the quantity and variety of written records was extremely limited. Most of the surviving economic records from the third millennium BCE concern state taxation and redistribution, and relatively few concern private transactions. In the course of the second millennium BCE, written records became more common and varied, and private records of transactions increased in number. In the first millennium BCE, the state finally began to document private transactions as well as state taxation and redistribution.

Older studies of the ancient Egyptian economy assumed that writing became the primary form of documenting economic activities after its invention, and that the surviving written documentation is representative of ancient economic activities. These studies have suggested that state redistribution dominated the ancient Egyptian economy in the earlier periods.[29] More recent studies have recognized that witnesses, memories, and oral testimonies continued to document economic activities alongside writings, that some activities were more likely to be documented in writing than others, and that the use of writing gradually increased through time. The surviving records are thus a biased sample, because the memories and oral testimonies of witnesses have not survived, except when they were committed to writing. These studies suggest that in the earlier periods the state chose not to document private transactions, and that the predominance of state taxation and redistribution in the surviving documentation from those periods overstates their role in the economy.[30]

Recent studies have also emphasized the limitations of the ancient Egyptian use of documentation. Chris Eyre observes that information collected in local documentation was rarely passed on to the central administration and if so only in summary form.[31] He asserts that the central authorities could not easily audit local documentary archives either, because they were rarely cataloged and indexed except in the memories of the local officials and transacting parties who possessed them.[32] Finally, he suggests that ancient Egyptian documents frequently required their scribes or possessors to authenticate them and interpret them, because they were effectively *aides-memoires* with little or no independent authority.[33]

This study, however, will argue that written documentation did preserve and transmit information that the state could use to hold its agents and subjects accountable and thereby enforce their transactions, despite all these shortcomings. The central administration may not have received much local documentation, but it was alerted to possible irregularities when agents or officials failed to meet their targets or when there were complaints against them, and when transacting parties signaled a dispute. The central authorities may not have been able to directly audit local documentary archives, but they could access them indirectly through audits of agents and officials and trials involving transacting parties, who would be obliged to produce them as evidence. Finally, the ancient Egyptians were well aware of the shortcomings of both written documentation and oral testimonies. They usually evaluated them together, and their judgments were based on the relative quality of both types of evidence.

This study will further argue that the Egyptian state always privileged the documentation and enforcement of state revenues over those of private property transfers, but the difference in documentation, enforcement, and transaction costs steadily decreased through Egyptian history, thereby reshaping the Egyptian economy. In the third millennium BCE, the state fostered the use of written documentation primarily to enforce the collection and redistribution of state revenues, because it increased the efficiency of extraction, which more than offset the additional costs of the written documentation. On the other hand, the state did not support written documentation of private transactions, perhaps because it had no effective means of taxing private transactions, and thus could not recapture the additional costs of written documentation. In turn, this differential use of writing, and the resulting difference in enforcement and enforcement costs, may have meant that "investment" in state redistributive networks, through state service for example, was less risky and more attractive than investment in property or participation in entrepreneurial property transfers. The predominance of state taxation and redistribution in the surviving documentation from the earliest periods may overstate its role in the economy, but it may also reflect its privileged, favored status.

In the second millennium BCE, the state began documenting individual rather than collective tax obligations, primarily to eliminate free riders and increase efficiency of tax collection. This documentation could also be used to enforce private title to property, but it did not regularly record transfers of title, and consequently was of limited use for enforcing private property transfers. Only in the early first millennium BCE did the state and its agents began to encourage written documentation of private transactions, through temple notaries. The differential use of writing for state and private transactions diminished, and with it the difference in enforcement and enforcement costs. Investment in property and entrepreneurial property transfers became more competitive with "investment" in state redistributive networks through state service, and hence became more common in both the archaeological and the written record. Increasing material investment in heavily built "tower houses" in the later first millennium BCE parallels increasing numbers of house sales in the same period.[34] Nonetheless, the state continued to privilege documentation and enforcement of state transactions over private ones, and the price of land remained relatively low throughout the pharaonic period.[35]

Chris Eyre has argued that the Egyptian state increasingly encouraged documentation of private transactions in the first millennium BCE, because the governing regimes were increasingly of foreign origin, Libyan, Nubian, Persian, and Greek, composed of military rather than scribal elites, who could not always speak Egyptian.[36] He suggests that it was the need for these colonial regimes to inform themselves about native custom in order to control native behavior that led to the social disembedding of native Egyptian written culture.[37] This study, however, will argue that the Egyptian state encouraged documentation of private transactions in response to changes in the media of exchange that allowed the state to tax and recapture the costs of documenting private transactions.

Media of Exchange

Most economists would agree that fluctuations in the money and credit supply have a profound effect on economic behavior. This study will argue that money is also a socially constructed economic institution, and that changes in its construction also affect both the money supply and economic behavior. Modern monies simultaneously serve at least three different functions, as a measure of value, a medium of exchange, and a store of wealth, but some ancient monetary systems employed many commodities for different purposes. Gold, silver, and copper only slowly came to fulfill all of these purposes simultaneously, and only gradually replaced most other commodities. This reduced some of the information costs of comparing the values of different commodities, and some of the search costs of finding parties with suitable commodities to exchange, because gold, silver, and copper served as measures of value, were always suitable to exchange, and could be stored indefinitely. The adoption of coinage further lowered information costs, because states used die stamps to certify and guarantee the weight and purity of individual pieces of gold, silver, and copper.

Some scholars assign the invention of coinage a privileged role in this development, associating it with major changes in economic behavior in the Aegean starting in the seventh century BCE. David Schaps links the invention of coinage with a growing reliance on market exchanges as a source of livelihood,[38] with increasing use of short-term rather than long-term contract labor, including mercenary soldiers,[39] and with the development of commercial credit.[40] Others, however, argue that the invention of coinage was only one step in the incremental development of money. Christine Thompson has collected archaeological evidence from the Levant dating from the twelfth to the seventh centuries BCE, showing that lumps of silver (*Hacksilber*) were sometimes placed together in bags, often of standard weights, and then sealed with stamped clay bullae to certify their weights. It was then a small additional step to stamp or seal lumps of silver of standard weights, rather than bullae attached to bags containing these lumps, and thus to invent coinage in Lydia in western Anatolia.[41] John Kroll has argued that lumps of silver were also used in the Aegean in seventh and sixth centuries BCE, prior to the widespread adoption of coinage.[42]

Still other scholars have noted that in the ancient Near East silver was used as a measure of value, a medium of exchange, and a store of wealth already in the late third millennium BCE, although not for every transaction nor in great quantities.[43] This use of silver increased through time. In the Neo-Assyrian empire, copper was more commonly used than silver in exchanges in the eighth century BCE, but silver became more common in the seventh century BCE, perhaps due to an influx of silver tribute following the great expansion of the empire.[44] In the Neo-Babylonian empire, Babylonian temples in the seventh and sixth centuries BCE regularly obtained silver through donations, payments of rents and tithes, and sale of commodities, and they regularly used it to pay dues to the crown, parts of salaries to personnel, and to purchase commodities.[45] In the Achaemenid and Seleucid empires, the amount of silver probably continued to increase in the sixth through first centuries BCE.[46] As the amount of silver in circulation increased, some economic changes attributed to the invention of coinage in the Aegean also occurred in the ancient Near East, before the widespread adoption of coinage. The development of tax farming, banking, and commercial credit in Babylonia, particularly from the seventh century BCE onward, is an example of this.[47]

For much of Egyptian history, the Egyptians used a variety of commodities as media of exchange, measures of value, and stores of wealth, which are the three main uses of money. Grain, cloth, and copper predominated in the third millennium BCE, while gold and especially silver gradually became more common in the course of the second and early first millennia BCE. The Greeks began bringing silver coins to Egypt in the sixth century BCE, and the Egyptians began minting imitations late in the fifth or early in the fourth century BCE. They began minting bronze coins in the late fourth century BCE, and their use spread in the course of the third, second, and first centuries BCE. Some Egyptologists have emphasized that commodities like grain performed all of the functions of money.[48] However, while grain and cloth were sometimes used as stores of wealth, they were obviously not as concentrated or durable as copper and especially silver and gold, and indeed were ultimately superseded by the latter as they became more common. There is, however, growing recognition among numismatists that the increased use of lumps of gold and especially silver in Egypt in the early first millennium BCE was transitional to the use of coinage in the later first millennium BCE, and that for several centuries the Egyptians treated Greek silver coins as convenient lumps of silver. This study will therefore emphasize the transformative role of the increased use of silver rather than the introduction of coinage. Increasing use of silver permitted the state to exact taxes on exchanges as a fraction of the value of the exchanges, and the state thereby acquired a fiscal interest in documenting, enforcing, and indeed encouraging private transactions, because it could recapture the costs of doing so and derive revenue from sales taxes. In turn, state documentation and enforcement of private transactions and transfers encouraged investment in property, by reducing title risks.

Redistribution, Markets, and Entrepreneurial Activity

Coase suggested that some transactions can be conducted more efficiently in markets, and some more efficiently in firms using nonmarket allocation systems, and that transaction costs determined the boundaries between the market and firms.[49] Williamson elaborated that simple and nonspecific transactions involving standardized, interchangeable commodities, or short-term labor contracts involving unskilled labor, tend to be efficient in markets, while complex and idiosyncratic transactions involving commissioned products, or long-term labor contracts involving skilled labor, tend to be efficient in firms.[50]

In the ancient Near East, there were no profit-maximizing corporations, and many state organizations, temples, and households were at best risk-minimizing and rent-seeking. Nonetheless, some state organizations, temples, and households did undertake entrepreneurial activities, and behaved like firms.[51] In Mesopotamia, patrilineal inheritance was dominant, some households were relatively long-lived, and a few were heavily capitalized, especially when their heads also held state or temple offices for successive generations. It is, therefore, often difficult to distinguish state and temple offices from the households of their office holders, causing some to debate whether Mesopotamian states were patrimonial societies with a bureaucratic veneer,[52] or bureaucracies incorporating patrilineal households.[53] In Egypt, patrilineal inheritance was less prominent than in Mesopotamia,[54] except during the twelfth through sixth centuries BCE as a result of Libyan cultural influence.[55] Most households were comparatively short-lived and lightly capitalized, except when their heads held state or temple offices, which they rarely did for more than a few generations,[56] except during the twelfth through sixth centuries BCE. Consequently royal palaces and temples more often undertook entrepreneurial activities than individual households, employing merchants, craftsmen, and laborers.

In ancient Egypt, low value and perishable commodities like grain, bread, and fish, as well as higher value and more durable goods like clothing and furniture, were both exchanged in markets and redistributed or donated, though redistribution and donation may have become less common in the late first millennium BCE, when the use of silver and bronze money and coinage became common. High value and immovable properties like land and houses were donated more often than they were exchanged, but exchanges became more common from the early first millennium BCE onward, as the increasing use of written title documentation and silver money lowered transaction costs in markets. Long-term employment for skilled labor with state organizations, temples, and households was common. Some long-term employment was only part time, however, giving the employing organizations partial claim upon their employees' skilled labor, and providing their employees with some income security, which allowed the employees to seek additional income from entrepreneurial activities. Long-term employment for unskilled labor occasionally occurred in temples and households, and it usually took the form of permanently bound labor or slavery. The state tended to use compulsory labor obligations to ensure that it had access to unskilled labor, however, without resorting to long-term employment. Individuals were compelled to provide a specified amount of labor to the state each year as a tax or service obligation, during which the laborers were fed. These individuals were expected to support themselves during the rest of the year. Short-term employment, aside from compulsory labor obligations, was rare until the late first millennium, when the use of silver and bronze money and coinage became common. Some of this short-term employment occurred regularly between the same employing organizations and employees, notably in commodity monopolies, where it may have replaced long-term part-time employment.

THE ORGANIZATION OF THIS STUDY

The ancient Egyptians usually measured time by the reigns and regnal years of each successive king. In the third century BCE, an Egyptian named Manetho wrote a history of Egypt in Greek that arranged the reigns of hundreds of these kings into thirty dynasties. In the nineteenth century CE, Egyptologists organized Manetho's dynasties into a series of periods. These four time measures provide relative dates with decreasing degrees of specificity, much like years, decades, centuries, and millennia in absolute dates. After 664 BCE, regnal years, reigns, dynasties, and periods can all be correlated with absolute dates. Before 664 BCE, however, absolute dates are only approximate, because fragmentary sources do not always preserve how many years each king reigned or in which order, to which dynasty they belonged, and whether the dynasties were successive or parallel. Consequently, this book will henceforth use the four relative time measures, supplemented with absolute dates after 664 BCE. The remainder of this book is organized into seven chapters corresponding to successive periods of ancient Egyptian history. These are:

1. The Early Dynastic Period	c. 3000–2686 BCE
2. The Old Kingdom and First Intermediate Period	c. 2686–2025 BCE
3. The Middle Kingdom and Second Intermediate Period	c. 2025–1550 BCE
4. The New Kingdom	c. 1550–1069 BCE
5. The Third Intermediate Period	c. 1069–664 BCE
6. The Saite and Persian Periods	664–332 BCE
7. The Ptolemaic Period	332–30 BCE

Each chapter begins by describing the sequence of dynasties and their main cities and cemeteries. A table lists by dynasty and chronological order the individual kings mentioned in each chapter, and a map indicates the sites named. The first half of each chapter discusses the various means of documenting and enforcing transactions known for the periods covered by the chapter. Enforcement is broken down into judicial and extrajudicial organizations responsible for prosecuting crimes against state revenues and finances like taxes, and those responsible for adjudicating disputes over property transfers like sales and inheritances. Documentation is similarly divided into records of objects of taxation such as agricultural fields, people, and livestock, records of bottleneck taxation like sales taxes, burial taxes, and customs duties, and records of property transfers. The second half of each chapter discusses the various media of distribution attested in the period covered by the chapter, the various modes of distribution, namely redistributive networks and exchanges, and entrepreneurial activities. It will be argued that changes and developments in enforcement, documentation, and the available media of distribution altered the transaction costs associated with redistribution and exchange respectively, and thereby shifted the boundaries between the two modes of distribution through time.

ONE

THE EARLY DYNASTIC PERIOD (c. 3000–2686 BCE)

The Early Dynastic Period consists of the First and Second Dynasties (c. 3000–2686 BCE). These dynasties ruled over Egypt from a royal court at the city of Memphis, but the kings of the First Dynasty continued to build tombs at their ancestral cemetery at Abydos in Upper Egypt, while those of the Second Dynasty alternated between Saqqara to the west of the Memphis, and Abydos. Nonetheless, many of the officials of the First- and Second-Dynasty kings built their tombs at Saqqara to the west of Memphis or at Helwan to the east of it. (See Map 1.1 and Table 1.1.)

The Early Dynastic Period witnessed the first relatively limited use of writing in Egypt. Short monumental inscriptions on stone stelae labeled the tombs of kings and courtiers; short inscriptions on ivory, bone, stone, and wooden tags labeled some objects in the tombs of kings and officials; short commemorative inscriptions appeared on some objects found in tombs and shrines at various sites; and names written inside a royal *serekh* were incised on pottery and stone vessels. Secondary evidence for writing consisted of impressions of inscribed cylinder seals left on clay used to seal various containers in the tombs of kings and officials, which did not require literacy on the part of the users.[1]

DOCUMENTATION AND ENFORCEMENT

There is little inscribed evidence concerning judicial administration in the Early Dynastic Period. The title of vizier, the highest official under the king

MAP 1.1. Egypt in the Early Dynastic Period

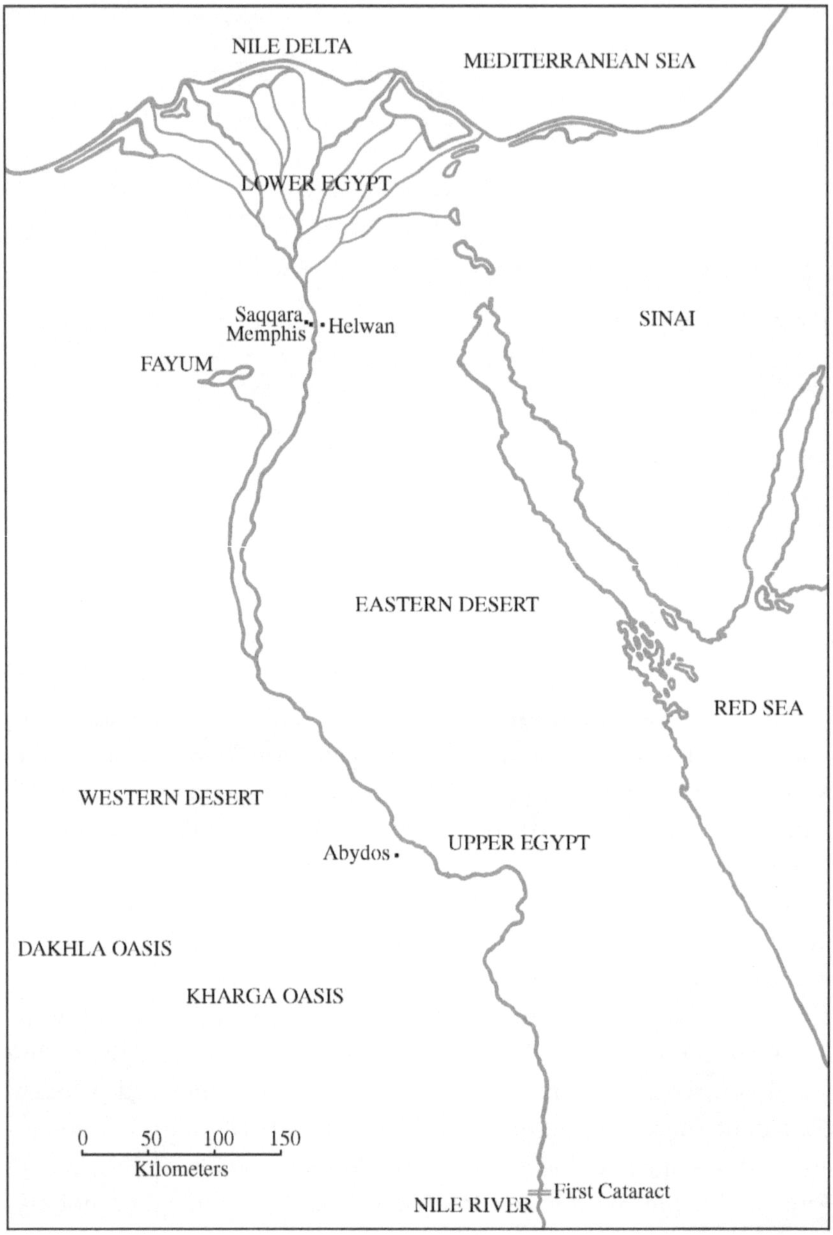

and the head of the central judicial administration in the Old Kingdom, may appear already in the Early Dynastic Period, but it is not securely attested until the Third Dynasty.[2] There is some evidence that the state made use of writing to document and enforce community tax obligations to the state, through surveys and censuses of objects of taxation. The limited use of writing, however,

TABLE 1.1. *The Early Dynastic Period*

Protodynastic Period (c. 3200–3000 BCE)
Owner of Tomb U-j
Iry-hor
Early Dynastic Period (c. 3000–2686 BCE)
Dynasty 1 (c. 3000–2890 BCE)
Narmer
Aha
Djer
Djet
Den
Queen Merneit
Anedjib
Semerkhet
Qaa
Dynasty 2 (c. 2890–2686 BCE)
Hetepsekhemwy
Raneb
Ninetjer
Weneg
Sened
Sekhemib-Peribsen
Khasekhemwy

Source: Dates after Ian Shaw (ed.), *The Oxford History of Ancient Egypt* (Oxford: University Press, 2000), pp. 479–483.

probably prevented it from being used more widely to document and enforce individual tax obligations or private transactions, for example.

Field Surveys and Censuses: Some evidence for surveys and censuses for tax purposes in the Early Dynastic Period comes from several fragments of royal annals. These royal annals record the names of successive years, which consisted of one or two significant events in each year. The annals were inscribed in the Fifth Dynasty at the earliest, but the year names were probably assigned in the Early Dynastic Period, because there are wooden and ivory tags and labels from the tombs of First Dynasty kings and officials at Abydos and Saqqara, respectively, that contain similar year names, suggesting that the royal annals accurately preserved older records.[3] In the best preserved fragment of royal annals known as the Palermo Stone, every second year entry in the fourth row on the recto is identified by a combination of two events: the Following of Horus (*šms Ḥr*), which was probably a religious ceremony or a royal procession through the country, and the fourth through tenth occasions of the count (*zp* X *ṯnwt*).[4] These entries are clearly labeled as belonging to King Ninetjer of the Second Dynasty. The term "count" in isolation is ambiguous, but every second year entry in the beginning of the fifth row on the recto of the Palermo Stone refers to a combination of the following of Horus and the sixth through eighth occasions of the count of gold and fields (*zp* X *ṯnwt nbw sḫt*).[5] These entries are not labeled but must belong to the king preceding Djoser, who should be either Khasekhemwy of the Second Dynasty or Nebka of the Third Dynasty if he precedes rather than follows Djoser. The qualification "of gold and fields" argues that these counts were fiscal. The count of gold could represent an inventory of existing wealth, but the count of fields probably represented a survey of income sources, from which revenue was collected at the harvest.

In the Second Dynasty, the occasion of the count is closely associated with the Following of Horus, but the Following of Horus is already attested in the First Dynasty. It appears without an accompanying occasion of the count already in every second year entry in the second row on the recto of the Palermo Stone, which is unlabeled but is often attributed to King Djer of the First Dynasty. Neither the Following of Horus nor the occasion of the count appears in the third row on the recto, which is also unlabeled and is often attributed to King Den of the First Dynasty. Some have suggested that the Following of Horus already included an inventory for tax purposes in the First Dynasty,[6] although if that were true it would hardly have been necessary to refer to the inventory separately as "the occasion of the count" alongside the Following of Horus in the Second Dynasty. Others argue that an inventory did not accompany the biennial Following of Horus until the Second Dynasty, when the count is explicitly mentioned alongside it on the Palermo Stone.[7] Wilkinson suggests that a census or survey may have grown out of the Following of Horus, since a ceremonial progress through the country would have been a good opportunity to assess its wealth,[8] but the limited use of writing in the Early Dynastic Period argues against countrywide censuses or surveys of individual people, fields, or other properties for tax purposes. Indeed, there is no evidence of registration of individual people or properties for tax purposes even in the following Old Kingdom, when there is far more extensive use of writing, only of estates (*ḥwwt*) and towns (*niwwt*) that were collectively responsible for taxes.

Estates: In the reign of Djer in the First Dynasty, clay container sealings and a few tags, labels, and vessel inscriptions from tombs of kings and officials at Abydos and Saqqara begin to bear the names of districts, whose determinatives categorize them as estates (*ḥwwt*). These names probably indicated the sources of the contents of the containers and vessels and the objects formerly associated with the tags.[9] Estates (*ḥwwt*) are well known from the following Old Kingdom, when they frequently appear along with towns (*niwwt*) in lists in royal and private funerary chapels, often personified as offering bearers in tomb scenes. The funerary attestations suggest that revenues from specific estates and towns were assigned to specific royal and private funerary cults.[10] Estates predominated in the early Old Kingdom, while towns became more common in the late Old Kingdom, suggesting a trend away from estates toward towns.[11] Inscriptions and scenes from late Old Kingdom tomb-chapels reveal that estates and towns were both managed by relatively low-ranking chiefs (*ḥkꜣw*), who were beaten for nonpayment of taxes.[12] Estates and towns were also the basis for unit formation in military service, which was a form of compulsory labor.[13] Estates and towns thus appear to have been collectively responsible for payment of harvest taxes and compulsory labor, and their representatives were held personally responsible for nonpayment.

DISTRIBUTION

Grave goods in tombs provide archaeological evidence that forms of distribution took place in Egypt for centuries before the appearance of writing shortly before the Early Dynastic Period. Nonetheless, the size and wealth of tombs of kings and officials started growing rapidly around the time that writing appeared, indicating that the systems of distribution were also developing and expanding in this period. The appearance and increasing complexity of written distribution records on grave goods in the Early Dynastic Period thus may track the development of these distribution systems, as well as the development of new applications for writing. These distribution records on labels and sealings attached to offering containers in tombs, and sometimes on the containers themselves, may preserve the names of the districts and institutions responsible for producing and distributing the offering goods. Texts do not seem to refer private transactions in this period, however. This is a logical consequence of the restricted use of writing in this period, which only later in the Old Kingdom spread beyond the royal court and its agents.

Tomb U-j: The earliest written records of distribution known from Egypt come from elite Tomb U-j at Abydos, which dates one or two centuries before the First Dynasty and which may have belonged to an anonymous chief or king of a proto-state centered on Abydos.[14] The tomb contained vessels inscribed with names written inside royal *serekhs*, possibly indicating the institutions responsible for the vessels;[15] impressions of nontextual cylinder seals in the clay used to seal vessels, possibly identifying the individuals responsible for the contents of the vessels;[16] and ivory, bone, and stone tags that were once attached to other now vanished grave goods, and that were incised with numbers or possible place names, perhaps indicating the origins of the goods.[17]

Tax-Marks and Other Inscriptions: From the reign of Iry-hor just before the First Dynasty to the reign of Den in the First Dynasty, some incised vessels, clay seal impressions, and incised tags and labels found in royal and private tombs bear inscriptions that have been called tax-marks. The tax-marks identify a type and quality of a product, most often oil, and describe it as received (*iw.t*), counted (*ipw.t*), brought (*inw*), delivered (*nḥb*, *ḏḥ3*), or food (*ḏf3*) from either Upper Egypt (*Šmꜥw*) or Lower Egypt (*Mḥw*). Tax-marks on tags and labels sometimes also include a year name with the names of the king and of an official. Other inscriptions from this period, however, simply give the name of the king and of an official.[18]

Royal Domains: In the reign of Djer in the First Dynasty, some jar sealings from royal and private tombs begin to name estates (*ḥwwt*), discussed previously, and institutions whose names were written inside a hieroglyph resembling a fortified wall.[19] The reading of the hieroglyph is uncertain, so these institutions have been called royal domains.[20] They should not be confused with the estates and later towns that have also been called domains.[21] Indeed, the royal domains may have received their revenues from estates and other sources, and may have been the institutional ancestors of the later royal mortuary temples.[22] In the reign of Den in the First Dynasty, sealings also start to give the names and titles of the officials who managed the royal domains, usually an administrator (*ꜥḏ-mr*) or controller (*ẖrp*) or executive (*ḥry-wḏ3*), each coupled with the name of the domain.[23]

Royal Palaces: In the reign of Djet in the First Dynasty, sealings and other inscriptions begin to attest to an institution known as the royal house (*pr-nzwt*) alongside the royal treasury (*pr-ḥḏ/pr-dšr*). It was probably responsible for supporting the king and his court at various palaces, analogous to the Residence in the Old Kingdom. A controller of the royal house (*ẖrp pr-nzwt*) is attested.[24]

Royal Treasuries: In the reign of Den in the First Dynasty, some sealings and other inscriptions from the tombs of kings and officials begin to refer to royal treasuries.[25] Tax-marks disappear at this time, but references to estates and domains continue, indicating that they were separate though possibly subordinate institutions. The royal treasuries were alternately named the white house (*pr-ḥḏ*) or the red house (*pr-dšr*). From the reign of Den it was known as the white house, and then from the reign of Anedjib through that of Ninetjer as the red house. It was renamed the white house again under Sekhemib-Peribsen, and the red house again under Khasekhemwy, until it finally became known as the double white house (*pr.wy-ḥḏ*) or double treasury in the Old Kingdom. It would be tempting to see the white and red houses as the component elements of the double treasury, perhaps representing Upper and Lower Egypt, except that they are never attested together in the same place or even the same reign.[26] In the Second Dynasty, the treasury appears to have contained a number of subdepartments. These included a workshop (*pr-šnꜥ*), a house of redistribution (*pr-ḥry-wḏb*), and a provisioning department (*iz-ḏf3*).[27] Royal seal-bearers or chancellors (*ẖtmw-bity*) may have managed the treasury and were probably the highest-ranking officials in the central administration below the king and the vizier, though the vizier is not securely attested until the Old Kingdom. An executive of the house of redistribution (*ḥry-wḏꜣ pr-ḥry-wḏb*) is attested in the Second Dynasty, as is a scribe of the provisioning department (*zẖ iz-ḏfꜣ*).[28]

ENTREPRENEURIAL ACTIVITIES

In addition to simply redistributing goods and services, the state sometimes used them to facilitate the future acquisition of raw materials or production of goods. This usually took the form either of expeditions beyond the populated areas under the control of the Egyptian state for warfare and booty, trade or mining, or of the foundation of institutions within the populated areas of Egypt.

Expeditions: The fragment of royal annals known as the Palermo Stone contains year names apparently commemorating military expeditions, such as "smiting the bowmen," in what is probably the reign of Den in the First Dynasty, and destroying two places called Shem-Re and Ha in the reign of Ninetjer in the Second Dynasty.[29] Wooden and ivory tags and labels from the tombs of First Dynasty kings and officials at Abydos and Saqqara also preserve year names apparently commemorating military expeditions. A label of King Den reads "first occasion of smiting the easterners."[30]

Foundations: The Palermo Stone also contains year names that commemorate the creation of statues, boats, and buildings, some of which may reflect the foundation of institutions if they were endowed with revenues. In the second row in what is probably the reign of Djer in the First Dynasty, there are references to planning (*ḥꜣ*) the building "Companion of the Gods" (*smn-nṯrw*) and creating (*ms.t*, literally giving birth to) images of the gods Iat, Min, and Anubis.[31] In the third row in what is probably the reign of Den in the First Dynasty, there are references to planning (*ḥꜣ*) pools (*šw*) in the northwest, planning (*ḥꜣ*) the building "Thrones of the Gods" (*sw.t-nṯrw*) as well as stretching the cord for its great door (*pḏ-šs ꜥꜣ wr*) and opening its pool (*wp.t-š*) in three successive years, and creating (*ms.t*) images of the gods Sed, Seshat, and Mafdet.[32] In the fourth row that is labeled the reign of Ninetjer in the Second Dynasty, there is a reference to stretching the cord (*pḏ-šs*) for the building "Door of Horus" (*r-n-Ḥr*), and in the fifth row in what is probably the reign of Khasekhemwy in the Second Dynasty, there are references to building in stone (*ḳd inr*) the building "the Goddess endures" (*nṯrt mn*), creating (*ms.t*) the statue "High is Khasekhemwy" (*ḳꜥ Ḫꜥ-sḫm.wy*), and "cutting the desert" (*šd dšrt*) in Duadjefa, which may refer to building a ship as it does in the reign of King Sneferu on the same annal fragment.[33]

CONCLUSIONS

In the Early Dynastic Period, very little is known about the state judicial administration or how written documentation affected enforcement. The state introduced the use of writing to document collection and redistribution of state revenues, presumably because the increased efficiency of extraction offset the costs of training and supporting the necessary scribes. Even so, the state probably only documented collective tax obligations. The limited use of writing, however, probably prevented it from being used more widely. The state does not appear to have used writing to document private property transfers. Such transactions were probably documented orally with local witnesses.

TWO

THE OLD KINGDOM AND THE FIRST INTERMEDIATE PERIOD (c. 2686–2025 BCE)

The Old Kingdom (c. 2686–2181 BCE) began with the Third Dynasty, which was transitional from the Early Dynastic Period. Its kings ruled Egypt from the royal court or Residence in the city of Memphis, and built their tombs at nearby Saqqara. The Fourth, Fifth, and Sixth Dynasties constitute the Old Kingdom proper, and continued to rule from Memphis. The kings of the Fourth Dynasty built their tombs at Meidum, Dahshur, and Giza, those of the Fifth and Sixth Dynasties at Saqqara and Abusir. Many officials of the Fourth, Fifth, and Sixth Dynasties built their tombs near those of the kings whom they served. Other officials represented the kings in the provinces and built tombs there.

The First Intermediate Period (c. 2181–2025 BCE) began with the Seventh and Eighth Dynasties, which continued to rule from Memphis, and retained control of Egypt at least as far south as Coptos where the provincial governors acknowledged them and acted on their behalf.[1] In the north, they were succeeded by the Ninth and Tenth Dynasties, which originated from Herakleopolis and controlled Lower and Middle Egypt as far south as Assiut, where the provincial governors acknowledged them and fought on their behalf against the provincial governors and kings farther to the south.[2] In the south, the provincial governors fought with one another for supremacy, until the provincial governors of Thebes eventually defeated the other Upper Egyptian provinces and styled themselves kings. This new Eleventh Dynasty then successfully warred against the Herakleopolite kings of the Ninth and

MAP 2.1. Egypt in the Old Kingdom and First Intermediate Period

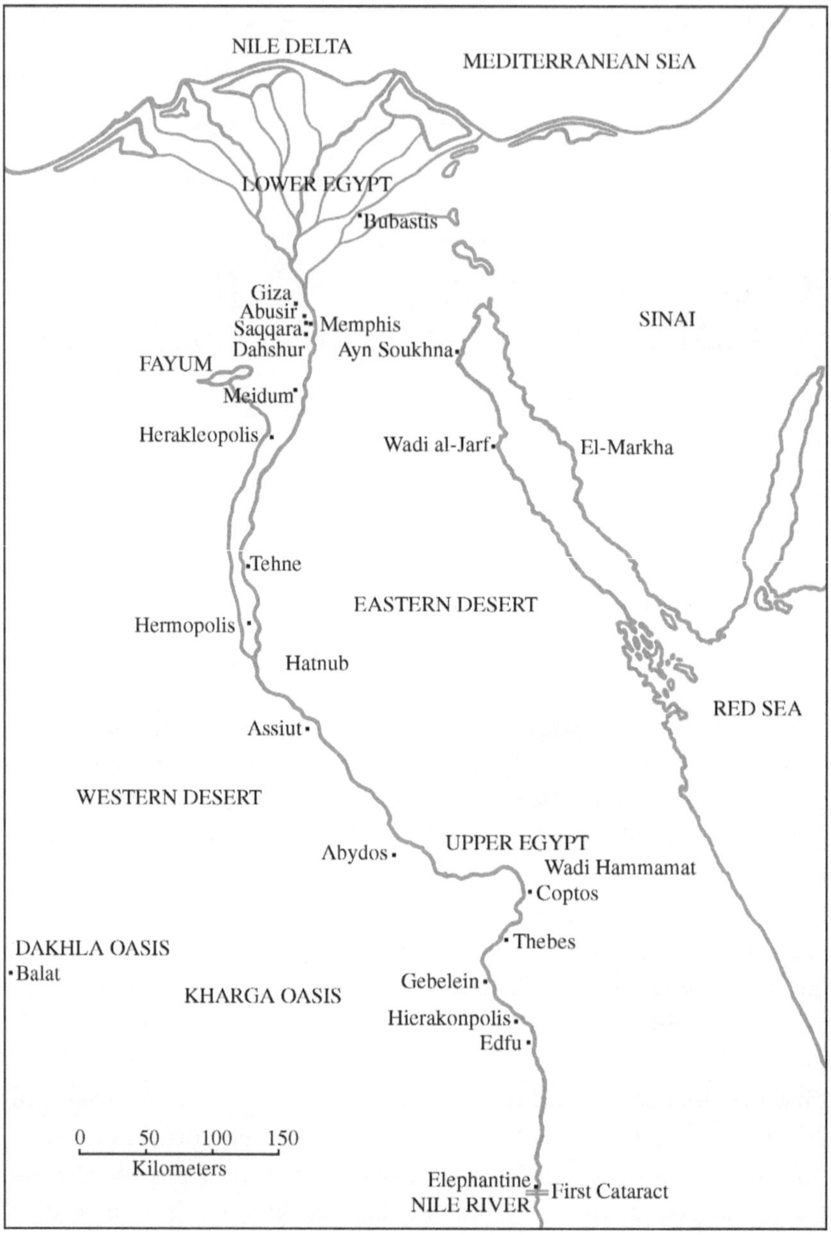

Tenth Dynasties. The reunification of Egypt marked the end of the First Intermediate Period, and the beginning of the Middle Kingdom. (See Map 2.1 and Table 2.1)

The Old Kingdom saw diversification of uses of writing compared to the preceding Early Dynastic Period. The first narrative texts appear in this period, in the form of religious texts inscribed in royal tombs (Pyramid

TABLE 2.1. *The Old Kingdom and First Intermediate Period*

Old Kingdom (c. 2686–2181 BCE)

Dynasty 3 (c. 2686–2613 BCE)
Nebka
Djoser
Sekhemkhet
Khaba
Sanakht
Huni

Dynasty 4 (c. 2613–2494 BCE)
Sneferu
Khufu
Djedefre
Khaefre
Menkaure
Shepseskaf

Dynasty 5 (c. 2494–2345 BCE)
Userkaf
Sahure
Neferirkare
Shepseskare
Neferefre
Niuserre
Menkauhor
Djedkare
Unas

Dynasty 6 (c. 2345–2181 BCE)
Teti
Userkare
Pepi I
Merenre
Pepi II

First Intermediate Period (c. 2181–2025 BCE)

Dynasties 7 and 8 (c. 2181–2160 BCE)
Qakare Ibi
Neferkaure
Neferkauhor
Demedjibtawy

Dynasties 9 and 10 (c. 2160–2025 BCE, Heracleopolis)
Khety
Merykare

Dynasty 11, before unification (c. 2160–2025 BCE, Thebes)
Mentuhotep I
Intef I
Intef II
Intef III

Source: Dates after Ian Shaw (ed.), *The Oxford History of Ancient Egypt* (Oxford: University Press, 2000), pp. 479–483.

Texts), biographies inscribed in the tombs of officials, and letters both royal and private, as well as agreements and even court proceedings. The first accounts also appear, taking the form of tables with horizontal and vertical lines demarcating rows and columns.[3]

CRIMINAL JUSTICE

In the Old Kingdom, the king, the vizier, and the great courts located at Memphis, seem to have had jurisdiction over crimes against the state wherever they occurred in Egypt, including interference with royal revenues. There are a number of royal decrees from this period that forbid administrative officials from taking goods from specific temples, or compelling their personnel to provide compulsory labor, except by royal decree. These decrees state that officials who violate the decrees will be sent to the great courts for sentencing.

In the Old Kingdom, the king was the head of the judicial administration. No evidence has survived from this period indicating that the king could hear and decide cases himself,[4] though he certainly had that privilege in later periods. However, there is evidence from the Old Kingdom that he could appoint officials to hear special cases, such as Weni's investigations of Queen Weretyamtes.

Stela Cairo CG 1435 (Autobiography of Weni), lines 10–13:[5]

When there was a secret charge in the royal harem against queen Weretyamtes, his majesty made me go in to hear it alone.

(11) No chief judge and vizier, no *sr*-official was there, only I alone; because I was worthy, because I was rooted in his majesty's heart; because his majesty had filled his heart with me.

Only I put it in writing (12) together with one other senior warden of Nekhen, while my rank was only that of overseer of royal tenants.

Never before had one like me heard a secret of the king's harem; but his majesty made me hear it, (13) because I was worthy in his majesty's heart beyond any *sr*-official of his, beyond any noble of his, beyond any servant of his.

The vizier was in charge of the entire central administration under the king, and in the early Old Kingdom he was usually a member of the royal family. In the later Old Kingdom, however, the vizier frequently came from outside the royal family, though he often married into it. Around the same time, starting in the mid-Fifth Dynasty, the central administration was formally divided into five departments, namely the great court, the scribes of royal documents, works, the granary, and the treasury. The vizier usually held special titles indicating that he was in charge of each of these five departments, such as "overseer of the six great courts," or "overseer of the scribes of royal documents." However, many of these departments also had their own overseer serving under the vizier, sometimes with titles subtly different from those of the vizier, such as "overseer of the great court" instead of "overseer of the six great courts."[6] The overseer of the great court was the official responsible for the central judicial administration under the vizier and was assisted by numerous scribes of the great court and their managers.[7] In addition, the overseer of scribes of royal documents was responsible for many paralegal matters, including outgoing correspondence such as royal decrees and incoming correspondence like petitions.[8]

There are several different names for what appear to be high or central courts, including great court (*ḥw.t wr.t*), great *ḏ3ḏ3.t*-court (*ḏ3ḏ3.t wr.t*), great *ḏ3ḏ3.t*-court of the great god (*ḏ3ḏ3.t wr.t nt ntr ꜥ3*), royal *ḏ3ḏ3.t*-court (*ḏ3ḏ3.t nswt*), broad hall (*wsḫ.t*), broad hall of Horus (*wsḫ.t Ḥr*), and *sḫw*-hall of Horus (*sḫw Ḥr*). Some of these different names may refer to the same institutions. The composition of these courts is unclear, but the autobiography of Weni suggests that some of them could include the vizier or his immediate subordinates.[9]

Stela Cairo CG 1435 (Autobiography of Weni), lines 2–4:[10]

While my office was that of – (3) his majesty made me senior warden of Nekhen, his heart being filled with me beyond any other servant of his. I heard cases alone with the chief judge and vizier, concerning all kinds of secrets.

(4) [I acted] in the name of the king for the royal harem and for the six great houses, because his majesty's heart was filled with me beyond any *sr*-official of his, any noble of his, any servant of his.

There is currently no evidence that the central court or courts served as a court of appeal for local courts.[11] The central court or courts are primarily attested in conjunction with royal decrees and royal revenues. Several royal decrees of the type called exemption decrees state that violations were to be tried in central courts. The royal decree of King Neferirkare from Abydos names the great court in this context.[12] Royal decrees B, C, and D of King Pepi II from Coptos refer to the *sḥw*-hall of Horus in a similar fashion.[13] Likewise, an official states in Letter 80A from the archives of the funerary temple of King Neferirkare at Abusir that the great court did not convict him of failure to deliver goods.[14]

The royal decrees known as exemption decrees are in fact also concerned with royal revenues, suggesting that this was a primary legislative and judicial interest of the central administration in the Old Kingdom. The exemption decrees legislated that the property and personnel of specific institutions, usually mortuary temples, *ka*-chapels, or temples of local gods, should be exempted or protected from demands by royal or provincial officials.

Stela Boston MFA 03.1896 (Decree of Neferirkare from Abydos):[15]

(1) Horus Userkhau (Neferirkare)

(2) A royal decree (to) the overseer of *ḥm-nṯr*-priests, Hemwer:

(3) "I do not empower any man (to do any of the following):

- (4) to take away any *ḥm-nṯr*-priest (5) who is in your nome (6) for the purpose of compulsory labor and any (other) work (7) of the nome, with exceptions for carrying out the cult rites (8) for his god in the temple where they take place, (9) and for maintaining the temples (10) in which they (the rites) are;
- (13) to levy the corvee for any work on (14) any god's field (15) on which priestly duty is done by (16) any *ḥm-nṯr*-priest;
- (17) to take away any dependents (*mrt*) who are on (14) any god's field (15) on which priestly duty is done by (16) any *ḥm-nṯr*-priest (18) for the purpose of doing compulsory labor and any (other) work of the nome.

(11) They are (all) exempted for all time (12) through the royal decree of the king of Upper and Lower Egypt Neferirkare; you do not have any legal claim against it with respect to any duty.

(19) With regard to any man of the nome who shall take away
- (20) any *ḥm-nṯr*-priest who is on (21) the land of the god who does priestly service in that nome;
- (25) the dependents (*mrt*) (26) who are on any god's field;

(22) for the purpose of compulsory labor and any work of the nome, (23) you shall send him to the great court and he shall be made to work in the stone quarry, (24) and to harvest barley and emmer wheat.

(27) (And with regard to) any *sr*-official, royal acquaintance, or person concerned with any reversionary offerings (28) who shall act counter to this decree of my majesty (29a) which has been registered in the great court, (29b) (his) house, land, people, and everything he owns shall be taken away and (30) he shall be put onto compulsory labor."

(30) Sealed in the presence of the king himself (on) the second month of the Shemu season, day 11+.

In some cases, the king approved the demands that royal officials made on other officials or institutions. For example, the provincial governor Harkhuf inscribed in his tomb near Elephantine a copy of a royal decree sent to him when he was returning from an expedition to Iam in Nubia with tribute for King Pepi II. The royal decree permitted Harkhuf to draw supplies from any royal official or institution in order to expedite the delivery of the tribute.

Autobiography of Harkhuf, lines D1-6, and 25–26:[16]

(1) The king's own seal, year of the second occasion, third month of Akhet, day 15: (2) a royal decree for the sole companion, lector priest and overseer of foreigners Harkhuf.

(3) "Note has been taken of the content of this letter of yours which you composed for the attention of the king at the palace, to let it be known that you have come back successfully (4) from Iam with the expedition which was with you.

What you have said in this letter of yours is that you have brought back (5) all sorts of great and wonderful tribute which Hathor, mistress of Imaau, has given to the *ka* of (6) the king of Upper and Lower Egypt Neferkare (Pepi II), may he live for ever and for eternity....

(25) Orders have been taken to (every) chief of a new settlement, companion, and overseer of *ḥm-nṯr*-priests to command that supplies be taken which are (26) in his charge from every estate storeroom and from every temple; I make no exemption therefrom."

In other cases, however, the king was apparently concerned that excessive demands by royal agents could adversely affect the ability of other royal agents or institutions to fulfill their own obligations to the king, the cults of the king's predecessors, or the gods. The king therefore issued exemption decrees that established exclusive rights for some agents or institutions to exploit the property and personnel assigned to them, presumably to protect them from the risk that another agent or institution would seize their produce.

The exemption decrees do not refer to individuals, however, except as royal and provincial officials. Because the central administration was otherwise very interested in protecting its revenue sources, the absence of references to individuals suggests that the central administration collected revenues through officials and institutions, but not directly from individuals. This interpretation is supported by other evidence discussed in this chapter, which suggests that in the Old Kingdom there was collective responsibility for taxes. It is crucial to note, however, that institutional and collective responsibility for taxation does not necessarily imply institutional or collective ownership of property. It merely means that the central administration lacked either the means or the interest to document individual tax obligations, and to adjudicate disputes arising therefrom.

PROPERTY DISPUTE RESOLUTION

Local courts appear to have had jurisdiction over private property disputes. Several property transfer contracts mention that a local court witnessed them, and a record of a trial that probably took place at a local court at Elephantine Island deals with the authenticity of a property transfer contract. Furthermore, local courts are never mentioned in conjunction with criminal cases, nor are the great courts are ever mentioned in connection with property disputes, so the great courts do not seem to have functioned as courts of appeal.

In the Old Kingdom, local remedies could begin with a letter of complaint to an individual authority requesting redress. An example of this is Papyrus Cairo CG 58043 (*Boulaq* 8),[17] a Sixth Dynasty letter from Saqqara. A female servant writes to her superior Mereri, complaining that one Mehu wrote a document obliging him to take care of her, but Mehu has not fulfilled his obligations to her. The servant requests Mereri to intervene on her behalf with Mehu.

In addition to individual authorities, there were also courts of local officials who could offer remedies. These courts were known as *ḏꜣḏꜣ.t*-courts, but they could also be described obliquely as "the *sr*-officials," though not every reference to *sr*-officials refers to a *ḏꜣḏꜣ.t*-court.[18] It is unknown whether letters of complaint could be sent directly to such judicial institutions or whether they had to be sent first to individual authorities who acted as gatekeepers. Both practices are known in later periods. Local *ḏꜣḏꜣ.t*-courts were concerned with property or contract laws. Contracts could be drawn up before such courts, such as house sale Stela JdE 42787 drawn up before the *ḏ3ḏ3.t*-court of the pyramid-town of Akhet-Khufu at Giza.

Papyrus Berlin P. 9010 comes from Elephantine Island and probably dates to the Sixth Dynasty.[19] It records the legal decision of an anonymous judicial institution, most likely a local *ḏ3ḏ3.t*-court. A man named Sobekhotep has brought a document purportedly made by Woser concerning his wife, his children, and all his property in his residence, possibly a reference to a testament (*wḏ.t-mdw*) or a transfer (*imy.t-pr*) document serving as a will. Woser's son Tjau, however, says that his father never made this document. The legal decision is that if Sobekhotep produces three witnesses who will take an oath swearing that the document contains the words of Woser, then these things will remain with Sobekhotep; but if he does not produce three such witnesses, then they will remain with Tjau.[20]

Papyrus Berlin P. 9010:

(1) … this Sobekhotep has brought a document that the royal noble and overseer of foreigners, Woser, caused to be made, that he (Woser) reckons to him (Sobekhotep) (2) his wife, his children, and all his property in his residence, until all the children (3) of this Woser are satisfied therewith, the older one treated according to his age, the younger one according to his youth.

This Tjau has said that (4) his father (Woser) has never made it in any place.

If this Sobekhotep brings three excellent witnesses who are believable concerning this, (5) who make (the oath) "May your manifestation be against him, god," that this document was indeed made according to that which this Woser has said is therein, (6) then they will remain in the residence of Sobekhotep, because he has brought these three witnesses who say these words in their presence, (7) "This Sobekhotep is the beneficiary."

If he does not bring three witnesses to say these words (8) in their presence, then everything in it of this Woser shall not remain with him, (but) shall remain with his son, the royal noble and overseer of foreigners, Tjau.

DOCUMENTATION OF OBJECTS OF TAXATION

One of the five departments of the central administration under the vizier was responsible for documentation. As previously noted, the overseer of scribes of royal documents was responsible for many paralegal matters.[21] In addition, there is some evidence that the central administration also documented the objects of taxation, in order to better enforce its revenue collection.

Field Surveys and Censuses: In the Old Kingdom, evidence for surveys and censuses for tax purposes comes from references to a biennial "occasion of the count." The occasion of the count (*zp ṯnwt*) is attested already in the Early Dynastic Period in the fragment of royal annals known as the Palermo Stone, in several year names from the reign of King Ninetjer of the Second Dynasty. An "occasion of the count of gold and fields" (*zp* X *ṯnwt nbw sḫt*) occurs in the same fragment of royal annals in several year names from a later reign immediately preceding that of King Djoser, belonging to either Khasekhemwy of the Second Dynasty, or Nebka of the Third Dynasty, if he preceded rather than followed Djoser.[22]

In the Old Kingdom, the Palermo Stone and related fragments also refer to the occasion of the count several times in the reigns of King Sneferu of the Fourth Dynasty, and Kings Userkaf, Sahure, and Neferirkare of the Fifth Dynasty.[23] Starting in the reign of Userkaf, these references take the form "the year of the Xth occasion of the count" (*rnpt zp X ṯnwt*), or "the year after the Xth occasion of the count" (*rnpt m-ḫt zp X ṯnwt*). In the reign of Userkaf, the occasion of the count is once qualified as "of cattle" (*iḥw*).[24] Another fragment of royal annals known as the South Saqqara Stone regularly refers to "the year of (or after) the Xth occasion of the count of cattle" (*rnpt (m-ḫt) zp X ṯnwt iḥw*) in registers referring to the reigns of Kings Teti, Merenre, and Pepi I of the Sixth Dynasty.[25] Such references to the year of (or after) the occasion of the count replaced the Early Dynastic system of year names, and became the standard means of identifying years in the Old Kingdom.[26] The count may not have been strictly biennial, however, because years of the count occur much more frequently than years after the count.[27]

This form of dating is also attested outside of the royal annals, though in most cases it was abbreviated to "the year of the Xth occasion" (*rnpt zp X*) or "the year after the Xth occasion" (*rnpt m-ḫt zp X*).[28] There are a few examples of a fuller writing, however. For example, the testament inscribed in the tomb of the vizier Nikaure at Giza, probably dating to the reign of King Menkaure of the Fourth Dynasty, refers to "the year of the twelfth occasion of accounting large and small cattle" (*rnpt zp 12 ipt iḥw ꜥwt*).[29] The exemption decree of King Shepseskaf of the Fourth Dynasty for the mortuary complex of King Menkaure at Giza is dated to "the year after the first occasion of accounting large and small cattle" (*rnpt m-ḫt zp tpi ipt iḥw ꜥwt*).[30] An inscription in the Sinai dated to King Pepi II of the Sixth Dynasty refers to "the second occasion of the count of all large and small cattle of Lower and Upper Egypt" (*rnpt zp 2 ṯnwt ihw ꜥwt nbt*).[31] In all of these cases the use of the terms "count" (*ṯnwt*) and especially "account" (*ipt*) suggest that the purpose of the cattle count was indeed fiscal and not purely ritual as some have suggested.[32] The fiscal interpretation seems to be supported by a passage in the autobiography of Weni.

Stela Cairo CG 1435 (Autobiography of Weni), line 36:[33]

I counted (*ip*) everything (*ḫt nb*) that is counted for the Residence in this Upper Egypt on two occasions, and all services (*wnwt nb*) that are counted for the Residence in Upper Egypt on two occasions.

The nature of the objects of the count strongly suggests that its purpose was a census of objects of taxation.[34] In later periods, land surveys and censuses of people and animals were the primary basis for taxation. Harvest taxes were collected on the basis of land surveys, and compulsory labor (and later capitation taxes) were collected on the basis of censuses of people and animals. Admittedly, the count is a very indirect witness of taxation, but there is more direct evidence for a census of objects of taxation from the Middle Kingdom, making it plausible that there was already some form of census for this purpose in the Old Kingdom. However, if there was a census in the Old Kingdom, it may have been less comprehensive than those in later periods. The indirect evidence for tax collection in the Old Kingdom (see Estates and Towns) suggests that responsibility may have been assigned collectively to estates and towns, rather than to individuals and their fields as in later periods. Such collective responsibility would have required less detailed surveys and censuses than those attested in later periods.

Estates and Towns: In the Old Kingdom, the Egyptian countryside continued to be organized at the local level into districts consisting of agricultural land and its cultivators, as it had been in the Early Dynastic Period. The names of the districts are often preserved in lists in royal and private funerary chapels. In the Early Dynastic Period, the names of the districts had only one type of determinative, categorizing them as estates (*ḥwwt*). In the Old Kingdom, however, the names of districts had two types of determinatives, categorizing them into estates (*ḥwwt*) and towns (*niwwt*). In the past, these districts have been collectively called funerary domains,[35] or just domains,[36] but in this study, the terms estates and towns are used instead. In the early Old Kingdom estates predominate, while in the late Old Kingdom towns become more common, suggesting a trend away from estates toward towns.[37] The funerary attestations suggest that revenues from specific estates and towns could be assigned to specific royal and private funerary cults.[38] Some have argued that the lists of estates and towns associated with funerary cults were fictions,[39] but this does not mean that estates and towns did not exist or did not supply revenues to funerary cults,[40] and in fact administrative papyri from the royal mortuary temples at Abusir occasionally refer to supplies arriving from specific estates and towns.[41]

Inscriptions and scenes from Fifth and Sixth Dynasty tomb-chapels reveal that estates and towns were both managed by relatively low-ranking chiefs (*ḥḳ3w*). Chiefs of estates were usually explicitly titled as such (*ḥḳ3w ḥwwt*), while chiefs of towns were sometimes just called chiefs (*ḥḳ3w niwwt* or just *ḥḳ3w*). Thus a scene from the mortuary chapel of the Sixth Dynasty vizier Khentika called Ikhekhi at Saqqara shows five chiefs of estates being beaten before Ikhekhi and two scribes of his funerary establishment (*sš n pr-ḏt*), presumably for failure to deliver revenues.[42] Similarly, a scene from the Fifth Dynasty mortuary chapel of Ti also at Saqqara shows three chiefs of towns being beaten before five scribes (*sš*) during accounting by the *ḏ3ḏ3.t*-court of a funerary establishment (*ip in ḏ3ḏ3.t n pr-ḏt*).[43] However, inscriptions in private tombs show that many high officials, including most provincial governors or nomarchs, also held the title of chief of an estate (*ḥḳ3 ḥwt*). One interpretation is that the term "chief of an estate" refers to owners of estates, who could vary considerably in status and rank, and who could be resident or absentee landlords.[44] A more widely accepted interpretation, however, is that estates were districts that could not be owned, though their revenues could be assigned to institutions and individuals.[45] The low ranking chiefs of estates were probably the headmen of these districts, while the high ranking holders of the title were either recipients of revenues, or, in the case of provincial governors or nomarchs, responsible for overseeing these districts in their provinces or nomes.[46] In this interpretation, estates and towns were collectively responsible for harvest taxes and compulsory labor, and their representatives were held personally responsible. This finds support in the Autobiography of Weni, which suggests that estates and towns were the basis for unit formation in military service, which was after all a form of compulsory labor.[47]

Stela Cairo CG 1435 (Autobiography of Weni), lines 13–18:[48]

When his majesty took action against the Asiatic Sand-dwellers, (14) his majesty made an army of many tens of thousands from all of Upper Egypt, from Elephantine to Medenyt; from Lower Egypt, from all of the Two-Sides-of-the-House (15) and from Sedjer and Khen-sedjru; and from Irtjet-Nubians, Medja-Nubians, Iam-Nubians, (16) Wawat-Nubians, Kaau-Nubians; and from Tjemeh-land.

His majesty sent me at the head of this army, (17) there being counts, royal seal-bearers, sole companions of the palace, chieftains (*ḥryw-tpw*) and chiefs of estates (*ḥḳ3w ḥwwt*) of Upper and Lower Egypt, companions, overseers of scouts, (18) overseers of priests of Upper and Lower Egypt, and overseers of districts at the head of the troops of Upper and Lower Egypt, from the estates (*ḥwwt*) and towns (*niwwt*) that they governed (*ḥḳ3*), and from the Nubians of those foreign lands.

DOCUMENTATION OF PROPERTY TRANSFERS

The surviving evidence for documentation of property transfers and exchanges in the Old Kingdom consists of written transcripts of verbal statements. The transcripts sometimes provide the names of witnesses who could be requested to authenticate the agreements, either individually,[49] or collectively as in the "*ḏ3ḏ3.t*-court of the pyramid-town of Akhet-Khufu" at Giza.[50] Many of the surviving transcripts do not provide the names of witnesses, but usually this was because the transcripts were intended as memoranda or reminders for the witnesses themselves. In contrast, the scribes who wrote the transcripts are never named, and thus could not be requested to authenticate the transcripts. Witnesses are similarly privileged over scribes in the court decision involving a disputed document in Papyrus Berlin P. 9010, discussed previously. The court called for witnesses to verify that the document contained the words of a verbal statement but made no mention of the scribe of the document. The implication is that verbal statements were the primary means of documenting agreements and that the memories of witnesses were the primary means of authenticating them. Written transcripts would seem to have had no authority independent of the verbal statements, because there was no way to authenticate them independently from the witnesses to the verbal statements. The primacy of verbal statements over written transcripts could suggest that many or even most agreements were never transcribed, but of course no records of such purely verbal agreements have survived. Nonetheless, written transcripts were sometimes made, apparently to function as public memoranda, to remind the contracting parties and witnesses of what was said in the verbal statements. There is no evidence that information about local property transfers was passed to the central administration, and consequently it lacked the information necessary to effectively intervene in local property disputes.

Exchanges: Among the surviving transcripts, there are a few transfers involving an exchange (*isw*) of property, the equivalent of a sale in a barter economy.[51] These include a sale (*in m isw*) of a house (*pr pn*) in exchange for cloth and a bed on Stela Cairo JdE 42787;[52] two sales (*di isw*) of houses (*pr*) in exchange for cloth (*ḥbs*) on Papyri Gebelein I verso B and VI;[53] a fragmentary sale (*in r isw*) of a funerary chapel (*ḥw.t-k3 tn*) in exchange for one-thirtieth of an aroura on Block Saqqara RM 22.11.1956;[54] a sale (*ir m isw*) of a door (*sb3 pn*) in exchange for a bolt of cloth (*d3iw*) in the Inscription of Khenemti on Doorlintel Cairo CG 1634 from Saqqara;[55] and the false door of *Tf-h3y*.[56]

Satisfaction seems to have been an important feature of these exchanges, in contrast to wills or testaments. Several of them contain an oath in which one anonymous party swears that they will uphold the agreement to the satisfaction of the other party. This oath is situated between the statements of the two exchanging parties, and it may have been applied to both parties. That was certainly the case with a similar oath of satisfaction in an exchange described in the Middle Kingdom petition *P. Kahun* II 1.

Stela Cairo JdE 42787 mentioned previously probably comes from Giza. It documents the sale of a house, perhaps that of one of the pyramid-builders whose village lay to the south of the royal necropolis. The inscription transcribes the speech of the buyer Serefka in the first person: "I have bought (*in.n.i r isw*) this house from the scribe Tjenti. I have given 10 shati for it." It is noted that the transaction was made in the presence of the *ḏꜣḏꜣ.t*-court of the pyramid-town of Akhet-Khufu at Giza and many witnesses. The payment is specified and the house is described. The seller Tjenti then swears an oath by the king: "As lives the king, I will cause that it is in order, because you should be satisfied with it ...." Finally, the names of four witnesses are given.

Stela Cairo JdE 42787:

(1) [... Seref]ka, (2) he says: "(I) have brought this house in exchange (*in m isw*) (3) from the scribe Tjenti. (4) (I) have given 10 shat for it."

(5) Sealed with the seal before (6) the *ḏꜣḏꜣ.t*-court of the pyramid-town Akhet-Khufu (and) many witnesses of Tjenti of the phyle of Kaemipu.

(7) (Description of payment:) 4 pieces of cloth: 3 shat. (8) A bed: 4 shat. (9) 2 pieces of cloth: 3 shat.

(10) (Description of house:) Built in stone, (11) unfinished roof (12) in sycamore (13) wood.

(14) He says: "As the king lives, I will cause that that there is justice, you will be satisfied on account of it, to bring into being everything which belongs to this house, (15) because you have completed these payments in exchange."

(16) The necropolis workman (*ẖrt-ntr*), Hema.

(17) The *ka*-servant, Ini.

(18) The *ka*-servant, Seben.

(19) The *ka*-servant, Heryankh.

Papyrus Gebelein I verso B and Papyrus Gebelein VI also mentioned earlier are two texts written on separate papyri in a small archive found in a wooden box in Gebelein, probably dating to the Fourth Dynasty. Both texts document sales of houses and share virtually identical formats. After the date (lines 1–2), the texts transcribe the speeches of the sellers in the first person (line 3): "I have given in exchange a house." The texts then transcribe the speeches of the buyers in the first person (line 5): "I have given in exchange a cloth." The texts also record an oath (line 4): "As lives the king, Netjerysen/I will cause that it is in order, because I am satisfied with it." Neither text gives the names of any witnesses, and it is possible that they were memoranda written by a witness to refresh his memory, because they were written among a variety of other texts, some on the same papyri.

Papyrus Gebelein I verso B:

(1) The year after the 3rd occasion of the counting of cattle in Upper and Lower Egypt, (2) 3rd month of Peret, day 26, in (the funerary estate) Inerty-Inpu.

(3) "(I) have given in exchange a house 16 cubits long by 15 cubits broad," (said) the royal servant (*ḥm-nswt*), Nefer.

(4) "As lives the king, Netjerysen will cause that it is in order, because (I) am satisfied with it."

(5) "(I) have given in exchange a cloth of 15 ½ cubits," (said) the royal servant (*ḥm-nswt*) and funerary estate member (*snw-ḏt*), Iru.

Papyrus Gebelein VI:

(1) [The year] after the 2nd occasion of counting the cattle [in Upper and Lower Egypt?] (2) [? month of] Akhet, day 20. Sealed [with the seal]

(3) "(I) have given in exchange a house 16 cubits long by 11 cubits broad," (said) the royal servant (*ḥm-nswt*), Iu[...].

(4) "As lives the king, (I) will cause that it is in order, because (I) am satisfied [with it]."

(5) "[(I) have given in exchange] a cloth of 24 cubits," (said) [...].

Testaments and Transfers: Most of the surviving transcripts of verbal agreements from the Old Kingdom are not exchanges (*isw*), however, but rather are testaments (*wḏ.t-mdw*) or transfers (*imy.t-pr*). All of the testaments and transfers explicitly identified as testaments and transfers survive as inscriptions in tomb-chapels or fragments thereof. Testaments labeled as such include the inscription of Wepemnofret from his tomb at Giza,[57] the inscription of Kaemnofret from Block Cairo CG 1432,[58] the inscriptions of Nika'ankh from his two tombs at Tehne,[59] and probably the inscription of the vizier Nikaure from his tomb at Giza.[60] The inscription of the vizier Nebkauhor from his tomb at Saqqara describes itself as both a testament and a transfer,[61] suggesting that the two terms can overlap.

These inscriptions usually establish rules for the mortuary cult of the deceased buried in the tomb-chapels. Most of the testaments and transfers omit the names of witnesses, presumably because the multiple hereditary mortuary priests who performed the mortuary cults in the tomb-chapels served to authenticate the documents. This appears to be confirmed by the fact that the one testament that does provide the names of fifteen witnesses also does not establish a mortuary cult, but merely gives a burial chamber in the tomb of the testator to his eldest son.[62] Testaments and transfers were effectively unilateral, and consequently satisfaction was not a feature of their transcripts, in contrast to exchanges. However, there is often a statement that the speaker was "alive and on his two feet,"[63] apparently the equivalent of English "of sound mind and body."

The Inscription of Kaemnofret mentioned above is typical. It survives on a loose block, Cairo CG 1432, which may come from Giza near the pyramid of Khaefre named "Great is Khaefre," and probably dates to the Fifth Dynasty. The inscription documents the testament (*wḏ.t-mdw*) of Kaemnofret, and transcribes his speech in the first person. The inscription notes that the speech was made while he was in good health, literally, "living on his two feet."

Block Cairo CG 1432 (Inscription of Kaemnofret):

(1) [Made while] he lived upon his two feet, as sole companion, chief of Nekheb, chosen for the guard for the king every day, the sole companion, chief of Nekheb, administrator (*ʿḏ-mr*) of (the domain of) *Dwꜣ-Ḥr-ḫnty-pt*, [Kaemnofret?] (2) [for?] this *ka*-priest of (my) funerary estate (*ḏt*) (3) ... according to every testament (*wḏt-mdw*) which I made concerning it.

I do not give authority to [my children, my brothers] (4) my sisters, any children of inspectors (*sḥḏ*) of *ka*-priests ... [... over fields], (5) people, anything which I have made for them for invocation-offerings for me therefrom, being their male servants, [their female servants], (6) their brothers, their sisters, except (*ḥꜣw*) for invocation-offerings [for me therefrom in the necropolis] (7) in (my) tomb of eternity which is of the pyramid "Great is Khaefre," according to the share (*mḏdt*) of fields, people, [everything which I have made for them for invocation-offerings] (8) therefrom.

I do not give authority to any *ka*-priest of (my) funerary estate (*ḏt*), to give fields, people, anything [which I have made for them for invocation-offerings] (9) therefrom in exchange (*rdi r isw*) with any person, (or) to give (it) with any transfer (*imy.t-pr*) to any person, except that they give [to their children] (10) of his division (*pšst=f*) together with the *ka*-priest who is established (*i.mn*) as this *ka*-priest.

As for any *ka*-priest of (my) funerary estate (*ḏt*), who shall disturb (*ḫnnt=f*) [fields, people, anything] (11) for invocation-offerings which the king has given to me to be revered (*imꜣḫ*), there shall be taken from him the share (*mḏdt*) in his possession [for the phyle in which he is].

(12) As for any *ka*-priest of (my) funerary estate (*ḏt*), who shall dispute (*šnt=f*) with his colleague, who shall make a case for ejecting him as *ka*-priest [so that he may seize the share (*mḏdt*)] (13) in his possession on account of it, there shall be taken from him fields, people, anything which I have given to him for invocation-offerings therefrom, [... the officials] (14) therein shall make for him an end, to not dispute (*šn*) before the

> officials (*srw*) [concerning fields, people, anything which I have made] (15) for any *ka*-priest of (my) funerary estate (*ḏt*) for invocation-offerings therefrom in (my) tomb of eternity in the necropolis of the pyramid "Great is Khaefre."
>
> [As for] (16) any *ka*-priest of (my) funerary estate (*ḏt*), who shall go forth to another official position before the officials (*srw*), [if] (17) the officials [permit], he shall go forth to the other official position, (but) the share (*mḏdt*) in his possession is for his phyle, in which he was. [I do not give authority to him to take anything] (18) of fields, people, anything which (I) made for them for invocation-offerings therefrom in (my) tomb [in the necropolis of the pyramid "Great is Khaefre"]. (19) He shall go forth with himself alone.
>
> As for the fields which the king gave to me to be a revered one (*imȝḫ*), [they belong to *ka*-priests] (20) for invocation-offerings for me therefrom in the necropolis.
>
> As for anything, which goes forth from that which I have given to them [it shall be divided with them in the place in which] (21) judgment is given. The share (*mḏdt*) divided for those who belong to these phyles is one-tenth. This shall be done ... (22) for invocation-offerings for me therefrom in the necropolis in (my) tomb of eternity of (the necropolis of) the pyramid "Great is Khaefre."
>
> [As for the towns] (23) of (my) funerary estate (*ḏt*), which the king gave to me to be a revered one (*imȝḫ*), and which are protected (*ḫwwt*) for invocation-offerings according to the list ..., [it is the *ka*-priests] (24) of (my) funerary estate (*ḏt*) who make invocation-offerings for me therefrom, in (my) tomb of eternity which is in the necropolis of "Great is Khaefre" with respect to fields, people] (25) anything which (I) made for them.
>
> As for the towns of my funerary estate (*ḏt*), which priests serve on account of it ...

There are also a number of transcripts of verbal agreements from the Old Kingdom that are not explicitly identified as testaments or transfers but nonetheless probably served the same purpose. Many of these also survive as inscriptions in tomb-chapels or fragments thereof, including the inscription of Metjen from his tomb at Saqqara, now Berlin 1105 and 1106,[64] the inscription of Penmeru from his tomb at Giza (G 2197),[65] the inscription of Sennuankh from his tomb at Saqqara (D 52),[66] the inscription of the mortuary priestess Pepi from Block Berlin 14108,[67] the inscription of Tjenti from Block Cairo JdE 57139,[68] and the inscription of Nyankhkhnum and Khnumhotep from their tomb at Giza.[69]

However, there are also two fragmentary transcripts preserved on clay tablets from Balat (Ayn Asil) in the Dakhla Oasis that appear to have served a similar purpose.[70] Clay tablets were used in Balat in the Old Kingdom in place of papyrus, presumably because papyrus plants did not grow there and papyrus was not regularly imported from the Nile Valley at that time. This suggests that similar documents may have been written on papyrus in the Nile Valley but have not survived. Indeed, the disputed document that was the subject of the legal decision in P. Berlin P. 9010 may have been just such a papyrus.

MEDIA OF EXCHANGE AND REDISTRIBUTION

Money can serve a variety of purposes, and can take a variety of forms. It can be a measure of value, a medium of exchange, and a store of wealth. Different forms of money do not have to serve all of these purposes at the same time, however, nor are they mutually exclusive. In the Old Kingdom, weights of metal served as a measure of value, but they are almost never attested as a medium of exchange. Instead, other commodities are more commonly attested as media of exchange, often cloth in exchange for real property, or grain and bread for other goods and commodities. Weights of metal or cloth were probably also used as stores of wealth, but only to a limited extent; if they had been readily available, they probably would have been used more often as media of exchange.

The limited availability of stores of wealth or sources of credit would not have inhibited transactions, which could have been made as barter exchanges; but it could have made it difficult to exact transfer taxes on the transactions. The lack of transfer taxes, in turn, helps explain why the central administration was not interested in documenting and enforcing property transfers outside of the royal revenue system, because the central administration had no way to recapture its costs.

Measures of Value: Weights of metal were clearly used as measures of value in one transaction in the Old Kingdom. Stela Cairo JdE 42787 documents the sale of a house, which is sold in exchange for ten shatis or rings of metal, which are then specified as a bed and two pieces of cloth worth four shatis, three shatis, and three shatis respectively. The shatis were thus never actually exchanged and served only as measures of value of the objects exchanged.[71] It has been suggested that Old Kingdom shatis were rings of copper, based on a careful examination of the determinative for shati.[72] In the Middle Kingdom, however, a shati was equivalent to one-twelfth of a Middle Kingdom deben of gold, as shown by Papyrus BM 10057–10058 (*Rhind Mathematical Papyrus*), Problem 62;[73] and in the New Kingdom, shatis were probably rings of silver weighing approximately one-twelfth of a New Kingdom deben or 7.6 grams.[74] Old Kingdom lists of metals mention silver before gold, and consequently it has been suggested that silver was originally rarer and more valuable than gold,[75] but no records expressing their relative values have survived from the Old Kingdom.

Media of Exchange: The use of shatis as a measure of value may have derived from real shatis used as a store of wealth and a medium of exchange. Again, however, only one transaction involving real shatis is known from the Old Kingdom, in which six shatis were exchanged for a length of cloth.[76] Pieces of cloth were apparently the type of material most commonly given in high value Old Kingdom exchanges. The value of the cloth is expressed in terms of shatis in Stela Cairo JdE 42787, but more often the value of the cloth is not indicated as in Papyrus Gebelein I verso B, in Papyrus Gebelein VI, and in the Inscription of Khenemeti. This raises the possibility that pieces of cloth were also used as a store of wealth and a medium of exchange.[77] Grain, bread, furniture, and utensils were frequently exchanged in lower value transactions, for bread, cakes, fruits, vegetables, fish, meat, clothing, and utensils.[78]

Stores of Wealth: Some media of exchange, such as metal and cloth, retain their value longer than others, such as grain and bread. Consequently, one would expect that more durable media would tend to be stored and accumulated for potential future high value transactions, while less durable media would tend to be used immediately for low value transactions. The limited evidence from the Old Kingdom conforms to this pattern (as detailed earlier).

REDISTRIBUTIVE NETWORKS

In the Old Kingdom, the state relied on a growing variety of institutions to collect, process, and redistribute revenues from estates and towns and other sources. Some of these institutions were primarily concerned with collection and storage of revenues, such as the royal granaries and treasuries. Others were concerned with processing and distributing revenues to royal building projects, various palaces, mortuary temples and sun temples, and even some private funerary chapels. Provincial administrators shared in the collection of revenues and commodities, and distributed them to local work projects and expeditions, royal *ka*-chapels, and the palaces and funerary chapels of the provincial administrators. Many of the beneficiaries were priests in rotation or laborers on work projects, for whom periodic state redistribution provided an economic cushion allowing them to engage in other periodic, seasonal, or speculative economic activities. State redistribution was better documented and enforced over long distances than private redistribution or exchanges. The central administration enforced long-distance transactions or property transfers if they were part of the royal revenue system, but the local judicial administrations could not enforce long-distance transactions or property transfers at all. Consequently, economic actors who wished to engage in high value long-distance transactions were encouraged to act within the state redistributive networks to reduce their exposure to risks, while low value local transactions dominated private redistributive networks and exchanges.

Granaries and Treasuries: The royal granaries and treasuries were primarily concerned with the collection and storage of revenues. From the middle of the Fifth Dynasty, the granary and the treasury were two of the five departments into which the central administration was formally divided, along with the great court, the scribes of royal documents, and works. The vizier often held the titles "overseer of the double granary" and "overseer of the double treasury" to indicate that he was in charge of these two departments. However, these departments sometimes had their own overseers serving under the vizier, bearing the titles "overseer of the granary" and "overseer of the treasury" in the Fifth Dynasty, and then "overseer of the double granary" and "overseer of the double treasury" in the Sixth Dynasty.[79]

Very little is known about the organization of the state granary, however. One would expect it to be a central office managing a dispersed network of central and local granaries, rather than a central group of granaries alone, in order to minimize the distance that grain was transported for collection and disbursement.[80] The local granaries were probably features of the districts known as estates and towns.[81] In fact, the accounts of the royal mortuary temples at Abusir known as the Abusir Papyri mention deliveries of bread from estates via the Residence, and Posener-Kriéger has suggested that such deliveries arrived at the Residence in the form of grain, where they were baked into bread before being delivered to the nearby mortuary temples.[82] Granaries are only occasionally mentioned in the Abusir Papyri,[83] perhaps because deliveries of bread and beer were more common than deliveries of grain,[84] and perhaps because most deliveries to the mortuary temples came from a variety of other royal institutions such as the Residence, a royal palace, a sun temple, or other mortuary temples.[85] Such royal institutions may have mediated disbursements from state granaries, as they did in the New Kingdom. Indeed, in the Old Kingdom some offering formulae in private tombs specifically request "an offering that the king gives" (*ḥtp-di-nswt*) consisting of invocation offerings from the Residence, emmer wheat and barley from the double granary, and linen from the double treasuries.[86]

Even less is known about the state treasuries in the Old Kingdom than about the state granaries, except that the treasuries handled commodities such as incense, oil, unguents and perfumes, and especially types of cloth.[87] Cloth was however the most common medium of exchange in high value exchanges in the Old Kingdom, as noted previously. By analogy with the state granary, one might expect the state treasury to be a central office managing a dispersed network of central and local treasuries, the latter perhaps being features of the districts known as estates and towns. Papazian has suggested that the redistribution office (*pr-ḥry-wḏb*) and the provisioning office (*is-ḏfꜣ*) were subordinate departments of the treasury concerned with the redistribution of commodities.[88]

Royal Works: The department of royal works was concerned with royal building projects. The office of overseer of all royal works (*imy-r kꜣt nbt nt nzwt*) is attested from the beginning of the Fourth Dynasty. By the middle of the Fifth Dynasty, royal works became one of the five departments of the central administration under the supervision of the vizier, and the title overseer of all royal works could be held by both the vizier and a subordinate in charge of the department, while other subordinates held the title overseer of royal works (*imy-r kꜣt nt nzwt*).[89] Tomb biographies of the holders of these titles reveal that the department was in charge of constructing monumental buildings such as palaces, temples, and *ka*-chapels, as well as canals.[90] Vymazalova argues that the department also organized the construction of pyramids, which was a nearly continuous project since construction of king's pyramid usually began shortly after he ascended the throne, and not long after work on the previous king's pyramid ceased.[91]

The department presumably recruited labor and arranged for provisions and equipment for construction projects, but administrative records for such projects have not survived.[92] Exemption decrees for temples, mortuary temples, and *ka*-chapels indicate that their personnel could be compelled to provide compulsory labor and other work, but it is unknown to what extent such labor was used in long-term construction projects in the Memphite region, for example.[93] Inscriptions left by workmen, however, reveal that they were divided into crews, gangs, phyles, and divisions.[94] Already in the Fourth Dynasty, Egyptian work crews were apparently divided into pairs of gangs (*ꜥprw*). One pair of gangs left masons' marks on blocks on the north and south sides respectively of the relieving chambers of the Great Pyramid of Khufu, while another pair of gangs left masons' marks on blocks on the north and south sides respectively of the mortuary temple of the pyramid of Menkaure. The masons' marks in the mortuary temple of Menkaure also show that each of the two gangs was divided into four phyles (*zꜣw*), and that the phyles were each divided into at least four divisions. If these worked in rotation like phyles and divisions in Fifth Dynasty royal mortuary cults, it was a very different kind of rotation with at least two phyles from each gang at work at the same time.[95] In the Fifth Dynasty, limestone tablets found in the rubble core of the sun temple of Userkaf at Abusir mention no gangs, but suggest that there were five phyles each divided into at least two divisions, which may have worked in rotation one month in ten like those in Fifth Dynasty royal mortuary cults.[96]

The Residence and Other Royal Palaces: In the Old Kingdom, the Egyptians often referred to aspects of their central administration in the singular: the Residence, the granary, and the treasury. However, these were probably collective terms, referring to any number of actual physical palaces, granaries, and treasuries, many but not all of which may have been located in and around

Memphis.[97] The administrative archives of the Fifth Dynasty royal mortuary temples of Kings Neferirkare and Neferefre at Abusir refer to the Residence as an important source of redistributed revenues, though these are often routed through a specific royal palace or sun temple.[98] Indeed, the palace "Extolled is the beauty of Sahure" (*Wṯs-nfrw-S3ḥw-Rˁ*) is known from dockets excavated from the royal mortuary temple of King Neferefre at Abusir.[99] The implication is that the royal mortuary temples lay outside of the Residence, and probably the sun temples and some royal palaces as well. Thus not every royal institution in and around Memphis was considered part of the Residence.

Provincial Administrators: By the Third Dynasty at the latest, a system of administration began to develop at the level of the Egyptian provinces known as nomes, to mediate between the central administration and local tax districts and production centers. Some have suggested that this provincial administration developed out of the estate administration and was superimposed on top of it, because at least one early estate has the same name as a later province or nome.[100] Others suggest that the provincial administration developed out of and alongside early royal institutions, because some of the earliest provincial governors held the same titles as domain administrators (*ˁḏ-mr*) in the Early Dynastic Period, but qualified by the name of a nome rather than a domain.[101] Still others argue that the provincial administration developed as the kings shared their authority with provincial elites, in return for their recognition of and cooperation with that authority.[102]

In the Third and Fourth Dynasties, the titles and duties of these provincial administrators had not yet been standardized. In Upper Egypt they bore the titles chief of the great estate (*ḥḳ3 ḥwt-ˁ3t*), overseer of missions (*imy-r wpwt*), and guide of the land (*sšm-t3*), while in Lower Egypt they bore the titles domain administrator (*ˁḏ-mr*) or chief of the great estate (*ḥḳ3 ḥwt-ˁ3t*). Many of these provincial administrators built tombs in the royal cemeteries around Memphis, which could imply that they spent parts of their careers at the court, or simply that they chose to be buried near the king.[103] In the Fifth Dynasty, increasing numbers of provincial administrators built tombs in the nomes that they administered. They continued to bear the same titles that they had in the Third and Fourth Dynasties, but in addition they also began to bear a new series of titles indicating new responsibilities, such as overseer of new towns (*imy-r niwwt m3wt*), overseer of fortresses (*imy-r mnnw*), and overseer of royal tenants (*imy-r niswtyw*).[104] In the Sixth Dynasty, most provincial administrators built tombs in the nomes that they administered, and the state began to standardize their duties and titles. Provincial governors in Upper Egypt bore the titles great chief (*ḥry-tp ˁ3*), overseer of Upper Egypt (*imy-r Šmˁ*), and overseer of *ḥm-nṯr*-priests (*imy-r ḥmw-nṯrw*).[105] The last title may refer to the priests of the *ka*-chapels that kings, royal family members, and royal officials began to establish in the nomes in the Sixth Dynasty, often in association with divine cults.[106]

Provincial administrators had access to and made increasing use of royal revenues to carry out their diversifying duties, and consequently their residences became local redistribution centers like the royal palaces and Residence at Memphis. One such provincial palace at Balat in the Dakhla Oasis was the residence of the ruler of the oasis (*ḥḳꜣ wḥꜣt*), who seems to have been equivalent to a provincial governor. Its archives of early hieratic texts inscribed on clay tablets were preserved when the palace burned and they were baked at the end of the reign of Pepi II. The archives largely consist of letter orders for disbursement of commodities to laborers, and inventories recording account balances. These would have been supplemented with verbal orders, and by sealings made when storerooms were opened and closed, which could have been used to cross-check the orders and inventories. Few of the texts explicitly mention the royal granary and the treasury, but the many storerooms in the palace probably functioned as local branches.[107]

Royal Mortuary Temples: In the Old Kingdom, the amount of funerary offerings deposited in and around the royal tomb declined rapidly after the Third Dynasty, and the corresponding growth of royal mortuary temples after the Third Dynasty suggests that many funerary offerings may have been redirected to the ongoing royal mortuary cults. Each royal mortuary temple was probably assigned revenues from a number of estates and towns. Personifications of these estates and towns were probably depicted in most royal mortuary temples, and have survived in those of Sneferu, Khufu, Userkaf, Sahure, Niuserre, Djedkare, Unas, and Pepi II.[108]

Papyri from the administrative archives of the Fifth Dynasty royal mortuary temples of Kings Neferirkare and Neferefre at Abusir reveal how the royal mortuary cults received the revenues from the estates and towns. The papyri from the mortuary cult of Neferirkare were discovered during illicit excavations in the 1890s, while those from the mortuary cult of Neferefre were discovered during scientific excavations in the 1980s.[109] Many of the papyri were monthly account-tables of regular temple revenues, and records of additional deliveries for festivals, which usually indicated the provenance of the revenues.[110] The revenues usually did not arrive directly at the royal mortuary temples from the estates and towns, but rather came by way of a variety of other royal institutions, such as the royal Residence, a royal palace at Abusir, a sun temple at Abusir, other royal mortuary temples, and occasionally even from divine temples such as the temple of Ptah.[111] Many of these revenues were apparently converted from raw materials like grain, cattle, and fowl into finished products like bread, beer, and meat portions at these royal institutions before being delivered to the royal mortuary temples, though the mortuary temples had some production facilities of their own.[112]

The papyri also reveal how the royal mortuary cults distributed their revenues from the estates and towns. Many of the papyri were monthly account-tables of regular ration distributions of bread, beer, and meat to temple personnel, or records of irregular distributions.[113] Distributions of cloth were accounted separately from rations of bread, beer, and meat.[114] There were also monthly rosters indicating the posts that the groups of personnel on duty were to guard each night,[115] and monthly inventories of temple equipment made when new groups of personnel came on duty.[116] The papyri indicate that the temple personnel were divided into five phyles (*wr*, *śṯ*, *w3ḏt*, *nḏś*, and *imy-nfrt*), which were each subdivided into two divisions. Each division performed the cult and received the cult offerings for one month once every ten months.[117] In the mortuary cult of Neferirkare each division consisted of about twenty men and one headman, so that the temple personnel consisted of about 220 men, while the mortuary cult of Neferefre was less than half that size.[118]

The temple personnel included *ḥm-nṯr*-priests, *wᶜb*-priests, lector priests (*ẖry-ḥbt*), *ẖnty-š*-farmers, and *ẖt*-servants, among others, who performed different aspects of the cult, and received different shares of the offering. The ten divisions consisted of *ḥm-nṯr*-priests and *ḏnty-š*-farmers and were headed by an inspector of *ḥm-nṯr*-priests (*śḥḏ ḥmw-nṯr*). The higher-ranking *ḥm-nṯr*-priests sometimes sent their *ḏt*-servants to perform their tasks, or delegated them to a *ẖnty-š*-farmer. The title *ḥm-nṯr*-priest frequently alternates with the title *wᶜb*-priest. One or more lector priests were permanently assigned to each pyramid temple to recite rituals during the daily services and monthly festivals. Aside from the lector priests, all these personnel only served one month in ten, and thus they were able to serve in multiple mortuary cults, or to engage in other economic activities. Officials at the royal court frequently also served as *ḥm-nṯr*-priests.[119]

Ka-chapels: The Third and Fourth Dynasties may have founded and administered cults of the royal *ka* in the countryside at small step pyramids scattered around Egypt. The later Fourth and Fifth Dynasties made no such foundations, but it has been suggested that the Fifth Dynasty sun temples played a similar role through association of the cult of the royal *ka* with the solar cult.[120] The Sixth Dynasty established both royal and nonroyal *ka*-chapels in the provinces, but associated them with the cults of local divinities, perhaps to integrate the latter into the royal economy.[121] Pepi I and Teti both established *ka*-chapels in Bubastis, associated with the cult of the goddess Bast.[122] Pepi I also established a *ka*-chapel for the royal mother Iput in Coptos, probably associated with the cult of the god Min,[123] and Pepi II ordered the establishment of *ka*-chapels for the governors of Dakhla Oasis at their palace in Balat (Ayn

Asil).[124] The Eighth Dynasty King Neferkauhor ordered the establishment of a *ka*-chapel for the vizier Shemai in Coptos,[125] and a successor of Neferkauhor, the Horus Demedjibtawy, mentions a *ka*-chapel of Shemai's son the vizier Idi in Coptos.[126] These *ka*-chapels may have been an attempt to extend the system of royal institutions from the area around Memphis into the provinces, and in some cases to integrate local temples into that system. The *ka*-chapels and their associated temples may have been assigned revenues from estates and towns, much like other royal institutions such as royal mortuary temples and sun temples. Indeed, kings made "exemption decrees" for some of these *ka*-chapels and temples,[127] just as they did for royal mortuary temples.[128]

Sun Temples: Sun temples appeared in the Fifth Dynasty and disappeared thereafter. Two sun temples are known archaeologically at Abusir, namely *Nḫn-Rᶜ* of Userkaf and *Sšp-ib-Rᶜ* of Niuserre. Texts however mention four more sun temples, namely *Sḫt-Rᶜ* of Sahure, *St-ib-Rᶜ* of Neferirkare, *Ḥtp-Rᶜ* of Neferefre, and *ꜣḫt-Rᶜ* of Menkauhor.[129] Each sun temple was probably assigned revenues from a number of estates and towns, much like the royal mortuary temples. References to such estates and towns have survived in the fragmentary foundation inscriptions of the sun temple of Niuserre.[130] The administrative archives of the royal mortuary temples of Neferirkare and Neferefre both mention the sun temple of *St-ib-Rᶜ* of Neferirkare as a source of revenues.[131] These revenues arrived at the sun temple in the form of grain, cattle, and fowl, and were transformed there into bread, beer, and meat portions before being sent to the royal mortuary temples.[132]

Private Funerary Establishments: From the beginning of Egyptian history, Egyptian funerary practices included both the deposition of funerary offerings at the time of burial in the tomb alongside the deceased and subsequent regular funerary offerings to the deceased in or in front of a tomb-chapel attached to the tomb. In the course of the Old Kingdom, however, royal and private funerary practices both placed increasing emphasis on expanding and perpetuating the postburial regular funerary offerings. Royalty could do this on a large scale by dedicating revenues from various estates and towns to provision the royal mortuary cults, because such revenues were securely documented and enforced by the central administration. Private individuals could also dedicate revenues from their private properties to provision their funerary establishments (*pr-ḏt*), as in the inscription of Metjen,[133] the inscription of Penmeru,[134] and the inscription of Tjenti.[135] The size and durability of funerary establishments composed of private properties was probably limited, however, because private property transfers were only documented and enforced locally. Consequently, among the surviving documentation the most commonly attested and presumably most effective solution was for high officials to obtain a perpetual endowment of royal revenues from various estates and towns as a grant of royal favor, literally "an offering which the king gives" (*ḥtp-di-nswt*). Indeed, endowments of royal revenues supplemented revenues from private properties in two of the three examples of private endowments cited earlier, those of Penmeru and Tjenti. Beneficiaries of such royal grants sometimes depicted the estates and towns in their tomb-chapels personified as offering bearers, just as kings did in their royal mortuary temples.[136] Whatever the source of revenues, the funerary offerings that they generated usually reverted to the mortuary priests who performed the offerings, and thus constituted a private redistributive network. In the case of a few very high-ranking men and women buried at Giza, Abusir, and Saqqara, the mortuary priests were organized into five phyles each with two divisions, each of which served once every ten months, much like the royal mortuary cults of Neferirkare and Neferefre at Abusir. Over half of the male beneficiaries were viziers, some of whom married king's daughters, and all of the female beneficiaries were royal wives, suggesting that these private mortuary cults consciously emulated the royal mortuary cults. In most cases, however, the mortuary cult probably consisted of a single mortuary priest and his descendants.[137]

EXCHANGES

In the Old Kingdom, there is limited evidence for both high and low value exchanges. High value exchanges of land, houses, and prebends were more likely to be documented than low value exchanges, but the range of uses of written documentation was restricted, so that many high value exchanges were probably documented only with witnesses, and consequently no written records of them have survived. Most of the surviving written records concern private local exchanges, no doubt because of the dependence on local witnesses for documentation and enforcement. Exchange partners probably found each other through social networks rather than anonymous markets, because the exchanges involved real estate and prebends. Economic actors may, therefore, have preferred to distribute and receive high value properties through state redistributive networks, especially over long distances, because many such transactions were documented in writing and were enforced by the state. Also, if the central administration only documented community tax obligations, then the tax obligations of individual properties may not have been well defined, further discouraging investment in private property.

There is somewhat more evidence for exchanges involving low value goods, such as fish, fruit, vegetables, clothing, and furniture. Low value exchanges were probably extremely common, but given the limited use of written documentation in the Old Kingdom, one would not expect to find it used for such transactions. In fact, most of the evidence for low value exchanges comes from representations of marketplaces in tombs and temples, rather than from direct written documentation of specific transactions. The hieroglyphic captions accompanying these scenes suggest anonymous markets, but it is not clear whether the participants were private individuals or institutional agents or a mixture of the two, nor whether the markets were local or regional. There is some evidence that they were policed, however.

Land: In the Old Kingdom, there are a few references to the purchase, sale, and inheritance of agricultural land, such as the purchase of 200 arourae of fields to establish a funerary foundation in the inscription of Metjen,[138] and the sale of a funerary chapel in exchange for one-thirtieth of an aroura of fields on Block Saqqara RM 22.11.1956.[139] Menu has suggested that these references actually refer to the purchase and inheritance of revenues from land, and that there was no truly private agricultural land in the Old Kingdom.[140] In this study, however, the ability to purchase, sell, or inherit revenue from a specific plot of agricultural land is treated as effectively private ownership of that land. It is also possible that some settlements engaged in semicommunal farming, in which settlements held their agrarian land collectively and redistributed it among its cultivators each year after the Nile flood, according to the quality of the land and the influence of the cultivators. Such semicommunal farming is attested in Egypt in the nineteenth century CE, and has been attributed to royal or public land in Egypt in the Ptolemaic and Roman Periods.[141] If it also occurred in the Old Kingdom, it would help account for the emphasis on taxing estates and towns rather than specific properties.

Houses: In the Old Kingdom, there are clear examples of the sale and inheritance of houses and tomb-chapels.[142] House sales include Stela Cairo JdE 42787[143] and Papyri Gebelein I verso B and VI.[144] Sales of tomb-chapels, or parts thereof, include the Block Saqqara RM 22.11.1956[145] and the inscription of Khenemti on Doorlintel Cairo CG 1634.[146] The inscription of Wepemnofret from his tomb at Giza provides evidence for the inheritance of part of a tomb.[147]

Prebends: Priestly positions took two forms, appointments in temples to the gods and deceased kings and appointments in private mortuary cults. Both forms of positions and the revenues therefrom were intended to be perpetual and inherited. The Inscriptions of Nika'ankh suggest that he arranged for his children to inherit shares of his position as priest of Hathor mistress of *Ra-int* and shares of his appointment as mortuary priest to Khenuka. However, he also appointed mortuary priests for his own mortuary cult, and he expected the children of his mortuary priests to inherit their appointments.[148]

Marketplaces: Some Old Kingdom tomb-chapels contain market scenes, which provide evidence of exchanges in marketplaces. Market scenes are attested in several Old Kingdom mastabas at Saqqara, as well as the Causeway of Unas.[149] The mastabas with market scenes include those of Ti, reign of Niuserre;[150]

Niankhkhnum and Khnumhotep, reign of Niuserre;[151] Djadjaemankh / Tepemankh, late Fifth Dynasty or early Sixth Dynasty;[152] the vizier Kagemni, reign of Teti;[153] and the vizier Ankhmahor, reign of Teti.[154] These market scenes depict both perishable commodities such as fish, fruit and vegetables, and imperishable goods,[155] which could suggest that they represent local markets.

ENTREPRENEURIAL ACTIVITIES

Redistributive networks and exchanges primarily describe systems of acquiring and distributing goods and services. In both systems, however, economic actors may choose to use existing goods and services to acquire new raw materials or to produce new goods, rather than simply redistributing or exchanging them. In the Old Kingdom, state entrepreneurial activities could take the form of expeditions beyond the populated areas under Egyptian control. The king and his agents were probably the only economic actors that could organize large expeditions and could afford to take large risks, and if they were successful they were better able to protect their newly acquired goods and resources than other economic actors due to the privileged status of royal revenues in the legal administration. State entrepreneurial activities also included founding new institutions within the populated areas under Egyptian control. Again the king and his agents were the only economic actors who could do so, because it involved reallocating state revenues.

Expeditions: During the Old Kingdom, the king often dispatched expeditions outside of the Nile Valley, by sea, by river, or overland. Sometimes officials from the central administration, such as the vizier, organized and led these expeditions on behalf of the king, and sometimes, especially in the Sixth Dynasty, provincial officials such as nomarchs did so. These expeditions were described in semimilitary terms, and sometimes they did engage in military conquest and pillage. Weni, who served in the central administration, described in his autobiography (lines 13–32) how he organized one such expedition against the Asiatics and Sand-dwellers and brought back great numbers of troops as captives. However, expeditions could also engage in activities such as quarrying stone, mining and smelting ore, or harvesting timber. Weni described in his autobiography how he quarried a sarcophagus in Ibhat (lines 37–38), a granite false door and lintel in Elephantine (lines 39–42), and an alabaster offering-table from Hatnub (lines 42–45), and harvested timber for barges in Nubia (lines 45–47).[156] Furthermore, expeditions sometimes engaged in trade by exchanging goods with foreign rulers. The expeditions then brought these goods and resources back to the Nile Valley, where they entered the Egyptian economy.[157] The king probably redistributed many of these goods and resources, but some could have been exchanged. Expeditions therefore represent a form of economic activity that could partake either of redistribution or exchange.

Expeditions to Nubia, to the south of Egypt, are well attested. The fragmentary royal annals on the Palermo Stone record an expedition to Nubia in the reign of Sneferu that brought back 7,000 captives and 200,000 small cattle.[158] Old Kingdom expeditions to Nubia are primarily known, however, from the tomb autobiographies of the provincial governors at Elephantine on the southern border of Egypt, who often conducted the expeditions for the king. For example, Pepynakht called Heqaib, who was a nomarch at Elephantine, described in his autobiography how he organized an expedition to Nubia and brought back prisoners and livestock.

Autobiography of Pepynakht called Heqaib, lines 4–9 (after Strudwick, pp. 334–335):[159]

The majesty of my lord sent me to devastate the land of Wawat and Irtjet. I did (5) what pleases my lord and killed a great number there, including the ruler's children and the commander of the excellent Nubian force. I brought a (6) great number of them to the Residence as prisoners, I being at the head of the expedition, a large and strong force, as one who is strong of heart, and my lord was delighted (7) with me, as (he was) with every mission on which he sent me.

The majesty of my lord sent me to subdue those foreign lands, (8) and I did it in such a way that my lord was immensely pleased with me. I brought to the Residence the two subdued chiefs of these foreign lands along with gifts of (9) live oxen and goats chosen for the benefit of the Residence, as well as their children and the two commanders of the Nubian forces which were with them.

Another nomarch of Elephantine, Sabni, possibly a son of Pepynakht called Heqaib, described how he harvested timber in Nubia to build barges to transport obelisks.

Autobiography of Sabni, lines 1–3 (after Strudwick, p. 339):[160]

The majesty of my lord sent me to construct two great barges (2) in Wawat so as to ship two great obelisks north to Heliopolis. I set out for Wawat with troops of five solders. The foreigners whom I had engaged were on the west and east of Wawat in order to bring back my troop of soldiers (3) successfully. I never permitted that the sandal or bread of any man be stolen. I constructed these two barges so that the majesty of my lord favored me for it.

Yet another nomarch of Elephantine, Harkhuf, described in his autobiography how he traded with the rulers of Nubia to bring back "tribute."

Autobiography of Harkhuf, lines R4-L9 (after Strudwick, pp. 330–331):[161]

The majesty of Merenre, my lord, sent me together with my father, the sole companion, lector priest, Iri, to Iam to open up the way to this

> foreign land. (R5) I made the trip in seven months, and I brought back all sorts of perfect and luxury items of tribute therefrom, I was favored very highly for it.
>
> His majesty sent me a second time, (6) only this time on my own. I took the Elephant road, and went out via Irtjet, Mekher, Tereres and Iertjetj in the space of eight months. I returned (7) having brought great amounts of tribute from these foreign lands, (8) the likes of which had never before been brought back to the land. I returned in the region of the house of the ruler of the lands of Setjau and Irtjet, (9) after having explored those foreign lands. I have not discovered that this was done by any companion and overseer of foreigners who went previously to Iam.
>
> (10) His majesty sent me a third time to Iam. (11) I went out from the Thinite nome upon the oasis road, and I found the ruler of Iam (12) had gone away to the land of the Tjemehu to drive them off (13) to the western corner of the sky. I followed him to the land of the Tjemehu. (14) I satisfied him just so that he might praise all the gods for the sovereign. (L1) [Then I sent off an official with a man of] Iam to the retinue of Horus to let the majesty of Merenre, my lord, know (2) that [I had gone to the land of the Tjemehu] in pursuit of the ruler of Iam. When I had satisfied the ruler of Iam, (3) [I came down through ...] south of Irtjet and north of Setjau, and I found the ruler (4) who had united Irtjet, Setjau and Wawat; with three hundred donkeys loaded with incense, ebony, *hekenu*-oil, *shesat*, (5) panther skins, elephant tusks, throw sticks, and all sorts of wonderful products did I travel. When the ruler of Irtjret, Setjau and (6) Wawat saw the strength and the number of the troop-contingent of Iam which was coming with me to the Residence, as well as (my own) expedition which was travelling with me, (7) this ruler then accompanied me, gave me cattle and goats, and led me on the hill-paths of Irtjet, due to the excellent manner in which I (8) had exercised vigilance, more so than any companion or overseer of foreigners who had previously been sent to Iam. Now when this servant had travelled north to the Residence, (9) the count, sole companion, overseer of the two cool rooms, Khuni was sent to greet me with ships laden with date-wine, cakes, bread and beer.

Expeditions to the Levant, to the northeast of Egypt, are poorly attested. An official named Khnumhotep mentioned in his autobiography in his tomb at Elephantine that he traveled to both Byblos and Punt,[162] presumably with maritime expeditions. Byblos and the Lebanon were the source of the pine and cedar wood used for the construction of large ships in Egypt.[163] Evidence for expeditions to the southern Levant is ambiguous: the location of the expedition against the Asiatics and Sand-dwellers described by Weni in his autobiography (lines 13–32) is uncertain, and could refer to the Sinai.[164]

Expeditions to the deserts east of Egypt, and to the Sinai Peninsula and Punt, are well known. Inscriptions and graffiti commemorate expeditions to

Hatnub located east of Amarna to quarry Egyptian alabaster, more properly called travertine, from the reign of Khufu in the Fourth Dynasty through that of Pepi II at the end of the Sixth Dynasty.[165] As previously mentioned, Weni described quarrying an alabaster offering-table from Hatnub in his autobiography (lines 42–45).[166] Expeditions to the Wadi Hammamat for greywacke are also attested.[167] At the beginning of the Fourth Dynasty in the reign of Sneferu, maritime expeditions began to depart from the Gulf of Suez port of Wadi al-Jarf located to the southeast Memphis.[168] This has been linked to mentions of shipbuilding in the reign of Sneferu in the fragmentary annals on the Palermo Stone.[169] Later in the Fourth and in the Fifth Dynasty, maritime expeditions also began to depart from the Gulf of Suez port of Ayn Soukhna, located due east of Memphis.[170] Ships were built in the Nile Valley, and were disassembled and carried to the ports where they were reassembled. Both sites contained rock-cut galleries where the disassembled ships were stored between expeditions. Some expeditions sailed east, landed on the El-Markha Plain opposite Wadi al-Jarf, and headed inland to the Wadi Maghara.[171] Other expeditions sailed south to Punt. The fragmentary royal annals on the Palermo Stone record an expedition to Punt in the last year of King Sahure's reign, which brought back electrum and malachite.[172] The return of this expedition is also depicted in the reliefs on the causeway of Sahure's mortuary complex, which show Sahure celebrating the bringing of frankincense (*ᶜnd*) trees.[173]

Expeditions to the deserts west of Egypt are poorly known. The fragmentary royal annals on the Palermo Stone record an expedition to Libya in the reign of Sneferu that brought back 1,100 captives and 23,000 small cattle.[174] Furthermore, donkey caravans appear to have been dispatched regularly from Balat in the Dakhla Oasis southwest along the Abu Ballas trail to the Gilf Kebir mountains. At several sites along the trail, caches of storage jars made in Balat were installed to hold water and grain for the donkey caravans,[175] and graffiti depicting water bags filled with the hieroglyphic signs for water marked the way.[176] The provincial governors at Balat presumably arranged for the jars to be cached, for them to be filled with water and grain ahead of the donkey caravans, and for the caravans themselves, much as the provincial governors at Elephantine organized and carried out many expeditions into Nubia. Indeed, the donkey caravan leaders probably engaged in trade much like the donkey caravans described in Harkhuf's autobiography.

During the First Intermediate Period, weakness and fragmentation of the state curtailed expeditions abroad and encouraged internal expeditions by fragments of the state against each other. The Seventh and Eighth Dynasties undertook only minor expeditions to the Wadi Hammamat in the Eastern Desert.[177] Under the Ninth and Tenth Dynasties, the governors of the fifteenth

Upper Egyptian province at Hermopolis sent expeditions to Hatnub in the Eastern Desert to quarry travertine, commemorated by inscriptions and graffiti,[178] while the tomb autobiographies of the governors of the thirteenth Upper Egyptian province at Assiut indicate that they fought against the provincial governors and kings farther to the south.[179] The tomb autobiography of Ankhtifi, the governor of the third Upper Egyptian province at Hierkonpolis, records that he took control of the second Upper Egyptian province at Edfu, that he controlled the first Upper Egyptian province at Ombos and Elephantine, and that he repelled attacks from the fourth and fifth Upper Egyptian provinces at Thebes and Coptos.[180] A stela at Gebel Tjauti states that the governor of the fifth Upper Egyptian province at Coptos opened the desert road after fighting the ruler of another province who had sealed the door to the desert.[181]

Foundations: During the Old Kingdom, kings established and endowed their mortuary complexes and cults at many sites in Egypt in the vicinity of the royal Residence at Memphis, such as Djoser and Sekhemkhet at Saqqara in the Third Dynasty;[182] Sneferu at Meidum and Dahshur, Khufu at Giza, Djedefre at Abu Roash north of Giza, Khaefre and Menkaure at Giza, and Shepseskaf at South Saqqara in the Fourth Dynasty;[183] Userkaf at Saqqara, Sahure, Neferirkare, Neferefre and Niuserre at Abusir, Djedkare at South Saqqara, and Unas at Saqqara in the Fifth Dynasty;[184] and Teti at Saqqara, and Pepi I, Merenre and Pepi II at South Saqqara in the Sixth Dynasty.[185] Most of these mortuary complexes included pyramids, whose construction consumed vast quantities of labor and material. However, their mortuary cults supported large numbers of personnel in rotation, who were able to engage in other economic activities when not on duty, even if those activities frequently consisted of participation in other royal mortuary cults or the private funerary cults of high officials, given the high concentration of such cults in the Memphite region. The kings of the Fifth Dynasty also established and endowed at least six sun temples at Abusir, which presumably also supported significant numbers of personnel.[186]

Outside of the Memphite region, the kings of the Third and Fourth Dynasties may have founded cults of the royal *ka* at small step pyramids scattered around Egypt, and the kings of the Sixth Dynasty certainly established and endowed both royal and nonroyal *ka*-chapels in the provinces, often associated with cults of local divinities.[187] The kings of the Sixth Dynasty also established governorates in the provinces, which may have managed provincial *ka*-cults, and certainly organized entrepreneurial expeditions on behalf of the kings. The governorates also supported personnel who were able to engage in other economic activities, stimulating economic specialization in provincial capitals characteristic of urban centers.

During the First Intermediate Period, weakness and fragmentation of the state limited internal foundations. The Seventh and Eighth Dynasties undertook only minor foundations such as the mortuary complex of King Qakare Ibi at South Saqqara,[188] and the Ninth and Tenth Dynasties left no known foundations. The governors of the fourth Upper Egyptian province at Thebes and later kings of the Eleventh Dynasty established mortuary complexes at Thebes,[189] and rebuilt temples throughout Upper Egypt as they gradually reunited Egypt.

Private Entrepreneurial Activities: Many private households throughout Egypt probably engaged in private entrepreneurial activities on a small scale, such as using agricultural slack times to produce handicrafts for exchange in local markets. Despite its small scale, however, this activity probably accounted for a considerable proportion of all Old Kingdom entrepreneurial activity, due to the numbers of households involved. However, there is virtually no written evidence for this activity, aside from a few market scenes depicted in Old Kingdom tombs.

CONCLUSIONS

In the Old Kingdom and the First Intermediate Period, the state judicial administration directly prosecuted crimes against the state such as interference with revenues and redistribution, but it allowed local courts and authorities to adjudicate property transfer disputes. This differential enforcement was the result of differential documentation. The state promoted the use of writing to document and enforce collection and redistribution of state revenues, presumably because the increased efficiency of extraction offset the costs of training and supporting the necessary scribes. Even so, the state only documented the collective labor and harvest tax obligations of districts known as estates and towns, probably because the state still lacked the scribal infrastructure to document labor obligations for individual people, and harvest taxes for individual plots of land. The state did not support written documentation of private property transfers, however, because it did not tax individual people and properties, and thus it had no way to recover the costs of documenting transfers of them. Individual ownership and transfers of land and property were primarily documented orally with local witnesses, and only rarely transcribed in writing.

The nature of the state documentation of revenues shaped state redistribution, even as the lack of state documentation of property transfers limited exchanges. The state frequently rewarded officials with redistributed state tax revenues to establish mortuary cults as a reward for service, but it rarely rewarded them with plots of land, which is not surprising because the state did not document them. The recipients of these redistributed state revenues were concentrated around the royal residence at Memphis, with its numerous palaces and private and royal funerary foundations, and in the provincial administrative centers. Only a very few higher value exchanges are known, involving land and houses, probably because such exchanges were much less secure than royal donations of revenue. At least some low value exchanges took place in markets, because they are depicted in tomb scenes. Indeed, such transactions may have been common, but most would have been documented orally, if at all.

THREE

THE MIDDLE KINGDOM AND THE SECOND INTERMEDIATE PERIOD (c. 2025–1550 BCE)

The Middle Kingdom (c. 2025–1773 BCE) was established when the kings of the later Eleventh Dynasty reunited Egypt under their rule. The Eleventh Dynasty continued to rule from Thebes, and built their tombs there as well, surrounded by those of their high officials. The Twelfth Dynasty rapidly succeeded the Eleventh Dynasty, and moved their residence from Thebes to Itjtawy near El-Lisht. The kings of the Twelfth Dynasty built their tombs at El-Lisht, Dahshur, El-Lahun, Hawara, as well as Abydos, and some of their high officials built their tombs alongside those of their kings. Provincial governors initially continued to represent the kings in the provinces and to build tombs there, but were later replaced by mayors.

The Second Intermediate Period (c. 1773–1550 BCE) began when the Twelfth Dynasty and the Middle Kingdom came to an end. The Thirteenth Dynasty initially ruled all of Egypt from Itjtawy and Thebes, but later lost control of the northeastern Delta. It was characterized by a large number of kings with very short reigns.[1] The Fourteenth Dynasty briefly ruled the northeastern Delta from Avaris at the same time as the later Thirtreenth Dynasty.[2] The Hyksos invaded northern Egypt from the Levant, ending the Fourteenth Dynasty and establishing the Fifteenth Dynasty that ruled Lower Egypt from Avaris.[3] The Kushites also invaded southern Egypt from Nubia, and together these invasions brought down the later Thirteenth Dynasty. It was replaced by the Sixteenth and Seventeenth Dynasties, which ruled Upper Egypt from

Thebes.[4] The Seventeenth Dynasty eventually conquered the Hyksos Fifteenth Dynasty and reunited Egypt, ending the Second Intermediate Period and beginning the New Kingdom. (See Map 3.1 and Table 3.1.)

The Middle Kingdom witnessed further diversification of uses of writing compared to the Old Kingdom. There are still narrative texts in the form of religious texts inscribed in tombs and on coffins (Coffin Texts), biographies inscribed in the tombs and on commemorative stelae of officials, letters, agreements, and court proceedings. However, these were now joined by the first literary texts, many of which were copied by scribes as part of their training.[5]

CRIMINAL JUSTICE AND PROPERTY DISPUTE RESOLUTION

The king, the vizier, and their local agents were responsible for adjudicating disputes involving state revenues as well as those arising from private property transactions. The head of the judicial administration was the king. In the late Middle Kingdom, petitions could be and were sent to the king, though in the surviving examples the king referred the petitions to the vizier. The surviving examples are Papyrus Brooklyn 35.1446, "Insertion B" and "Insertion C,"[6] two early Thirteenth Dynasty royal decrees to the vizier in Thebes ordering him to deal with two petitions submitted at the Residence, presumably Itjtawy. Upon arrival in Thebes, the two royal decrees were copied or "inserted" into blank spaces on an administrative papyrus kept in the office of giving people located in the office of the vizier. The contents of the petitions are fragmentary, but may concern compulsory labor.[7]

> **P. Brooklyn 35.1446 recto, Insertion B:**
>
> (1) Regnal year 5, third month of Peret, day 20+
>
> (2) Copy of a royal decree that was brought to the office of (3) the reporter of the Southern City.
>
> (4) Royal decree to the overseer of the city, the vizier, the overseer of the six great courts, (5) Ankhu:
>
> "Behold, one has brought to you this decree of the king (6) in order to cause that you know that (7) the elder of the portal, Yebiy'aw son of Remeny'ankhe, has petitioned (8) saying: '... has been done in ... (9) the servant ... from among the people (10) who committed a violation against the fugitive. Cause that I live, (11) my (lord),[8] by causing that one bring him to the Residence (12) and that one question him concerning the violation that he committed.' (13) So he said.
>
> Behold, it has been heard. (14) Cause that one bring him under guard to (15) the Residence. (16) Then shall you take action against him.
>
> (17) Behold, the king, may he live, prosper and be healthy, communicates."

MAP 3.1. Egypt in the Middle Kingdom and Second Intermediate Period

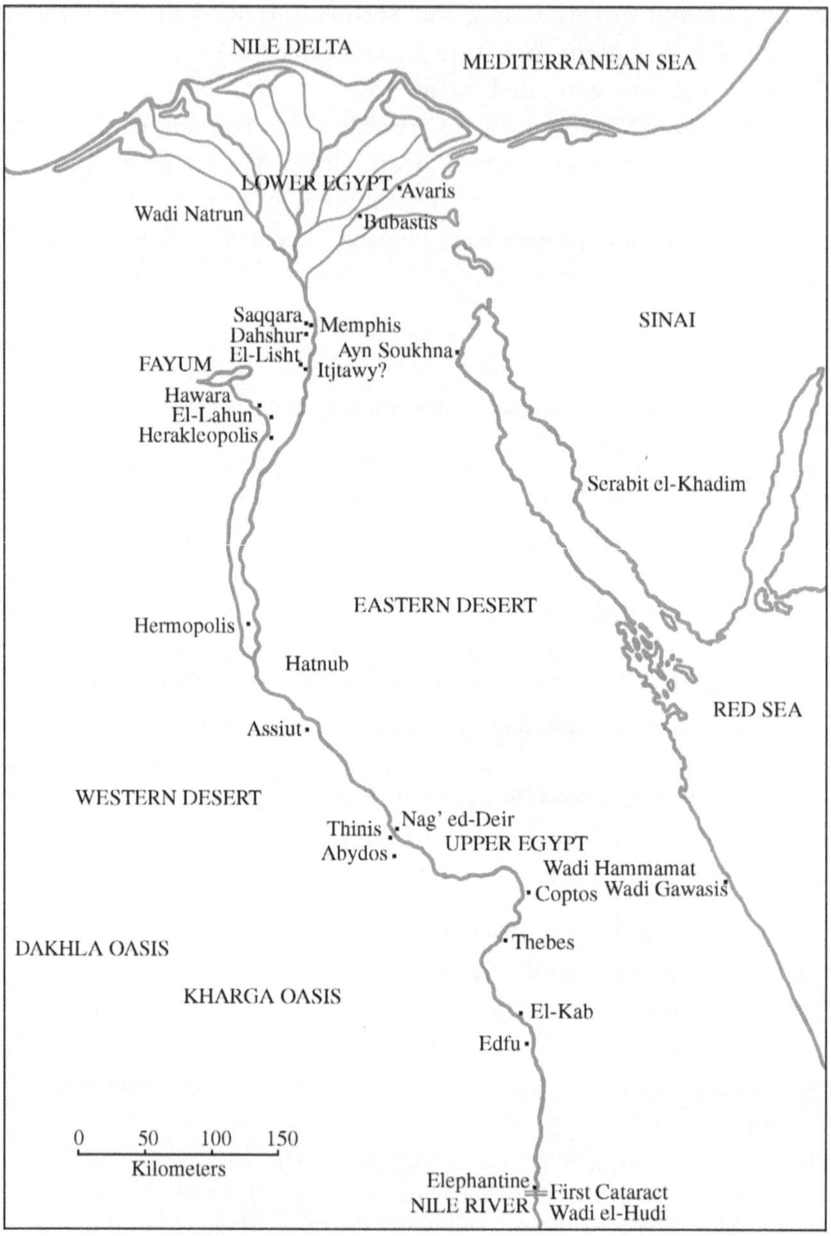

P. Brooklyn 35.1446 recto, Insertion C:

(1) Regnal year 6, third month of Peret, day 3

(2) Copy of another royal decree that was brought to the office of the reporter of the Southern City.

(3) Royal decree to the overseer of the city, the vizier, the overseer of the six great courts, Ankhu:

TABLE 3.1. *The Middle Kingdom and Second Intermediate Period*

The Middle Kingdom (c. 2025–1773 BCE)	
Dynasty 11, after unification (c. 2025–1985 BCE)	
Montuhotep II	
Mentuhotep III	
Mentuhotep IV	
Dynasty 12 (c. 1985–1773 BCE)	
Amenemhat I	
Senusert I	
Amenemhat II	
Senusert II	
Senusert III	
Amenemhat III	
Amenemhat IV	
Queen Sobekneferu	
The Second Intermediate Period (c. 1773–1550 BCE)	
Dynasty 13 (c. 1773–1650 BCE, Itjtawy and Thebes)	*Dynasty 14 (c. 1773–1650 BCE, Avaris)*
Sekhemre-Khutawy	Nehesy
Sekhemkare	
Ameny-Qemau	
Awibre Hor	
Khendjer	
Merhetepre	
Dynasty 15 (Hyksos, c. 1650–1550 BCE, Avaris)	*Dynasties 16 and 17 (c. 1650–1550 BCE, Thebes)*
Khyan	Nebirerau I
Apepi	Sobekemsaf I
Khamudi	Intef VI
	Intef VII
	Intef VIII
	Sobekemsaf II
	Senakhtenre Ahmose
	Seqenenre Tao
	Kamose

Source: Dates after Ian Shaw (ed.), *The Oxford History of Ancient Egypt* (Oxford: University Press, 2000), pp. 479–483.

"Behold, one has brought to you this decree of the king (4) to cause that you know that the treasurer of the king of Lower Egypt, the overseer of fields of the Southern City, [?Ha'ankhef?], son of Yebiya'u, has petitioned (5) saying: '... from the office of giving people of the Residence in the seizure? under the charge of? my estate-workers? (6) who were? given to me from the office of giving people. Cause that I live, my lord, by causing that one give (them) to me as replacements.'[9] So he said.

(7) Behold, what has been done has been heard. Behold the decrees pertaining thereto: Let him who is in the Residence come. Then you shall

cause a directive to be issued? concerning (8) the people thereof. Let him who is in the Southern City come. Then you shall act against him.

Behold, the king, may he live, prosper and be healthy, communicates with you likewise."

Although the king referred these petitions to the vizier, he probably could hear and decide cases himself, if he chose. In the Second Intermediate Period, the king issued a decree concerning a case of sacrilege that was recorded in the Coptos Stela of Intef VII.[10] There is no surviving evidence from the Middle Kingdom or the Second Intermediate Period that he could appoint officials to hear special cases, though he had that privilege in the Old and New Kingdoms.

In the Middle Kingdom, the vizier was ostensibly still in charge of the entire central administration under the king, but he shared considerable authority with the chancellor or treasurer (lit. overseer of sealed things, *imy-r ḫtmt*), and the chief steward (*imy-r pr wr*).[11] In the Second Intermediate Period, the vizier played a major role in the Thirteenth and Sixteenth Dynasties in Upper Egypt, whereas the chancellor or treasurer was prominent in the Fourteenth and Fifteenth Dynasties in the Delta.[12] In the Middle Kingdom, the central administration was divided into several sectors, including the palace, the treasury, the office of the vizier, and the military. The vizier and the office of the vizier dealt with judicial administration and documentation. The office of the vizier contained two departments, an office of fields and the office of giving people (also known as the great prison), which were concerned with documenting the two types of objects of taxation, namely agricultural lands and people.[13] The vizier himself was responsible for judicial administration, and to indicate this he bore the Old Kingdom title "overseer of the six great courts," even though the great court seems to have been abolished or subsumed within the office of the vizier. According to the "Duties of the Vizier," a New Kingdom text probably composed in the Middle Kingdom, the vizier was generally responsible for hearing petitions (lines 27–28).[14] The vizier was apparently assisted in these judicial tasks by the overseer of inquiries (*imy-r šn.t*),[15] and by a number of reporters (*wḥmw*) who represented him locally.[16]

Duties of the Vizier, lines 27–28:[17]

(27) ... It is he who makes every investigation (?).

It is he who hears every appeal (?), when a man goes to dispute with his second.

It is he who appoints anyone to be appointed (28) at the palace-gate (*ᶜryt*);

Anyone to be questioned comes to him in the royal house.

It is he who hears every decree.

It is he who hears cases of loss for every temple estate.

It is he who fixes all fixed dues as supplies for recipients.

Petitions could also be directed to local officials, who served as agents of the king or the vizier. Local courts of *sr*-magistrates were sometimes available to advise these officials. It is not clear if these courts were related to the *ḏꜣḏꜣt*-courts and *ḳnbt*-courts that are mentioned in Middle Kingdom sources.[18] In the Middle Kingdom literary text, "The Eloquent Peasant," which is set in the First Intermediate Period, a farmer on the estate of the chief steward Meru's son Rensi robbed a peasant while the latter was passing through the estate. The peasant, therefore, petitioned the chief steward for justice. The chief steward discussed the case with the *sr*-magistrates who were with him, and with the king, before responding to the petition.

In the *Stèle juridique de Karnak*, a petition is submitted to the office of a reporter, which is said to be in the office of the vizier, and the dispute is resolved there before the reporter. Stela Cairo JdE 52453 (*Stèle juridique de Karnak*) is a record of a dispute resolution from Thebes, dating to Year 1 of King Nebirerau I of the Sixteenth Dynasty.[19] The record cites a transfer document (*imy.t-pr*, lines 4–12) and an exchange document (*swnt*, lines 13–14), as well as the petition (*spr*, lines 16–18) and settlement (lines 19–22) that caused them to be drawn up. These texts were all inscribed in hieroglyphs on a stela that was erected in the temple of Karnak at Thebes. The stela thus represents an alternative method of documentation based on monumentality and publicity, supplementing the methods used in the documents it cites.

The petitioner Sobeknakht addresses the reporter (*wḥmw*) of the northern district Kamose, and complains that he has loaned 60 deben of gold to Kebsi, who has not repaid it. There is no mention that the loan was documented, suggesting that documentation was not a prerequisite for a hearing. The stela also records the mediation of the reporter (*wḥmw*) and the litigants in lines 19–22. Kebsi says that the gold has "perished" and cannot be repaid, but offers to transfer his office of mayor (*ḥꜣty-ꜥ*) of El-Kab to Sobeknakht as compensation. This case may have been somewhat irregular. Kebsi was the son of the vizier, the reporter in whose office the dispute was resolved was a subordinate of the vizier, and the vizier himself witnessed the documents that settled the dispute.

Stela Cairo JdE 52453 (*Stela juridique de Karnak*), lines 4–22:

[Transfer]

(4) Year 1, fourth month of Akhet, day 30 under the majesty of this god.

The transfer (*imyt-pr*) that was made by the officer of the ruler's crew (*ꜣtw n ṯt ḥḳꜣ*), Kebsi, for his kinsman the king's son, seal-bearer of the king of Lower Egypt, overseer of the temple, Sobeknakht: (5) "There is my office of mayor of El-Kab, that came to me as office of my father, the mayor of El-Kab, Iymeru [...] which reached my father out of the things of his maternal brother, the mayor of (6) El-Kab, Iy the younger, who died without children; it is for my kinsman, the king's son, overseer of the temple, Sobeknakht, from son to son, from heir to heir. One shall give him its bread, its beer, (7) its meat, its provisions, its *ka*-servants, its servants, its building, without allowing anybody to oppose himself against it, for he has given me its price: 60 *deben* gold in all kinds of things.

As for anyone who will go to make a petition to the *sr*-official or to the (vizier) who hears (8) the (king's) orders saying: 'this office comes to me,' one shall not listen to him; one shall give this office of mine to my kinsman, the king's son, overseer of the temple, Sobeknakht, from son to son, from heir to heir. One shall not listen (9) to anyone who makes a petition about it, for it is an office of my father: I have made its instructions for my kinsman, the king's son, overseer of the temple, Sobeknakht. If any son or daughter comes, any brother or sister, any relative of mine, saying: (10) 'this office comes to me,' one shall not listen to them; one shall give it to this brother of mine, the king's son, overseer of the temple, Sobeknakht."

This transfer (*imyt-pr*) was made in the presence of the overseer of the city, vizier, overseer of the six great courts, Sobeknakht, the dignitary, (11) Nebsumenu, and the *ḥm-nṯr*-priest of Horus of Nekhen, Sobeknakht, by the dignitary, Renseneb. If anyone attacks this transfer (*imyt-pr*) or if one delays to act according it: one shall not have it interfered with by anyone, ever.

Made by the office of the reporter (*wḥmw*) (12) of the Northern District. Said to the scribe of the prison (*ẖnrt*), Amenhotep, being the proxy of the scribe of the reporter (*wḥmw*) of the Northern District. Made for him in conformity with the law (*hp*), after his (Iy's) death, ... (13) . . .

[Exchange]

Year 1, fourth month of Akhet, day 30 under the majesty of this king.

Exchange (*swnt*) of the king's son, seal-bearer of the king of Lower Egypt, overseer of the temple, Sobeknakht with the officer of the ruler's crew, Kebsi, son of the vizier Iymeru.

(14) That which this king's son, seal-bearer of the king of Lower Egypt, overseer of the temple, Sobeknakht has given to this officer of the ruler's crew, Kebsi: 60 *deben* gold, in gold, bronze, grain and clothes.

[Petition]

(15) It has been found that a document (*snn*) was brought to the office of the reporter of the Northern District, in the office of the vizier, in Year 1 in the time of the "Protector of Egypt," life, prosperity, health (l.p.h.) This document (*snn*) is in the words of the *ḥm-nṯr*-priest of Horus of Nekhen, (16) Sobeknakht, and the officer of the ruler's crew, Kebsi. It was brought to the office of the reporter of the Northern District, in the office of the vizier, in Year 1 in the time of the "Protector of Egypt" l.p.h.

The petition (*spr*) says: "I have come (17) as representative of the king's son, overseer of the temple, Sobeknakht, in order to say: I have given 60 deben gold, in gold, bronze, clothes and grain belonging to me through assignment, to the officer of the ruler's crew, Kebsi: He has not given it back. I petition (*spr*) against him (that) (18) one exacts it from him for me." So he said.

One discussed it in the office of the reporter of the Northern District and placed it before the officer of the ruler's crew, Kebsi, who entered into it likewise, and said: "(These 60 *deben*) have perished in my hand."

[Adjudication]

(19) One addressed him (Kebsi), saying: "See you are as one who stands against the *ḥm-nṯr*-priest of Horus of Nekhen, Sobeknakht, as representative of the mayor of El-Kab".

This is what he (Kebsi) said: "I shall replace (these 60 *deben*) for him with my office of mayor of El-Kab, which reached me out of the things of my father, (20) the overseer of the city and vizier, Iymeru; which came to him out of the things of his maternal brother, Iy the younger, who died without children; which is the office that my father, the vizier, Iy, made for [me] by means of a transfer (*imyt-pr*) in Year 1, at the time of the king Merhetepre, justified."

One placed this (21) likewise before the *ḥm-nṯr*-priest of Horus of Nekhen, Sobeknakht, who is the representative of the mayor of El-Kab, Sobeknakht, and who was satisfied (*hr*) with it likewise. One caused that they swear upon it with an oath by the Lord, l.p.h., lest they go back on it, ever. (22) This oath was made in the presence of Kamose, the reporter of the Northern District, on this same day, and one registered? (*ꜣw.t-ꜥ*) it in the office of the vizier.

Private Social Control: In most societies, most individuals belong to a variety of social networks, consisting of family, friends, neighbors, colleagues, patrons, and clients. Individuals can often employ such social networks to enforce agreements and resolve disputes, in addition to state judicial administrations. Social networks may serve as alternatives to state judicial administration, but they may also use state adjudication to reinforce private social control.[20]

Most of the evidence from Middle Kingdom Egypt comes from state sources, but nonetheless there are some hints of private social control. In a Middle Kingdom literary text set in the First Intermediate Period, "The Eloquent Peasant," an individual named Nemtynakht robs a peasant who was on his way to market. The peasant petitions the Chief Steward Meru's son Rensi for redress, but the Chief Steward's *sr*-magistrates advise him not to hear the petition, saying:

The Eloquent Peasant, B1 lines 44–49 (Parkinson 75–80):

"Surely it is a peasant of his (i.e. of Nemtynakht) who has gone to someone else beside him. (45) That is what they do to peasants of theirs who go to others beside them. That is what they do. Should one punish this Nemtynakht for a trifle of natron and a trifle of salt? If he is ordered to replace it, he will replace it."

In other words, the magistrates suggest that Nemtynakht and the peasant are part of a local social network, and that the state should not intervene in their dispute. The peasant, however, ultimately persuades the chief steward that it is his duty to adjudicate.

DOCUMENTATION OF OBJECTS OF TAXATION

In the Middle Kingdom, there is clear and direct evidence that the central administration documented the objects of taxation in order to better enforce its revenue collection, in contrast to the indirect evidence for taxation from the Old Kingdom. The Middle Kingdom evidence for the documentation of objects of taxation includes field surveys, presumably to calculate harvest taxes, and censuses of people, presumably to calculate compulsory labor services. Furthermore, the Middle Kingdom evidence suggests that there was individual or household responsibility for taxes, rather than the collective community responsibility suggested by the Old Kingdom evidence.

In the short run, collective responsibility for taxes can be attractive for a state, because it reduces its management costs and risks. The state deals with a limited number of community representatives rather than a large number of individuals, thereby reducing its management costs. Furthermore, if some individuals fail to pay their share, then others in their communities must make up their shortfalls, thereby guaranteeing the state its revenues. However, collective responsibility can also discourage individuals from trying to increase their productivity, because they may just end up paying a larger share of their community's taxes, particularly if others slack off or "free ride." In the long run, this disincentive for growth can cost the state significant amounts of potential revenues. The ancient Egyptians seem to have come to this conclusion already by the Middle Kingdom.

Towns: In the Middle Kingdom, the Egyptian countryside continued to be organized at the local level into districts consisting of agricultural land and its cultivators, as it had been in the Old Kingdom. In the Old Kingdom, the names of the districts had two types of determinatives, categorizing them into estates (*ḥwwt*) and towns (*niwwt*). In the Middle Kingdom, however, the category of estate appears to have been abandoned, and the countryside may have been divided solely into towns with their hinterlands. This may have been the natural conclusion of the trend for kings in the later Old Kingdom to establish increasing numbers of towns and decreasing numbers of estates.[21] In the Middle Kingdom, estates (*ḥwwt*) are only mentioned in an archaizing literary text set in the First Intermediate Period, the Instructions for Merikare (lines P 106–109), in which the future king Merikare is instructed to establish estates in the Delta.[22]

Similarly, the title chief of an estate (*ḥḳꜣ ḥwt*) seems to have largely fallen out of use by the late Middle Kingdom.[23] It is used in an archaizing literary text, the Eloquent Peasant (lines B I 117–118, 220–221 and 223–224), but in one instance (line B I 220–221) the chief of an estate is said to rule a town (*niwt*).[24] The title chief of an estate also appears in the Instructions to the Vizier (lines R 9–13, R 21–22, R 24–25, and R 32), paired with the title mayor (*ḥꜣty-ꜥ*).[25] The Instructions to the Vizier survive only in New Kingdom copies, but may date to the late Middle Kingdom.[26] The title chief of an estate may thus have survived the disappearance of estates as a term for rulers of smaller villages and towns, in contrast to mayors (*ḥꜣtyw-ꜥ*).[27] Nomarchs frequently used the title mayor (*ḥꜣty-ꜥ*) as an indicator of rank in the late Old and early Middle Kingdoms, but after the disappearance of nomarchs in the late Middle Kingdom, the title came to designate the rulers of larger towns.[28]

Middle Kingdom towns were thus the administrative successors to Old Kingdom estates and towns, but they played rather different roles in the state redistributive networks. In the Old Kingdom, the estates and towns may have been collectively responsible for harvest taxes and compulsory labor, and their headmen may have been held responsible for their estates and towns. In the Middle Kingdom, however, individuals were held directly responsible for their harvest taxes and compulsory labor, through field surveys and censuses. Nonetheless, towns remained important nodes in the state redistributive networks, as the sites of institutions like royal palaces, royal mortuary temples, and temples of divinities, and the seats of provincial administrators like nomarchs and mayors.

Field Surveys: The evidence for field surveys includes the "Duties of the Vizier." The vizier was responsible for hearing petitions concerning fields (lines 17–19) and concerning field boundaries (line 20), and for registering the field boundaries and calculating their taxes (lines 26–27). The vizier apparently shared these responsibilities with the overseer of fields, the *ḏꜣḏꜣt*-court of the mat (*ṯmꜣ*), and the scribes of the mat (*ṯmꜣ*).

Duties of the Vizier, lines 17–19:[29]

(17) ... Now as for any messenger to whom the vizier sends concerning any petitioner, he should permit access to him.

Now as for anyone petitioning the vizier concerning fields, he is to order him to him, in addition to hearing by (18) the overseer of fields and the *ḏꜣḏꜣt*-court of the mat (*ṯmꜣ*).

He may apply a delay for it of two months for his fields in Upper or Lower Egypt, but for his fields which are adjacent to the Southern City [and the Residence], he is to apply a delay for it of three days in (19) accordance with the rule, and should hear any official in accordance with this rule which is with him.

Duties of the Vizier, line 20:[30]

(20) It is he who applies the neighboring-land for every plot of land.

As for any petitioner who would say "our boundaries have moved," then it is checked that they are under the seal of officials.

If it has happened, then he is to take the plot of the *ḏ3ḏ3t*-court that moved them.

Duties of the Vizier, lines 26–27:[31]

(26) ... It is he who dispatches the army of scribes of the mat (*ṯm3*)

to calculate the expenditure of the Lord.

District (*sp3t*) records are to be in his bureau for hearings on any fields.

It is he who makes the boundaries for every district, every marshland (?), every temple estate (?), every sealed land (?)

The evidence for field surveys also includes Papyrus Harageh 3, a late Middle Kingdom fragment of a daybook of a tax-assessor from the site of Harageh, east of El-Lahun.[32] The scribe labels his work as "assessing for him the dues (*ḫbi inw*) in the office of fields of the Northern District" (line 14), and "registering (*snhy*) in the office of the treasurer of the King and overseer of fields of the Northern District" (line 15). The scribe works with officials titled "scribes of the fields" (lines 2, 12, 16 and 18), "scribe of the mat" (line 17), "holder of the cord" (lines 6 and 21) and "stretcher of the cord" (lines 5 and 22). The cord was probably used to measure fields, because a few New Kingdom tomb-chapels have a scene showing a cord being stretched alongside a field, usually next to a scene showing the field being harvested.[33]

Individuals like Hekanakht probably held and cultivated some of these fields, and paid a harvest tax to the state. Officials cultivated other fields for the king, however, using compulsory labor. The Reisner Papyri record stewards (*imy-r pr*) cultivating *ḫbsw*-lands using teams of *mny*-laborers who received rations during their service. The chief steward (*imy-r pr wr*) may have been in charge of these stewards and the royal agricultural estates that they cultivated.[34]

Censuses: There is considerable evidence for censuses of people from the Middle Kingdom, perhaps reflecting a great demand for compulsory labor to cultivate royal agricultural estates. The evidence includes the "Duties of the Vizier," which states that the vizier was responsible for registering people for compulsory labor and punishing those who failed to perform (lines 13–15).[35]

Duties of the Vizier, lines 13–15:[36]

(13) Now, as for any action of the vizier in hearing cases in his office, as for anyone [in]efficient in any [mission?] whom he will hear concerning it, or anyone whose (labor) duty he will not remove (14) when his hearing comes to it, then it is to be added to the roll of transgressors that is in

> the great prison (*ẖnrt wr*), and likewise for any official of his in ... whose duty he will not remove.
>
> If their case arises again, the entry on the roll of transgressors should be reported (15) with a summary of the case for which they were added on the roll concerning their failing.

Four Middle Kingdom documentary texts from El-Lahun, labeled household documents (*wpwt*), suggest that the vizier may have shared these tasks with local officials and courts, who were responsible for registering the people and passing the information on to the office of the vizier, as they did with field surveys. The household documents record the occupational title, name and father's name of the head of household, as well as the names of other individuals forming part of the household. Their names are always preceded by their relationship to the head of household or one of the other household members, either by marriage, birth or dependent status, and are sometimes followed by their occupational title or status. Each of these household documents contains information for only one household, but they seem to imply the existence of a central register or census.[37] They could represent individual household census returns, but they more likely represent extracts made for heads of households to help establish their rights,[38] because three household documents for the same household were found together,[39] and one is explicitly said to be a copy (*mity*).[40] The central register or census was probably used to record people for compulsory labor.[41] Two of the household documents state that they were made in the office of the vizier,[42] who was also responsible for punishing those who failed to perform their labor.

One of the household documents is Papyrus UC 32166 (*Kahun* IV 1), dated to Year 3 of King Sekhemre-Khutawy of the early Thirteenth Dynasty.[43] It records the household of the lector-priest Senusert's son Khakauresneferu called Sneferu. His household included his son and daughter, as well as the extended families of three unrelated female members of his estate. The other three household documents are Papyri UC 32163–32165 (*Kahun* I 3–5), which record the composition of the household of Hori and his son Sneferu at three different stages in its development.[44] The best preserved of the three household documents is the last, UC 32163 (*Kahun* I, 3), dated to Year 5 of King Sekhemkare of the early Thirteenth Dynasty, in which Sneferu takes over the household of his father Hori. The document is said to have been sworn in the office of the vizier (line 9), but to have been made in the office of fields (line 11), before witnesses (lines 12–13), including a scribe of the *ḏꜣḏꜣt*-court (line 14). It is not clear whether this was a local *ḏꜣḏꜣt*-court or not. The office of the vizier was presumably the final destination for the information. The office of fields could have been a local office, which collected the information and forwarded it to the office of the vizier, but it could also have been a division of the office of the vizier.

Papyrus UC 32164 (*Kahun* I 4):[45]

(1) [... the second (unit?)] of troops installed? [in the Northern District ...]

(2) [... *wꜥb*-priest] of Sopdu Lord of the East, Shef?-[...]

(3) [... transfer] document.

Verso

(1) [Made? in the office] of the vizier, in the section for household documents (*wpwt*) [...]

(2) [in the presence? of the great one] of the tens of Upper Egypt, Sery,

(3) by the overseer of the estate, accountant of cattle, Nebipu son? of Kef?-[...]

(4) scribe of the judge, Seneb ... baker, Sen?-...

(5) guard of the estate, Senbu ...

(6) The household document (*wpwt*) of the warrior Djehuty's son Hori, [being on] the second (unit?) of troops installed? [in the Northern District].

(7) His wife Satsopdu's daughter Shepset	woman of Gesiab
(8) His son Sneferu	infant

Papyrus UC 32165 (*Kahun* I 5):[46]

(1) The household document (*wpwt*) of the warrior Djehuty's son Hori, [being on] the second (unit?) of troops installed? in the [Northern] District.

(2) His wife Satsopdu's daughter Shepset		woman of Gesiab
(3) His son Sneferu		child
(4) His mother Harekheni		her daughter Iset
(5) Her daughter Qatsenut	her daughter Rudet	child
(6) Her daughter Meket	her daughter Sneferu	child

Papyrus UC 32163 (*Kahun* I 3):[47]

(1) Year 3, fourth month of Akhet, day 15 under the majesty of the king of Upper and Lower Egypt Sekhemkare, may he live forever and ever.

(2) Copy of the household document (*wpwt*) of the warrior (*ꜥḥꜣwty*) Hori's son Sneferu, his father being on the second (unit?) of troops.

(3) His mother Satsopdu's daughter Shepset — *wꜥbt*-priestess of Gesiab

(4) Mother of his father Harekheni — orphan (*nmhyt*) of the cemetery workers of the Northern District (*wꜥrtw*)

(5) Sister of his father Qatsenut	ditto
(6) Sister of his father Iset	ditto

(7) Sister of his father Satsneferu ditto

(8) Entered under the household document of his father of Year 2

(9) Swearing of this household in the office of the vizier in Year 5, first month of Peret, day 8

(10) being the household of a dead man?

(11) Made in the office of fields of the Northern District (*wꜥrtw*) Scribe of the army, Sanehat, of the Northern District

(12) in the presence of the great one of the tens of Upper Egypt, Montuemhat son of Imyerkhenret,

(13) by the overseer of the estate, accountant of cattle, Senebeni, of the Northern District

(14) Scribe of the *ḏꜣḏꜣt*-court, Senbef son of Aau, ditto

The "Duties of the Vizier," lines 13–15, mentions a "roll of transgressors that is in the great prison (*ẖnrt wr*)," and in fact one of these rolls may have survived. Papyrus Brooklyn 35.1446, "Text A," is a late Middle Kingdom list of seventy-nine men and one woman whom a *ḏꜣḏꜣt*-court had ordered to be imprisoned in the Great Prison for fleeing from their compulsory labor service, and whose relatives were ordered to be released. The implication is that the relatives of those who failed to perform their compulsory labor were thrown into the Great Prison, until the fugitives themselves were caught.

Papyrus Brooklyn 35.1446 Text A, line 63:

a) The [daugh]ter of Sianhur, Teti,
b) (of) the scribe of the fields of Thinis,
c) woman:
d) (An order) was issued to the Great Pri[son] (in) Regnal year 31, third month of Shemu, day 9, to release (her people) in the *ḏꜣḏꜣt*-court, being (an order) issued in order to execute against her the law pertaining to one who runs away without performing his service.
e) Here (check mark)
f) Statement by the scribe of the vizier, Deduamun: "It is completed."
g) Case closed.

The list was almost certainly kept in the office of the vizier, probably in the office of giving people, because several royal decrees to the vizier were copied into blank spaces in the list ("Insertions B and C," described earlier). The identity of the *ḏꜣḏꜣt*-court that released the prisoners is disputed, however. Quirke argued that it was a higher court, possibly associated with the vizier, because he believed that local *ḏꜣḏꜣt*-courts were no longer attested in Middle Kingdom.[48] However, Philip-Stéphan has suggested that they were indeed local *ḏꜣḏꜣt*-courts, which appear to be synonymous with local *ḳnbt*-courts, as in leather roll Berlin P. 10470.[49]

DOCUMENTATION OF PROPERTY TRANSFERS

The surviving evidence for the documentation of property transfers and exchanges in the Middle Kingdom consists of written transcripts of verbal statements, as it did in the Old Kingdom. Witnesses remained the primary means of authenticating the written transcripts. Many transcripts provide the names of witnesses who could be requested to confirm that the writing reflected the verbal agreements. Some transcripts omit the names of witnesses, perhaps because they were intended as memoranda or reminders for the witnesses themselves. The contracts of Hapidjefa are an example of the latter phenomenon. Hapidjefa was nomarch of Assiut under Senusert I, and concluded ten agreements with priests and officials in Assiut to endow his funerary cult. He then had these contracts inscribed in his tomb-chapel, as a reminder for his *ka*-servant/funerary priest, who was supposed to enforce them. The contracts omit the names of witnesses, but the *ka*-servant/funerary priests may have been a witness to the agreements, and their monumentality served as a kind of authentication as well.

In contrast to the Old Kingdom, however, the Middle Kingdom also saw the appearance of scribal notarization and even registration. Some written transcripts give the names of scribes, or at least the names of the offices where the scribes produced the transcripts, but not the names of witnesses. There are also written transcripts that provide both the names of scribes and of witnesses. In these cases, the scribes could be requested to authenticate agreements alongside the witnesses, or even instead of them. Significantly, the occasional use of the names of the scribal offices rather than the names of the scribes themselves, suggests that the office rather than the individual could be requested to authenticate the written transcripts, presumably by consulting an archival copy of the transcript. This would mean that the transcript could be authenticated long after the memories of the scribes and witnesses had faded. And in fact one Middle Kingdom transcript cites a copy of another transcript registered in the office of a scribe, showing that such transcripts were treated as authenticated legal documents independent of the testimony of scribes or witnesses.

Evidence for local registration of property transfers can be seen in Papyrus UC 32055 (*Kahun* II 1), a petition from El-Lahun dating to the late Twelfth Dynasty.[50] The petitioner first explains that his father drew up a transfer document (*imy.t-pr*) for an exchange of property. Rather than provide a copy of the transfer, the petitioner describes the procedure for making the transfer in lines 2–14. The transacting parties appeared before the overseer of the fields, who represented the *srw*-officials of El-Lahun. The two parties each named the property that they wished to exchange (*isw*). The value of the properties was not discussed, but the official asked the two parties whether they were satisfied (*hr*) with the exchange, and then had them swear that they were satisfied. The names of the witnesses follow. The petitioner then makes his petition proper, in lines 15–20. The petitioner explains that the other party to the transaction never fulfilled his part of the exchange, and that his father, on his deathbed, told his son to make this petition.

Papyrus UC 32055 (*Kahun* II 1):

(1) [....] of Gesiab, Senebebu [....] (the town) Hetep-Senusert-true-of-voice [...] position

(2) This is what his son said:

"My father made a transfer (*imyt-pr*) consisting of (the office of) *wꜥb*-priest and chief of the phyles of Sopdu Lord of the East belonging to him, (3) for the scribe and chief of the seal of the town of Gesiab, Iyemiatib.

He said to my father: (4) 'I will give to you the capital (*tp*), and every delivery of income (*ꜣt wꜣwꜣw*) belonging to you,' so he said.

(5) Then my father was asked by the overseer of fields Mersu who was acting as deputy for the officials, (6) saying: 'Are you satisfied (*hr*) with the giving to you of the capital (*tp*) mentioned above and [every delivery (*ꜣt*)?] (7) of income (*wꜣwꜣw*) reckoned (*ipw*) to you in exchange (*m-isw*) for your (office of) *wꜥb*-priest and [chief of the phyles]?'

(8) Then my father said: 'I am satisfied (*hr*).'

That which the officials said: (9) 'The two men are to swear (*r rdi.t ꜥrḳ*) saying: 'We are satisfied (*hr*).'

(10) Then the two men were asked to (swear by) the life (*ꜥnḫ*) of the Lord, l.p.h. before the mayor [....] (11) and overseer of fields Mersu acting as deputy for the officials.

(12) List of the names (*imy-rn=f*) of witnesses in whose presence this was made:

The scribe Iyem-[...]

(13) ...[...]nu

(14) Ar[...]

(15) Now my father petitioned (*spr*) [...]: (16) 'he has [not removed] the impediments from the capital (*tp*).' Moreover, my father said to me when he was ill: (17) '[If] the capital (*tp*) which the scribe and chief of the seal Iyemiatib swore to me is not given to you, (18) [then] you should petition (*spr*) for it to the official who will hear it. Then (19) the capital (*tp*) will be given to you,' so he said.

This is the petition that I make [...] belonging to [...] (20) that which the scribe Iyemiatib has reached at this moment."

Papyrus UC 32037 (*Kahun* VII 1) is a transfer document (*imy.t-pr*) from El-Lahun, dated to Year 39, probably of Amenemhat III.[51] After the date (line 1), and the names of the contractors (lines 2–3), the papyrus transcribes the speech of the donator Meri in the first person (lines 3–9): "I give my office ... to my son Intef ... as my 'staff of old age' since I have become old ..." There then follows the list of the names of three witnesses (lines 10–13).

> **Papyrus UC 32037 (*Kahun* VII 1):**
>
> (1) Year 39, fourth month of Akhet, day 29.
>
> (2) A transfer (*imyt-pr*) that the controller of the phyle, Intef's son Meri called Kebi made for (3) his son Meri's son Intef called Iuseneb.
>
> "I give my (4) (office of) controller of the phyle to my son Mery's son Intef called Iuseneb for (being my) 'staff of old age' (5) because I have become old. Cause that he is appointed (*dhnt=f*) at once.
>
> (6) As for the transfer (*imyt-pr*) that I made for his mother previously, (I turn my) back to it.
>
> (7) As for my house which is in the district Hut-ma'at, it is for my (8) children born to me by the daughter of (9) the phyle-member and district councillor Sobekemhat's daughter Nebetneninisu, together with all that is in it."
>
> (10) List of the names (*imy-rn=f*) of witnesses in whose presence the transfer (*imyt-pr*) was made:
>
> (11) The controller of the phyle, Sabastet's son ditto,
>
> (12) The [libationer?], Senusert's son Senbubu,
>
> (13) [...]
>
> Verso
>
> (1) The transfer (*imyt-pr*) that (2) the controller of the phyle, Intef's son (3) Meri made for his son (4) Meri's son Intef (5) called Iuseneb.

Papyrus UC 32058 (*Kahun* I 1) contains two transfer documents (*imy.t-pr*) from El-Lahun.[52] It is part of a private family archive that also included Papyrus UC 32167 (*Kahun* I 2) discussed later, and perhaps also the household documents Papyri UC 32163–32165 (*Kahun* I 3–5) discussed previously.[53] Text A is a copy of a transfer document (*imy.t-pr*) dating to Year 44, probably of Amenemhat III. After the label (line 1), the date (line 2), and the names of the contractors (line 3), the papyrus transcribes the speech of the donator Anchren in the first person (lines 4–5): "All my property in country and town is for my brother ..." There then follows the statement that it was placed as a record (*snn*) in the office of the second reporter (*wḥmw*) of the south. Text B is a transfer document (*imy.t-pr*) dating to Year 2, probably of Amenemhat IV. After quoting a previous transfer document (*imy.t-pr*) (Text A, lines 1–5), the date (line 6), and the names of the contractors (line 7), the papyrus transcribes the speech of the donator Wah in the first person (lines 7–14): "I make a transfer (*imy.t-pr*) for my wife ..." There then follows in a second column the list of the names of the three witnesses (column ii, lines 1–4). The transfer from husband to wife in Text B has been interpreted as being functionally similar to later Demotic annuity contracts, because it guaranteed the wife's income independently from the marriage.[54]

Papyrus UC 32058 (*Kahun* I 1):

[Text A]

(1,1) Copy (*mity*) of the transfer (*imyt-pr*) that the trusted seal-bearer and controller of construction, Anchren, made.

(2) Year 44, second month of Shemu, day 13.

(3) The transfer (*imyt-pr*) that the trusted seal-bearer and controller of construction of the Northern District (*w*^{c}*r.t*), Shepset's son Ihyseneb called Anchren, made.

(4) "All my property (*ḫt*) in the country and in town is for my brother, the *w*^{c}*b*-priest and chief of the phyles of Sopdu Lord of the East, Shepset's son Ihyseneb called Wah; (5) and all my dependants are for this brother of mine."

This was placed as a record (*snn*) in the office of the second reporter of the South in Year 44, second month of Shemu, day 13.

[Text B]

(6) Year 2, second month of Akhet, day 18.

(7) The transfer (*imyt-pr*) that the *w*^{c}*b*-priest and chief of the phyles of Sopdu Lord of the East, Wah, made.

"I make a transfer (*imyt-pr*) for my wife (8) a woman from Gesiabet, Satsopdu's daughter Sheftu called Teti, being all the property (*ḫt*) which my brother, (9) the trusted seal-bearer and controller of construction Anchren, gave to me, concerning every object in its place (i.e. wherever they are), being everything that he gave me. She shall give it (10) to anyone she desires among her children that she shall bear for me.

I give to her the four Asiatics (11) which my brother the trusted seal-bearer and controller of construction Anchren gave to me. It is she who shall give them to anyone she wishes of her children.

(12) As for my tomb: may I be placed in it with my wife, without allowing anyone to interfere with it.

(13) As for the chambers which my brother the trusted seal-bearer and controller of construction Anchren built for me: may my wife be therein, without allowing that she be cast out (lit. placed on the ground!) from them (14) by anyone."

[Second hand] "It is the deputy Gebu who shall act as child-educator (*šd-n-ḫn*) for my son."

[First hand] (2,1) List of the names (*imy-rn=f*) of the persons in whose presence this was done:

(2) the scribe of the fisherman, Kemeni.

(3) the doorkeeper of the temple, Ankhtifi 's son Ipu.

(4) the doorkeeper of the temple, Seneb's son Seneb.

Verso

(1) The transfer (*imyt-pr*) (2) that (3) the *wꜥb*-priest and chief of the phyles (4) Wah made.

In other cases, however, there is no list of witnesses, and the transcripts may have been notarized by the office in which they were written, as in the case of the copy of a transfer document (*imyt-pr*) cited in *P. Kahun* I 1 previously, and in *P. Kahun* I 2. Papyrus UC 32167 (*Kahun* I 2) is an exchange document (*swnt*) from El-Lahun, dating to Year 29, probably of Amenemhat III.[55] The two contractors are probably the same as those in *P. Kahun* I 1A, and the four slaves are probably the "Asiatics" mentioned in *P. Kahun* I 1B, discussed previously. After the date (line 1), the contractors are said to have made the exchange (*swnt*) in the office of the vizier, before the vizier (lines 2–5). The document (*hnn*) is said to have been made by the scribe of the town.

Papyrus UC 32167 (*Kahun* I 2):

(1) Year 29, third month of Akhet, day 7.

(2) Made in the office of the vizier, before the overseer of the city and vizier, Khety (3) by the scribe, the overseer of the seal of the office of giving people, Amenemhat's son Ameny:

(4) Exchange (*swnt*) of the assistant of the overseer of the seal of the Northern District, Shepset's son Ihyseneb, (5) with the *wꜥb*-priest, the chief of the phyles of Sopdu Lord of the East, Shepset's son Ihyseneb.

(6) Agreement (*hnn*) of the scribe of this town, Ptahwenenef's son Sehetepibre.

(7) The female Asiatic Akhiatef Kemeteni;

(8) Kemeni Sopduemmeri;

(9) Meshy 2 (years?) 3 months;

(10) [...]am [...]benu.

The exchange document *P. Kahun* I 2 seems suspiciously abbreviated, and not just because of the lack of witnesses. The contemporary petition *P. Kahun* II 1 discussed subsequently suggests that it was necessary in exchanges for both parties to swear that they were satisfied with the exchanges, as was the case in Old Kingdom exchanges, yet no such oath is mentioned in *P. Kahun* I 2. Perhaps such standard clauses were omitted from notary copies.

State Registration: Property transfers were sometimes registered locally, as was previously shown, but the information may have been passed on to the central administration as well. In such cases the central administration would have possessed some of the information required to intervene in property disputes, but it does not seem to have done so, suggesting that it collected the information to enforce taxation rather than property taxes. The Middle Kingdom evidence for the central registration of property transfers includes the "Duties of the Vizier," which states that the district *ḳnbt*-courts were responsible for providing the documents to the vizier, who then sealed them (line 19).[56]

Duties of the Vizier, line 19:[57]

(19) ... Now he is the one who fetches the district councillors (*ḳnbtyw nw ww*).

He is the one who sends them out, and they report to him the state of their districts (*ww*).

He is brought every transfer document (*imyt-pr*) and it is he who seals (*ḫtm*) them.

Middle Kingdom documentary texts, however, reveal that while local courts could witness property transfers, one member of the court, the local reporter, was actually responsible for recording them and passing the information on to the office of the vizier. This can be seen in leather roll Berlin P. 10470,[58] a late Middle Kingdom document of unknown provenance, most likely either Elephantine or Thebes. It records the correspondence between the reporter of Elephantine and the office of the vizier, the latter probably located at Thebes. The first section records a petition to the reporter at Elephantine requesting that a servant woman be transferred from one party to another at Elephantine. The second section records the response of the vizier to the petition, instructing the reporter how to proceed. A third badly damaged section probably recorded the response of the reporter to the vizier, and a fourth section records further instructions of the vizier. The fifth section records the registration of the transfer by the reporter, witnessed by the local court.

It has been observed that leather roll Berlin P. 10470 does not resemble any Middle Kingdom transfer document (*imy.t-pr*) or exchange document (*swnt*), and that it does not mention any such document. However, it does describe the oral procedures that apparently formed the basis for such documents. Both transacting parties were asked if they were satisfied (*hr*) with the transfer, and then were asked to swear that they were, before witnesses. Presumably this was the information that the reporter was supposed to record and to pass on to the vizier.

Leather Roll Berlin P. 10470:

[Petition for transfer]

(1,1) ... (1,2) the reporter (*wḥmw*) of Elephantine Hekaib: "Look ... in order to cause that you know that (1,3) the chief of the mat Itefseneb son of Hekaib [said to] them, saying: 'Senbet daughter of Senmut is a servant woman (*ḥmt*) of the tenants (*ḏt*) of the people of Elephantine, (1,4) but she is (also) a servant woman who covers, a royal servant. Cause that I live, my lord, and cause that one give her estate [to me], (1,5) to the city, as her owners are satisfied (*hr*).' [So he said]. The conclusion is that it shall be done as her owners are satisfied (*hr*). (1,6) So runs what he reported (*smi*). This was sent [to cause] that they know it. You should act accordingly, so that the royal domain ..."

[Orders of the vizier]

(1,7) Copy of the leather roll that was brought from the office of the vizier, that the chief of the mat Itefseneb brought on this day....

(1,8) The overseer of the city, the vizier, overseer of the six great courts, Amenemhat. An order to the reporter of Elephantine Hekaib, saying (1,9) that: "An order was issued for the office of the vizier in Year 1, first month of Shemu, day 27 of the time of Khubak, l.p.h. (1,10) The order concerns the petition that the chief of the mat Itefseneb son of Hekaib made, saying 'Senbet daughter of Senmut is a servant woman of the tenants (1,11) of the people of Elephantine, but she is also a servant woman who covers, a royal servant. Cause that I live (1,12) my lord, and cause that one give her to me, to the city, as her owners are satisfied (*hr*)'. So he said. The conclusion is that it shall be done (1,13) as her owners are satisfied (*hr*). So run the orders. Look, the leather roll has been brought to you from the Office of the Vizier in order that every instruction in it may be known ... (1,14) ...

Look, they have been questioned (*wšd*) about it, and they have also approved (*hnn*) of it. They were caused to swear concerning it. (1,15) Look, what has been ordered has been put before the servant woman Senbet. Look, one has sent to cause that (1,16) the mayor of Elephantine know it ... This was sent to cause that they know it. You should act according to all that has been ordered, and you should act according to (1,17) ... that which this leather roll reported ..."

[Response of the reporter]

(2,2) "... such is what has been found. This is to inform you about it."

[Report of the vizier]

(2,3) A report (*smi*) on this leather roll has been brought from the office of the vizier, (2,4) stating "Look, the agents (*rwḏw*) of the people (2,5) about whom you wrote have been questioned. They said, 'We are satisfied (*hr*) (2,6) with the giving of the servant woman Senbet to the city [as her owners] are satisfied (*hr*), (2,7) in accordance with the petition that our brother the chief of the mat (2,8) Itefseneb has made concerning her.'

Look, they were caused to swear concerning it, and (2,9) that which has been ordered has been put before the servant woman Senbet. (2,10) You should act accordingly in the office of the reporter of Elephantine."

[Registration of the transfer]"

(2,11) The reporter of Elephantine Hekaib said, "I have heard (2,12) what you have sent to me about her from the office of the vizier, stating 'Look

(2,13) orders have been put before the servant woman Senbet ... (2,14) ... the people have been questioned ... (2,15) ... they were caused to swear it,' saying 'We are satisfied (*hr*) with the giving ...'"

(3,1-2) ... (3,3) district of Elephantine ... (3,4) chief of the mat Hekaib's son Itefseneb ... (3,5) district of Elephantine, Hekaib, son of Bebisenbet, (3,6) have been addressed, saying "Are you satisfied (*hr*) with the (3,7) giving of the servant woman Senbet to the city in accordance with the petitions (*sprw*) of (3,8) your brother the chief of the mat Hekaib's son Itefseneb about her?" (3,9) They said, "We are satisfied (*hr*) with it." Then they were made to take the oath about it. (3,10) ... they ... about it. Then what had been ordered was put (3,11) before the servant woman Senbet also. Names of the *d3d3t*-court (3,12) of judges (*sdmw*): the reporter of Elephantine, ...

MEDIA OF EXCHANGE AND REDISTRIBUTION

In the Middle Kingdom, weights of gold appear to have served as standard measures of value. Copper, cloth, grain, and other commodities were much more frequently used as media of exchange, however. Gold was presumably too valuable or too rare to use as a medium of exchange in the majority of transactions.

Limited availability of gold would have inhibited the collection of regular taxes in gold, and the variety of commodities used as media of exchange could have discouraged the collection of property transfer taxes as a fraction of the value of property transferred. An inability to collect property transfer taxes in turn could have prevented the central administration from recapturing costs associated with documenting and enforcing property transfers, and may help explain why the central administration reduced its role in documentation and enforcement in the New Kingdom.

Measures of Value: Weights of metal were used as measures of value in the Middle Kingdom and the Second Intermediate Period, particularly the deben, which weighed about 13.6g in the Middle Kingdom, and 91g in the New Kingdom. Stela Cairo JdE 52453 (*Stela juridique de Karnak*), line 7, states that Sobeknakht has given to Kebsi "60 deben of gold being everything (*m ḫt nb*)," but line 14 states more explicitly that Sobeknakht has given to Kebsi "60 deben of gold, in gold, bronze, grain and clothes, "in other words commodities worth 60 deben of gold.[59] Shatis or rings of metal may also have been used as a measure of value in the Middle Kingdom, as they were already in the Old Kingdom.[60] Papyrus BM 10057–10058 (*Rhind Mathematical Papyrus*), Problem 62, supposes that a bag containing gold, silver, and lead has been bought for 84 shatis. A deben of gold is given for twelve shatis, a deben of silver for six shatis, and a deben of lead for three shatis, making twenty-one shatis. Twenty-one goes into 84 four times, so there must be $4 \times 12 = 48$ shatis of gold, $4 \times 6 = 24$

shatis of silver, and 4 × 3 = 12 shatis of lead in the bag.[61] The copyist of the *Rhind Mathematical Papyrus*, a scribe named Ahmose, stated that this papyrus was written in Year 33 of the Hyksos king Auserre (Apepi), as a copy of an old writing made in the reign of King Nimaatre (Amenemhat III).[62] The papyrus therefore dates to the end of the Second Intermediate Period, just before the beginning of the New Kingdom, but the text apparently dates back to the Middle Kingdom. Problem 62 in the *Rhind Mathematical Papyrus* clearly shows that the Middle Kingdom shati was equivalent to one-twelfth of a Middle Kingdom deben of gold. In contrast, Old Kingdom shatis may have been of copper,[63] and New Kingdom shatis were probably rings of silver weighing one-twelfth of a New Kingdom deben or 7.6 grams.[64] Problem 62 also shows that in the Middle Kingdom, four deben of lead were worth two deben of silver, which were worth one deben of gold.[65] If silver had once been worth more than gold, as has been suggested,[66] it was no longer so.

Media of Exchange: Copper and especially cloth and grain appear to have been the most common media of exchange in the Middle Kingdom, as in the Old Kingdom. Hekanakht mentions all three in his correspondence with his household.[67] In a letter to his mother Ipi, Hekanakht writes to Merisu and Heti's son Nakht that he has sent twenty-four deben of copper with which to lease land (P. Hekanakht 2 verso, line 1), but then adds that they should arrange to lease twenty arourae of land by paying rent in copper, cloth, grain, or anything (P. Hekanakht 2 verso, lines 2–3). In a letter to Merisu, Hekanakht also writes that he should arrange to lease twenty arourae of land with cloth that has been woven (P. Hekanakht 1 recto, lines 4–6), but adds that he should pay rent in grain instead if he can get a good price for it (P. Hekanakht 1 recto, lines 5–6). Hekanakht writes to the overseer of Lower Egypt Herunefer that he is owed grain, but may be repaid in oil at a rate of one *hbnt*-measure of oil for two *ẖꜣr*-sacks of barley or three *ẖꜣr*-sacks of emmer, though he would prefer to be repaid in barley (P. Hekanakht 3 recto, line 8 – verso, line 1).

Stores of Wealth: Some media of exchange, such as cloth and especially copper, store value better than others, such as grain and oil. Hekanakht clearly understood this, because in his letter to Merisu he berates him for sending him dry old barley instead of good new barley (P. Hekanakht 1 verso, lines 1–4). Hekanakht also preferred to be paid in barley rather than oil if possible (P. Hekanakht 3 verso, line 1), which Baer suggested was because oil could turn rancid. Baer has suggested that Hekanakht "seems to have tried to keep his financial condition as liquid as possible, and apart from emergencies, this will have resulted in a steady increase in his stocks of the durable commodities that composed his capital."[68] Nonetheless, Hekanakht appears to have been willing to use his stocks of copper and cloth if they could get a better exchange than grain.

Credit: Hekanakht's accounts record considerable quantities of grain that were apparently on loan to others. One account lists quantities of barley and emmer that were "outside" (*r-hntw*), specified by individual by his name (P. Hekanakht 5 recto, lines 37–54). Another account lists quantities of barley that were "with" (*m-ꜥ*) various individuals and households in villages in the district Perhaa (P. Hekanakht 6). In the New Kingdom, property that is described as being "with" (*m-ꜥ*) someone was in fact on loan to them.[69] This was undoubtedly also the case in Hekanakht's accounts, because the account that uses this phrase (P. Hekanakht 6) is paralleled by another account of emmer and barley in a letter to the overseer of Lower Egypt Herunefer, which also specifies how Hekanakht wishes to be repaid (P. Hekanakht 3 recto, line 6 – verso, line 1).

REDISTRIBUTIVE NETWORKS

In the Middle Kingdom, the state employed treasuries and granaries to receive and redistribute revenues and commodities. The revenues and commodities were processed and distributed to support royal projects and dockyards, palaces and mortuary temples associated with the royal residences at Thebes and Itjtawy, as well as provincial administrators' palaces and funerary chapels, and local temples and their integrated royal *ka*-chapels. Some high officials were full-time beneficiaries of these redistributed revenues and were relatively wealthy on account of them, but many low-ranking officials, priests in rotation, and compulsory laborers were part-time beneficiaries who received modest incomes that nonetheless allowed them to engage in other economic activities, particularly those generating highly periodic, fluctuating, entrepreneurial, and market-dependent incomes. State redistribution remained better documented and enforced over long distances than private redistribution or exchanges. High value exchanges were documented in writing more often than in the Old Kingdom, and state agents sometimes made records of them, but they were still dependent on local witnesses for authentication, and thus state redistribution remained the choice mode of distribution for long-distance transactions.

Granaries and Treasuries: In the Middle Kingdom, the chancellor or treasurer (lit. overseer of sealed things, *imy-r ḫtmt*) was the highest ranking official after the king and the vizier, and he is believed to have administered the dispersed networks of central and local granaries and treasuries that presumably existed, since he sometimes also bore the title overseer of the double treasury.[70] There is, however, very little evidence for what happened to tax revenues between collection and disbursement. One exception is Inscription G61 in the Wadi Hammamat of the reporter Ameny son of Montuhotep, which commemorates a thirty-day quarrying expedition in Year 38 of King Senusert I, consisting of 18,538 men, including 17,000 corvee laborers (*ḥsb*). It records (lines 19–21) that their bread and beer were supplied from the granary of the lord, l.p.h., that meat was supplied from the storeroom of the lord, l.p.h., and that other equipment was supplied from the treasury of the lord, l.p.h.[71] The text thus confirms that state granaries and treasuries existed in the Middle Kingdom, and that they provided supplies for state expeditions at least. One might expect that the residence and other royal palaces also drew and disbursed supplies from state granaries and treasuries, but the evidence is ambiguous. Papyrus Boulaq 18 contains the accounts of a royal palace at Thebes for twelve days in the early Thirteenth Dynasty, including both deliveries and outpayments of provisions. These came from three sources or accounts, namely the district of the head of the south (*wꜥrt tp-rsy*), the office of giving people (*ẖꜣ n dd rmt*, a subdivision of the office of the vizier concerned with corvee labor), and the treasury (*pr-ḥḏ*).

The Residence and Other Royal Palaces: There were probably several royal palaces at any given time in the Middle Kingdom and Second Intermediate Period. The Eleventh Dynasty probably possessed one in Thebes, and the Twelfth Dynasty established another at Itjtawy, which became part of the Residence.[72] The Thirteenth Dynasty maintained the Residence at Itjtawy, but also used a royal palace at Thebes. In the Second Intermediate Period, there were separate palaces associated with the Hyksos at Avaris, and with the Seventeenth Dynasty at Thebes.

The Thirteenth Dynasty royal palace at Thebes is the palace best known as a redistributive institution, because the Hieratic papyrus Boulaq 18 preserves its accounts for twelve days in a Year 3 of an unnamed early Thirteenth Dynasty king.[73] It records deliveries as well as outpayments of provisions. The deliveries were broken down into special and regular deliveries. The latter consisted of 1630 loaves of bread and 130 *ds*-jars of beer daily, from three separate sources or accounts, namely the district of the head of the south (*wꜥrt tp-rsy*), the office of giving people (*ẖꜣ n dd rmt*), and the treasury (*pr-ḥḏ*).

The outpayments were similarly broken down into regular outpayments for personnel, offerings and travelling officials, and special outpayments for rewards and the like. Authorization was apparently not needed for regular outpayments for personnel, offerings, and travelling officials. Authorization was usually recorded, however, for changes to regular outpayments of provisions, and for special outpayments. In most cases, authorization took the form of a verbal command from one of the superiors of the scribe, the scribe of the great prison (*sš n ẖnrt wr*) Neferhotep, in whose tomb the papyrus was found.[74] In the example cited below, Reneferemib orders Neferhotep to disburse provisions to a visiting party of Medjay.

Hieratic Papyrus Boulaq 18, Column 29, 2, lines 1–8:

1) (The commission) concerning which the interior overseer of the Inner Palace (*imy-r ꜥẖnwty n kꜣp*) Renefemib came, being (the commission) concerning which he went forth:

2) Cause that one give to the Medjay who arrived yesterday.
3) Done according to this commission, 4) reward today according to decree.
5–8) [List of provisions for the Medjay]

In some cases, however, authorization for special outpayments of provisions took the form of a written order from an authority, which was carefully copied into the accounts. In the example cited below, Senebef writes an order to provide provisions to the same group of Medjay as in the previous example. The written orders usually specify that the outpayments come from three different sources, namely the district of the head of the south, the bureau (of giving people), and the treasury. This suggests that there may have been separate institutional accounts within the palace granaries and stores.

Hieratic Papyrus Boulaq 18, Column 29, 2, lines 9–15:

9) Copy of the letter to 10) the districts, by the keeper of the chamber of service staff (*imy-r ꜥ.t n wršw*) Senebef:

11) Year 3, third month of Akhet, day 3.

12) Cause that the sledge (? *r n ḏri.t*) be brought on the third month of Akhet, day 4.

13–15) [List of provisions to be provided by the district of the head of the south, the bureau (of giving people), and the treasury]

Provincial Administrators: During the early Middle Kingdom, the system of provincial administration continued to be based on nomes. Provincial governors in Upper Egypt bore the title great chief (*ḥry-tp ꜥꜣ*), as well as mayor (*ḥꜣty-ꜥ*) and overseer of *ḥm-nṯr*-priests (*imy-r ḥmw-nṯrw*).[75] During the late Middle Kingdom, however, the system of provincial administration based on provincial governors of nomes was deemphasized in favor of a system based on mayors and overseers of *ḥm-nṯr*-priests or temples, and on towns and villages.[76] In the early Middle Kingdom, the office or institution of mayor possessed an estate, which was official or institutional property. Hapidjefa the provincial governor of Assiut indicates on several occasions in his funerary inscriptions that he is using property from his father's estate (*pr-it.f*) to establish his private funerary endowment, not property of the mayor's estate (*pr-ḥꜣty-ꜥ*).[77] Mayors apparently received harvest taxes from the mayors' estates (*pr-ḥꜣty-ꜥ*),[78] which were presumably sent to the mayors' magazines (*šnꜥ n ḥꜣty-ꜥ*). Mayors also received a portion of the offerings of local temples, perhaps in their capacity as overseer of *ḥm-nṯr*-priests.[79] These revenues are explicitly sent to the mayors' magazines (*šnꜥ n ḥꜣty-ꜥ*).[80] In the later Middle Kingdom, mayors and overseers of temples continued to receive a considerable portion of the revenues of local temples, for example at the royal mortuary temple of Senusert II, as shown by Papyrus Berlin P. 10005.

Royal Dockyards: In the Middle Kingdom, royal dockyards played an important role in managing materials and labor for state enterprises. An archive of four papyri containing accounts of a royal dockyard (*wḫrt*) in the Thinite nome is contained in the Reisner Papyri. They were found by George Reisner in 1904 on top of three wooden coffins in Tomb N 408 at Nag' ed-Deir, a cemetery of the ancient town of Thinis.[81] The oldest of the papyri, Papyrus Reisner II, has dates with regnal years 15–18, probably of Senusert I.[82] The papyrus contains copies of three administrative orders from the overseer of the city, the vizier, the overseer of the six great mansions, Intefiqer, to seven stewards of the palace (*imy-r-pr n pr-ꜥꜣ*) in the Thinite nome, including Iey's son Anhurhotep, each of whom is in charge of an *imw*-boat and thirty crewmen. The first orders a shipment of wooden materials, presumably from the dockyard; the second orders a shipment of grain and bread downstream to the residence, presumably at Itjtawy; and the third orders another shipment of wooden materials, and instructs the stewards to inform him if their craftsmen are seized at the dockyard.[83] The papyrus also contains accounts of copper, wood, and leather material and equipment received at the dockyard of the palace (*wḫrt nt pr-ꜥꜣ*), some of which are to be used to outfit an *imw*-boat to send south with craftsmen to Thebes; and daily accounts of the dockyard of provisions for men of the steward Iey's son Anhurhotep from the *ḫbsw*-lands of others.[84] Papyrus Reisner III has dates with regnal years 22–23, also probably of Senusert I.[85] It contains daily accounts of provisions for *mny*-laborers who were in Thinis from the *ḫbsw*-lands of the steward Iey's son Anhurhotep,[86] who may have been divided into seven crews (*ṯst*) who were assigned to make and transport mudbricks to construct parts of buildings in Thinis.[87] Papyrus Reisner I has dates with regnal years 24–25, again probably of Senusert I.[88] It includes daily accounts of *mny*-laborers who were in Coptos, the days they spent travelling, working, and being absent, and their rations;[89] accounts of *mny*-laborers who were in Thinis from the *ḫbsw*-lands of the steward Iey's son Anhurhotep, including 149 men divided into 16 crews, and 167 men divided into 14 crews, together with their rations;[90] accounts of materials like stone, hides, and mats, and provisions like fish, bread, and fowl;[91] and accounts of labor used to construct various parts of a temple.[92] Papyrus Reisner IV contains accounts of men divided into crews and their rations. Dates with regnal years 7–8 occur in an older account of cloth distributions, partially preserved as a palimpsest.[93]

More evidence concerning the role of dockyards is provided by a stela found in the Wadi Gawasis on the Red Sea coast, which states that King Senusert I ordered the overseer of the city, the vizier, the overseer of the six great mansions, Intefiqer, to build (*ḳd*) a fleet at the dockyard (*wḫrt*) of Coptos to send to the mining region of Punt, while the reporter Ameny son of Montuhotep and 3,756 others built (*ḳd*) the fleet on the sea shore, presumably after they had been disassembled and transported across the Eastern Desert from Coptos in the Nile Valley.[94] The same reporter Ameny later directed the quarrying expedition in the Wadi Hammamat in Year 38 of King Senusert I described previously.

Military and Police: In the Middle Kingdom, the army probably consisted in part of professional soldiers and *medjay*-police who regularly received redistributed revenues, and in part of reserve soldiers who only received revenues while on campaigns, expeditions, or garrison duty. The Middle Kingdom evidence is highly equivocal, however, because much of it comes from titles rather than narrative texts.

One exception is Stela Manchester Museum 3306, from Abydos and dated to the reign of Senusert III. It contains the autobiography of Khusobek called Djaa, which records that he was born in Year 27 of Amenemhat II, that he trained as a warrior (*ꜥḥ3wty*) alongside Senusert III at the Residence, and that he was appointed to the royal guard (*šmsw n ḥḳ3*) and given sixty men. He served with the king on campaign in Nubia, and was subsequently promoted to inspector of the guard (*sḥḏ šmsw*) and given 100 men. He also served with the king on campaign in the Levant, and was made chief officer of a town regiment (*3ṯw ꜥ3 n niwt*). A graffito from near the Nubian border fortress at Semna from Year 9 of Amenemhat III reveals that he was subsequently promoted to officer of a royal crew (*3ṯw n ṯt ḥḳ3*).[95]

The previously mentioned stela found in the Wadi Gawasis on the Red Sea coast, dated to the reign of Senusert I, provides evidence that soldiers also participated in paramilitary expeditions. It states that the reporter Ameny son of Mentuhotep was accompanied by 3,756 men, including 50 royal guards (*šmsw n nb ꜥ.w.s.*), 500 soldiers of a royal crew (*ꜥnḫw n nb ꜥ.w.s.*), and 3,200 soldiers of a town regiment (*ꜥnḫw n niwt*).[96] Similarly, the previously mentioned quarrying inscription of Ameny son of Mentuhotep in the Wadi Hammamat, dated to Year 38 of Senusert I, states that the expedition consisted of 18,538 men, including 30 royal guards (*šmsw n nb ꜥ.w.s.*), and warriors (*ꜥḥ3wty*), namely 300 soldiers of a royal crew of Thebes (*ꜥnḫ n ṯt nt ḥḳ3 W3st*) and 700 soldiers of a provincial regiment (*ꜥnḫ n sp3t*), as well as 17,000 corvee laborers (*ḥsb*). The royal guards each received thirty loaves of bread over thirty days, while the warriors each received only fifteen loaves.[97]

The Hieratic papyri British Museum 10752 and 10753 sheet 3 (The Semnah Despatches) provide evidence that soldiers also served on garrison duty. They contain a series of reports from the Nubian border fortress at Semna to the vizier at Thebes, dated to the reign of Amenemhat III. They mention warriors (*ꜥḥ3wty*), guards (*šmsw*), officers (*3ṯw*), and soldiers of a town regiment (*ꜥnḫw n niwt*).[98]

Other stelae, graffiti, scarab sealings and papyri confirm the existence of several varieties of guards (*šmsw*),[99] officers (*3ṯw*),[100] and soldiers (*ꜥnḫw*).[101] Soldiers were subdivided into soldiers of a town regiment (*ꜥnḫw n niwt*) and soldiers of a royal crew (*ꜥnḫw n ṯt ḥḳꜣ*), just as officers were divided into (chief) officers of a town regiment (*ꜣṯw (ꜥꜣ) n niwt*) and officers of a royal crew (*ꜣṯw n ṯt ḥḳꜣ*).[102] Warriors (*ꜥḥꜣwty*) may be another grade of soldier,[103] or more likely a generic term equivalent to soldier (*ꜥnḫw*).[104] Berlev has argued that the officers and soldiers of a town regiment were infantry, and that officers and soldiers of a royal crew were marines.[105] In contrast, Franke has argued that officers and soldiers of a town regiment served as town garrisons, while officers and soldiers of a royal crew served directly under the king, like guards.[106] If Franke is correct, then soldiers of a town regiment (*ꜥnḫw n niwt*) may have been reserve soldiers under the command of professional officers, who could be called to serve on campaigns, paramilitary expeditions, or periodic garrison duty. This could help explain why in the New Kingdom Wilbour Papyrus, the same term (*ꜥnḫw n niwt*) is reapplied to female holders of plots corresponding to those held by reserve soldiers (*wꜥw*) and stable-masters (*ḥry iḥw*).[107]

Royal Mortuary Temples: Several Middle Kingdom royal mortuary temples are known archaeologically, including the mortuary complex of Montuhotep II at Deir el-Bahri at Thebes, several pyramid complexes built in the region around Itjtawy, and the mortuary temple of Senusert III at Abydos. The role of these mortuary temples as redistributive institutions, however, is best seen in the papyri from the valley temple of Senusert II at El-Lahun known as Sekhem-Senusert, which was distinct from the adjoining town known as Hetep-Senusert.[108] The papyri constituted the archive of the temple scribe Horemsaef. They include letters, most often to the temple scribe (*sš ḥwt-nṯr*) and steward (*imy-r pr*) Horemsaef, most often from the mayors (*ḥꜣty-ꜥ*) and overseers of the temple (*imy-r ḥwt-nṯr*), who served to link the royal mortuary temple to the provincial administration.[109] The papyri also include a large number of accounts, many of them unpublished.[110] The best known account is Papyrus Berlin P. 10005. It records the daily income of the temple as 410 loaves of bread, 63 *sḏꜣ*-jars of beer, and 172 *ḫpnw*-jars. Of these, 340 loaves, 28 *sḏꜣ*-jars, and 56 ½ *ḫpnw*-jars were the divine offering, which then reverted to the funerary priests (*ḥmw-kꜣ*). The remainder, 70 loaves, 35 *sḏꜣ*-jars, and 115 ½ *ḫpnw*-jars, were divided among twenty members of the staff of the temple according to their rank. The mayor and overseer of the temple received nearly one-quarter of the remainder, 16 2/3 loaves, 8 1/3 *sḏꜣ*-jars, and 27 2/3 *ḫpnw*-jars. In contrast, the temple scribe received only 2 2/9 loaves, 1 1/9 *sḏꜣ*-jars, and 3 31/45 *ḫpnw*-jars.[111] However, only two members of the staff, the mayor and overseer of the temple, and the chief lector priest, were permanently on duty. The other eighteen members, including the temple scribe, belonged to one of four phyles (*sꜣw*) that served for one month every four months.[112] Each phyle had to report on the status of the temple inventory when it began and ceased duty, and had to provide a list of the phyle members present.[113] Because these staff members only served one month in four, they were able and indeed were probably obliged to engage in other economic activities.

Divine Temples: The Eleventh Dynasty revived the Sixth Dynasty practice of associating royal *ka*-chapels with temples of local divinities, and built or rebuilt several temples incorporating royal *ka*-chapels.[114] The presence of royal *ka*-chapels in the temples allowed them to function as local agents of the kings, alongside and probably subordinate to the provincial administration, much like the royal mortuary temple of Senusert II.

The funerary inscriptions of Hapidjefa, the provincial governor of Assiut, reveal the organization of one temple of a local divinity, Wepwawet of Assiut, and its relation to the provincial administration. The temple of Wepwawet in Assiut included a group of hour-priests (*wnwtyw ḥwt-nṯr*) or *wᶜb*-priests (the terms seem interchangeable in these texts), with whom Hapidjefa made three contracts.[115] The temple of Wepwawet also included a group of ten members of the staff of the temple, known collectively as the *ḳnbt*-court of the temple (*ḳnbt nt ḥwt-nṯr*). The staff included the overseer of *ḥm-nṯr*-priests (*imy-r ḥmw-nṯr*), a reporter (*wḥmw*), a wardrobe-keeper (*šnḏwty*), an overseer of the storeroom (*imy-r šnᶜ*), an overseer of the *ka*-chapel (*imy-r ḥwt-kꜣ*), and a temple scribe (*sš ḥwt-nṯr*), among others. Hapidjefa concluded one contract collectively with the *ḳnbt*-court,[116] one contract with the wardrobe-keeper,[117] and one contract with the overseer of *ḥm-nṯr*-priests,[118] who was Hapidjefa himself, combining the offices of provincial governor, mayor, and overseer of *ḥm-nṯr*-priests. These last three contracts concerned a total of twenty-seven days of temple service and their associated revenues. Hapidjefa explained:[119] "Look, as for a temple day, it is 1/360th of a year. You divide the rations of everything that enters this temple, being bread, beer or meat, because a daily ration is that which occurs as 1/360th of the bread, of the beer, of everything that enters into this temple, for each one of these temple days that I have given to you."

Private Funerary Establishments: In the Old Kingdom, most private funerary establishments for which the source of their revenues is known relied on grants of royal revenues, although a few relied on revenues from private properties, or combined them with grants of royal revenues. Royal revenues were apparently the preferred revenue source, perhaps because they were institutional and hence perpetual, at least in theory. In the Middle Kingdom, the private funerary establishment about which the most is known is that of Hapidjefa, a provincial governor of Assiut under Senusert I. The sources of its revenues were the temples of Wepwawet and Anubis in Assiut, and a few officials associated with the necropolis. The preference for institutional revenues thus continued, but temples rather than the state were now the preferred institutions, at least for Hapidjefa. Hapidjefa's funerary establishment is known because he inscribed his rock-cut tomb above Assiut with ten contracts that record how he endowed his funerary cult.[120] In each of these contracts, Hapidjefa exchanged specific revenue sources belonging to him as a private individual or as a mayor, for other revenues from the temples of Wepwawet and Anubis in Assiut or from necropolis officials in perpetuity. These revenues from the temples were to be offered to his statue in the temples of Wepwawet and Anubis in Assiut, and then would revert to his *ka*-priest and his heirs, who managed his funerary cult. The *ka*-priest and his heirs thus had a personal interest in ensuring the contracts were fulfilled in perpetuity, and Hapidjefa states that is why he had them inscribed in his tomb for his *ka*-priest.[121]

EXCHANGES

In the Middle Kingdom, there is slightly more evidence than in the Old Kingdom for high value exchanges involving land, houses, slaves, and prebends. The increased use of writing as well as witnesses to document high value exchanges means that more records have survived, and the participation of state agents in documenting and enforcing high value exchanges made them more secure, more attractive, and consequently more numerous than in the Old Kingdom. Most of the surviving written records concern local exchanges, because even written documents were still dependent on local witnesses for enforcement. Exchange partners usually found each other through social networks rather than anonymous markets. Institutions could engage in exchanges as well as private individuals, acting through authorized agents, though there seems to be some ambiguity whether individual office holders could legitimately alienate property belonging to the perpetual endowment of an institution or office. State redistributive networks may thus have remained the preferred mode of distribution for high value properties over long distances. There is somewhat less evidence for exchanges involving low value goods than in the Old Kingdom, but this is because fewer scenes and descriptions of marketplaces have survived. For the most part, low value exchanges were not directly documented with writing in either the Old or the Middle Kingdom, because the additional security was not worth the additional costs.

Land: There is very little evidence from the Middle Kingdom about either institutional or private ownership of agricultural land. Some private individuals had the right to lease their land to others, suggesting private ownership. Thus in the Hekanakht papyri, Hekanakht exhorts Merisu, "You should find land, 10 arouras of land (to be planted) with emmer and 10 arouras with barley, which must be good land of Khepeshit. Don't go down onto the land of (just) anybody, but ask Hau the younger; and if you find that he has none, then you should go before Herunefer and he will put you on well-watered land of Khepeshit" (P. Hekanakht 1 recto, lines 7–10). Three of Hapidjefa's contracts transfer land inherited from his father to various officials in exchange for regular contributions of bread and beer and lamp wicks for his funerary statue cult.[122]

Houses: Papyrus UC 32037 (*Kahun* VII 1) is a transfer (*imyt-pr*) in which Meri gives his office of Controller of the phyle to his son Iuseneb, and his house to his children by his wife Nebetneninisu, who may or may not include his son Iuseneb.[123] Papyrus UC 32058 (*Kahun* I 1), Text A, is a copy of a transfer (*imyt-pr*) in which Anchren gives all of his property to his brother Wah. Text B is a transfer (*imy.t-pr*) in which Wah gives this property, including his house that his brother built, to his wife, who may then dwell there without fear of being cast out.[124] Papyrus Cairo CG 91061 is a letter in which a scribe writes to another scribe to let him know that his house has been given to a third party, a *wꜥb*-priest, but the context is obscure.[125]

Slaves: Papyrus UC 32167 (*Kahun* I 2) records an exchange (*swnt*) of four Asiatic slaves from Ankhren to his brother Wah.[126] Papyrus UC 32058 (*Kahun* I 1), Text A, is a copy of a transfer (*imy.t-pr*) in which Ankhren gives all of his property to his brother Wah. Text B is a transfer (*imy.t-pr*) in which Wah then gives his brother's property, including the slaves, to his wife, who may then give them to any of their children.[127]

Prebends: There is some evidence from the Middle Kingdom that official positions or prebends could be treated as private capital, that is to say they could be bought and sold as well as inherited. Three of Hapidjefa's contracts exchange his days of service in the temple of Wepwawet, inherited from his father, to various officials in the temple of Wepwawet, in return for contributions of meat, bread, beer, and lamp wicks for his funerary statue cult.[128] Papyrus UC 32055 (*Kahun* II 1) is a petition in which a son says that his father made a transfer (*imyt-pr*) giving his office of *wꜥb*-priest and chief of the phyles of Sopdu Lord of the East to one Iyemiatib, in exchange (*m isw*) for the capital (*tp*) and delivery of income (*fꜣt wꜣwꜣw*).[129] Stela Cairo JdE 52453 (*Stela juridique de Karnak*) contains a transfer (*imyt-pr*) in which Kebsi transfers his office of mayor of El-Kab to Sobeknakht, and an exchange (*swnt*) in which Kebsi exchanges the office with Sobeknakht as payment for a debt of sixty gold deben.[130]

Institutional Exchange Partners: In the Middle Kingdom, there is some evidence that institutions could participate in exchanges through authorized agents. In four of Hapidjefa's contracts, Hapidjefa as mayor exchanges revenues belonging to the office of mayor to the temples of Wepwawet and Anubis, in return for contributions of bread for his funerary statue cult.[131] In two of these contracts, Hapidjefa warns that it would not be good for any future mayors to revoke these donations to the temples, implying that they could do so.[132] In another contract, Hapidjefa exchanges his private days of service in the temple of Wepwawet with himself as overseer of *ḥm-nṯr*-priests of the temple, in return for contributions of meat, bread, and beer belonging to the office of overseer of *ḥm-nṯr*-priests, for his funerary statue cult.[133]

Marketplaces: A market scene may be attested in the Middle Kingdom tomb of Djari (TT 366) at Thebes, but it is unpublished.[134] In the Middle Kingdom literary text "The Eloquent Peasant," set in the First Intermediate Period, a peasant of the Wadi Natrun loads his donkeys with local products and travels south toward Herakleopolis, in order to obtain food for his household, presumably through exchange at a marketplace though this is never explicitly stated. The peasant does not appear to be involved in a redistributive or social network, however, because he has no recourse to them when a local official seizes the peasant's donkeys and goods, and the peasant must petition the official's superior for justice.

Ports of Trade: Stela Berlin 14753 of Year 8 of Senusert III, from the fortress of Semna at the southern border of Egypt in Nubia, states that no Nubians are to be allowed to travel north across the border, unless they come to trade at Mirgissa, or with a message.[135] The town of Mirgissa thus appears to have been a port of trade, to which trade was funneled. In the Saite and Persian Periods, customs duties were levied on goods entering and leaving Egypt through such ports of trade, but there is no evidence for customs duties or bottleneck taxation of any kind in earlier periods in Egypt, though taxes related to the transport of commodities are attested in Mesopotamia already in the second millennium BCE, in the Old Babylonian and Middle Assyrian Periods, when they were collected in both silver and kind.[136] In the absence of similar evidence from Egypt, however, in the Middle Kingdom such ports of trade may have been created to give the state first or sole access to high value goods entering Egypt. State expeditions beyond the populated areas of Egypt to acquire high value goods like hard stones from the Eastern Desert or incense from Punt for redistribution served to validate the state project in addition to procuring raw materials for the economy. The state then had an obvious interest in preventing high value goods from entering the Egyptian economy outside of the state redistributive networks.

ENTREPRENEURIAL ACTIVITIES

Economic actors may choose to use existing goods and services in excess of immediate needs to acquire new raw materials or produce new goods, rather than simply hoarding, redistributing, or exchanging them. In the Middle

Kingdom, the state and its agents undertook major entrepreneurial activities, such as expeditions beyond the populated areas under Egyptian control, or foundations of new institutions within the populated areas under Egyptian control. There is no evidence that the temples undertook such activities on behalf of the state in the Middle Kingdom, but they did not yet command the resources that they would in the New Kingdom. There is, however, evidence for some private individuals undertaking such activities, albeit on a smaller scale.

Expeditions: During the Middle Kingdom, expeditions beyond the populated areas under Egyptian control included military expeditions to acquire booty and prisoners by force, and paramilitary expeditions to obtain materials through mining, quarrying, or trade. Expeditions to Nubia are primarily known from royal foundations there, together with a few inscriptions. Kings Montuhotep II and Amenemhat I appear to have campaigned in Lower Nubia, allowing the latter's successor Senusert I to establish the border at Buhen. King Senusert III seems to have campaigned in Upper Nubia, allowing him to move the border southward to Semna. Senusert III reports capturing women and bringing back inhabitants from Upper Nubia in his stelae of Year 16, but otherwise there is little mention of booty.[137]

Expeditions to the Levant are known from a few inscriptions that chance has preserved. Two reused red granite blocks from the Temple of Ptah at Memphis preserve fragments of official Annals of Amenemhat II, probably dating from Year 45 of Senusert I and Year 3 of Amenemhat II, the last year of their coregency; and Year 4 of Amenemhat II, the first year of his sole reign. They record the return of an expedition to the Sinai, and the departure and return of two expeditions to Lebanon and possibly Syria respectively, as well as the metals, minerals, wood, and other materials that they brought back.[138] A fragmentary biographical inscription from the tomb of the vizier and chief steward Khnumhotep at Dahshur may refer to an Egyptian military expedition against Byblos in the reign of Senusert III, after the ruler of Byblos interfered with Egyptian trade for cedar at the neighboring town of Ullaza.[139] Some of the rulers of Byblos give themselves the Egyptian title "mayor" (*ḥ3ty-ˁ*) in Egyptian-language inscriptions in their tombs, but it is uncertain whether the Egyptians had subjugated them, or whether they were emulating Egyptian elites.[140]

Expeditions to the deserts east of Egypt, and to Punt and the Sinai Peninsula, are well known from inscriptions and graffiti. Expeditions were regularly sent into the Eastern Desert to quarry stone. The Wadi Hammamat, located to the east of Coptos, was a source for Egyptian greywacke.[141] The vizier Ameny who probably later became King Amenemhat I led one expedition to the Wadi Hammamat in the reign of Mentuhotep IV that was marked by several miraculous occurrences.[142] The reporter Ameny led another expedition to the Wadi Hammamat in the reign of Senusert I consisting of over 18,000 men.[143] The Hatnub quarries located east of Amarna were a source of Egyptian alabaster, more properly called travertine,[144] and the Wadi el-Hudi, located to the east of Aswan, was a source for amethyst.[145] Beginning in the reign of Montuhotep III, the kings of the Middle Kingdom dispatched expeditions overland through the Wadi Hammamat to the port of Sauu at the mouth of the Wadi Gawasis on the Red Sea coast, and thence by sea to Punt.[146] At the Wadi Gawasis, caves were excavated to store dismantled ships between expeditions, expedition leaders and staff left commemorative stelae, and notes on potsherds indicated the source of supplies for some of the expeditions.[147] Beginning in the reign of Montuhotep IV, the kings of the Middle Kingdom regularly sent expeditions overland to the port of Ayn Soukhna on the coast of the Gulf of Suez, whence they traveled by sea to the turquoise and copper mines around Serabit el-Khadim in the southern Sinai Peninsula.[148] At Ayn Soukhna, caves excavated in the Old Kingdom were reused to store dismantled ships between expeditions, and commemorative stelae were erected. At Serabit el-Khadim, Senusert I founded a temple of Hathor, which was enlarged by later kings, and which was fronted by numerous stelae erected by expedition leaders and their staff.[149] Expeditions to the deserts west of Egypt, in contrast, are known from one literary reference. King Senusert I was campaigning against the Libyans in the Western Desert when his father Amenemhat I died, according to the tale of Sinuhe.

In the early Second Intermediate Period, weakness of the state curtailed expeditions abroad, and eventually encouraged foreign military expeditions against Egypt. In the late Second Intermediate Period, the division of Egypt between the Fifteenth Dynasty at Avaris and the Seventeenth Dynasty at Thebes led to internal expeditions, such as those described on Stela Cairo TR 11/1/35/1 (The First Stela of Kamose) and Tablet Cairo JdE 41790 (Carnarvon Tablet I),[150] on Stela Luxor J 43 (The Second Stela of Kamose),[151] and on a Third Stela of Kamose.[152]

Foundations: During the Middle Kingdom, state entrepreneurial activities also included founding temples and settlements within populated areas under Egyptian control, in both Egypt and Lower Nubia. Such foundations usually involved at least some redistributed revenues for temple and mortuary cults and their personnel or for administrators and garrisons. Redistributed revenues provided various levels of support for some inhabitants: those with more generous support could themselves support economically specialized dependents, while those with less generous support could engage in additional economic activities to supplement their redistributed revenues, ensuring that such foundations supported a wide range of economic specializations.

Amenemhat I founded a new royal residence at Itjtawy, near El-Lisht to the south of Memphis. Middle Kingdom kings established and endowed their own mortuary complexes and cults at several sites in Egypt, such as Montuhotep II at Thebes, Amenemhat I and Senusert I at El-Lisht, Amenemhat II at Dahshur, Senusert II at El-Lahun, Senusert III at Dahshur and Abydos, and Amenemhat III at Dahshur and Hawara.[153] They sometimes also founded a number of towns in Egypt associated with their mortuary cults, such as Hetep-Senusert associated with the mortuary cult of Senusert II at El-Lahun,[154] and Wah-sut associated with the mortuary cult of Senusert III at Abydos.[155] Middle Kingdom kings founded the town of Avaris in the northeastern Delta, and they rebuilt and possibly reendowed many local temples in Egypt, some of which incorporated *ka*-chapels.[156] They probably also reclaimed at least some of the Fayum basin.

Amenemhat I built the "Walls of the Ruler" on the northeastern border of Egypt. Montuhotep II's and Amenemhat I's campaigns to the south brought Lower Nubia under Egyptian control as far as the Second Cataract. Sometime during the early Twelfth Dynasty, a campaign palace was built at Kor just south of Buhen, and later Senusert I built the fortress-town of Buhen itself.[157] Senusert III's campaigns in Upper Nubia extended Egyptian control to Semna, and in his Year 16 he erected Stela Berlin 1157 at Semna and Stela Khartoum 3 at Uronarti to mark the border.[158] He built a campaign palace at Uronarti, frontline fortresses at Kumma, Semna, and Semna South, and supporting fortresses at Uronarti, Shalfak, and Askut.[159] Senusert III also built a new fortress-town at Mirgissa, south of the old fortress-town of Buhen, and in his Year 8 set up Stela Berlin 14753 at the fortress of Semna in Nubia, forbidding any Nubians to travel north except to trade at Mirgissa.[160]

During the Second Intermediate Period, the Thirteenth Dynasty undertook only minor foundations, such as the mortuary complex of Ameny-Qemau at South Dahshur, the subsidiary burial of Awibre Hor at Dahshur, and the mortuary complex of Khendjer at South Saqqara.[161]

Private Entrepreneurial Activities: Hekanakht's letters and accounts clearly indicate that he was using existing reserves of commodities to accumulate greater reserves of commodities in the future.[162] Some of this activity employed members of his household in Nebesyt, which was in or near the district Perhaa, which may have been in the Memphite region. In his letter to his mother Ipi, Hekanakht includes a list of the food rations that he has set for each of the members of the household, consisting of quantities of grain (P. Hekanakht 2 recto, lines 7–23). The rations decrease down the list, presumably with decreasing seniority because Ipi heads the list. Hekanakht concludes this list by saying, "Look, the entire household is like [my] children, everything belongs to me" (P. Hekanakht 2 recto, lines 25–26). The use of the comparative "like" confirms that several members of the household were not immediate family members. Heti's son Nakht was certainly not, and Allen has suggested that Merisu, Sihathor and Sinebnut were not either, being tenant farmers instead.[163] Hekanakht then addresses Merisu and Heti's son Nakht in the same letter, stating that they should only give these rations to those who are working (P. Hekanakht 2 recto, lines 29–30). Taken at face value, this statement might suggest that Hekanakht administered his household as a firm with contract labor, and render bitter sarcasm indeed to his preceding statement that the entire household was like his children. It seems unlikely however that Hekanakht would have withheld rations for lack of work from his mother Ipi, his mistress, or the young men Anup and Snefru, especially because Hekanakht assigns them no tasks, except Snefru whom Merisu is told to let do what he wants (P. Hekanakht 2 recto, lines 35–37). Moreover, even for those members of the household who are assigned specific tasks, there is no mention of piecework payment.

Other activity, however, took place in the district Tjauwer, which may have been in the Thinite nome, and in any case was distant from Perhaa.[164] One of Hekanakht's accounts records quantities of emmer and bundles of flax that were in the district Tjauwer, in various storehouses and private houses (P. Hekanakht 7 recto, lines 1–7), including some "with" (*m-ꜥ*) the woman Sitnebsekhtu (P. Hekanakht 7 recto, lines 8–14). Allen argues that Hekanakht supplied the flax bundles to Sitnebsekhtu for her and her workshop to process into yarn, and that the quantities of emmer represented rations for Sitnebsekhtu and her workshop.[165] This interpretation is supported by the final line of the account, which indicates when Neferabdu should begin the rations (P. Hekanakht 7 recto, line 15). Another account records quantities of barley and bundles of flax that are in the district Tjauwer (P. Purches recto lines 1–5, verso line 1), including quantities of barley that might be "due to" (*int n*) Neferabdu and various individuals, and one occupation, shepherding (P. Purches recto, lines 6–19). Allen suggests that Hekanakht may have given responsibility for organizing the cultivation and harvest of flax in the Tjauwer district, including giving rations, as well as supplying flax to Sitnebsekhtu to turn into yarn.[166]

CONCLUSIONS

During the Middle Kingdom and the Second Intermediate Period, the state judicial administration began to adjudicate some property transfer disputes, as well as prosecuting crimes against state revenues. Enforcement, however, was directly dependent upon the quality of written documentation. The state began documenting labor obligations for individual people, and harvest taxes for individual plots of land, rather than collectively holding districts responsible for them. Presumably the state expected to increase its labor and harvest taxes by reducing the free-riding that inevitably derives from collective responsibility, and it expected the enhanced efficiency to offset the costs of training and supporting additional scribes necessary for individual documentation. The state also began registering some private property transfers, though it probably did so primarily to track changes in individual tax obligations, rather than specifically to enforce the property transfers. The state could expect to recoup the former costs through increased tax revenues, but not the latter in the absence of transfer taxes. An increasing number of private transactions were documented in writing, but most were probably still documented orally with local witnesses.

State documentation and enforcement of labor obligations and tax revenues was thus more consistent than that of property transfers, rendering title to royal grants of state tax revenues and land more secure than property transfers, especially for higher value properties and across long distances. Most of the beneficiaries of state redistribution, however, were probably concentrated around the royal residences at Thebes and Itjtawy, with their accumulations of palaces and royal and private funerary foundations, and in the provincial administrative centers with their temples. The state seems to have institutionally cultivated many plots of land using officials overseeing compulsory labor, as in the Reisner and Brooklyn papyri. Other plots of land may have been assigned to temples and provincial officials and like Hapidjefa, while individuals like Hekanakht cultivated still other plots and presumably paid a harvest tax to the state. Compulsory labor and presumably institutional cultivation therefore play a larger role in Middle Kingdom documentation than in other periods, while royal donation of land was rare, which probably limited the amount of land with secure title available to exchange. High value exchanges are attested, but they primarily involved revenues associated with state or temple offices, rather than land. At least some and probably many low value exchanges took place in markets, but most of these exchanges were probably documented orally, if at all. Palaces, funerary foundations, and temples provided long-term employment for some, but underemployment was common, possibly encouraging entrepreneurial activity. The state demanded short-term compulsory labor from individuals.

FOUR

THE NEW KINGDOM (c. 1550–1069 BCE)

The New Kingdom consists of the Eighteenth through the Twentieth Dynasties (c. 1550–1069 BCE). The Eighteenth Dynasty succeeded the Seventeenth Dynasty in Upper Egypt, and defeated the Hyksos or Fifteenth Dynasty in Lower Egypt, thereby reuniting the country. The Eighteenth Dynasty royal court probably alternated between Thebes in Upper Egypt and Memphis in Lower Egypt, except during the reign of Akhenaten when a new royal city and necropolis were established and then abandoned at El-Amarna in Middle Egypt. The Nineteenth Dynasty established a new royal city called Pi-Ramesses on the site of the Hyksos capital at Avaris in northeastern Egypt, but the royal court probably also met at Thebes and Memphis. The royal tombs were located at Thebes throughout the New Kingdom, except during the Amarna Period. (See Map 4.1 and Table 4.1.)

CRIMINAL JUSTICE

High officials and high courts located at Thebes and Memphis seem to have had jurisdiction over crimes against the state, including state revenues, and they seem to have applied a body of law established by royal decrees. These same officials and courts, however, also served as courts of referral for property disputes heard by local officials and local courts.

In the New Kingdom, the head of the judicial administration was the king, who could and often did hear and decide cases himself. There are several references to the king adjudicating disputes that concerned his tomb-builders at Deir el-Medina, frequently about the authority of officials over state property.[1] For example, Hieratic Ostracon British Museum 5631, from Deir el-Medina in the Nineteenth Dynasty, records that an official demanded that the writer hand over some copper tools belonging to pharaoh, and when the writer refused, the official seized twelve servants belonging to the writer's family instead. The writer's father then appealed to pharaoh, and he caused that the writer and the servants were set free.[2] Similarly, the Hieratic letter Papyrus Geneva D191 verso, lines 8–11, from Thebes dated in the late Twentieth Dynasty, records that one Prewenemef contended in a *ḳnb.t*-court with the addressee's father in the presence of the king, that the king caused the addressee's father to be justified against him, and that the king ordered the *sr*-officials to make an examination of his men in order to give them to him. And the king said, "Give to him people as is fitting."[3]

The king could also appoint officials to hear special cases on his behalf, as in Hieratic Papyrus Turin 1875 (The Turin Judicial Papyrus), from Thebes from the end of the reign of Ramesses III, in which Ramesses III appointed a tribunal of officials to investigate and pass judgment on those accused of plotting the Harem Conspiracy.[4] Admittedly, Ramesses III may have been dead when he made the appointment, if he perished in the Harem Conspiracy, but if so it was presumably a plausible legal fiction.

Papyrus Turin 1875 (The Turin Judicial Papyrus), lines 1,1-2,9:[5]

(I,1) [King Usermare-Meriamun, l.p.h., son of Re Ramesses] Ruler of Heliopolis [life, prosperity, health (l.p.h.), said] ... (lines 2–9) ... they being (II,1) the abomination of the land.

I commissioned the overseer of the treasury Montemtowe; the overseer of the treasury Pefrowe; (2) the standard-bearer Kara; the butler Paibese, the butler Kedendenna; the butler Baalmahar; (3) the butler Peirswene; the butler Dhutrekhnefer; the king's adjutant Penernute; the clerk Mai; (4) the clerk of the archives Preemhab; the standard-bearer of the infantry Hori; (5) saying:

"As for the matters which the people – I do not know who – have plotted, go and examine them."

(6) And they went and examined them, and they caused to die by their own hands those whom they caused (so) to die, (7) though [I] do not know [wh]o, [and they] also punished [the] others, though I do not know who. But (8) [I] had charged [them strictly], saying:

"Take heed, have a care lest you allow that [somebody] be punished (9) wrongfully [by an official] who is not over him." Thus I spoke to them again and again.

The viziers, however, were more regularly responsible for hearing serious cases. In the New Kingdom, there were usually two viziers serving at the same time

MAP 4.1. Egypt in the New Kingdom

under the king responsible for Upper and Lower Egypt respectively, until the end of the reign of Ramesses III after which there was only one vizier based in Thebes.[6] Viziers could receive petitions, such as Papyrus British Museum 10055 (P. Salt 124), in which Amennakht accused Paneb of many crimes at Deir el-Medina,[7] and perhaps Papyrus Turin 1887 (the Turin Indictment Papyrus), in which Qakhepesh denounced Penanukis at Elephantine.[8] Viziers

TABLE 4.1. *The New Kingdom*

The New Kingdom (c. 1550–1069 BCE)
Dynasty 18 (c. 1550–1295 BCE)
Ahmose I
Amenhotep I
Thutmose I
Thutmose II
Queen Hatshepsut
Thutmose III
Amenhotep II
Thutmose IV
Amenhotep III
Amenhotep IV / Akhenaten
Smenkhare
Tutankhamun
Ay
Horemheb
Dynasty 19 (1295–1186 BCE)
Ramesses I
Seti I
Ramesses II
Merneptah
Amenmesse
Seti II
Siptah
Queen Tausret
Dynasty 20 (1186–1069 BCE)
Sethnakht
Ramesses III
Ramesses IV
Ramesses V
Ramesses VI
Ramesses VII
Ramesses VIII
Ramesses IX
Ramesses X
Ramesses XI

Source: Dates after Ian Shaw (ed.), *The Oxford History of Ancient Egypt* (Oxford: University Press, 2000), pp. 479–483.

could investigate cases with the assistance of subordinate scribes of the vizier,[9] and the viziers could apparently decide cases on their own as well, as in the fragmentary Hieratic Papyrus Génève D409 + Turin 2021, from Thebes and dated to the late Twentieth Dynasty.[10]

Alternatively, the viziers and their subordinate scribes of the vizier could investigate and decide cases together with the great *ḳnb.t*-courts, on which they sat and over which they presided. The Decree of Horemheb, discussed subsequently, states that the king established two (great) *ḳnb.t*-courts in the two great cities of Upper and Lower Egypt (line 4 right), and other sources reveal that they were associated with the two viziers, one at Thebes and one at Heliopolis or Memphis. Like the king, the viziers and the great *ḳnb.t*-courts appear to have been particularly concerned with state property and revenues, especially the theft of state property and revenues, or the abuse of authority over them by officials, as exemplified by the Tomb Robbery papyri. Such cases were almost never handled by the local judicial administrations.[11] The great *ḳnb.t*-court at Thebes is mentioned once in the Tomb Robbery papyri from Year 16 of Ramesses IX, in Papyrus British Museum 10221 (P. Abbot), column 7, lines 1–16, where the vizier and the *srw*-magistrates are explicitly called the great *ḳnb.t*-court.[12] The same group of people appear in other Tomb Robbery papyri of nearly the same date, such as Papyrus Amherst (VI), column 3, lines 7–9, and Papyrus British Museum 10054 verso, column 1, lines 1–3, but they are not called the great *ḳnb.t*-court,[13] perhaps because they were examining suspects rather than passing judgment on them. The same pattern also occurs in later Tomb Robbery papyri from Year 1 of Repeating Births, such as Papyrus Mayer A, column 1, lines 1–10, and Papyrus British Museum 10052, column 5, lines 2–3, where the vizier and the magistrates examine suspects but are not called the great *ḳnb.t*-court.[14] The vizier and the great *ḳnb.t*-courts also occasionally adjudicated disputes over private property, though local *ḳnb.t*-courts more usually handled such cases, often with oracular consultations. The great *ḳnb.t*-court at Heliopolis is mentioned several times together with the vizier in the record of the trials of Mes, inscribed in his tomb in Saqqara in the reign of Ramesses II.[15] The great *ḳnb.t*-courts sometimes also served as witnesses to transactions, though again local *ḳnb.t*-courts more often performed this service. In the Hieratic Papyrus Génève D409 + Turin 2021, from Thebes and dated to the late Twentieth Dynasty, the vizier persuades some heirs to accept the will of their father, and then orders that this decision be made known in the great *ḳnb.t*-court of Thebes.[16]

Several royal decrees also confirm that royal revenues were a primary legislative and judicial interest of the central administration in the New Kingdom, much as in the Old Kingdom. Some of these royal decrees prohibited officials from interfering with temples and mortuary temples, much like the exemption decrees in the Old Kingdom. In the New Kingdom, however, it is clear that the king used temples as royal agents, to collect royal revenues on behalf of the king, and to produce and collect temple revenues upon which the king could draw as needed and desired. The king therefore had an interest in protecting temples from officials seeking to fulfill their obligations to the king by seizing property and personnel assigned to other officials and institutions. Examples of these protection decrees include the Nauri decree of Seti I, the Kanais decrees of Seti I, the Hermopolis decree of Seti I,[17] the Armant decree of Ramesses II from Hermonthis,[18] the Karnak decree of Seti II,[19] and the Elephantine decree of Ramesses III.[20]

The Kanais Decree of Seti I, for example, was inscribed in the temple of Seti I at Kanais in the Wadi Mia or Wadi Abbad near the Eastern Desert gold mines.[21] It preserves a royal decree that specifically protected the personnel of the mortuary temple of Seti I at Abydos engaged in mining, washing, and transporting gold from the Eastern Desert. The Nauri Decree of Seti I, however, inscribed on a cliff at Nauri in Nubia, is the longest (128 lines) and best preserved of these protection decrees.[22] It contains a royal decree protecting all of the personnel and property belonging to the mortuary temple of Seti I at Abydos throughout Egypt, with qualifications specific to Nubia suggesting a local adaptation of a general decree. The text was presumably inscribed at Nauri because the mortuary temple had interests nearby in the gold mines of the Wadi Allaqi. After an introduction enumerating Seti I's benefactions for the gods and especially Osiris of Abydos (lines 1–29), the decree begins by outlining its scope (lines 30–42), protecting any people, boats, fields, livestock, fishers and fowlers, and other temple personnel. It then lists specific violations and their resulting punishments, against people, boats, fields, fishers and fowlers, and property (lines 42–55), against livestock and herdsmen (lines 55–82), against boats bringing tribute from Nubia (lines 82–97), and against temple priests and workers (lines 97–119).

Nauri Decree, lines 30–42 (after Edgerton):[23]

His Majesty has commanded to cause that the House of Millions of Years of the King of Upper and Lower Egypt, Menmaatre (Seti I), "The Heart Is at Ease in Abydos," to be protected on water (and) on land throughout the nomes of Upper (31) and Lower Egypt,

in order to prevent wrong being done to any person belonging to the foundation, who is in the whole land, man or woman,

in order to prevent wrong being done to any goods belonging to (32) this estate (*pr*) which are in the whole land,

in order to prevent any person belonging to this estate (*pr*) being taken by capture (*m kfꜥw*) from one district for another district by corveé (*m brt*) or by forced labor (*m bḥw*) for plowing or by forced labor (*m bḥw*) for harvesting by any viceroy, (33) any commandant, any mayor, any agent, or any person sent on a mission to Kush,

in order to prevent their boat (*im*) being detained (*šnꜥ*) on (the) water by any patrol (*šnꜥy*),

in order to prevent wrong being done to any fields of the (34) foundation in rural districts [- – – – -] – - by any viceroy, any commandant, any agent of (the) House of Agents of the King's Estate (or any) person sent on mission to Kush, in order to prevent cattle, (35) asses, swine, goats (or other) animals [belonging to the] Foundation being taken by robbery (*m ḥwrꜥ*) or by way of liberty by any viceroy, any commandant, any mayor, (36) [any] charioteer, any stable-[chief], any chief of Nubians, [any agent of the King's Estate], any person sent on mission to Kush,

in order to prevent wrong being done to any catcher (*wḥꜥ*) belonging to the foundation (37) on his trapping marshes, on his fishing waters, (or) on fields which he has – ed,

in order to prevent any fisherman belonging to the foundation being driven (38) from his fishing-pools (*swnw.f n ḥꜣm*) which are in the whole land of Kush, by any viceroy, any commandant, any mayor, any agent belonging to the whole land of Kush,

in order to prevent wrong being done to any personnel (*smdt*) of the (39) foundation who are in the land of Kush, men or women, guardians of fields (*ḫwyw ꜣḥt*), agents, beekeepers, cultivators, gardeners, vintners, (40) bargers, packers, foreign traders, (the) staff of gold-washing, carpenters (*wḫr*), (or) anyone who carries on his occupation in the foundation,

but they shall be (41) privileged and protected (*ḫwy mky*) while every man of them carries on his occupation which is carried on in the foundation, without letting them be interfered with by any viceroy (42) of Kush, any commandant, any magistrates, any charioteer, any stable-chief, any standard-bearer, any soldier of the army (*wꜥw n mšꜥ*) (or) any person sent on mission to Kush.

The royal Decree of Horemheb,[24] however, included a first section prohibiting officials from interfering with individuals contributing to the royal revenues (lines 13–3 right). Individuals were conspicuously absent from the exemption decrees in the Old Kingdom, probably because the state did not collect any revenues directly from individuals. Starting in the Middle Kingdom, however, the state began to require compulsory labor from individuals and harvest taxes from individual plots rather than from institutions and communities. Consequently, the state acquired a fiscal interest in protecting individuals' abilities to produce revenues from royal officials seeking to fulfill their obligations by seizing irregularly private property and private persons. For example, the first paragraph of this first section (lines 13–16) prohibits any official from seizing a boat that a private individual (*nmḥy*) has made to transport goods of the king. Offenders will have their noses cut off and will be exiled to Tjaru (Sile).[25] The second paragraph (lines 16–21) states that if the boat of a private individual (*nmḥy*) has been seized, he will be given the boat of another so that he may fulfill his obligations, and he will be given wood.[26] The third paragraph (lines 21–23) states that if royal servants of the offering storerooms irregularly seize servants of private individuals (*nmḥy*) to harvest plants, the royal servants will have their noses cut off, will be exiled to Tjaru (Sile), and the days of labor of the servants of the private individuals will be exacted from them.[27] The fourth paragraph (lines 23–27) states that if soldiers took the hides of deceased cattle for their own use, thereby preventing the overseer of cattle of pharaoh from collecting them, the people (*rmṯ*) should not be held responsible, and the soldiers should to be punished.[28]

The royal Decree of Horemheb also included a second section describing the composition of the central and local judicial courts (lines 3 right – 7 right). Royal interest in local courts was also conspicuously absent in the Old Kingdom, again probably because the state did not collect any revenues from individuals. Once the state started collecting taxes from individuals in the Middle Kingdom, however, the state had to protect individuals' abilities to produce revenues, not just from royal officials as discussed previously, but also from other individuals. The king did not personally take responsibility for adjudicating disputes between individuals, but he did take responsibility for the judges who did so. This second section of the Decree of Horemheb thus states that the king has established (great) *ḳnb.t*-courts in the two great cities of Upper and Lower Egypt (line 4 right). He has instructed the judges not to accept recompense, but if there are exactions of silver or gold (line 5 right), the king has ordained that they shall be suppressed, in order to prevent exactions (line 6 right). The second section also states that the king has established (local) *ḳnb.t*-courts consisting of temple priests (*ḥm-nṯr, wꜥb*) and mayors (*ḥꜣty-ꜥ*) in the cities (line 7 right).[29]

PROPERTY DISPUTE RESOLUTION

In the New Kingdom, local *ḳnbt*-courts seem to have had primary jurisdiction over property disputes and personal injuries, and they seem to have applied a body of law supplied and possibly codified by pharaoh. Local *ḳnb.t*-courts may have been ubiquitous in New Kingdom Egypt. The village of Deir el-Medina, with no more than five hundred inhabitants, had its own *ḳnb.t*-court, though it was probably exceptional in this and many other matters. Local *ḳnb.t*-courts consisted of the notables of a community described collectively as *sr*-officials, and the courts are sometimes identified simply as "the *sr*-officials." The Decree of Horemheb stated that local *ḳnb.t*-courts should consist of temple priests and mayors (line 7 right), but at Deir el-Medina it usually consisted of the foremen and the scribes of the gang of workmen. The composition of the court at Deir el-Medina was not fixed, however, and could include high officials or their agents, such as the scribes of the vizier and the chiefs of police. These presumably conveyed information to the vizier and ensured that he and other high officials investigated and adjudicated the most serious cases.[30]

The *ḳnb.t*-courts could themselves give judgment, or could consult the motion oracle of a local god, whose statue was carried by his priests, usually the notables of the community. When the local *ḳnb.t*-courts gave judgment without recourse to an oracular consultation, the cases most often concerned economic transactions, especially disputes over payment.[31] Records of trials from Deir el-Medina give the impression that the *ḳnb.t*-courts often heard disputes involving the same properties or transactions on multiple occasions, sometimes handing down the same judgment repeatedly, presumably because it had previously not been enforced.[32]

A record of a dispute before a local *ḳnb.t*-court survives on a papyrus from the archive of the herder Mesi, Hieratic Papyrus Berlin P. 9785, from Gurob and dated to Year 4 of Amenhotep IV.[33] In it, the herder Mesi claimed that Hat came to him and gave him a female slave in exchange for two cows and two calves worth two deben and four rings of silver. Hat then confirmed this claim, and swore an oath of Pharoah. Finally, the *ḳnb.t*-court said "Mesi is correct, Hat is false," suggesting that Hat had previously contested Mesi's claim. The papyrus concludes with a list of the members of the *ḳnb.t*-court.

Another record of a dispute before a local *ḳnb.t*-court is partially preserved on a Hieratic papyrus found in Theban Tomb 48, Papyrus Cairo Museum JdE 65739, dated early in the reign of Ramesses II.[34] In the surviving portion, the citizeness Erenofre claimed that she has purchased the female Syrian slave Gemnihiamente from the merchant Reia with various clothes that she apparently wove herself and with objects that she has borrowed from named individuals, worth a total of four deben and one kite of silver. Erenofre denied that she used any objects belonging to the citizeness Bekmut, suggesting that Bekmut had previously claimed that Erenofre used objects belonging to Bekmut without her permission. The *ḳnb.t*-court then demanded that Erenofre take an oath of the sovereign that she should be beaten 100 times and be deprived of her slave if witnesses testify against her, and Erenofre took the oath. The *ḳnb.t*-court then told the soldier Nakht to produce the six witnesses that he claimed would testify against Erenofre. He did so, but the papyrus breaks off before they testify.

P. Cairo JdE 65739, lines 15–17, and 19–21:

(15) Said by the *ḳnb.t*-court of judges to the citizeness Erenofre:

"Take an oath by the Lord, saying: 'If witnesses (16) establish against me that there was anything belonging to the citizeness Bekmut within the silver which I gave for this servant, and I have concealed it, (17) I shall receive 100 strokes, while I am deprived of her'."

(19) ... Said by the *ḳnb.t*-court of judges to the soldier Nakhi:

(20) "Place before us the witnesses whom you said that they knew that this silver belonged to the citizeness Bekmut which was given in order to buy the slave (21) Gemnihiamente'.

Yet another record of a dispute before a local *ḳnb.t*-court is located on Hieratic Papyrus Berlin P. 3047 from Thebes and dated to Year 46 of Ramesses II.[35] After the date, the papyrus records the composition of the court, and then states that the scribe of the royal offering table Neferabe claimed a share of a plot of land that the chief scribe of the storehouse (*šnꜥ*) of Amun Niay managed as representative or agent (*rwḏ*) of the sibling coheirs, and offered the court a papyrus documenting his claim. Niay's response is broken, but the *ḳnb.t*-court ordered Niay to recognize Neferabe's claim, and further ordered Neferabe to lease the land to the *ḥm-nṯr*-priest Wennefer of the estate of Mut, for reasons either not given or not preserved.

The second section of the Decree of Horemheb states that the king gave the judges of the *ḳnb.t*-courts both instructions to their faces (*tp-rd m-ḥr.sn*) and laws in their journals (*hpw m hrwyt.sn*) (line 4 right),[36] and there is evidence for a corpus of law in the New Kingdom called the law of pharaoh. The contents of the corpus are unknown, because the corpus is only attested through a few references and citations. Some have speculated that this corpus may have been contained in the forty *šsmw* mentioned in the Instruction of the Vizier,[37] and depicted in the tomb of the Vizier Rekhmire,[38] but evidence that the Instruction to the Vizier was a Middle Kingdom composition could argue against this.[39]

One citation of the law of pharaoh occurs in the Hieratic Papyrus Cairo Museum JdE 58092 (*P. Boulaq* 10), from Deir el-Medina and dated to the late Nineteenth and early Twentieth Dynasties.[40] A plaintiff addresses the *ḳnb.t*-court of Deir el-Medina and the oracle of the deified King Amenhotep I about a disputed inheritance. The plaintiff presents the facts of the case, and cites the law of pharaoh, "May property be given to the one who buries." Then he asks the oracle of the deified King Amenhotep to make the right decision, and reminds him and the *ḳnb.t*-court of a previous decision of his in a similar case. Another citation of the law of pharaoh may occur in Hieratic Papyrus Génève D409 + Turin 2021, Col. 3, lines 4–5, from Thebes and dated to the late Twentieth Dynasty.[41] It states, "Pharaoh habitually says, 'Give the dowry? (*sfr*) (5) of every woman to her.'" There is some evidence for a law code in the New Kingdom that could be identical to the corpus of law known as the law of pharaoh. Ostracon DeM 764, from Deir el-Medina and dating to the Ramesside Period, describes how family property should be divided if the husband and wife separate.[42] The phraseology consists of prescriptive if-then statements reminiscent of later Demotic law codes, suggesting that this ostracon may be a citation of a New Kingdom law code.

Ostracon DeM 764:

(1) If there are small (2) children, make the property into three parts, one (3) for the children, one for the man, (and) one (4) [for] the woman.

If he will be in charge of (5) the property of the children, give to him the two-thirds of (6) all the property, while the one-third is for the (7) woman.

Oracular Consultations: The local *ḳnb.t*-court of Deir el-Medina made frequent use of oracular consultations for judicial purposes, particularly in disputes over real property.[43] Oracular consultations are first unambiguously attested in Egypt in the early New Kingdom.[44] The earliest examples involve the pharaohs Hatshepsut, Thutmose III, and Thutmose IV consulting the great gods, but nonroyal oracular consultations of local gods became common later in the New Kingdom. Most nonroyal oracular consultations occurred during processions and other appearances of divine images, because at other times the god was inaccessible to the public.[45] The processions and appearances may have been organized specifically for judicial oracular consultations, because their dates usually do not coincide with known festivals. During oracular consultations, the petitioner approached the divine image and presented it with a verbal or written statement or choice of statements, which some scholars call "oracle petitions." The god then expressed its approval, disapproval, or choice through movements transmitted by the bearers of the divine image.[46] The entire process of petition and answer was sometimes recorded, which some scholars call "oracle protocols." The approved or chosen statements were sometimes recast as the speech of the god, both within "oracle protocols" and in independent texts sometimes called "oracle decrees."[47]

On Hieratic Papyrus Cairo Museum JdE 58092 (*P. Boulaq* 10), discussed previously,[48] the undated recto of the papyrus records an oracle petition of Hay, son of Huy, to his good lord, probably the deified King Amenhotep I. Hay states that his father Huy provided his grandmother Tgemy and his grandfather Huynufe with coffins for burial without any assistance from Huy's siblings, but nonetheless Huy's siblings have claimed a share of their parents' property as inheritance. Hay cites the law of pharaoh, "May property be given to the one who buries," and asks the oracle to do the right thing in the presence of the *sr*-officials, that is the *ḳnb.t*-court. Finally, Hay reminds the oracle of a precedent, a previous oracular consultation in which the deified Amenhotep I granted the property of the woman Tanehasy to her son Sawadjyt because he alone buried her. The god evidently did the right thing, because the verso of the papyrus, dated to Year 8 of Ramesses III, records Hay's public division of his inherited property among his children.

Papyrus Cairo JdE 58092 (*P. Boulaq* 10), recto, lines 10–15:

May property be given (11) to the one who buries, says the law of pharaoh. My good Lord, (12) see I am before the officials (*srw*), cause that the good thing is done. (13) See the place of Tanehasy was given to Sawadjyt, when she was buried, (14) when he gave her his coffin. One gave him her half-share (*pš.t*) before the officials (*srw*), (15) because it was King Amenophis who gave it to him in the *ḳnb.t*-court.

Private Social Control: Individuals could use private social networks to help document and enforce agreements and to resolve disputes, in addition to adjudication by *ḳnb.t*-courts. There is evidence for informal horizontal social networks consisting of extended family and friends. Evidence for formal horizontal social networks such as private associations is less clear. Patronage was a kind of vertical social network that is well attested in New Kingdom Egypt. The petition of Amennakht (P. Salt 124 or P. BM 10055), from Deir el-Medina and dating to the late Nineteenth Dynasty, describes a clear example of patronage.[49] In the petition, the workman Amennakht wrote to the new vizier Hori to denounce the chief workman Paneb, reciting a list of his crimes stretching sixty-seven lines. Amennakht began his petition by stating that when his brother the chief workmen Neferhotep was killed, the previous vizier Preemhab passed over Neferhotep and appointed Paneb chief workman instead, after Paneb gave Preemhab five servants belonging to Amennakht and Neferhotep's father. Amennakht thus implies that Paneb had become a client of the vizier Preemhab. Amennakht did not need to explain to Hori that the vizier received petitions and headed the great *ḳnb.t*-court of Thebes, that Paneb had also become a member of the local *ḳnb.t*-court of Deir el-Medina by virtue of his appointment as chief workman, and that together Paneb and Preemhab controlled all local access to the local and central judicial administrations. It is therefore not surprising that Amennakht waited until the vizier Hori succeeded Preemhab before submitting his petition to denounce Paneb. It is also not surprising that Paneb had acted as if he was legally untouchable, by virtue of his position and his client relationship to the vizier. There is no way of knowing whether any or all of Amennakht's accusations were true. But the fact that he wrote them in a petition to the vizier suggests that they were at least somewhat plausible.

> **Papyrus BM 10055 (P. Salt 124), recto, lines 1,1–1,6:**[50]
>
> (1) [The workman] Amennakht [says]:
>
> "I am the son of the chief-workman Nebnufer. My father died (2) [and the chief-workman] Neferhotep, my brother, [was put] in his place. And the enemy killed Neferhotep (3) [and (although) I am?] his brother, Paneb gave five servants of my father to Preemhab who was then vizier (4) ... [and he put him in the place of?] my father, although indeed, it was not his place. And when the burial of all the kings was made, (5) [I reported?] Paneb's theft of the things of king Sety Merenptah. The list of them: (6) ... storehouses of the king Sety Merenptah, which were found in his possession after the burial."

DOCUMENTATION OF OBJECTS OF TAXATION

In the New Kingdom, the central administration documented objects of taxation in several ways. The king and the temples each conducted surveys of the lands that owed taxes to them. The king also conducted a census of people, probably to account for the compulsory labor owed to him, and a census of livestock, to account for the royal cattle contribution. Finally, the king periodically conducted inventories of temples, ostensibly to restore their endowments and increase their offerings, but perhaps also for the purpose of royal exactions from the temples, which are known to have occurred.

Field Surveys: In the New Kingdom, the king ceded a great deal of agricultural land to temples to provide them with revenues, but also retained considerable amounts of *ḫꜣ-tꜣ*-land, *mint*-land, and other types of land to provide royal revenues. The king and the temples cultivated some of their lands directly, thereby receiving the entire harvest. The king sometimes also assigned plots of royal *ḫꜣ-tꜣ*-land to temples without ceding the land to them, in order that the temples cultivate the land on his behalf as his agents. Finally, the king and the temples both assigned some of their lands to individual cultivators, in return for a share of the harvest, here called the harvest tax. Some families cultivated the same lands for generations, and in a very few cases, plots of land were sold, suggesting that the designation of land as "of pharaoh" or "of a temple" could simply indicate the primary tax obligation of the land rather than institutional ownership and cultivation, though as noted previously institutions did sometimes cultivate lands directly.[51] The king and the temples, therefore, each conducted surveys of the lands that they cultivated directly or which owed them their primary tax obligations.

Royal Land: Evidence for royal surveys of land is provided by Stela Brooklyn 69.116.1, from Kom el-Lufi north of Hermopolis, dated to Year 1 of Seti I,[52] and Stela CG 34502, from the Fayum, dated to Year 2,[53] both of which record royal decrees to make a land survey register (*ipw*).[54]

> **Stela Brooklyn 69.116.1:**
>
> (1) Year 1 under the majesty of the King of Upper and Lower Egypt Menmaatre, Son of Re (2) Seti (I) Merneptah, given life. Decree of his majesty l.p.h. (3) to make an inventory of these fields, established and enduring (4) south of the estate of Re, north of the middle of ...

The field surveys of royal land are known to have been kept in the offices of the royal granaries and treasuries. The scribes of the royal granaries and treasuries undoubtedly made the field surveys for the purpose of calculating and collecting the harvest or the harvest tax from royal land, and consequently they recorded the institutions or individuals who were responsible for the harvest or harvest tax from their fields. In many cases, these institutions or individuals were effectively the owners of the plots, or at least of the right to cultivate them, and in these cases the field surveys could serve as a kind of title record. An example of this occurs in Papyrus Sallier I, 9,2–9,9, which is a Late Egyptian Miscellany from the literary archive of Inena.[55] It purports to be a letter from the chief of the record-keepers of the royal treasury to a treasury scribe, informing him that an official has been wrongly deprived of land, that he should be assigned royal land, and that the assignment should be recorded in the royal granary.

Papyrus Sallier I, 9,2–9,9 (after Caminos):

The chief of the record-keepers of the treasury of pharaoh l.p.h. Amenemone speaks to the scribe Pentwere. This letter is brought to you (9,2) to the effect that Amenemuia, son of Amenemope, the stable-master of the Great Stable of Ramesse-miamun l.p.h. of the Residence, has reported to us, saying: "30 arouras of (9,3) fields have been given to me <to> make into fodder for the horse-team of pharaoh l.p.h. which is in my charge; and now, look, they have been taken away from me and given to Nodjme, the steward of (9,4) the Mansion of the King of Upper and Lower Egypt Usimare-setpenre l.p.h. in the House of Amun." Further, when my letter reaches you you shall cause these 30 arouras of fields to be released very speedily and at once to (9,5) Amenemuia, son of Amenemope, the stable-master of the Great Stable of Ramesse-miamun l.p.h. of the Residence. (9,6) And after the copy reaches you you shall demarcate for him fields of the estates of pharaoh l.p.h., (9,7) of enclosures of pharaoh l.p.h., of property of pharaoh l.p.h., of *mint*-fields of pharaoh l.p.h., of *ḫꜣ-tꜣ*-fields of pharaoh l.p.h., of harvest-tax lands of pharaoh l.p.h., and of domain-lands of pharaoh l.p.h., provided they are untended, wherever (9,8) he desires. And you shall cause to be brought to us a copy of whatever you shall do in the guise of an incontestable legal document, and it shall be recorded in writing (9,9) in the office of the granary of pharaoh l.p.h.

The Trial of Mose provides further evidence for royal documentation of land. The Trial of Mose records the court trial of a land dispute, which Mose had inscribed in his tomb at Saqqara after the court vindicated his claims in the reign of Ramesses II. According to Mose, King Ahmose I granted a plot of land to a certain Neshi as a reward, perhaps for military services during the reunification of Egypt at the beginning of the Eighteenth Dynasty. In subsequent generations, the land was divided and subdivided among Neshi's heirs, with one of them appointed as administrator (*rwḏw*). One such administrator, Khay, refused to acknowledge Mose's mother Nubnofret as an heir, so Nubnofret called upon the registers from the royal treasury and granary, which she presumably expected to show her as payer of the harvest tax. Unfortunately for her, they did not, setting the stage for another final trial in which Mose was vindicated.

The Trial of Mose, lines N4-9 (after Gardiner):[56]

(N4) ... Now the king Ahmose I had [given x arourae of land] as a reward to Neshi my father. And further, since king Ahmose I this land was held by one (heir) after another until [this day]. (N5) Then Hui, my father, and his mother Urnero pleaded (*sḫnw*) [together with their] brothers and sisters before the great *ḳnb.t*-court and the *ḳnb.t*-court of Memphis ... writing. [Then my father? Hui] died. And Nubnofret my mother came to till the portion of (N6) Neshi my father, but she was not allowed to till (it). Then she complained (*smi*) against the administrator Khay, and they [caused them to appear before?] the vizier [in] Heliopolis in Year 14 + x of King Rameses II. [Then ... complained saying?]: "Of a truth I am cast forth from this land of Neshi my (N7) father." Then she said: "Let there be brought to me the registers from the Treasury, and likewise from the department of the granary of pharaoh. For I am well pleased to say, that I am the daughter of Neshi. They divided (*psš.t.w*) (the property) for me together with them, but the administrator Khay does not know? my [right?] as a sister?" The administrator Khay complained (*smi*) in the great *ḳnb.t*-court in Year 18, and they sent forth (N8) the priest of the litter Amenemiopet, who was an officer of the great *ḳnb.t*-court, together with him, having a false register in his hand, (whereby) I ceased to be a child of Neshi. And they made the administrator Khay [administrator] for his brothers and sisters in the place of my heirship, although [I was] an heir of Neshi my (N9) father.

Temple Land: Temples documented the land that the king had ceded to them, whether they cultivated it directly or assigned it to cultivators, and temples also documented the land that the king had assigned to them to cultivate but had not ceded to them. The Wilbour papyrus (P. Brooklyn 34.5596) is a cadastral survey of such lands in northern Middle Egypt dating to Year 4 of Ramesses V. Text A of the papyrus lists about 2,800 plots of land in 279 paragraphs, giving their institutional affiliations, either to a temple or to a royal estate. Temple affiliations include the Theban temples, the Heliopolitan temples, the Memphite temples, and the smaller temples. Royal estate affiliations include the royal treasury, royal dockyards, harems and queens' estates, and royal fields, *mint*-lands, and *ḫ3-t3*-lands. Royal estate affiliations probably do not represent all of the royal land in Middle Egypt, rather only the small proportion of royal land assigned to temples to cultivate.[57]

Of the 2,800 plots in 279 paragraphs, 156 paragraphs are characterized as being nonapportioning, meaning that all the harvest went to the institution with which they were affiliated. In this study, it is assumed that temples cultivated the nonapportioning plots either directly or through anonymous local tenant cultivators.[58] 2,245 plots in 116 paragraphs are characterized as being apportioning, meaning that the harvest was "apportioned" between the institution with which they were affiliated, and a named individual who appears to have been responsible for the plot.[59] In this study, it is assumed that the cultivators of the apportioning plots were effectively private landowners, albeit with a harvest tax obligation to royal or temple institutions, analogous to the privately owned temple lands and the allotments of machimoi and clerouchs in the Saite, Persian, and Ptolemaic Periods.[60] This analogy is supported by the identity of the individuals responsible for the apportioning plots, who are for the most part titled stable-masters (22.3 percent), soldiers (12.0 percent), priests (11.8 percent), women (10.8 percent), and cultivators (9.7 percent). Furthermore, there is evidence in the Wilbour papyrus itself that the apportioning plots could be held hereditarily for multiple generations, in statements that the named holder of a plot was dead and it was in the possession of his children, or that the landholder held it with his siblings.[61]

The Great Harris Papyrus (BM EA 9999), dating to Year 32 of Ramesses III, provides more evidence concerning the documentation of temple land in the New Kingdom. It lists endowments made by Ramesses III for the gods of Egypt and their temples, categorized either as Theban temples, Heliopolitan temples, Memphite temples, or smaller independent temples, as in the Wilbour Papyrus. The amount of land assigned to the new temples was 1,071,780 arouras or about 3,000 square kilometers, out of a total cultivated area of between 16,500 and 22,400 square kilometers for Ramesside Egypt, or between 13 percent and 18 percent. These figures do not include the land held by the older temples, though some of the land assigned to new temples may have been reassigned from older institutions.[62] Thus the total amount of land held by the temples in Ramesside Egypt may have been considerably higher than these figures.

Censuses: The evidence for censuses of people in the New Kingdom consists of twenty-two fragmentary papyri in Turin from Deir el-Medina, dating to the Twentieth Dynasty, which contain lists of households and their members.[63] Each household (*pr*) is described as being of (*n*) the male head of household, whose name, father's name, and mother's name are given. In most cases there follow the names, patronyms, and matronyms of other members of the household, preceded by their relationship to the head of household by marriage or birth. Most of the fragmentary lists preserve the names of members of multiple households, suggesting that the complete lists would have been registers of some or all of the inhabitants of Deir el-Medina, rather than returns or extracts for individual households like the Middle Kingdom household documents (*wpwt*) from Lahun. The presence of both a patronym and a matronym and the absence of occupational titles further distinguish these New Kingdom registers from Middle Kingdom household documents. On the other hand, two potsherds from Deir el-Medina contain lists of members of individual households, Ostracon Liverpool County Museum M 13624 verso, and Ostracon Uppsala Victoria Museum 3001.[64] Like the Middle Kingdom household documents, these were perhaps returns prepared to update the registers, or extracts for private use. Unlike the registers, but like the Middle Kingdom household documents, both provide the occupational titles of the heads of household, and omit the patronyms and matronyms of the household members.

Registers of inhabitants like those from Deir el-Medina may have served a variety of administrative purposes. For example, two of the Tomb Robbery Papyri from the end of the Twentieth Dynasty preserve lists of houses on the west bank at Thebes, which may have been used in conjunction with registers of inhabitants, or may have been derived from them.[65] Papyrus BM 10054 verso, pages 2–3, is labeled "every man belonging to every house ... from the temple of Seti I as far as the temple of Ramesses III," and records people to whom grain was given to make bread.[66] Papyrus BM 10068 verso, pages 2–8, is labeled "town register of the west of Thebes from the temple of Seti I to the settlement of Maiunehes," and records households (*pr*) by the occupational title, name, and father's name of the heads of household.[67] Similarly, two potsherds from Deir el-Medina also preserve lists of houses in the village by the names of their heads of household. Ostracon Stockholm MM. 14126, dated to the reign of Ramesses II, records a distribution to houses of volumes, probably of water,[68] while Ostracon DeM 258, dated to the end of the Nineteenth Dynasty, records a list of clothes, probably laundry, by house.[69]

Registers of inhabitants by households could also have been used to record people for compulsory labor services, though the inhabitants of Deir el-Medina, whence the New Kingdom registers come, are likely to have been protected from such demands in order to expedite their work on the royal tombs. The Nauri Decree of Seti I reveals that there were two kinds of compulsory labor in the New Kingdom, corvée (*brt*), and forced labor (*bḥw*) for plowing and harvesting. The forced labor was presumably used for direct cultivation of royal lands that had not been assigned to private individuals or to temples. Certain royal officials were apparently empowered to take people for compulsory labor under certain conditions, because the Nauri Decree only punishes those who did so "by capture" (*m kfꜥw*), that is irregularly (lines 42–45). Other royal officials, however, were punished for taking people for compulsory labor without qualification, under any circumstances (lines 45–47).[70] The Decree of Horemheb likewise punishes royal servants who capture and seize servants for a harvest (lines 21–23).[71]

Nauri Decree, lines 42–47 (after Edgerton):[72]

As for any viceroy of Kush, any commandant, any mayor, (43) any agent, or any other person who shall take any person belonging to the foundation by capture (*m kfꜥw*) from one district for another district by corvée (*m brt*) or by (44) forced labor (*m bḥw*) for plowing or forced labor (*m bḥw*) for harvesting,

likewise the one who shall take any woman of any person belonging to the foundation, likewise their slaves (*ḥmw*), by capture (*m kfꜥw*) to do any task (45) which is in the whole land,

> likewise any charioteer, any stable-chief, or any other person belonging to the King's Estate sent on any mission of pharaoh who shall take any person belonging to the foundation (46) from one district for another district by corvée (*m brt*) or by forced labor (*m bḥw*) for plowing or by forced labor (*m bḥw*) for harvesting, likewise to do any task,
>
> punishment shall be done to him by beating him with two hundred blows and five pierced wounds, (47) together with exacting the work (*bꜣkw*) of the person belonging to the foundation from him for every day that he shall spend with him, to be given to the foundation.

Cattle Counts: In addition to censuses of people, there were also censuses of livestock in the New Kingdom, which appear to have been used to collect a cattle tax or levy. In the Decree of Horemheb, dating to the late Eighteenth Dynasty, the fourth paragraph of the first section (lines 23–27) states that the overseer of cattle of pharaoh was supposed to conduct a census of cattle (*irt irw iḥw*) in the entire land, and to take the hides of deceased cattle. If soldiers took the hides of deceased cattle for their own use, however, thereby depriving the crown, the people (*rmṯ*) should not be held responsible, and the soldiers should to be punished.[73] The hieratic letter Papyrus Cairo CG 58058, dated to the early Nineteenth Dynasty, also refers to an inventory of the contribution of cattle (line 2: *sipt*[*y*] *pꜣ nḥb iḥw*), and to making a census (line 6: *irt irw*), presumably of cattle.[74]

Temple Inventories: In addition to surveys of land and censuses of people and livestock, there were also royal inventories of temples and their property in the New Kingdom. References to royal inventories sometimes state that their purpose was to purify, restore, and rebuild the temples of the gods, and to increase their offerings. This motivation is not surprising, because the king's obligation to satisfy the gods was one of the main ideological justifications of pharaonic rule. Such royal inventories would also have provided the kings with the information that they needed to revise the endowments of temples,[75] and to exact levies from them, both of which are well attested in the New Kingdom.

In the Eighteenth Dynasty, Akhenaten presumably had access to an inventory of temples and their property in order to facilitate his transfer of the latter to the cult of the Aten. Likewise, King Tutankhamun probably had access to or created an inventory to coordinate the return of property to the temples in his reign, as described in his Restoration Stela.[76] In conjunction with the restoration, Tutankhamun issued a royal decree partially preserved on Stela Liverpool University E. 583, dated to his Year 8.[77] In it, Tutankhamun decreed that the hereditary prince, the count, the fanbearer on the right hand of the king, the royal scribe, the overseer of the treasury, Maya, tax (*ḥtri*) the entire land, and establish divine offerings (*wꜣḥ ḥtpw-nṯr*) for all of the gods of Egypt, from Elephantine to Semanebbehedet. In the Nineteenth Dynasty, King Merneptah issued a royal decree commissioning the royal scribe, lector, and chief steward Itewy to make a great inventory (*irt sipty wr*) of all the gods and goddesses of Upper and Lower Egypt. Two short inscriptions refer to the decree, one in the temple of Amun at Medinet Habu dated to Year 2, the other at Deir el-Bahri dated to Year 3.[78]

In the Twentieth Dynasty, King Ramesses III issued a royal decree for making a great inventory (*irt spy wr*), to purify (*swᶜb*) all the sanctuaries of Upper Egypt, and to inspect (*sip*) treasuries and granaries.[79] At least six inscriptions refer to the decree. Two virtually identical inscriptions at Tod and Karnak have lost their dates, but were probably once dated to Year 15. They cite the decree, and enigmatically add that it was in accordance with what was said in Year 5.[80] Another probably related inscription at Tod is clearly dated to Year 15. It does not cite the decree, but merely states that the chief of the guardians of writings of the royal treasury, Penpata, was commissioned to inspect the temples from Memphis to Elephantine.[81] There is a similar inscription at El-Kab, which has lost its date.[82] An inscription at Edfu is also dated to Year 15. It cites the decree, and adds that the chief of the guardians of writings, Penpata, was commissioned.[83] A similar inscription at Elephantine has lost its date.[84] Stela Turin 2682, found at Heliopolis, contains fragments of a temple inventory.[85] Its date is uncertain, but some scholars read a Year 15, and Pierre Grandet would assign it to Ramesses III, seeing it as part of his temple inventory program.[86] It preserves a royal decree commissioning the god's father and chief of secrets of Re-Horakhty, Ramaakheru son of Amememope, and the god's father and chief of secrets of Re-Horakhty, Nebmes son of Amenemope, to make an inventory (*ir sipt*) of the temple of Hathor.[87]

The results of these inventories and purifications of temples may be briefly summarized in the Double Stela of Karnak, dated to Year 20 of Ramesses III, which describes in the right hand text the benefactions that the king made for the gods of Egypt.[88] The Great Harris Papyrus (Papyrus BM EA 9999), dated to Year 32 of King Ramesses III, contains a more complete list of these benefactions, and again may be the result and summary of the inventories, purifications and restorations of the temples of Egypt ordered by Ramesses III.[89] One section of the papyrus described the monuments that the king made for the gods Amun-Re, Mut, and Khonsu of Thebes, consisting of temples, chapels and other buildings, statues, and other temple equipment (cols. 3–9). There follow lists of temple endowments, such as people, livestock, gardens, fields, workshops, and cities (List A, cols. 10–11); goods from annual taxes, tribute, and temple production (List B, col. 12); goods donated by the king (List C, cols. 13–16); grain offerings (List D, col. 16); bread, meat, fowl, and other food offerings (List E, cols. 17–21); and materials for making statues (List F, col. 21). These included 86,486 people, 421,362 livestock, and 864,168 ¼ arouras of fields.[90] Another section of the papyrus described the monuments made for the gods Re-Horakhty,

Atum, Iusaas, and Hathor of Heliopolis (cols. 25–30), followed by similar lists of endowments (Lists A-E, cols. 31–41). These included 12,963 people, 45,544 livestock, and 160,084 ¾ arouras of fields.[91] A third section of the papyrus described monuments made for the gods Ptah, Sakhmet, and Nefertem of Memphis (cols. 44–50), followed by similar lists of endowments (Lists A-E, cols. 51–56). These included 3,079 people, 10,047 livestock, and 10,154 arouras of fields.[92] A fourth section of the papyrus described monuments made for the gods Onuris-Shu of Thinis, Thoth of Hermopolis, Osiris of Abydos, Wepwawet of Assiut, Sutekh (Seth) of Ombos, Horus-Khenty-Shety of Athribis, and Sutekh (Seth) of Pi-Ramesses (cols. 57–60), followed by similar lists of endowments (Lists A-D, cols. 61–66). These included 5,811 people, 13,433 livestock, and 36,012 arouras of fields.[93] These four sections were followed by a fifth section summing up all of the temple endowments that Ramesses III had donated to the gods of Egypt (cols. 67–74), totaling 113,433 people, 490,386 livestock, and 1,071,780 arouras of fields.[94]

DOCUMENTATION OF PROPERTY TRANSFERS

Much of the surviving evidence for the documentation of property transfers and exchanges in the New Kingdom consists of written transcripts of verbal statements. In many cases, particularly on ostraca from Deir el-Medina, the transcripts provide neither the names of witnesses to the transactions, nor the names of the scribes who wrote the transcripts. The transcripts simply record the properties exchanged, lent, or borrowed, their values in weights of gold, silver, or most often copper, the date, and the names of one or both of the transacting parties. These transcripts presumably served as private reminders for their authors, who were either one of the transacting parties, or witnesses to the transactions. The authors could cite these transcripts if they testified in a dispute, because they could authenticate the transcripts themselves. These transcripts are probably not copies or drafts of official records, however, because they lack the information that such records would require to authenticate them independently of their authors.[95]

Hieratic Ostracon Vienna Nationalbibliothek Aeg. 2:[96]

(1) Year 3, fourth month of Shemu, day 5,

This day of bringing (*in*) the (2) ox of Amenkhau by the policeman (3) Amenkhau.

What was given to him (*rdi.tw n=f*):

1 wooden coffin (4) for a woman, decorated, makes (5) *deben* 35;

Verso

(6) 1 *rwḏ*-garment, makes *deben* 7;

(7) 1 pair of men's sandals, makes *deben* 2; total (*deben*) 44.

In some cases, particularly on papyri, the transcripts give the names of witnesses to the transactions, who could presumably authenticate the transcripts. In these cases, the transactions were often conducted in the presence of a local *ḳnb.t*-court, which witnessed the transaction, and could authenticate the transcript, and would adjudicate a dispute arising from the transaction. Sometimes the transcripts also provide the names of the scribes who wrote the transcripts, and who could also authenticate them, as in the case of the Hieratic Papyrus Berlin P. 9784, lines 14–19, from the archive of the herdsman Mesi from Gurob, dated to Year 2 of Amenhotep IV;[97] or the famous Hieratic Papyrus Ashmolean 1945.97 (The Will of Naunakhte), from the archive of the workman Amennakhte from Deir el-Medina, dated to Year 3 of Ramesses V.[98]

Hieratic Papyrus Berlin P. 9784, lines 14–19:

(14) Year 2, month x of Peret, day 27, under the majesty of this [good] god [the king of Upper and] Lower Egypt, (Neferkheperure Waenre), l.p.h. (Son of Re (15) Amenhotep IV), divine ruler of Thebes, may he live forever and ever, like his father Re every day.

On this day of approaching again that (16) Nebmehy did to the herder Mesi, [saying: "Cause that] one give to me a cow for (17) the exchange (*swnt*) of 3 arouras of field."

Then Mesi gave to him a cow worth ½ (silver) deben, before (18) numerous witnesses, before Ahmose (and) his son Nebamun, before Itjetj (19) (and) his son Iufankh, before Hay (and) before Nun.

The scribe Tjetj made (it) today.

With few exceptions, the information contained in such transcripts does not seem to have been registered with or otherwise passed on to the central judicial administration, and even when the central administration had access to such documentation, it did not always make use of it, either to adjudicate disputes or to update its documentation of objects of taxation. In the trial of Mes, he mentioned that his mother Nubnofret and her opponent Khay brought written records to an earlier trial in Year 18 of Ramesses II, but the vizier rejected them because the disputing parties had written them. Nubnofret then proposed consulting tax records from the treasury and the granary to identify the owners of the disputed property, but she was not listed in them, and so the vizier and the great *ḳnb.t*-court denied her claim.[99]

In general, the central administration seems to have privileged witnesses and state documentation, including records of previous cases decided by the great *ḳnb.t*-court. In the trial of Mes, the great *ḳnb.t*-court consulted a record of another earlier trial involving the same property that took place before the vizier and the great *ḳnb.t*-court in Year 59 of King Horemheb, and then the great *ḳnb.t*-court called upon witnesses who testified that Mes was heir to the property, which was restored to him.[100] In the Hieratic Papyrus Génève D409 + Turin 2021, from Thebes and dated to the late Twentieth Dynasty, the vizier persuaded some heirs to accept the will of their father, and then ordered that this decision be made known in the great *ḳnb.t*-court of Thebes, presumably in case the heirs would challenge it later.[101]

Property transfers to or from the king and the temples were documented directly by the state and the temples, in contrast to private transfers. Furthermore, inscriptions on stelae were increasingly used to publicize donations of land by the king or the viceroy of Nubia to soldiers and officials, or to the cults of deities and royal statues.[102] Many royal donations of land to cults indicated that a specific official and his heirs should manage their revenues, and a few imply that the king made the donation on behalf of the official in exchange for the revenues. Some of these donation stelae indicate that they were boundary stelae for the donated parcels of land.[103] The boundary stelae of Akhetaten, the capital city and district founded by Akhenaten at El-Amarna, might also fall into this category.[104] Other donation stelae record that a specific royal scribe, overseer of the treasury, or overseer of the double granary "came on account of it" (*iw ḥr.s*),[105] presumably to witness the transfer and record it in the state or temple field surveys. The use of donation stelae thus supplemented and reinforced state and temple documentation of objects of taxation, which doubled as title documentation.

MEDIA OF EXCHANGE AND REDISTRIBUTION

In the New Kingdom, weights of silver and copper and occasionally volumes of grain served as standard measures of value. A much wider variety of commodities served as media of exchange, however. Gold and silver were occasionally used as stores of value, but presumably they were too valuable or too rare to use as media of exchange in the majority of transactions.

Limited availability of gold and silver would have discouraged the state from trying to collect regular taxes in gold and silver, and the wide variety of commodities used as media of exchange could have discouraged the collection of property transfer taxes as a fraction of the value of property transferred. An inability to collect property transfer taxes in turn could have discouraged the state from investing more effort in documenting and enforcing property transfers, because of the difficulty of recapturing the additional costs.

Measures of Value: In the New Kingdom, values were usually expressed as weights of metal. The metal was most often silver, frequently copper, and very rarely gold, measured with the deben of 91 grams subdivided into ten kite of 9.1 grams, or occasionally into twelve silver shatis of 7.6 grams. A small number of records expressing the relative values of metals reveal that they did fluctuate. Copper fluctuated between 96, 100, and 104 deben per deben of silver in the Eighteenth and Nineteenth Dynasties, and 60 deben per deben of silver in the Twentieth Dynasty. Silver fluctuated from one and two-third deben of silver per deben of gold in the Eighteenth Dynasty, to two deben of silver per deben of gold in the Twentieth Dynasty. In the Middle Kingdom and Second Intermediate Period, silver had also been valued at two deben per deben of gold.[106]

Values of commodities were sometimes expressed as volumes of grain, rather than as weights of metals. The grain was usually barley, measured with the *ẖꜣr*-sack of 76.56 liters subdivided into four oipe or hekats of 19.14 liters or 40 hin, or with the hin of 0.47 liters.[107] Payments in actual barley were therefore sometimes specified as "barley as barley," to distinguish them from payments in other commodities valued in terms of barley. Records expressing the relative value of emmer indicate that it rose from one deben of copper per *ẖꜣr*-sack in the Nineteenth Dynasty and the early Twentieth Dynasty, to one and one-third deben of copper and then two deben of copper per *ẖꜣr*-sack in the early Twentieth Dynasty. The value continued to rise to four deben of copper per *ẖꜣr*-sack in the middle of the Twentieth Dynasty, spiking at eight deben of copper per *ẖꜣr*-sack. The value then fell to two deben of copper per *ẖꜣr*-sack in the late Twentieth Dynasty. Černý attributed some unusually high values to short-term scarcity immediate before the harvest, but he attributed the general rise and subsequent fall in values to unfavorable political circumstances in the middle of the Twentieth Dynasty.[108] Records expressing the relative value of barley indicate that it rose from two and one-fifth deben of copper per *ẖꜣr*-sack, to eight deben of copper per *ẖꜣr*-sack in the middle of the Twentieth Dynasty, spiking at twenty-four deben of copper per *ẖꜣr*-sack. The price then fell to three and a half deben of copper per *ẖꜣr*-sack, and then to two deben of copper per *ẖꜣr*-sack in the late Twentieth Dynasty.[109]

Media of Exchange: Purchases were most often made with one or more objects said to be worth a certain weight of metal, in exchange for one or more other objects said to be worth the same weight of metal. Sometimes metal objects were used in such exchanges, such as copper utensils, and they were said to be worth their weight in metal.[110] Nonetheless, lumps of precious metal were occasionally used as media of exchange, as well as measures of value. Seniu or shati, meaning "rings," are mentioned as media of exchange as well as measures of value in some Hieratic papyri. The existence of such rings is confirmed by their presence in the El-Till hoard from El-Amarna, along with bars of gold and bits of silver.[111] The rings in the El-Till hoard vary considerably in weight, but in the Hieratic papyri they are treated as uniform, one-twelfth deben or 7.6 grams each, which could suggest that they were in effect abstract tokens used as a medium of exchange.[112] It is also possible, however, that the rings were kept in sacks and that it was their overall weight that was significant in transactions, not the weight of individual rings.

Stores of Wealth: Lumps of precious metal were also occasionally used as stores of wealth, as well as media of exchange. The El-Till hoard consisted of gold and silver buried in a pottery jar in a residential quarter of El-Amarna. It contained twenty-three crude bars of gold, weighing 3,375 grams or thirty-seven deben, as well as silver rings, figurines, and other bits weighing 1,086 grams or twelve deben. This hoard clearly indicates that gold and silver could occasionally serve as a store of wealth, at least among a privileged elite.[113] The Tell Basta hoard or hoards were found on two occasions during railway construction near the site of Bubastis. Some of the objects are inscribed and date to the thirteenth and twelfth centuries BC, but they may have been deposited later, possibly much later. The finds consisted of gold and silver bowls, jars, jugs, situlae, wine strainers, jewelry, vessel parts, and scrap, for the most part of unknown weight.[114]

Credit: Given the rarity of lumps of gold, silver and even copper, it is not surprising that there is little evidence for the use of money credit. There was, however, probably a system of open credit to expedite barter exchange of property. Buyers often lacked sufficient property to make a desired exchange, or lacked specific property that a seller desired in exchange, and therefore they had to borrow other property from family, friends, and neighbors. The latter extended credit because they would eventually need similar credit themselves sometime, and then the favor would be returned and the credit repaid.[115]

REDISTRIBUTIVE NETWORKS

In the New Kingdom, the state employed a number of royal institutions to manage its redistributive networks. The royal granaries and treasuries and their branches appear to have received, disbursed, and kept accounts of state revenues, but they generally do not appear to have authorized or otherwise determined disbursements. The royal palaces and dockyards, on the other hand, frequently authorized disbursements from the royal granaries and treasuries and other storage institutions to individuals and personnel, as well as to other dependent institutions, gangs, and crews. Some of these disbursements consisted of food for immediate consumption, while others consisted of materials for further processing and transportation. Dependent institutions like bakeries, work gangs like the royal tomb-builders at Deir el-Medina, and ships' crews did most of the actual production, processing, and transportation. They were dependent on royal palaces, dockyards, or high officials like the vizier, who provided them with rations and raw materials. The state increasingly used the larger temples as agents, in addition to or instead of the provincial administrators it had used in the Old and Middle Kingdoms. The state could exact levies from the temples if needed, however, so that they served to some extent as branches of the royal treasuries and granaries. Temples also distributed taxes, labor, and commodities to numerous categories of personnel, from *ḥm-nṯr*-priests to regular *wꜥb*-priests in rotation and laborers, many of whom were able to engage in additional economic activities, thanks to the secure base salaries provided by the state or the temples. The central administration carefully documented and enforced both state and temple redistribution, privileging them over private redistribution and exchanges, which for the most part were dependent on local documentation and enforcement.

Royal Granaries and Treasuries: The primary task of royal granaries and treasuries appears to have been accounting for state revenues, when they were collected, and while they were stored, until they were disbursed. In some cases, scribes of the granary and the treasury may have been directly involved with harvesting state land. Papyrus Sallier I, 4,5–5,4 is a Late Egyptian Miscellany from the literary archive of Inena, which purports to be a report of a treasury scribe overseeing the harvest of state *ḫꜣ-tꜣ*-land for his superior, the chief of the record-keepers of the royal treasury.[116] In other cases, however, scribes may have simply received the harvest from state cultivators and accompanied it to a royal granary. Papyrus Louvre E. 3171 is probably from Memphis and dates to a Year 9 in the Eighteenth Dynasty.[117] It records that the cultivator Mahu, son of Amenhotep, delivered a total of 1,000 sacks of grain from one village to two ships, that the cultivator Nebnufe delivered 656 ½ sacks from another village, and that the cultivator Amenmose delivered a total of 1,421 sacks from yet another village to two other ships at three different locations, all of which were accompanied by the scribe Penroy to the granary of Memphis, presumably a royal granary.

The scribes of the granary and the treasury definitely recorded the arrival of shipments of harvests and harvest taxes at the royal granaries, however. Papyrus Louvre E. 3226 is probably from Thebes, and dates to Years 28–34 of Thutmose III.[118] It preserves two running accounts of a branch of the royal double granary. Text A is an account of dated deliveries of grain, said to be from named ships, various places, or other granaries, with periodic totals. Text B is an account of dated deliveries of dates, with periodic totals. The rectos of Texts A and B were written by the scribe Hapu of the overseer of the double granary Minnakht, while the versos were written by the scribe My of the overseer of the double granary Tjenuna. The rectos and versos are virtually identical parallel texts, presumably intended as checks on each other. The scribes of the granary and treasury may have also kept accounts of the revenues from royal *ḫꜣ-tꜣ*-land that temples cultivated on behalf of the state, and whose harvests they collected and stored on behalf of the state. The Turin Taxation Papyrus (Papyrus Turin

1895+2006), dating to Year 12 of Ramesses XI, records that the overseer of the granaries of pharaoh and viceroy of Kush, Panehesy, ordered the *ḥm-nṯr*-priests of the temples of Upper Egypt to hand over grain from the *ḫꜣ-tꜣ*-land of pharaoh to the scribe of the Necropolis, Dhutmose.[119]

Royal Palaces: The royal palaces appear to have managed the production, processing, transport, and distribution of commodities after the royal granaries and treasuries had collected, stored, and accounted for them. In some cases the palaces simply consumed or distributed the commodities, but in other cases they arranged for them to be processed further prior to consumption or distribution. Some accounts of a royal palace are preserved on Papyri Bibliotheque Nationale 203–213, 237 (P. Rollin 1882, 1884–86, 1889) and Papyrus Amherst XI, which are part of a papyrus archive from Memphis dating to Years 2 and 3 of Seti I.[120] P. Bibl. Nat. 203 is an account of deliveries of birds from various sources for the bird pens of Seti I. P. Bibl. Nat. 204–208 are accounts of disbursements of flour from various granaries to various bakeries, and of the bread loaves consequently delivered to the royal palace Per-Aakheperkare in Memphis, as well as the intervening wastage. P. Bibl. Nat. 209–213 and P. Amherst XI are accounts of shipbuilding wood and other materials with individuals and institutions in Memphis. Other accounts from another royal palace are preserved on a series of papyri from the royal harem at Mi-wer (Gurob), dating to the Nineteenth or Twentieth Dynasty.[121] The largest papyrus is a scribal journal recording receipt of deliveries and distributions of fish, oil, bread, and beer, as well as copies of correspondence. Other fragments record the delivery and branding of cattle, and the distribution of garments, for example.

Royal Dockyards: Royal dockyards also managed the production, processing, transport, and distribution of certain commodities, like the royal palaces. Some accounts of a royal dockyard are preserved on Papyrus BM 10056 and Papyrus Ermitage 1116A and B, which may be part of a papyrus archive from Memphis. Papyrus BM 10056 dates to Year 52 of Thutmose III,[122] and contains accounts listing measured pieces of wood issued to craftsmen for building boats at a royal dockyard called Perunefer.[123] The location of Perunefer is disputed, some placing it at Memphis, while others identify it with Tell el-Daba.[124] Papyrus Ermitage 1116A and B was divided and their rectos reused for New Kingdom copies of Middle Kingdom literary texts, "The Instruction to King Merikare" and "The Prophecies of Neferti" respectively. Papyrus Ermitage 1116B verso appears to date to Year 1 or 2 of Amenhotep II,[125] and contains accounts of wood issued to craftsmen to make various objects, some for the royal palace Per-Menkheperre.[126] Papyrus Ermitage 1116A verso mentions grain of a Year 18, and contains accounts of grain disbursements for both individuals and institutions, including an institution called Per-Duat.[127]

Military and Police: In the New Kingdom, the army primarily consisted of reserve soldiers who supported themselves when off duty by cultivating plots of land received as rewards or inheritances. Frequent campaigns and numerous garrisons, however, meant soldiers spent much time on duty, and consequently often received redistributed revenues. The *medjay*-police were also regular recipients of redistributed revenues, as previously.

The Decree of Horemheb specified that reserve soldiers served in the royal bodyguard in rotation. It also specified that soldiers serving in the royal bodyguard received regular rations from the state Double Granary, as well as provisions from the palace and rewards from the king himself. This may have been an innovation of Horemheb, or a reestablishment of earlier practices that had lapsed during the Amarna Period.[128]

Reserve soldiers probably also served in garrisons in rotation, given the numerous troop commanders (*ḥry-pḏ.t*), stable-masters (*ḥry-iḥw*), commanders of fortresses (*imy-r ḫtmw*), and garrison commanders (*imy-r iwʿy.t*) who served abroad, sometimes for years, but returned to Egypt to continue their careers and erect monuments and tombs for themselves. They were supposed to receive rations while in garrison, and most fortresses outside of Egypt contained granaries to supply their garrisons and armies on campaign. These granaries were in turn probably supplied with tribute from the regions in which they were located.[129]

Reserve soldiers called up to serve on campaigns could probably also draw rations and requisition personnel and supplies from various state institutions and temples. Consequently royal decrees sometimes prohibited military encroachment on royal interests. For example, the Nauri Decree of Seti I repeatedly forbids requisitioning anything from the Nubian properties and personnel of the mortuary temple of Seti I at Abydos, by any viceroy of Kush, any troop commander (*ḥry-pḏ.t*), any mayor, any agent, or by any charioteer (*kḏn*), any stable-master (*ḥry-iḥw*), any standard-bearer (*ṯꜣy-sr*), any soldier of the army (*wʿw n mšʿ*).[130] Similarly, the Decree of Horemheb legislated against soldiers who took the hides of deceased royal cattle.[131]

Off-duty reserve soldiers were expected to support themselves, however, and thus held and cultivated plots of land between campaigns and other duties. In the late New Kingdom, defeated Sea Peoples known as Sherden were settled in Egypt and assigned lands as reserve soldiers, and served in the Egyptian army under Ramesses II at the Battle of Kadesh.[132] Later, Libyans known as Meshwesh were also settled in Egypt and formed increasing proportions of Egyptian armies.[133] The Wilbour papyrus (P. Brooklyn 34.5596), dating to Year 4 or Ramesses V, hints at the number of off-duty reserve soldiers in Egypt, and the sizes of the plots that they held. It recorded the harvest obligations of around 2,800 plots of land in Middle Egypt. Institutions directly held about 555 plots, while individuals held around 2,245 plots with tax obligations to institutions. The names and titles of about 2,110 individual plot holders are preserved, of whom 471 (22.3 percent) were stable-masters (*ḥry iḥw*), 253 (12.0 percent) were soldiers (*wꜥw*), 59 (2.8 percent) were Sherden (*Šrdn*), 47 (2.2 percent) were charioteers (*kṯ*), and 24 (1.1 percent) were standard-bearers (*ṯꜣy-sryt*).[134] Stable-masters usually held plots of five arouras, and soldiers plots of three arouras, with few exceptions.[135] Sherden and standard-bearers most frequently held plots of five or ten arouras, and charioteers plots of ten or twenty arouras, but other plot sizes were not uncommon.[136] An additional 228 plot holders (10.8 percent) were women titled "citizeness" (*ꜥnḫ n niwt*) who usually held plots of three or five arouras, and were probably wives or mothers of soldiers or stable-masters.[137] Altogether, reserve soldiers and their wives represented 51.3 percent of the plot holders in the Wilbour Papyrus.

Dependent Institutions, Gangs, and Crews: Royal palaces and dockyards managed the production, processing, and transport of commodities, but dependent institutions, gangs, and crews appear to have done much of the actual work. The latter institutions seem to have had limited agency. The royal palaces and dockyards assigned them their rations, materials and tools, and production goals. As previously mentioned, the royal dockyard of Thutmose III issued materials to craftsmen to build boats, and the royal palace of Seti I issued flour to bakeries to produce bread, which was then delivered to the palace.

Some of this work may have occurred within the palaces and dockyards, but some definitely took place offsite, such as the transportation of commodities. Papyrus Leiden I 350 verso is a ship's log from Memphis dating to Year 52 of King Ramesses II.[138] It is part of a papyrus archive from the estate of the *sm*-priest of Ptah, Prince Khaemwaset, which included several magical and literary texts (P. Leiden I 343–359), and correspondence (P. Leiden I 360–368). The ship's log is preserved on the verso of a literary text, a "Hymn to Amun." The presence of the ship's log in the archive, references to sailors of the *sm*-priest among the crew (col. V, 3, 14), and frequent references to letters dispatched from the ship to the *sm*-priest in Memphis (col. I, 9; III, 1, 26; IV, 10, 19; V, 23), all suggest that the ship was attached to the estate of Prince Khaemwaset. The first part of the ship's log (cols. I-V) is organized into daily entries covering eleven days. The dates for the first two entries are lost, but the remaining nine days run from Year 52, second month of Peret, day 26, to third month of Peret, day 4. The ship was moored at Pi-Ramesses until it departed in the night of third month of Peret, day 1, and it arrived at Heliopolis in the evening of third month Peret, day 4. Each complete daily entry listed what was given (*rdyt*) as rations (*m ꜥḳw*) to the crew of the ship, which varied from day to day from twenty-five to forty people. Some daily entries broke down the crew into "sailors of the *sm*-priest" (*nfw n sm*), "people of the regiment" (*rmt/sdmw pꜣ sꜣw*), "personnel of the temple" (*rmt/smdt (n) ḥwt-ntr*), "personnel of the estate" (*rmt pꜣ pr/pr pn*), sometimes specified as "of Prince Ramesses" (*n pr sꜣ-nswt Rꜥ-ms-sw*), "sailors" (*nfw*), and "scribes" (*sšw*). The daily entries also record the departure of various people for various purposes, most often with a letter for the *sm*-priest. Two scribes were imprisoned for several days, and were sent rations until they were released. The daily entries also list deliveries (*inw*) by various people, including the charioteer Esse, the lady Isinofre daughter of Merenptah, the charioteer Ramessesnakht son of the general, the general himself, the servant Ptahptenro, one Tashowe, and one Htore. The deliveries consisted of loaves of bread, sacks of grain, jars of meat, milk, wine and beer, preserved fish, live fowl, bundles of firewood, and charcoal. The quantities were relatively small, apart from 1,210 preserved fish, but nonetheless they were probably not rations for the crew, which consisted almost exclusively of bread and herbs. By analogy with ship's log Papyrus Turin 2008 + 2016, they were probably small consignments of freight. The second part of the ship's log (col. VI) contained a separate summary of deliveries (*inw*), which largely disagreed with those listed in the daily entries.

The gang of the necropolis (*tꜣ is.t n pꜣ ḫr*) is the single best known gang of dependent craftsmen in ancient Egypt, but in many ways it was unique. For most of the New Kingdom, the gang's primary task was to excavate and decorate the royal tombs in the Valley of the Kings to the west of Thebes. The gang worked for the king, but it was under the direct supervision of the Vizier. During most of this period, the gang resided in a separate village community at Deir el-Medina, located in the low desert to the west of Thebes near the Valley of the Kings, though under Akhenaten it may have been relocated to the new royal residence of Akhetaten at El-Amarna.[139] At the end of the Twentieth Dynasty, however, royal tombs ceased to be constructed at Thebes, and rather than being disbanded the gang was assigned new tasks, such as campaigning in Nubia or recycling funerary equipment in the Theban necropolis. The gang was also increasingly supervised by and ultimately came to serve the high priest of Amun, as the authority of the king and the vizier at Thebes diminished.[140] The gang (*tꜣ is.t*) is best known during the Ramesside Period, when it usually consisted of about forty regular workmen, divided into two "sides" (*rwiꜣ.t*) of about twenty workmen. Occasionally the size of the gang was increased to up to 120 workmen, to expedite work on the royal tombs.[141] The two sides of the gang were each led by a chief-workman or foreman of the gang (*ꜥꜣ n is.t*),[142] and a deputy of the gang (*idnw n tꜣ is.t*) who was counted as one of the regular workmen.[143] There was one senior scribe of the necropolis (*sš n ḫr*), sometimes assisted by a chief draftsman (*ḥry sš-ḳd*).[144] The chief-workmen and the senior scribe received larger rations than the regular workmen and scribes. They were also regular members of the village *ḳnb.t*-court, making them leaders of the larger village community as well as of the gang. Positions in the gang were limited, as were houses in the village, which were linked to the positions.

Nonetheless, households included the wives, sons, and daughters of the workmen. Sons could inherit the positions and houses of their fathers, subject to approval of the vizier, or the positions and houses of other workmen who had no sons of their own, or they could leave the community to live and work elsewhere. Sons who remained in the community without a position of their own were called boys (*ᶜḏd*), and were collectively known as the children of the necropolis (*msw ḫr*). If the vizier promoted them to a position, they became known as young men (*mnḥ*), and initially received a smaller ration than regular workmen.[145]

The rations of the community of workmen consisted of monthly distributions (*diw*) of grain; regular daily, weekly, or monthly deliveries (*ḥtri*) of water, fuel, fish, and pottery by the "personnel of the outside" (*smdt n bnr*); regular deliveries (*ḥtri*) of cakes, dates, and beer by various mortuary temples to the west of Thebes; and irregular deliveries (*mkw*) of salt, oil, meat, natron, garments, and sandals from high officials.[146] The state normally provided the monthly distributions of grain to the community of workmen. Late in Twentieth Dynasty, grain sometimes also arrived from temple granaries, such as those of Maat, of Mut, of Amun, and of Hapy, but it could have come from state accounts at those granaries. In the Turin Taxation Papyrus (Papyrus Turin 1895 + 2006), the Viceroy of Kush and Overseer of the Granary Panehesy ordered the scribe of the necropolis Dhutmose to collect grain for the workmen originating from royal *ḫꜣ-tꜣ*-land but stored in various temple granaries in Upper Egypt. The grain supplies were normally delivered to a granary located near Deir el-Medina. It was known variously as "the granary" (*tꜣ šnwt*), "the granary of the necropolis" (*tꜣ šnwt (n) pꜣ ḫr*), and "the granary of the enclosure of the necropolis" (*tꜣ šnwt (n) pꜣ ḫtm n pꜣ ḫr*). This granary was probably also known as "the granary of pharaoh," suggesting that it was a branch of the state granary system.[147] The monthly distributions of grain were often distributed from the granary of the necropolis to the workmen in several installments. The initial distribution was called *diw* whether it was complete or partial, and all further installments were called *dni* (*diw*). The chief workmen and the senior scribe received monthly rations of five and a half *ẖꜣr*-sacks of emmer and two *ẖꜣr*-sacks of barley, while the regular workmen received four and a half *ẖꜣr*-sacks of emmer and one and a half *ẖꜣr*-sacks of barley, and young men received one and a half or two *ẖꜣr*-sacks of emmer and half, one and a half, or even two *ẖꜣr*-sacks of barley.[148] Delays and interruptions to the monthly distributions of grain in Year 29 of Ramesses III stimulated the workmen to repeatedly stop work and demonstrate in front of the mortuary temples in the west of Thebes, as described in the Turin Strike Papyrus (Papyrus Turin 1880).[149]

The state also arranged for the community of workmen to receive regular deliveries (*ḥtri*) of water, firewood, vegetables, fish, pottery, and so forth from small groups of water-carriers, woodcutters, gardeners, fishermen, potters, laundrymen, and gypsum-makers, who were collectively known as the personnel of the outside (*smdt n bnr*) or the personnel of the necropolis (*smdt n pꜣ ḫr*). The personnel did not reside with the workmen at Deir el-Medina, though their work regularly brought them there. The state provided them with rations, but they usually were not distributed with those for the workmen, and they were usually much less generous, three-quarters or one *ẖꜣr*-sack of grain per person. Some households of personnel served the community of workmen for several generations. The vizier once proposed to assign a number of former workmen to be personnel of the outside after the size of the gang had been reduced, though they would have lacked the skills for many of the tasks.[150] Each side of the gang was assigned six or twelve water-carriers (*inw-mw*), led by a chief water-carrier (*ḥry inw-mw*). Deliveries were measured in *ẖꜣr*-sacks, and deficits were recorded, suggesting that there were daily quotas for each worker. The water-carriers occasionally delivered other goods to the community of workmen, such as grain, rations, wood, copper, and so forth. The water-carriers frequently hired donkeys from the workmen to assist in the deliveries of water and other products, and even in plowing.[151] There were between two and six woodcutters (*šꜥd-ḫt* or *inw-ḫt*) divided between the two sides of the gang, depending upon the size of the gang. They were required to deliver several hundred units of firewood or several dozen sacks of dung each ten days. Records usually indicated the quota (*bꜣkw*) assigned, the amount actually delivered, which was often less than the quota, and the resulting deficit. The woodcutters frequently hired donkeys belonging to the workmen to help deliver the firewood.[152] There were usually eight fishermen (*wḥꜥw*) assigned to provide fish to the gang, four for each side. Each of the twenty workmen and the scribe on each side was supposed to receive four deben of fish a day, and the chief workman eight deben, for a total of ninety-two deben of fish per side per day. This was the target or quota assigned to the fishermen, which was cumulative. Actual deliveries took place irregularly every few days, and sometimes specified the weight of fish in deben; or the number, type and size of fish, and whether they were fresh, gutted, dried, or whole; or occasionally both. Deficits in the weight of fish delivered were recorded and were cumulative. Deliveries of fish were immediately distributed to the workmen, unlike grain that was stored in the granary.[153] Similarly, there were usually two potters (*ḳdw*) assigned to produce pots for the gang. It is unclear whether they were divided between the two sides of the gang, and whether they hired donkeys to deliver the pots. The potters were assigned quotas (*bꜣkw*) of several kinds of pots each ten days, usually on the tenth, twentieth, and thirtieth of each month. The most common types were big *ḳbw*-pots, and smaller *ṯ(ꜣ)b*-pots, usually ten times as many as *ḳbw*-pots. Deficits in deliveries were recorded, and were cumulative.[154] There were two or three washermen (*rḫty*) assigned to the community of workmen, one or two for each side of the gang. Each washerman was assigned to do the laundry for several households each day. Scribes or workmen sometimes made lists of the types and number of garments they gave to the washermen and their condition, or occasionally they simply made drawings of them. The washermen presumably took the laundry to the riverbank for washing, which gave them the opportunity to do errands for the workmen. There is no evidence that they made extensive use of donkeys for transport.[155]

The community of workmen also received regular deliveries (*ḥtri*) of cakes (*šꜥt-bit*) and beer from mortuary temples on the west bank of Thebes. These deliveries may have been reversions of temple offerings, because cakes and beer were both part of the daily cult ritual and the festival offerings in the mortuary temples.[156] Finally, the workmen sometimes received extra provisions (*mkw*) or rewards (*ḥsw* or *fḳꜣ*) during festivals or when high officials visited. These extra provisions often consisted of valuable commodities, such as meat, oil, salt and garments, as well as extra bread and beer. Some but certainly not all of these extra provisions may have been in exchange for private commissions carried out for high officials.[157]

Temples: In the New Kingdom, temples could also manage redistributive networks. Temples possessed endowments (*ḥtpw-ntr*, literally "divine offerings") of land, people, and cattle and other sources of revenue. Some of the revenues were offered to the gods (*ḥtpw-ntr*) and then were redistributed to the priests and other personnel as rations, while other revenues were used as rations and raw materials for dependent craftsmen and personnel.[158] Temple endowments varied greatly in size from temple to temple and through time, and were not necessarily linked to the physical size of a temple's architecture, as resources could be diverted from older temples to newer ones. Temples also varied greatly in agency. Some temples possessed a large amount of autonomy and managed their own endowments and revenues, while other temples had some aspects of their endowments and revenues managed for them, operating as dependent branches except with regard to their divine offerings.

In the New Kingdom, kings continued to build and endow royal mortuary temples, called "temples of millions of years" (*ḥw.t nt ḥḥw m rnpw.t*). Most were located in Thebes on the west bank of the Nile, opposite the temple of Amun-Re on the east bank, but some were located elsewhere, such as those of Seti I and Ramesses II at Abydos. Older mortuary temples seem to have remained economically autonomous, though sometimes parts of their endowments may have been transferred to newer mortuary temples. For example, it has been suggested that much of the endowment of the mortuary temple of King Ramesses II, the Ramesseum, was transferred to the mortuary temple of King Ramesses III at Medinet Habu. Similarly, parts of their endowments may occasionally have been transferred to divine temples. At the beginning of the Nineteenth Dynasty, the mortuary temple of King Seti I at

Abydos operated gold mines in Nubia and the Eastern Desert, but by the end of the Twentieth Dynasty the temple of Amun-Re at Thebes operated these or similar gold mines.[159]

In the New Kingdom, kings also continued to build and endow divine temples, on a greater scale than ever before. The temple of Amun-Re at Karnak in Thebes in particular benefited from building programs and donations of land and booty following successful military campaigns in the early Eighteenth Dynasty and especially under Thutmose III. Akhenaten stripped many temples of their endowments to benefit the cult of the Aten, but Tutankhamun and his successors abandoned the cult of the Aten and restored the endowments to the traditional temples. The Great Harris Papyrus (Papyrus BM EA 9999) shows that Ramesses III continued to favor the cult of Amun above all others, but many of his donations to Amun were actually to his own mortuary temple, which was described as being "in the estate of Amun."[160] Indeed, the Great Harris Papyrus and other Ramesside sources use the epithet "in the estate of Amun" to link together the temples of Amun-Re, Mut, and Khonsu as parts of the estate or domain of Amun, together with most of the royal mortuary temples to the west of Thebes, and even some temples in Nubia. Likewise, the temples of Re-Horakhty, Atum, Iusaas, and Hathor in Heliopolis and some temples in Nubia appear to be linked together as the estate or domain of Re, and the temples of Ptah, Sakhmet, and Nefertem in Memphis and some temples in Nubia as the estate or domain of Ptah.[161] Some have argued that the designation "in the estate" of a god indicated that a temple was administratively and economically subordinate to a larger divine institution.[162] Haring however argues that the designation represented administrative cooperation, in tax collection for example, but not economic subordination, which was indicated by the epithets "on the provision" (*ḥr sḏfꜣ/sdf*) or "in the retinue" (*imy-ḫt*) of another temple.[163]

As temples grew, so did their administrations, especially that of the temple of Amun-Re at Karnak. In the early New Kingdom, the administrative head of the temple of Amun-Re was a steward (*imy-r pr*) or chief steward (*imy-r pr wr*), who was sometimes also high priest but more often a civil administrator.[164] In the Ramesside Period, however, the high priest of Amun-Re became the administrative as well as religious head of the temple.[165] In the early New Kingdom, the temple of Amun-Re also possessed officials and scribal staff in charge of a granary and a treasury to store revenues and account for them until they were disbursed, as well as officials in charge of temple fields and cattle, production centers (*šnꜥ*) and craftsmen.[166] In the Ramesside Period, the domain of Amun also organized the collection of grain harvest taxes for several cooperating or dependent temples. Papyrus Baldwin (Papyrus BM EA 10061) + Papyrus Amiens (Papyrus Musée de Picardie 88.3.5) are the accounts of a flotilla of ships belonging to the domain of Amun, which sailed down the

Nile stopping periodically along the way to pick up grain harvest tax payments from endowment lands belonging to several temples associated with the domain of Amun.[167]

Some temple staff and personnel worked onsite, such as *ḥm-nṯr*-priests and *wꜥb*-priests, but other personnel worked offsite, such as temple ship crews, herdsmen, fishermen and fowlers, and miners in the deserts, just as many dependent gangs and crews worked offsite from the royal palaces or estates to which they were attached. The Nauri Decree (lines 36–40) provides a long list of dependent personnel working in Kush but attached to the mortuary temple of Seti I at Abydos, including fishers and fowlers, guardians of fields, beekeepers, cultivators, gardeners, vintners, bargers, packers, staff of gold-washing, and carpenters. Admittedly, some of these may have been directly attached to dependent institutions located in Nubia, and thus only indirectly attached to the mortuary temple of Seti I. Papyrus Baldwin (Papyrus BM EA 10061) + Papyrus Amiens (Papyrus Musée de Picardie 88.3.5) record the rations given to the crews of the flotilla of ships assigned to collect grain harvest taxes for the temple of Amun, as well as the taxes that were collected.

In the New Kingdom, the king could exact levies from temples, as well as endow them.[168] Some of these levies represented revenues from royal assets that the king had assigned to temples to exploit, and whose revenues the temples collected on behalf of the king. Other levies, however, seem to represent revenues from temple assets that the king had definitively donated to the temples and their gods. Papyrus BM 10401, dated to the late Twentieth Dynasty, records that a royal chief taxing master exacted various commodities from temples in Elephantine, Kom Ombo, Edfu, Hierakonpolis, and Esna.[169] In the Twentieth Dynasty, in Papyrus Cairo A-E, dating early in the reign of King Ramesses IX, the king sends a letter to the high priest of Amun at Karnak, Ramessenakht, ordering him to send galena to the royal residence (Text B), and another letter from a high official makes a similar demand of the scribe and chief physician of the temple of Amun (Text E).[170] Slightly later in the Twentieth Dynasty, in an inscription in the temple of Amun at Karnak dated to Year 10 of King Ramesses IX, the king praised another high priest of Amun, Amunhotep son of Ramessesnakht, for delivering tribute (*inw*) from the temple to the king.[171] The Turin Taxation Papyrus (Papyrus Turin 1895+2006), dating to Year 12 of Ramesses XI, records that the overseer of the granaries of pharaoh and viceroy of Kush, Panehesy, ordered the *ḥm-nṯr*-priests of the temples of Upper Egypt to hand over grain from the *ḫꜣ-tꜣ*-land of pharaoh to the scribe of the Necropolis, Dhutmose.[172]

Private Funerary Establishments: In the Old Kingdom, most private funerary establishments relied on grants of royal revenues, though a few also employed revenues from private properties. In the Middle Kingdom, however, Hapidjefa founded his funerary establishment with revenues from temples and necropolis officials, after he transferred private revenue sources to them. In the New Kingdom, private funerary establishments were usually supplied with revenues from temples or royal cult statues, in exchange for donations of private property to the temples and cult statues.[173]

There are a few examples from the New Kingdom of the king simply giving revenues from endowment fields of temples or royal statues to individuals to found a private funerary establishment. Stela Cairo CG 34021, from Thebes and dated to Thutmose IV, states that it is "the southeastern boundary of the donation-field (*ḥnk*) of the statue of the King of Upper and Lower Egypt, the Lord of the Two Lands, Menkheperure, given life, which was given as praise (*ḥswt*) from the king to the *wꜥb*-priest, the chief of the craftsmen of Amun, Khaut ..., a field being 5 arouras of *nḫb*-land of Tanetshenau in the divine offering (*ḥtp-ntrw*)."[174] Stela Cairo CG 34186, from Memphis and dated to Tutankhamun, states that "His majesty decrees that one give a donation-field (*sꜣḥ*) to the god's father of Ptah, Merymery, his donation-field being 40 arouras upon the field of the estate of Ptah. Has come on account of it, the royal scribe Merymery."[175]

There are also examples of the king, or the viceroy in Nubia, giving fields to the endowments of temples or royal statues, and their revenues to individuals for their private funerary establishments. This became the standard pattern for donation stela in the Third Intermediate Period. In such cases, it is probable that the king or the viceroy was merely acting as an intermediary between men and the gods, and that the private individuals actually provided the fields for the donation. Stela Cairo TR 5/12/35/1 and Stela Cairo JdE 65834, both from Abu Simbel and dating to Ramesses II, are boundary stela for the same donation. They depict the viceroy Paser before Amun, while their texts read "donation-field (*ḥnk*) for the support (*wḏb*) of Amun King of the Gods of the Two Lands, which is in the endowment (*sḥtp-nṯrw*) of the letter-scribe Khay son of Seba, from son to son, heir to heir, a field being 7 *khet*, south of the field of pharaoh, its north in water, its east in a private (*nmḥ*) field, its west in water."[176] A stela in Stuttgart, dated to Ramesses III, states that "His Majesty, l.p.h., has ordered the demarcation of a donation-field (*ꜣḥt ḥnk*) in/being ... *ḳdby*-field (and) pasture field for cattle for the statue of (Ramesses Heqaiunu) son of Ptah, beloved like Seth. His Majesty proceeded to the temple of (Ramesses Meryamun) beloved of his army, because it is the divine offering under the chief of the *thrw*, Amunkhau, of the fortress of (Ramesses Meryamun) beloved of his army, in the hand of his wife, the musician of Ptah, Isis, from son to son, heir to heir."[177]

In a few cases private individuals made it explicit that they presented their property directly to the endowment of a temple, supporting the thesis that the king usually only played a ritual role as intermediary between men and the gods. Stela Strasbourg 1378, dated to Year 1 of Ramesses I, depicts Ramesses I offering to Amun-Re, but the text states "On this day, the saying of words by the chief of bowmen, overseer of the fortress, Ay: 'I have given a field of 50 arouras to the endowment (*ḥtp-ntrw*) of Amun of the Pylon. I am giving a field of 21 arouras for my endowment (*mꜣwḏ*), likewise a field of X arouras for the endowment (*mꜣwḏ*) of Hatay son of ....'"[178] In the reign of Ramesses II, the scribe and counter of cattle of the temple of Amun-Re, King of the Gods, Simut called Kyky, had inscribed in his tomb-chapel, Theban Tomb 409 at Qurna, that he had donated all of his property to Mut and the temple of Mut, presumably to found a funerary establishment.[179]

There is one example of the king giving revenues from a temple to an individual who then in turn gave property to the endowment of a statue of the king, suggesting a reciprocal arrangement represented as a royal gift. Similar arrangements could also underlie some of the aforementioned royal gifts to private individuals. In the reign of Amenhotep III, the chief steward Amenhotep inscribed on a statue found at Memphis that the king donated to him revenues from the temple of Ptah for a chapel, which presumably contained the statue. Amenhotep then adds, however, that he donated all of his property in writing to the statue of the king in the temple of Ptah, suggesting that the royal donation was in fact an exchange.[180]

EXCHANGE

In the New Kingdom, there is limited evidence for high value exchanges involving land, houses, and slaves. Few high value exchanges appear to have been formally documented in writing as well as with witnesses, and consequently few records of such exchanges have survived. Those records that have survived are of private local exchanges, because even written records relied on local witnesses for authentication, and exchange partners usually found each other through social networks rather than anonymous markets. State and temple redistributive networks may have been the preferred mode of distribution for properties and goods over long distances, because of their superior documentation and enforcement by the central administration.

In contrast to high value exchanges, there is considerable evidence for numerous low-to-medium value exchanges whose values are measured in copper or occasionally grain, primarily from the site of Deir el-Medina. The frequency of such low value exchanges is not surprising, but their written documentation is, because low value transactions are rarely worth documenting in writing. However, most low value exchanges at Deir el-Medina were not formally documented in writing, only with witnesses. The witnesses at Deir el-Medina frequently kept personal written memoranda of the exchanges that they witnessed, which had no legal value independent from the testimony of the witnesses. Low-to-medium value exchanges at Deir el-Medina were usually private local exchanges through social networks, but institutions sometimes engaged in long distance exchanges through anonymous markets, by sending ships up and down the Nile to exchange at riverside marketplaces.

Land: There is some evidence for exchanges involving land in the New Kingdom, but most examples involve "donations" of land to temples or royal statues in exchange for "donations" of institutional revenues for private funerary establishments. In some cases, private donors explicitly record that they made a donation of fields in return for institutional revenues for their funerary cult, as in Stela Strasbourg 1378 of the chief of bowmen, overseer of the fortress, Ay, dated to Year 1 of Ramesses I,[181] discussed previously. In other cases, inscriptions recording private donations of land to temples omit reference to a corresponding gift of institutional revenues, but such revenues are nonetheless strongly implied by the funerary context of the inscriptions, as in Theban Tomb 409 of Simut called Kyky, dated to Ramesses II,[182] discussed previously.

More often, however, private donors of fields emphasize the role of the king or the viceroy in Nubia as donor to a god or a royal statue on their behalf, and the role of the king as donor of institutional revenues to the private donors of fields, thereby partially obscuring the underlying exchange, as in the statue of chief royal steward Amenhotep, dated to Amenhotep III,[183] or boundary stelae Cairo TR 5/12/35/1 and Cairo JdE 65834, dated to Ramesses II,[184] or the stela in Stuttgart, dated to Ramesses III,[185] also discussed previously. One could also mention the stela of the steward of Amun, Senenmut, dated to Year 3 or 4 of Thutmose III, which records a royal decree ordering the transfer of eight arouras of land that Senenmut had previously received as a royal reward and two slaves to the temple of Amun at Karnak, so that bread and beer would be offered first to the god and then to the statue of Senenmut in the temple; and the transfer of five arouras of land and two slaves to the mortuary temple of Hatshepsut, so that bread would be offered at the tomb of Senenmut.[186]

There is, however, one example of an exchange of land for silver in a small archive of four papyri from Gurob, dating from the end of the reign of Amenhotep III and the beginning of the reign of Amenhotep IV, belonging to the herder Mesi. These papyri contain transcripts of several verbal agreements that Mesi made, most for the purchase or lease of days of slave labor, as well as a court case arising from a dispute over payment.[187] One of them, however, Papyrus Berlin P. 9784, lines 14–19, dated to Year 2 of Amenhotep IV, also contains an agreement to purchase three arouras of field in exchange for a cow worth one-half (silver) deben.[188] This is the oldest price for land attested in Egypt.[189]

Houses: There is limited evidence for exchanges involving houses in the New Kingdom, though this may be in part because Deir el-Medina dominates the evidence. In the community of workmen in the royal necropolis of Thebes, each man who held a position as workman received a stipend of grain and other commodities, and the use of a set of places (*swt*), consisting of a house (*pr*) in the village of Deir el-Medina, a hut (*ꜥt*) near the Valley of the Kings, and a tomb (*ꜥḥꜥ.t*) and a courtyard (*ẖnw*) near the village.[190] These places were described as being of pharaoh, that is they belonged to the state, but workmen usually held them lifelong, unless the gang of workmen was downsized. Like their positions and stipends, the places were usually hereditary but not partible, and hence usually passed through patrilineal succession.

Nonetheless, even at Deir el-Medina, the workmen could also construct their own buildings, which were true private properties that could be transferred or divided. Hieratic Papyrus Cairo Museum JdE 58092 (*P. Boulaq* 10) verso, from Deir el-Medina and dated to Year 8 of Ramesses III, records a public division of several inherited properties consisting of a shrine (*ḥbt*), a pyramid (*mr*), two huts (*ꜥt*), a piece of land (*iwtn*), and a cellar (*štyt*).[191] Hieratic Ostracon Petrie 61, also from Deir el-Medina,[192] illustrates the distinction between property associated with a position and private property. The workman Baki threatens to cast Tanetdjesert out of his house, which is an idiom for divorcing her.[193] Tanetdjeseret apparently cannot make a claim to part of Baki's house (*pr*), because it belongs to the state and Baki only has use of it because of his position.[194] Therefore, Tanetdjeseret's father Horemwia offers her part of his storeroom (*wḏꜣ*), which he built himself and which is therefore his private property.[195]

> **Hieratic Ostracon Petrie 61:**
>
> The workman Horemwia, he says to the citizeness Tanetdjeseret, his daughter: "You are my good daughter. If the workman Baki casts you out of the house, I will act. As for the house, it is what belongs to pharaoh, l.p.h., but you may dwell in the anteroom to my storehouse because it is I who made it. No one in the world will cast you out of there."

Slaves: There is some evidence for exchanges involving slaves in the New Kingdom. For example, Papyrus Cairo JdE 65739, a hieratic papyrus found by Winlock in a tomb in western Thebes, records a trial before a *ḳnb.t*-court about ownership of a slave.[196] The woman Erenofre claimed that she purchased the Syrian slave Gemnihiamente with linen that she had woven herself, and with objects lent to her as credit. The woman Bekmut protested that Erenofre used objects that had not been lent to her. Likewise, one of the papyri from the archive of the herder Mesi from Gurob, Papyrus Berlin P. 9785, dated to Year 4 of Amenhotep IV, records the purchase of a female slave in exchange for two cows and two calves, which later resulted in a dispute over payment and a trial before a *ḳnb.t*-court.[197] There is also some evidence for the lease or hire of slaves in the New Kingdom. This suggests that some purchases of slaves were entrepreneurial, that is they were made with the intention of obtaining future revenue. For example, the papyrus archive of Mesi from Gurob contains several records of the purchase or lease of days of slave labor. Papyrus Berlin P. 9784, lines 1–13, dated to Year 27 of Amenhotep III, records the purchase of two days of service each of two female slaves; and lines 20–33, dated to Year 3 of Amenhotep IV, record the purchase of two days of service of a female slave.[198] Papyrus Gurob II,1, dated to Year 33 of Amenhotep III, records the purchase of seventeen days of service of one female slave, and four days of service of another female slave; and Papyrus Gurob II,2, also dated to Year 33 of Amenhotep III, records the purchase of six days of service of a female slave.[199]

Donkeys: There is considerable evidence for exchanges involving donkeys in the New Kingdom. Twelve secure examples are known from Deir el-Medina.[200] There is also considerable evidence for the lease or hire of donkeys in the New Kingdom, with thirty-three secure examples from Deir el-Medina.[201] The donkeys were almost always owned by workmen of the gang of the necropolis, who usually leased or hired them out to water-carriers and other personnel of the outside. Water-carriers received a small salary to regularly transport water to Deir el-Medina, which required the help of donkeys to carry the heavy water-filled jars. The personnel of the outside could not easily afford to purchase donkeys, but some workmen could and did and then hired or leased them to the water-carriers.[202] Again, this suggests that some of the purchases of donkeys were entrepreneurial, with the intention of obtaining future revenue.

Cattle, Small Cattle, Pigs, and Fowl: There is some evidence for exchanges involving cattle. Statue Cairo CG 42121 of the royal butler Neferperet, dated to Thutmose III, records his donation of cattle and a milk jar to the mortuary temple of Thutmose III. The presence of the inscription on the statue implies that in exchange Neferperet received offerings for his statue in the temple.[203] As previously mentioned, one of the papyri from the archive of Mesi from Gurob, Papyrus Berlin P. 9784, lines 14–19 dated to Year 2 of Amenhotep IV, contains an exchange of three arouras of field for a cow worth one-half deben (of silver).[204] Likewise, Papyrus Berlin P. 9785 from the same archive, dated to Year 4 of Amenhotep IV, records an exchange of a female slave for two cows and two calves that led to a dispute before a *ḳnb.t*-court.[205] Several texts from Deir el-Medina also record sales of cattle.[206] Other texts mention small cattle, that is sheep and goats;[207] pigs;[208] and fowl.[209]

Marketplaces: In the New Kingdom, as in the Old Kingdom, tomb scenes demonstrate persuasively that marketplaces existed. Market scenes are attested in several New Kingdom tombs at Thebes: Siuser (? TT A4), Eighteenth Dynasty; Kenamun (TT 162), reign of Amenhotep III; Khaemhat (TT 57), reign of Amenhotep III; Ipuy (TT 217), reign of Ramesses II; and Huy and Kenro (TT 54), early Nineteenth Dynasty.[210] They are also mentioned in texts from Deir el-Medina, and in ships' logs. The texts from Deir el-Medina reveal that the workmen sometimes exchanged their surplus goods at the marketplaces, suggesting that they were in part local markets. However, the market scenes in the tombs of Kenamun, Khaemhat, and Ipuy depict ships moored at riverbanks next to the marketplaces, and there are indications that the ships were the source of some of the goods in the marketplaces, suggesting that they may not have been purely local markets. The role of the riverbanks as interregional markets is confirmed by the ship's logs Papyrus Leiden I 350 verso and Papyrus Turin 2008 + 2016. There it appears that ships owned by the king, by temples, and even by private individuals sailed up and down the Nile, buying and selling goods at the riverbanks (*mrwt*).[211]

ENTREPRENEURIAL ACTIVITIES

In the New Kingdom, as in earlier periods, the state undertook expeditions beyond the populated areas under Egyptian control, including royal military campaigns to bring back booty and tribute from foreign lands, as well as paramilitary expeditions to mine and quarry in the deserts or to trade with distant lands. The state also undertook foundations of new institutions within the populated areas under Egyptian control, organized production of commodities for future use, redistribution, or exchange, and facilitated the distribution of goods through entrepreneurial exchange. The kings increasingly assigned responsibility for exploiting mineral resources to temples, however, and allowed them to organize paramilitary mining expeditions to exploit them. Temples also organized production of goods for future use, redistribution, or exchange, and participated in the distribution of goods through entrepreneurial exchanges. Private households also engaged in entrepreneurial production for exchange.

State Expeditions: During the New Kingdom, expeditions included both military expeditions to plunder and take slaves, and paramilitary expeditions to acquire commodities through mining, quarrying, or trade. Military expeditions became particularly common in the New Kingdom, and the king frequently took personal responsibility for leading them, and for redistributing his share of the plunder and slaves, usually to temples. In contrast, paramilitary expeditions to exploit mineral resources were increasingly organized by temples rather than state officials, especially in the Ramesside Period.

Expeditions to Nubia were frequent early in the New Kingdom, after King Ahmose conquered the Hyksos capital at Avaris in the eastern Delta and reunited Egypt, and after he captured the city of Sharuhen in the Southern Levant, thereby securing Egypt's northeastern border. Ahmose then began campaigning in Nubia, and his successor Amenhotep I campaigned in Nubia as far as the Third Cataract. Amenhotep I's successor Thutmose I campaigned in Nubia as far as the Fourth Cataract in his Years 1, 3, and 4, destroying the native Nubian state at Kerma and securing Egypt's southern border. The autobiography of Ahmose son of Ebana in his tomb at El-Kab recounts his roles in the Nubian campaigns of Kings Ahmose, Amenhotep I, and Thutmose I.[212] He received slaves as booty during each of the campaigns, and was rewarded with gold and land in Egypt afterward. After these campaigns, the Egyptian kings ruled Nubia through an official known as the King's Son or Viceroy of Kush, and Nubia primarily became a source of tributary income rather than military plunder, though later kings continued to conduct campaigns to suppress revolts. Thutmose II defeated a revolt in Nubia, Thutmose III campaigned once in Nubia in his Year 50, and his successor Amenhotep II may have done so as well. Akhenaten campaigned in Nubia,[213] and Seti I defeated a revolt there in his Year 8. Egypt's control over Nubia ended in the late Twentieth Dynasty, when the King's Son or Viceroy of Kush, Panehesy, invaded Egypt to suppress the high priest of Amun at Thebes, Amenhotep,[214] and then in turn was driven out of Egypt by another high priest of Amun, Piankh.[215]

Expeditions to the Levant were frequent throughout the New Kingdom. King Ahmose captured the Hyksos capital at Avaris in the eastern Delta, and spent three years besieging Sharuhen in the southern Levant. Ahmose and his successors Amenhotep I and Thutmose I then campaigned in Nubia, securing Egypt's southern border, before Thutmose I campaigned in the Levant again as far as the Euphrates in his Year 2. The autobiography of Ahmose son of Ebana in his tomb at El-Kab also recounts his roles in the Levantine campaigns of Kings Ahmose and Thutmose I.[216] Further campaigns ensured that the Levant became a source of tributary income, but it also continued to be a source of military plunder because of the destabilizing presence of powerful states beyond the Levant. During much of the Eighteenth Dynasty, the Mitanni were the main threat to Egyptian control of the Levant. Thutmose I's successor Thutmose II also campaigned in the Levant, and Thutmose III campaigned sixteen times in the Levant between his Year 21, when he fought the Battle of Megiddo, and his Year 42, when he fought at Tunip. He thereby defeated most of the states in the Levant and made them tributary vassals.[217] His successor Amenhotep II campaigned in the Levant in his Year 3, described on nearly identical stelae at Amada and Elephantine,[218] and in his Years 7 and 9, described on stelae at Memphis and Karnak.[219] During the late Eighteenth and early Nineteenth Dynasties, the Hittites replaced the Mitanni as the main threat to Egyptian control of the Levant. King Seti I campaigned in the Levant in Years 1 and 9?, and defeated a revolt in Nubia in Year 8. These campaigns were documented on the hypostyle hall at Karnak, in the Seti I temples at Abydos and at Qurna in Thebes, in the temple at Kanais, and on stelae erected at Beth Shan, Tell es-Shihab, and Qadesh.[220] King Ramesses II campaigned in the Levant in his Years 4, 5 (Qadesh), 7, 8, and 9. The Battle of Qadesh in his Year 5 was commemorated in the Poem, the Bulletin and Reliefs; the South, Middle, and North Stelae at Nahr Kelb; and a stela at Beth Shan.[221] In the Twentieth Dynasty, King Ramesses III defeated an attempted invasion of Egypt by the Sea Peoples in his Year 8, but many of them settled in the Levant and eroded Egyptian control there.[222] This campaign was documented in the reliefs on the walls of Medinet Habu.

Expeditions to the deserts east of Egypt, and to the Sinai Peninsula and Punt, were common. Expeditions were sent to quarry quarzite at Gebel el-Ahmar, limestone at Tura, sandstone at the Wadi Shatt el-Rigal and at Gebel el-Silsileh, and granite at Aswan and Sehel. Expeditions were also sent to the Wadi Hammamat to quarry greywacke, siltstone, and breccia, as well as steatite, serpentine, and granite.[223] Expeditions were also sent to the Wadi Hammamat, to Kanais in the Wadi Mia or Wadi Abbad, and to the Wadi Allaqi to mine for gold, and to Gebel el-Zeit to mine lead.[224] In the Ramesside Period, however, the kings usually assigned the rights to exploit the gold and lead mines to various temples and mortuary temples (see Temple Expeditions). Expeditions were frequently sent to the copper and malachite mines in the Wadi Maghâra and at Serabit el-Khadîm, commemorated by numerous inscriptions around the mines and at the Hathor temple at Serabit el-Khadîm.[225] During the Ramesside Period, expeditions were also sent to the copper mines in the Wadi Timna, but were commemorated by only one inscription dated to Ramesses III, and a small Hathor chapel.[226] Queen Hatshepsut sent one expedition to Punt in her Year 9, which was commemorated by reliefs in her mortuary temple at Deir el-Bahri.[227]

Expeditions to the deserts west of Egypt were uncommon, except to repel Libyan invasions, or to preemptively attack them. In the Nineteenth Dynasty, King Merneptah defeated a coalition of Libyans and Sea Peoples in his Year 5 and captured thousands of prisoners and took large quantities of gold, silver, weapons, furniture, and cattle, which were documented on black granite Stela Cairo JdE 31408 (Israel Stela) from his mortuary temple at Thebes,[228] on the Athribis Stela, and on his "Great Karnak Inscription." In the Twentieth Dynasty, King Ramesses III conducted campaigns against the Libyans in his Year 6 and Year 11 and again took thousands of prisoners, which were documented in reliefs on the walls of his mortuary temple at Medinet Habu.[229]

State Foundations: During the New Kingdom, state entrepreneurial activities included founding temples and settlements within the populated areas under Egyptian control, as well as fortresses and garrisons at their margins. These foundations were usually endowed with land or redistributed revenues to provide some support for administrators, temple cults and priests, or garrisons and soldiers, who could engage in additional economic activities to supplement their incomes.

The Egyptian kings conquered the native Nubian state at Kerma at the beginning of the Eighteenth Dynasty, and subsequently remade much of Nubia in Egypt's image. They founded numerous temples in Nubia and endowed them with local estates.[230] Under King Seti I, these Nubian temples sent revenues to the Seti I's mortuary temple at Abydos, as described in the Nauri Decree of Seti I. Presumably the king could then access these revenues through his mortuary temple, as later kings are known to have done. During the early Eighteenth Dynasty, after the Egyptians conquered the kingdom of Kush in Nubia, the Egyptians rebuilt and expanded the Middle Kingdom fortress at Buhen, and built new fortresses at Sai Island, and perhaps Tombos at the Third Cataract, and Napata at the Fourth Cataract. They also reestablished settlements and temples at many of the other Middle Kingdom fortresses.[231] During the late Eighteenth Dynasty, they added fortresses at Sesebi and Kawa, and perhaps at Napata if they had not already done so, and established settlements and temples at Sedeinga, Soleb, and Tombos.[232] During the Nineteenth Dynasty, the Egyptians added a fortress at Amara West to those at Sai Island, Sesebi, Kawa, and Napata, all of which remained in use until the Egyptians abandoned Nubia at the end of the Twentieth Dynasty.[233]

The Egyptian kings conquered much of the Levant by the middle of the Eighteenth Dynasty, but for the most part they left the local settlements and institutions intact and exacted tribute from them. During the early Eighteenth Dynasty, the Egyptians built a palatial fortress at Avaris and a fortress at Tjaru (Sile), and established garrisons at Sharuhen (Tell el-Ajjul) and perhaps Gaza in the southern Levant.[234] During the late Eighteenth Dynasty, after Thutmose III established an Egyptian empire in the Levant, the Egyptians possibly added garrisons at Megiddo, Byblos, and Ullaza, and way stations along the northern Sinai coast at Bir el-Abd and Deir el-Balat.[235] During the Nineteenth Dynasty, after Seti I and Ramesses II defended the Egyptian empire in the Levant against the Hittites, the Egyptians added a border fortress at Tjeku (Tell er-Retabah) to that at Tjaru (Sile), and added garrisons at Tell el-Farah, Tel Sera, Tell el-Hesi, Gezer, Ashdod, Aphek, Jaffa, and Beth Shan to those at Gaza, and perhaps Sharuhen.[236] During the Twentieth Dynasty, they added a border fortress at Kom el-Qulzoum to those at Tjaru and Tjeku, and they maintained garrisons at Gaza, Tell el-Farah, Tel Serah, and Beth Shan until the Egyptian empire in the Levant was abandoned after the reign of Ramesses III.[237]

In the Western Deserts during the Nineteenth Dynasty, the Egyptians built a line of fortresses stretching westward from Kom Abu Billo, to Kom el-Hisn, Kom Abu Girg, El-Gharbaniyat, El-Alamein, and ultimately to Zawiyet Umm el-Rakham. These fortresses remained in use through at least the beginning of the Twentieth Dynasty.[238]

State Production and Exchange: State institutions such as royal palaces and dockyards sometimes undertook the production of goods for eventual use, redistribution, or entrepreneurial exchange. The dockyard at Perunefer under Thutmose III and the palace of Per-Aakheperkare at Memphis under Seti I both appear to have arranged for the construction of ships, and the palace of Prince Khaemwaset at Memphis under Ramesses II used one such ship to transport and exchange commodities.

Temple Expeditions: In both the Old and Middle Kingdoms, the king frequently ordered royal officials such as viziers and provincial governors to exploit mines and quarries in the deserts. In the New Kingdom, however, the king frequently assigned the rights to exploit desert mines to various temples and mortuary temples, especially in the Ramesside Period.[239] In the Nineteenth Dynasty, King Seti I apparently assigned gold mines in both the Eastern Desert and in Nubia to his mortuary temple at Abydos. The Kanais Decrees of Seti I in his temple at Kanais near the Eastern Desert gold mines specifically protect personnel engaged in mining, washing, and transporting gold for his mortuary temple at Abydos.[240] The Nauri Decree of Seti I on a cliff at Nauri in Nubia protects all property and personnel belonging to the mortuary temple of Seti I at Abydos. Nauri is located near the gold mines in the Wadi Allaqi in Nubia, however, and the decree mentions gold miners (line 40), and tribute of Kush including gold (lines 82–97).[241]

In the Twentieth Dynasty, King Ramesses III assigned or reassigned gold mines in the Eastern Desert and Nubia to the temple of Amun at Karnak and to his mortuary temple at Medinet Habu. His successors appear to have maintained this arrangement. The Great Harris Papyrus, dated to Year 32 of King Ramesses III, states that the Theban temples received gold from both the Eastern Desert and from Nubia (List B in P. Harris I, 12a, 6–9). The former, known as gold of the desert of Coptos, constituted 61.3 deben a year, while the latter, known as gold of Kush, was 290.8 deben per year.[242] Papyrus IFAO A+B, dated to the middle of the Twentieth Dynasty, is an account of a series of expeditions to mine and wash gold and to find galena in the Eastern Desert by personnel of the temple of Amun at Karnak, a temple of Re, and the mortuary temple of Ramesses III at Medinet Habu, under the leadership of a chief of the desert (*ꜥꜣ n ḫꜣst*). The gold and galena were delivered to the high priest of Amun of Karnak and the scribe of the treasury of Amun, to a temple of Ptah, and to the scribes of the tomb.[243] Papyrus Cairo A-E is a possibly related papyrus dated to the reign of Ramesses IX that preserves correspondence related to the temple of Amun at Karnak. In a pair of texts, the high priest of Amun at Karnak, Ramessesnakht, writes to a troop of Nubians charged with guarding the gold miners and washers belonging to the temple of Amun, and asks them to remain there to receive deliveries (Texts C and D). The mines were probably located in the Eastern Desert (cf. Text A).[244]

Temple Production and Exchange: In addition to organizing expeditions to mines and quarries, temples supported dependent gangs of laborers who exploited fisheries and tended livestock and fowl, as described in the Nauri Decree of Seti I for his mortuary temple at Abydos. Other dependent gangs of craftsmen may have produced commodities like cloth and papyrus. The temples used their agricultural surpluses to support such dependent gangs, who then delivered quantities of goods to the temples. In this way laborers and craftsmen were insulated from market fluctuation, while the temples could convert agricultural surplus to more durable goods. The kings may have collected a portion of this production already in the New Kingdom, as they did in later periods.

Temples also supported dependent crews of ships, who transported surplus commodities for exchange, possibly entrepreneurial exchange. Temple ships may have been a preferred mode of transport, because the Decree of Horemheb (lines 13–21) implies that boats belonging to private individuals were not protected from seizure and expropriation,[245] except when they were carrying cargo for the state or temples, whereas the Nauri Decree of Seti I (lines 30–34, 82–97) states that ships belonging to temples were protected from seizure and expropriation at all times.[246]

Papyrus Turin 2008 + 2016 is a ship's log from Thebes dating to a Year 7 late in the Twentieth Dynasty.[247] It is part of a large collection of papyri now in Turin mostly relating to the workmen's community at Deir el-Medina, and it is unclear how it became part of that collection. The ship is described as "the great ship of the august staff of Amun" (recto I, 14; and II, 24), and "the ship of the high priest of Amun" (recto IIIA, 1; verso I, 1; and III, 15), clearly indicating that it was attached to the temple-estate of Amun of Thebes.

The first part of the ship's log (recto I, 1 – III, 28) is organized into daily entries covering seventeen days. The first preserved entry is dated Year 7 first month of winter, day 17, said to be the second month since the departure from Thebes; and the last preserved entry is Year 7, second month of winter, day 3, said to be the second month and 17th day since the departure from Thebes. The first daily entry records the departure from Heliopolis and arrival at Memphis. The twelfth daily entry records the departure from Memphis and arrival at "The Pylons of the House of Osiris," where the ship stayed for the remainder of the log. The daily entries do not list the ship's crew and their rations, unlike Papyrus Leiden I 350 verso. They do however record the departure of various people for various purposes. Notably, a total of nine people were sent on second month of winter, days 1 and 3 to search for the scribe Praemhab and nine or ten other people, who had been away for one month and eleven days. This suggests that the crew of the ship numbered well over twenty, like the ship in Papyrus Leiden I 350 verso.

The daily entries also list deliveries (*inw*) by various people. A few small deliveries were said to be rations, but a delivery of preserved fish of a cup-bearer appears to have been a consignment of freight, and a delivery of oil in exchange (*irt šwy*) for a quantity of cloth appears to have been a barter exchange of freight. The second part of the ship's log (recto IIIA, 1 – verso III, 15) consists of a separate account of the freight carried by the ship. The freight included jars of oil, wine and olives, sacks of emmer wheat, gourds and salt, bundles of rushes, sedge and papyrus, papyrus rolls, papyrus ropes, and preserved fowl and fish. These appear to have belonged variously to the crew, the guard Amenkhau, the steward of the estate of Amun Ramessesnakht, and a royal cup-bearer. One of the daily entries indicated that the guard Amenkhau obtained the jars of oil belonging to him in exchange for a quantity of cloth, as previously noted. The accounts indicate that other jars of oil, sacks of emmer wheat and gourds, and papyrus rolls were also exchanged for cloth, and that some of the preserved fish and fowl were off-loaded as food for laborers for the high priest of Amun.

Private Entrepreneurial Activities: In the New Kingdom, private individuals and households sometimes also undertook entrepreneurial activities, notably production and exchange. Admittedly, much private production and exchange was not entrepreneurial, and was destined for consumption or to obtain goods for consumption. But some private production and exchange was entrepreneurial, and was intended to accumulate surplus durable goods, which could eventually be exchanged for revenue producing commodities, like slaves or donkeys that could be hired out. In order to maximize accumulation of surplus durable goods, private individuals and households often supplemented their primary revenues from agriculture or state or temple service by exchanging their surplus labor for commodities, or producing commodities for exchange.

The community of royal tomb-builders at Deir el-Medina illustrates this entrepreneurial behavior. The state provided the gang of workmen settled at Deir el-Medina with tools and deliveries of rations and clothing for its work cutting and decorating the royal tombs in the Valley of the Kings. In their spare time, however, members of the gang also carved and decorated funerary equipment for each other and for individuals outside of Deir el-Medina, in exchange for compensation.[248] The workmen wrote numerous memoranda documenting these exchanges, mostly on limestone flakes or ostraca. These memoranda were reminders rather than independent legal documents, though workmen undoubtedly consulted them before testifying in legal disputes. Cooney has identified three categories of memoranda involving the manufacture and exchange of funerary equipment: workshop records, receipts, and transaction receipts. Workshop records documented exchanges made by a producer of funerary equipment. The producer usually named himself, listed what he made for whom and its worth, and what he received from whom and its worth. In many cases the other parties were other craftsmen at Deir el-Medina for whom the producer provided skills and labor for a project involving multiple craftsmen. Simple receipts documented exchanges made by a purchaser of funerary equipment. The purchaser often did not name himself, but listed which goods he gave to whom and their worth, and which products he received from whom and their worth. Transaction receipts differed from simple receipts because they documented complex exchanges of goods and products among multiple parties, some of which involved funerary equipment. In addition to memoranda, letters occasionally mentioned commissions of funerary equipment, and official journal records occasionally mentioned that workmen were engaged in commissions. Finally, legal records documented disputes involving funerary equipment, such as the price agreed upon, whether payment occurred, or whether heirs provided funerary equipment for their parents and thus were eligible to inherit their property, which were presumably the reason that workmen made the memoranda.[249]

These documents reveal that all kinds of craftsmen at Deir el-Medina engaged in production of funerary equipment, including draftsmen, scribes of the tomb, chief workmen or foremen, ordinary workmen, and carpenters. The craftsmen were organized into one or more informal workshops, to which individual craftsmen contributed specialized labor. Objects often passed from one craftsman to another, as they worked on the objects in succession. Workshop records documented who worked on objects requiring multiple craftsmen, while receipts and transaction receipts documented the departure of objects from the workshop. Most funerary equipment was commissioned through the social networks to which the craftsmen belonged, sometimes by their superiors. Consequently, these superiors sometimes allowed craftsmen to work on funerary equipment while "on duty" in the Valley of the Kings, rather than in their "spare time." In this way, social networks blurred the distinction between "state" and "private" work. Cooney argues that commissioned work was not "entrepreneurial," taking the latter to be speculative production for the open market without commission.[250] However, the accumulation of durable commodities through commissioned work could be speculative, if the intention or desire was to eventually exchange them. Craftsmen rarely documented the source or cost of tools and supplies for funerary equipment, or the amount of time required to produce funerary equipment. However, they did record the value of their work, when they bought and sold objects. Furthermore, they often bought and sold incomplete objects, thereby recording their contribution to objects requiring the skills and labor of multiple craftsmen.[251] In theory, craftsmen could earn as much as or double what they received from the state, if they regularly obtained multiple commissions for funerary equipment each month, thereby doubling or tripling their incomes. In practice, however, they probably obtained commissions only once every few months.[252]

Some of the production and exchange at Deir el-Medina was used to accumulate durable goods or capital, and some of these goods were probably used to acquire slaves or donkeys, which their owners then leased out to other workmen or to the service personnel attached to the community to generate revenue. This pattern was probably not unique to the tomb-builders at Deir el-Medina. Similar entrepreneurial behavior can be seen in Hieratic Papyrus Cairo Museum JdE 65739 from Thebes, which records a trial before a *ḳnb.t*-court discussed previously (in "Property Dispute Resolution").[253] The trial occurred because the citizeness Bekmut claimed that the citizeness Erenofre purchased the slave Gemnihiamente using objects belonging to Bekmut without her permission. Erenofre's testimony suggests that her husband, the overseer of the district Simut, probably provided the primary revenue for his household, but Erenofre also wove cloth that she accumulated and eventually used to purchase the slave Gemnihiamente, together with additional commodities supplied by others. Erenofre may have intended to recompense the others with revenue generated by hiring out the slave.

P. Cairo JdE 65739, lines 2–14:

Said by the citizeness Erenofre: (2) "[I am the wife of the overseer of the district, Simut] and I happened to sit in his house, and I worked [...] (3) and provided my clothes. And in Year 15, seven years after I had entered into the house of the overseer of the district, Simut, (4) the merchant Reia approached me with the Syrian slave Gemnihiamente, she being a young girl and (5) he said to me: 'Bring (*ini*) this young girl for you and give me her exchange (*swn*)' So he said to me. And I received (*šsp*) the young girl and gave him (6) her exchange (*swn*). Behold, I state the exchange (*swn*) that I gave for her before the officials (*srw*):

1 shawl (of thin cloth) makes 5 kite of silver, (7) 1 sheet (of thin cloth) 3 ⅓ kite of silver, 1 cloak (of thin cloth) 4 kite of silver, 3 loincloths (of fine thin cloth) 5 kite of silver, (8) 1 skirt (of fine thin cloth) 5 kite of silver.

1) Brought from (*ini m* ꜥ) the citizeness Kafy: 1 *gꜣy*-vessel of bronze, weighing 18 deben (9) 1 ⅔ kite of silver
2) Brought from (*ini m* ꜥ) the head of the storehouse of Pyiay: 1 *gꜣy*-vessel of bronze, weighing 14 deben 1 ½ kite of silver
3) Brought from (*ini m* ꜥ) the priest Huy – (10) – Pinhas: 10 deben of beaten bronze, 1 kite of silver
4) Brought from (*ini m* ꜥ) the priest Aniy: 1 *gꜣy*-vessel of bronze, weighing 16 deben (11) 1 ½ kite of silver and 1 *mnt*-vessel of honey ... 5 kite of silver
5) Brought from (*ini m* ꜥ) the citizeness Tjuiay: 1 *kꜣhꜣnꜣ* of bronze, (12) weighing 20 deben 2 kite of silver
6) Brought from (*ini m* ꜥ) the steward Tetia of the house of Amun: 1 *kb.t*-vessel of bronze, weighing 20 deben 2 kite of silver (13) and ... 4 kite of silver.

Total 4 deben and 1 kite of silver consisting of all things. And I gave it to the merchant Reia, there being in it no (14) article belonging to the

> citizeness Bekmut. And he gave me this young girl, and I gave her the name Gemnihiamente."

Such behavior may have been widespread. Throughout Egypt, farmers probably used agricultural slack times to produce handicrafts like furniture or cloth in order to exchange for goods that they could neither grow nor make themselves. No doubt many acquired such goods for consumption, but some probably hoped to accumulate them to acquire new sources of revenue, such as slaves or cattle.

CONCLUSIONS

During the New Kingdom, the state judicial administration prosecuted crimes against state revenues and redistribution throughout Egypt, and adjudicated many property disputes. The differing quality of documentation for redistribution and exchange, however, determined the relative effectiveness of their enforcement. The state continued to document labor obligations for individual people and harvest taxes for individual plots of land, but the state increasingly shared responsibility for documentation of harvest tax obligations with temples, which served as state agents. The state and the temples ceased registering private property transfers, but recognized that documentation of individual harvest tax obligations could serve as a form of title to plots of land. Authenticated written documents were rare, and private transactions were still primarily documented orally with local witnesses, who often made written records for their own use.

Superior documentation therefore appears to have lowered transaction costs for royal and temple redistribution more than for exchange, especially for high value properties and across long distances. Many of the beneficiaries of state and temple redistribution, however, were concentrated around the great aggregations of temples and palaces at Thebes, Memphis, Pi-Ramesses, and briefly Akhetaten at El-Amarna. The state continued to institutionally cultivate some plots of land, but the state increasingly donated land to temples to institutionally cultivate, and also entrusted state land to them to cultivate, without relinquishing title. The state also frequently rewarded officials and soldiers for service with plots of state or temple land to cultivate, in return for a harvest tax. The state thus seemed to deliberately give up shares of the harvest on many plots, in order to outsource the administrative costs and harvest risks to temples and private individuals. The increasing amount of land given by kings to private individuals may have stimulated exchanges of such land. High value exchanges of land as well as state and temple revenues become more common, though many of these exchanges were portrayed as donations to the king or the gods in return for donations by the king of revenues for mortuary cults. This undoubtedly reflects the fact that royal donation was still the most secure form of property title. Exchanges of houses, slaves, and animals are also attested, but they were not portrayed as donations, probably because the title security was less important. Again, at least some and probably many low value exchanges took place in markets, which are depicted in tomb scenes. Most of these low value exchanges were probably documented orally, if at all, but an increasing number were documented in writing, in the ostraca from Deir el-Medina. Palaces and temples provided long-term employment, but underemployment was common, encouraging entrepreneurial activity. The state demanded short-term compulsory labor from individuals.

FIVE

THE THIRD INTERMEDIATE PERIOD (c. 1069–664 BCE)

The early Third Intermediate Period (c. 1069–850 BCE) began when the Twenty-first Dynasty built a new royal city at Tanis in the northeastern Egyptian Delta, centered on a temple to Amun. The new city reused a great deal of stonework from the Nineteenth and Twentieth Dynasty royal city at Pi-Ramesses, which had apparently been abandoned, possibly due to a shift in the course of the Nile. Meanwhile, the high priests of Amun at Thebes essentially ruled Upper Egypt, though they acknowledged the kings at Tanis. The Twenty-second Dynasty also ruled from Tanis, but temporarily reestablished royal authority in southern Egypt by appointing royal sons to be high priests of Amun at Thebes. The Twenty-first and Twenty-second Dynasty kings built modest tombs inside the enclosure wall of the temple to Amun at Tanis.[1]

The late Third Intermediate Period (c. 850–664 BCE) began when a collateral branch of the Twenty-second Dynasty attempted to establish control over Thebes and Upper Egypt, and met with opposition and civil war. It is debated whether Manetho's Twenty-third Dynasty refers to this collateral branch,[2] or to another set of kings who may have briefly succeeded the Twenty-second Dynasty at Tanis.[3] Other local lineages were effectively autonomous but continued to acknowledge the Twenty-second Dynasty, until one based at Sais took control of the northwestern Egyptian Delta and founded the Twenty-fourth Dynasty. The Nubian kings of Napata then invaded Egypt and subjugated or eliminated the Twenty-second, Twenty-third, and Twenty-fourth Dynasties, establishing the Twenty-fifth or Kushite Dynasty, which endured until the Assyrians in turn invaded from the north and drove the Nubians out of Egypt.[4] (See Map 5.1 and Table 5.1.)

CRIMINAL JUSTICE

During the Third Intermediate Period, responsibility for criminal justice and enforcing state finances was frequently divided between competing dynasties of kings, and autonomous local rulers like the high priests of Amun at Thebes, who produced most of the surviving evidence for the criminal justice system in this period. In the early Third Intermediate Period, during the Twenty-first Dynasty, the high priests of Amun provided criminal justice in the south of Egypt, some of them adopting the title of vizier.[5] They conducted trials concerning crimes against the state, or against the gods, which were inscribed on the walls of the temple of Amun at Karnak. The high priests of Amun frequently employed oracular consultations with Amun and the other gods in these trials. Oracular consultations had been used for judicial purposes already in the Ramesside Period, but at that period they are best known from local judicial administrations, like the *ḳnb.t*-court of Deir el-Medina. In the Twenty-first Dynasty, however, the high priests of Amun used special oracular consultations called "divine audiences" (*pḥ-nṯr*), held within the temple of Amun at Karnak in the "Floor of Silver," possibly in the court of the Tenth Pylon. There the high priests consulted Amun about important political and judicial affairs, and received divine sanction for their authority.[6] For example, the Banishment Stela Louvre C.256 from Thebes records that the high priest Menkheperre consulted Amun-Re in a Year 25 before recalling exiles from the Oases.[7] Similarly, an inscription near the Tenth Pylon of the Temple of Amun at Karnak records that the high priest Pinudjem II presided over consultations with Amun-Re in Years 2, 3, and 5 of an unnamed king in the investigation and acquital of the scribe Thotmose son of Suawyamun.[8] During the early Twenty-second Dynasty, however, the kings reestablished some control over the south of Egypt. They appointed their sons as high priests of Amun, and other individuals as viziers in Upper Egypt.[9]

In the late Third Intermediate Period, under the later Twenty-second or Twenty-third Dynasties, Upper Egyptian viziers drawn from local families may have administered criminal justice,[10] along with the warring high priests Osorkon (B) and Harsiese (B) under Kings Takelot II and Shoshenq III. Once again, Osorkon and Harsiese both employed oracular consultations. The Chronicle of Prince Osorkon records an oracular consultation of Amun by Osorkon when he was in control of Thebes in the reign of Takelot II.[11] The Karnak Oracular Text against Harsiese records an oracular consultation in which the *wꜥb*-priests of Amun, Mut, and Khonsu petition the great god Amun-Re, King of the Gods, to prevent administrators from depriving them of

MAP 5.1. Egypt in the Third Intermediate Period

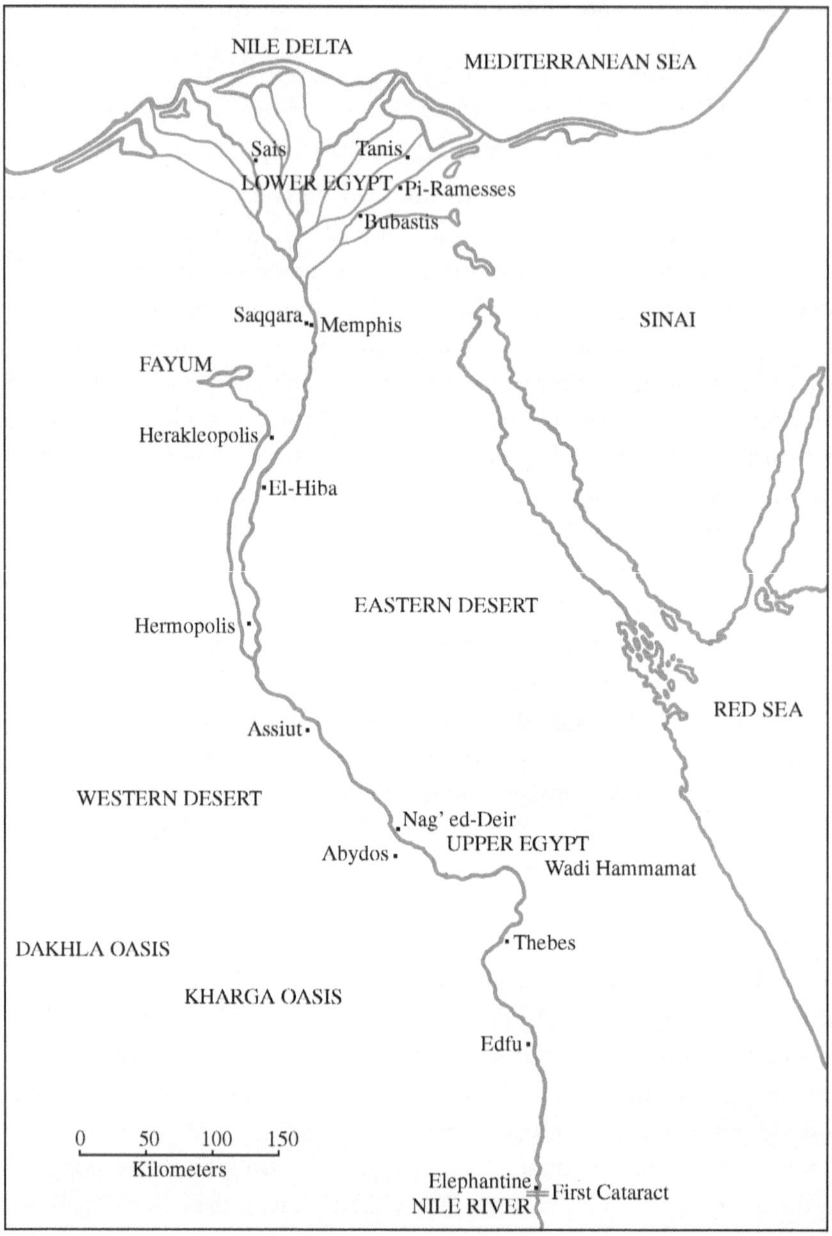

their revenues. Harsiese, the Magnate of the Ten of Upper Egypt, and probably the high priest of Amun, is summoned to enforce the decision of Amun-Re in favor of the petitioners. The petitioners propose to withhold the cloth that is usually taken to the treasury of the high priest of Amun, and Amun-Re agrees.[12] During the latest Twenty-second or Twenty-third and Twenty-fifth Dynasties, however, kings reestablished control over the south of Egypt. They

TABLE 5.1. *The Third Intermediate Period*

Third Intermediate Period (c. 1069–664 BCE)	
Dynasty 21 (c. 1069–945 BCE, Tanis)	*Dynasty 21, High Priests of Amun (c. 1069–945 BCE, Thebes)*
Smendes I	Herihor
Amenemnisut	Piankh
Psusennes I	Pinedjem I
Amenemope	Masaharta
Osorkon the Elder	Menkheperre
Siamun	Smendes II
Psusennes II	Pinedjem II
	Psusennes III
Dynasty 22 (c. 945–735 BCE, Tanis)	*Dynasty 22, collateral branch (c. 850–735 BCE, Thebes)*
Shoshenq I	Harsiese
Osorkon I	Takelot II
Shoshenq II	Petubast I
Takelot I	Iuput I
Osorkon II	Osorkon III
Shoshenq III	Takelot III
Shoshenq IV	Rudamun
Pimay	Iny
Shoshenq V	
Dynasty 23 (c. 735–715 BCE, Tanis)	*Dynasty 24 (c. 727–715 BCE, Sais)*
Petubast II	Tefnakht
Osorkon IV	Bakenrenef
Dynasty 25 (c. 747–664 BCE)	*Dynasty 26, before unification (c. 672–664 BCE, Sais)*
Piye	Necho I
Shabaka	
Shebitku	
Taharqa	
Tanwetamani	

Source: Dates after Ian Shaw (ed.), *The Oxford History of Ancient Egypt* (Oxford: University Press, 2000), pp. 479–483.

countered the authority of the high priests of Amun by enhancing the office of god's wife of Amun and appointing their daughters to this office, and by supporting local dynasties of Upper Egyptian viziers,[13] who seem to have presided over a great *ḳnbt*-court at Thebes.[14]

PROPERTY DISPUTE RESOLUTION

During the early Third Intermediate Period, local courts continued to conduct trials concerning property disputes, most commonly disputes over payment for property transfers. The names and natures of these courts are unknown, except that they frequently used oracular consultations for judicial purposes, continuing the tradition established in Ramesside Period *ḳnbt*-courts. Records of local court trials include the oracular consultations of Hemen and Khonsu in P. Brooklyn 16.205 from Thebes; the oracular consultation of Sutekh in the larger Dakhla Stela Ashmolean 1894.107a from the Dakhla Oasis; and the oracular consultations of Horus-of-the-Camp and Horus-khau from El-Hiba and/or Nag' ed-Deir. The oracular consultation of Hemen and Khonsu is known from Hieratic Papyrus Brooklyn 16.205.[15] It probably comes from Thebes and dates to a Year 4 after a Year 49, which can only refer to Psusennes I or the high priest of Amun Menkheperre in the Twenty-first Dynasty.[16] The text takes the form sometimes called an "oracle protocol," and records the use of an oracular consultation to resolve a dispute over payment, namely whether the payment had been made or not. Note that in this oracular consultation the gods Hemen and Khonsu were probably presented with two written alternatives, and did no more than indicate which of the two proposals they prefered. Nonetheless, their choices were then paraphrased as their speech.

P. Brooklyn 16.205, column 2, line 2 – column 3, line 10:

(2,2) They disputed again today about payment for the sections of (3) field of citizeness Ipip, which Peneferher son of Harsiese, (4) her male kinsman, sold to Ikeni.

They went (5) before Hemen of Hefat, and Hemen said to the two written claims: "Right is (6) Ikeni! He paid her money to Peneferher (in) the (bad) time. (7) It is closed." So Hemen said before all the witnesses.

(3,1) (Year) 4, second month of Shemu, day 8, day of going before Khonsu by the boatman (2) Pesmentawy, together with the god's father Anan son of Harsetitef (and) the god's father (3) Hemensankh son of Harsetitef, total two (persons), about payment for the 5/8 (aroura) of field (4) which is by the well of Ikeni.

The god's father Anan and his brother Hemensankh said: (5) "Verily their father has not received (any) money (6) (of) Ikeni."

The boatman Pesementawy said: "Verily (7) Harsetitef received two oipe of emmer – one oipe (equalling) a loincloth – in Year 49. (8) The scribe (also) received two loincloths, total four."

They made two written claims and they placed them before (9) Khonsu-in-Thebes and he said: "Right is Ikeni! He did give the two oipe and the two *rwd*-cloths, (10) total four, to Harsetitef." Right before many numerous witnesses.

Similar oracular consultations include those of Sutekh in the larger Dakhla Stela Ashmolean 1894.107a from the Dakhla Oasis;[17] and of Horus-of-the-Camp and Horus-khau from El-Hiba and/or Nag' ed-Deir.[18] The latter include two Hieratic papyri formerly in Boston and now in Berkeley that provide examples of two written alternatives. They were excavated at Nag' ed-Deir, and probably date to the late Twentieth or Twenty-first Dynasties. They take the form sometimes called "oracle petitions," and appear to be intended to resolve another dispute about payment.

> **P. Berkeley inventory number unknown, Petition A, lines 1–8:**
> (1) Horus-of-the-Camp, my good lord! Concerning this (2) cow of which Teuhrai said: "Karsasi (3) son of Hartenu gave it to Pameshem in (4) return for its price, and Pameshem (5) gave him the first installment of its price, and (he) withheld the remainder." (6) You say: "Pameshem is right! He (7) completed the payment of the price for this cow of (8) Karsasi to him."
>
> **Petition B, lines 1–7:**
> (1) Horus-of-the-Camp, my good lord! Concerning (2) this cow of which Teuhrai said: "Karsasi (3) son of Hartenu gave it to Pameshem (4) in return for its price, and Pameshem gave (5) its price likewise (sc. in part)." You say: "Karsasi is right! (6) Pameshem did not give him the (full) price (7) in return for his cow."

During the late Third Intermediate Period, there are references to Halls of Writings, which seem to be courts that heard cases concerning property disputes. The oath in Abnormal Hieratic contracts has the first contractor swear that the title is clear from claims by children and siblings. In the event that such a claim should arise, however, the Halls of Writings are instructed not to hear the claim, suggesting that responsibility for enforcement lay with them.[19] Their name suggests that they may have privileged written documentation as evidence. Access to these courts, however, may have been restricted. Among the comparatively few documents surviving from the Late Third Intermediate Period is an Abnormal Hieratic public protest (*šꜤr*), namely Papyrus Cairo CG 30884 + 30864 + 31182 from Thebes, dated to Year 5, probably of Taharqa (686 BCE).[20] In the Demotic legal system, public protests could be used to prevent others from obtaining clear title to a piece of property. If one made a public protest each year for three years, the dispute would be heard by a court.[21] The only other way to bring a dispute to court was to petition a high official, who acted as a gatekeeper for frivolous disputes. The Abnormal Hieratic legal system is less well known than the Demotic, but the Abnormal Hieratic public protest may have been used in similar ways, suggesting that access to the courts may have been similarly restricted. Furthermore, one of the references to the great *ḳnb.t*-court of Thebes occurs in the archive of Petubast from Thebes, in Abnormal Hieratic Papyrus Louvre E. 3228c, dated to Year 6 of Taharqa (685 BCE).[22] In it, two parties are said to have disputed before the great *ḳnb.t*-court, and the judges of the court and the chief scribe of documents have ordered the first party to write for the second party that they no longer have a claim to the object of dispute, and the result is the quitclaim contract on the papyrus. It is very significant that the court has ordered the loser of the dispute to write a quitclaim, because this would have served as a proof of clear title, preventing further dispute over payment, and making the decision far more decisive than the nonbinding decisions of local *ḳnb.t*-courts in earlier periods.[23]

P. Louvre E. 3228c (*RdE* 6, 1951, p. 159–161), lines 5–12:

> I have disputed with you before the great ones of the great *ḳnb.t*-court of Thebes and before the chief scribe of documents, (6) concerning the 2 deben of silver, part of 6 deben of silver, that you have given to us for the delivery of (7) the slave, whom I have purchased, whom I (8) and my sister have sold, (9) for 4 deben of silver, making 6 deben of silver. The chief scribe of documents (10) and the great ones of the great court of Thebes, they have said, "Write (it) for him, I no (longer) have (11) any claim on the slave, (12) for whom you have given us 6 deben of silver".... They say, "As Amun lives and as pharaoh lives, (22) may he be healthy and may Amun give victory to him, there does not belong to us a son or daughter, a brother or sister, or any man (23) on the entire earth, who is able to claim them, ever. As for the one who (24) will claim them, his deposition will not be heard in any hall of writings."

During the late Third Intermediate Period, the great *ḳnbt*-court and the Halls of Writings may have applied traditional Egyptian property laws, but there is currently no manuscript known to date from the Third Intermediate Period that contains a law code. It has been suggested that a manuscript dating to the early Ptolemaic Period contains a law code that in part dates back to the late Third Intermediate Period, but this dating is disputed. The language and script of the Demotic Legal Code of Hermopolis West are typical of the third century BCE, but the manuscript seems to place the harvest before the third month of Akhet, day 30 (Hathyr 30). In the third century BCE, Hathyr 30 fell in January and February, which is much too early for the harvest. Pestman argued that the harvest should have taken place in May and June, and that therefore some elements of the Legal Code may date back to the late ninth or early eighth centuries BCE, when Hathyr 30 fell in those months. If so, there must have been subsequent recensions that replaced Hieratic legal vocabulary such as *nꜥ*, "smooth," with Demotic equivalents such as *wꜥb*, "pure."[24] Lippert has argued that the harvest should have taken place in April and May, and that therefore the Legal Code need only date back to the late seventh or early sixth centuries BCE, to the Saite Period when Demotic legal vocabulary was beginning to replace Hieratic,[25] but Ritner points out that *nꜥ* continued to be used into the Persian Period.[26]

DOCUMENTATION OF OBJECTS OF TAXATION

The kings and the temples continued to conduct field surveys and censuses to calculate harvest taxes and compulsory labor requirements despite the fragmentation of the state in the Third Intermediate Period, demonstrated by several papyri preserving field surveys from southern Egypt, and references to taxes on professions suggesting the existence of censuses. The New Kingdom practice of appointing temples to administer royal lands on behalf of the king allowed the documentation of objects of taxation to continue without interruption while local rulers became autonomous or usurped royal privileges, and may even have facilitated the fragmentation of authority in this period.

Field Surveys: Several fragmentary papyri preserve field surveys in the 10th Upper Egyptian nome. The papyri were probably found together, but were subsequently dispersed by dealers to different collections in the 1880s. The papyri include P. Berlin P. 3063 (Papyrus Reinhardt);[27] P. Ashmolean 1945.94 (Griffith Fragments), + P. Louvre AF 6345, 6346–6347;[28] and P. Prachov. Papyrus Reinhardt is the most studied of these papyri. It contains a reference to a temple of Mut founded by King Psusennes I, which requires the papyrus to date after the early Twenty-first Dynasty. For each field, the owning institution is named, together with the official responsible for the field, the status of the field, and the cultivator of the field. There follows the dimensions of the field, and a calculation of its area (paragraphs of Type-a). In separate lists, the expected yields of each field are calculated (paragraphs of Type-b). These papyri, then, seem to deal with land equivalent to the apportioning paragraphs of the Wilbour papyrus, that is, land cultivated by individuals who had a tax obligation to institutions. If these individuals could transfer their rights to cultivate this land, as is likely, then it was effectively private land. The papyri do not seem to deal with significant amounts of land cultivated by institutions themselves. Such land probably existed, but was simply not recorded by Papyrus Reinhardt, the Griffith fragments, and related papyri.

In the Third Intermediate Period, agricultural land is sometimes designated as institutional land, most often as temple endowment land, though state land is also attested. These two designations seem to have indicated the administrative affiliations of the land, rather than its owners or cultivators. They probably indicated the institutions that calculated and received the harvest tax from the owners and cultivators of the land, though in some cases an institution appears to have administered land affiliated with another institution. Both institutional designations appear in Stela Cairo JdE 31882 (Apanage Stela), which records an oracular decree by the god Amun-Re for the high priest of Amun Iuwerot, confirming Iuwerot and his son Khaenwase in possession of the estate that Iuwerot created in Year 10 of King Osorkon I.[29] Some of the fields comprising the estate were part of the temple domain of Amun, while others were fields of pharaoh. Nonetheless, Iuwerot paid the purchase silver to the cultivators of the fields, rather than to the domain of Amun or to pharaoh, suggesting that the cultivators were effectively the owners of the fields, rather than the domain of Amun or pharaoh. When Iuwerot purchased the fields, he caused that the land-registers (*nꜣ dny.w*) of the fields of the domain of Amun that were with the granary scribes of the domain of Amun were brought, and he caused that their former owners cede them, whether they were in the domain of Amun, or fields of pharaoh.[30] He then caused that the administrators of the domain of Amun register them as his possessions in their places of writing. These sentences seem to confirm that the institutional designation concerned administration, rather than ownership. Furthermore, the reference to the fields of in the domain of Amun being with the granary scribes of the domain of Amun strongly suggests that the administration concerned the harvest tax. Finally, the absence of any reference to land-registers (*nꜣ dny.w*) or administrators of pharaoh suggests that the domain of Amun administered the fields of pharaoh on behalf of the king.

> **Stela Cairo JdE 31882 (Apanage Stela), lines 1–8:**
>
> (1) Amun-Re King of the Gods, the very great god from the beginning of time, said:
>
> "Concerning this establishment of fields which was founded by the first *ḥm-nṯr*-priest of Amun-Re King of the Gods, the general, the great chief, Iuwerot, justified, who was at the head of the great armies (2) of the south as far as the district of Assiut, which (establishment) is located in the district of high land to the northwest of the island which is called Iat-neferet, when he was young in the time of his father the king Meriamun Osorkon, (3) in Year 10, fourth month of Shemu, day 30:
>
> These 556 arouras of clear private fields with their wells, their trees, their (4) small and large cattle, which he purchased from the private people of the land, with satisfied heart, without any leaving aside a remainder. He has caused that they bring the land-registers (*nꜣ dny.w*) of the fields of the (5) domain of Amun which are with the granary scribes of the domain of Amun in all the districts of the south, and he has caused that they ceded the fields which he has bought among the fields of the domain of Amun, the allotment of (6) fields of pharaoh likewise.
>
> They gave to him these 556 arouras of clear private fields, with their wells and their trees, they made them in writing (7) with the administrators of the domain of Amun in their places of writing according to the manner of giving them to him which their owners made, with the name of every person among those who had sold a field, and the manner (8) in which he bought them."

A transfer of fiscal affiliation may be implied in Stela Hermitage 5630, dated to Year 10 of Shoshenq IV, which records the donation of ten arouras of land of pharaoh to the gods Shu and Tefnut by the great chief of the Libu, Niumateped A. Presumably these ten arouras previously paid taxes to the state ("pharaoh"), but subsequently paid taxes to a temple of Shu and Tefnut.[31]

Censuses: There are no surviving census documents from the Third Intermediate Period, but there are references to compulsory labor (*bḥw*),[32] which could have been collected using registers of liable individuals, as in other periods of Egyptian history after the Old Kingdom. There are also references to the collective taxation of certain professions or occupations in various localities that could imply the existence of censuses recording the professions of individuals who could be held accountable for these taxes.

For example, the granite altar Cairo JdE 39410 from Herakleopolis records how prince Namlot persuaded his father Shoshenq I to restore the daily ox-offering to Harsaphes in his temple in Herakleopolis.[33] Shoshenq I issued a royal decree ordering the cities, towns, and settlements (*nꜣ niwt, dmi.w, wḥ(ꜣ).w*) of Herakleopolis to contribute 365 oxen a year for the offering. In the list that follows, however, individual military officials contribute approximately six months of oxen, individual priests and officials of Harsaphes contribute two months, at least twenty-six towns contribute three months, and various professions contribute one month. The professions include (lines 27–28): "the coppersmiths and the harpists, 1 ox; the gardeners and the washers, 1 ox; the chariot craftsmen 1 ox; the chariot warriors, 1 ox; the stone masons, 1 ox; the potters and the builders, 1 ox."

Similarly, the Stela Cairo JdE 36861 records a donation by Taharqa to a shrine of Amun-Re in the Memphite region, which seems to have been managed by the temple of Ptah.[34] The donation included a deben of cooked meat, six loaves daily, and beer from the estate of Ptah; the produce of "The Canal of the Army" in the estate of Ptah; twenty oxen and one bull and thirty geese to be pastured in "The Canal of the Army"; 467 ½ arouras of other fields, including 120 arouras in the estate of Amun-Re; thirty deben of silver from the fishermen of Memphis, equivalent to thirty-eight oxen; and twenty-three hin of oil a month from the harbor of Memphis from the chief merchants. The thirty deben of silver equivalent to thirty-eight oxen owed by the fishermen of Memphis is the earliest attested Egyptian tax calculated in money.

These professional or occupational taxes appear to have been collective taxes, because the amounts were fixed without reference to the number of individuals liable for them. There is no information about how the collective liabilities were allocated among members of professional or occupational groups, but there must have been some way of documenting who the members were, or the taxes would have been unenforceable. One possibility is that professions or occupations were recorded in a census register. Some Middle and New Kingdom census documents included the occupations of heads of households,[35] Herodotus recorded that the Saite king Amasis required every

Egyptian man to declare the source of his livelihood to the provincial governor each year,[36] and the Ptolemies organized their censuses according to household (Gr. *kat' oikian*) and according to the occupations of the heads of households (Gr. *kat' ethnos*).[37] The Ptolemaic trade or occupational taxes, however, were probably imposed on each of the members of a trade or profession at a fixed rate per individual.[38]

DOCUMENTATION OF PROPERTY TRANSFERS

In the Third Intermediate Period, most property transfer agreements were probably oral and were documented only by witnesses. In the early Third Intermediate Period, a few such agreements were further documented with written transcripts. Property transfers to temples were often inscribed on stelae. Some transfers were further documented by elaborate oracular property decrees, which were then inscribed on temple walls or stela. Oracular property decrees were probably introduced because of a demand for better documentation and enforcement of property transfers, but they were only conducted by the central administration and hence their use was limited. In the late Third Intermediate Period, however, oracular consultations ceased to be used for documentation. Instead, temple notaries were established to make written transcripts of oral agreements more widely available. The increased use of silver as a medium of exchange may have made it possible to levy a registration tax on property transfers, and to thereby recapture some of the additional costs of documentation and enforcement.

Many property transfer agreements, particularly those involving lower value goods, were probably oral and were documented only by witnesses. The value of the goods would not have justified the costs of documenting the transactions with written transcripts. Evidence for this can be gleaned from the records of local court trials discussed previously. Two of these records concerned disputes over payments in property transfers, namely the oracular consultations of Hemen and Khonsu in P. Brooklyn 16.205 from Thebes;[39] and the oracular consultations of Horus-of-the-Camp and Horus-khau from El-Hiba and/or Nag' ed-Deir.[40] If there had been any written documentation at all of the property transfer agreements, then such disputes could have been resolved by consulting the documentation, rather than by consulting a divine oracle.

Some oral property transfer agreements were probably further documented by written transcripts, particularly those involving higher value goods. Some written transcripts omitted the names of the witnesses, because they were intended as memoranda or reminders, for the witnesses or for the public. One such public record has survived, Stela Cairo JdE 70218 found in the ruins of Fustat, dating to Year 16 of Siamun in the late Twenty-first

Dynasty.[41] It records that Ity has purchased two arouras of fields from Ankhefenkhonsu for two deben and two kite of silver. This simple public record of the transaction and the amount paid might have deterred disputes about payment, which seem to have been common, but it did not guarantee the title in any way.

> **Stela Cairo JdE 70218, lines 2–9:**
> (2) On this day of giving silver which the overseer of the treasury of Ptah, Ity, (3) did for the *wꜥb*-priest of Ptah, Ankhefenkhonsu son of the chief of the bookkeepers (4) who are in the granary of Ptah, Pasebty, in exchange for a field of 2 arouras in the district of (5) Pabaht at Memphis, to the west of (6) the garden of Taiat. "I am giving to him (7) 2 deben and 2 kite of silver."
>
> Again in exchange for a field which is in (8) Pabaht at Memphis, belonging to the *wꜥb*-priest of Ptah, Harsekhty, (9) a field of 2 arouras. "I am giving 1 deben of silver."

In the Twenty-first and early Twenty-second Dynasties, the high priests of Amun introduced a new method of documenting property transfers, called here oracular property decrees. The high priest or senior clergy of Amun conducted an oracular consultation with Amun and the other gods at Karnak, to confirm that a specified individual had acquired certain properties legally. The confirmation was then inscribed on the walls of the Temple of Amun, or on a stela. Oracular property decrees thus closely resembled in form the special judicial oracular consultations orchestrated by the high priests in the temple of Amun at Karnak, and one oracular property decree may be explicitly called a "divine audience" (*pḥ-nṯr*).[42] Unlike judicial oracular consultations, however, oracular property decrees were intended to prevent title disputes from occurring, rather than resolving them after they had arisen.

Oracular property decrees were not written transcripts of verbal agreements. They were written confirmations that property transfer agreements had been fulfilled, that the current owner had paid or otherwise satisfied the previous owners, and that the property title was clear. They usually also declared that the owner will pass the property to their heir or other designate. The current owner therefore wished to confirm that the title was clear for the new owner, to protect them from challenges to their title.[43] They typically also declared that anyone who defied or challenged the title will incur a wrathful manifestation of the gods.[44] This was the ostensible means by which the title was guaranteed for the owners. Their proofs of legal acquisition, however, together with their statement of intent to transfer to heirs, would have been difficult to dispute. And their monumental semipublic format on stelae standing in the courts of temples, or inscribed on the walls of the temples, would have made them hard to ignore.

The use of oracular property decrees was very limited, restricted to a privileged few. There are four well preserved examples of oracular property decrees, for Menkheperre; for Henettawy daughter of Istemkheb; for Maatkare daughter of King Psusennes II; and for Iuwerot and his son Khaenwase. All of the beneficiaries were high priests of Amun, or their immediate family members. Menkheperre was a high priest of Amun; Henettawy was the daughter of the high priest of Amun Menkheperre, and the wife of the high priest of Amun Smendes II;[45] Maatkare was daughter of King Psusennes II, wife of King Osorkon I, and mother of the high priest of Amun Shoshenq II;[46] and Iuwerot was a son of King Osorkon I, and the high priest of Amun who succeeded Shoshenq II.[47]

The Oracular Property Decree for the high priest of Amun Menkheperre was inscribed on a column in the temple of Khonsu at Karnak.[48] The god Amun-Re confirms Menkheperre's purchase and ownership of fields, and threatens any sellers who deny that they have been paid in full. Menkheperre asserts that Amun-Re will give sixty copper deben per silver deben, and that he will give forty copper deben above them, making 100 copper deben per silver deben. He also asserts that he will give five sacks of emmer per shawl, though the countryside customarily gives three sacks. The amount of fields is never given, only the amount of money paid for them, and the names of the people to whom the money was given. This includes 305 deben making 30 ½ shawls for the heirs of Tanetserer; 905 deben for the "heirs-of-burial" of Tanet[...], the three inheritances in the possession of Painebenadjed, chief of the miners of the estate of Amon; 305 deben making 30 ½ shawls for Iryaa; and so on.

The Oracular Property Decree for Henettawy daughter of Isemkheb was inscribed on the Tenth Pylon of the Temple of Amun at Karnak, and is dated to Years 5, 6, and 8 of an unnamed king.[49] The high priest of Amun Pinudjem II son of Menkheperre, and the third (later second) *ḥm-nṯr*-priest of Amun Tjanefer petition Amun-Re King of the Gods to confirm the properties that Henettawy has purchased for herself and for her daughter Isemkheb; the division of the properties of Henettawy's mother Isemkheb that Smendes II made for his daughters Neskhonsu and Isemkheb; and the properties that Isemkheb purchased for her daughter Henettawy.

The Oracular Property Decree for Maatkare daughter of King Psusennes II was inscribed on the Seventh Pylon of the Temple of Amun at Karnak. The introduction and date are lost.[50] Amun-Re King of the Gods, Mut and Khonsu confirm all the properties that Maatkare daughter of King Psusennes II has purchased or inherited; her ownership of them; and her children and grandchildren's ownership of them.

The Oracular Property Decree for the high priest of Amun Iuwerot and his son Khaenwase was inscribed on red granite Stela Cairo JdE 31882 (Apanage

Stela) found at Karnak.[51] Amun-Re states that Iuwerot has acquired 556 arouras of land in Year 10 of his father King Osorkon I, that he acquired these fields by purchase, and that he has registered the sales with the temple of Amun according to the names of the sellers and the amount that he paid for them. There follows a list of fields, with the names of their sellers, and the amount they received for their land. Amun-Re then confirms the fields in possession of Iuwerot's son Khaenwase, and thereafter Khaenwase's children and grandchildren, and that Iuwerot's siblings and other children shall not share in this inheritance.

Oracular consultations were also used in some donation stelae to guarantee title for property donated to temples for funerary and other pious foundations. Donation stelae appeared already in the New Kingdom, but the majority date to the Third Intermediate Period, from the end of the Twenty-first Dynasty onward.[52] Oracular consultations occur in some of the early Third Intermediate Period examples, such as the red granite Donation Stela Cairo JdE 66285 of the future king Shoshenk I for his father Nemrat, found at Abydos.[53] An unnamed king, perhaps Psusennes II, petitions Amun-Re King of the Gods, that Shoshenk shall succeed his father Nemrat; and that Amun-Re shall slay anyone who interferes with the pious foundation for a statue of Nemrat son of Mehetenweskhet. The king then orders the statue sent to Abydos, and a stela bearing the decree to be erected in the temple of Osiris at Abydos. The stela concludes with a list of the properties and servants assigned to the pious foundation of the statue of Nemrat, and the amounts paid for them to the treasury of the temple of Osiris at Abydos.

Stela Cairo JdE 66285, lines 2–5:

> Then his (majesty) spoke again in the presence of this great god: "My good lord, you shall kill the (3) chief of the army, the officer, the scribe, the agent, any messenger, any one sent on a mission to the fields, who shall seize property belonging to this statue of the Osiris, the great chief of the Ma, Nemrat son of Mehetenweskhet, which is in Abydos, and (4) any people who shall take from its divine endowment, to its land, its people, its cattle, its garden, any of its offerings, any of its endowments. You shall exercise your great and terrible manifestation against them and against their wives (5) and their children." This great god assented. Thereupon his majesty kissed the ground before him.

An oracular consultation also occurs in the Donation Stela Cairo JdE 45327 of Nimlot for Djedptahiuefankh, found at Tell el-Minia wa el-Shorafa, fifteen kilometers south of Helwan.[54] It begins with the date, Year 16 of Osorkon II, followed by the specifications of the field being presented to Ptah. Then Nimlot son of Osorkon II states that he has donated the field for Djedptahiuefankh, and that Ptah shall slay anyone who interferes with the pious foundation. The great god (or the priests carrying his statue) agrees.

Stela Cairo JdE 45327, lines 2–9:

(2) This day of giving of a field of [42 ½] arouras ... (3–5) ... which was done by the *ḥm-nṯr*-priest of Harsaphes king of the two lands, the great chief of [Per]-Sekhemkheper[re], the chief of the army, the commander, Nimlot, son of the lord of the two lands Meryamun son of Bastet Osorkon II, his mother being (6) Djedmutiuesankh, when he reported it before Ptah, the great god, saying: "My good lord, you shall receive the *ka*-service of the field which I have given to you for (7) the god's father of a god's father, the *ḥm-nṯr*-priest, the chief of secrets of Ptah, the temple scribe, the scribe of the cattle of the estate of Ptah, Djedptahiuefankh, being a good gift from my hand. You shall give me its exchange of life, prosperity, health, long life, a great old age (8) and he shall keep? it forever and ever." Then this great god assented very greatly. Again he (Nimlot) said: "My good lord, you shall kill any people, any associates (9) on the entire earth who shall transgress it, which is forever and ever, you shall cut off their name on the entire earth, while Sakhmet is after their wives, and Nefertem is after their children." Then this great god assented very greatly.

Donation stelae continued to be used to document and publicize increasing numbers of donations of both royal and especially private property to temples in the late Third Intermediate Period, but they ceased to employ oracular consultations. Such stelae usually depicted the local king or prince making the donation as intermediary between men and the gods, but the texts record no response from the gods, making it unlikely that any oracular consultation took place. Instead, emphasis was placed on a statement that the gods would inflict unpleasant and obscene punishments on the person and families of anyone who interfered with the pious foundation.[55] Many donation stelae from the late Third Intermediate Period were inscribed in Hieratic, even though Hieroglyphs were normally used for monumental inscriptions on stone.[56] Some used Hieroglyphic labels for figures in the donation scenes above the text, but Hieratic for the text proper, indicating that the use of Hieratic was deliberate. Ritner has therefore suggested that the Hieratic inscriptions were copies of Hieratic texts on papyri. Indeed, one donation stela from Thebes depicts a beneficiary holding a papyrus in the donation scene.[57] The use of donation stela thus apparently supplemented other forms of title documentation, such as the state and temple tax field surveys.

During the Late Third Intermediate Period, there was a major shift in the documentation of private property transfers. The use of oracular property decrees was abandoned. Instead, a system of temple notaries was created, to write down oral agreements using the Abnormal Hieratic system of contracts in Upper Egypt, and probably the Demotic system of contracts in Lower Egypt, though none have survived from this period. Because many parties to such agreements were illiterate, the temples also provided literate witnesses, who would listen to the oral agreements of the parties, and who then signed the contract to certify that the written transcript was an accurate representation of the parties' words. The written transcript or contract was then given to one of the parties as proof of title. These contracts were thus guarantees of title, much like the earlier oracular property decrees. Unlike the latter, however, they were available to anyone who could afford them. These contracts indicate that title disputes were to be heard in the new Halls of Writings. Furthermore, the contracts indicate that the losers of disputes in the Halls of Writings had to write contracts giving up all future claims to the properties in question.

The Abnormal Hieratic system of contracts was developing already in the Theban Twenty-third Dynasty, in the late ninth or early eighth century BCE. Evidence for this is provided by a group of abstracts of Hieratic contracts preserved on P. Berlin 3048 verso, one of the Takelothis papyri. The Takelothis papyri come from Thebes, and are dated to the reign of a king named Takelot son of Isis Meryamun, one of the three kings named Takelot. The epithet "son of Isis" does not occur in the name of Takelot I,[58] so this must be Takelot II or III, dating to late ninth or early eighth centuries respectively.[59] P. Berlin 3048 verso contains thirty-seven separate texts, most of which are as yet unpublished.[60] One of the few published texts (number 36) consists of abstracts of marriage contracts,[61] which contained an oath by a contractor swearing to fulfill his obligations, thereby guaranteeing the contract. The use of oaths was not standard in the abstracts of contracts on P. Berlin 3048 verso, however, because another published text (number 5) consists of a loan contract without an oath.[62]

> **P. Berlin 3048 verso, Text 36, lines 11–19:**
> (11) On this day of entering the house of the god's father of Amun-Re King of the Gods PN1 (12) which did the *ḥm-nṯr*-priest of Amun and the overseer of the treasury of pharaoh, Bakenamun son of [PN2 to make the woman PN3 his daughter as] (13) wife. The list of the things which he said he shall give them to her (as her gift) of a woman: (14) 10 deben silver, emmer wheat 1000. He said: "As Amun lives, as pharaoh lives, as the first *ḥm-nṯr*-priest of Amun lives, may Amun give to him victory, (15) before the *ḥm-nṯr*-priest of Amun-Re King of the Gods, the overseer of the treasury of pharaoh, Djedmontefonch son of Auefenmut son of Harsiese (16–19) ... I am the one who shall give to her the things which are written above."

The oldest actual Abnormal Hieratic contracts, as opposed to abstracts, date to the late eighth century BCE, under the Twenty-fifth Dynasty. These Abnormal Hieratic contracts were based on a verbal statement made by the first contracting party to the second contracting party. A contract scribe made a transcript of the statement of the first contracting party, and a number of literate witnesses then copied the transcript, to certify that it agreed with the verbal statement in the event that one or both contracting parties were illiterate, and to guarantee the identities of the contracting parties.[63] Occasionally the first contracting party also signed the transcript.[64] The second contracting party assented to the statement by accepting the transcript of it.[65]

In the Abnormal Hieratic Papyrus Leiden F 1942/5.15, dated to Year 21 of Piye (726 BCE), the seller first confirms that he has received payment for a slave, thereby deterring disputes over whether payment had actually been made. The seller then swears an oath that no one else has a claim to the slave, thereby guaranteeing that the title to the slave is clear.[66] Note that the seller identifies those most likely to challenge the title of the new owner as his children and siblings, much as in the oracular property decree for Iuwerot and Khaenwase. The seller should know better than anyone else who such heirs might be, and whether they indeed had any unsatisfied claims, therefore it was quite logical to require the seller to guarantee that the title was clear.

> **P. Leiden F 1942/5.15 (*OMRO* 61, 1980, p. 10), lines 3–9:**
>
> "I have received from you the 3 deben and 1 kite of silver of the treasury (4) of Harsaphes as money for Paneferou, the man from the north. (5) I have given him to you in exchange for it."
>
> He (the seller) said: "As Amun lives, as pharaoh lives, (6) may he be healthy, I do not have a son, daughter, brother, sister (or) any person in the world, (7) who will be able to have a claim on him (the slave). Anyone who would have a claim, (8) his deposition shall not be heard in any hall of writings, tomorrow (and) after (9) tomorrow."

Several types of Abnormal Hieratic contracts are known already in the late Third Intermediate Period. Types include marriage contracts,[67] inheritance division contracts,[68] slave sales contracts,[69] money and grain loan contracts,[70] land lease contracts,[71] quitclaim or cession contracts,[72] and public protests.[73] Types of contracts known from multiple examples usually employed standardized terminology, which continued to be used for the same types into the Saite Period.

It is uncertain whether Abnormal Hieratic contract scribes made separate archival records of contracts in the Late Third Intermediate Period. P. Berlin 3048 verso contains abstracts of a group of Hieratic contracts, such as one would expect in an archival register. On the other hand, P. Berlin 3048 verso also contains many other types of short texts that one might not expect in an archival record, prompting one editor to characterize it as a "scribbling-pad," and indeed the texts were written on the blank verso of a papyrus containing a Hieratic hymn to Ptah and a prayer for the protection of Ramesses IX.[74]

MEDIA OF EXCHANGE AND REDISTRIBUTION

In the Third Intermediate Period, weights of silver and occasionally quantities of cloth served as standard measures of value. Cloth and especially silver appear to have increasingly served as media of exchange as well, along with weights of gold and copper, and volumes of grain. The range of commodities used as media of exchange seems to have been more limited than in the preceding New Kingdom, when virtually any commodity could be used in an exchange. Presumably silver was either more desirable as a medium of exchange than in earlier periods, or more readily available. The robbery of royal tombs at the end of the New Kingdom may have injected considerable quantities of gold and silver into the Egyptian economy.[75]

The first regular taxes in silver appear in this period, no doubt as a result of the wider use of silver as a medium of exchange. These taxes appear to have targeted occupations that were likely to use silver, though they were still collected through censuses rather than at bottlenecks. Curiously, there is no evidence for the collection of property transfer taxes on exchanges from this period, even though it would have been a logical means of recapturing the costs of the many innovations in documentation and enforcement of property transfers in this period.

Measures of Value: Weights of silver and quantities of cloth served as standard measures of value in the Third Intermediate Period. Quantities of cloth, measured as shawls (*dr*), apparently replaced copper and grain as the standard measures of lower values, though weights of copper were sometimes "equated" to weights of silver, and volumes of grain "equated" to quantities of cloth. For example, the Oracular Property Decree for the high priest of Amun Menkheperre[76] records the sellers of properties to Menkheperre as saying (line 13) "We have received the 5 [*ẖꜣr*-sacks] of emmer per [shawl evaluated at 100] copper [deben] per deben of silver [...]." Menkheperre says (lines 27–28) "Let the silver payment be great from Amun-Re, King of the Gods, the great god. Give it, per deben of silver, at 60 deben of copper, and I shall give the 40 (deben) over and above them. I shall give 5 *ẖꜣr*-sacks of emmer [per] shawl, though it is 3 *ẖꜣr*-sacks that the country gives per shawl – an excess of 2 *ẖꜣr*-sacks." Finally, in the list of payments (lines 32–52), 305 deben are repeatedly said to amount to 30 ½ shawls. These equivalences imply that 100 deben of copper made fifty *ẖꜣr*-sacks of emmer wheat, made ten shawls (*dr*), and made one deben of silver. Similarly, Hieratic Papyrus Brooklyn 16.205,[77] dated to a Year 4 after a Year 49 that can only refer to King Psusennes I or the high priest of Amun Menkheperre,[78] records a judicial oracular consultation with Khonsu about a disputed payment, about which is said (column 3, lines 6–8) "Verily Harsetitef received two oipe of emmer – one oipe (equalling) a shawl – in Year

49. The scribe (also) received two shawls, total four." An oipe was one-quarter *ḏꜣr*-sack, so that these equivalences imply that one-quarter *ḏꜣr*-sack of emmer wheat made one shawl (*dr*).

Media of Exchange: It appears that payment could be made with a variety of commodities in the Third Intermediate Period. Some texts state that payment consisted of a quantity of commodities "worth" another quantity of commodities, usually one of the standard measures of value like silver or cloth, as was common in New Kingdom records from Deir el-Medina. Thus in the Oracular Property Decree for Menkheperre cited earlier, the list of payments (lines 32–52) consistently states that payments were in deben, and several times clarifies "305 deben amounting to 30 ½ shawls." These payments must have been in copper deben, as described previously, and 30 ½ shawls must have been their value according to a standard measure. Likewise, in Hieratic Papyrus Brooklyn 16.205, cited earlier, payment consisted of two oipe of emmer and two shawls, so the payment was worth four shawls according to a standard measure.

Other texts, however, state that payment consisted simply of one of the standard measures of value, most often a weight of silver. For example, Stela Cairo JdE 70218,[79] dated to Year 16 of Siamun, records the purchase of two fields, each measuring two arouras, one for two deben two kite of silver, and the other for one deben of silver. Similarly, Stela Cairo JdE 66285 includes a list of the property and services that the future king Shoshenq I purchased in order to endow the cult of a statue of his father Nemrat.[80] The list (lines 9–26) includes 100 arouras of fields purchased for ten deben of silver, a garden for two deben of silver, ten oxen for two deben of silver, eleven people for six deben and one kite of silver, and the services of twelve and a quarter people from the temple of Osiris at Abydos for eight deben and seven and four-thirds kite of silver. Likewise, Stela Cairo JdE 31882 (Apanage Stela),[81] dated to Year 10 of Osorkon I, records (lines 8–23) the purchase of a total of 556 arouras of fields from sixteen groups of cultivators for a total of eighteen deben and four and three-fourth kite of silver, as well as thirty-five slaves for a total of fifteen deben and one-third kite of silver. Finally, Stela Cairo JdE 37888,[82] dated to Year 8 of Tanwetamani, records the transfer of ten arouras of high fields from the chantress of the Residence of Amun, Ankhnesites, for an unknown number of gold deben and ten red cloths.

The simplest explanation for the absence of commodities other than silver, gold, or cloth in these texts is that payment was actually made in silver, gold, or cloth. This would suggest that silver was increasingly being used as a medium of exchange as well as a measure of value in the Third Intermediate Period, compared to the New Kingdom. An alternative explanation is that payment was still made with a variety of commodities, but it was no longer felt necessary to indicate the commodities, only their value in a standard measure like silver. This would indicate nothing about the use of silver as a medium of exchange, but would still suggest that silver was increasingly being used as a measure of value.

Further evidence that some exchanges were made with silver may be found in Abnormal Hieratic contracts from the late Third Intermediate Period that refer to payment of weights of silver of the treasury of Harsaphes. The earliest attestations occur in the abstracts of an Abnormal Hieratic loan contract and an unpublished Abnormal Hieratic house sale contract, both preserved in Papyrus Berlin P. 3048 verso.[83] The loan contract is dated to a Year 13, either of King Takelot II in the late ninth century BCE, or of King Takelot III in the early eighth century BCE, as previously described. Some have suggested that these weights of silver had to meet purity standards set by the temple treasury of Harsaphes.[84] Others have suggested that these weights of silver had to be in a form of proto-coinage, that is actual silver ingots marked with the sign of the temple treasury of Harsaphes.[85] Still others have suggested that these weights of silver were merely weighed according to the temple treasury standard.[86] The last suggestion is the most likely, because there is no physical evidence that stamped ingots existed, and because parallels from the Persian Period seem to refer to a weight standard (see Chapter 6).

Stores of Wealth: A bullion hoard illustrates the increasing use of silver as a store of wealth in the late Third Intermediate Period. The Elephantine hoard consisted of a small ceramic vessel stylistically dated to the Twenty-fifth or early Twenty-sixth dynasties (750–600 BC), which contained three linen packets and 118 pieces of cut silver fragments (*Hacksilber*) weighing together 39.45 grams. It has been suggested that the packets each weighed approximately 13.15 grams, and that this was a standard weight.[87]

Credit: Loans of both grain and money are attested in Late Third Intermediate Period Egypt. Two grain loans are known. In the archive of Petebast from Thebes, Abnormal Hieratic Papyrus Louvre E. 3228b (Choix I 1), dated to a Year 13, probably of Shabaka (703 BCE), was a grain loan for which twenty-two and a half sacks were to be repaid after one month, suggesting a principal of fifteen sacks and 50 percent interest.[88] Abnormal Hieratic Tablet MMA 35.3.318 recto from Thebes, dated to a Year 5 possibly of Taharqa (686 BCE), was a grain loan of thirty sacks of barley, for which forty-five sacks were to be repaid eight months later, indicating 50 percent interest.[89]

Two money loans have are also known. Hieratic Papyrus Berlin P. 3048 verso Text 5 from Thebes, dated to a Year 13 probably of Takelot II or III (late ninth or early eighth century BCE), was an abstract of a loan of five silver deben, for which ten silver deben were to be repaid one year later, indicating 100 percent interest.[90] Abnormal Hieratic Tablet MMA 35.3.318 verso from

Thebes, dated to a Year 3 possibly of Taharqa (688 BCE), was a money loan of two and a half silver deben, to be repaid with interest when the lender desired. The interest was specified as one kite for each deben each month, which is 10 percent per month or 120 percent annually.[91]

REDISTRIBUTIVE NETWORKS

In the Third Intermediate Period, branches of royal granaries and treasuries continued to receive state revenues, and palaces and estates continued to redistribute these revenues, though not necessarily on behalf of a single royal authority. Temples also continued to cultivate land or collect harvest taxes, and to redistribute revenues to officials, priests, and dependent personnel. The fragmentation of the state limited its ability to enforce state and temple redistribution, however, especially over long distances, making them comparatively less secure and attractive than in the New Kingdom, while the increasing involvement of temples in documenting high-value exchanges made them relatively more secure and attractive than previously.

Royal Granaries and Treasuries: Royal granaries and treasuries probably continued to exist throughout the Third Intermediate Period and to account for state revenues, though at times various branches may have served different kings and authorities. For example, during the Twenty-first Dynasty, the temple of Amun at Karnak probably continued to manage or cultivate much royal land in Egypt on behalf of the king, and to collect and store its harvest taxes in state accounts, as it had in the late New Kingdom. However, it was probably the high priest of Amun who controlled the accounts in the Twenty-first Dynasty, rather than the king or his agents. During the early Twenty-second Dynasty, however, when the king reasserted his authority over Upper Egypt, control of the accounts probably reverted to the king. Stela Cairo JdE 31882 (Apanage Stela), dated sometime after Year 10 of King Osorkon I, refers to fields in the domain of Amun, as well as those in the allotment of pharaoh, showing that the fiscal and administrative distinction still existed.

Military and Police: In the Third Intermediate Period, the army still consisted primarily of reserve soldiers who supported themselves when off duty, but they spent less time on duty because there were fewer campaigns and fewer permanent garrisons, and thus they received fewer redistributed revenues. The relatively impoverished and frequently fragmented state simply had fewer resources to redistribute to soldiers on duty, aside from booty and spoils after a successful campaign. The *medjay*-police, who had previously been regular recipients of redistributed revenues, also disappeared in this period. Many of the reserve soldiers were now probably descendants of Libyans settled in Egypt at the end of the New Kingdom. These Libyans were probably organized and mobilized according to segmentary lineages, in which soldiers served their chiefs or great chiefs rather than the king. Consequently, some chiefs and great chiefs were effectively autonomous, and a few even declared themselves kings, thereby helping create the politically fragmented landscape of the late Third Intermediate Period.[92]

Dependent Institutions, Gangs, and Crews: The fragmentation of royal authority in the Third Intermediate Period probably resulted in some dependent institutions, gangs, and crews shifting their allegiances or having their allegiances shifted in exchange for continued support. For example, at the end of the Twentieth Dynasty, the authority of the king and his vizier in Upper Egypt diminished, and royal tombs were no longer constructed at Thebes. The high priest of Amun at Karnak became the dominant authority in Upper Egypt, and he offered new tasks to the gang of the necropolis formerly settled at Deir el-Medina, such as campaigning in Nubia or recycling funerary equipment in the Theban necropolis.[93]

Temples: From the Third Intermediate Period onward, separate royal mortuary temples ceased to be built. Royal burials were usually located within the walled precincts of major divine temples, and the royal mortuary cults probably became subsidiary to those temples. Divine temples, however, continued to flourish and grow in the Third Intermediate Period. Donation stelae record the donation of fields to a god or gods and their temples by kings and private individuals alike. In either case, the stela often depict a king symbolically offering the hieroglyph for fields to the gods, because in theory the king was the chief priest of the gods, though in practice he was represented by the local priesthood. In the Third Intermediate Period, local rulers are sometimes depicted making the offering rather than the king, reflecting the diminished status of kings in this period. Private donors are usually depicted standing behind the king or local ruler who makes the offering on their behalf. The fields are sometimes designated to support a private funerary cult (see the following subsection), but they are sometimes assigned to the divine cult proper.

Temples may have been subject to state levies in the Third Intermediate Period, as in earlier periods. By the reign of Osorkon I, the office of manager (*mr-šn*) of a temple domain starts to appear among the titles of some priests.[94] These attestations reveal little about the nature of the office, but later in the Persian Period the priests of each temple selected a temple manager annually subject to state approval,[95] and in the Ptolemaic Period the state held the temple manager (*mr-šn*, Gr. *lesōnis*) accountable for shortfalls in temple revenues and perhaps also for state levies on temples.[96] If the temple manager held similar responsibilities already in the Third Intermediate Period, the introduction of the office may represent an attempt by the early Twenty-second Dynasty to assert more control over temple finances, after the autonomy of the high priests of Amun at Thebes in the Twenty-first Dynasty.

Private Funerary Endowments: Private funerary endowments are well attested in the later Third Intermediate Period from donation stelae. Revenue sources, usually fields, were donated to a god or gods for the funerary cult of the deceased. In some cases, the deceased's mortuary priests may have managed the revenue sources on behalf of the gods' temple, while in other cases the gods' temple managed the revenue sources and delivered bread, beer, and other commodities as offerings for the deceased and rations for the mortuary priests. Evidence for both arrangements can be seen in the red granite Stela Cairo JdE 66285 from Abydos, known as the donation stela of Shoshenk I.[97] In it, an unnamed king petitions the god Amun-Re to confirm the endowment of a funerary statue cult by the chief of the Meshwesh and future king Shoshenk I for his father Nemrat at Abydos. The stela ends with a list of the properties and people that Shoshenq acquired for the endowment, and the amount of silver paid for them (lines 9–26). Some of the properties and people were apparently assigned directly to the endowment, such as 100 arouras of fields, a farmer and four servants, ten oxen and their herdsman, a garden and gardener, and two weavers and two servants (lines 9–16). However, the services of other people were provided in perpetuity by the temple of Osiris at Abydos, in return for silver given to the temple treasury (lines 16–26).

Stela Cairo JdE 66285, lines 16–26:

Bee-keepers: 5 men, each one 6 ⅔ kite per person, making in silver 3 ⅔ deben, paid into the treasury of Osiris, and ½ hin of honey passes out (17) daily from the treasury of Osiris to the sacred property of the Osiris, great chief of the Meshwesh, Nemrat, justified, for ever and ever, as the contribution of these <5> bee-keepers whose silver has been paid into the treasury of Osiris, so that they shall never die, so that they shall never be missing.

Thurifer(s): (18) 5 men, each one 6 ⅔ kite, making in silver 3 ⅔ deben, paid into the treasury of Osiris, and the 5 kite of incense passes out daily from the treasury of Osiris to the sacred property of the Osiris, great chief of the Meshwesh, Nemrat, justified, whose mother is Mehetemweskhet, for ever and ever, as (19) the contribution of the 5 thurifers whose silver has been paid into the treasury of Osiris, so that they shall never die, so that they shall never be missing.

Oil-man: 1 man, making in silver 6 ⅔ kite, paid into the treasury of Osiris, and ½ hin of (20) lamp oil passes out daily from the treasury of Osiris for the lamp of the Osiris, great chief of the Meshwesh, Nemrat, justified, whose mother is Mehetemweskhet, for ever and ever, as the contribution of the oil-man, whose silver has been paid into the treasury of Osiris, so that he shall never die, so that (21) he shall never be missing.

> One man's gift: brewer(s): 2 men, each one 6 ⅔ kite of silver; confectioner: ¼ man, making in silver 1 kite; paid into the treasury of Osiris, and this barley and spelt passes out daily as bread and beer of the store-house from (22) the granary of Osiris and the brewery of Osiris to the sacred property of the Osiris, great chief of the Meshwesh, Nemrat, justified, whose mother is Mehetemweskhet, for ever and ever, as the contribution of this cellar of the brewery and of the confectioner whose silver has been paid into the treasury of Osiris (23) ... together with the harvests of this land from the 100 arouras which go into the granary of Osiris in the course of the year, so that they shall never die, so that they shall never be missing.
>
> Total, the silver of the people which has been paid into the treasury of Osiris: (24) 8 deben 7 4/3 kite of silver, making in men 12 ¼, whose contributions shall pass out from the treasury of Osiris to the sacred property of the Osiris, great chief of the Meshwesh, prince of princes, Nemrat, justified, son of the great chief of the Meshwesh, Shoshenk, justified, whose mother is Mehetemweskhet, for ever (25) and ever.
>
> Total, the sacred property of the statue of the Osiris, great chief of the Meshwesh, justified, Nemrat, justified, son of Mehetemweskhet, which is in Abydos: land, 100 arouras; men and woman, 25; garden, 1; silver altar, 1; service-vessel, 1; libationer (26) ... making in silver ... deben ...

In contrast, evidence that mortuary priests sometimes assumed primary responsibility for managing funerary endowments might be seen in a group of Abnormal Hieratic lease contracts from Thebes, probably dating to the reign of Taharqa, involving choachytes and endowment fields.[98] In three of these lease contracts, P. Louvre E. 7856 verso, and P. Louvre E. 7851 recto and verso, various choachytes lease endowment fields from other parties, two of them women, to cultivate them for a share of the harvest. These leases could have been a method of entrusting the endowment fields to the choachytes, but more likely they represent choachytes leasing them out to other choachytes.[99]

EXCHANGES

In the Third Intermediate Period, there is abundant written evidence for exchanges of relatively high-value goods like land, slaves, and cattle, whose values were measured in silver, much more so than in the preceding New Kingdom. This probably reflects both an increased use of written documentation, and an increase in the number of high-value exchanges. Most of these were private local exchanges, because enforcement was still dependent on local witnesses. Exchange partners usually found each other through social networks rather than anonymous markets. Fragmentation of the state and temple redistributive networks in this period may have reduced their ability to participate in long distance distribution, and may have made exchanges comparatively more secure and attractive than in the New Kingdom. There is, however, less evidence for exchanges of low value goods whose values were measured in cloth, copper, and grain in the Third Intermediate Period than in the New Kingdom. Low value exchanges, however, are often not worth documenting in writing, so such underrepresentation is not surprising. The case of Deir el-Medina in the New Kingdom, with frequent written documentation of low value exchanges, was exceptional.

Land: Some exchanges of land in the Third Intermediate Period consisted of "donations" of land to temples in exchange for "donations" of institutional revenues for private funerary establishments, as in the New Kingdom. Many donation stela imply that a king or local prince donated land on behalf of an individual to provide revenues for the individual's funerary establishment.[100] Other exchanges, however, recorded on Hieroglyphic inscriptions and Hieratic papyri discussed previously, mention multiple sales of land for cloth, copper, or silver. Many of these purchases appear to have been intended to create estates to generate revenues for this life, or for funerary cults for the afterlife.[101] The Oracular Property Decree for the high priest of Amun Menkheperre in the temple of Khonsu at Karnak records that he purchased several plots of land from specified individuals in exchange for copper.[102] Hieratic Papyrus Brooklyn 16.205, from Thebes and dated to a Year 4 after a Year 49 in the middle of the Twenty-first Dynasty,[103] records two disputes about payment that arose from two purchases of land, and which were resolved through the use of two oracular consultations with the gods Hemen and Khonsu.[104] Hieroglyphic Stela Cairo JdE 70218, from Fustat and dated to Year 16 of King Siamun in the late Twenty-first Dynasty, records that the Overseer of the Treasury of Ptah, Ity, purchased two arouras of fields from the *wᶜb*-priest of Ptah, Ankhefenkhonsu, for two deben and two kite of silver, as well as two arouras of fields from the *wᶜb*-priest of Ptah, Harsekhty, for one deben of silver.[105] The Oracular Property Decrees for Henettawy daughter of Isemkheb, inscribed on the Tenth Pylon at Karnak,[106] and for Maatkare daughter of King Psusennes II, inscribed on the Seventh Pylon at Karnak,[107] both mention unspecified purchases of land. Red granite Donation Stela Cairo JdE 66285 from Abydos records the oracular consultation by an unnamed king with the god Amun-Re to confirm the foundation of a funerary statue cult by the chief of the Meshwesh and future king Shoshenk I for his father Nemrat at Abydos.[108] The stela ends with a list of the properties and people comprising the foundation, including 100 arouras of fields worth ten deben of silver, and twenty-five people and ten oxen worth sixteen deben and two and two-third kite of silver, presumably indicating the price paid for them or their services. The Oracular Property Decree for the high priest of Amun Iuwerot and his son Khaenwase, inscribed on red granite Stela Cairo JdE

31882 (Apanage Stela), found at Karnak and dated to Year 10 of Osorkon I, records that the high priest of Amun Iuwerot purchased a total of 556 arouras of fields from sixteen groups of cultivators for a total of eighteen deben and four and three-quarter kite of silver, as well as thirty-five slaves for a total of fifteen deben and one-third kite of silver.[109] The fields were said to be part of the temple domain of Amun-Re, and paid their harvest taxes to the granary of Amun-Re, but the purchase silver was paid to the cultivators of the fields. This suggests that the cultivators were effectively the owners of the fields, rather than the temple domain, which only received a harvest tax.

Stela Cairo JdE 31882, lines 8–23:

Their list: – The place of the *wꜥb*-priest of Amon, Neskhons, deceased, son of Hori, deceased, son of Ankhefenkhonsu, deceased, 137 arouras of clear private fields (*ꜣḥ nmḥ.w nꜥ*) (9) and 99 arouras of – fields (*ꜣḥ šꜣ.w tnj*), total 236 arouras, 1 well (*šd*), 8 sycamores, 6 fruit trees, which makes 8 deben ¾ kite of silver.

The place of the tenant (*mnḥ*) Djedmutefankh, deceased, son of Iken, deceased, (10) 66 arouras of clear private fields and 5 arouras of – fields, total 71 arouras, 3 wells, 26 large fruit trees and 50 small ones, 3 sycamores, which makes 4 deben ⅔ ¾ kite of silver.

The tenant (*mnḥ*) Ahmose, (11) deceased, son of Djedmutefankh, deceased, with the children of Pashenmut, deceased, son of Djedmutefankh, deceased, 64 arouras of – fields and 5 arouras of clear private fields, total 69 arouras, (12) which make 1 deben 5 kite of silver.

The soldier (*ḳrꜥ*) Penamon, deceased, son of Paikesh, deceased, and the tenant Nesmerihor, deceased, son of Djedkhonsuefankh, deceased, 30 arouras of – fields, which makes 6 kite of silver.

The citizeness (*ꜥnḫ-n-niw.t*) Ta- (13) shereniah, the wife of the *wꜥb*-priest of Amun Shaimenimef, deceased, 10 arouras of – fields, which makes 1 kite of silver.

The tenant (*mnḥ*) Remenpouf, deceased, son of Kaimen, deceased, 14 arouras of clear private fields (14) and 23 arouras of – fields, total 37 arouras, which make 1 deben and 1 ¼ kite of silver.

The rower (*ẖnw*) Tjaiouiou, deceased, of the director of the livestock of Amun, 3 arouras of – fields, which make ⅔ (kite) of silver.

(15) The tenant (*mnḥ*) Hor, deceased, son of Shemeg, deceased, with this wife of Penamon, deceased, daughter of Shemeg, deceased, 45 arouras of – fields, which make 8 kite of silver.

The soldier (*ḳrꜥ*) Iahweben, deceased, son of Pete- (16) khons, deceased, 8 arouras of clear private fields and 2 arouras of – fields, total 10 arouras, makes 3 ⅔ kite of silver.

The tenant (*mnḥ*) Kenmathel, deceased, son of Iken, deceased, 1 aroura of field, which makes ½ kite of silver.

(17) The tenant (*mnḥ*) Djedhorefankh, deceased, son of Nestanetereten, son of Hor, 3 arouras of clear private fields and 2 arouras of – fields, total 5 arouras, makes 1 ⅔ kite of silver.

The tenant (*mnḥ*) Paoun, deceased, son of Iken, deceased, (18) 15 arouras of clear private fields, which makes 6 kite of silver.

The citizeness (*ꜥnḫ-n-niw.t*) Neskhons, daughter of Iken, deceased, with his son Thotmes, deceased, his son Petekhons, deceased, and his son Kenmathel, deceased, 8 arouras of clear private fields (19) and 2 arouras of – fields, total 10 arouras, which makes 3 ⅔ kite of silver.

The tenant (*mnḥ*) Djedkhons, deceased, son of Iken, deceased, 1 aroura of clear private field and 1 aroura of – field, total (20) 2 aroura, makes ⅔ (kite) of silver.

The tenant (*mnḥ*) Nesy, deceased, (daughter of) Iouwkasar, deceased, 5 arouras of clear private fields and 2 arouras of – fields, total 7 arouras, and 1 well, which makes 2 (21) ⅔ kite of silver.

The tenant (*mnḥ*) Djedmutefankh, deceased, son of Iken, deceased, 5 arouras of clear private fields, which makes 2 ½ kite of silver.

These male and female servants which he has purchased from the private people of the land (22) likewise: 32 men and women, which make 15 deben and ⅓ kite of silver, and likewise these 3 servants from the north which he acquired.

Total: 556 arouras of diverse fields and 35 men and women, their wells, their trees, (23) and their small and large cattle.

Houses: An unpublished abstract of an Abnormal Hieratic sales contract is preserved in Papyrus Berlin P. 3048 verso, and records the purchase of a house for two silver deben.[110]

Slaves: Two Hieroglyphic inscriptions mention the purchase of multiple slaves along with fields to help cultivate them, or to provide specialized artisanal labor for institutions. These purchases seem to have been intended to transfer the services of the slaves with their fields, however, rather than to actually move the slaves. Red granite Donation Stela Cairo JdE 66285 confirms the foundation of a funerary statue cult by the future king Shoshenk I for his father Nemrat at Abydos.[111] It records the purchase of a farmer and four servants to work 100 arouras of purchased land, a herdsman to herd ten purchased oxen, a gardener to work a purchased garden, and two weavers and two servants (lines 9–16). The stela also records the purchase of the services of five bee-keepers, five thurifers, one oil-man, two brewers and a quarter confectioner from the temple of Osiris at Abydos. A total of eight deben and seven and four-thirds kite of silver was paid to the treasury of Osiris to ensure that the people never died and were never missing (lines 16–26). The first group of people were apparently purchased with the land and cattle that they tended, while only the services of the second group of people were purchased, albeit in perpetuity. The Oracular Property Decree for the high priest of Amun Iuwerot and his son Khaenwaset, inscribed on red granite Stela Cairo JdE 31882 (Apanage Stela), found at Karnak and dated to Year 10 of Osorkon I, may also record the purchase of people with the land they worked:[112] "These male and female servants which he has purchased from the private people of the land likewise: 32 men and women, which makes 15 deben and ⅓ kite of silver, and likewise these 3 servants from the north which he acquired" (lines 21–22).

In contrast, several Abnormal Hieratic papyri document sales of individual slaves for silver, which appear to have resulted in the actual movement of slaves from one household to another. Abnormal Hieratic sales contract P. Leiden K 128, dated to Year 21 of Piye (726/5 BCE), records the sale of Pneferiu, "the man from the north," from one party to another.[113] Likewise, Abnormal Hieratic sales contract P. Vatican 2038C, dated to Year 22 of Piye (725/4 BCE), similarly records the sale of Bentuiut, "the man from the north," from one party to another.[114] In the Archive of Petubast from Thebes, Abnormal Hieratic Papyrus Louvre E 3228e (*Choix* I 6), dated to Year 10 Shabaka (706/5 BCE), records the sale of Montuirties, "the man from the north," from one party to Petubast, and Abnormal Hieratic Papyrus Louvre E 3228d (*Choix* I 7), dated to Year 3 of Taharqa (688/7 BCE), records the sale of Udjahor, "the man from the north," from one party to a second.[115] Abnormal Hieratic Papyrus Louvre E 3228f, dated to Year 5 of Taharqa (686/5 BCE), records the sale of Udjahor and two other slaves by the son of that second party to Petubast.[116] In Abnormal Hieratic Papyrus Louvre E 3228c, dated to Year 6 of Taharqa (685/4 BCE), the son of the second party cedes Irturetj, "the man from the north," to Petubast, after losing a lawsuit.[117]

Cattle: A pair of oracle petitions from Nag' ed-Deir, P. Berkeley inventory number unknown A and B, concern a dispute about a sale of a cow. One of the petitions says that full payment was made, the other states that only partial payment was made. The petitions were addressed to the deity Horus-of-the-Camp, who was supposed to choose the correct petition. Donation Stela Cairo JdE 66285, of Shoshenq for his father Nemrat, records the purchase of ten oxen for two deben of silver.

ENTREPRENEURIAL ACTIVITIES

In the Third Intermediate Period, periodic fragmentation of the state limited the ability of kings and their agents to undertake military expeditions to populated areas beyond the borders of Egypt, though paramilitary expeditions into the unpopulated deserts around Egypt to quarry and mine still took place. The divisions within the state also limited the resources available for new settlements and foundations, even as it encouraged kings and agents to shift local populations and revenues to found or expand local settlements and institutions to serve new seats of authority. Under these circumstances, accumulation of private property may increasingly have been seen as a more reliable investment than royal service and participation in state redistributive networks.

Expeditions: In the early Third Intermediate Period, the early Twenty-first Dynasty kings at Tanis in Lower Egypt had little authority over the high priests of Amun at Thebes in Upper Egypt, preventing either of them from undertaking military expeditions abroad. The later Twenty-first Dynasty and early Twenty-second Dynasty kings reasserted control over the high priests of Amun, however, allowing them to launch a major military expedition in the southern Levant. King Shoshenq I campaigned against King Rehoboam of Judah, after King Jeroboam led the secession of Israel from Rehoboam, and carried off the treasures of the temple and the palace in Jerusalem.[118] The campaign is also known from lists of conquered place names inscribed on the Bubastite Portal at Karnak,[119] and from a fragment of a stela of Shoshenq I found at Megiddo.[120]

In the late Third Intermediate Period, however, the later Twenty-second Dynasty at Tanis was joined by the Twenty-third Dynasty, and the Twenty-fourth Dynasty at Sais, which discouraged further Egyptian expeditions abroad, and indeed made Egypt the target of foreign military expeditions. The Kushite king Piye invaded Egypt from Nubia, subjugated the kings of the Twenty-second and Twenty-third Dynasties, and established the Kushite Twenty-fifth Dynasty. The campaign is recorded on Stela Cairo JdE 48862 + 47086–47089 (Victory Stela of Piye), found in 1862 in the temple of Amun at Gebel Barkal in Nubia, and dated to Year 21 of King Piye.[121] Piye's successor Shabaka campaigned in Lower Egypt, subjugated the Twenty-fourth Dynasty, and brought "men of the north" to Thebes as slaves. Shabaka's successor Shebitku sent his brother and later successor Taharqa to campaign in the southern Levant against the Assyrians, who had already subjugated the kingdom of Israel. Together with King Hezekiah of Judah, Taharqa defeated the Assyrians at the battle of Eltekeh.[122] King Assurbanipal of Assyria subsequently invaded Egypt from the Levant, and drove Taharqa's successor Tanwetamani out of Egypt, ending the Kushite Twenty-fifth Dynasty. Assurbanipal also sacked Thebes, and established as his client King Psammetichus I of Sais, founding the Twenty-sixth Dynasty.

Foundations: At the end of the New Kingdom, the royal residence and city of Pi-Ramesses was abandoned, probably due to a shift in the course of the Pelusaic branch of the Nile. Consequently the kings of the Twenty-first and Twenty-second Dynasties built a new royal residence at the site of Tanis, together with a temple complex devoted to Amun, and a royal cemetery within the temple enclosure. During the Twenty-first Dynasty, the high priests of Amun at Thebes founded the fortress town of El-Hiba at the northern end of their domain. In the Twenty-second Dynasty, Shoshenq I built a new temple to Amun at El-Hiba, Osorkon I and Osorkon II built a new temple complex devoted to Bastet at the site of Bubastis, and Osorkon I also developed the fortress town of Per-Sekhemkheperre at Herakleopolis. The Twenty-fourth Dynasty kings established a new royal residence at Sais.

Private Entrepreneurial Activities: In the Third Intermediate Period, some private individuals and households accumulated surplus durable goods in order to exchange them for revenue producing properties, as they had in the New Kingdom. The surplus durable goods increasingly consisted of silver rather than cloth, however, and the revenue producing properties more often included land in addition to slaves. The Oracular Property Decrees for the high priests of Amun Menkheperre and Iuwerot explicitly document the acquisition of large estates through purchase with copper or silver. The Oracular Property Decrees for Henettaway daughter of Isemkheb and Maatkare daughter of King Psusennes II imply similar acquisitions through purchase as well as inheritance. Together, these sources give the impression of a trend toward investment in land in this period. There are no statistics to support this or any other impression, but the development of Oracular Property Decrees in this period, a new judicial procedure to help protect title to large estates, suggests that there was a trend toward investment in land and a need to protect such investments. It is noteworthy that this trend occurred at a moment in Egyptian history when the authority of the state was at a low ebb. Previously it has been suggested that the relative security of state redistributive networks compared to exchanges attracted investment to the state sector. This suggests a corollary that decreasing security of state redistributive networks may have driven investment to the private sector. Other private individuals and households leased lands and cultivated them for a share of the harvest, in some cases probably for subsistence, in other cases possibly to accumulate surpluses that could be exchanged for revenue producing properties. A group of Abnormal Hieratic lease contracts from Thebes, probably dating to the reign of Taharqa, and involving choachytes and endowment fields, has already been mentioned.[123]

CONCLUSIONS

In the Third Intermediate Period, the state fragmented, and temples assumed responsibility for adjudicating property disputes, at first using oracular consultations, and later courts associated with temples. Fragments of the state and the temples continued to document labor obligations for individual people and harvest taxes for individual plots of land. Temples also developed new forms of written documentation of transfers of land and property, however. Temples first used oracular property decrees to document transfers, and then temple notaries documented them. Temples may have introduced these measures to counteract weak documentation and enforcement of royal donations by state fragments.

Improved documentation of property transfers and increased use of silver as a medium of exchange in turn lowered transaction costs for high-value exchanges. Dependence on local courts and witnesses still limited the range of enforcement of such exchanges, but the fragmentation of the state also limited the range of state and temple redistribution, making investment in property more competitive with state service than in previous periods. Private donations of land to temples in exchange for revenues for mortuary cults continued, but high-value exchanges increasingly involved plots of land and silver, and many were documented with written contracts. Many low value exchanges probably took place in markets, but most of these were not documented in writing. Long-term employment with state or temple organizations was common, as was short-term compulsory labor for the state.

SIX

THE SAITE AND PERSIAN PERIODS (664–332 BCE)

The Saite Period consists of the Twenty-sixth or Saite Dynasty (664–525 BCE). The Saite Dynasty succeeded the Twenty-fourth Dynasty based at Sais in northwestern Egypt, and came to power as allies of the Assyrians after the latter expelled the Kushites from Egypt. When the Assyrians in turn departed, the Saites expanded to fill the resulting power vacuum, and reunited Egypt by appointing their daughters to be the god's wives of Amun at Thebes. The Saite royal court seems to have alternated between Sais and Memphis. The Persian Period (525–332 BCE) includes the Twenty-seventh Dynasty or First Persian Period, the native Egyptian Twenty-eighth, Twenty-ninth, and Thirtieth Dynasties, and the Second Persian Period. The First Persian Period began when the Persian kings defeated the Saite Dynasty and added Egypt to their empire. It saw several unsuccessful revolts against Persian rule, until a successful revolt established the Egyptian Twenty-eighth Dynasty, rapidly followed by the Twenty-ninth and Thirtieth Dynasties. The Persians finally reconquered Egypt and established the Second Persian Period ten years before Alexander the Great's invasion. The Persians ruled Egypt through a provincial governor known as a satrap, based at Memphis, and they introduced Aramaic as an administrative language alongside Egyptian. (See Map 6.1 and Table 6.1).

MAP 6.1. Egypt in the Saite and Persian Periods

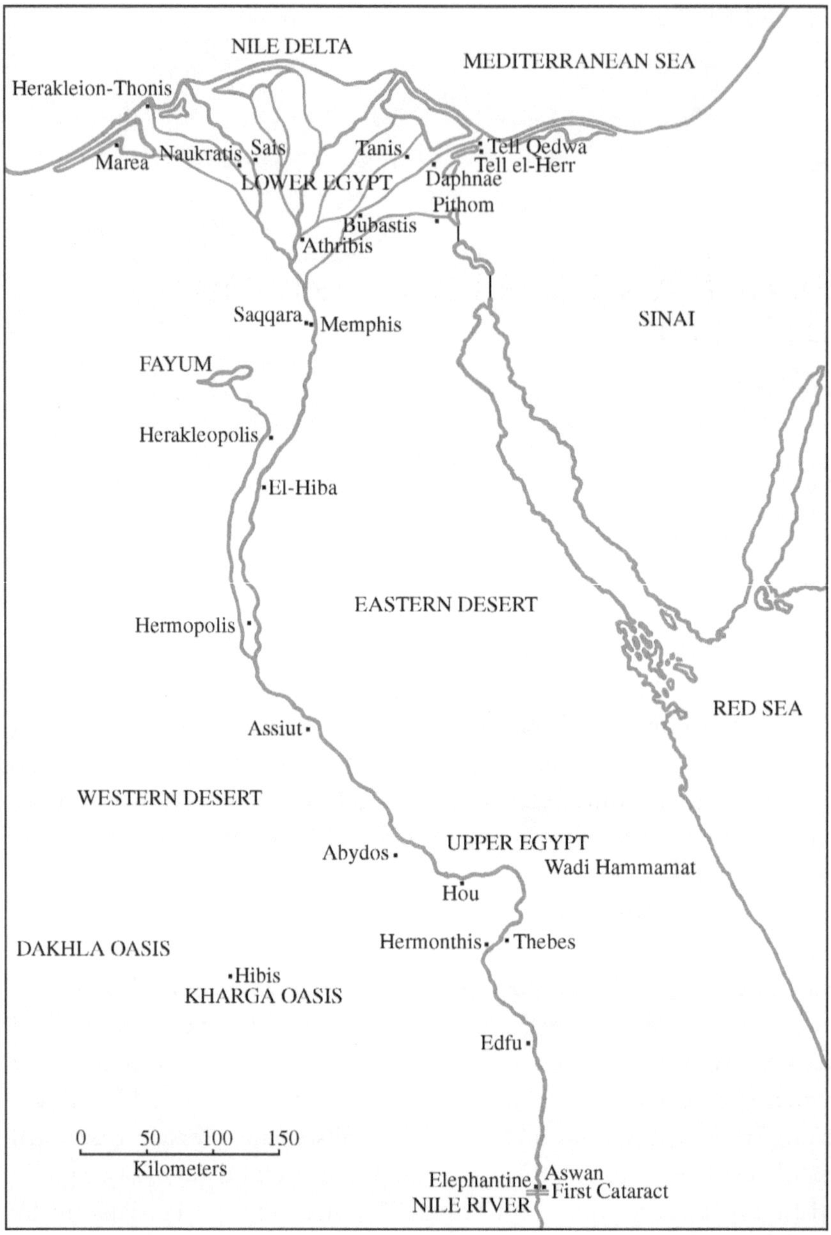

CRIMINAL JUSTICE

In the Saite and Persian Periods, crimes against the state, and against state finances, fell under the jurisdiction of the criminal justice system. In the Saite Period, this system consisted of the king, the viziers and later the chief finance minister, the shipping master at Herakleopolis, and various military

TABLE 6.1. *The Saite and Persian Periods*

The Saite Period (664–525 BCE)
Dynasty 26, after unification (664–525 BCE)
Psammetichus I (664–610 BCE)
Necho II (610–595 BCE)
Psammetichus II (595–589 BCE)
Apries (589–570 BCE)
Amasis (570–526 BCE)
Psammetichus III (526–525 BCE)
The Persian Period (525–332 BCE)
Dynasty 27, first part (525–404 BCE)
Cambyses (530/525–522 BCE) – Conquered Egypt in 525 BCE
Darius I (522–486 BCE) – Revolt of Psammetichus IV (486 BCE)
Xerxes I (486–465 BCE)
Artaxerxes I (465–424 BCE) – Revolt of Inaros (c. 460–454 BCE)
Darius II (424–405 BCE)
Artaxerxes II (405–404/358 BCE) – Lost Egypt in 404 BCE
Dynasty 28 (404–399 BCE)
Amyrtaeus (404–399 BCE)
Dynasty 29 (399–380 BCE)
Nepherites (399–393 BCE)
Hakoris (393–380 BCE)
Dynasty 30 (380–343 BCE)
Nectanebo I (380–362 BCE)
Teos (362–360 BCE)
Nectanebo II (360–343 BCE)
Dynasty 27, second part (343–332 BCE)
Artaxerxes III (358/342–338 BCE) – Reconquered Egypt in 342 BCE
Arses (338–336 BCE) – Revolt of Khababash (338–336 BCE)
Darius III (336–332 BCE)

Source: Dates after Ian Shaw (ed.), *The Oxford History of Ancient Egypt* (Oxford: University Press, 2000), pp. 479–483.

commanders who enforced their decisions locally. In the Persian Period, the criminal justice system consisted of the satrap or governor of Egypt, the chief finance minister, and the garrison commanders who served as their local agents.

The Saite reunification of Egypt reduced the number of kings in Egypt to one, and restored to him ultimate judicial and administrative authority. Nonetheless, subjects could come to the house of pharaoh and petition the king to hear their complaints, and on occasion he did hear and decide judicial cases himself. The Petition of Petiese records that in Year 31 of King Psammetichus I, several priests in El-Hiba murdered Petiese I's grandsons. Petiese I complained to the shipping master in Herakleopolis, who sent a general and soldiers to arrest the priests. Petiese I accompanied the priests downstream to the house of pharaoh, where he accused them before the king, and the king had them punished.[1] Then in Year 4 of King Psammetichus II, the supervisor of Herakleopolis seized Petiese II's priesthoods in El-Hiba, and Petiese II went downstream to the house of pharaoh to complain, but he was told that the king was too ill to hear him.[2]

Subjects could also bring their complaints to the king's officials, in either the central or the local administrations. As a result of the reunification, however, the Saite kings inherited a number of high officials appointed when Egypt had been divided into multiple principalities. Rather than abruptly replace all of these high officials, the Saite kings often let them hold office until they died, and then did not appoint successors. Thus immediately after the reunification the Saite kings were served by at least two viziers, one in Upper Egypt and at least one in Lower and Middle Egypt. In the course of the Saite Period, however, first the Upper Egyptian vizier was eliminated, and later the Lower Egyptian vizier as well. By the end of the Saite Period, a new official, the chief financial minister (Dem. *snty*), replaced the viziers.[3]

The Saite Period Upper Egyptian vizier, Nespaqashuty D, was the son of the vizier Nespamedu and the grandson of the vizier Nespaqashuty C. Both Nespamedu and Nespaqashuty C had served under the Kushite kings, residing at Abydos where they were buried.[4] Nespaqashuty D lived and was buried at Thebes, and was not replaced after his death in the reign of King Psammetichus I.[5] It is unclear whether these Upper Egyptian viziers had any judicial authority. An Abnormal Hieratic quitclaim contract from Thebes under the Kushite kings refers to a dispute "before the great ones of the great *ḳnb.t*-court of Thebes and before the chief scribe of documents."[6] In the New Kingdom the viziers presided over the great *ḳnb.t*-courts, but at the time this Abnormal Hieratic contract was written they seem to have resided at Abydos rather than Thebes.

Several Lower Egyptian viziers are known. Bakenrenef served under King Psammetichus I and was buried at Saqqara. Sasobek also served under King Psammetichus I, and is known from his sarcophagus in the British Museum (EA 17), possibly from Sais. A vizier Psamtikmerineith appears to have served under King Amasis.[7] The Lower Egyptian viziers seem to have had some judicial authority. Two Demotic contracts from El-Hiba in Middle Egypt from the reign of King Psammetichus I state "the man who shall come against you to take you to the vizier and the judges."[8] Likewise, in the Petition of Petiese, when King Psammetichus II was too ill to adjudicate Petiese's dispute, Petiese petitioned "the vizier and the judges."[9] It is unclear whether the judges mentioned in these phrases belonged to an otherwise unattested high court over which the vizier presided, as in the New Kingdom; or whether they belonged to the local courts or "Houses of Judgment" associated with temples.

After the Persian conquest of Egypt, the Persian King of Kings became the titular king of Egypt. However, a Persian governor or satrap resident in Egypt assumed many of the administrative functions of the king, and the chief financial minister had absorbed some of the vizier's functions, such as hearing petitions. The most famous Persian Period petition is the so-called Petition of Petiese (P. Rylands 9), which was addressed to the chief financial minister. It was found together with a number of documentary texts pertaining to the family of the petitioner, suggesting that that copy was never sent, and that it was a real petition despite having many literary features.

In the Saite Period, provincial governors and generals served as local agents of the king and the criminal justice system. The provincial governors and generals received complaints, and allocated them to the appropriate jurisdictions. They themselves dealt with alleged criminal offences, personal injuries, and property damages. Under the Persians, garrison commanders, often Persian or Aramaic-speaking foreigners, represented the Persian satrap in Memphis or the distant Persian king, and performed functions similar to provincial governors and generals.

The Saite reunification of Egypt brought a variety of local authorities under royal control. In Lower and Middle Egypt these included local Libyan lineage chiefs, whose authority was hereditary and was not dependent on the kings. Consequently, the Saite kings gradually reassigned their roles in local judicial administration to provincial governors and generals, who were appointed by and owed their authority to the kings.[10]

At the beginning of the Saite Period, the shipping masters (*ꜥꜣ n mry.t*) of Herakleopolis served as the king's primary representative for all of Middle and Upper Egypt. The first shipping master, Petiese son of Ankhsheshonq, served until Year 18 of King Psammetichus I. His son, Sematawytefnakht son of Petiese, served until at least Year 31 of King Psammetichus I. In that year, a criminal complaint of murder in El-Hiba in the Herakleopolite nome was brought to him, and he dispatched a Libyan lineage chief known as the chief of the Ma to protect the petitioner,[11] as well as a general to investigate and make arrests. Those arrested were sent to the house of pharaoh, and the king passed judgment on them.[12]

By the middle of the Saite Period, however, the office of shipping master had disappeared, and his judicial authority had been reassigned. In Year 4 of King Psammetichus II one finds instead a supervisor (*ḥry*) of Herakleopolis acting as the king's local representative.[13] He was apparently a kind of provincial governor, since his authority extended to El-Hiba in the same nome, and thus he may have been paralleled by other provincial governors in other nomes.[14] Thus near the end of the Saite Period, in Year 15 of King Amasis, a complaint about property damages in El-Hiba was directed to the supervisor of Herakleopolis, and to a general who was in the Herakleopolite nome, who both sent men to investigate and make arrests. Ultimately, the supervisor of Herakleopolis persuaded the petitioner to drop the charges in return for ten deben of silver.[15]

After the Persians conquered Egypt, they stationed several garrison commanders and their troops at strategic locations in Egypt, and these garrison commanders seem to have served as local agents for the Persian satrap in Memphis and the distant Persian king, who received complaints on their behalf. It is not known, however, whether the Persians retained the Egyptian provincial governors in the rest of the country, or whether they replaced them with their own agents, as the Ptolemies eventually did after Alexander the Great conquered Egypt from the Persians.

PROPERTY DISPUTE RESOLUTION

In the Saite and Persian Periods, private property disputes arising from contracts written in Egyptian fell under the jurisdiction of the Egyptian court system, which applied traditional Egyptian property laws. These were local courts known as Houses of Judgment, which were associated with local temples. In the Persian Period, however, contracts written in Aramaic were recognized alongside those written in Egyptian, though private property disputes arising from such Aramaic contracts were adjudicated by courts composed of local Aramaic-speaking officials, such as garrison commanders, rather than by the Egyptian courts associated with temples.

Egyptian Courts: The Saite reunification of Egypt brought the Upper Egyptian court system in line with that of Lower and Middle Egypt. At the end of the Third Intermediate Period, under the Kushite kings, the local judicial administration in Upper Egypt appears to have consisted of the great *ḳnb.t*-court in Thebes, and the Halls of Writings. In the Saite and Persian Periods, however, there are no longer any references to either great *ḳnb.t*-courts or local *ḳnb.t*-courts. Instead, there are references to the "houses of judgment" (*ᶜ.wy.w n wpy*). These houses of judgment were composed of boards of judges (*wp.w* or *wpty.w*), and were associated with temples in major provincial towns, perhaps the same temples with which contract notaries were associated.[16] As in the preceding period, unsuccessful litigants continued to be required to cede all further claims to disputed property. Cession or quitclaim contracts were extremely rare prior to the Ptolemaic Period (332–30 BCE), however. During the Saite (664–525 BCE) and First Persian (525–404 BCE) periods, one finds only Papyrus Rylands 4, dated to Year 2 of Amasis (569 BCE),[17] Papyrus BM 10792 and perhaps also Papyrus Cairo CG 50059, both dated to Year 8 of Cambyses (522 BCE),[18] Papyrus Louvre AF 9761 *(Tsenhor* 15), dated to Year 28 of Darius I (494 BCE),[19] and Papyrus Loeb 43 (*Hou* 8), dated to Year 2 of Psammetichos III (485 BCE).[20] During the Twenty-eighth, Twenty-ninth, and Thirtieth Dynasties (404–342 BCE) and the Second Persian (342–332 BCE) period, one finds *Papyrus Cairo CG dem.* 50150 + 50155, probably to be dated to the reign of Nectanebo I (380–362 BCE),[21] Papyrus Louvre 2430, dated to Year 2 of Darius III (334 BCE),[22] and perhaps Papyrus Sorbonne 1277, dated to the reign of Artaxerxes III (342–338 BCE).[23]

Egyptian courts probably adjudicated disputes arising from Egyptian language agreements according to Egyptian law. There is currently no manuscript known to date from the Saite and Persian Periods that contains an Egyptian law code, but it has been suggested that two manuscripts dating to the Ptolemaic Period contain law codes that in part date back to the Saite and Persian Periods. As previously mentioned, the Demotic manuscript of the Legal Code of Hermopolis West dates to the third century BCE, but at least some elements of the text date back at least to the late seventh or early sixth centuries BCE, that is the Saite Period, if not earlier.[24] The Demotic manuscript of the Zivilprozessordnung is probably also from Hermopolis, and probably also dates to the third or second century BCE. One of the fragments of the manuscript refers to King Amasis, however, and in the following line to a Year 29. Another fragment refers to a Year 43, which can only refer to Psammetichus I or Amasis. This suggests that elements of the text of the Zivilprozessordnung also date back at least to the reign of Amasis.[25]

Access to these courts could presumably be obtained by petitioning an authority for redress, as in *P. Rylands* 9, from El-Hiba dated to 513 BCE. Perhaps one could also make three public protests in three years to obtain a court hearing. Public protests are not attested in the Saite and Persian Periods, but are in the preceding and following periods. The remedy of first resort, however, was the first contractor. The Demotic contract formulary has the first contractor promise that the title is clear from claims by children and siblings, much like the oath in Abnormal Hieratic contracts. However, Demotic contracts also make the first contractor explicitly liable for clearing the title of any such claim that should arise, as in *P. Rylands dem.* 1, dated to 644 BCE.

> ***P. Rylands dem.* 1, lines 3–7:**
>
> You have caused (4) my heart to agree to the silver of these three shares (of property) which are above.
>
> No children nor siblings nor any man in the land nor myself likewise shall be able to exercise authority over them without you, from Year 21 of pharaoh Psammetichus onwards until any year, including (5) children, siblings or any man in the land.
>
> The man who shall come against you on account of these shares which are above, I will cause that he is smooth for you in any dispute in the land, together with children and siblings, until any silver, grain, anything (6) in the whole land which shall enter into your heart, while these three shares which are above belong to you forever.

> The man who shall come against you to take you to the vizier and the judges in the name of the shares which are above, (7) he shall not say "produce a signing witness" except in the town in which the witness is.
>
> "As Amun lives, as pharaoh lives, I shall not be able to say 'false' to any word which is above, I shall not be able to withdraw a word thereof."

Aramaic Courts: The Persians maintained the Egyptian "houses of judgment" introduced in the Saite Period, but they also allowed communities of Aramaic-speaking officials and garrison soldiers stationed in Egypt, at Elephantine for example, to have separate courts that adjudicated cases arising from contracts written in their own languages, according to their own contract or property laws. The judges in these courts may have been local high ranking Aramaic-speaking Persian officials, such as the *fratarka* and the garrison commander at Elephantine.[26] These officials could adjudicate a dispute by imposing an oath on a disputant; if the disputant swore the oath, they were justified. The Jews in the garrison at Elephantine swore such oaths in Aramaic by Yahweh, and several have survived on papyri.[27]

Private Social Control: Individuals undoubtedly resorted to private social networks to help document and enforce agreements and to resolve disputes, in addition to arbitration by agents of the king or the satrap and by local Egyptian and Aramaic courts. Extended family and friends constituted informal horizontal social networks, to which most individuals belonged. For example, the Petition of Petiese records that the shipping master in Herakleopolis Petiese appointed his cousin Petiese I to be priest in the temple of Amun of Teudjoi at El-Hiba in Year 4 of Psammetichus I,[28] and that Petiese I turned to the shipping master's son and successor Sematawytefnakht for assistance in capturing the rival priests who killed his grandsons in Year 31 of Psammetichus I.[29] The Petition of Petiese also implies that one or more provincial supervisors (*ḥry*) eventually replaced the office of shipping master. When Petiese I's grandson and heir Petiese II went on campaign in the Levant with Psammetichus II in his Year 4, the priests of Amun of Teudjoi persuaded the new supervisor of Herakleopolis, Horudja son of Harkheb, to reassign some of the positions in the temple of Amun of Teudjoi from Petiese II to his own son Ptahnefer son of Horudja, a priest of Sobek.[30] When Petiese II returned to El-Hiba from the Levant, he tried to recover his positions. First he went to the pharaoh, but he did not receive him because he was ill. Then he reported to the vizier and the judges, and they decided against him. They brought Ptahnefer son of Horudja, and they wrote their explanations in the house of judges, saying "Ptahnefer, this portion which he received while his father was supervisor of Herakleopolis, is the portion of the pharaoh."[31] Petiese II then sought the help of his relatives in Thebes. They gave him ten deben of silver, and said "Behold, when it is said that Pharaoh has died, we will send to the house of pharaoh about everything that these priests of Amun have done to you. You should report to the vizier (and) those who have written their explanations in the house of judges with this priest of Sobek who has taken your share. They will not be able to avoid doing a good deed for you at that time."[32] Petiese II then returned to El-Hiba, where he was told "There is no profit to go to the house of judges. Your opponent is richer than you. Even if you had 100 silver deben he would win against you."[33]

Private associations were a more formalized kind of horizontal social network, which is first attested in Egypt in the sixth century BCE,[34] though the earliest preserved association rules dates from the early fourth century BCE.[35] Better preserved association rules from the Ptolemaic Period show similarities to contemporary Greek association rules, with provisions for regular social gathering and drinking, funds for the collective care and burial of association members and their families, and fines for antisocial behavior between association members, including instigating formal legal proceedings against other members of the association before first attempting to resolve the dispute within the association.[36]

Elsewhere in the Near East, private associations known as *marzēaḥ* date back to the third millennium BCE,[37] but the comparatively late appearance of private associations in Egypt compared to the rest of the Near East may be due to the existence there of local *ḳnb.t*-courts until the seventh century BCE, which filled many of the roles of local private associations elsewhere. The disappearance of local *ḳnb.t*-courts by the Saite Period in turn may have created a social and judicial void, which was then filled by private associations. The private associations recreated a local forum where communities, or parts thereof, could attempt to negotiate, mediate, arbitrate, or otherwise resolve local disputes, without resorting to regional authorities such as the houses of judgment. As noted earlier, other studies of transaction costs have noted a preference for resolving local disputes locally.[38]

Patronage was a kind of vertical social network that is well attested in Saite and Persian Egypt. Patrons were expected to provide legal protection (*nḫt*) for their clients, in return for favors.[39] For example, the Petition of Petiese records that in Year 15 of Amasis, the overseer of fields (*mr ꜣḥ*) confiscated certain fields from the priests of Amun of Teudjoi.[40] The priests of Amun of Teudjoi then asked the courtier Khorkhonsu son of Hor to protect them and to return their fields to them. In return, Khorkhonsu demanded that his brother be made a *ḥm-nṯr*-priest in the temple of Amun.[41] The priests of Amun then approached Necho son of Ptahnefer, the grandson of the former supervisor of Herakleopolis, Horudja son of Horkheb, and asked him either to provide them protection, or to assign his *ḥm-nṯr*-priesthood in the temple of Amun to Khorkhonsu's brother, so that Khorkhonsu would protect them. Necho agreed to transfer his *ḥm-nṯr*-priesthood, and Khorkhonsu agreed to protect them.[42]

Khorkhonsu then brought the overseer of fields before pharaoh, and compelled him to reassign some fields to the priests of Amun.[43]

DOCUMENTATION OF OBJECTS OF TAXATION

In the Saite and Persian Periods, there were several officials who may have been responsible for economic documentation. Prior to the Saite Period this task belonged to viziers, but already by Year 4 of King Psammetichus I responsibility for economic documentation in Upper Egypt had been assigned to the shipping master (*ꜥꜣ n mry.t*) in Herakleopolis, Petiese son of Ankhsheshonk.[44] In Year 18 of Psammetichus I, he died,[45] and was succeeded by his son Sematawytefnakht son of Petiese.[46] In the Petition of Petiese, it is said about the shipping master that "it is he who inspects from the southern guard post to Aswan,"[47] and "it is he who administers the southern land, and who causes to come into being its silver and its emmer."[48] Pharaoh says to the shipping master, "You inspect the southern land, I will cause that they count it with you."[49] By the middle of the Saite Period, however, the office of shipping master had disappeared, and his judicial authority was reassigned to a supervisor or provincial governor (*ḥry*), while his economic authority was assigned to the overseer of royal boats (*imy-r ꜥḥꜥ.w nsw*).[50]

By the end of the Saite Period, and throughout the Persian Period, responsibility for economic documentation in both Upper and Lower Egypt belonged to a new official, the chief financial minister (Demotic *snty*).[51] There may have been multiple chief financial ministers serving at the same time in these periods, each responsible for a portion of Egypt.[52] The duties of the chief financial ministers are suggested by the additional titles that they held. Some of these additional titles were also borne by individuals who did not bear the title chief financial minister, and who were possibly their subordinates. One title frequently held by the chief financial minister was "chief of inundatable lands" (Egyptian *(pꜣ) ḥry idb*).[53] The same title is applied to gods and kings in Ptolemaic and Roman Egyptian temples in contexts concerning the measurement of fields and the documentation of their harvest.[54] A bearer of this title who did not also bear the title chief financial minister was responsible for nominating candidates for the position of manager (Dem. *mr-šn*) in each temple for approval by the Persian satrap.[55] A related title frequently held by the chief financial minister was "overseer of fields" (Eg. *mr ꜣḥ*).[56] A bearer of this title who did not also bear the title chief financial minister seems to have had the power to assign and reassign rights to cultivate fields.[57] Another title frequently borne by the chief financial minister is "overseer of the scribes of the council (Eg. *mr sšw ḏꜣḏꜣt*).[58] It may be a variant of the title "overseer of the scribe(s) who account(s) for everything" (Eg. *mr sš ḥsb ḫt nbt*), also frequently held by the chief financial minister. The probably subordinate title "scribe who accounts for everything which is of the royal domain" (Eg. *sš ḥsb ḫt nbt nt pr-nswt*) is reminiscent of a phrase in the Naukratis stela of Nectanebo I, in which a tenth of everything "which is accounted to the royal domain" is donated to the goddess Neith.[59] These titles therefore suggest duties involving the documentation or registration of people and objects, possibly for tax purposes.

The titles "overseer of the scribes of the council" and "overseer of the scribe(s) who account(s) for everything" suggest that the chief financial minister was assisted by local agents, who may have been the institutional antecedents of the royal scribes, district scribes, and village scribes of the Ptolemaic Period. Indeed, the family that held the office of royal scribe in the Thebaid in the early Ptolemaic Period performed some of the same functions just prior to the conquest of Egypt by Alexander the Great.[60]

The documentation or registration of objects of taxation, such as fields, people, and animals, probably took the form of a survey of fields and a census of people and animals, as in earlier periods.[61] No actual field surveys or census lists have survived from the Saite and Persian Periods, in contrast to the preceding New Kingdom and Third Intermediate Period, and the following Ptolemaic Period, but institutional continuity makes it very likely that they existed, as do references to field surveys in other documents.

Field Surveys: In the Saite and Persian Periods, agricultural land is usually designated as institutional land, most often as temple endowment land, though state land may also be attested. This designation mainly appears to indicate the institution that received the harvest tax, rather than the owner or the cultivator of the land. The owners appear to have been free to cultivate and harvest their land, or to lease their land to another party for a share of the harvest, or even to donate or sell their land, as long as they, or the lessee, or the new owner paid the harvest taxes.[62] The state and the temples may have each conducted surveys and censuses of and collected the harvest taxes from their own fields and cultivators, as they did in the preceding Third Intermediate Period.

No field surveys survive from the Saite and Persian Periods, but other documents indicate that temple scribes measured the fields held by private individuals in the temple endowment in order to calculate their harvest tax obligations, and that the private individuals then paid their harvest taxes to the temples and their granaries. Leases of privately held land in temple endowments often allot responsibility between the lessor and the lessee for payment of harvest taxes to a temple domain, and usually specify that temple scribes will measure the field in the name of the lessor.[63] Receipts provide direct evidence for payment of harvest taxes to a temple domain.[64]

There was also state land alongside temple endowment land, though it is much less well attested. Royal scribes probably measured the fields held by private individuals in state land, and private individuals may well have paid their harvest taxes to the state and its granaries.[65] Demotic Papyrus Loeb 45 (*Hou*

5), dated to Year 25 of Darius (497 BCE), may be a lease of privately held state land. It does not explicitly designate the land as state land, but it does declare that the scribes of pharaoh will measure the fields in the name of the lessor, and it suggests that they may collect the harvest tax as well, in the same way that temple scribes are supposed to measure fields in temple endowments and collect their harvest taxes.

Censuses: Herodotus wrote in the mid-fifth century BCE that in the reign of the mid-sixth century BCE King Amasis there were 20,000 inhabited towns in Egypt, that Amasis required that every Egyptian man should declare each year before the nomarch or provincial governor the source of his livelihood, and that failure to do so was punishable by death.[66] Pseudo-Aristotle wrote in the mid-fourth century BCE that the Athenian general Chabrias advised King Teos to raise money for a military expedition by demanding contributions by household (Gr. *oikia*) and by individual (Gr. *sōma*).[67] Herodotus' and Pseudo-Aristotle's accounts could imply the existence of censuses organized by households, and by the occupations of the heads of households. This is not implausible because some census documents included such information already in the earlier Middle and New Kingdoms,[68] and separate censuses organized according to household (Gr. *kat' oikian*) or occupation of heads of household (Gr. *kat' ethnos*) are known from the following Ptolemaic Period.[69] Herodotus did not state the purpose of Amasis' census, but censuses were used in Egypt to exact compulsory labor requirements from the Middle Kingdom onward, and may have been used to collect occupational or trade taxes in kind and money from the Third Intermediate Period onward. Pseudo-Aristotle says that Chabrias advised King Teos to levy a capitation or poll tax using a census, but does not say that Teos actually did so, and the first evidence for the collection of a capitation tax in money dates to the immediately following Ptolemaic Period.

DOCUMENTATION OF BOTTLENECK TAXATION

In the Saite and Persian Periods, the state and its agents the temples also began collecting taxes in money alongside those in kind and in labor. In contrast to harvest taxes calculated from measurements of fields or labor taxes from censuses of people, however, these new money taxes were only levied when potential objects of taxation passed through notional checkpoints or bottlenecks monitored by the state and its agents. For example, sales taxes were exacted when contractors went to a temple notary to draw up a property transfer contract, burial taxes had to be paid when mortuary priests brought the dead to temple controlled cemeteries to inter them, and customs duties were collected when traders brought goods to borders to import them. Potential objects of taxation that avoided the bottlenecks and taxation were usually subject to some form of legal sanction to discourage tax evasion. For example, property transfer contracts that lacked a receipt for the payment of sales taxes might be viewed unfavorably in a temple court, and imported goods that lacked a receipt for customs duties might be seized. Receipts could also serve as a means for the state to check the records of its agents and then hold them accountable, since revenues from these bottleneck taxes were not as predictable as harvest taxes calculated from measurements of fields or labor taxes calculated from censuses of people.

Sales Taxes: The earliest bottleneck money taxes were sales taxes on real estate transfers. The use of silver as a medium of exchange appears to have spread through Egyptian society through trade and from the top down, and was thus initially restricted to merchants and traders, and to expensive transactions like real estate transfers, so it is logical that the first money taxes were levied on these transactions. Already in the late Third Intermediate Period, by ninth or early eighth century BCE, temples had established notaries to record real property transfers. Beginning in the Saite Period, by the late seventh century BC, the temples used these notaries as a bottleneck to collect the tenth of scribes and representatives, which was 10 percent of the value of the property involved in the transfer.[70] A statement that this tax had been paid to the temple of Amun, serving as a receipt, was incorporated in two Abnormal Hieratic contracts from Thebes, Papyrus Turin 2118A (246) (*Choix* I 9), dated to Year 30 of Psammetichus I (635 BC), and Papyrus Turin 2120 (247) (*Choix* I 10), dated to Year 45 of Psammetichus I (620 BC);[71] and on two Demotic contracts from Thebes, Papyrus British Museum 10117 (Reich), dated to Year 29 of Amasis (542 BC),[72] and Papyrus Louvre E. 7128 (*Tsenhor* 10), dated to Year 12 of Darius I (510 BC).[73] This was effectively a 10 percent sales tax on any property that was sufficiently valuable to require a title document to protect the new owner's rights to that property. Pseudo-Aristotle wrote that the general Chabrias advised King Teos to demand a tax of one obol on the sale of each artaba of grain, and one-tenth of the profits from shipping and manufactures.[74]

Burial Taxes: In the Saite and Persian Periods, temples seem to have administered and controlled access to the cemeteries in the neighboring deserts. Beginning in the Saite Period, by the seventh century BCE, burial plots had to be purchased from temples, and by the sixth century BCE, temples started collecting a money tax on the burial of the dead in these cemeteries, which served as a bottleneck. These were not death taxes, because there was no requirement that the dead be buried in these cemeteries, only the desire of Egyptians for a good burial. Furthermore, the temples collected the tax from mortuary priests, who buried and performed rituals for the dead, and who received a significant contribution from the deceased's relatives for doing so. Already in the

Saite Period, temple officials known as the overseer of the necropolis received payments in silver for the purchase of tombs, or the plots of land on which they were built, and issued receipts for said payments. In the Demotic Stela Louvre C. 101, dated to Year 8 of Psammetichus I (657 BCE), the overseer of the necropolis declares to a tomb owner that he is satisfied with the money for a tomb that a mason has built.[75] In the hieroglyphic Stela Florence 1658 (2536), dated to Year 4 of an unnamed king, the overseer of the necropolis declares to a tomb owner that he has received the money for a tomb.[76] In Demotic Papyrus Louvre E. 7128 (*Tsenhor* 10), dated to Year 12 of Darius (510 BCE), the overseer of the necropolis declares to a choachyte that his heart is satisfied with the money for a plot of land.[77] The overseer of the necropolis also received payments for the right to bury individual mummies in tombs, above the cost of the tombs themselves. In the Demotic Papyrus Louvre E. 7850, dated to Year 38 of Amasis (533 BCE), the overseer of the necropolis acknowledges to his superior the receipt of a red bull as payment for the burial of an individual.[78] Demotic Papyrus Cairo CG 50062, dated to Year 6 of Cambyses (524 BCE), records a series of payments of a half silver kite, apparently for burials.[79]

Customs Duties: In the Saite and Persian Periods, the state started directly collecting customs duties levied at the border on goods entering Egypt. To facilitate this, the state may have required foreign merchants and traders to enter Egypt only at designated points, thereby creating bottlenecks at which it could collect customs duties on goods. Physical bottlenecks at the borders of Egypt were not new in these periods. Already in the Middle Kingdom, King Senusert III set up Stela Berlin 14753 at the fortress of Semna in Nubia, forbidding any Nubians to travel north except to trade at Mirgissa.[80] Some have argued that the fortress of Tjaru (Sile) on the northeastern border of Egypt played a similar role in the New Kingdom.[81] There is no evidence that customs duties were collected at such bottlenecks in Egypt before the Saite and Persian Periods, though bottleneck taxes related to the transport of commodities are attested in Mesopotamia already in the second millennium BCE, in the Old Babylonian and Middle Assyrian Periods, when they were collected in both silver and kind,[82] and again in the seventh through fourth centuries BCE, in the late Neo-Assyrian, Neo-Babylonian, and Achaemenid Periods, when they were increasingly paid in silver.[83]

The Egyptian state also appears to have instituted some kind of border control in the Saite Period. The Greek historian Herodotus wrote that King Amasis (570–526 BC) allowed the Greeks to settle at the site of Naukratis, located in the Egyptian Delta on the Canopic branch of the Nile.[84] He also wrote that in earlier times, presumably meaning before his own time in the Persian Period, Naukratis was the only emporion or trading port in Egypt, and that ships that came to any other branch of the Nile were required to sail on to the Canopic branch to Naukratis.[85] Herodotus described this concentration of trade at Naukratis as a privilege, but it could also have served as a bottleneck at which customs duties could be levied, though there is no direct evidence for customs duties in the Saite Period.[86]

The earliest direct evidence for customs duties dates to the Persian Period, the time of Herodotus, when Naukratis was no longer the only trading port in Egypt. The Aramaic Papyrus Berlin P. 13446 A-H, K-L + Papyrus Cairo Museum JdE 43502, from Elephantine at the southern border of Egypt, contains a version of the literary story of Ahiqar. It also contains a palimpsest text of a register of customs duties collected in money from Ionian and Phoenician ships and cargoes.[87] The incoming cargoes primarily consisted of wine, oil, bronze, iron, wool, and wood, while the outgoing cargoes consisted primarily of natron. The customs duties consisted of 10 percent of the cargo payable in kind, and a money tax called "silver of the men" payable in gold or silver.[88] Although the papyrus was found in Elephantine, it does not name that site, and most of the ships named on it came from Ionia or Phoenicia, so scholars have argued that the papyrus was originally written at a northern site like Memphis, Naukratis, or most likely Herakleion-Thonis, and was only later brought to Elephantine.[89]

Herakleion-Thonis was located at the mouth of the Canopic branch of the Nile, downstream from Naukratis, and served as its harbor. The role of Herakleion-Thonis as the customs collection point for Naukratis is confirmed by a pair of nearly identical basalt stelae erected at the two sites by King Nectanebo I in his Year 1 (380 BCE). The stela from Herakleion-Thonis dedicates 10 percent of the harbor customs duties and local tax revenues to the temple of Neith at Sais, while the stela from Naukratis dedicates 10 percent of local tax revenues.[90] These dedications were not a tax of 10 percent, but rather 10 percent of the total tax revenues, while the state kept the other 90 percent.[91]

DOCUMENTATION OF PROPERTY TRANSFERS

In the Saite and Persian Periods, property transfers continued to be documented by a variety of authorities, as they had been in the preceeding Third Intermediate Period. In the Saite Period the authorities were predominantly contract scribes associated with Egyptian temples, who employed the Abnormal Hieratic system in Upper Egypt or the Demotic system in Lower Egypt, until the latter eventually superseded the former and was used throughout Egypt. Then in the Persian Period, the Egyptian temple contract scribes using the Demotic system were joined by Persian officials and soldiers who employed an Aramaic system.

Egyptian Documentation: As in the preceding Late Third Intermediate Period, contract scribes attached to temples continued to transcribe the verbal statements of one of the contracting parties, and several literate witnesses attached to the same temples continued to certify that the written transcript agreed with the verbal statement, though now the witnesses usually only signed the transcript, rather than recopying it.[92] The first contracting party continued to give the resulting contract to the second contracting party as an authenticated record of the agreement, and the second contracting party assented to the agreement by accepting the transcript of it. Temple contract scribes did not document all transactions, however. Some minor transactions consisted of letter contracts, which the first contracting party wrote for the second contracting party. These letter contracts may have been known in Demotic as *šʿt*-contracts.[93] Other minor transactions consisted of verbal agreements witnessed by community members, and relied on social pressure for enforcement.

In the Saite Period, Hieroglyphic stelae continued to be used to document donations of property to temples, but Abnormal Hieratic and Demotic contracts were used for most other transactions. The Demotic script and documentation system probably developed in Lower and Middle Egypt, while the Abnormal Hieratic script and documentation system had developed in Upper Egypt.[94] The two scripts and documentation systems used different contract formulae, but both employ traditional Egyptian legal terminology, and both use essentially the same contract types, suggesting that the underlying transaction law was similar in both scripts and systems. They probably developed while Egypt was fragmented into the parallel Twenty-second, Twenty-third, and Twenty-fourth Dynasties in the Late Third Intermediate Period. The parallel dynasties presumably patronized separate networks of notaries and courts, allowing different scripts and practices to develop in different regions and networks. After the Saite Dynasty reunified Egypt, however, these regional networks of notaries and courts answered to the same royal court, and the differences in documentation began to diminish. Demotic contracts coexisted alongside Abnormal Hieratic contracts for most of the Saite Period, but gradually replaced them throughout Egypt by the Persian Period. The replacement was subtle, because Abnormal Hieratic and Demotic contracts could be written by different members of the same families of contract notaries, usually attached to temples in major provincial towns.[95]

Aramaic Documentation: During the Persian Period, the Persian Empire stationed various officials and soldiers in Egypt, and many of these used Aramaic as their primary written language. These officials and soldiers, therefore, documented agreements among themselves in the Aramaic language and script, and some of these documents have survived, notably from the Jewish garrison on Elephantine Island. The Aramaic documentation used in Egypt at Elephantine, however, shows some similarities to Demotic documentation. This initially led some scholars to postulate possible Aramaic influence on Demotic transaction law.[96] However, more recent studies have shown that some of the shared features of Elephantine Aramaic and Demotic documentation have long roots in Egyptian legal tradition, but lack antecedents in Aramaic, making it likely that Elephantine Aramaic practice was adapted to work with the native Demotic practice.[97]

State Registration: In the Saite and Persian Periods, there is no evidence of state registration. Local temple notaries documented property transfers in the Egyptian language, and collected the tenth of scribes and representatives. The temple notaries may have kept local registers of the documents that they produced and taxed, but there is no evidence that this information was passed to the central administration in the Saite and Persian Periods. The earliest evidence for state registration of local Egyptian documentation of property transfers dates to the early Ptolemaic Period. The Legal Manual of Hermopolis may also support a relatively late date for the introduction of state registration for Egyptian documents. The main text of the Legal Manual required property owners only to be in possession of a title document to obtain clear title,[98] and the additional requirement that said title document be registered appears to be a later addition.[99]

MEDIA OF EXCHANGE AND REDISTRIBUTION

In the Saite Period, weights of silver became the standard measures of value, to the exclusion of other metals and commodities. Weights of silver appear to have served increasingly as media of exchange as well, while the use of other commodities apparently diminished, creating a partial unity of measures of value and media of exchange. In the Persian Period, Egyptian texts equated foreign weight and coin terms with Egyptian weights, theoretically allowing imported coins to be treated as abstract tokens. In hoards, however, imported coins were cut and otherwise treated as bullion until and even after the introduction of locally minted coins in the fourth century BC. Silver was probably simply more widely available than in earlier periods, judging from the increase in numbers of hoards of silver used as stores of wealth. The increased availability of silver in turn allowed the state and temples to collect sales taxes on exchanges as a fraction of the value of the exchange; customs duties on imported goods as a fraction of the value of the goods; and occupational taxes as a surcharge on specific occupational activities. These taxes not only targeted occupations that were likely to use silver, they were collected at point of use bottlenecks.

Measures of Value: In the Saite and Persian Periods, Abnormal Hieratic and Demotic texts usually measure value as weights of silver. Weights of copper are almost never used, in contrast to the New Kingdom. The weights of silver are almost always either the deben of 91 grams, or the kite of 9.1 grams.

In the Persian Period, Demotic texts sometimes also refer to staters equated to two kite, or five to the deben. These staters are also described as Ionian staters, and are thought to reflect Athenian tetradrachms, the most common coins in Persian Period Egypt, which weighed 17.2 grams on average.[100] In the Persian Period, Aramaic texts from Egypt refer to the silver karsh, shekel, zus, and hallur.[101] The karsh consisted of ten shekels, and the shekel of two zuz or of forty hallurs.[102] Three Aramaic texts equate two shekels with one stater, and one adds that the stater is of the "silver of Yavan" (Ionia). This stater is also thought to reflect the Athenian tetradrachm.[103] This implies that in Persian Period Egypt, the Aramaic karsh was equivalent to the Egyptian deben, and the Aramaic shekel was equivalent to the Egyptian kite. One Aramaic text, a register of customs duties, also refers to gold staters, which are equivalent to slightly less than a shekel.[104]

Media of Exchange: In the Saite and Persian Periods, Abnormal Hieratic and Demotic texts usually express payments as weights of silver, but occasionally as commodities, or as commodities worth a weight of silver. A payment expressed as a commodity occurs in Papyrus Louvre E. 7850, from Thebes, dated to Year 38 of Amasis (533 BCE), which is a receipt for payment of a red bull as "the substitute for the things which are given to the Overseer of the Necropolis," for an individual who presumably to be buried.[105] The value of the red bull is not indicated, but Papyrus Cairo CG 50062, from Assiut, dated to Year 6 of Cambyses (524 BCE), records a series of payments of a half silver kite per burial (*ḳ(r)s.t*).[106] Payments expressed as commodities worth weights of silver occur in Papyrus CG 50060, from Assiut from the same archive as the preceding papyrus, dated to Year 5 of Cambyses (525 BCE), which is a receipt (*isw*) for silver that the Overseer of the Necropolis has given to the temple manager (*mr-šn*). There follows a list of quantities of wine and beer and their values in silver, or in some cases simply weights of silver, which are said to be in the possession of the temple manager and other individuals.[107]

After the Third Intermediate Period, Abnormal Hieratic contracts cease to refer to payment of weights of silver of the treasury of Harsaphes. In the Saite Period, Abnormal Hieratic and Demotic contracts refer to payment of weights of silver of the treasury of Thebes, and in the Persian Period Demotic contracts refer to weights of silver of the treasury of Ptah. As in the Late Third Intermediate Period, there has been debate whether this meant that the silver had to meet purity standards set by the temple treasuries,[108] or that it had to consist of ingots marked with the sign of the temple treasuries,[109] or whether it was merely weighed according to the temple treasury standard.[110] The last is almost certainly the correct interpretation, however. In the Persian Period, Aramaic texts refer twice to payment in silver weighed out on the balance,[111] many times to payment in silver weighed according to the "stones of the king,"[112] or in one or two cases according to the "stones of Ptah."[113] The latter is surely the same standard of the treasury of Ptah mentioned in Demotic contracts. Furthermore, stamped ingots are conspicuously absent from Saite and Persian Period hoards, which consist almost exclusively of lumps of silver and imported Greek coins.

Coins appear in Egypt in the Saite Period, but the first references to Greek coins in Egyptian texts are Ionian staters, which appear in the Persian Period,[114] as do the first references to Ionian staters in Aramaic texts.[115] The first coins minted in Egypt were unmarked imitations of Athenian tetradrachms, possibly dating from the late fifth century BC, or more likely from the early fourth century BC onward, after Egypt successfully revolted from Persian rule. There are also a number of fractions imitating Athenian types, some marked with the hieroglyphic legend *w3ḥ*, others with the Greek legend NAY, presumably for Naucratis.[116] Dies for producing unmarked imitations of Athenian tetradrachms have been found at several locations in Egypt, suggesting decentralized production.[117] In the mid-fourth century BC, the Egyptian king Teos (362–360 BC) minted a gold coin of Athenian design but on the daric standard marked with the Greek legend TAΩ, and his successor King Nectanebo II (360–343 BC) probably produced a series of gold coins on the daric standard with the hieroglyphic text *nb nfr*, "good gold."[118] In the late fourth century BC, after the Persians reconquered Egypt, King Artaxerxes III (343–338 BC) produced a series of imitation Athenian tetradrachms and fractions thereof marked with the Demotic label "pharaoh Artaxerxes." At the same time, the Egyptian satraps Sabakes (c. 340–333 BC) and Mazakes (333–332 BC) produced imitation tetradrachms and fractions marked with the Aramaic labels "Sabakes" and "Mazakes."[119] There is considerable debate whether some or all of these Egyptian issues were intended primarily for Greek mercenaries who demanded payment in coins, or whether they may have had a wider circulation.[120]

Stores of Wealth: Saite and Persian Period hoards illustrate the use of silver as a store of wealth as well as a medium of exchange. These hoards can consist of ingots, jewelry, and chopped fragments of silver (*Hacksilber*), as in earlier periods, or of coins, or of a combination of the two. Hoards without coins can be difficult to date, and in Egypt they are usually assumed to date before coins began to appear at the end of the sixth century BC. Three such hoards are known from Egypt,[121] including one from Tell el-Atrib (Athribis) found in 1924 that contained fifty kilograms of silver.[122] Hoards with coins appear in Egypt from the end of the sixth century BC. From the Archaic Period (to 480 BC), thirteen coin hoards are known from Egypt, containing at least 428 coins.[123] Five of these hoards included cut or fragmented coins. These five hoards also contained cake ingots or *Hacksilber*, and in one hoard from

Mit Rahinah (Memphis) found in 1860 the ingots and *Hacksilber* weighed seventy-three kilograms, dwarfing the twenty-three coins accompanying them.[124] From the Classical Period (480–332 BC), twenty-eight coin hoards are known from Egypt, containing at least 8,827 coins, though one hoard from Tell el–Maskhuta (Pithom) found in 1947-48 accounts for at least 6000 of them.[125] Nine of these hoards included cut or fragmented coins, and nine hoards (not all the same ones) contained cake ingots and or *Hacksilber*.[126] Hoards containing ingots and *Hacksilber* as well as coins continued into the fourth century BC, even after locally minted coins became available. The numerous cut and fragmented coins may represent tests of quality, suggesting that the coins were valued for their silver rather than for their nominal values. Similarly, the ingots may also represent a test of quality, because the Classical authors record that molten silver bubbled a certain way when it was at least 97 percent pure.[127] Such tests of quality are more likely to be performed when media are actively exchanged than when they are passively being stored, suggesting that the coins and the ingots were used as media of exchange as well as stores of wealth.[128]

Textual sources also provide some insight into the use of weights of silver as stores of wealth. For example, in Type C marriage contracts, brides usually give their husbands a very substantial sum of thirty deben of silver, equivalent to 600 drachmas or 150 tetradrachms, in return for maintenance for the rest of her life. The wife can terminate the marriage by asking for the sum back, but the husband cannot unilaterally give it back. The sum probably represents passive storage of years of savings, passed intact from father to daughter, from bride to husband, and from father to daughter again.

Credit: Loans of both grain and money are attested in Saite and Persian Period Egypt. Three grain loans have survived, two of them in Demotic and one in Aramaic. Demotic Papyrus Louvre E. 9293 (Choix I 3) from Thebes, dated to Year 24 of Darius (498 BCE), was a grain loan of one sack of barley, for which one and a half sacks were to be repaid two months later, which is 50 percent interest. If it was not repaid, additional interest would accrue at one sack of barley per ten sacks per month, which is 10 percent per month and 120 percent per year.[129] In the archive of the gooseherds from Hou, Demotic Papyrus Strasbourg 4 (Hou 13), dated to Year 35 of Darius (487 BCE), was a grain loan for which twenty-seven sacks of barley were to be repaid when the lender desired, suggesting a principal of eighteen sacks and 50 percent interest.[130] In the archive of Ananiah son of Azariah from Elephantine, Aramaic Papyrus Brooklyn Museum 47.218.93 (Kraeling 11), dated to Year 4 of Artaxerxes (402 BCE), was a grain loan of six seahs or two artabas of emmer, to be repaid with 100 percent interest one month later.[131]

Seven money loans have survived, three of them in Demotic and four in Aramaic. Abnormal Hieratic Papyrus BM 10113 (Choix I 2) from Thebes, dated to Year 20 of Apries (570 BCE), was a money loan for one silver deben to be repaid six months later. If it was not repaid, additional interest would accrue at one-third kite for each deben each month, which is 3.3 percent per month and 33 percent per year.[132] In the archive of the gooseherds from Hou, Demotic Papyrus Loeb 48+49A (Hou 12), dated to Year 35 of Darius (487 BCE), was a money loan for three or four silver kite for eight months. The amount to be repaid was six silver kite, implying an interest rate of 100 percent per eight months if the principle was three kite, or 50 percent per eight months if the principle was four kite. If it was not repaid, additional interest would accrue at one-tenth kite per kite per month, which is 10 percent per month and 120 percent per year.[133] Demotic Papyrus Berlin P. 3110 (Choix I 5) from Thebes, dated to Year 35 of Darius (487 BCE), was a loan of a cow rather than money, but failure to return the cow would result in a fine of five silver kite, which would accrue interest at one-tenth kite per kite per month.[134] Aramaic Papyrus Bodleian Library MS Heb. c. 59 P (Cowley 11) from Elephantine, dated to a Year 36 (c. 487 BCE), was a money loan for four shekels or kite by the stones of Ptah or of the Treasury of Ptah. Interest was two hallurs per shekel per month, which is 5 percent per month and 60 percent per year.[135] In the archive of Ananiah son of Azariah from Elephantine, the Aramaic Papyrus Berlin P. 13491 (Cowley 10), dated to Year 9 of Artaxerxes (456 BCE), was a money loan for four shekels for one year. Interest was two hallurs per shekel per month, which is 5 percent per month and 60 percent per year.[136] Aramaic Papyrus Cairo JdE 43487 (Cowley 29) from Elephantine, dated to Year 17 of Darius (407 BCE), was a money loan for which one karsh and four shekels or seven staters were to be repaid nine months later.[137] Aramaic Papyrus Berlin P. 13476 (Cowley 35) from Elephantine, dated to Year 5 of Amyrtaeus (400 BCE), was a money loan for which two shekels or one stater were to be repaid one month later.[138]

REDISTRIBUTIVE NETWORKS

In the Saite and Persian Periods, royal granaries and treasuries received, disbursed, and kept accounts of state revenues, while a variety of institutions and officials drew upon and distributed these revenues. The revenues were used to support provincial officials, soldiers, and police, as well as gangs and crews who processed and transported commodities. Temples continued to manage redistributive networks of their own, using their own revenue sources. State and temple redistributive networks probably remained the preferred modes of distribution over long distances, following the reunification of Egypt at the end of the Third Intermediate Period, but the growing availability and use of written documentation for high-value exchanges probably made them increasingly competitive.

Royal Granaries and Treasuries: The Saites and Persians probably possessed a dispersed network of royal granaries, which collected and kept track of harvest taxes in grain deposited in local branches, so that surpluses could be transported when needed. Such dispersed storage systems were safer than centralized ones, because risks were distributed, and they minimized unnecessary transportation. Such a system existed already in the Old and New Kingdoms, one still existed in the Ptolemaic Period, and the Nitokris Adoption Stela discussed later suggests that some such system also existed in the Saite Period. The Saites may have also possessed a dispersed network of treasuries, and the Persians certainly did so, since there are references to a royal storehouse or treasury in the garrison town of Elephantine at the southern border of Egypt that dealt with payments in both grain and money.[139] This network could have collected and transported state taxes in money such as customs duties,[140] as well as levies from temples, which collected sales and burial taxes in money.[141]

Some deposits of money tax revenues at local branches of the treasury may have been considered tribute. Herodotus states that the annual tribute of the satrapy of Egypt and Cyrenaica under the Persian king Darius was 700 Babylonian talents or 833 Euboean talents of silver, in addition to 120,000 unspecified units of grain for the Persians stationed in Memphis and their foreign mercenaries (*epikouroi*).[142] It has been suggested that most tribute was used locally. Since grain consumed in Egypt was considered tribute,[143] some or all of the tribute in silver may also have been spent in Egypt. The Aramaic-speaking mercenaries garrisoned at Elephantine received salaries in both grain and money distributed from the local storehouse or treasury, for example.[144] Others, however, question whether Herodotus' figures have any value at all.[145]

Palaces and Officials: In the Saite Period, the Nitokris Adoption Stela illustrates some of the ways that palaces and officials drew upon and distributed state revenues. Stela Cairo JdE 36327 was found at Karnak and is dated to Year 9 of King Psammetichus I.[146] It records the adoption of Nitokris daughter of King Psammetichus I as heir and successor to the god's wife of Amun Shepenwepet II, replacing Shepenwepet II's former heir designate Amunirdis daughter of the Kushite king Taharqa. The stela describes how Nitokris sailed south from Psammetichus I's palace to Thebes, and messengers preceded her to arrange for provisions along the way, which were supplied by the nomarch or governor of each nome or province through which she passed (lines 7–10). The nomarchs may have drawn on state revenues, as had been done for state messengers and expeditions since the Old Kingdom. After reaching Thebes sixteen days later (lines 10–15), Shepenwepet II and her former heir Amunirdis drew up a written testament (*imy.t-pr*) donating the office and all of its property to Nitokris, witnessed by all of the *ḥm-nṯr*-priests and *wꜥb*-priests and companions of the temple (lines 15–17).

The stela concludes with a list of properties and revenues given to Nitokris, presumably for her household or palace in Thebes. These properties and revenues included 1,900 arouras of fields in seven nomes or provinces of Upper Egypt; 600 deben (or 54.6 kilograms) of bread daily from the temple of Amun from the first, third, and fourth *ḥm-nṯr*-priests of Amun, and from the mayor of Thebes and overseer of Upper Egypt, Montuemhat and his wife and his son; 1,500 deben (or 136.5 kilograms) of bread from fifteen temples in Lower Egypt; and 1,400 arouras of fields in four nomes or provinces of Lower Egypt (lines 17–31). Nitokris and her household need not have personally collected the harvests from her estates, however; the harvests may have been deposited at local granaries, and an equivalent amount withdrawn from other granaries at Thebes. The bread from Lower Egyptian temples may have been supplied in a similar manner, and even the bread from the temple of Amun was probably simply credited to Nitokris' accounts at the temple from those of the named *ḥm-nṯr*-priests and officials, rather than being delivered to her from them daily.

After the Persian conquest of Egypt, the Persian kings were sometimes portrayed as pharaohs on monuments, but they were rarely resident in Egypt. Their local representatives, the satraps and their estates and officials, however, undertook some activities that royal palaces and officials had previously performed. For example, in one of a group of leather letters found in a bag, the satrap Arsames wrote an open letter ordering various officials in and outside of Egypt to provide rations for his new estate manager Nehtihur while he travelled from Babylon to Egypt,[147] as had been done for traveling officials in Egypt since the Old Kingdom. In another leather letter, the satrap Arsames wrote to his new estate manager Nehtihur and ordered to guard his domestic staff and goods and increase the number of craftsmen among the domestic staff, as the previous estate managers Pshamshek and his father Ahhapi had done,[148] implying that his estate processed commodities for redistribution or exchange like palaces and in both the Old and New Kingdoms. Indeed, a leather letter from Arsames to another Persian official to return some Cilician slaves that had been seized during a revolt suggests that some of the domestic staff on Arsames' estate may have oil-pressers,[149] while another leather letter from Arsames to his estate manager Nehtihur orders him to have a sculptor make a statue.[150]

Royal Dockyards: The Saites and Persians appear to have developed an Egyptian navy, though the nature of its warships is debated.[151] Herodotus records that Necho II had triremes built, some for the Mediterranean Sea and others for the Red Sea.[152] Those for the Mediterranean were presumably based in Egypt, because it had limited control over the Levant, and Herodotus says that Apries engaged in a naval battle with Tyre.[153] Herodotus also says that Amasis was the first to conquer the island of Cyprus,[154] which would have required ships based in Egypt because the Neo-Babylonians had conquered the Levant by his reign. Herodotus further records that the Persian fleet that Xerxes gathered for the invasion of Greece (480 BCE) consisted of 1,207 ships, including 200 Egyptian ships as well as 300 Phoenician and 150 Cypriot ships,[155] indicating that there were ships based in Egypt independent of the Levant and Cyprus. Finally, during the Twenty-eighth, Twenty-ninth, and Thirtieth Dynasties the Egyptians apparently built a fleet for use against the Persians, because Hakoris supposedly sent fifty triremes to aid the revolt of Evagoras of Cyprus,[156] and Teos later placed Chabrias the Athenian in charge of an Egyptian fleet.[157] These fleets were probably built with supplies from the royal and satrapal treasuries. In a papyrus letter from Elephantine dated to Year 12 of Darius (411 BCE), the satrap Arsames ordered the official Wahpremahi to release wood and other materials to a carpenter to repair a boat, after the boatmen requested treasury accountants and carpenters to inspect the boat, and after they submitted a list of necessary materials.[158] These fleets may have been built in royal and satrapal dockyards, as was done in the preceding Middle and New Kingdoms. If so, at least some of the dockyards were probably located at Herakleion-Thonis at the mouth of the Canopic branch of the Nile, downstream from Sais and Naukratis. Herakleion-Thonis became the main Egyptian port in the Saite and Persian Periods, until Alexandria replaced it in the early Ptolemaic Period. The pottery from the underwater site dates from the Saite through the middle of the Ptolemaic Period,[159] and the shipwrecks as well.[160] Redistributed revenues for shipwrights and sailors associated with royal and satrapal dockyards, together with those for priests associated with recently founded temples, could have stimulated the growth of the new port.

Military and Police: During the Saite and Persian Periods, the majority of the army still consisted of reserve soldiers who supported themselves when off duty, but more frequent campaigns and more numerous garrisons meant that they were on duty more often than in the Third Intermediate Period. Furthermore, a growing proportion of the army consisted of foreign mercenaries who were permanently on duty, and regularly received redistributed revenues, increasingly in money as well as in kind.

Herodotus states that the Saite king Psammetichus I established garrisons at three border fortresses, at Elephantine in the south, Daphnae in the northeast, and Marea in the northwest.[161] Additional Saite frontier fortresses are known from excavations, such as Tell Qedwa in the Sinai[162] and Dorginarti in Lower Nubia.[163] Herodotus reports that under Psammetichus I, the garrison at Elephantine revolted when it was not relieved for three years, implying that rotation was the ideal if not the norm.[164] By the reign of Apries, the garrison at Elephantine may have included foreign mercenaries, who may have revolted according to the autobiography of an Egyptian general.[165]

Herodotus also states that Psammetichus I settled Ionian and Carian mercenaries (*epikouroi*) in camps (*stratopeda*) in the eastern Delta, and gave them land in which to dwell.[166] It is not clear whether they also received land to cultivate or stipends.[167] Apries employed 30,000 of the descendants of these Ionians and Carians to try to suppress a revolt of Egyptian soldiers led by Amasis.[168] Amasis was victorious and made himself king,[169] however, and transferred the Ionians and Carians to Memphis to serve as his bodyguard.[170] In Memphis they were presumably permanently on duty and received stipends rather than land to cultivate.

The Persians also maintained garrisons at border fortresses, such as Daphnae and Elephantine,[171] as well as at the satrapal capital at Memphis. Additional Persian frontier fortresses are known from excavations, such as Tell el-Herr in the Sinai,[172] which seems to have replaced the Saite fortress at nearby Tell Qedwa.[173] The garrisons consisted of Persians and their foreign mercenaries (*epikouroi*), who were predominantly Aramaic-speakers rather than Ionians and Carians. They lived permanently in their garrisons with their families, and probably received stipends. Herodotus records that the Egyptian tribute to the Persians included 120,000 unspecified units of grain annually for these garrisons.[174] Aramaic papyri from the garrison at Elephantine indicate that it consisted of at least four units called degals, each of which were subdivided into four units called centuries.[175] The degals may have nominally held and cultivated land, but individual soldiers certainly did not.[176] Instead they received monthly stipends of grain and silver from the local branch of the treasury. The grain rations varied from one to two and a half artabas of barley per month.[177] Some soldiers were able to use surpluses from their stipends to engage in subsidiary entrepreneurial activities, such as investing in loans and real property.[178]

During the Twenty-eighth, Twenty-ninth, and Thirtieth Dynasties (404–342 BCE), when Egypt became independent from the Persian Empire, the Egyptian kings also employed foreign mercenaries, but primarily Greeks rather than Aramaic-speakers. King Hakoris (393–380 BCE) recruited a large number of Greeks, as well as Chabrias the Athenian to lead them.[179] King Teos (362–360 BCE) recruited 10,000 Greek mercenaries, including the Spartan king Agesilaus to lead them, and Chabrias the Athenian to lead the fleet.[180] These mercenaries were almost certainly paid in money as well as food rations, possibly with gold and silver coins bearing hieroglyphic inscriptions that appear around this time.[181] Indeed, the Egyptian kings may have introduced a number of tax reforms to provide the necessary revenues in money.[182]

The Saites also maintained a large body of reserve soldiers, who were expected to support themselves until they were called up to serve on campaigns. Herodotus used the Greek term "warriors" or *machimoi* to describe these reserve soldiers. He claimed that in the Saite Period they constituted one of seven Egyptian castes, that sons inherited their status from their fathers, and that they were forbidden to engage in any profession other than military activities. He stated that those known as Kalasiries came from the western Delta and numbered 160,000, while those known as Hermotybies came from the eastern Delta and the Thebaid and numbered 250,000.[183] Herodotus also claimed that each solder received twelve arouras of tax-free land to cultivate.[184] Egyptian *machimoi* continued to act as reserve soldiers in the Persian Period. Herodotus states that the Persian army at Plataia in 479 BCE included both Kalasiries and Hermotybies.[185]

Modern scholars have identified Herodotus' *machimoi*, Kalasiries and Hermotybies with *rmt-ḳnḳn*, *gl-šr.w*, and *rmt-ḏm.w* respectively in Egyptian documents,[186] though they reject Herodotus' attribution of a caste structure to the ancient Egyptians and to the *machimoi*.[187] Some scholars also question whether the Egyptian state could support the large numbers of *machimoi* reported by Herodotus,[188] but because they only received state support when on active duty, there was no practical limit to their number, only to the number called to serve at one time. Many *machimoi* may have been descendants of Libyans who settled or were settled in Egypt in the late New Kingdom and the Third Intermediate Period.[189] Papyrus Rylands 9 indicates that some Kalasiries (*gl-šr*) were subordinate to the Shipping Master in Herakleopolis and a local Chief of the Ma,[190] that some Hermotybies (*rmt-ḏm*) were subordinate to a nome supervisor (*ḥry*) and a general (*mr-mšʿ*) in Herakleopolis,[191] and that both groups could be called up to perform police duties in addition to military activities. Other documents show that they held and cultivated land, though not the equal-sized tax-free plots described by Herodotus, and engaged in commercial activities such as cattle sales.[192]

Temples: Donation stelae record the donation of fields to a god or gods and their temples by kings and private individuals alike. In either case, the stela often depict a king symbolically offering the hieroglyph for fields to the gods, because in theory the king was the chief priest of the gods, though in practice he was represented by the local priesthood. The fields are sometimes designated to support a private funerary cult (see Private Funerary Endowments), but they are sometimes assigned to the divine cult proper, often to provide oil for a lamp-offering,[193] or occasionally beer for beer-offerings.[194] Papyrus Bibliotheque National 215, dated to the Early Ptolemaic Period, contains several texts from earlier periods, including a royal decree in which Cambyses rescinds the regular state donations to temples established by Amasis, with the exception of those for the temple of Ptah in Memphis and two others.[195] Temple endowments (Dem. *ḥtp-ntr*, lit. "divine offering") generated revenues, which were first offered (Dem. *ḥtp*) to the gods (Dem. *ntr*) of the temple, and then were redistributed to temple personnel, such as *ḥm-nṯr*-priests and *wꜥb*-priests, as described in the "Petition of Petiese" from El-Hiba, dated to Year 9 of Darius I (513 BCE).

> **P. Rylands 9, col. xiii, lines 7–8:**
> (7) ... I possess 4 stipends (Dem. *ḥtp*) in the name of the share of the *ḥm-nṯr*-priest of Amun, (and) I possess another 16 stipends in the name (8) of the (other) gods for whom I serve as *ḥm-nṯr*-priest, totalling 20 stipends. There are 20 *wꜥb*-priests per phyle ... (and) 1 phyle of *wꜥb*-priests makes 1/5 of the temple endowment revenues.

There were four phyles of *wꜥb*-priests in each temple, until the addition of a fifth phyle by Ptolemy III in 238 BC. In the Temple of Amun of El-Hiba described in the "Petition of Petiese," these four phyles each contained twenty *wꜥb*-priests, making eighty *wꜥb*-priests in total. These *wꜥb*-priests each received one stipend (Dem. *ḥtp*), together accounting for four-fifths of the temple endowment revenues. The *ḥm-nṯr*-priest of Amun and an unknown number of *ḥm-nṯr*-priests of the other gods of the temple received the remaining twenty stipends, which accounted for the remaining one-fifth of the temple endowment revenues.

There is little explicit evidence that kings exacted levies from temples until the end of the Saite and Persian Periods, when Greek sources record that the kings of the Thirtieth Dynasty tried to raise revenues in gold and silver by taxing priests and temples in order to pay for Greek mercenaries.[196] Pseudo-Aristotle wrote that King Teos lacked money for war against the Persians, so his Athenian general Chabrias encouraged him to tell the priests that he would have to suppress some temples and many priests to pay for the wars. The priests therefore volunteered the money, to preserve their temples and positions.[197] Nonetheless it is likely that the state exacted levies in kind from temples throughout the Saite and Persian Periods. Such levies were attested in the preceding New Kingdom, illustrated by Papyrus BM 10401,[198] and in the following Ptolemaic Period the kings continued to exact levies in kind from temples, demonstrated by the remission of arrears of such taxes in the Memphis Decree of Ptolemy V recorded on the Rosetta Stela.[199] The temple manager (*mr-šn*) may have been responsible for delivering such levies to the state. It seems to have been an undesirable office at times, because there is a letter from a Persian satrap to the priests of the temple of Khnum at Elephantine chastising them for nominating a slave to be temple manager, and exhorting them to nominate someone of worth.[200] In the Ptolemaic Period, in the archive of Milon from Edfu, the temple manager seems to have been personally responsible for shortfalls in the payment of temple revenues to the state, which could explain why the office was at times undesirable, and why the state wanted someone of worth to fill the position.[201]

Private Funerary Endowments: In the Saite Period, private funerary endowments are attested both from donation stelae and from papyri. In donation stelae, fields were donated to a god or gods for the funerary cult of the deceased. Often the fields were placed under the authority of a specific individual, presumably the deceased's mortuary priest. In papyri, fields could be donated to a god, to the deceased, or even to the mortuary priests of the deceased. In the Persian Period, donation stelae disappear, and fields are only donated to mortuary priests in papyri. The harvests from the fields could at least theoretically be offered to the deceased before reverting to the mortuary priest, and texts refer to such revenues as "rations of Osiris" (*ꜥḳ n Wsir*) or "choachyte rations" (*ꜥḳ n wꜣḥ-mw*).[202]

The Abnormal Hieratic Papyrus Turin 2121 [old 248], from Thebes, dated to Year 47 of Psammetichus I (618 BCE), records the donation of ten arouras of fields to Osiris to serve as endowment for the funerary cult of the deceased Petiese son of Wenamun, under the authority of the choachyte Pefheryhesy son of Inaros. The subject of the papyrus is thus identical to many donation stelae from the late Third Intermediate and Saite Periods, but the papyrus frames the donation as a contract between the deceased's wife and children on the one hand, and the god Osiris and the deceased on the other. The papyrus became part of the archive of the choachyte Pefheryhesy, who presumably represented the interests of Osiris, the deceased, and himself.[203]

P. Turin 2121 [248] (*Choix* I 18, p. 117–124), Thebes, 618 BC:

(1) Year 47, third month of Shemu, day 18 of pharaoh Psammetichus (I), (2) (On) this day have said the woman, Reru daughter of Hemkhonsu, the wife of the *ḥm-nṯr*-priest of Amun Prince of Thebes, the overseer of *ḥm-nṯr*-priests in Thinite Abydos, Petiese son of Wenamun, (3) and Wenamun son of Petiese, and Hemkhonsu son of Petiese, and all their brothers, before Osiris Foremost of the Westerners, Lord of Abydos, (and?) (4) the *ḥm-nṯr*-priest of Amun-Re King of the Gods, overseer of *ḥm-nṯr*-priests in Thinite Abydos, fourth *ḥm-nṯr*-priest of Osiris, Horus, and Isis of Abydos, Prince of Thebes, Petiese (5) son of the god's father of Amun, Wenamun:

"We offer to you the 10 arourae of high private land which are in the Domain of Amun, in 'The Southern District of Thebes,' which are in the high land of Hermonthis; (6) which the *ḥm-nṯr*-priest of Amun, Petiese son of Wenamun, our father, purchased from the carpenter of the Domain of Amun, Ipy son of Harudja (7) (in) Year 45 of pharaoh Psammetichus (I).

We have caused that it is established for you as an offering for you forever, in the hands of the choachyte and slave Pefheryhesy (8) son of Inaros. We have caused that it is established forever. They belong to you, your fields of offerings, from today.

There is no man on the entire earth who shall be able (9) to exercise authority over them, except for you. The one who shall cause that you are established, he shall possess the favor of Amun-Re and Ptah, and his son shall be established after him.

(10) As for the one who shall overturn them, he shall be for the sword of Amun-Re and Ptah, he shall be for the fire of Sekhmet, and his son [shall not be established] after him. We have given them to you today, (11) with satisfied heart.

There does not belong to us any claim against them from today onward."

They say, "As Amun lives and as pharaoh lives, may he be healthy and may Amun give victory to him, (12) we will not be able to say 'False' regarding any plan which is above. There does not belong to us a son or daughter, a brother or sister, a lord or mistress, any man on the entire earth, who will be able to (13) exercise authority over them, except for you. We have offered them to you. We have given their old documents and their new documents, which were made (for) (14) the *ḥm-nṯr*-priest of Amun, Petiese, regarding them, together with the annual share, without any word which is said against you."

In writing, (15) Wenamun son of Petiese. (16) In writing, Hemkhonsu son of the *ḥm-nṯr*-priest of Amun-Re King of the Gods, Prince of Thebes, Petiese son of Wenamun, he having witnessed every word which (17) is above in Year 47, third month of Shemu, day 18 of pharaoh Psammetichus (I), may he live forever like Re.

In some cases, the temple or its tenants may have managed the cultivation of the fields, while the mortuary priests received bread and beer from the temples as offerings and rations, nominally from the donated fields. More often in the Saite and Persian Periods, however, the mortuary priests or their tenants may have managed the cultivation of the fields, remitting taxes to the temples. The archive of the choachyte and woman Tsenhor contained two papyri in which fields for the funerary cults of the deceased were given directly to choachytes.[204] In one, P. Louvre E. 10935 (Tsenhor 1), dated to Year 15 of Amasis (556 BCE), eleven arouras of land were given to Tsenhor's father to serve as the endowment for the cult of the donor's mother. In another, P. Louvre E. 3231a (Tsenhor 14), dated to Year 25 of Darius I (497 BCE), four arouras of land were given to Tsenhor's daughter for the funerary cult of a woman.

P. Louvre E. 3231a (*Tsenhor* 14), Thebes, 497 BC:

(1) In Year 25, second month of Shemu under pharaoh Darius. Has said the god's [father, the *ḥm-nṯr*-priest of Amun-Re] king of the gods, Ankhefenkhonsu son of Nespaiutawy, scribe of sacred books, to the woman choachyte Ruru daughter of Psenese, her mother is Tsenhor:

"I have given to you the 4 arouras of land (2) which are within my land on the high fields of the 'Stable of the milkpot of Amun' as the [endowment (*tꜣ ḥtp*) for] (the mummy of) the woman Tateipuwer daughter of the god's father Hor, her mother is Taouher.

The neighbours of the 4 arouras of land, (mentioned) above: their south, the land of the hair-dresser; their north, my land (3) [...]; their west, the land of [...] son of Sheshonk; their east, the land of Namenechamun, son of Peteratawy. Yours are the 4 arouras of land above together with their trees. I have no claim whatsoever in the world to them."

In writing by the god's father of Mont lord of Thebes, Ipy son of Teos.

(4) In writing by the god's father, the *ḥm-nṯr*-priest of Amun-Re king of the gods, Ankhefenkhonsu son of Nespaiutawy, scribe of sacred books, himself.

Names of 7 witnesses (on the back).

Mortuary priests who managed the cultivation of endowment fields sometimes leased the fields to tenants in return for a share of the harvest, allowing the mortuary priests to devote themselves to their mortuary cult duties. The archive of the choachytes Djekhy and his son Ituredj contains six leases of fields.[205] Two of these, P. Louvre E. 7836,[206] dated to Year 35 of Amasis (536 BCE), and P. Louvre E. 7839,[207] dated to Year 37 of Amasis (534 BCE), are leases of endowment fields by choachytes to cattle-keepers and bee-keepers as tenants.

P. Louvre E. 7839, Thebes, 534 BC:

(1) Year 37, second month of Shemu, under pharaoh Amasis. Has said the bee-keeper of the domain of the temple of Mont (2) lord of Hermonthis, Petetum son of Peteneferhotep, his mother is Tary, to the choachyte (3) of the valley, Ituredj son of Djekhy:

"You have committed (*sḥn*) to me your endowment land (*ꜣḥ ḥtp*) (4) which was given to you for the mouth (*rꜣ*) of the chapel of the *ḥm-nṯr*-priest of Amun, Djekhy son of Besmut, (5) its south being the place of Nesamun; its north the place of Amunemtesneb; its west (6) the place of Efau; its east the dike of (the domain) 'The canals of the scorpion';

(8) in order to cultivate it from year 37 to year 38. When the harvest (*šmw*) occurs in year 38 (8) I shall pay the harvest-tax (*šmw*) of the temple of Amun for your land, and I shall give you the remainder (9) of the harvest (*šmw*) that will occur, as the harvest (*šmw*) of your land. I shall go away (10) from your land and keep myself far from it from year 38, (11) second month of Peret, onwards, without discussing any legal title."

In writing by Neshor son of (12) Petehorresnet, the overseer of the necropolis.

Name of one witness (on the back).

EXCHANGES

In the Saite and Persian Periods, there is abundant evidence for exchange of relatively high-value goods like land, houses, tombs, slaves, cattle, and prebends, as in the Third Intermediate Period. This reflects the availability and use of formal written documentation for high-value exchanges, making them secure and attractive. Most of these high-value exchanges were local and private, and used social networks rather than anonymous markets to identify exchange partners. State and temple redistributive networks were probably once more the preferred mode of distribution for high-value properties over long distances. There is limited evidence for exchanges of low-value goods. As in the Third Intermediate Period, such low-value exchanges were simply not worth documenting in writing.

Land: Several Abnormal Hieratic and Demotic papyri directly document sales of agricultural land for silver, while several others document donations of land that refer to previous purchases and sales to establish a chain of clear title. Admittedly, many of these purchases were investments to establish revenue-producing endowments for private funerary cults, but other Demotic and Aramaic papyri document leases of land, indicating that there was a wider demand for land. In the archive of Pefheryhesy, Abnormal Hieratic Papyrus Turin 2118A (246), dated to Year 30 of Psammetichus I (635/4 BCE), and Abnormal Hieratic Papyrus Turin 2120 (247), dated to Year 45 of Psammetichus I (620/19 BCE), record successive sales of the same ten arouras of land for silver. Abnormal Hieratic Papyrus Turin 2119 (244) records harvest tax payments for the ten arouras for Years 33–38 and 41–42 of Psammetichus I. Abnormal Hieratic Papyrus Turin 2121 (248), dated to Year 47 of Psammetichus I (618/7 BCE), records the donation of the same ten arouras of land by the wife and children of the last purchaser, Petiese son of Wenamun, to the god Osiris and the now deceased Petiese son of Wenamun to serve as the endowment for his funerary cult. The donation contract put the choachyte Pefheryhesy in charge of the funerary cult and endowment. Presumably all of the papyri were then given as proof of title to the choachyte Pefheryhesy, so that he could protect the interests of Osiris, the deceased, and himself.[208] In the archive of Tsenhor from Thebes, Demotic Papyrus Louvre E. 10935 (Tsenhor 1), dated to Year 15 of Amasis (556 BCE), records the donation of eleven arouras of land to Tsenhor's father to serve as the endowment for the cult of the donor's mother. The papyrus also recounts as proof of title three previous sales of the plot of land, once in Year 3 of Apries (587 BCE), and twice in Year 14 of Amasis (557 BCE). Demotic Papyrus Louvre E. 3231a (Tsenhor 14), dated to Year 25 of Darius I (497 BCE), records a similar donation of four arouras of land to Tsenhor's daughter as endowment for the funerary cult of a woman.[209]

Houses and Tombs: Several Hieroglyphic and Demotic stela and papyri record the sale of tombs by a temple agent known as the Chief of the Necropolis to private individuals, which have been discussed previously as possible taxes on the use of the necropolis. These include Demotic Stela Louvre C. 101, dated to Year 8 of Psammetichus I (657/6 BCE),[210] Hieroglyphic Stela Florence 1658 (2536), dated to Year 4 of an unspecified pharaoh,[211] and Demotic Papyrus Louvre E. 7128 (*Tsenhor* 10), dated to Year 12 of Darius I (510 BCE).[212] However, Hieroglyphic Stela Florence 1639 (2507), dated to Year 4 of Apries (586/5 BCE), may be a transcription of a Demotic document, and records the sale of a tomb to a lector priest by a choachyte, suggesting that there was a market in tombs.[213] Furthermore, several Aramaic papyri directly document sales of houses, while others document donations that refer to previous sales and purchases to establish a title chain, showing that there was a market in houses. In the archive of Mibtahiah daughter of Mahseiah from Elephantine, Aramaic Papyrus Cairo Museum JdE 37108 (Cowley 13), dated to Year 19 of Artaxerxes I (446 BCE), records the sale of a house that Mahseiah had previously purchased to his daughter Mibtahiah in exchange for goods worth a certain amount of silver.[214] In the archive of Ananiah son of Azariah from Elephantine, Aramaic Papyrus Brooklyn Museum 47.218.95 (Kraeling 3), dated to Year 28 of Artaxerxes I (437 BCE), was a purchase of a house with silver by Ananiah from Bagazusht and his wife Ubil. Aramaic Papyrus Brooklyn 47.218.91 (Kraeling 4), dated to Year 31 of Artaxerxes I (434 BCE), records that Ananiah gave half of the same house to his wife Tamut. Further, Aramaic Papyri Brooklyn 47.218.32 (Kraeling 6), dated to Year 3 of Darius II (420 BCE); Brooklyn 47.218.92 (Kraeling 9), dated to Year 1 of Artaxerxes II (404 BCE); and Brooklyn 47.218.88 (Kraeling 10), dated to Year 3 of Artaxerxes II (402 BCE), all record that Ananiah gave part of the same house to his daughter Jehoishma. Finally, Aramaic Papyrus Brooklyn Museum 47.218.94 (Kraeling 12), dated to Year 4 of Artaxerxes II (402 BCE), was a sale of the remainder of the house for silver by Ananiah to his son-in-law Ananiah son of Haggai, husband of Jehoishma.[215]

Slaves: Several Demotic and Aramaic papyri document sales of slaves for silver, but many of them are self-sales, or sales with the consent of the slave, suggesting that slaves were not as commoditized as in earlier periods. For example, Demotic bowl Louvre E 706 (Bakir, pls. 17–18), dated to Year 4 of Psammetichus II (592/1 BCE), records a self-sale into slavery. In the archive of Petiese from El-Hiba, Demotic Papyrus Rylands 3, dated to Year 2 of Amasis (569/8 BCE), is a self-acknowledgment of slavery by Peftjawykhons to a first party. Demotic Papyrus Rylands 4, also dated to Year 2 of Amasis (569/8 BCE), then records the cession of Peftjawykhons to a second party. Demotic Papyrus Rylands 5, also dated to Year 2 of Amasis (569/8 BCE), is a self-acknowledgment of slavery by Peftjawykhons to that second party. A year later, Demotic Papyrus Rylands 6, dated to Year 3 of Amasis (568/7 BCE), records the self-sale of Peftjawykhons to the same second party, and several years later Demotic Papyrus Rylands 7, dated to Year 8 of Amasis (563/2 BCE) records another self-acknowledgment of slavery by Peftjawykhons to the second party. In the archive of Djekhy and his son Iturudj from Thebes, Demotic Papyrus Louvre E. 7832, dated to Year 32 of Amasis (539 BCE) records a self-sale to be a son. The formula is very similar to many self-sales into slavery.[216] In the archive of Tsenhor from Thebes, Demotic Papyrus Turin 2122 (*Tsenhor* 7), dated to Year 5 of Darius I (517 BCE), records the sale of the slave Psenpkote from one party to another. Demotic Papyrus Bibl. Nat. 223 (*Tsenhor* 8), dated to Year 6 of Darius I (516 BCE), then records the sale of the same slave Psenpkote from the second party to a third, with the consent of the slave.[217] Finally, Aramaic Papyrus Cairo Museum ASR 1576 (Segal 8), probably from Elephantine and dated to the late fourth century BCE, is a sale of slaves.[218]

Cattle and Fowl: Many Saite and Persian archives contain papyri relating to the ownership and sale of cattle.[219] The archive of the gooseherds of Hou, dating to the reigns of Darius I and Psammetichus IV, contains four papyri relating to the ownership of geese. It also contained three papyri concerning cattle, including one sale, and two papyri concerning donkeys, including one sale.[220]

Priestly Positions or Prebends: Shares of appointments in temples together with their revenues or prebends were sometimes transferred in the Saite and Persian Periods, but there are no examples of them being sold for silver. Papyrus Rylands 1, from the archive of Petiese from El-Hiba, dated to Year 21 of Psammetichus I (644 BCE), records a transfer of a position and several shares of offices and their revenues.[221] An archive from Assiut, dating from Year 28 of Amasis (543 BCE) to Year 8 of Cambyses (522 BCE), records several transfers of priestly prebends,[222] as does the archive of Horudja from Elephantine, dating from Year 12 of Darius I (510 BCE) to Year 5 of Artaxerxes I (460 BCE).[223] Shares of appointments in private mortuary cults together with their incomes were sometimes also transferred in this period. For example, Papyrus Louvre E. 7843 from the archive of Djekhy and his son Ituredj, dated to Year 35 of Amasis (536 BCE), is a contract for sharing revenues from a private mortuary cult,[224] while Papyrus Turin 2127 (Tsenhor 16) from the archive of Tsenhor, dated to Year 31 of Darius I (491 BCE), is a transfer of a share of revenues.[225]

ENTREPRENEURIAL ACTIVITIES

In the Saite and Persian Periods, Egypt was unified again, but nonetheless was frequently unable to mount successful military expeditions to populated areas beyond its borders, either because of the appearance of large and militarily powerful states beyond its borders, or because it had been subjugated by one of these states, namely the Persian Empire. The unified Egyptian state established many new settlements, foundations, and institutions in the Saite Period and the Twenty-eighth, Twenty-ninth, and Thirtieth Dynasties, but fewer in the Persian Period, when resources were diverted to Persia as tribute. In both the Saite and the Persian Periods, however, state service and participation in state redistributive networks once again became highly lucrative investments alongside accumulation of private property.

Expeditions: In the Saite Period, the Egyptian state was able to mount expeditions beyond areas under Egyptian control, but was constrained by the strength of Egypt's neighbors. Nubia to the south was home to the Napatan Kingdom, Libya to the west was the site of a number of Greek colonies in Cyrenaica, and the Levant to the east lay first within the Assyrian Empire and then within the Babylonian Empire. Psammetichus I (664–610 BCE) reunited Egypt as a client of the Assyrian Empire, but nonetheless campaigned in the southern Levant which was nominally under Assyrian control, besieging the city of Ashdod (Azotos) for twenty-nine years until he took it.[226] He also campaigned in Libya, according to a stela from Saqqara dated to Year 11.[227] Psammetichus I's successor Necho II (610–595 BCE) also campaigned in the southern Levant and conquered Migdol (Magdolos) and Gaza (Cadytis).[228] Necho II sent an army north to aid his Assyrian allies when the Babylonians revolted, and defeated and killed King Josiah of Judah at Megiddo (609 BCE) when Josiah refused to give his army passage north.[229] The Babylonians defeated the Assyrians at Harran (608 BCE), but the Egyptians retained control of the Levant. Necho II deposed Josiah's son Jehoahaz and appointed his brother Jehoiakim king of Judah, and demanded 100 talents of silver and one talent of gold as tribute.[230] The Babylonians then defeated the Egyptians at Carchemish on the Euphrates (605 BCE), drove them out of the Levant, subjugated Judah, and unsuccessfully tried to invade Egypt (601 BCE). Necho II's successor Psammetichus II (595–589 BCE) sent an expedition to Nubia (Ethiopia).[231] This expedition is known from a stela from Shellal dated to Year 3,[232] a parallel stela from Karnak,[233] and from Stela Cairo JdE 67095 from Tanis dated to Year 3.[234] The Shellal stela records the capture of 4,200 prisoners, while the Tanis stela records that king of Kush was killed in his residence. Psammetichus II also personally led an expedition to the Levant in his Year 4, accompanied by priests bearing the bouquets of Amun.[235] This expedition may have persuaded Judah to revolt against Babylon. Psammeticus II's successor Apries (589–570 BCE) continued to campaign in the Levant, attacking Sidon by land and Tyre by sea.[236] However, Babylon reasserted itself in the Levant, destroying Jerusalem (587 BCE), and besieging Tyre for thirteen years (586–573 BCE). Apries also sent an unsuccessful expedition against the Greek cities in Cyrenaica, and the expedition revolted and placed Amasis on the throne.[237] Amasis (570–526 BCE) was the first to conquer Cyprus.[238] He also defeated a Babylonian invasion in Year 4 that attempted to restore Apries, according to the Amasis Stela of Year 4.[239]

In the First Persian Period (525–404 BCE), Egypt was constrained from organizing independent military expeditions abroad after Cambyses (525–522 BCE) invaded, deposed Amasis' successor Psammetichus III (526–525 BCE), and made Egypt a satrapy of the Persian Empire, due to the risk of revolt, though paramilitary expeditions to quarry stone in the Wadi Hammamat in the Eastern Desert still occurred.[240] Indeed, King Psammetichus IV led a revolt of Egypt from the Persian Empire at the end of the reign of Cambyses' successor Darius I (522–486 BCE),[241] and Darius I's successor Xerxes I (486–465) had to suppress it. King Inaros son of Psammetichus led another revolt of Egypt in the reign of Xerxes I's successor Artaxerxes I (465–424 BCE), with the assistance of the Athenian navy.[242] Egypt revolted yet again after the death of Artaxerxes I's successor Darius II (423–405 BCE), and became independent of the Persian Empire for sixty years. During the Twenty-eighth, Twenty-ninth, and Thirtieth Dynasties (404–343 BCE), the constant threat of an attack from the Persian Empire prevented Egypt from mounting military expeditions abroad, except for preemptive attacks on the Persian Empire. In the Twenty-ninth Dynasty, King Hakoris (393–380 BCE) prepared to attack the Persians, by gathering mercenaries and engaging the Athenian Chabrias.[243] In the Thirtieth Dynasty, King Teos (362–360 BCE), the son and successor of King Nectanebo I (380–362 BCE), launched a campaign against the Persians in the Levant, with the Athenian Chabrias in charge of the fleet and the Spartan king Agesilaus in charge of the mercenaries, but the Egyptian army revolted and appointed Teos' cousin as King Nectanebo II (360–343).[244] In the Second Persian Period (343–332 BCE), Artaxerxes III (343–338 BCE) finally conquered Egypt again and returned it to the Persian Empire. Egypt revolted once again under Artaxerxes III's successor Arses (338–336 BCE), however, under the leadership of King Khababash.[245]

Foundations: In the Saite Period, the state established many new foundations. The Saite kings embellished their dynastic residence at Sais, and the temple of Neith there. They built a massive palace at Memphis to the north of the temple of Ptah, and they founded a new city, temple complex, and sometime royal residence at Defenneh (Daphnae) on the Pelusiac branch of the Nile, at the eastern edge of the Nile Delta. The Saite kings also established three border fortresses at Elephantine, Daphnae, and Marea.[246] Psammetichus I also settled Ionian and Carian soldiers along the Pelusaic branch of the Nile to the east of Bubastis, until Amasis removed them to Memphis.[247] Necho II began building a canal from the Pelusiac branch of the Nile to Pithom (Patumos) and thence to the Red Sea, but he abandoned the project before it was completed.[248]

Necho II supposedly also sent a Phoenician fleet from the Red Sea to circumnavigate Africa.[249] Amasis granted Naukratis to the Greeks;[250] in earlier times, anyone who came to Egypt by sea was obliged to sail to the Canopic branch of the Nile and thence to Naukratis.[251]

In the First and Second Persian Periods, the state established relatively few new foundations. The Persians reused the royal palace at Memphis as the satrapal residence, and they maintained the border fortresses at Elephantine and Daphnae that the Saites had established.[252] Darius I completed the canal from the Pelusaic branch of the Nile to the Red Sea. Darius' canal was commemorated by four or five quadrilingual stelae inscribed in Hieroglyphs, Persian, Elamite, and Babylonian.[253] Darius I also completed the temple of Amun at Hibis in the Kharga Oasis. During the Twenty-eighth, Twenty-ninth, and especially the Thirtieth Dynasties, however, the state once again established many new foundations. Nectanebo began reclaiming the Fayum.

Private Entrepreneurial Activities: State service and participation in redistributive networks could be a lucrative form of entrepreneurial activity. According to the Petition of Petiese, in Year 4 of Psammetichus I, the shipping master at Herakleopolis restored the temple of Amun of Teudjoi at El-Hiba, by returning its revenues that had been diverted away from it.[254] The returned revenues were then used to support priests and craftsmen, so that this act could be seen as a form of investment. Admittedly, the shipping master derived his authority from being an agent of the king in Middle and Upper Egypt, so this was hardly a pure case of private investment. On the other hand, the shipping master then wrote documents appointing a close relative, Petiese I, to hold the highest positions in the reestablished temple,[255] and to receive 20 percent of its revenues,[256] so the shipping master was hardly operating solely as an uninterested agent of the king. State service was also useful for retaining wealth. In the Petition of Petiese, one or more provincial supervisors eventually replaced the office of shipping master. Then in Year 4 of Psammetichus II, while Petiese I's grandson Petiese II was on campaign with the king in the Levant, the new supervisor of Herakleopolis appointed his own son to Petiese II's positions in the temple. After his return, Petiese II petitioned the king and vizier and the judges to recover his position, but despite his documents he was unsuccessful, at least in part because he no longer had any relatives in high state service.[257]

Nonetheless, accumulation and exploitation of revenue-producing properties remained a popular form of entrepreneurial activity alongside state service. In the late Saite Period, the archive of the choachytes Djekhy and his son Ituredj from Thebes contains six leases of fields.[258] Two of these, Demotic Papyrus Louvre E. 7836,[259] dated to Year 35 of Amasis (536 BCE), and Demotic Papyrus Louvre E. 7839,[260] dated to Year 37 of Amasis (534 BCE), are leases of endowment fields by choachytes to cattle-keepers and bee-keepers as tenants. Early in the Persian Period, the Aramaic Papyrus Bauer-Meissner, dated to Year 7 of Darius I (515 BCE), is a land lease from Korobis in the Oxyrhynchite nome.[261] Later in the Persian Period, the satrap Arsames held a large estate in Egypt, which could have been associated with his position. There were, however, at least two other Persians who held estates in Egypt at the same time, Warohi,[262] and Warfis,[263] and neither was a satrap. Arsames, Warohi, and Warfis were not always resident on their Egyptian estates, and all employed Egyptian estate managers. Both Arsames and Warohi extracted at least some rental income for use beyond the estate, and indeed beyond Egypt. In two leather letters, both Arsames and Warohi wrote to Arsames' estate manager Nehtihur ordering him to send to Babylon the rents that Warohi's estate manager Hatubasti had failed to send, along with those from Arsames's estate.[264] Arsames assigned at least some of his estate to tenant farmers in return for rent, though inheritance of tenancy was subject to Arsames' approval. In a leather letter, Arsames ordered Nehtihur to appoint Petosiris son of Pamun to cultivate his father's fields, as long as he paid the land tax.[265] It is unclear how much if any of Arsames' estate was cultivated directly. Arsames' estate included craftsmen among the domestic staff, as was mentioned previously. Warfis' estate may have as well, based on a leather letter from Warfis to Arsames' estate manager Nehtihur, ordering him to restore the Cilician slaves, wine, and other goods that Warfis' officer and possibly estate manager Maspata claims he has stolen, and to stay away from Warfis' domestic staff.[266]

CONCLUSIONS

In the Saite and Persian Periods, the reunified state prosecuted crimes against state finances across Egypt, and collaborated with local Egyptian temple courts to adjudicate private property transfer disputes. Enforcement of state finances and private property transfers was dependent on written documentation. The state continued to document labor obligations for individual people and harvest taxes for individual plots of land, and to share with temples responsibility for documentation of harvest taxes on temple endowments. Local temple notaries continued to be responsible for documenting private property transfers, but they now also documented sales taxes on these transfers, allowing them to recapture their documentation costs. Temples also documented burial taxes, while the state documented customs duties.

Written documentation and the increased use of silver as a medium of exchange reduced transaction costs for redistribution and especially exchange, but the reunified state could enforce royal redistribution across larger distances than the local temples could enforce exchanges, due to their reliance on local witnesses. Donations of land continued to be used as royal rewards for officials and soldiers, and some salaries in kind began to be supplemented with payments in silver. Land was still donated to temples in exchange for revenues for mortuary cults, but most high-value exchanges involved silver, and many were documented with written contracts. Many low-value exchanges probably took place in markets, but most of these were not documented in writing. Long-term employment with state or temple organizations was common, as was short-term compulsory labor for the state.

SEVEN

THE PTOLEMAIC PERIOD (332–30 BCE)

The Ptolemaic Period began when Alexander the Great defeated the Persians in Egypt in 332 BCE. After he died in 323 BCE, his generals divided up his empire and Ptolemy took Egypt. Initially the generals ruled in the name of Alexander's heirs, but Ptolemy proclaimed himself king in 305 BCE. He and his successors continued to rule Egypt until the Romans conquered it in 30 BCE, suppressing several revolts including one in Upper Egypt, 205–186 BCE. The Ptolemies initially ruled from Memphis but soon moved the royal court to Alexandria, which Alexander the Great had founded on the northwest coast of Egypt. They also introduced Greek as an administrative language alongside Egyptian. (See Map 7.1 and Table 7.1).

CRIMINAL JUSTICE

In the Ptolemaic Period, as in earlier periods, interference with royal revenues was handled by the criminal justice system, which applied a body of law established by royal decrees. The king was the head of the criminal justice system, and indeed of the entire judicial administration, and could and did hear cases himself. In earlier periods, however, kings usually distanced themselves from the routine activities of the judicial administration by delegating them to a vizier and a high court. In contrast, the Ptolemaic kings presented themselves as personally responsible for the judicial administration, without the formal

MAP 7.1. Egypt in the Ptolemaic Period

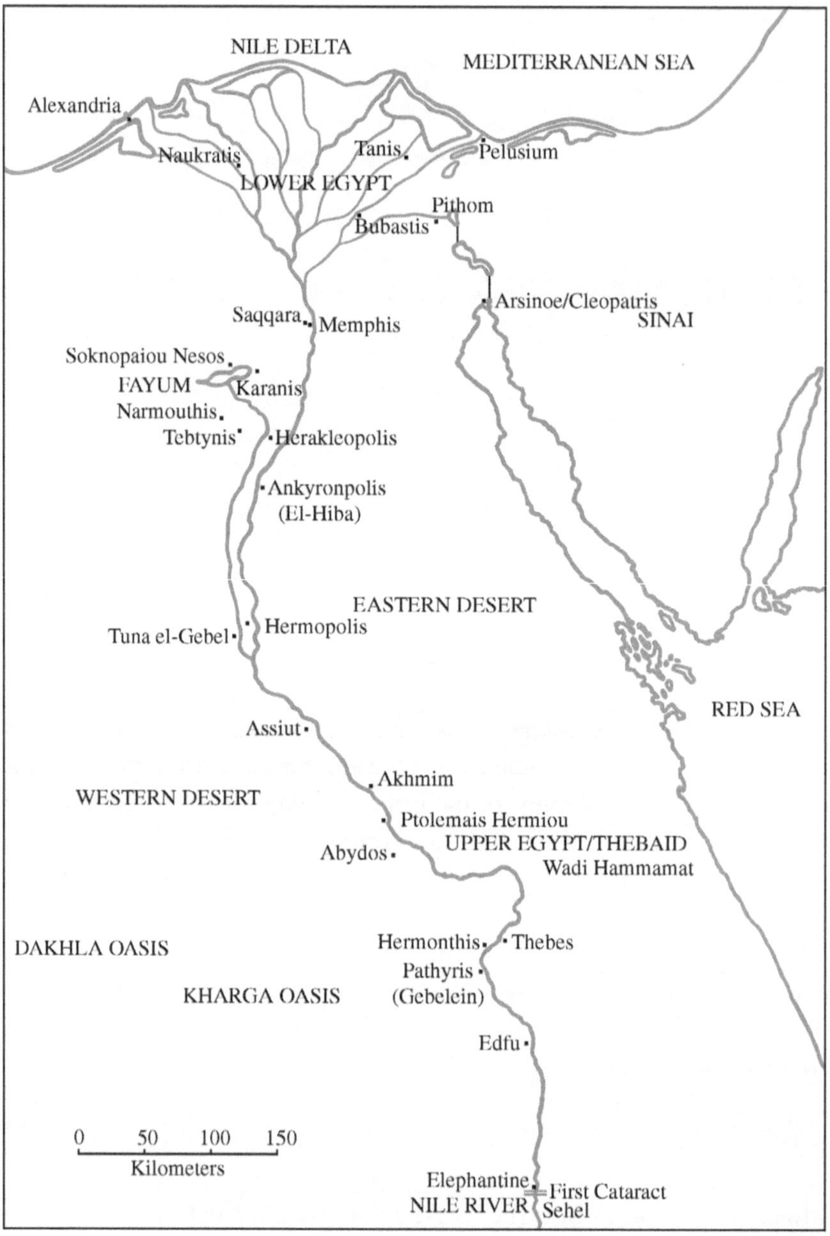

assistance of a vizier or a high court. In doing so, the Ptolemies acted in accordance with the Macedonian model of kingship, in which the king embodied the state in his own person.[1]

As in earlier periods, subjects could air their grievances with a letter of complaint to the king or one of his officials. However, the Macedonian model of kingship encouraged subjects to approach their king for justice, and

TABLE 7.1. *The Ptolemaic Period*

The Ptolemaic Period (332–30 BCE)
Macedonian Dynasty (332–305 BCE)
Alexander "the Great" (332–323 BCE)
Philip Arrhidaeus (323–317 BCE)
Alexander IV (317–310/305 BCE) – Died in 310 BCE, nominal ruler until 305 BCE
Ptolemaic Dynasty (305–30 BCE)
Ptolemy I (305–285 BCE)
Ptolemy II (285–246 BCE)
Ptolemy III (246–221 BCE)
Ptolemy IV (221–205 BCE)
Ptolemy V (205–180 BCE) – Revolt of Haronnophris (205–199 BCE), and Chaonnophris (199–186 BCE)
Ptolemy VI (180–145 BCE) – Joint reign with Ptolemy VIII (170–163 BCE)
Ptolemy VIII (145–116 BCE) – Joint reign with Cleopatra II (131–116 BCE) and Cleopatra III (124–116 BCE)
Cleopatra III and Ptolemy IX (116–107 BCE)
Ptolemy X (107–88 BCE) – Joint reign with Cleopatra III (107–101 BCE)
Ptolemy IX (88–80 BCE)
Ptolemy XII (80–51 BCE)
Cleopatra VII (51–30 BCE)

Source: Dates after Ian Shaw (ed.), *The Oxford History of Ancient Egypt* (Oxford: University Press, 2000), pp. 479–483.

consequently just under half of all letters of complaint were addressed to the king (173 out of 402 examples).[2] Letters to the king were known as petitions (*enteuxeis*), and were written in Greek. The address was not always a formality, because petitioners could and sometimes did personally deliver petitions directly to the king, if they happened to be near the place where the king was.[3] Furthermore, the king did at least sometimes personally read the petitions that were personally delivered to him, even if he then delegated the cases to one of his agents, such as the local provincial governor (*stratēgos*).[4] More often, however, petitioners addressed their petitions to the king but delivered them to one of his local agents, usually a provincial governor, who dealt with it on his behalf.[5]

Beneath the king, the Ptolemaic state administration was divided into three sections. One section was concerned with maintaining order and enforcing the law, and consisted of the regional governor (*epistratēgos*), the provincial governors (*stratēgoi*) and their local commissioners (*epistatai*), and the provincial police commissioners (*epistatai phylakitōn*) and their local chiefs of police (*archiphylakitai*) and policemen (*phylakitai*).[6] Another section was concerned with economic documentation. The royal scribes (*basilikoi grammateis*, Egyptian *sẖ pr-ꜥꜣ*) in each province, and the district scribes (*topogrammateis*, Egyptian *sẖ mꜣꜥ*) and village scribes (*kōmogrammateis*, Egyptian *sẖ tmy*) under them, made cadasters of land and censuses of people and livestock, and calculated the harvest and money taxes that they owed the state. The royal scribes and their auditors or checking scribes (*antigrapheis*) also checked the books of tax collectors, and supervised payments subsequently made by royal granaries and banks.[7] The third section was concerned with economic management. The provincial managers (*oikonomoi*, Egyptian *sḥn*) in each province auctioned off the rights to collect money taxes to tax collectors on the basis of the censuses and cadasters. The sections concerned with economic documentation and management both reported to the chief finance minister (*dioikētēs*, Egyptian *snty*) and to the under finance ministers (*hypodioikētai*), who in turn reported to the king.[8] It was the section concerned with maintaining law and order that received petitions to the king and dealt with them on his behalf. The provincial governors could give decisions or delegate cases to the courts, and they could order their subordinates to enforce the decisions.

In earlier periods of Egyptian history, subjects often approached the vizier and other officials for justice, rather than the king, and this practice continued under the Ptolemies. Letters addressed directly to agents of the king account for just over half of all letters of complaint (229 out of 402 examples). To distinguish them from petitions to the king (*enteuxeis*), these letters were known either as memoranda or reminders (*hypomnēmata*, Egyptian *mḳmḳ*) or short reports or declarations (*prosangelmata*). Most were written in Greek (196 examples), but some were written in Demotic (33 examples).[9] Memoranda or reminders were submitted to higher-ranking officials, while short reports or declarations were directed at lower-ranking officials. In the late Ptolemaic Period, the distinction between petitions and memoranda began to fade, and the distinction between memoranda and reports as well, ultimately giving rise to the more uniform Roman petitions.[10] Most memoranda and reports were addressed to officials primarily concerned with maintaining law and order, such as the regional governor (*epistratēgos*), the provincial governors (*stratēgoi*) and their local commissioners (*epistatai*), and the provincial police commissioners (*epistatai phylakitōn*) and their local chiefs of police (*archiphylakitai*). Nonetheless, a significant number were also addressed to officials in other sections of the state administration, such as the chief finance minister (*dioikētēs*), the under finance ministers (*hypodioikētai*), the provincial managers (*oikonomoi*), and the village scribe (*kōmogrammateis*), presumably because the complaints were thought to fall under their purview.[11]

Higher officials who received petitions often delegated responsibility to lower officials, who frequently engaged the local police (*phylakitai*). Local police could also investigate suspected criminal activity on their own initiative, as well as at the request of their superiors. They conducted searches, seized property, and interrogated and arrested suspects. Suspects were then brought or summoned to examinations (*episkepseis*) before one or more officials who delivered judgment.[12] Officials also assigned local police, wayfarers (*ephodoi*), and various kinds of guards (*phylakes*) to protect state fiscal interests, violation of which was clearly considered criminal. They guarded crops before and during the harvest, as well as harvest taxes afterward. They were present at state auctions of property and tax farming contracts, and assisted tax farmers with the collection of money taxes. They also patrolled the river, canals, paths, and deserts, and helped collect tolls at guard posts.[13] Local police and wayfarers were state agents, who received a salary or sometimes a grant of land.[14] Guards were often part-time state agents or private employees.[15]

PROPERTY DISPUTE RESOLUTION

In the Ptolemaic Period, private property disputes that did not involve royal revenues were usually handled by the court system, which applied traditional Egyptian and Greek property laws. There were in fact two sets of courts in Ptolemaic Egypt. The provincial Houses of Judgment (*nꜣ ꜥwy.w wpy*) were linked to local Egyptian temples, and remained the primary courts of Egyptian judges (*laokritai*) through the Ptolemaic Period. The Ptolemies also established courts of Greek judges (*chrēmatistai*) for the benefit of Greek immigrants, alongside the courts of Egyptian judges. The relationship between these two sets of courts is discussed in one of a set of royal decrees issued in 118 BCE after the civil wars among Ptolemy VIII, Cleopatra II, and Cleopatra III. Official copies of the decrees were circulated throughout the country, and one official in Tebtynis made a personal copy that became *P. Tebt.* I, 5. The copy seems to be corrupt, because the phrase "Egyptians against Greeks" is repeated twice in the first paragraph. If the second occurrence of the phrase is corrected to "or Egyptians against <Egyptians, and Greeks> against Greeks," the decree can be read to state that disputes arising from notarized contracts written in Demotic should be judged by the Egyptian judges (*laokritai*), while disputes arising from contracts written in Greek should be judged by the Greek judges (*chrēmatistai*), and that the ethnicity of the parties involved was irrelevant. This reading of the decree would provide for a return to earlier practice after irregularities during the civil wars, rather than introducing a new practice.[16]

***P. Tebt.* I, 5, re-edited as *Corp. Ord. Ptol.* 53, lines 207–220:**

(207) And they have decreed, both concerning suits brought by Egyptians against Greeks, and concerning (suits) by Greeks against Egyptians, or Egyptians against Greeks, of all classes

(210) – with the exception of those who farm royal land and those who lease royal monopolies, and the others who are involved with the state revenues –

> that the Egyptians who have made contracts in Greek with Greeks shall give and receive satisfaction before the Greek judges (*chrēmatistai*), while the Greeks (215) who have concluded contracts in Egyptian (sc. with Egyptians) shall give satisfaction before the Egyptian judges (*laokritai*) in accordance with the laws of the country (i.e. Egyptian laws).
>
> The suits of Egyptians against Egyptians shall not be taken by the Greek judges (*chrēmatistai*) to their own courts, but they shall allow them to be decided before the Egyptian judges (*laokritai*) in accordance with the (220) laws of the country.

Egyptian Courts: Ptolemaic Egyptian courts are relatively well known, thanks to a family archive from Assiut, which contains thirteen Demotic papyri, including a record of a court trial.[17] In 170 BCE, the woman Chratianch sued her brother-in-law Tefhape to obtain his share of his father's property. The Demotic Papyrus British Museum 10591 records the composition of the court, the written arguments and documents submitted to the court, and the court's decision in favor of Tefhape, who received the court record. The papyrus describes the composition of the court as the judges (*nꜣ wpty.w*) of the priests (*nꜣ wꜥb.w*) of the god Wepwawet and the deified Ptolemies, being three men who sat in the House of Judgment of Assiut (*pꜣ ꜥ.wy wpy n Sywt*). A Greek state representative called the introducer (*eisagōgeus*, Egyptian *pꜣ ꜣysws*) sat with them, and brought the lawsuit before them.[18]

Egyptian courts judged property disputes arising from Egyptian documents according to Egyptian property law. Several papyri from the Ptolemaic Period preserve fragments of Egyptian property law codes, including the Legal Code of Hermopolis West, dated to the third century BCE;[19] the Zivilprozeßordnung from Hermopolis, dated to the third or second century BCE;[20] P. Berlin P. 23757 recto from Akhmim, dated to the third century BCE;[21] P. Florence Istituto Papirologico "G. Vitelli" + P. Carlsberg 301 from Tebtynis, dated to the first century BCE;[22] and P. Berlin P. 23890 and P. Carlsberg 628.[23] The texts on these papyri may be much older than the papyri themselves, however, dating back at least to the Saite Period,[24] if not earlier.[25] These law codes are phrased as a series of prescriptive if-then statements that describe hypothetical situations, and then the legal procedures and formulae to be used in these situations. This has led some scholars to suggest that they were legal manuals rather than law codes, but such a distinction seems unlikely. The ancient Egyptians regularly expressed mathematical, medical, and even philosophical principles as prescriptive or didactic if-then statements, and thus would probably have expressed law codes in the same way. This seems to be confirmed by the lawsuit of Chratianch, which also cites laws in the form of prescriptive if-then statements,[26] suggesting that this was indeed the manner in which the ancient Egyptians codified their laws.

The largest, best preserved and best studied fragment of an Egyptian law code is the so-called Legal Code of Hermopolis West.[27] It was found during excavations at Tuna el-Gebel, a necropolis of Hermopolis, and probably dates to the third century BCE. It preserves several groups of hypothetical situations and prescriptions, which display a thematic organization.

Legal Code of Hermopolis West:

Lines 1,1-2,11: Rules for leases of fields.

Lines 2,12-22: Rules for using a public protest to prevent someone from obtaining clear title.

Lines 2,23-3,2: Rules for using leases to obtain clear title.

Lines 3,2-4,6: Rules for leases other than fields.

Lines 4,6-5,31: Rules for annuity contracts.

Lines 6,1-7,17: Rules for establishing proof of title.

Lines 7,18-8,29: Rules for construction.

Lines 8,30-9,26: Rules for intestate inheritance.

Lines 9,26-29: Additional rules for using leases to obtain clear title.

Another important fragment of an Egyptian law code is the so-called Zivilprozeßordnung, probably from Hermopolis, and probably dating to the third or second century BCE.[28] It contains at least two groups of hypothetical situations and prescriptions. The best preserved group concerns disputes about transactions, thereby giving the Zivilprozeßordnung its name.

P. Berlin 13621 + P. Giessen UB 101.3 recto, column 2, lines 1–18:

(1) [...] (2) Number 13. Concerning a document, which one will take. (3) Makes 43 its year.

(4) [The] person who writes concerning something, and [the] person for whom he makes the *sẖ*-document: writes concerning something (means) he will be far from the law of the *sẖ*-document, which he has made for him.

(5) [The] person, who complains [against a man, saying] "he has seized a house, agricultural land, or cattle/an office belonging to me": If one of the people brings a *sẖ*-document concerning it, saying: "He has written concerning [the thing ...]" (6) one will cause that he is far from him. [If he says]: "I have not written," one will cause that he swears after his statement upon it (the *sẖ*-document), "I am after you [...]" (7) upon it [...]

(8) If a person complains [against a person] saying: "he made for me a *šʿ.t*-document ... money for me. He has not given it to me." If the person against whom he complains [says: ...] (9) If he says: "I have not made it for him," one will cause that he swears. The *šʿ.t*-document possesses no witness. If it happens that it possesses witnesses [...] (10) the one who will do it.

> (11) The person who complains verbally, gives to them an oath, the one that they will make him, according to their words.
>
> (12) The person who complains against a person, and whose law is drawn up, if it happens that they are before the judges, if it happens that they read [...]
>
> (13) [The person] who complains against his companion, saying: "He seized something belonging to me until Year 20 before today," one will not listen to him. If it happens that ...
>
> (14) If a person complains against a person concerning money, while he says: "I will give it to him in such-and-such a town." If the person against whom he complains [...] (15) in the town in which he complained against him.
>
> (16) If [a person] complains against a person, saying: "he has seized such-and-such a document belonging to me," while he says "I have not taken it," one will cause that he swears, saying: ["the document which he says 'you have taken it from me,'] (17) I have not taken it, I have not caused that one take it, I have not done anything on the earth to cause that one take it, I have not destroyed it, [I have not caused that one destroy it, I have not done anything on the earth to cause] (18) that one destroy [it, I have not erased it, I have not] caused that one erased [it, I have not done] anything [on the earth to cause that one erased it ..."]

The Zivilprozeßordnung suggests that provincial Houses of Judgment could hear cases arising from all kinds of Demotic documents, and not just contracts authenticated by temple scribes and witnesses and state notaries. However, the Zivilprozeßordnung and the lawsuit of Chratianch suggest that such contracts were given precedence over other Demotic documents, and all documents were given precedence over oral testimony. The same preference for written over oral testimony appears in the expanded title guarantee in Demotic contracts. The Zivilprozeßordung suggests that provincial Houses of Judgment required oaths to support unauthenticated documents and oral testimony. Failure to take an oath discredited such documents and testimonies, giving the oaths a decisive character. Such decisive oaths were often used to resolve accusations of adultery or theft during marriage.

Greek Courts: By the third century BCE, the Ptolemaic kings organized a series of state courts (*kritēria*) in the provinces consisting of three Greek judges (*chrēmatistai*), to which the state representative called the introducer (*eisagōgeus*) could bring cases involving Greek contracts.[29] It has been argued that these state courts gradually superseded a series of locally organized courts (*dikastēria*), composed of local Greek judges (*dikastai*) for Greek cases and Egyptian judges (*laokritai*) for Egyptian cases, and mixed courts (*koinodikia*) for cases involving both Greeks and Egyptians, which disappeared in the second century BCE.[30] This interpretation should be rejected, however, because it erroneously privileges distinctions in Greek terminology over similarities in useage, because the state introducer (*eisagōgeus*) also brought cases before the "local" Greek judges (*dikastai*) and the Egyptian judges (*laokritai*). The "local" courts (*dikastēria*) and "local" Greek judges (*dikastai*) were probably just the generic terms for the state courts (*kritēria*) and Greek judges (*chrēmatistai*). The generic terms probably gradually dropped out of use as the technical terms came into more general use.

Private Social Control: Individuals frequently turned to private social networks to document and enforce agreements and to resolve disputes, as well as to agents of the king and local Greek and Egyptian courts. Most individuals participated in at least one horizontal social network, such as their extended family or their local community, and usually they belonged to several. Members of such networks could serve as witnesses to verbal or written agreements, and they could apply social pressure to fellow members to enforce the agreements, and to resolve disputes arising from them.

Private associations were a more formalized form of horizontal social network. Private associations in Ptolemaic Egypt typically drew up rules regulating the behavior of their members for one year, after which time the associations drew up new rules and could change members. These rules required members to pay annual dues, to participate in and make contributions for periodic religious ceremonies and social drinking, and to aid fellow members in need and behave civilly toward each other. The rules also required members to pay fines when they transgressed any of the rules.[31] Some of these rules and fines were clearly intended to help the association enforce agreements and resolve disputes among members, as in *P.Assoc. Cairo* 30605, lines 19–20, from Tebtynis dating to 145 BCE.[32] These rules fined members who disputed with other members before consulting with the association, and fined them more if they continued to dispute after consulting the association.

> ***P.Assoc. Cairo* 30605, lines 19–20:**
>
> (19) The man among us who will give trouble to a man among us before the military or civil authorities, (who) will interfere, (who) has not complained before the members of the association previously, his fine will be 50 deben.
>
> The man among us who will complain ..., after the law has been made for him (20) in the association, after he has complained about it in it, his fine will be 100 deben.

Monson has suggested that the members of private associations were relatively well off, because the dues and fines sometimes exceeded the annual income of average farmers.[33] He notes that the membership of associations sometimes included priests, but did not exclusively consist of them.[34] He also argues that the dues and fines were high to encourage commitment to the associations and to thereby help build trust, much like the mandatory joint participation in religious ceremonies and social drinking. He emphasizes that the resulting trust would have enhanced the ability of private associations to enforce agreements and resolve disputes among members, beyond the rules and the fines.[35]

Some individuals also participated in vertical social networks that created bonds of mutual obligation that can be described as patronage.[36] The officials or institutions providing this patronage were expected to protect their clients from other authorities.[37] Officials did so by using their authority to intervene on behalf of their clients in disputes,[38] while temples provided asylum to their clients.[39] Some royal decrees grant the right of asylum to specific temples, while other royal decrees prohibit officials and temples from giving protection to specific categories of individuals, suggesting that the state recognized patronage as a formal relationship.[40]

DOCUMENTATION OF OBJECTS OF TAXATION

As previously noted, one of the three sections of the Ptolemaic state administration was primarily concerned with economic documentation. This section of the administration consisted of village scribes (*kōmogrammateis*), who collected information locally and reported it to district scribes (*topogrammateis*), who summarized it and reported it to the royal scribes (*basilikoi grammateis*) in each province. The royal scribes then further summarized the information and reported it to the chief finance minister (*dioikētēs*) and under finance ministers (*hypodioikētai*) in Alexandria.[41] In some form, this section of the administration probably dates back to the Saite and Persian Periods. The office of chief finance minister is attested in both the late Saite and Persian Periods,[42] and the family that held the office of royal scribe in the Thebaid in the early Ptolemaic Period performed some of the same functions prior to the conquest of Egypt by Alexander the Great.[43] In the Ptolemaic Period, one of the tasks of this section of the administration was the documentation of objects of taxation, such as people, animals, and fields. As in earlier periods, the Ptolemaic documentation of objects of taxation took two main forms, a survey of fields, and censuses of people and animals.[44]

Field Surveys: Fragmentary Demotic and Greek papyri preserve portions of several Ptolemaic field surveys and related documents dating to the third and second centuries BCE. The field surveys were used to calculate harvest taxes, as in earlier periods. There were two surveys each year. The village scribes conducted the first survey after the Nile inundation had subsided in the Nile Valley, or in September in the Fayum, but in either case before the fields were sown. They measured all of the land in each village, cultivated or not, and recorded its owners and its category or use. The village scribes conducted the second survey in February, a couple of months before the harvest. They measured all of the cultivated land in each village, and recorded its owners and category or use.[45] In Upper Egypt, they sometimes also issued a receipt of measurement (*r-rḫ=w* text) to the landowners. The second survey was used to calculate the harvest taxes on the fields, which were collected during the harvest in April or May. The amount of taxes was proportional to the amount of land cultivated at the time of survey, rather than the actual amount of the harvest. This protected the state from the risks of bad harvests and harvest fraud. Some receipts of measurement also include a calculation of the taxes owed.[46]

In previous periods, the state took responsibility for surveying and collecting harvest taxes from state agricultural lands, and assigned to temples the responsibility for surveying and collecting harvest taxes on temple lands. Initially, the early Ptolemies continued this arrangement. On the one hand, the state directly administered and taxed the grain-producing agricultural land known as royal land (*basilikē gē*), and taxed other grain-producing agricultural land that had been entrusted to officials as gift estates (*dōreai*), and to reserve soldiers or cleruchs (*klērouchoi*) as cleruchic land (*klerouchikē gē*). It also taxed orchards and vineyards on private land (*idiōtikē gē*). On the other hand, the temples continued to administer and tax the grain-producing agricultural land as well as orchards and vineyards classified as temple land (*hiera gē*).[47]

In the course of the Ptolemaic Period, however, the state assumed responsibility for surveying and collecting harvest taxes from temple as well as state lands. Papyrus Revenue Laws, columns 24–38, reveals that the state began administering and taxing orchards and vineyards on temple land in Year 23 of Ptolemy II (263 BCE). It indicates that responsibility for surveying orchards and vineyards on temple as well as state lands was assigned to the royal scribe (*basilikos grammateus*) in each nome or province (columns 33 and 36–37). The responsibility for collecting the one-sixth or one-tenth harvest tax on wine produced from orchards and vineyards was assigned to the provincial manager (*oikonomos*) (columns 31 and 33). The tax could be paid either in wine or in money, but the provincial manager auctioned off any wine that was collected so that the money value of the entire tax could be subject to tax farming. The revenues from this tax were then dedicated to the cult of the deceased and deified Queen Arsinoe II Philadelphus, which was carried out in the temples. This no doubt made the state diversion of these revenues more acceptable to the temples.[48]

Papyrus Revenue Laws, column 33:[49]

(33) The [provincial manager (*oikonomos*)] shall examine the [wine], as much as remains, and taking with him the tax-farmer, the checking-scribe (*antigrapheus*) and his agent, shall jointly with them sell the wine, giving the [tax-farmers (?)] time in which to settle their accounts, and exacting

> payment of the [amounts] he shall put them down in the account of the tax-contract to the credit of the tax-farmers.
>
> The royal scribes (*basilikoi grammateis*) shall, within ten days from the day on which they proclaim the auction, notify to the tax-farmers how many vineyards or orchards there are in each nome, with the number of arouras (which they contain), and how many vineyards or orchards belonging to persons on the tribute list paid the tax to the temples before the twenty-second year. If they fail to make out the list, or if they are discovered to have made it out incorrectly, if convicted in a suit, they shall pay to the tax-farmers for every mistake of which they are convicted 600 drachmas and twice the amount of the loss (incurred by them). All owners of vineyards or gardens on the tribute list who paid the sixth to the temples before the twenty-first year, shall henceforth pay it [to (Arsinoe) Philadelphos (?)]

In the course of the late third and early second centuries BCE, the state also assumed responsibility for surveying grain-bearing lands belonging to temples, and for collecting their harvest taxes at state rather than temple granaries. In exchange, the state granted an allowance (*syntaxis*) to the temples. This process began in the late third century BCE, around 223 BCE under Ptolemy III, when the state began confiscating temple land entrusted to private individuals who owed the state taxes. This land was then sold at royal auction, and henceforth was administered by the state rather than the temple. The revolt of Upper Egypt in 205 BCE, and its subsequent suppression in 186 BCE under Ptolemy V, may have allowed the state to assume administration of still more temple land. The results of this process can be seen in the Memphis Decree of Ptolemy V dated to 196 BCE, which contains the first mention of the allowance (*syntaxis*).[50] The decree purports to confirm the endowments of the temples, but it no longer describes them as land that produced revenues for the gods and their temples, but rather as allowances that were given to the temples by the king, and the gods' shares of the revenues from vineyards and orchards collected by the state.

The Memphis Decree of Year 9 of Ptolemy V (196 BCE), Rosetta lines 8–9:[51]

> He ordered concerning the endowments of the gods, and the money and the grain that are given as allowances to their (9) [temples] each year, and the shares that belong to the gods from the vineyards, the orchards, and all of the rest of the property which they possessed under his father, that they should remain in their possession.

The state assumption of responsibility for collecting harvest taxes from vineyards, orchards, and grain-bearing lands belonging to temples in exchange for subventions to the temples in theory could mean that the state assumed the risk of poor harvests. In practice, however, the state and its agents might not pay the subvention, thereby shifting the risk back to the temples. The latter is attested on a red granite stela erected by the priests of Khnum on Elephantine, recording a royal letter from Cleopatra III and Ptolemy IX dated to 115 BCE ordering the provincial governor (*stratēgos*) Phommous to give the priests of Khnum their subvention, in response to the priests' petition.[52]

Censuses: Portions of several Ptolemaic censuses and other documents related to censuses have survived on fragmentary Demotic and Greek papyri, mostly from the third century BCE.[53] The Ptolemaic census of people took two forms, a census according to household (*kat' oikian*) and a census according to the occupation of the heads of household (*kat' ethnos*).[54] The census of animals was separate from those of people.[55] Village scribes compiled the censuses with the assistance of written declarations (Gk. *apographai*) submitted to the authorities by heads of households.[56]

The Ptolemies continued to use the censuses of people to collect compulsory labor requirements for men, as in earlier periods.[57] Men were required to move thirty *naubia*-measures (Gk. *naubia*, Dem. *nby*) of earth a year, and received Demotic and Greek receipts on ostraca confirming that they had fulfilled their requirements. Those who could not or did not want to perform this duty could pay a compulsory labor tax (Gk. *leitourgikon*, Dem. *ḥḏ ꜥrt*) of two kite or four drachmas, for which they also received a receipt.[58] Ptolemaic censuses organized according to the occupations of the heads of households (Gr. *kat' ethnos*) were also used to collect trade or occupational taxes. In contrast to the Third Intermediate Period, however, the Ptolemaic trade taxes were probably imposed on each of the members of a trade or profession at a fixed rate per individual.[59]

The Ptolemies also used the censuses of people to collect new capitation taxes in money. Numerous Demotic receipts on ostraca reveal that from Year 1 to Year 21 of Ptolemy II (285–263 BCE), a new capitation tax known as the yoke tax (*ḥḏ nḥb*) was levied on men, paralleling the old compulsory labor requirement. Men paid up to four kite or eight drachmas annually,[60] possibly in monthly installments.[61] In Year 22 of Ptolemy II (263 BCE), the capitation taxes in money were reformed, and the revenues therefrom were subject to tax farming, like the one-sixth or one-tenth harvest tax on wine. The yoke tax was replaced by a new capitation tax known as the salt tax (Gk. *halikē*, Dem. *ḥḏ ḥmꜣ*), which was levied on both men and women. Demotic and Greek receipts on ostraca show that it was initially levied at an annual rate of three-quarter kite or one drachma three obols for men, and a half kite or one drachma for women, payable in semiannual installments. Then in Year 31 of Ptolemy II (254 BCE) the annual rate was lowered to a half kite or one drachma for men, and one-fourth kite or three obols for women. Finally, in Year 5 of Ptolemy III (243 BCE) the annual rate was lowered again to one-third kite or four obols for men, and one-eighth kite or one and a half obols for women, until Year 5 of Ptolemy IV (217 BCE) when the salt tax ceases to be attested.[62]

After the capitation taxes were reformed, the Ptolemies also used the censuses to collect the income of a server tax (Dem. *ʿḳ rmt iw=f šms*), the guard tax (*ʿḳ rsy*), and other taxes on some men, and the wool tax (Gk. *erea*, Dem. *ḥḏ inw*) on some women alongside the salt tax. Receipts on ostraca indicate that the income of a server tax appeared in Year 23 of Ptolemy II (262 BCE) at a rate of three obols, and from Year 27 (258 BCE) at three and three-quarter obols. The guard tax appeared in Year 33 of Ptolemy II (253 BCE) at a rate of one obol, and from Year 38 (248 BCE) it began to be collected together with the income of a server tax and other taxes at a rate of five and three-eighth obols. Combined receipts for the salt, income of a server, guard and other taxes appear in Year 5 of Ptolemy III (243 BCE).[63] The wool tax was introduced in Year 31 of Ptolemy II (254 BCE) at a rate of three and three-quarter obols. Combined receipts for the salt and wool taxes appear in Year 5 of Ptolemy III (243 BCE).[64]

After Year 5 of Ptolemy IV (217 BCE), Greek and Demotic receipts for capitation taxes in money ceased to be issued, though these or similar taxes were undoubtedly still collected, because censuses and tax registers continued to be compiled into the second century BCE.[65] By the first century BCE, the capitation taxes had certainly changed. Censuses or tax registers (*laographia*) from Theogonis near Tebtynis in the southern Fayum record monthly installment payments by individuals for two capitation taxes called the contribution (*syntaxis*) and the police tax (*epistatikon*).[66] Tax accounts and petitions to the governor of the Herakleopolite province mention two more capitation taxes, a grain levy tax (*sitonion*) and a stater tax (*statērismos*), assessed in money on each village as a lump sum that was then divided among the populations.[67] And ostraca from Karanis in the northeastern Fayum contain tax receipts for installment payments by individuals for the contribution, the police tax, and the grain levy tax.[68]

DOCUMENTATION OF BOTTLENECK TAXATION

In the Ptolemaic Period, the state and the temples continued to collect taxes in money at bottlenecks, alongside the taxes in money and kind collected from sources measured with field surveys and counted by censuses.

Sales Taxes: At the beginning of the Ptolemaic Period, as in the Saite and Persian Periods, temple notaries documented property transfers in the Egyptian language and Demotic script and collected a property transfer tax known as the tenth of scribes and representatives, which was 10 percent of the value of the property being transferred. Temple notaries sometimes incorporated a statement in contracts that payment of the tenth was the responsibility of the purchaser, and sometimes separate Demotic receipts on papyrus were issued to the buyer. The state began to collect an additional transfer tax of two and a half kite or five drachmas on each property transfer from the reign of Alexander IV onward. Separate Demotic receipts on papyrus were issued for this tax, and Demotic receipts on ostraca for the house tax (*ḥḏ ᶜ.wy*) may represent partial payments for this tax.[69]

In the reign of Ptolemy II, a fragmentary tax law papyrus reveals that sales and other transfers of slaves in the Greek language had to be registered at the state registry (*agoranomion*), and a transfer tax had to be paid to a royal bank. Also about this time, starting in Year 21 of Ptolemy II (264 BCE), Demotic contracts began to receive Greek subscriptions indicating that they had been received (*peptōken*) and registered (*echrēmatisen*), in some cases by a tax farmer (*telōnēs*).[70]

Near the end of the third century BCE, the tenth of scribes and representatives and the two and a half kite tax on Demotic property transfers disappeared, and were replaced in Year 12 of Ptolemy IV (210 BCE) by the enrollment tax (Gr. *enkyklion*, Dem. *ꜣggryn*) levied at a rate of eight drachmas two and a quarter obols per 100 drachmas (8.375 percent), and the copper tax (Gr. *chalkiaia*) at a rate of four drachmas one and one-eighth obols per 100 drachmas (4.188 percent). In one case a Demotic receipt was subscribed on a contract, in another case a Greek receipt was subscribed, and in a third case a separate Greek receipt was issued. The new taxes had to be paid at a tax office (*telōnion*) or a royal bank, and thus the state took control of the revenues from taxes on Demotic property transfers away from the temples, though the temples may have still received a share of the revenues.[71]

Burial Taxes: In the Ptolemaic Period, temples continued to administer and control access to cemeteries in the deserts. Burial plots had to be purchased from temples, and a money tax had to be paid on the burial of the dead in these cemeteries. The burial tax or tax of the overseer of the necropolis (*ḥḏ/tny mr ḫꜣst*) is attested from numerous Demotic receipts on ostraca from Thebes. It was collected at a rate of half silver kite or one drachma per burial from Year 2 of Alexander IV (315 BCE) through Year 6 of Ptolemy III (241 BCE). By Year 13 of Ptolemy III (234 BCE) until the beginning of the reign of Ptolemy IV (222 BCE), however, the rate was raised to half silver kite and one obol or seven obols per burial.[72]

The burial plot tax or price of a burial plot is also attested from Demotic receipts on ostraca from Thebes, and was collected at a rate of two and a half kite or five drachmas per burial plot from Year 2 of Alexander IV (315 BCE) until the beginning of the reign of Ptolemy IV (222 BCE).[73] The earliest of these receipts, from Years 2 and 7 of Alexander IV (315 and 310 BCE) and on papyri rather than ostraca, refer instead to the tax of the tomb-chapel (*tny tꜣ s.t* or *tny tꜣ štꜣ*), which is reminiscent of the house tax (*ḥḏ ꜥ.wy*). This suggests that the burial plot tax may have been viewed as a transfer tax on tombs.[74] Support for this interpretation may be found in Demotic receipts on ostraca from Edfu from the second century BCE, which give permission for burials because the payment of the one-tenth has been received. These are clearly burial tax or burial plot tax receipts, but the one-tenth is the traditional name for the transfer tax exacted by temples. Similar Demotic receipts occur from Thebes from the second or first century BCE, but omit the reference to the one-tenth.[75]

The Theban mortuary priests usually paid the burial tax and the burial plot tax to the temple on behalf of their clients, and at least sometimes they also contracted with the temple to farm the taxes as well. Demotic Papyrus British Museum 10528 (Glanville), from Thebes and dated to Year 14 of Ptolemy I (291 BCE), is a promissory contract in which a mortuary priest writes that he has promised to pay five deben (or fifty kite) in exchange for the money of the overseer of the necropolis and the two and a half kite that are given for tombs, and that he will not bother the other mortuary priests or the temple manager (*mr-šn*) for this money.[76] A series of Demotic receipts on ostraca for the money or monies of document (*ḥḏ/ḥḏ.w n bꜣk*) may represent partial payment for the farmed taxes. The temple at Edfu collected similar taxes already in the third century BCE, called the tax of the necropolis (*tny ḫꜣst*) or the mummification tax (Gr. *taricheia*), and these appear to have been farmed by temple priests. A series of Demotic receipts on ostraca appear to record payments by the tax-farming priests to the temple, and a Greek letter on papyrus (P. Eleph. gr. 8) from the archive of Milon appears to be a promise by the tax-farming priests to make payments that were in arrears.[77]

Customs Duties: The Ptolemaic state exacted customs duties on goods imported into Egypt, as had been done in the preceding Persian Period. The duties had to be paid on the cargoes of ships arriving at Alexandria and Pelusium before the cargoes were offloaded. Papyrus Tebtunis I 5, lines 22–333, from Tebtynis, preserves a copy of an amnesty and regulation decree of Year 52 of Ptolemy VIII, Cleopatra II, and Cleopatra III (118 BCE), which specifies that goods may not be seized unless the officials of the customs-house (*pylē*) find something on the wharf at the harbors of Alexandria, on which the duty has not been paid, or of which the importation is forbidden. It also specifies that the seized goods should be brought to the chief finance minister (*dioikētēs*).[78]

The Ptolemaic duties were calculated as a percentage of the declared value of the goods and were paid in money, in contrast to the Persian practice of collecting some duties in kind as a percentage of the cargo. Fortunately, one papyrus happens to preserve the percentage rates of customs duties on a small selection of goods. Papyri Cairo CG (P.Cair.Zen. I) 59012–59014 date to Year 27 of Ptolemy II (259 BCE), and are from the archive of Zenon, the estate manager of the chief finance minister (*dioikētēs*) Apollonios. They form a dossier concerning goods imported into Egypt for Apollonios and others on ships captained by Patron and Herakleides. Papyrus Cairo CG 59012 is a copy of the declared valuation (*timēsis*) and the calculated customs duties and other taxes paid at Pelusium on the goods carried by the two ships,[79] while Papyrus Cairo CG 59013 records the portage (*phoretron*) for Apollonios' goods on Herakleides' ship, and Papyrus Cairo CG 59014 the portage for those on Patron's ship.[80] The customs duties in Papyrus Cairo CG 59012 were calculated at 50 percent (*hēmisu*) for sweet wine (*glykys*), filtered wine (*sēstos*), vinegar (*oxos*), and white oil; at 33 percent (*tritē*) for Chian and Thasian jars of wine and dried figs; at 25 percent (*tetartē*) for honey, cheese, salt fish and meats, and nuts; and at 20 percent (*pemptē*) for washed wool.[81]

Ptolemaic customs duties were particularly heavy on commodities produced in Egypt under monopolies, such as oil, presumably to protect the commodity monopolies from foreign competition. Papyrus Revenue Laws, dated to Year 27 of Ptolemy II (259 BCE), forbade the importation of oil to Egypt for sale, and levied a duty on oil imported for personal use.[82]

> **Papyrus Revenue Laws, col. 52:**
> [It shall not be lawful] to bring [foreign oil] into the country for sale, either from Alexandria or Pelusium or any other place. Whoever does so shall be deprived of the oil, and shall in addition pay a fine of 100 drachmas for each *metrētēs*, and for more or less in proportion. If any persons carry with them foreign oil for their personal use, those who bring it from Alexandria shall declare it in Alexandria, and shall pay down 12 drachmas for each *metrētēs*, and for more or less in proportion, and shall obtain a receipt before they bring it inland. Those who bring it from Pelusium shall pay the tax in Pelusium and obtain a receipt. The collectors in Alexandria and Pelusium shall place the tax to the credit of the province to which the oil is brought.

The Ptolemaic state probably also exacted tolls on goods transported within Egypt that passed by strategically located guard posts (*phylakai*), one of which was located at Memphis.[83]

DOCUMENTATION OF PROPERTY TRANSFERS

Two institutions participated in the documentation of property transfers, semiautonomous local notaries, and state registries. Initially, when Alexander the Great arrived in Egypt, notaries associated with Egyptian temples documented property transfers and collected transfer taxes. Then under Ptolemy I, Greek immigrants to Egypt also began drawing up property transfers in Greek. Ptolemy II therefore instituted a state registry (*agoranomion*) to register and collect transfer taxes on Greek property transfers. These state registries then slowly took over ever more tasks from the Egyptian temple notaries and Greek scribes, until the latter were finally abolished shortly after the Roman conquest.

Egyptian Documentation: As in the preceding periods, Ptolemaic contract scribes attached to temples continued to transcribe the verbal statements of one of the contracting parties, and several literate witnesses attached to the same temples continued to certify that the written transcripts agreed with the verbal statements. The witnesses usually only signed the transcripts, though in the Early Ptolemaic Period some of the witnesses also recopied the transcripts. The first contracting parties continued to give the resulting contracts to the second contracting parties as an authenticated record of the agreement, and the second contracting parties continued to assent to agreements by accepting the transcripts of them. These transcripts written by contract scribes attached to temples may have been known in Demotic as *sẖ*-contracts.[84]

Temple contract scribes did not document all transactions, however. Some minor transactions consisted of letter contracts, which the first contracting party wrote for the second contracting party. These letter contracts may have been known in Demotic as *šʿt*-contracts.[85] Other minor transactions consisted of verbal agreements witnessed by community members, and relied on social pressure for enforcement. Evidence for such verbal agreements can be found in memoranda not unlike those from Deir el-Medina in the New Kingdom. Occasionally these verbal agreements were transcribed with the names of the witnesses, and may have been known in Demotic as *hn*-agreements.[86]

Greek Documentation: The Greeks who settled in Ptolemaic Egypt introduced the six-witness contract or double document, which contained two copies of the same contract on the same papyrus, one above the other. The upper copy (*scriptura interior*) was rolled up and sealed with the signatures of six witnesses written around the seals, while the lower copy (*scriptura exterior*) was left exposed. The contract was deposited with a private individual (*syngraphophylax*), who guarded it until it needed to be consulted during a dispute.[87]

Starting in the early second century BCE, however, the state registry (*agoranomion*) began to function as a notary as well as a registry for some Greek contracts. The state registry produced agoranomic contracts, which also had a scriptura interior and a scriptura exterior, but unlike the six-witness contract or double document, the two were not copies. Instead, the scriptura interior was an abstract of the contract in the scriptura exterior, which was copied into the archives of the state registry. The abstract in the state registry served to authenticate the agoranomic contract, and consequently it needed no witnesses. The agoranomic contract did not however replace the older double document, which coexisted alongside it.[88]

State Registration: At the very beginning of the Ptolemaic Period, as in the preceding periods, there is no evidence of state registration. Temple notaries documented property transfers in Demotic, and collected the tenth of scribes and representatives, while the state collected an additional transfer tax of two and a half kite or five drachmas on each property transfer.[89] Early Greek immigrants to Egypt documented agreements in the Greek language with "six-witness" contracts that they themselves drew up and kept, and presumably they paid no property transfer taxes on these entirely private agreements.

In the reign of Ptolemy II, however, a fragmentary tax law papyrus reveals that sales and other transfers of slaves in the Greek language had to be registered at the state registry (*agoranomion*), and a transfer tax had to be paid to a royal bank.[90] Several registers containing summaries of Greek six-witness contracts or double documents are attested in the early Ptolemaic Period.[91] At the same time, temple notaries may also have been required to register the documents that they drew up with the state registry, because Egyptian contracts begin to receive Greek registration subscriptions in the reign of Ptolemy II.[92] A register containing summaries of Demotic contracts is also attested in the early Ptolemaic Period, but it is unclear whether a temple notary or a state registry produced it.[93]

Starting in the early second century BCE, the state registry (*agoranomion*) began to function as a notary for Greek agoranomic contracts. Perhaps for this reason, by the mid-second century BCE it became known as the writing office (*grapheion*) as well as the state registry (*agoranomion*).[94] Ptolemy VIII then introduced a new state registration requirement for Egyptian contracts at the very beginning of his sole reign in 145 BCE. The requirement survives in copy of a royal decree circulated to state registry officials. The writing offices (*grapheia*) were ordered to make abstracts of Egyptian contracts, before giving them Greek subscriptions and returning them to the contractors.[95] The results of this decree are preserved in a group of documents from Tebtynis in the early first century BCE, which contain registers of summaries of Demotic contracts, along with the separate abstracts of contracts ordained by the decree.[96]

Ptolemy VIII or Cleopatra III also introduced another new state registration requirement for Greek contracts sometime between 130 and 113 BCE. Previously, Greeks could draw up their own Greek six-witness contracts and subsequently register them at the state registries, or they could have the state registry draw up agoranomic contracts for them. Now Greeks had to let the state registries draw up the six-witness contracts as well as the agoranomic contracts, and to make abstracts of them, before giving them Greek subscriptions and returning them to the contractors. As a result, the upper copy (*scriptura interior*) of the six-witness contract became an abstract rather than a copy, as in the agoranomic contract; but the six-witness contract retained its witness signatures, thereby remaining distinct from the agoranomic contracts.[97] There is a register of copies of Greek agoranomic contracts from the state registry (*agoranomion*) in Pathyris (Gebelein) from 111–110 BCE.[98]

MEDIA OF EXCHANGE AND REDISTRIBUTION

In the Ptolemaic Period, weights of silver continued to be the standard measures of value, alongside volumes of hard wheat used for harvest taxes in kind. At the same time, coins minted in silver and bronze rapidly replaced weights of lump silver as media of exchange. Coins were, however, equated with specific weights of silver, thereby preserving the partial unity of measures of value and media of exchange achieved in the preceding Saite and Persian Periods. Silver was probably even more widely available in the Ptolemaic Period than in the Saite and Persian Periods, because the numbers of hoards of silver coins used as stores of wealth continued to increase. The increased availability of silver in turn allowed the state to use censuses to collect capitation taxes in silver, in addition to the sales taxes, customs duties, and surcharges on occupational activities already collected in the Saite and Persian Periods.

Measures of Value: In the early Ptolemaic Period, the standard measures of value in official accounts were weights of silver or copper, and occasionally volumes of hard wheat. Payments in gold or copper were usually reckoned into silver in early Ptolemaic official accounts, and payments in gold or silver were reckoned into copper in late Ptolemaic official accounts. Payments in various grains and legumes were usually reckoned into hard wheat in official accounts, but silver or copper was the standard measure of value for virtually all other commodities and purposes. In Egyptian texts, weights of silver or copper were measured in deben, kite, and fractions of kite, while in Greek texts weights of silver or copper were measured in drachmas, obols, and chalkoi. Egyptian texts measured grain in artabas, chous, and hin, while Greek texts measured grain in artabas, chous, and choinixes.[99]

There seems to have been an increase in the amount of silver in Egypt during the Third Intermediate, Saite, and Persian Periods. In New Kingdom Egypt, the value of a weight of gold relative to the same weight of silver was usually about 2:1.[100] After Alexander the Great conquered Egypt in 332 BCE, however, he minted gold coins in Egypt that were valued at 10:1 against silver coins.[101] This suggests that the value of gold in Egypt had increased relative to silver during the Third Intermediate, Saite, and Persian Periods. This could have occurred through a decrease in the amount of gold, making it scarcer and more valuable; but is more likely to be the result of an increase in the amount of silver, making it more common and less valuable. There is evidence for an increase in the silver supply in the many hoards of predominantly Greek silver coins dating to the Saite and Persian Periods that have been found in Egypt, presumably as result of trade with Greece.

Media of Exchange: Gold, silver, and bronze coins were minted in Ptolemaic Egypt, and silver and bronze coins were certainly used as media of exchange, probably to the exclusion of the lumps of silver used in the Saite and Persian Periods. Stray silver and copper coins are frequently found in archaeological excavations, suggesting that they were used as media of exchange in day-to-day transactions rather than as stores of wealth, and the small denominations of some silver and copper coins suggests the same. The supply of coinage undoubtedly increased during the Ptolemaic Period, but the demand for payment in coinage by the state also increased, and Von Reden has argued persuasively that the coinage supply was unable to keep pace, requiring the use of many different kinds of credit to stretch the coinage supply. Hard wheat, emmer wheat, barley, and vetch were also accepted media of exchange, but primarily for payment of agricultural taxes, and for repayment of grain loans. The state sometimes paid nominally money salaries partly in kind, and the temples regularly paid salaries in kind.

Stores of Wealth: Egyptian coin hoards again illustrate the use of coins as stores of wealth in Ptolemaic Egypt. Sixteen coin hoards containing more than 16,329 coins are known from the beginning of the early Ptolemaic Period (332–264 BCE).[102] Twenty coin hoards containing more than 1,295 coins are known from the end of the early Ptolemaic Period (264–200 BCE).[103] Seven coin hoards containing more than 539 coins are known from the middle Ptolemaic Period (200–118 BCE).[104] Sixteen coin hoards containing 2,210 coins are known from the late Ptolemaic Period (118–30 BCE).[105] This is a total of fifty-nine coin hoards containing over 20,373 coins, a considerable increase over the preceding Saite and Persian Periods, from which thirty-one coin hoards are known containing over 8,412 coins. However, the vast majority of these hoards date to the early Ptolemaic Period, suggesting that there may have been a decrease in the availability of coinage in the late Ptolemaic Period.

Again, the very existence of these hoards suggests that one use of these coins was passive storage of wealth. In contrast to the hoards, however, increasing numbers of stray coins found in archaeological excavations argues for their increasing circulation in exchange for commodities and services. The denominations of coins available in Ptolemaic Egypt also give some insight into the use of coinage. There was a full range of gold coins, large denomination silver tetradrachms, small denomination silver coins, and bronze coins. This suggests that the economy was more monetized than in the Saite and Persian Periods, and that coinage was used for a wide range of transactions by all levels of society.

Credit: Some scholars have distinguished between credit for investment and credit for consumption, and have argued that only the former is evidence for economic rationality.[106] In fact, credit for investment and credit for consumption are both perfectly economically rational responses to a lack of liquidity or a shortage of coinage. Indeed, outside of subsistence economies, some sort of credit for consumption is virtually required for occupations with cyclical variations in income, such as agriculture. However, Von Reden has argued persuasively that shortage of coinage was endemic in Ptolemaic Egypt. The Ptolemies did increase the supply of coinage in Egypt, but they also increased the demand for payment in coinage, requiring the extensive use of a wide variety of credit to free up the limited supplies of coinage.[107]

Formal loans of both grain and money are well attested in Ptolemaic Egypt. Von Reden argues that the Ptolemies developed a legal infrastructure that protected creditors by expediting execution, and protected debtors by limiting interest on cash loans, and thus encouraged formal lending by lowering transaction costs.[108] The interest rate for grain loans was 50 percent due after the next harvest, the same as in the preceding Late Third Intermediate, Saite, and Persian Periods. The maximum interest rate for money loans seems to have been 30 percent per year (2.5 percent per month) until the end of the reign of Ptolemy II, and 24 percent per year (2 percent per month) thereafter.[109] Both rates were a considerable decrease from 100 percent per year (in one case)[110] or 100 percent per six months (in one case)[111] in the Late Third Intermediate, Saite, and Persian Periods. Higher value formal loans were usually based on written contracts, and were often secured by mortgaging real estate. Lower value formal loans were probably often based on oral agreements, and were secured by pledges or by third party guarantees.[112]

Many formal loans, however, were actually embedded in other transactions, and may have been intended to generate liquidity. Formal loans that were secured by sales of mortgaged real estate could become prepayments for purchase of the real estate. Formal loans could also be combined with leases of real estate to provide prepayments of rent (often called prodomatic or antichretic leases). Formal loans could also be combined with future commodity sales to provide prepayments for the commodities.[113] Furthermore, many transactions involved credit without formal loans. Sales of commodities on credit and prepayment for commodities were common.[114] Many labor contracts also involved prepayment of salaries, so that the contractors could in turn prepay subcontractors.[115] These informal credit transactions often took place in patronage relationships, which served to secure them.[116]

Finally, Von Reden has argued that while the Ptolemaic system of royal banks and their local branches was meant to collect taxes on behalf of the royal treasury, it was also meant to keep coinage in circulation locally, and not simply to siphon it all off to Alexandria. The annual tax payments to royal banks and their branches were underwritten and guaranteed by tax farmers, so that the banks could pay salaries in advance of the tax payments, thereby allowing individuals to pay their taxes.[117] Ptolemaic banks did not, however, become independent sources of credit for private individuals. Royal banks and private banks did hold individual deposits and accounts, and did make loans and payments to individuals, but these individuals were often state officials and their clients, or tax farmers and their employees.[118]

REDISTRIBUTIVE NETWORKS

The Ptolemies used royal granaries and banks to receive and disburse state revenues in kind and in money, and a variety of high officials were responsible for authorizing and tracking outpayments. Disbursements often provided salaries for local officials, soldiers, and police. The state, however, increasingly contracted out to private entrepreneurs much processing and transportation of commodities that previously would have been done by gangs and crews directly salaried by the state institutions. Temples continued to manage redistributive networks, though they were increasingly dependent on the state for revenue collection. The Ptolemies were able to do this with the help of improved documentation, discussed previously, which gave them greater accountability and control over their local agents.[119]

Royal Granaries: The Ptolemies inherited from the Saites and Persians a system for documenting and transporting harvest taxes in grain, which kept track of grain deposited in local granaries so that surpluses could be transported as needed. The lack of detailed information about the Saite and Persian system, however, makes it difficult to determine the degree to which the Ptolemies modified it. In the Ptolemaic Period, one or more grain accountants (*sitologoi*) and a checking scribe (*antigrapheus*) representing the royal scribe usually administered a granary (Gk. *thēsauros*, Dem. *pꜣ rꜣ*). These officials held long-term appointments typical of state officials.[120] In the Fayum, several village granaries (*thēsauroi*) were often treated as branches of a district granary (*ergastērion*). The grain accountants (*sitologoi*) and checking scribe (*antigrapheus*) were attached to the district granary (*ergastērion*), rather than to the individual village granaries (*thēsauroi*).[121] A provincial grain accountant (*sitologos*) kept track of grain stocks in the village and district granaries, and determined from which ones outpayments and transfers should be made, including the annual transfer of a portion of the harvest tax to Alexandria.[122] Local granaries thus could apparently serve as branches of district and provincial granaries, and ultimately also of a single dispersed royal granary, both for tax collection and other inpayments, and for outpayments.

The local granaries were filled primarily through the collection of harvest taxes. The grain accountants often issued tax receipts to taxpayers in Upper Egypt, and occasionally in the Fayum as well.[123] The grain received as harvest taxes could then be paid out locally, as loans of seed grain for local farmers, as the grain or bread portions (*sitometria*) of salaries for local officials, garrison soldiers, and police, or as subventions (*syntaxeis*) for local temples. Grain could also be transferred from one local granary to another, if local outpayments exceeded local inpayments, or more often from local granaries to the royal granaries in Alexandria. Most transfers were made by ship. Such outpayments and transfers usually required a provincial official, either a manager (*oikonomos*) or later a governor (*stratēgos*), to issue orders for payment to the provincial and local granary accountants, and to the royal and local checking scribes who countersigned the orders.[124] In the case of transfers by ship, the person in charge of the ship (*nauklēros*) also issued a kind of written loading receipt known as a *nauklēros*-receipt to the delivering grain accountant. The delivering grain accountant retained these orders and receipts, to adjust their accounts.[125] Such transfers probably also required the delivering grain accountant to issue a written loading receipt for the receiving grain accountant, and sometimes a duplicate receipt for a superior. The receiving grain accountant and his superior kept these receipts, to adjust their accounts, and consequently they are never found together with the orders and receipts for the delivering grain accountant.[126]

A few ancient references hint at the quantity of harvest tax revenues in kind collected in Egypt.[127] Jerome gave Ptolemy II's annual income as 1.5 million artabas of grain,[128] which is usually thought to be too low. Aurelius Victor wrote that Egypt supplied 6 million artabas of grain under the Emperor Augustus,[129] while the Emperor Justinian gave the annual wheat assessment of Egypt as 8 million artabas.[130]

Royal Banks: The Ptolemies also inherited a system for documenting and transporting taxes in money from the Saites and Persians, though in the Saite and Persian Periods money taxes were limited to sales taxes and burial taxes collected by temples and customs duties collected by the state. In contrast, the Ptolemies introduced widespread state taxes in money,[131] and therefore they greatly modified the Saite and Persian system. The Ptolemies initially used a network of local treasury or tax offices (*logeutēria*) to collect taxes in money. These were probably later integrated into a network of royal banks that appeared around the middle of the reign of Ptolemy II. The royal banks in each province functioned as dispersed branches of the royal treasury. State taxes and other revenues were deposited into separate treasury accounts, and state employees were paid out of these accounts.[132] In addition, however, many royal banks also accepted private accounts, deposits, and withdrawals, made transfers from one account to another, and provided credit or loans.[133]

It is usually assumed that the institutional models for the Ptolemaic royal banks were Classical Greek public chests or treasuries and private banks. Claire Préaux and Jean Bingen argued that Ptolemies must have introduced banking from Greece to Egypt, because they believed that banking required coinage and that the Egyptians had no coinage before Alexander.[134] Raymond Bogaert also maintained that Ptolemaic royal banks were based on Greek models, though he admitted that the Egyptians used imported Greek coins, locally produced imitations, and some local issues already in the fifth and fourth centuries BCE.[135] In the previous chapter, however, it was argued that weighed silver bullion and scrap or *Hacksilber* functioned much like coinage long before and after the first Greek coins were imported and imitated in Egypt. It was also argued that the Saites and the Persians had a system for collecting some taxes and paying some salaries in silver, as well as a network of branch granaries, which could also have inspired the Ptolemaic royal banks. Indeed, Friedrich Preisigke has observed that the administrative systems of the royal and later public banks in Ptolemaic and Roman Egypt showed many similarities to the administrative systems of royal and later public granaries.[136] If Ptolemaic royal banks were a purely Greek institution transplanted to Egypt, one might not expect to find such similarities to traditional Egyptian institutions like granaries.

There were three types of royal banks in Ptolemaic Egypt, those located in provincial capitals, local banks, and tax offices (*logeutēria*) located in villages. A royal banker (*trapezitēs*, rarely *basilikos trapezitēs*) administered the royal bank (*basilikē trapeza*) located in each provincial capital. There were also local banks in some villages that served as branches of royal banks. Such banks could be called the bank (*trapeza*) of a named village, and their bankers could be described as the subordinate of (*ho para*) a royal banker. In addition to local banks, there were also tax offices (*logeutēria*) in some villages, which served as local branches of royal banks purely for tax collection purposes. The directors of tax offices (*logeutēria*) were also called bankers (*trapezitai*), and were also described as subordinates of (*ho para*) a royal banker or of a local banker.[137] In addition to royal banks, the Ptolemies also leased out the right to operate concessionary banks, and tolerated private banks. Concessionary banks were granted a monopoly on money-changing, and they flourished while the state demanded payment of taxes in silver rather than copper. However, private banks drove them out of business after the silver standard was abandoned in 210 BCE. These banks also accepted private accounts, deposits, and withdrawals, made transfers from one account to another, and provided credit or loans.[138]

The royal banks probably received most money tax payments. State officials associated with early treasury or tax offices (*logeutēria*) may have issued receipts for payments of the yoke tax, the capitation tax introduced at the end of the reign of Ptolemy I or at the beginning of the reign of Ptolemy II (c. 285 BCE). The receipts do not indicate the institutions at which the payments were made, but the scribes who signed them held long-term appointments, which were typical of state officials.[139] State officials associated with tax offices (*logeutēria*), local banks and royal banks probably received payments of the salt tax, the capitation tax that replaced the yoke tax in the middle of the reign of Ptolemy II (c. 263 BCE). Occasionally these officials issued receipts for the payment of these and other taxes.[140] More often, however, the state required the tax farmers who farmed these taxes to hire scribes to issue receipts, and these scribes held short-term annual appointments corresponding to the tax farming lease.[141] The money received by tax offices, local banks, and royal banks could be paid out locally, as the cash portions (*opsōnia*) of salaries for local officials, garrison soldiers, and police.[142] Money could also be transferred from tax offices and local banks to royal banks and from there to the royal treasury in Alexandria.[143] As with grain, these money outpayments and transfers required a provincial official, either a manager (*oikonomos*) or later a governor (*stratēgos*), to issue an order for payment to a banker,[144] and to a royal scribe who countersigned the order.[145] In some cases, the bankers required the recipients of outpayments to write receipts, perhaps because there was no order for payment.[146]

A few ancient sources provide figures for the money revenues of the Ptolemies, some or all of which may ultimately derive from records kept by the Ptolemies.[147] Jerome gave Ptolemy II's annual income from Egypt as 14,800 Ptolemaic talents or 12,000 Attic talents of silver, in addition to 1.5 million artabas of grain.[148] Diodorus wrote that the annual income of Ptolemy XII was 6,000 talents of silver,[149] while Strabo gave it as 12,500 talents according to a lost oration of Cicero.[150] The ancient sources do not specify what these numbers represent, however, so it is possible that both figures given for Ptolemy XII are correct. Preaux speculated that Diodorus omitted revenues from Alexandria, while Rostovtzeff suggested that Strabo gave the revenues in debased currency, and Diodorus their real value.[151]

Palaces, Officials, and Commodity Monopolies: In earlier periods, state salaries were predominantly paid in kind rather than in money, and consequently royal palaces and officials commissioned dependent institutions, gangs, crews, and individuals to process and transport commodities for future redistribution to state employees. In the Ptolemaic Period, however, state salaries were increasingly paid in money rather than in kind, and palaces no longer served as institutional state agents. Nonetheless, the state and its officials continued to commission individuals to process and transport commodities, now for sale as well as for redistribution to state employees. Sometimes there may have been little distinction between sale and redistribution, however, when the state provided employees with commodities instead of wages: it would have been easy for the state to book the distribution simultaneously as payment of wages and as payment for commodities.

State production and distribution of many commodities were subject to so-called monopolies, such as the oil monopoly (*elaikē*) described in Papyrus

Revenue Laws cols. 38–72, or the cloth monopoly (*othoniēra*) apparently described in cols. 87–107. The revenues generated by the sale of such commodities were farmed out at auction to the highest bidders in each district, much like taxes. The winning contractors then assumed the risk that revenues might be less than their bid, and any profit from revenues greater than their bid.[152]

The state and its officials, however, were heavily involved in the actual production and sale of the commodities. For example, the rules for the oil monopoly in Papyrus Revenue Laws specify that the oil seed harvest be bought from farmers at fixed prices (col. 39), and that the resulting oil be sold at fixed prices (col. 40). It indicates that the provincial manager pay set wages to the oil makers and set payments to the contractors according to the quantity of oil produced (col. 45), that he lock up the oil presses and other tools when not in use by the oil makers (col. 46), and that he make arrangements with the dealers and retailers to distribute and sell the oil produced (cols. 47–48). Finally, each month an auditor appointed by the provincial managers would balance the amounts paid for oil seed, the wages of the oil makers, the costs of jars, and transportation of the oil against the amounts received for the oil produced, and the contractors would receive their payments from the profits (cols. 54–55). All of these payments were presumably made to and from the account of the oil monopoly contract at a royal bank.[153]

The state and its officials were also heavily involved in the distribution of the commodities. Demotic papyri Cairo CG 31219 and 31225, from Tebtynis and dated to Years 17 and 24 of Ptolemy III (230 and 223 BCE), are letters from oil dealers to provincial managers confirming receipt of quantities of oil to sell, and promising payment to a royal bank of the price of the oil within five days of request.[154] Demotic papyri Lille II 50 and 51, from Ghoran and dated to Year 24 of Ptolemy III (223 BCE), are letters from individuals to provincial managers providing payment surety bonds for oil dealers, promising to pay part of the price of the oil to a royal bank if the oil dealers failed to do so.[155] Finally, numerous Demotic ostraca from Thebes in the third century BCE contain receipts for the price of oil paid by consumers, presumably issued by oil dealers.[156]

The rules for the cloth monopoly in Papyrus Revenue Laws are poorly preserved, but other sources indicate that the state was involved in cloth production and distribution in a manner similar to the oil monopoly. Greek papyri Hibeh I 67 and 68, from El-Hiba and dated circa 228 BCE, are orders to a royal banker to pay weavers at Ankyronpolis (El-Hiba) fixed prices in money for the cloth that they had woven.[157] Greek papyrus Tebtunis III 703, from Tebtynis and dated to the late third century BCE, contains instructions from a chief finance minister to a provincial manager, and lines 87–117 concern the cloth monopoly.[158] The provincial manager is told that the weavers should meet their quotas, that they should be charged fixed prices for any shortfalls, and that the looms should be locked up when not in use. Finally, Demotic papyri Cairo CG 31161, 31216, and 31246–31248, from Tebtynis and dated to Year 22 of Ptolemy III (225 BCE), are letters from cloth dealers confirming receipt of quantities of cloth, with subscriptions confirming payment in money.[159]

Royal Dockyards: The Ptolemies built a massive fleet after Ptolemy II's defeats in the First Syrian War (274–271 BCE), and subsequently Ptolemy II and III were able to successfully contest with the Seleucids and the Macedonians for control of the Eastern Mediterranean and the Aegean. Athenaeus records that Ptolemy II possessed a fleet of 336 warships, which were rated according to the number of banks of oars they possessed. It included 112 larger warships including two "thirties," one "twenty," four "thirteens," two "twelves," fourteen "elevens," thirty "nines," thirty-seven "sevens," five "sixes," and seventeen "fives." There were also 224 "fours," "threes," and *triemioliai*. Athenaeus states that Ptolemy II also sent more than 4,000 ships to the islands and the other cities that he ruled and Libya, so the 336 warships appear to have been the Alexandrian fleet, exclusive of ships stationed elsewhere or belonging to allies.[160] The cost of maintaining this fleet would have been enormous. If the 112 larger warships employed 300 men each, and the 224 smaller warships 200 men each, this fleet would have required at least 78,400 crewmen, and possibly many more. Assuming that they were paid one drachma a day, they would have cost at least 4,800 talents a year just in salaries. Alternatively, if each ship cost approximately 10,000 drachmas a month (an attested figure), the fleet would have cost 6,700 talents a year.[161] These figures are comparable to those required for the Ptolemaic army, and together the fleet and army would have consumed much of the Ptolemies' money revenues during the reigns of Ptolemy II and III.[162] This level of spending was not sustainable, however, and was not maintained after Ptolemy III's victories in the Third Syrian War (246–241 BCE). The Ptolemaic fleet was probably built and maintained at least in part in the royal dockyards at Alexandria. Consequently, these dockyards must have been a major source of redistributed revenues to shipwrights, sailors, and oarsmen during the reigns of Ptolemy II and III,[163] which probably contributed significantly to the spectacular growth of the then young city, together with redistributed revenues from the royal court and palaces established there under Ptolemy I.

Military and Police: During the Ptolemaic Period, much of the army still consisted of reserve soldiers who supported themselves when off duty by cultivating plots of land received as rewards or inheritances. An increasingly large proportion of the army, however, consisted of standing soldiers who regularly received state redistribution, which was largely paid in money rather than in kind.

The Ptolemies maintained a number of standing soldiers as elite troops and bodyguards at the royal court.[164] The royal *agēma*-infantry (*agēma para tois basileusin*) numbered 3,000 at the Battle of Raphia (217 BCE). The household infantry (*therapeia*), the guard at the court (*phylakeia peri tēn aulēn*), and the picked *machimoi* at the court (*epilektoi machimoi peri tēn aulēn*) were probably comparable in number to the royal *agēma*-infantry. Their officers were known as chief bodyguards (*archisōmatophylakes*) and bodyguards (*sōmatophylakes*), and they included swordbearers (*machairophoroi*) and spearbearers (*lonchophoroi*). The cavalry at the court (*hippeis peri tēn aulēn*) numbered 700 at the Battle of Raphia. Together these elite troops and bodyguards may have represented as much as a tenth of all of the soldiers available to the Ptolemies.

The Ptolemies also maintained a number of standing soldiers at garrisons. In the early Ptolemaic Period, the main garrisons were located at Alexandria, Pelusium, and Elephantine. In the late Ptolemaic Period, however, after the Great Theban Revolt (205–186 BCE), garrisons were located throughout Middle and Upper Egypt. These garrisons were probably manned with recently recruited mercenaries and reserve soldiers who served in rotation.[165] The early Ptolemies preferred to recruit Macedonian and Greek veterans with international experience, but the later Ptolemies increasingly preferred to recruit untrained Egyptians. Before the Battle of Raphia (217 BCE), Ptolemy IV recruited 11,000 Greek, Thracian, and Galatian infantry mercenaries from abroad, and 2,000 Greek cavalry mercenaries. He also locally recruited 23,000 Egyptian and Libyan infantry, and 2,300 Libyan cavalry. Together, these recent recruits represented half of the Ptolemaic army at Raphia.

Much of the Ptolemaic army consisted of reserve soldiers who supported themselves when off duty. These were usually former standing soldiers and mercenaries and their descendants. When they were demobilized, they were often rewarded with hereditary land allotments (*klēroi*) to buy their loyalty, to give them a means of support, and to make them reserve soldiers or cleruchs (*klērouchoi*).[166] The early Ptolemies offered Macedonian and Greek veterans large land allotments to obtain and retain their loyalty as reserve soldiers. Cavalry received allotments of one hundred, eighty, or seventy arouras, while infantry received thirty or twenty-five arouras. In contrast, they offered Egyptian infantry small allotments of ten, seven, or five arouras, because there was little competition for their services. Terminology reflected these ethnic distinctions. Foreign holders of allotments (*klēroi*) were called cleruchs (*klērouchoi*), while Egyptian holders were called *machimoi*. The later Ptolemies, however, increasingly recruited untrained Egyptians, including many of Greek descent, and offered them medium-sized land allotments as reserve soldiers, in part because they were less likely to transfer their loyalty, and in part because there was less land to give. New cavalry recruits were offered between seventy and ten arouras depending on their status, new infantry recruits between ten and five arouras, and policemen between twenty-four and ten arouras. Terminology increasingly reflected status rather than ethnic distinctions. Privileged cavalry were called *katoikoi hippeis* and unprivileged cavalry *machimoi hippeis*, while *machimoi* became a term for infantry.[167] At the Battle of Raphia (217 BCE), Ptolemy IV had 36,000 infantry cleruchs, including 3,000 *agēma*-infantry, and 700 cavalry cleruchs, consisting of the cavalry at the court. Together, these cleruchs represented just under half of the Ptolemaic army at Raphia.

All of these soldiers received state redistribution while on duty, so the cost of maintaining an army on campaign would have been enormous. Polybius records that Ptolemy IV's army at the Battle of Raphia (217 BCE) consisted of 75,000 men. There were 70,000 infantry, including 11,000 recently hired Greek, Thracian, and Galatian mercenaries and 23,000 Egyptians and Libyans, as well as 36,000 cleruchs. There were also 5,000 cavalry, including 2,000 recently hired Greek mercenaries and 2,300 Libyans, and 700 cleruchs.[168] If each infantryman was paid one drachma a day, each cavalryman two drachmas, and their officers (about 1 percent of the troops) ten drachmas, this army would have cost at least 5,300 talents a year just in salaries. The Ptolemies did not conduct major land campaigns every year, however, so normally the cost of the military would have been less. Most cleruchs did not have to be paid except for elite troops and bodyguards, and there would have been fewer recent recruits except to serve in garrisons, so the annual cost may have been around 2,000 talents a year in salaries.[169]

State Employees: The Ptolemaic state supported large numbers of personnel through redistribution, in the form of salaries and wages for state officials, soldiers on duty, workers in commodity monopolies, and other employees. The Ptolemaic state typically paid salaries and wages in a combination of money (*opsōnia* or *misthoi*) and grain or bread (*sitometria*), and frequently also in oil (*elaiometria*), clothing (*himatismos*), and wine. Payments in kind were often accounted in money and deducted from money wages, however, blurring the distinction between sale and redistribution of commodities.[170] State officials were expected to support themselves and their immediate subordinates from their salaries, as well as purchase office supplies such as papyri.[171] Apparently they were subject to audits, because they frequently kept records of payments and expenses in both money and kind.[172] Soldiers received salaries only when on duty, but they usually received grants of land to support themselves off duty after their first tour of duty. Workers in commodity monopolies were paid only during their contracts for the commodities that they produced. Some workers were paid in advance and shortfalls in production were treated as debts.[173]

State officials, from the chief finance minister (*dioikētēs*) to royal scribes (*basilikoi grammateis*) and village scribes (*kōmogrammateis*), were also frequently assigned vacant lands to bring under cultivation and provide the state with their harvest taxes. Payment of these harvest taxes was a condition of holding office.[174] In the third century BCE, the Ptolemies frequently assigned large gift estates (*dōreai*) to high officials for the duration of their service,[175] and to "ten-thousand aroura men" (*myriarouroi*, Egyptian *ꜥ3-n-10,000*).[176] These officials were expected to develop their estates through irrigation projects, by founding and building towns to attract and house settlers, by hiring agricultural labor to work the newly cultivable land or by renting it to tenant farmers, and by organizing state monopolies to supply the settlers with various commodities, so that when the state reclaimed the gift estates at the end of their recipients' careers, they would be more valuable than when they were assigned. The recipients of these large gift estates tended to employ existing state redistributive networks. State taxes and other revenues were paid into the local branches of the state granaries and royal banks, and the estate holders used them for irrigation and construction projects, for seed loans to tenant farmers, and for the salaries of local officials, hired agricultural labor, and workers in commodity monopolies,[177] both in money (*opsōnia*) and in kind (*sitometria*).[178] Such large gift estates became much less common after the third century BCE, however, presumably because most of the land that could be developed in this way already had been.[179]

Temples: As in previous periods, the Ptolemies continued to use temples as their institutional agents in the redistributive economy, particularly for older revenue sources such as sales taxes in money and harvest taxes in kind. Admittedly, the Ptolemies transferred responsibility for collecting some revenues away from the temples to the state, but they usually compensated the temples with similar revenues from the state. For example, they initially allowed the temples to survey and collect the harvest taxes from agricultural lands in their temple endowments, in return for giving the state a share of the harvest taxes. Later, however, they assigned to state agents the responsibility for surveying and collecting harvest taxes from temple lands, from which a share was given to the temples. Similarly, they initially allowed the temples and their associated notaries to collect the sales taxes on property transfers, but later required the sales taxes to be paid to the state banking system. Furthermore, the Ptolemies allowed the temples to retain responsibility for collecting some revenues. For example, the temples managed the necropoles, and collected fees from mortuary priests in return for allowing them to build tombs and inter individuals there. Thus the Ptolemies appear to have been primarily interested in controlling revenue collection, rather than in suppressing the temple redistributive networks.

Indeed, the Ptolemies had several reasons to maintain the temple redistributive networks. Perhaps most importantly, temple revenues provided offerings to the gods of the temples, which then reverted to the temples and their priests to serve as their incomes. Maintenance of these offerings was one of the ideological justifications for Egyptian kingship, and maintenance of the incomes of the priests ensured their continued ideological support for the Ptolemaic monarchy. In contrast to state salaries, however, priestly incomes seem to have been paid primarily in kind. The state therefore permitted the temples to continue to produce a number of commodities for redistribution to priests and temple employees, such as linen, oil, and beer. The state forbade anyone to sell these commodities, however, presumably to avoid competition with the state commodity monopolies.

Papyrus Revenue Laws, cols. 51–52:[180]

When they wish to manufacture sesame oil in the temples, they shall call in the manager of the contract and the agent of the provincial manager (*oikonomos*) and the checking-scribe (*antigrapheus*) and make the oil in their presence; and they shall manufacture within two months the amount which they declared that they would consume in the year. But the castor oil which they use they shall obtain from the contractors at the fixed price.

The provincial manager and the checking-scribe shall write down the amounts of castor oil and sesame oil used by each temple and send the list to the king, and shall also give one to the chief finance minister (*dioikētēs*). It shall not be lawful to sell to any person any of (52) the oil manufactured for the temples; whoever does so shall be deprived [of the oil], and shall in addition forfeit [100 drachmas] for each *metrētēs*, and for more or less in proportion.

Despite this regulation, priests often leased their positions and their incomes for cash payments, especially in the second and first centuries BCE.[181] The Ptolemies also continued to exact some levies on temple commodity production. This can be seen in the Memphis Decree of Ptolemy V dated to 196 BCE, which capped or abolished some of these levies and remitted back payments, primarily for the state's share of linen produced by temple personnel. Curiously, the decree also remitted the back payments of the state share of harvest taxes from temple lands, for which the state was now responsible for collecting.

The Memphis Decree of Year 9 of Ptolemy V (196 BCE), Rosetta, lines 9–10:[182]

Moreover, he ordered concerning the priests that they should not pay their tax on becoming priests above what they used to pay up to Year 1 under his father; he released the people (10) [who hold] the offices of the temples from the voyage they used to make to the Residence of Alexandria each year; he ordered that no rower should be impressed into service; and he renounced the two-thirds share of the fine linen that used to be made in the temples for the Treasury.

The Memphis Decree of Year 9 of Ptolemy V (196 BCE), Rosetta, lines 16–18:[183]

> He remitted the arrears (17) that were due to the King from the temples up to Year 9, and amounted to a large total of money and grain; likewise the value of the fine linen that was due from the temples from what is made for the Treasury, and the verification fees(?) of what had been made up to that time; moreover, he ordered concerning the artaba of wheat per aroura of land, which used to be collected from the fields of the endowment, and likewise (18) for the wine per aroura of land from the vineyards of the god's endowments, he renounced them.

The Ptolemies thus had multiple incentives to encourage efficient management of the temple redistributive networks. The temple manager (*mr-šn*, Gr. *lesōnis*) was now held personally responsible for managing temple activities and revenues, if that was not already the case in earlier periods. If the temple failed to raise enough revenues to make the requisite offerings to the gods and subsequently fully pay the incomes of the priests, and to deliver the required revenues to the king, then the temple manager was expected to make up the difference from his own possessions. This can be seen in the Archive of Milon from Elephantine, consisting of twenty-two Greek and ten Demotic papyri dating from 225 to 222 BCE. Previously, several members of the same priestly family had served as temple manager of the temple of Horus in Edfu, during which time there had been deficits in the collection of land taxes and linen production. The archive reveals that the Greek official Milon then began to auction off the property of the priestly family in order to recover the shortfalls in revenue.[184]

Private Funerary Endowments: In the Ptolemaic Period, numerous private funerary endowments are known from the private archives of mortuary priests. These archives frequently refer to inheriting and even buying and selling tombs and mummies, which was shorthand for transferring the funerary cult service obligations for these tombs and mummies as well as the rations and incomes received for performing said service obligations.

The private archives of mortuary priests do occasionally refer explicitly to the rations and incomes associated with tombs and mummies. The inheritance contract Papyrus BM 10827 (Andrews 14), line 4, from Thebes, dated to Year 13 of Ptolemy II (270 BCE), donates a number of tombs and mummies "and their rations of Osiris."[185] The account Ostracon Universität Zürich 1869 (*O. Taxes* 2, 156), from Thebes, dated to the third century BCE, is a list of rations or loaves of bread given to several mortuary priests.[186]

The private archives of mortuary priests never refer to the actual revenue sources, however. Presumably revenue sources were now exclusively donated to temples, and were no longer placed directly in the care of the mortuary priests, as was frequently done in the preceding Saite and Persian Periods. Records of private donations of revenue sources to temples to establish such funerary cults have not survived, however. Donation stelae were no longer used, and temple archives are rare.

The private archives of mortuary priests do occasionally preserve contracts appointing the mortuary priests to serve a particular tomb. Prior to the Ptolemaic Period, labor or service contracts were rarely governed by written contracts, so these service contracts usually adapt traditional property transfer contracts with additional clauses governing the mortuary priests' service of the tomb in question. Different types of property transfer contracts were adapted, depending on who supplied the tomb, and how.

Papyrus BM 10240 (Reich), from Thebes, dated to Year 20 of Ptolemy III (228 BCE), is one such appointment of choachyte contract, in which the choachyte supplied the tomb and retained ownership.[187] The initial clause is "You are my choachyte of this tomb," followed by the identification of the tomb by specifying its neighbors, and the fact that the choachyte had previously purchased it. The second contractor is then said to be the choachyte of the aforementioned tomb for ninety-nine years, along with his children and grandchildren until eternity. The second contractor may not place another mummy in the tomb without the permission of the first contractor, while the first contractor may not appoint another choachyte to the tomb, subject to a penalty of twenty silver deben or 100 staters. There is other evidence that choachytes sometimes supplied the tombs for their clients. The burial plot receipt O. BM 66383 (Andrews 13), was issued to one Harsiesis son of Amenothes, who is known from P. BM 10240 (Reich) to have been a choachyte. The burial plot receipt says "that he built for the exalted one Psenthotes," presumably a client of his.[188]

Papyrus Philadelphia 24, from Thebes, dated to Year 21 of Ptolemy III (227 BCE), is another appointment of choachyte contract, adapted from a traditional lease contract, in which the choachyte's client supplied the tomb by leasing it to the choachyte.[189] The initial clause is "I have leased to you this chapel upon the necropolis of Djeme in the west of Thebes," followed by the identification of the tomb by specifying its neighbors and the fact that the choachyte's client had previously purchased it from the manager (*mr-šn*) of the temple of Amun, who made him a lease (*sḥn*) for it. Then, instead of the regular series of clauses giving the rights and obligations of the contractors as lessor and lessee, there are a series of clauses giving the rights and obligations of the contractors as choachyte and client, similar to those in Papyrus BM 10240 (Reich), except that the penalty is ten silver deben or fifty staters. There is evidence that many contracts between choachytes and their clients were leases. In P. Louvre 2429bis (*Schreibertradition* 5), dated to Egyptian year 13 of Ptolemy I, Pchorchonsis son of Panas sells all of his property to his wife Neschonsis daughter of Teos, including "my occupation of choachyte of Hermonthis, concerning which the priests of Mont lord of Hermonthis of the 4 phyles made a lease for me."[190] Similarly, in P. Louvre 2428 (*Schreibertradition* 108), dated to Egyptian year 8 of Ptolemy II, the same Pchorchonsis son of Panas gives up claim to all of his property in favor of his wife Neschonsis daughter of Teos, including "my occupation (as) choachyte of Hermonthis and the leases which were made for me in the temple (and) the town."[191]

Papyrus BM 10388 (Andrews 2), from Thebes, dated to Year 24 of Ptolemy III (223 BCE), is yet another appointment of choachyte contract, adapted from a traditional sales contract, in which the choachyte supplied the tomb and sold it to the client.[192] The initial clause is "You have satisfied my heart with the money of the price of ...," followed by the identification of the plot by specifying its neighbors, and the fact that the choachyte had previously purchased the plot from the god Amun. Then comes the regular series of clauses giving the rights and obligations of the contractors as buyer and seller, followed by a series of clauses giving the rights and obligations of the contractors as choachyte and client, similar to those in Papyrus BM 10240 (Reich), except that the penalty is ten silver deben or fifty staters.

EXCHANGES

Rostovtzeff and Preaux once argued largely on the basis of Greek papyri from the Ptolemaic Fayum such as the Papyrus Revenue Laws, the Menches Archive, or the Zenon Archive, that the Ptolemaic kings claimed ownership of all agricultural land in Egypt. They granted the temporary use of some land to temples as temple land (*hiera gē*), some to officials as gift estates (*dōreai*), some to cleruchs (*klērouchoi*) as cleruchic land (*klērouchikē gē*), and leased the rest as royal land (*basilikē gē*) to the predominantly Egyptian population, which became known as royal farmers (*basilikoi geōrgoi*). However, as the true owners of the agricultural land, the Ptolemaic kings decided which crops would be sown where, and received a considerable share of the harvest as taxes.[193]

It is now believed, however, because of Demotic papyri from the Nile Valley, that outside of the Fayum the proportion of royal land (*basilikē gē*) was relatively small, and the proportion of temple land (*hiera gē*) relatively large. These papyri also show that temple land was usually treated as private property with a tax obligation to the temples, rather than as institutionally cultivated land. Furthermore, reexamination of Greek papyri from the Fayum and elsewhere have revealed that cleruchic land (*klērouchikē gē*) was effectively also treated as private property with a tax obligation to the state, and only rarely reverted to the state. Consequently, a very significant proportion of agricultural land in Ptolemaic Egypt was effectively private property over which the state had relatively little direct control.[194] As long as the effective owners of such property fulfilled their harvest tax and service obligations to the state or temples, the effective owners were free to dispose of their property or its surplus agricultural produce as they wished, either through redistribution or through market exchange. Similarly, individuals owed personal and occupational taxes and service obligations to the state, but once they paid them they were free to dispose of their surplus labor as they liked.

At least some of this privately owned property and labor was distributed through exchange rather than redistribution. Redistributive networks rarely distribute goods and services exactly where they are desired, in precisely the quantities desired. Consequently, there is a general tendency for redistributive networks to generate or feed into exchange networks, which further redistribute the goods and services. Furthermore, in Ptolemaic Egypt redistributive networks frequently operated in money rather than in kind. This would have increased the interdependence of redistribution and exchange, because individuals had to exchange goods and services to obtain money for taxes to the state, and they had to exchange state payments in money to obtain desired goods and services. There is less direct evidence from Ptolemaic Egypt for exchange than for redistribution, however, because the state did not document exchanges as thoroughly as redistribution. There is very little direct evidence for relatively low value property transfers, because such transfers were rarely documented, but there is some direct evidence for relatively high value property transfers, because the state encouraged local documentation and helped enforce the transfers.

Marketplaces: Marketplaces are convenient locations for exchanges, because they bring together potential buyers and sellers, and allow them to compare wares and exchange offers. Riverbanks probably continued to serve as marketplaces in the Ptolemaic Period, as they had in the New Kingdom, though there are no tomb scenes or ship's logs to confirm this. There are, however, numerous references to ships owned by institutions such as temples or by royal family members,[195] as well as to privately owned ships.[196] Most of the references concern the transportation of grain taxes and monopolized commodities,[197] but the ships could also have carried private goods, especially outside of the harvest tax season. This is supported by receipts for freight charges or transportation fees (Greek *porthmis*, *porthmika*, or *diagōgē*; Demotic *hm.t*),[198] which suggest that ships transported cargos for exchange and not just for redistribution, since taxes on the transportation of taxes would be redundant even by Ptolemaic standards.

Exchanges do not have to take place in marketplaces, however. For example, the Ptolemaic state usually used auctions to sell confiscated properties,[199] tax-farming contracts, and the products of production monopolies of commodities like oil or cloth. In contrast, the operators of retail monopolies of oil and cloth employed itinerant retailers to take small quantities directly to potential buyers, rather than wait for them to visit a market place. Operators of combined production and retail monopolies of bulky commodities like beer, however, sold their wares at their breweries due to the cost of transportation. Likewise, real estate markets existed without a physical marketplace.

Land: Evidence for land ownership and transfer in the Ptolemaic Period (332–30 BCE) primarily comes from two sources, namely the Fayum and Upper Egypt. Early studies of the Ptolemaic economy, notably those of Preaux and Rostovtzeff, relied heavily on Greek textual evidence from the Fayum, and particularly from the archive of Zenon, manager of the large gift-estate of Apollonios, who was probably the architect of Ptolemy II's tax reforms.[200] They were also influenced by the rhetoric of Classical Greek authors such as Herodotos and Isocrates, who claimed that Near Eastern monarchs treated their kingdoms as their personal property and their subjects as slaves, in contrast to free private-property owning Greek citizens. Extrapolating from these sources, Preaux and Rostovtzeff argued that the early Ptolemies, like the Persians and the Egyptian kings before them, treated Egypt as their personal property. The native Egyptians were reduced to landless tenants on royal land, while Greek cleruchs and officials were generously granted the use but not the ownership of their cleruchic land and gift-estates during their lifetimes. Only the weakness of the later Ptolemies led to the emergence of effectively private property in Egypt, which in turn led to the rise of a bourgeois middle class, free markets, and market forces, based on the models developed earlier in Greece.[201]

Subsequent studies of the economy of Ptolemaic Egypt, notably by Manning, have used the Egyptian sources from Upper Egypt to complement the picture provided by Greek textual sources from the Fayum. These Egyptian sources show that the land held by traditional Egyptian temples could in fact be inherited, bought, and sold by private individuals, and should be considered as effectively private property, albeit with tax obligations to temples. Similarly, cleruchic land should also be considered as effectively private property, with an obligation to serve in the army when called up, and restrictions on the inheritance and transfer of the land to those unable to serve. Thus only holders of royal land should be described as landless tenant farmers. Consequently, Manning has argued that there was a much lower proportion of royal land and much higher proportion of temple land in the Nile Valley than in the Fayum.[202] Unfortunately, the only quantitative source for the proportion of private land (including both clerouchic land and temple land) to royal land in the Ptolemaic Period comes from the Fayum, where it was approximately 1:1. However, in the succeeding Roman Period there are quantitative sources for both the Nile Valley and the Fayum, and the proportion of private land to royal or public land was between 4:1 and 3:1 in the Nile Valley, and 1:1 in the Fayum.[203]

Monson has argued that at least some royal land in Ptolemaic Egypt was actually managed locally and semicommunally by villages, rather than centrally by the state as Rostovtzeff had assumed. Monson also suggested that there was more private land relative to semicommunal royal land in the Nile Valley than in the Fayum because the Nile Valley had been settled much longer than the recently reclaimed Fayum, and was consequently more densely populated, discouraging semicommunal land-holding.[204]

Houses: Evidence for house ownership and transfer in Ptolemaic Egypt is provided by numerous Demotic and Greek sale and inheritance contracts concerning houses and shares of houses. Partible inheritance frequently fragmented ownership of houses, resulting either in physical division of properties or in shared ownership of undivided properties. Both outcomes encouraged sales and other transfers as well as strategic marriages in order to reunite divided portions or dispersed shares of houses.[205] Some transfers and marriages probably required little or no money, but the sales taxes paid on some house sales suggest that they were cash transactions.[206]

Priestly Positions or Prebends: Shares of appointments in temples were sometimes transferred in the Ptolemaic Period, but the form of payment is rarely specified. For example, the Demotic and Greek archive of Totoes son of Smanres, dating from 194 BCE to 100 BCE, records several transfers of days of service in the temple of Hathor at Deir el-Medina and other chapels in western Thebes, together with their corresponding revenues.[207] Similarly, a group of Demotic papyri from Soknopaiou Nesos records four transfers of shares of service days in a chapel of Harpsenesis, dating between 122 BCE and 42 BCE.[208] Other documents that appear to record transfers of chapels or parts thereof may implicitly include their priestly appointments and revenues.[209] The archive of Amenothes called Zoilos son of Horos, dated from 198 BCE to 176 BCE, documents several transfers of parts of a sacred ibis catacomb in western Thebes,[210] while three Greek and Demotic wooden tags dating to 255 BCE may record an earlier state sale of a half share of the same sacred ibis catacomb for cash.[211] Temple priests sometimes also leased their days of service and their corresponding incomes in kind in return for cash payments.[212] Transfers of shares of appointments in private mortuary cults also occurred frequently. Such transfers were often described as donations, sales, and cessions of tombs or mummies, but there was an obligation to perform their cult in return for their revenues or incomes, usually implicit but sometimes explicit.[213]

ENTREPRENEURIAL ACTIVITIES

Goods and services may be redistributed or exchanged, but they may also be invested as capital and labor to produce other more desirable goods and services. The state engaged in a variety of entrepreneurial activities. There were military campaigns and paramilitary expeditions. There were also numerous infrastructure projects, and the production and sale of various commodities. The Ptolemies restricted the roles of temples in entrepreneurial activities, however, which were usually limited to production and distribution of commodities. Private entrepreneurs, on the other hand, were encouraged to share the risks of state production and distribution of commodities for a share of the potential profits.

Expeditions: The Ptolemies conducted major military campaigns, both by land in the Levant, and by sea in the Eastern Mediterranean. Initiating these military campaigns incurred additional costs beyond the regular redistributive costs of maintaining an army or navy. For example, cleruchs (*klērouchoi*) and salaried soldiers (*misthophoroi*) formed the core of Ptolemaic armies, but the Ptolemies always supplemented them with newly recruited mercenaries, and all of these had to be paid and supplied during the campaign.[214] In contrast, impressed merchant ships served primarily as transports, while the core of the Ptolemaic navies consisted of warships that had to be built or refitted specifically for a campaign, and whose crews had to be paid and supplied during the campaign.[215] These campaigns were therefore expensive, but if they were successful they also brought in revenues, both in the short and in the long term. Short-term revenues consisted of booty, as much as 1,500 silver talents after the capture of Seleucia and the sack of Antioch by Ptolemy III. Long-term revenues included taxes from provinces added to the Ptolemaic Empire, such as Cyprus, Cyrenaica, and Syro-Palestine, estimated to have been between 4,000 and 8,000 talents annually. It is these revenues that allow military campaigns to be considered "entrepreneurial."[216] The early Ptolemies also mounted paramilitary expeditions to the southern coast of the Red Sea to capture elephants for their armies. These expeditions required the construction of special ships (*elephantigoi*) to transport captured elephants back to ports on the Egyptian coast of the Red Sea.[217]

Foundations: The Ptolemies and their agents founded and refounded many settlements. I would argue that they frequently did so by establishing one or more redistributive institutions in the new settlements, such as garrisons of salaried soldiers (*misthophoroi*), or Egyptian temples, or even the royal court and dockyards in Alexandria. Such redistributive institutions guaranteed that the new settlements would have had an initial group of inhabitants with disposable incomes that could then attract other settlers. The foundations of some settlements may have also included land grants, particularly those in the Fayum, which would have attracted further agrarian settlers. Other settlements included harbor facilities, as at Alexandria and the Red Sea ports, which would have attracted merchant settlers. Most of these settlements, if successful, would have generated revenues for the state, which meant that the initial assignment of state revenues to redistributive institutions and infrastructural projects was a state entrepreneurial activity.

Alexandria: Alexander the Great is usually credited with founding Alexandria, though there is growing evidence that there were already some harbor facilities there before he arrived. The foundation flourished in part due to the establishment of the Ptolemaic court and royal dockyards there, and their redistributive networks. However, Alexandria also benefitted from several early Ptolemaic infrastructure projects, such as the breakwaters, the heptastadion linking Pharos Island with the city, and the harbors that they formed, not to mention the Pharos lighthouse, which together with the royal court made Alexandria a focus of international trade.[218]

The Fayum: The early Ptolemies are credited with reclaiming large amounts of land in the Fayum basin. They presumably built dikes to prevent the annual Nile flood from reaching the Fayum basin, in order to allow the level of Lake Moeris to fall to expose more cultivable land. They presumably also dug canals around the rim of the Fayum basin, to supply water that no longer arrived with the annual Nile flood. The Ptolemies then assigned the reclaimed land to various agents, either nomarchs or myriarourai, who were expected to develop it.[219] The Ptolemies then gave the land to officials as gift estates (*dōreai*) and to cleruchs (*klērouchoi*) as allotments (*klēroi*), or leased it to royal farmers (*basilikoi geōrgoi*). However, they may also have assigned some of the land as endowments for older temples, such as that of Isis-Hermouthis at Narmouthis (Medinet Madi), or to establish new temples to serve as nuclei for new settlements in reclaimed areas where there were no older settlements.[220]

The Nile Valley: Middle and Upper Egypt were densely populated in the Ptolemaic Period, so there was less scope for new foundations there than in other areas. Nonetheless, in Upper Egypt, Ptolemy I is credited with founding the city of Ptolemais Hermiou,[221] and the provincial governor (*stratēgos*) Boethos founded the city of Euergetis in the mid-second century BCE.[222] Furthermore, the Ptolemies also rebuilt or enlarged a number of temples in Upper Egypt, and after the Upper Egyptian Revolt of 205–186 BCE they established several garrisons of salaried soldiers there, of which Pathyris (Gebelein) is the best known.

Nubia: The Ptolemies conquered and controlled the northern portions of Lower Nubia known as the Dodekaschoinos or the Triakontaschoinos, though they lost control of them during the Upper Egyptian Revolt of 205–186 BCE, and possibly again toward the end of the Ptolemaic Period.[223] The Ptolemies founded several temples in Lower Nubia, at Debod, Talmis (Kalabsha), Pselkis (Dakka), and Primis (Qasr Ibrim), and probably a garrison at Primis as well, which may have served as nuclei for new settlements.[224] A Greek honorific decree on Sehel Island dedicated to Ptolemy VI and the provincial governor (*stratēgos*) Boethos records that the latter founded two such new settlements, Philometoris and Kleopatra, somewhere in the Lower Nubia.[225]

The Red Sea: The early Ptolemies and their agents built roads and wells in the Eastern Desert in order to supply mining expeditions in the Eastern Desert with food and water. They also established several harbors on the Egyptian coast of the Red Sea, of which Berenike was the most successful, in order to supply elephant hunting expeditions to the southern Red Sea. They extended the roads and wells to reach these harbors, and they even restored a canal through the Wadi Tumilat to the harbor of Arsinoe/Cleopatris in the Gulf of Suez. The early Ptolemies also established harbors and inland hunting bases farther south nearer to the elephant hunting grounds proper, but these were more ephemeral because the hunting grounds were regularly exhausted and new ones had to be found. After the elephant hunts ceased, the later Ptolemies used Berenike to support trade with South Arabia, and later with India after the monsoon winds were discovered.[226]

State Production and Sale of Commodities: The early Ptolemies also sponsored entrepreneurial production and sale of certain commodities like vegetable oil, cloth, papyrus, beer, and so forth, through a system of commodity monopolies. In theory, the state auctioned the right to produce and sell specific commodities in specific districts to private entrepreneurs. In practice, however, the private entrepreneurs merely underwrote the state production and sale of these commodities. Some commodities, such as oil and cloth, were divided into separate production and sale monopolies; while others, such as beer, combined the two. In production monopolies, the state usually sold the raw materials to the entrepreneurs at a fixed price, such as vegetable seeds for oil, or flax for linen. The state also provided machinery to the entrepreneurs, such as oil presses or weaving looms. The state also fixed the wages that the entrepreneurs paid to laborers, and required the laborers to produce bonds ensuring their presence at work. The only variable left to the entrepreneurs was the number of laborers that they hired. The point of this was to allow entrepreneurs to closely calculate their costs, and thereby encourage relatively high bids for the commodity monopolies. In sale monopolies, the state provided commodities to merchants, who had to produce bonds guaranteeing that they would not abscond with the valuable commodities. The merchants then sold these commodities.

Private Entrepreneurial Activities: Private entrepreneurial activities took many forms. A few wealthy and powerful individuals like the chief finance minister (*dioikētēs*) Apollonios and the provincial governors (*stratēgoi*) Boethos and Kallimachos undertook infrastructure projects such as founding cities and temples. However, these individuals all held important state offices, and can be seen as state agents. Much private entrepreneurial activity probably took the form of underwriting the state collection of taxes through tax farming; or underwriting the state production and sale of monopolies through commodity monopolies; or underwriting state administrative activities by leasing banks and registries. Lesoneis appear to have similarly underwritten temple economies,[227] but there may have been fewer opportunities to make a profit and more opportunities to incur a loss, judging from the difficulties in finding individuals to undertake the task in the Persian Period. Priestly households received much of their salaries from the temples in kind, and thus they frequently sold their surplus scribal labor,[228] or even leased their positions and their revenues in return for money.[229] The majority of Egyptian households probably engaged in agricultural activities that primarily produced revenues in kind, and consequently the need to pay capitation taxes in money must have forced many of them to sell their surplus labor or to engage in small scale entrepreneurial activities.

CONCLUSIONS

In the Ptolemaic Period, the state prosecuted interference with royal revenues throughout Egypt, and cooperated with local Egyptian temple courts and Greek provincial courts to adjudicate disputed private property transfers. Enforcement relied heavily on written documentation. The state continued to document harvest taxes for individual fields, but reclaimed from temples the responsibility for documenting harvest taxes on temple endowments. The state continued to document labor obligations for individual people, to which were added capitation taxes in money. Local temple notaries remained responsible for documenting private property transfers and associated sales taxes, but the state began registering such property transfers and sales taxes as well, as it began to take back responsibility for documentation from temples. Temples continued to document burial taxes, however, while the state continued to document customs duties.

Written documentation and the increased use of coinage reduced transaction costs for both redistribution and exchange, but state enforcement of royal redistribution had a longer reach than local temple or provincial court enforcement of exchanges. The state encouraged the use of coinage, but limited supplies required the use of various forms of money credit, and helped preserve redistribution and exchange in kind. Donations of land continued to be used as royal rewards for officials and soldiers for service, but salaries were increasingly paid in coin rather than kind. Higher value exchanges frequently involved coinage, and many were documented with written contracts. Many low value exchanges probably took place in markets, but most of these were not documented in writing. Short-term employment for payment in coinage appears for the first time alongside short-term compulsory labor for the state, but long-term employment with state and temple organizations was still common.

CONCLUSION

Diachronic examination of the history of the ancient Egyptian economy from c. 3000 BCE to 30 BCE has shown strong correlations between changes in social and legal institutions and changes in the economy proper. The spread of the use of writing for documentation and enforcement of revenue collection and property transfers, together with the increasing use of metallic money as media of redistribution and exchange, affected the transaction costs associated with different allocation systems, and thereby shifted the boundaries between the different modes of distribution in the ancient Egyptian economy. This result appears to validate the use of an institutional approach to the ancient Egyptian economy.

Throughout ancient Egyptian history, the state judicial administration privileged enforcement of state revenue collection and redistribution over enforcement of private property transfers. From the late third millennium BCE, from the Old Kingdom onward, the state judicial administration was usually involved directly in cases of alleged interference with state revenues and other crimes against the state, but it often allowed local agents and representatives to adjudicate private property transfer disputes. In the late third millennium BCE, in the Old Kingdom, local courts and authorities appear to have dealt with property transfer disputes, without reference to the higher state judicial administration. In the second millennium BCE, in the Middle and New Kingdoms, local courts and representatives of the state judicial administration judged property disputes as well as minor crimes. In the early first millennium BCE, in the Third Intermediate Period, the state fragmented and temples assumed responsibility for adjudicating property disputes, though later in the first millennium BCE, from the Saite Period onward, the reunified state increasingly collaborated with temples to enforce private property transfers.

The enforcement of state revenue collection and redistribution, as well as of private property transfers, was also influenced by the gradual development of written documentation of revenue sources and property transfers. This was the result of the steady discovery and exploitation of new documentary applications for writing from the early third millennium BCE, from the Early Dynastic Period onward, and not a response to increased foreign cultural influence and political control in Egypt in the first millennium BCE, as has been proposed.[1] In the third millennium BCE, in the Early Dynastic Period and the Old Kingdom, the state began applying written documentation to the collective tax obligations of districts known as estates and towns. It did not document individuals, their property, or property transfers, however. At the beginning of the second millennium BCE, in the Middle Kingdom, the state extended its written documentation from collective to individual tax obligations. This not only reduced the opportunities for free riding, but it also allowed the state to enforce private property title, if it wished. Indeed, the state also tried to document private property transfers, though its motive was probably to track transfers of individual tax obligations, rather than to enforce private property title. In the early first millennium BCE, from the Third Intermediate Period onward, however, temples began documenting private property transfers, at first instead of the fragmented state, and then on behalf of the reunified state. Later in the first millennium BCE, in the Ptolemaic Period, the state finally began documenting private property transfers alongside the temples.

The increased documentation of private property transfers in the first millennium BCE was also a response to the growing stocks of silver in Egypt, and their increasing use in exchanges, which facilitated bottleneck taxation like sales taxes and customs duties, which in turn allowed the temples and the state to recoup the costs of documenting property transfers. Already in the late third millennium BCE, in the Old Kingdom, the advantages of using standard commodities like copper or cloth as measures of value were understood, even if they were not conceptualized as reducing information costs. And already in the early second millennium BCE, in the Middle Kingdom, Hekanakht understood the advantages of durable commodities like copper or cloth as stores of wealth, compared to perishable commodities like grain or oil. Nonetheless, throughout the third and second millennia BCE, a wide variety of commodities continued to be used as media of exchange, because the available stocks of durable commodities were insufficient to meet demand. By the late second millennium BCE, in the New Kingdom, however, references to the use of silver in exchanges appear. By the early first millennium BCE, in the Third Intermediate Period, they become common, and by the mid-first millennium BCE, in the Saite and Persian Periods, silver was the standard medium of exchange in high value transactions. It is probably not a coincidence that bottleneck taxes on property transfers also appear in Egypt in the mid-first millennium BCE, in the Saite Period, because the preferred medium of payment of such taxes in Egypt was always silver. Bottleneck taxes related to transport of commodities are attested earlier in Mesopotamia, in the second millennium BCE, in the Old Babylonian and Middle Assyrian Periods,[2] but they were increasingly paid in silver in the seventh through fourth centuries BCE, in the late Neo-Assyrian, Neo-Babylonian, and Achaemenid Periods,[3] when silver stocks in Mesopotamia also increased.[4] The invention of coinage in Lydia in western Anatolia in the seventh century BCE and its subsequent adoption in the Aegean also occurred about the same time that silver became a unified measure of value, store of wealth, and medium of exchange in Egypt, and around the time that bottleneck transfer taxes were introduced as well. The idea of coinage was manifestly not responsible for these developments in Egypt, however. The ancient Egyptians continued to treat some imported Greek coinage as lump silver through the Saite and Persian Periods, into the early fourth century BCE. They were clearly much less impressed with the idea of coinage than many modern numismatists. Indeed, it is possible that many of the economic developments in the Aegean that have been attributed to the invention or idea of coinage,[5] are actually mostly the result of the vast increase in stocks of silver extracted from mines in the Aegean in the seventh to fourth centuries BCE, that just happened to take the form of coins rather than ingots or *Hacksilber*. But that is a subject for another book.

The increasing use of writing to document and enforce state revenue collection and redistribution, and private property transfers, together with the growing use of silver as a medium of exchange, reduced transaction costs in the course of ancient Egyptian history. Transaction costs fell at different rates for redistribution and exchange, however, at different times and for different goods and services, which helped determine the shifting boundaries between market and nonmarket allocation systems. From the beginning of Egyptian history, relatively low value, perishable or portable commodities and goods were often exchanged in markets, because title security was not a significant transaction cost. Such commodities and goods were often also redistributed to employees, however, due to limited stocks of durable commodities serving as media of exchange. The distribution of the same types of commodities and goods through both market and nonmarket allocation systems affected market price formation and fluctuation, persuading some scholars that market price formation did not exist,[6] and others that the state consciously intervened in the market to regulate prices and prevent speculation and inflation.[7] High value immovable properties were rarely exchanged in markets in the third and second millennia BCE, but more often in the first millennium BCE. Royal donation was the only effective title security in the late third millennium BCE, in the Old Kingdom. State documentation of individual properties for tax purposes in the second millennium BCE, in the Middle and New Kingdoms, provided another form of title, but intermittent documentation and enforcement of title transfers limited its effectiveness, and royal donation remained the most effective title security. Perhaps for this reason, some property exchanges were framed as reciprocal royal donations. Limited stocks of durable, concentrated stores of wealth and media of exchange like silver were also a significant transaction cost in the second millennium BCE, in the Middle and New Kingdoms. Regular documentation of private property transfers in the first millennium BCE, from the Third Intermediate Period onward, however, and the increased availability of silver as a medium of exchange lowered transaction costs and increased private property exchanges. Labor markets were slow to develop in ancient Egypt. The state and temples regularly offered skilled labor long-term employment, even after silver money and coinage became a common medium of exchange in the late first millennium BCE, in the Ptolemaic Period. The state usually compelled groups and individuals to provide unskilled labor for short periods, while temples and households instead resorted to bound labor, when it was available.

The Ptolemaic Period came to an end and the Roman Period began when Octavian, the future Emperor Augustus, conquered Egypt in 30 BCE, and incorporated it into the Roman Empire as an imperial province. This transition initiated fundamental changes in the organization of the Egyptian economy, making the coming of Rome to Egypt an appropriate end to this study.

On the one hand, the Roman state in Egypt took a greater responsibility for documenting and enforcing private property transfers. The Romans abolished the Ptolemaic system of Egyptian temple courts and Greek provincial courts for adjudicating disputes arising from private property transfers. The Roman prefect and his local agents continued to acknowledge Egyptian and Greek legal traditions concerning private property, but they assumed responsibility for prosecuting all crimes and adjudicating all property disputes in Roman Egypt.[8] The Romans also dispensed with Egyptian temple notaries for documenting Egyptian private property transfers. Instead, the state made registry offices responsible for notarizing as well as registering Egyptian as well as Greek private property transfers, for maintaining local copies of that documentation, and for sending further copies to the central record office in Alexandria.[9] At the same time, the Romans also eliminated the use of temple witnesses to accommodate illiterate Egyptian contractors, and instead required contractors or their representatives to provide autograph Greek subscriptions to their private property transfers, thereby shifting some of the costs of literacy from the state and its agents to its subjects.

On the other hand, the Roman state in Egypt transferred much responsibility for managing the economy from the state and the temples to private households. The Romans drastically reduced the amount of redistribution in Egypt through officials, commodity monopolies, and temples, and thus also the amount of support for households of administrative elites, craftsmen and priests.[10] The Romans also lowered the harvest tax rates on land in Egypt, however, encouraging investment in real property and the creation of a new landowning elite to replace the old administrative elites.[11] This new Egyptian landowning elite was expected to perform some administrative tasks as uncompensated compulsory service obligations or liturgies, thereby shifting some of the costs of administration from the state and its agents to its subjects.[12] Some of these landowning elites and their estates may have taken over some of the roles of state commodity monopolies and temples in providing management and long-term employment to skilled labor,[13] though many were probably content with rent-seeking.[14] In time, these large estates also became responsible for collecting taxes from small holders on behalf of the emperor,[15] and for managing the cultivation of some imperial estates on behalf of the emperor,[16] much as Egyptian temples had once cultivated royal land and collected royal harvest taxes on behalf of the crown.

NOTES

INTRODUCTION

1 A. Smith, *An Inquiry into the Nature and Causes of the Wealth of Nations* (1776), chapter 2.

2 For example, K. Baer, "An Eleventh Dynasty Farmer's Letters to his Family," *JAOS* 83 (1963), pp. 1–19.

3 B. Menu, "Le système économique de l'Égypte pharaonique," in B. Menu, *Égypte pharaonique. Nouvelles recherches sur l'histoire juridique, économique et sociale de l'ancienne Égypte* (Paris: L'Harmattan, 2004), pp. 210–212; and B. Menu, "Deir el-Médîna au crible de l'économie politique," in B. Menu, *Égypte pharaonique. Nouvelles recherches sur l'histoire juridique, économique et sociale de l'ancienne Égypte* (Paris: L'Harmattan, 2004), pp. 217–220.

4 D. Warburton, "Keynes'sche Überlegungen zur altägyptischen Wirtschaft," *ZÄS* 118 (1991), pp. 76–85; D. Warburton, *State and Economy in Ancient Egypt: Fiscal Vocabulary of the New Kingdom* (Orbis Biblicus et Orientalis 151. Freiburg & Göttingen: 1997), pp. 326–338; D. Warburton, "Before the IMF: The Economic Implications of Unintentional Structural Adjustment in Ancient Egypt," *JESHO* 43 (2000), pp. 65–131; D. Warburton, *Macroeconomics from the Beginning. The General Theory, Ancient Markets, and the Rate of Interest* (Civilisations du Proche-Orient. Série IV. Histoire – Essais 2. Neuchâtel: 2003); idem, "Economics, Anthropological Models and the Ancient Near East," *Anthropology of the Middle East* 4 (2009), pp. 65–90.

5 M. Weber (translated by R.I. Frank), *The Agrarian Sociology of Ancient Civilizations* (London: 1976); M. Weber (translated by Guenther Roth – Claus Wittich), *Economy and Society: An Outline of Interpretive Sociology* (Berkeley: University of California Press, 1978); K. Polanyi, *The Great Transformation* (New York: Farrar and Rinehart, 1944); K. Polanyi – C.M. Arensberg – H.W. Pearson (eds.), *Trade and Markets in the Early Empires* (Glencoe IL: Free Press, 1957); M.I. Finley, *The Ancient Economy*, 2nd ed. (Berkeley: University of California Press, 1985).

6 J.J. Janssen, *Commodity Prices from the Ramessid Period. An Economic Study of the Village of Necropolis Workmen at Thebes* (Leiden: E. J. Brill, 1975), pp. 539–562.

7 J.J. Janssen, "Prolegomena to the Study of Egypt's Economic History during the New Kingdom," *SAK* 3 (1975), pp. 127–185.

8 J.J. Janssen, "Gift-Giving in Ancient Egypt as an Economic Feature," *JEA* 68 (1982), pp. 253–258; E. Bleiberg, "The King's Privy Purse During the New Kingdom: An Examination of *INW*," *JARCE* 21 (1984), pp. 155–167; E. Bleiberg, "The Redistributive Economy in New Kingdom Egypt: An Examination of *B3kw(t)*," *JARCE* 25 (1988): pp. 157–168; and E. Bleiberg, *The Official Gift in Ancient Egypt (Inw)*, (Norman, 1996).

9 J. Černý, *A Community of Workmen at Thebes in the Ramesside Period* (BdÉ 50. Cairo: IFAO, 1973), pp. 93–97; and J.J. Janssen, *De Markt op de Oever* (Inaugural Professorial Lecture. Leiden, 1980).

10 J.J. Janssen, *Two Ancient Egyptian Ship's Logs, Papyrus Leiden I 350 verso and Papyrus Turin 2008 + 2016* (Oudheidkundige Mededelingen uit het Rijksmuseum van Oudheden te Leiden, Supplement op 42. Leiden: E.J. Brill, 1961); V. Condon, "Two Account Papyri of the Late Eighteenth Dynasty (Brooklyn 35.1453 A and B)," *RdÉ* 35 (1984), pp. 57–82; J.J. Janssen, "Two Variant Accounts?," *Varia Aegyptiaca* 1 (1985), pp. 109–112; V. Condon, "'Two Variant Accounts?' by Janssen? (VA 1,3, 109–112)," *Varia Aegyptiaca* 2 (1986), pp. 23–29; and M. Römer, "Der Handel und die Kaufleute im Alten Ägypten," *SAK* 19 (1992), pp. 257–284.

11 W. Scheidel – S. von Reden (eds.), *The Ancient Economy* (Edinburgh: University Press, 2002), pp. 1–4; I. Morris – J.G. Manning, "Introduction," in J.G. Manning – I. Morris (eds.), *The Ancient Economy: Evidence and Models* (Stanford: University Press, 2005), pp. 6–14.

12 M. Granovetter, "The Strength of Weak Ties," *The American Journal of Sociology* 78, Issue 6 (May, 1973), pp. 1360–1380; M. Granovetter, "Economic Action and Social Structure: The Problem of Embeddedness," *The American Journal of Sociology* 91, No. 3 (November, 1985), pp. 481–510; M. Granovetter, "Comment on Liverani and Bedford," in J.G. Manning – I. Morris (eds.), *The Ancient Economy: Evidence and Models* (Stanford: University Press, 2005), pp. 84–88.

13 B. Kemp, *Ancient Egypt, Anatomy of a Civilization* (London, 1989), pp. 232–260 (chapter 6, "The birth of economic man"); K.M. Cooney, *The Cost of Death: The Social and Economic Value of Ancient Egyptian Funerary Art in the Ramesside Period* (EU 22. Leiden: NINO, 2007), pp. 8–16; A.P. Zingarelli, *Trade and Market in New Kingdom Egypt, Internal Socio-Economic Processes and Transformations* (BAR International Series 2063. Oxford: Archaeopress, 2010), pp. 113–115.

14 For example, A. Bresson, *L'économie de la Grèce des cités (fin VIe – Ier siècle a.C.)*, 2 vols. (Paris: Armand Colin, 2007), esp. vol. 1, pp. 23–36, and vol. 2, pp. 7–71.

15 R. Coase, "The Nature of the Firm," *Economica* 4, no. 16 (1937), pp. 386–405.

16 D.C. North – R.P. Thomas, *The Rise of the Western World: A New Economic History* (Cambridge, 1973), p. 93, pp. 135–136; D.C. North, *Structure and Change in Economic History* (New York, 1981), pp. 36–37.

17 D.C. North, "Markets and Other Allocation Systems in History: The Challenge of Karl Polanyi," *Journal of European Economic History* 6 (1977), pp. 703–716.

18 D.C. North, *Structure and Change in Economic History* (New York, 1981), pp. 3–12.

19 D.C. North – R.P. Thomas, *The Rise of the Western World: A New Economic History* (Cambridge, 1973), pp. 19–24.

20 D.C. North – R.P. Thomas, *The Rise of the Western World: A New Economic History* (Cambridge, 1973), pp. 91–101.

21 D.C. North, "Government and the Cost of Exchange in History," *Journal of Economic History* 44, 2 (1984), pp. 255–264; D.C. North, "Transaction Costs in History," *Journal of European Economic History* 14 (1985), pp. 557–576.

22 P.R. Milgrom – D.C. North – B.R. Weingast, "The Role of Institutions in the Revival of Trade: The Medieval Law Merchant, Private Judges, and the Champagne Fairs," *Economics and Politics* 2, Issue 1 (March 1990), pp. 1–23; A. Greif, "Contract Enforceability and Economic Institutions in Early Trade: Lessons from the Commercial Revolution," *American Economic Review* 82 No. 2 (May 1992), pp. 128–133, esp. 131–132.

23 A. Greif, "Contract Enforceability and Economic Institutions in Early Trade: Lessons from the Commercial Revolution," *American Economic Review* 82 No. 2 (May 1992), pp. 128–129; A. Greif – P. Milgrom – B.R. Weingast, "Coordination, Commitment and Enforcement: The Case of the Merchant Gild," *Journal of Political Economy* 102, No. 4, (Aug. 1994), pp. 745–776; A. Greif, *Institutions and the Path to the Modern Economy: Lessons from Medieval Trade* (Cambridge: University Press, 2006), pp. 91–123 (chapter 4. Securing Property Rights from the Grabbing Hand of the State: The Merchant Guild).

24 A. Greif, "Reputation and Coalitions in Medieval Trade: Evidence on the Maghrebi Traders," *Journal of Economic History* 49, no. 4 (Dec. 1989), pp. 857–882; A. Greif, "Contract Enforceability and Economic Institutions in Early Trade: The Maghribi Traders' Coalition," *American Economic Review* 83, No. 3 (June 1993), pp. 525–548; A. Greif, *Institutions and the Path to the Modern Economy: Lessons from Medieval Trade* (Cambridge University Press, 2006), pp. 58–90 (chapter 3. Private-Order Contract Enforcement Institutions: The Maghribi Traders' Coalition).

25 A. Greif, "Contract Enforceability and Economic Institutions in Early Trade: Lessons from the Commercial Revolution," *American Economic Review* 82 No. 2 (May 1992), 129–131; A. Greif, "Cultural Beliefs and the Organization of Society: A Historical and Theoretical Reflection on Collectivist and Individualist Societies," *The Journal of Political Economy* 102, No. 5, (Oct. 1994), pp. 912–950.

26 D. Charpin (translated by J.M. Todd), *Reading and Writing in Babylonia* (Harvard, 2010), pp. 105–114, pp. 154–177.

27 M. Van de Mieroop, "Why Did they Write on Clay?," *Klio* 79, 1 (1997), pp. 7–18; P.

Steinkeller, "The Function of Written Documentation in the Administration Praxis of Early Babylonia," in M. Hudson – C. Wunsch (eds.), *Creating Economic Order. Record-Keeping, Standardization, and the Development of Accounting in the Ancient Near East* (International Scholars Conference on Ancient Near Eastern Economies 4. Bethesda MD: CDL Press, 2004), pp. 65–88.

28 M. Jursa, "Accounting in Neo-Babylonian Institutional Archives: Structure, Usage, and Implications," in M. Hudson – C. Wunsch (eds.), *Creating Economic Order. Record-Keeping, Standardization, and the Development of Accounting in the Ancient Near East* (International Scholars Conference on Ancient Near Eastern Economies 4. Bethesda MD: CDL Press, 2004), pp. 145–198.

29 W. Helck, *Wirtschaftsgeschichte des Alten Ägypten im 3. und 2. Jahrtausend vor Chr.* (Handbuch der Orientalistik, Band 1, Abschnitte 5. Leiden-Köln: Brill, 1975), pp. 134–135.

30 C.J. Eyre, "Feudal Tenure and Absentee Landlords," in S. Allam (ed.), *Grund und Boden in Alägypten, Akten des internationalen Symposions Tübingen 18–20. Juni 1990* (Untersuchungen zum Rechtsleben im Alten Ägypten 2. Tübingen, 1994), pp. 107–133; C.J. Eyre, "Peasants and 'Modern' Leasing Strategies in Ancient Egypt," *JESHO* 40, 4 (1997), pp. 367–390; C.J. Eyre, "The Village Economy in Pharaonic Egypt," in A.K. Bowman – E. Rogan (eds.), *Agriculture in Egypt, from Pharaonic to Modern Times* (Proceedings of the British Academy 96. Oxford: University Press, 1999), pp. 33–60.

31 C.J. Eyre, *The Use of Documents in Pharaonic Egypt* (Oxford: University Press, 2013), pp. 194–201.

32 C.J. Eyre, *The Use of Documents in Pharaonic Egypt* (Oxford: University Press, 2013), pp. 342–347.

33 C.J. Eyre, *The Use of Documents in Pharaonic Egypt* (Oxford: University Press, 2013), pp. 101–102.

34 B.P. Muhs, "Property Title, Domestic Architecture, and Household Lifecycles in Egypt," in M. Muller (ed.), *Household Studies in Complex Societies, (Micro) Archaeological and Textual Approaches* (Oriental Institute Seminars 10. Chicago: Oriental Institute, 2015), pp. 321–347.

35 K. Baer, "The Low Price of Land in Ancient Egypt," *JARCE* 1 (1962), pp. 25–45; and A. Monson, *From the Ptolemies to the Romans. Political and Economic Change in Egypt* (Cambridge: University Press, 2012), pp. 191–199.

36 C.J. Eyre, *The Use of Documents in Pharaonic Egypt* (Oxford: University Press, 2013), pp. 115–124.

37 C.J. Eyre, *The Use of Documents in Pharaonic Egypt* (Oxford: University Press, 2013), pp. 1–15.

38 D.M. Schaps, *The Invention of Coinage and the Monetization of Ancient Greece* (Ann Arbor: University of Michigan Press, 2003), pp. 111–123.

39 D.M. Schaps, *The Invention of Coinage and the Monetization of Ancient Greece* (Ann Arbor: University of Michigan Press, 2003), pp. 138–162.

40 D.M. Schaps, *The Invention of Coinage and the Monetization of Ancient Greece* (Ann Arbor: University of Michigan Press, 2003), pp. 175–193.

41 C.M. Thompson, "Sealed Silver in Iron Cisjordan and the 'Invention' of Coinage." *Oxford Journal of Archaeology* 22 (2003), pp. 67–107.

42 J.H. Kroll, "Weighed Bullion in Archaic Greece," in W.V. Harris (ed.), *The Monetary Systems of the Greeks and Romans* (Oxford: University Press, 2008), pp. 12–37.

43 X. Ouyang, *Monetary Role of Silver and Its Administration in Mesopotamia during the Ur III Period (c. 2112–2004 BCE): A Case Study of the Umma Province* (Biblioteca del Próximo Oriente Antiguo 11. Madrid: Consejo Superior de Investigaciones Científicas, 2013), pp. 17–21, and 153–161.

44 K. Radner, "Money in the Neo-Assyrian empire," in J.G. Dercksen (ed.), *Trade and Finance in Ancient Mesopotamia (MOS Studies 1): Proceedings of the First MOS Symposium, Leiden 1997* (PIHANS 84. Istanbul: Nederlands historisch-archaeologisch Instituut, 1999), pp. 128–129.

45 A.C.V.M. Bongenaar, "Money in the Neo-Babylonian institutions," in J.G. Dercksen (ed.), *Trade and Finance in Ancient Mesopotamia (MOS Studies 1): Proceedings of the First MOS Symposium, Leiden 1997* (PIHANS 84. Istanbul: Nederlands historisch-archaeologisch Instituut, 1999), pp. 164–172.

46 R.J. Van der Spek, "The 'Silverization' of the Economy of the Achaemenid and Seleukid Empires and Early Modern China," in Z.H. Archibald – J.K. Davies – V. Gabrielsen (eds.),

The Economies of Hellenistic Societies, Third to First Centuries BC (Oxford: University Press, 2011), pp. 402–420.

47 M. Jursa, "Accounting in Neo-Babylonian Institutional Archives: Structure, Usage, and Implications," in M. Hudson – C. Wunsch (eds.), *Creating Economic Order. Record-Keeping, Standardization, and the Development of Accounting in the Ancient Near East* (International Scholars Conference on Ancient Near Eastern Economies 4. Bethesda MD: CDL Press, 2004), pp. 145–198; M. Jursa, "Agricultural Management, Tax Farming and Banking: Aspects of Entrepreneurial Activity in Babylonia in the Late Achaemenid and Hellenistic Periods," in P. Briant – F. Joannès (eds.), *La transition entre l'empire achéménide et les royaumes hellénistiques (vers 350–300 av. J.-C.)* (Persika 9. Paris: De Boccard, 2006), pp. 157–169.

48 B. Menu, "Deir el-Médîna au crible de l'économie politique," in B. Menu, *Égypte pharaonique. Nouvelles recherches sur l'histoire juridique, économique et sociale de l'ancienne Égypte* (Paris: L'Harmattan, 2004), pp. 217–219.

49 R. Coase, "The Nature of the Firm," *Economica* 4, no. 16 (1937), pp. 386–405.

50 O.E. Williamson, "Transaction Cost Economics: The Governance of Contractual Relations," *Journal of Law and Economics* 22, 2 (Oct. 1979), pp. 233–261.

51 M. Jursa, *Aspects of the Economic History of Babylonia in the First Millennium BC* (Alter Orient und Altes Testament: Veröffentlichungen zur Kultur und Geschichte des Alten Orients und des Alten Testaments 377. Münster: Ugarit-Verlag, 2010), pp. 282–315.

52 D. Schloen, *The House of the Father as Fact and Symbol, Patrimonialism in Ugarit and the Ancient Near East* (Studies in the Archaeology and History of the Levant 2. Winona Lake IN: Eisenbrauns, 2001); S.J. Garfinkle, "Was the Ur III state bureaucratic? Patrimonialism and bureaucracy in the Ur III Period," in S.J. Garfinkle – J.C. Johnson (eds.), *The Growth of an Early State in Mesopotamia: Studies in Ur III Administration* (Biblioteca del Próximo Oriente Antiguo 5. Madrid: Consejo Superior de Investigaciones Cientificas, 2008), pp. 55–61.

53 N. Postgate, *Bronze Age Bureaucracy: Writing and the Practice of Government in Assyria* (Cambridge: University Press, 2013), p. 2.

54 P.W. Pestman, "The Law of Succession in Ancient Egypt," in J. Brugman – M. David – F.R. Kraus – P.W. Pestman – M.H. van den Valk (eds.), *Essays on Oriental Laws of Succession* (Studia et Documenta ad Iura Orientis Antiqui Pertinentia 9. Leiden: E.J. Brill, 1969), pp. 58–77.

55 A. Leahy, "The Libyan Period in Egypt: An Essay in Interpretation," *Libyan Studies* 16 (1985), pp. 51–65; R.K. Ritner, "Fragmentation and Re-Integration in the Third Intermediate Period," in G.P.F. Broekman – R.J. Demarée – O.E. Kaper (eds.), *The Libyan Period in Egypt, Historical and Cultural Studies into the 21st – 24th Dynasties: Proceedings of a Conference at Leiden University, 25–27 October 2007* (EU 23. Leiden – Leuven: NINO – Peeters, 2009), pp. 327–340.

56 J.J. Shirley, "Crisis and Restructuring of the State: From the Second Intermediate Period to the Advent of the Ramesses," in in J.C. Moreno García (ed.), *Ancient Egyptian Administration* (HdO 104. Leiden: Brill, 2013), pp. 572–576.

1. THE EARLY DYNASTIC PERIOD (c. 3000–2686 BCE)

1 J. Baines, *Visual and Written Culture in Ancient Egypt* (Oxford: University Press, 2007), pp. 117–145 (chapter 5, "Writing and society in early Egypt").

2 T.A.H. Wilkinson, *Early Dynastic Egypt* (London, New York: Routledge, 1999), pp. 137–139; E.-M. Engel, "The Organisation of a Nascent State: Egypt until the Beginning of the 4th Dynasty," in J.C. Moreno García (ed.), *Ancient Egyptian Administration* (HdO 104. Leiden: Brill, 2013), p. 32.

3 T.A.H. Wilkinson, *Early Dynastic Egypt* (London: Routledge, 1999), pp. 218–220, and fig. 6.7. (Year labels).

4 T.A. Wilkinson, *Royal Annals of Ancient Egypt. Palermo Stone and Its Associated Fragments* (London: Kegan Paul International, 2000), p. 120.

5 T.A. Wilkinson, *Royal Annals of Ancient Egypt. Palermo Stone and Its Associated Fragments* (London: Kegan Paul International, 2000), p. 130.

6 T.A.H. Wilkinson, *Early Dynastic Egypt* (London: Routledge, 1999), pp. 113–114, 220–221.

7 E. Endesfelder, "Zu einigen Aspekten der ökonomischen Entwicklung in der Frühdynastischen

Zeit Ägyptens," *Altorientalische Forschungen* 7 (1980), pp. 5–7.

8 T.A.H. Wilkinson, *Early Dynastic Egypt* (London: Routledge, 1999), pp. 113–114, 220–221; T.A. Wilkinson, *Royal Annals of Ancient Egypt. Palermo Stone and Its Associated Fragments* (London: Kegan Paul International, 2000), pp. 120, 130.

9 T.A.H. Wilkinson, *Early Dynastic Egypt* (London: Routledge, 1999), pp. 116–120, 123–124, and fig. 4.2; E.-M. Engel, "The Organisation of a Nascent State: Egypt until the Beginning of the 4th Dynasty," in J.C. Moreno García (ed.), *Ancient Egyptian Administration* (HdO 104. Leiden: Brill, 2013), pp. 27–28.

10 H.K. Jacquet-Gordon, *Les noms des domaines funéraires sous l'Ancien Empire Égyptien* (BdÉ 34. Cairo: IFAO, 1962), pp. 125–455; W. Helck, *Wirtschaftsgeschichte des Alten Ägypten im 3. und 2. Jahrtausend vor Chr.* (HdO 1, Abschnitte 5. Leiden-Köln: Brill, 1975), pp. 45–72.

11 H.K. Jacquet-Gordon, *Les noms des domaines funéraires sous l'Ancien Empire Égyptien* (BdÉ 34. Cairo: IFAO, 1962), pp. 3–25; M. Atzler, "Einige Bemerkungen zu *ḥw.t* und *niw.t* im Alten Reich," *CdÉ* 47 (1972), pp. 17–44; W. Helck, *Wirtschaftsgeschichte des Alten Ägypten im 3. und 2. Jahrtausend vor Chr.* (HdO 1, Abschnitte 5. Leiden-Köln: Brill, 1975), pp. 34–44.

12 T.G.H. James and M.R. Apted, *The Mastaba of Khentika Called Ikhekhi* (London: EES, 1953), p. 45 and pl. 9; H. Wild, *Le tombeau de Ti, fascicule 3. La chapelle (deuxième partie)* (MIFAO 65. Cairo: IFAO, 1966), pl. CLXVIII, details on pl. CXLIV.

13 C.J. Eyre, "Village Economy in Pharaonic Egypt," in A.K. Bowman and E. Rogan (eds.), *Agriculture in Egypt, from Pharaonic to Modern Times* (Proceedings of the British Academy 96. Oxford: University Press, 1999), pp. 37–38.

14 E.-M. Engel, "The Organisation of a Nascent State: Egypt until the Beginning of the 4th Dynasty," in J.C. Moreno García (ed.), *Ancient Egyptian Administration* (HdO 104. Leiden: Brill, 2013), pp. 23–25.

15 G. Dreyer, U. Hartung, and F. Pumpenmeier, *Umm el-Qaab I: das prädynastische Königsgrab U-j und seine frühen Schriftzeugnisse* (Archäologische Veröffentlichungen 86. Mainz: Philipp von Zabern, 1998), pp. 47–91.

16 G. Dreyer, U. Hartung, and F. Pumpenmeier, *Umm el-Qaab I: das prädynastische Königsgrab U-j und seine frühen Schriftzeugnisse* (Archäologische Veröffentlichungen 86. Mainz: Philipp von Zabern, 1998), pp. 108–112.

17 G. Dreyer, U. Hartung, and F. Pumpenmeier, *Umm el-Qaab I: das prädynastische Königsgrab U-j und seine frühen Schriftzeugnisse* (Archäologische Veröffentlichungen 86. Mainz: Philipp von Zabern, 1998), pp. 113–145.

18 E. Endesfelder, "Zu einigen Aspekten der ökonomischen Entwicklung in der Frühdynastischen Zeit Ägyptens," *Altorientalische Forschungen* 7 (1980), pp. 7–12; J. Kahl, "Zur Problematik der sogenannten Steuervermerke im Ägypten der 0.-1. Dynastie," pp. 168–176 in C. Fluck, L. Langener, and S. Richter (eds.), *Divitiae Aegypti: Koptologie und verwandte Studien zu Ehren von Martin Krause* (Wiesbaden: L. Reichert Verlag, 1995); E.-M. Engel, "The Organisation of a Nascent State: Egypt until the Beginning of the 4th Dynasty," in J.C. Moreno García (ed.), *Ancient Egyptian Administration* (HdO 104. Leiden: Brill, 2013), pp. 25–27.

19 E. Endesfelder, "Zu einigen Aspekten der ökonomischen Entwicklung in der Frühdynastischen Zeit Ägyptens," *Altorientalische Forschungen* 7 (1980), pp. 12–15.

20 T.A.H. Wilkinson, *Early Dynastic Egypt* (London: Routledge, 1999), pp. 116–123, and fig. 4.1; P. Andrássy, *Untersuchungen zum ägyptischen Staat des Alten Reiches und seinen Institutionen* (IBAES 11. London, Golden House Publications, 2008), pp. 14–15; E.-M. Engel, "The Organisation of a Nascent State: Egypt until the Beginning of the 4th Dynasty," in J.C. Moreno García (ed.), *Ancient Egyptian Administration* (HdO 104. Leiden: Brill, 2013), pp. 28–29.

21 H.K. Jacquet-Gordon, *Les noms des domaines funéraires sous l'Ancien Empire Égyptien* (BdÉ 34. Cairo: IFAO, 1962), p. 3 n. 1.

22 P. Andrássy, *Untersuchungen zum ägyptischen Staat des Alten Reiches und seinen Institutionen* (IBAES 11. London: Golden House Publications, 2008), pp. 14–15; H. Papazian, *Domain of Pharaoh. The Structure and Components of the Economy of Old Kingdom Egypt* (HÄB 52. Hildesheim: Gebrüder Gerstenberg, 2012), pp. 37–50; E.-M. Engel, "The Organisation of a Nascent State: Egypt until the Beginning of the 4th Dynasty," in J.C. Moreno García (ed.), *Ancient Egyptian Administration* (HdO 104. Leiden: Brill, 2013), pp. 28–29.

23 T.A.H. Wilkinson, *Early Dynastic Egypt* (London: Routledge, 1999), pp. 118–124;

P. Andrássy, *Untersuchungen zum ägyptischen Staat des Alten Reiches und seinen Institutionen* (IBAES 11. London: Golden House Publications, 2008), pp. 12–16; E.-M. Engel, "The Organisation of a Nascent State: Egypt until the Beginning of the 4th Dynasty," in J.C. Moreno García (ed.), *Ancient Egyptian Administration* (HdO 104. Leiden: Brill, 2013), pp. 29–31.

24 T.A.H. Wilkinson, *Early Dynastic Egypt* (London: Routledge, 1999), p. 133; E.-M. Engel, "The Organisation of a Nascent State: Egypt until the Beginning of the 4th Dynasty," in J.C. Moreno García (ed.), *Ancient Egyptian Administration* (HdO 104. Leiden: Brill, 2013), p. 30.

25 E. Endesfelder, "Zu einigen Aspekten der ökonomischen Entwicklung in der Frühdynastischen Zeit Ägyptens," *Altorientalische Forschungen* 7 (1980), pp. 15–18.

26 T.A.H. Wilkinson, *Early Dynastic Egypt* (London: Routledge, 1999), pp. 125–128; E.-M. Engel, "The Organisation of a Nascent State: Egypt until the Beginning of the 4th Dynasty," in J.C. Moreno García (ed.), *Ancient Egyptian Administration* (HdO 104. Leiden: Brill, 2013), pp. 31–32; H. Papazian, "The Central Administration of Resources in the Old Kingdom: Departments, Treasuries, Granaries and Work Centers," in J.C. Moreno García (ed.), *Ancient Egyptian Administration* (HdO 104. Leiden: Brill, 2013), pp. 70–73.

27 T.A.H. Wilkinson, *Early Dynastic Egypt* (London: Routledge, 1999), pp. 128–131, but see H. Papazian, *Domain of Pharaoh. The Structure and Components of the Economy of Old Kingdom Egypt* (HÄB 52. Hildesheim, Gebrüder Gerstenberg, 2012), pp. 63–73, who notes that the workshop (*pr-šn'*) was not simply a storehouse.

28 T.A.H. Wilkinson, *Early Dynastic Egypt* (London: Routledge, 1999), pp. 128–133, but see H. Papazian, *Domain of Pharaoh. The Structure and Components of the Economy of Old Kingdom Egypt* (HÄB 52. Hildesheim, Gebrüder Gerstenberg, 2012), pp. 63–73; E.-M. Engel, "The Organisation of a Nascent State: Egypt until the Beginning of the 4th Dynasty," in J.C. Moreno García (ed.), *Ancient Egyptian Administration* (HdO 104. Leiden: Brill, 2013), p. 34.

29 T.A. Wilkinson, *Royal Annals of Ancient Egypt. Palermo Stone and Its Associated Fragments* (London: Kegan Paul International, 2000), pp. 106, 125–126.

30 T.A.H. Wilkinson, *Early Dynastic Egypt* (London: Routledge, 1999), pp. 156–157.

31 T.A. Wilkinson, *Royal Annals of Ancient Egypt. Palermo Stone and its Associated Fragments* (London: Kegan Paul International, 2000), pp. 98–99, 100–101.

32 T.A. Wilkinson, *Royal Annals of Ancient Egypt. Palermo Stone and Its Associated Fragments* (London: Kegan Paul International, 2000), pp. 108–115, 118–119.

33 T.A. Wilkinson, *Royal Annals of Ancient Egypt. Palermo Stone and Its Associated Fragments* (London: Kegan Paul International, 2000), pp. 121, 132–135.

2. THE OLD KINGDOM AND THE FIRST INTERMEDIATE PERIOD (c. 2686–2025 BCE)

1 W.C. Hayes, "Royal Decrees from the Temple of Min at Coptus," *JEA* 32 (1946), pp. 3–23; W. Schenkel, *Memphis · Herakleopolis · Theben: die epigraphischen Zeugnisse der 7.-11. Dynastie Ägyptens* (ÄA 12. Wiesbaden: Harrassowitz, 1965), pp. 11–24.

2 D. Franke, "Zwischen Herakleopolis und Theben: Neues zu den Gräbern von Assiut." *SAK* 14 (1987), pp. 49–60.

3 J. Baines, *Visual and Written Culture in Ancient Egypt* (Oxford: University Press, 2007), pp. 95–116 (chapter 4. Literacy, social organization, and the archaeological record: the case of early Egypt).

4 A. Philip-Stéphan, *Dire le droit en Égypte pharaonique* (Connaissance de l'Égypte Ancienne 9. Bruxelles, Éditions Safran, 2008), pp. 21–23.

5 K. Sethe, *Urk.* I 98–110; M. Lichtheim, *Ancient Egyptian Literature, Volume I: The Old and Middle Kingdoms* (Berkeley: University of California Press, 1973), pp. 18–23; N. Strudwick, *Texts from the Pyramid Age* (SBL Writings from the Ancient World. Atlanta: SBL, 2005), pp. 352–357 (Text 256).

6 N. Strudwick, *The Administration of Egypt in the Old Kingdom: The Highest Titles and their Holders* (Studies in Egyptology. London: Kegan Paul International, 1985), pp. 337–344.

7 N. Strudwick, *The Administration of Egypt in the Old Kingdom: The Highest Titles and Their Holders* (Studies in Egyptology. London: Kegan Paul International, 1985), pp. 176–198; A. Philip-Stéphan, *Dire le droit en Égypte pharaonique* (Connaissance de l'Égypte Ancienne

9. Bruxelles, Éditions Safran, 2008), pp. 311–312 (II. Charges à la Grande Cour: Service scribal de la Grande Cour).

8 N. Strudwick, *The Administration of Egypt in the Old Kingdom: The Highest Titles and Their Holders* (Studies in Egyptology. London: Kegan Paul International, 1985), pp. 199–216; A. Philip-Stéphan, *Dire le droit en Égypte pharaonique* (Connaissance de l'Égypte Ancienne 9. Bruxelles, Éditions Safran, 2008), p. 55, pp. 311–322.

9 A. Philip-Stéphan, *Dire le droit en Égypte pharaonique* (Connaissance de l'Égypte Ancienne 9. Bruxelles, Éditions Safran, 2008), pp. 24–38.

10 K. Sethe, *Urk.* I 98–110; M. Lichtheim, *Ancient Egyptian Literature, Volume I: The Old and Middle Kingdoms* (Berkeley: University of California Press, 1973), pp. 18–23; N. Strudwick, *Texts from the Pyramid Age* (SBL Writings from the Ancient World. Atlanta: SBL, 2005), pp. 352–357 (Text 256).

11 A. Philip-Stéphan, *Dire le droit en Égypte pharaonique* (Connaissance de l'Égypte Ancienne 9. Bruxelles, Éditions Safran, 2008), pp. 104–123.

12 K. Sethe, *Urk.* I 170–172; N. Strudwick, *Texts from the Pyramid Age* (SBL Writings from the Ancient World. Atlanta: SBL, 2005), pp. 98–101 (Text 17).

13 Decree B: K. Sethe, *Urk.* I 280–283; N. Strudwick, *Texts from the Pyramid Age* (SBL Writings from the Ancient World. Atlanta: SBL, 2005), pp. 107–109 (Text 24). Decree C: K. Sethe, *Urk.* I 284–288; N. Strudwick, *Texts from the Pyramid Age* (SBL Writings from the Ancient World. Atlanta: SBL, 2005), pp. 109–111 (Text 25). Decree D: K. Sethe, *Urk.* I 288–293; N. Strudwick, *Texts from the Pyramid Age* (SBL Writings from the Ancient World. Atlanta: SBL, 2005), pp. 112–113 (Text 26).

14 P. Berlin 11301: P. Posener-Kriéger, *Les Archives du Temple Funeraire de Neferirkare-Kakai (Les Papyrus d'Abousir) Traduction et Commentaire I et II* (BdÉ 65. Cairo: IFAO, 1976), pp. 451–465 (Letter 80A); A. Philip-Stéphan, *Dire le droit en Égypte pharaonique* (Connaissance de l'Égypte Ancienne 9. Bruxelles, Éditions Safran, 2008), pp. 29–30, 297–298 (Text 90).

15 K. Sethe, *Urk.* I 170–172; N. Strudwick, *Texts from the Pyramid Age* (SBL Writings from the Ancient World. Atlanta: SBL, 2005), pp. 98–101 (Text 17).

16 K. Sethe, *Urk.* I 120–131; M. Lichtheim, *Ancient Egyptian Literature, Volume I: The Old and Middle Kingdoms* (Berkeley: University of California Press, 1973), pp. 23–27; N. Strudwick, *Texts from the Pyramid Age* (SBL Writings from the Ancient World. Atlanta: SBL, 2005), pp. 328–333 (Text 241).

17 A. Mariette, *Les Papyrus Egyptiennes du Musee de Boulaq, Tome Premier, Papyrus Nos 1–9* (Paris: Librairie A. Franck, 1871), p. 10 and pl. 39; K. Baer, "A Deed of Endowment in a Letter of the Time of Ppjj I?," *ZÄS* 93 (1966), pp. 1–9; H. Goedicke, "Ein Brief aus dem Alten Reich (Pap. Boulaq 8)," *MDAIK* 22 (1967), pp. 1–8 and pl. I.

18 A. Philip-Stéphan, *Dire le droit en Égypte pharaonique* (Connaissance de l'Égypte Ancienne 9. Bruxelles, Éditions Safran, 2008), pp. 47–49, 51–52.

19 Generalverwaltung, *Hieratische Papyrus aus den Koniglichen museen zu Berlin, Dritter Band: Schriftstucke der VI Dynastie aus Elephantine, Zauberspruche fur Mutter und Kind, Ostraka* (Leipzig: J. C. Hinrichs'sche Buchhandlung, 1911); K. Sethe, "Ein Prozessteil aus dem alten Reich," *ZÄS* 61 (1926), pp. 67–79; M. Green, "A Means of Discouraging Perjury," *GM* 39 (1980), pp. 33–39; N. Strudwick, *Texts from the Pyramid Age* (SBL Writings from the Ancient World. Atlanta: SBL, 2005), pp. 186–187 (Text 103).

20 A. Philip-Stéphan, *Dire le droit en Égypte pharaonique* (Connaissance de l'Égypte Ancienne 9. Bruxelles, Éditions Safran, 2008), pp. 124–135.

21 N. Strudwick, *The Administration of Egypt in the Old Kingdom: The Highest Titles and Their Holders* (Studies in Egyptology. London: Kegan Paul International, 1985), pp. 199–216; A. Philip-Stéphan, *Dire le droit en Égypte pharaonique* (Connaissance de l'Égypte Ancienne 9. Bruxelles, Éditions Safran, 2008), p. 55, pp. 311–322.

22 A.H. Gardiner, "Regnal Years and Civil Calender in Pharaonic Egypt," *JEA* 31 (1945), p. 13; T.A. Wilkinson, *Royal Annals of Ancient Egypt. Palermo Stone and its Associated Fragments* (London: Kegan Paul International, 2000), pp. 120, 130.

23 T.A. Wilkinson, *Royal Annals of Ancient Egypt. Palermo Stone and its Associated Fragments* (London: Kegan Paul International, 2000), pp. 143–146, 153–158, 160–166, 171, 177–178, 217–218, 233.

24 A.H. Gardiner, "Regnal Years and Civil Calender in Pharaonic Egypt," *JEA* 31 (1945),

pp. 13–14; for the use of the year after the count already in the reign of Userkaf, see T.A. Wilkinson, *Royal Annals of Ancient Egypt. Palermo Stone and its Associated Fragments* (London: Kegan Paul International, 2000), pp. 217–218.

25 M. Baud – V. Dobrev, "De nouvelles annales de l'ancien émpire égyptien: une 'Pierre de Palerme' pour la VIe dynastie," *BIFAO* 95 (1995), pp. 23–92, esp. pp. 46–47; cf. M. Baud – V. Dobrev, "Le verso des annales de la VIe dynastie, Pierre de Saqqara-Sud," *BIFAO* 97 (1997), pp. 35–42.

26 A.H. Gardiner, "Regnal Years and Civil Calender in Pharaonic Egypt," *JEA* 31 (1945), pp. 11–16.

27 A.J. Spalinger, "Dated Texts of the Old Kingdom," *SAK* 21 (1994), pp. 275–319; J.S. Nolan, "The Original Lunar Calendar and Cattle Counts in Old Kingdom Egypt," in S. Bickel – A. Loprieno (eds.), *Basel Egyptology Prize 1: Junior Research in Egyptian History, Archaeology, and Philology* (Aegyptiaca Helvetica 17. Basel: Schwabe & Co. AG, 2003), pp. 80–82.

28 A.J. Spalinger, "Dated Texts of the Old Kingdom," *SAK* 21 (1994), pp. 275–319; J.S. Nolan, "The Original Lunar Calendar and Cattle Counts in Old Kingdom Egypt," in S. Bickel – A. Loprieno (eds.), *Basel Egyptology Prize 1: Junior Research in Egyptian History, Archaeology, and Philology* (Aegyptiaca Helvetica 17. Basel: Schwabe & Co. AG, 2003), pp. 95–97.

29 K. Sethe, *Urk.* I, 16, line 14; N. Strudwick, *Texts from the Pyramid Age* (SBL Writings from the Ancient World. Atlanta: SBL, 2005), p. 200 (Text 111).

30 K. Sethe, *Urk.* I, 160; N. Strudwick, *Texts from the Pyramid Age* (SBL Writings from the Ancient World. Atlanta: SBL, 2005), pp. 97–98 (Text 16).

31 K. Sethe, *Urk.* I, 112–113; A.H. Gardiner, "Regnal Years and Civil Calender in Pharaonic Egypt," *JEA* 31 (1945), p. 15; N. Strudwick, *Texts from the Pyramid Age* (SBL Writings from the Ancient World. Atlanta: SBL, 2005), pp. 139–140 (Text 62).

32 J.S. Nolan, "The Original Lunar Calendar and Cattle Counts in Old Kingdom Egypt," in S. Bickel – A. Loprieno (eds.), *Basel Egyptology Prize 1: Junior Research in Egyptian History, Archaeology, and Philology* (Aegyptiaca Helvetica 17. Basel: Schwabe & Co. AG, 2003), pp. 78–80.

33 K. Sethe, *Urk.* I 98–110; M. Lichtheim, *Ancient Egyptian Literature, Volume I: The Old and Middle Kingdoms* (Berkeley: University of California Press, 1973), pp. 18–23; N. Strudwick, *Texts from the Pyramid Age* (SBL Writings from the Ancient World. Atlanta: SBL, 2005), pp. 352–357 (Text 256).

34 M. Verner, "The System of Dating in the Old Kingdom," pp. 23–43 in H. Vymazalová – M. Barta (eds.), *Chronology and Archaeology in Ancient Egypt (The Third Millennium B.C.)* (Prague: Czech Institute of Egyptology, Faculty of Arts, Charles University in Prague, 2008), pp. 40–41, contra J.S. Nolan, "The Original Lunar Calendar and Cattle Counts in Old Kingdom Egypt," in S. Bickel – A. Loprieno (eds.), *Basel Egyptology Prize 1: Junior Research in Egyptian History, Archaeology, and Philology* (Aegyptiaca Helvetica 17. Basel: Schwabe & Co. AG, 2003), p. 80.

35 H.K. Jacquet-Gordon, *Les noms des domaines funéraires sous l'Ancien Empire Égyptien* (BdÉ 34. Cairo: IFAO, 1962), p. 3 n. 1.

36 H. Papazian, *Domain of Pharaoh. The Structure and Components of the Economy of Old Kingdom Egypt* (HÄB 52. Hildesheim, Gebrüder Gerstenberg, 2012), pp. 37–39.

37 H.K. Jacquet-Gordon, *Les noms des domaines funéraires sous l'Ancien Empire Égyptien* (BdÉ 34. Cairo: IFAO, 1962), pp. 3–25; M. Atzler, "Einige Bemerkungen zu *ḥw.t* und *niw.t* im Alten Reich," *CdÉ* 47 (1972), pp. 17–44; W. Helck, *Wirtschaftsgeschichte des Alten Ägypten im 3. und 2. Jahrtausend vor Chr.* (HdO 1, Abschnitte 5. Leiden-Köln: Brill, 1975), pp. 34–44.

38 H.K. Jacquet-Gordon, *Les noms des domaines funéraires sous l'Ancien Empire Égyptien* (BdÉ 34. Cairo: IFAO, 1962), pp. 125–455; W. Helck, *Wirtschaftsgeschichte des Alten Ägypten im 3. und 2. Jahrtausend vor Chr.* (HdO 1, Abschnitte 5. Leiden-Köln: Brill, 1975), pp. 45–72.

39 J.C. Moreno Garcia, *Ḥwt et le milieu rural égyptien du IIIe millénaire. Économie, administration et organisation territoriale* (Bibliothèque de l'école des hautes études sciences historiques et philologiques 337. Paris, Librairie Honoré Champion, 1999), pp. 63–117.

40 H. Papazian, *Domain of Pharaoh. The Structure and Components of the Economy of Old Kingdom Egypt* (HÄB 52. Hildesheim, Gebrüder Gerstenberg, 2012), pp. 37–39.

41 P. Posener-Kriéger – M. Verner – H. Vymazalová, *Abusir X. The Pyramid Complex*

of Raneferef: The Papyrus Archive (Prague: Czech Institute of Egyptology, 2007), pp. 353–354.

42 T.G.H. James – M.R. Apted, *The Mastaba of Khentika Called Ikhekhi* (London: EES, 1953), p. 45 and pl. 9.

43 H. Wild, *Le tombeau de Ti, fascicule 3. La chapelle (deuxième partie)* (MIFAO 65. Cairo: IFAO, 1966), pl. CLXVIII, details on pl. CXLIV.

44 P. Piacentini, "On the titles of the *ḥq3w ḥwt*," in S. Allam (ed.), *Grund und Boden in Alägypten, Akten des internationalen Symposions Tübingen 18.-20. Juni 1990* (Untersuchungen zum Rechtsleben im Alten Ägypten 2. Tübingen, 1994), pp. 235–236.

45 J.C. Moreno Garcia, *Ḥwt et le milieu rural égyptien du IIIe millénaire. Économie, administration et organisation territoriale* (Bibliothèque de l'école des hautes études sciences historiques et philologiques 337. Paris, Librairie Honoré Champion, 1999), pp. 193–194. Also K. Baer, *Rank and Title in the Old Kingdom, the Structure of the Egyptian Administration in the Fifth and Sixth Dynasties* (Chicago: University of Chicago Press, 1960), pp. 21 and 170.

46 É. Martinet, *Le Nomarque sous l'Ancien Empire* (Paris, 2011), pp. 196–197.

47 C.J. Eyre, "Work and the Organization of Work in the Old Kingdom," in M.A. Powell (ed.), *Labor in the Ancient Near East* (American Oriental Series 68. New Haven: American Oriental Society, 1987), pp. 18–20; C.J. Eyre, "Village Economy in Pharaonic Egypt," in A.K. Bowman – E. Rogan (eds.), *Agriculture in Egypt, From Pharaonic to Modern Times* (Proceedings of the British Academy 96. Oxford: University Press, 1999), pp. 37–38.

48 K. Sethe, *Urk.* I 98–110; M. Lichtheim, *Ancient Egyptian Literature, Volume I: The Old and Middle Kingdoms* (Berkeley: University of California Press, 1973), pp. 18–23; N. Strudwick, *Texts from the Pyramid Age* (SBL Writings from the Ancient World. Atlanta: SBL, 2005), pp. 352–357 (Text 256).

49 The Inscription of Wepemnofret, published in H. Goedicke, *Die privaten Rechtsinschriften aus dem Alten Reich* (Beihefte zur Wiener Zeitschrift für die Kunde des Morgenlandes 5. Wien: 1970), pp. 31–43; and Stela Cairo JdE 42787, published in H. Goedicke, *Die privaten Rechtsinschriften aus dem Alten Reich* (Beihefte zur WZKM 5. Wien: 1970), pp. 149–173; and B. Menu, "Ventes de maisons sous l'ancient empire égyptien," in eadem, *Recherches sur l'histoire juridique, économique et sociale de l'ancienne Égypte 2* (BdÉ 122. Cairo: 1998), pp. 274–278.

50 Stela Cairo JdE 42787, op. cit.

51 B. Menu, "Ventes de maisons sous l'ancient empire égyptien," in eadem, *Recherches sur l'histoire juridique, économique et sociale de l'ancienne Égypte 2* (BdÉ 122. Cairo: 1998), pp. 271–287.

52 K. Sethe, *Urk.* I 157–158; H. Goedicke, *Die privaten Rechtsinschriften aus dem Alten Reich* (Beihefte zur WZKM 5. Wien: 1970), pp. 149–173; B. Menu, "Ventes de maisons sous l'ancient empire égyptien," in eadem, *Recherches sur l'histoire juridique, économique et sociale de l'ancienne Égypte 2* (BdÉ 122. Cairo: 1998), pp. 274–278; N. Strudwick, *Texts from the Pyramid Age* (SBL Writings from the Ancient World. Atlanta: SBL, 2005), pp. 205–206 (Text 121).

53 P. Posener-Kriéger, "Le prix de étoffes," in M. Görg – E. Pusch (eds.), *Festschrift Elmar Edel* (ÄAT 1. Bamberg: 1979), pp. 318–331; P. Posener-Kriéger, *I papyri di Gebelein – scavi G. Farina 1935* (Studi del Museo Egizio di Torino 1. Torino: 2004); N. Strudwick, *Texts from the Pyramid Age* (SBL Writings from the Ancient World. Atlanta: SBL, 2005), pp. 185–186 (text 102).

54 H. Goedicke, *Die privaten Rechtsinschriften aus dem Alten Reich* (Beihefte zur WZKM 5. Wien: 1970), pp. 174–177.

55 H. Goedicke, *Die privaten Rechtsinschriften aus dem Alten Reich* (Beihefte zur WZKM 5. Wien: 1970), pp. 178–181; N. Strudwick, *Texts from the Pyramid Age* (SBL Writings from the Ancient World. Atlanta: SBL, 2005), pp. 191–192 (Text 107).

56 H. Goedicke, *Die privaten Rechtsinschriften aus dem Alten Reich* (Beihefte zur WZKM 5. Wien: 1970), pp. 182–185.

57 H. Goedicke, *Die privaten Rechtsinschriften aus dem Alten Reich* (Beihefte zur WZKM 5. Wien: 1970), pp. 31–43; N. Strudwick, *Texts from the Pyramid Age* (SBL Writings from the Ancient World. Atlanta: SBL, 2005), p. 203 (Text 116).

58 K. Sethe, *Urk.* I 11–15; H. Goedicke, *Die privaten Rechtsinschriften aus dem Alten Reich* (Beihefte zur WZKM 5. Wien: 1970), p. 44–67; N. Strudwick, *Texts from the Pyramid Age* (SBL Writings from the Ancient World. Atlanta: SBL, 2005), pp. 189–191 (Text 106).

59 K. Sethe, *Urk.* I 24–32, 161–162; H. Goedicke, *Die privaten Rechtsinschriften aus dem Alten Reich* (Beihefte zur WZKM 5. Wien: 1970), pp. 131–148; N. Strudwick, *Texts from the Pyramid Age* (SBL Writings from the Ancient World. Atlanta: SBL, 2005), pp. 195–199 (Text 110).

60 K. Sethe, *Urk.* I 16–17; *wḏ.t-mdw* restored by H. Goedicke, *Die privaten Rechtsinschriften aus dem Alten Reich* (Beihefte zur WZKM 5. Wien: 1970), pp. 21–30; N. Strudwick, *Texts from the Pyramid Age* (SBL Writings from the Ancient World. Atlanta: SBL, 2005), p. 200 (Text 111).

61 H. Goedicke, *Die privaten Rechtsinschriften aus dem Alten Reich* (Beihefte zur WZKM 5. Wien: 1970), pp. 81–103; N. Strudwick, *Texts from the Pyramid Age* (SBL Writings from the Ancient World. Atlanta: SBL, 2005), pp. 187–188 (Text 104).

62 The Inscription of Wepemnofret, H. Goedicke, *Die privaten Rechtsinschriften aus dem Alten Reich* (Beihefte zur WZKM 5. Wien: 1970), pp. 31–43.

63 The Inscriptions of Wepemnofret, H. Goedicke, *Die privaten Rechtsinschriften aus dem Alten Reich* (Beihefte zur WZKM 5. Wien: 1970), pp. 31–43; of Kaemnofret, K. Sethe, *Urk.* I 11–15; H. Goedicke, *Die privaten Rechtsinschriften aus dem Alten Reich* (Beihefte zur WZKM 5. Wien: 1970), pp. 44–67; of Nika'ankh, K. Sethe, *Urk.* I 24–32, 161–162; H. Goedicke, *Die privaten Rechtsinschriften aus dem Alten Reich* (Beihefte zur WZKM 5. Wien: 1970), pp. 131–148; and of Nikaure, K. Sethe, *Urk.* I 16–17; H. Goedicke, *Die privaten Rechtsinschriften aus dem Alten Reich* (Beihefte zur WZKM 5. Wien: 1970), pp. 21–30.

64 K. Sethe, *Urk.* I 1–7; H. Goedicke, *Die privaten Rechtsinschriften aus dem Alten Reich* (Beihefte zur WZKM 5. Wien: 1970), pp. 5–20; N. Strudwick, *Texts from the Pyramid Age* (SBL Writings from the Ancient World. Atlanta: SBL, 2005), pp. 192–194 (Text 108).

65 H. Goedicke, *Die privaten Rechtsinschriften aus dem Alten Reich* (Beihefte zur WZKM 5. Wien: 1970), pp. 68–74; N. Strudwick, *Texts from the Pyramid Age* (SBL Writings from the Ancient World. Atlanta: SBL, 2005), pp. 200–201 (Text 112).

66 K. Sethe, *Urk.* I 36–37; H. Goedicke, *Die privaten Rechtsinschriften aus dem Alten Reich* (Beihefte zur WZKM 5. Wien: 1970), pp. 75–80; N. Strudwick, *Texts from the Pyramid Age* (SBL Writings from the Ancient World. Atlanta: SBL, 2005), pp. 201–202 (Text 114).

67 K. Sethe, *Urk.* I 35; H. Goedicke, *Die privaten Rechtsinschriften aus dem Alten Reich* (Beihefte zur WZKM 5. Wien: 1970), pp. 108–112; N. Strudwick, *Texts from the Pyramid Age* (SBL Writings from the Ancient World. Atlanta: SBL, 2005), p. 201 (Text 113).

68 K. Sethe, *Urk.* I 163–165; H. Goedicke, *Die privaten Rechtsinschriften aus dem Alten Reich* (Beihefte zur WZKM 5. Wien: 1970), pp. 122–130; N. Strudwick, *Texts from the Pyramid Age* (SBL Writings from the Ancient World. Atlanta: SBL, 2005), pp. 202–203 (Text 115).

69 A.M. Moussa – H. Altenmüller, *Das Grab des Nianchchnum und Chnumhotep* (Archäologische Veröffentlichungen 21, Deutsches Archäologisches Institut, Abteilung Kairo. Mainz: Philipp Von Zabern, 1977), pp. 87–88, Taf. 28, Abb. 11; N. Strudwick, *Texts from the Pyramid Age* (SBL Writings from the Ancient World. Atlanta: SBL, 2005), p. 194 (Text 109).

70 A. Philip-Stéphan, *Dire le droit en Égypte pharaonique* (Connaissance de l'Égypte Ancienne 9. Bruxelles, Éditions Safran, 2008), pp. 260–261 (Documents 55 and 56).

71 B. Menu, "Ventes de maisons sous l'ancient empire égyptien," in eadem, *Recherches sur l'histoire juridique, économique et sociale de l'ancienne Égypte 2* (BdÉ 122. Cairo: 1998), p. 274.

72 H.G. Fischer, "Notes on the Mo'alla Inscriptions and Some Contemporaneous Texts," *WZKM* 57 (1961), pp. 60–64 (2. "Copper" as an expression for one's "means").

73 T.E. Peet, *The Rhind Mathematical Papyrus, British Museum 10057 and 10058* (London: Hodder & Stoughton Ltd., 1923; reprinted Nendeln Liechtenstein: Kraus, 1970), pp. 104–107 and pl. R.

74 E.W. Castle, "Shipping and Trade in Ramesside Egypt," *JESHO* 35 (1992), pp. 256–273, contra T.E. Peet, "The Unit of Value *šꜥty* in Papyrus Boulaq 11," in *Mélanges Maspero* I (MIFAO 66/1. Cairo: IFAO, 1935–38), pp. 185–199, who argues for pieces not rings.

75 J. Černý, "Prices and Wages in Egypt in the Ramesside Period," *Cahiers d' histoire mondiale* 1 (1954), p. 904.

76 A.M. Moussa – H. Altenmüller, *Das Grab des Nianchchnum und Chnumhotep* (Archäologische Veröffentlichungen 21, Deutsches

Archäologisches Institut, Abteilung Kairo. Mainz: Philipp Von Zabern, 1977), p. 85.

77 P. Posener-Kriéger, "Le prix de étoffes," in M. Görg – E. Pusch (eds.), *Festschrift Elmar Edel* (ÄAT 1. Bamberg: 1979), pp. 318–331.

78 S.I. Hodjash – O.D. Berlev. "A Market-Scene in the Mastaba of *Ḏ3ḏ3-m-ᶜnḫ* (*Tp-m-ᶜnḫ*)," *Altorientalische Forschungen* 7 (1980), pp. 46–48.

79 N. Strudwick, *The Administration of Egypt in the Old Kingdom: The Highest Titles and Their Holders* (Studies in Egyptology. London: Kegan Paul International, 1985), pp. 337–344.

80 N. Strudwick, *The Administration of Egypt in the Old Kingdom: The Highest Titles and Their Holders* (Studies in Egyptology. London: Kegan Paul International, 1985), pp. 267–268.

81 H. Papazian, "*The Central Administration of Resources in the Old Kingdom: Departments, Treasuries, Granaries and Work Centers*," in J.C. Moreno García (ed.), *Ancient Egyptian Administration* (HdO 104. Leiden: Brill, 2013), pp. 61–66.

82 P. Posener-Kriéger, "Les papyrus d'Abousir et l'économie des temples funéraires de l'ancien empire," in E. Lipiński (ed.), *State and Temple Economy in the Ancient Near East*, Vol. 1 (OLA 5. Leuven: Department Oriëntalistiek, 1979), pp. 141–144.

83 N. Strudwick, *The Administration of Egypt in the Old Kingdom: The Highest Titles and Their Holders* (Studies in Egyptology. London: Kegan Paul International, 1985), p. 268; and P. Posener-Kriéger, *Les Archives du Temple Funeraire de Neferirkare-Kakai (Les Papyrus d'Abousir) Traduction et Commentaire I et II* (BdÉ 65. Cairo: IFAO, 1976), pp. 329–331.

84 P. Posener-Kriéger, *Les Archives du Temple Funeraire de Neferirkare-Kakai (Les Papyrus d'Abousir) Traduction et Commentaire I et II* (BdÉ 65. Cairo: IFAO, 1976), pp. 232–239 (bread), pp. 239–242 (beer and other liquids), and pp. 252–253 (grain).

85 P. Posener-Kriéger, *Les Archives du Temple Funeraire de Neferirkare-Kakai (Les Papyrus d'Abousir) Traduction et Commentaire I et II* (BdÉ 65. Cairo: IFAO, 1976), pp. 257–272, 619–624; P. Posener-Kriéger – M. Verner – H. Vymazalova, *Abusir X. The Pyramid Complex of Raneferef: The Papyrus Archive* (Prague: Czech Institute of Egyptology, 2007), pp. 381–384, p. 386; H. Vymazalová, "The Abusir Papyrus Archives and the Fifth Dynasty Royal Funerary Cults in M. Dolinska and H. Beinlich (eds.), *8. Ägyptologische Tempeltagung: Interconnections between Temples* (Königtum, Staat und Gesellschaft früher Hochkulturen 3/3. Wiesbaden, 2010), pp. 199–202.

86 N. Strudwick, *The Administration of Egypt in the Old Kingdom: The Highest Titles and Their Holders* (Studies in Egyptology. London: Kegan Paul International, 1985), pp. 269–270.

87 N. Strudwick, *The Administration of Egypt in the Old Kingdom: The Highest Titles and Their Holders* (Studies in Egyptology. London: Kegan Paul International, 1985), pp. 293–294; H. Papazian, "The Central Administration of Resources in the Old Kingdom: Departments, Treasuries, Granaries and Work Centers," in J.C. Moreno García (ed.), *Ancient Egyptian Administration* (HdO 104. Leiden: Brill, 2013), pp. 70–73.

88 H. Papazian, "The Central Administration of Resources in the Old Kingdom: Departments, Treasuries, Granaries and Work Centers," in J.C. Moreno García (ed.), *Ancient Egyptian Administration* (HdO 104. Leiden: Brill, 2013), pp. 76–82.

89 N. Strudwick, *The Administration of Egypt in the Old Kingdom: The Highest Titles and Their Holders* (Studies in Egyptology. London: Kegan Paul International, 1985), pp. 236–240.

90 N. Strudwick, *The Administration of Egypt in the Old Kingdom: The Highest Titles and Their Holders* (Studies in Egyptology. London: Kegan Paul International, 1985), pp. 240–244.

91 H. Vymazalova, "The Administration of Royal Funerary Complexes," pp. 177–195 in J.C. Moreno García (ed.), *Ancient Egyptian Administration* (HdO 104. Leiden: Brill, 2013), pp. 177–182.

92 C.J. Eyre, "Work and the Organisation of Work in the Old Kingdom," in M.A. Powell (ed.), *Labor in the Ancient Near East* (American Oriental Series 68. New Haven: American Oriental Society, 1987), p. 15.

93 C.J. Eyre, "Work and the Organisation of Work in the Old Kingdom," in M.A. Powell (ed.), *Labor in the Ancient Near East* (American Oriental Series 68. New Haven: American Oriental Society, 1987), pp. 18–20.

94 A.M. Roth, *Egyptian Phyles in the Old Kingdom, the Evolution of a System of Social Organization* (SAOC 48. Chicago: Oriental Institute, 1991), pp. 119–124.

95 A.M. Roth, *Egyptian Phyles in the Old Kingdom, the Evolution of a System of Social Organization* (SAOC 48. Chicago: Oriental Institute, 1991), pp. 124–133.

96 A.M. Roth, *Egyptian Phyles in the Old Kingdom, the Evolution of a System of Social Organization* (SAOC 48. Chicago: Oriental Institute, 1991), pp. 133–142.

97 Cf. S. Quirke, "The Residence in Relations between Places of Knowledge, Production and Power: Middle Kingdom evidence," pp. 111–130 in R. Gundlach – J.H. Taylor (eds.), *Egyptian Royal Residences, 4. Symposium zur ägyptischen Königsideologie / 4th Symposium on Egyptian Royal Ideology* (Königtum, Staat und Gesellschaft früher Hochkulturen 4,1. Wiesbaden: Harrassowitz, 2009). Quirke argues that the Twelfth and Thirteenth Dynasty Residence was "unilocal" and located in Itjtawy, but not associated with any specific building or structure.

98 P. Posener-Kriéger, *Les Archives du Temple Funeraire de Neferirkare-Kakai (Les Papyrus d'Abousir) Traduction et Commentaire I et II* (BdÉ 65. Cairo: IFAO, 1976), pp. 257–272, 282–283, 619–624; and H. Vymazalová, "The Abusir Papyrus Archives and the Fifth Dynasty Royal Funerary Cults," in M. Dolinska – H. Beinlich (eds.), *8. Ägyptologische Tempeltagung: Interconnections between Temples* (Königtum, Staat und Gesellschaft früher Hochkulturen 3/3. Wiesbaden, 2010), pp. 199–200.

99 P. Posener-Kriéger, *Les Archives du Temple Funeraire de Neferirkare-Kakai (Les Papyrus d'Abousir) Traduction et Commentaire I et II* (BdÉ 65. Cairo: IFAO, 1976), p. 620; P. Posener-Kriéger – M.Verner – H.Vymazalova, *Abusir X. The Pyramid Complex of Raneferef: The Papyrus Archive* (Prague: Czech Institute of Egyptology, 2007), p. 319, pp. 332–333, 358–359; H.Vymazalová, "The Abusir Papyrus Archives and the Fifth Dynasty Royal Funerary Cults," in M. Dolinska – H.Beinlich (eds.), *8.Ägyptologische Tempeltagung: Interconnections between Temples* (Königtum, Staat und Gesellschaft früher Hochkulturen 3/3. Wiesbaden, 2010), p. 200; and H. Vymazalová, "The Economic Connection between the Royal Cult in the Pyramid Temples and the Sun Temples in Abusir," in H. Strudwick – N. Strudwick (eds.), *Old Kingdom: New Perspectives on Egyptian Art and Archaeology, 2750–2150 B.C.* (Oxford, 2011), pp. 302–303.

100 W. Helck, *Wirtschaftsgeschichte des Alten Ägypten im 3. und 2. Jahrtausend vor Chr.* (HdO 1, Abschnitte 5. Leiden-Köln: Brill, 1975), pp. 34–44; P. Andrássy, *Untersuchungen zum ägyptischen Staat des Alten Reiches und seinen Institutionen* (IBAES 11. London, Golden House Publications, 2008), pp. 14–15.

101 T.A.H. Wilkinson, *Early Dynastic Egypt* (London: Routledge, 1999), pp. 139–142.

102 J.C. Moreno García, "Introduction. Élites et états tributaires: le cas de l'Égypte pharaonique," pp. 11–50 in J.C. Moreno García (ed.), *Élites et pouvoir en Égypte ancienne. Actes du colloque Université Charles-de-Gaulle-Lille 3, 7 et 8 juillet 2006* (CRIPEL 28, 2009–2010. Lille: Université Charles-de-Gaulle-Lille 3, 2009).

103 E. Martin-Pardey, *Untersuchungen zur ägyptischen Provinzialverwaltung bis zum Ende des Alten Reiches* (HÄB 1. Hildesheim: Gebrüder Gerstenberg, 1976), pp. 41–78; É. Martinet, *Le Nomarque sous l'Ancien Empire* (Paris, 2011), pp. 111–141; J.C. Moreno Garcia, "The Territorial Administration of the Kingdom in the Third Millennium," in J.C. Moreno García (ed.), *Ancient Egyptian Administration* (HdO 104. Leiden: Brill, 2013), pp. 87–107.

104 E. Martin-Pardey, *Untersuchungen zur ägyptischen Provinzialverwaltung bis zum Ende des Alten Reiches* (HÄB 1. Hildesheim: Gebrüder Gerstenberg, 1976), pp. 78–108; É. Martinet, *Le Nomarque sous l'Ancien Empire* (Paris, 2011), pp. 143–176; J.C. Moreno Garcia, "The Territorial Administration of the Kingdom in the Third Millennium," in J.C. Moreno García (ed.), *Ancient Egyptian Administration* (HdO 104. Leiden: Brill, 2013), pp. 107–121.

105 E. Martin-Pardey, *Untersuchungen zur ägyptischen Provinzialverwaltung bis zum Ende des Alten Reiches* (HÄB 1. Hildesheim: Gebrüder Gerstenberg, 1976), pp. 109–125; É. Martinet, *Le Nomarque sous l'Ancien Empire* (Paris, 2011), pp. 177–231; J.C. Moreno Garcia, "The Territorial Administration of the Kingdom in the Third Millennium," in J.C. Moreno García (ed.), *Ancient Egyptian Administration* (HdO 104. Leiden: Brill, 2013), pp. 121–146.

106 E. Martin-Pardey, *Untersuchungen zur ägyptischen Provinzialverwaltung bis zum Ende des Alten Reiches* (HÄB 1. Hildesheim: Gebrüder Gerstenberg, 1976), pp. 126–143.

107 L. Pantalacci, "Balat, a Frontier Town and Its Archive," pp. 197–214 in J.C. Moreno García (ed.), *Ancient Egyptian Administration* (HdO 104. Leiden: Brill, 2013).

108 H.K. Jacquet-Gordon, *Les noms des domaines funéraires sous l'Ancien Empire Égyptien* (BdÉ

34. Cairo: IFAO, 1962), pp. 125–199; H. Vymazalová, "The Abusir Papyrus Archives and the Fifth Dynasty Royal Funerary Cults," in M. Dolinska – H. Beinlich (eds.), *8. Ägyptologische Tempeltagung: Interconnections between Temples* (Königtum, Staat und Gesellschaft früher Hochkulturen 3/3. Wiesbaden, 2010), p. 199.

109 P. Posener-Kriéger – M. Verner – H. Vymazalova, *Abusir X. The Pyramid Complex of Raneferef: The Papyrus Archive* (Prague: Czech Institute of Egyptology, 2007), pp. 20–23.

110 P. Posener-Kriéger, *Les Archives du Temple Funeraire de Neferirkare-Kakai (Les Papyrus d'Abousir) Traduction et Commentaire I et II* (BdÉ 65. Cairo: IFAO, 1976), pp. 255–295; P. Posener-Kriéger – M. Verner – H. Vymazalova, *Abusir X. The Pyramid Complex of Raneferef: The Papyrus Archive* (Prague: Czech Institute of Egyptology, 2007), pp. 390–394; and H. Vymazalová, "The Abusir Papyrus Archives and the Fifth Dynasty Royal Funerary Cults," in M. Dolinska – H. Beinlich (eds.), *8. Ägyptologische Tempeltagung: Interconnections between Temples* (Königtum, Staat und Gesellschaft früher Hochkulturen 3/3. Wiesbaden, 2010), p. 198.

111 P. Posener-Kriéger, *Les Archives du Temple Funeraire de Neferirkare-Kakai (Les Papyrus d'Abousir) Traduction et Commentaire I et II* (BdÉ 65. Cairo: IFAO, 1976), pp. 257–272, 619–624; P. Posener-Kriéger – M. Verner – H. Vymazalova, *Abusir X. The Pyramid Complex of Raneferef: The Papyrus Archive* (Prague: Czech Institute of Egyptology, 2007), pp. 381–384, p. 386; H. Vymazalová, "The Abusir Papyrus Archives and the Fifth Dynasty Royal Funerary Cults," in M. Dolinska – H. Beinlich (eds.), *8. Ägyptologische Tempeltagung: Interconnections between Temples* (Königtum, Staat und Gesellschaft früher Hochkulturen 3/3. Wiesbaden, 2010), pp. 199–202.

112 P. Posener-Kriéger – M. Verner – H. Vymazalova, *Abusir X. The Pyramid Complex of Raneferef: The Papyrus Archive* (Prague: Czech Institute of Egyptology, 2007), pp. 385–386; H. Vymazalová, "The Economic Connection between the Royal Cult in the Pyramid Temples and the Sun Temples in Abusir," in H. Strudwick – N. Strudwick (eds.), *Old Kingdom: New Perspectives on Egyptian Art and Archaeology, 2750–2150 B.C.* (Oxford, 2011), pp. 302–303.

113 P. Posener-Kriéger, *Les Archives du Temple Funeraire de Neferirkare-Kakai (Les Papyrus d'Abousir) Traduction et Commentaire I et II* (BdÉ 65. Cairo: IFAO, 1976), pp. 288–295, 405–412; P. Posener-Kriéger – M. Verner – H. Vymazalova, *Abusir X. The Pyramid Complex of Raneferef: The Papyrus Archive* (Prague: Czech Institute of Egyptology, 2007), pp. 387–388, 394–398; and H. Vymazalová, "The Abusir Papyrus Archives and the Fifth Dynasty Royal Funerary Cults," in M. Dolinska – H. Beinlich (eds.), *8. Ägyptologische Tempeltagung: Interconnections between Temples* (Königtum, Staat und Gesellschaft früher Hochkulturen 3/3. Wiesbaden, 2010), p. 198.

114 P. Posener-Kriéger – M. Verner – H. Vymazalova, *Abusir X. The Pyramid Complex of Raneferef: The Papyrus Archive* (Prague: Czech Institute of Egyptology, 2007), pp. 398–403.

115 P. Posener-Kriéger – M. Verner – H. Vymazalova, *Abusir X. The Pyramid Complex of Raneferef: The Papyrus Archive* (Prague: Czech Institute of Egyptology, 2007), pp. 210–215.

116 P. Posener-Kriéger – M. Verner – H. Vymazalova, *Abusir X. The Pyramid Complex of Raneferef: The Papyrus Archive* (Prague: Czech Institute of Egyptology, 2007), pp. 242–264.

117 A.M. Roth, *Egyptian Phyles in the Old Kingdom, the Evolution of a System of Social Organization* (SAOC 48. Chicago: Oriental Institute, 1991), pp. 77–89.

118 P. Posener-Kriéger – M. Verner – H. Vymazalová, *Abusir 10 The Pyramid Complex of Raneferef: The Papyrus Archive* (Prague: Czech Institute of Egyptology, Faculty of Arts, Charles University in Prague, 2006), pp. 364–369.

119 P. Posener-Kriéger – M. Verner – H. Vymazalová, *Abusir 10. The Pyramid Complex of Raneferef: The Papyrus Archive* (Prague: Czech Institute of Egyptology, Faculty of Arts, Charles University in Prague, 2006), p. 365, pp. 369–374; H. Vymazalova, "The Administration of Royal Funerary Complexes," in J.C. Moreno García (ed.), *Ancient Egyptian Administration* (HdO 104. Leiden: Brill, 2013), pp. 182–195.

120 H. Papazian, "Perspectives on the Cult of Pharaoh during the Third Millennium B.C.: A Chronological Overview," in H. Vymazalová – M. Barta (eds.), *Chronology and Archaeology in Ancient Egypt (The Third Millennium B.C.)* (Prague: Czech Institute of Egyptology, Faculty of Arts, Charles University in Prague, 2008), pp. 74–77.

121 H. Papazian, "Perspectives on the Cult of Pharaoh during the Third Millennium B.C.: A

Chronological Overview," in H. Vymazalová – M. Barta (eds.), *Chronology and Archaeology in Ancient Egypt (The Third Millennium B.C.)* (Prague: Czech Institute of Egyptology, Faculty of Arts, Charles University in Prague, 2008), pp. 77–79.

122 L. Habachi, *Tell Basta* (Supplément aux ASAE 22. Cairo: IFAO, 1957), pp. 14–18, and figs. 2–3; A. el-Sawi, *Excavations at Tell Basta: Report of Seasons 1967–1971 and Catalogue of Finds* (Prague: Charles University, 1979), pp. 75–76, and figs. 164–167; N. Strudwick, *Texts from the Pyramid Age* (SBL Writings from the Ancient World. Atlanta: SBL, 2005), pp. 92–93 (Text 13).

123 K. Sethe, *Urk.* I 214; N. Strudwick, *Texts from the Pyramid Age* (SBL Writings from the Ancient World. Atlanta: SBL, 2005), pp. 105–106 (Text 21).

124 L. Pantalacci, "Un décret de Pépi II en faveur des gouverneurs de l'oasis de Dakhla," *BIFAO* 85 (1985), pp. 245–254; N. Strudwick, *Texts from the Pyramid Age* (SBL Writings from the Ancient World. Atlanta: SBL, 2005), p. 115 (Text 28).

125 K. Sethe, *Urk.* I 302–304; N. Strudwick, *Texts from the Pyramid Age* (SBL Writings from the Ancient World. Atlanta: SBL, 2005), pp. 119–120 (Text 33).

126 K. Sethe, *Urk.* I 304–306; N. Strudwick, *Texts from the Pyramid Age* (SBL Writings from the Ancient World. Atlanta: SBL, 2005), pp. 123–124 (Text 39).

127 Decree of Teti for the temple of the god Khentimentiu at Abydos: K. Sethe, *Urk.* I 207–208; N. Strudwick, *Texts from the Pyramid Age* (SBL Writings from the Ancient World. Atlanta: SBL, 2005), pp. 102–103 (Text 19). Decree of Pepi I for the ka-chapel of the royal mother Iput at Coptos: K. Sethe, *Urk.* I 214; N. Strudwick, *Texts from the Pyramid Age* (SBL Writings from the Ancient World. Atlanta: SBL, 2005), pp. 105–106 (Text 21). Decree B of Pepi II for the temple of the god Min at Coptos: K. Sethe, *Urk.* I 280–283; N. Strudwick, *Texts from the Pyramid Age* (SBL Writings from the Ancient World. Atlanta: SBL, 2005), pp. 107–109 (Text 24). Decree C of Pepi II for the temple of the god Min at Coptos: K. Sethe, *Urk.* I 284–288; N. Strudwick, *Texts from the Pyramid Age* (SBL Writings from the Ancient World. Atlanta: SBL, 2005), pp. 109–111 (Text 25).

128 Decree of Shepseskaf for the mortuary temple of Menkaure at Giza: K. Sethe, *Urk.* I 160; N. Strudwick, *Texts from the Pyramid Age* (SBL Writings from the Ancient World. Atlanta: SBL, 2005), pp. 97–98 (Text 16). Decree of Pepi I for the pyramid towns of Sneferu at Dahshur: K. Sethe, *Urk.* I 209–213; N. Strudwick, *Texts from the Pyramid Age* (SBL Writings from the Ancient World. Atlanta: SBL, 2005), pp. 103–105 (Text 20). Decree of Pepi II for the pyramid town of Menkaure at Giza: K. Sethe, *Urk.* I 277–278; N. Strudwick, *Texts from the Pyramid Age* (SBL Writings from the Ancient World. Atlanta: SBL, 2005), pp. 106–107 (Text 23).

129 M. Nuzzolo, "The Sun Temples of the Vth Dynasty," *SAK* 36 (2007), pp. 217–247; H. Vymazalová, "The Abusir Papyrus Archives and the Fifth Dynasty Royal Funerary Cults," in M. Dolinska – H. Beinlich (eds.), *8. Ägyptologische Tempeltagung: Interconnections between Temples* (Königtum, Staat und Gesellschaft früher Hochkulturen 3/3. Wiesbaden, 2010), pp. 200–201.

130 H. Vymazalová, "The Economic Connection between the Royal Cult in the Pyramid Temples and the Sun Temples in Abusir," in H. Strudwick – N. Strudwick (eds.), *Old Kingdom: New Perspectives on Egyptian Art and Archaeology, 2750–2150 B.C.* (Oxford, 2011), pp. 297–298, p. 301.

131 P. Posener-Kriéger, *Les Archives du Temple Funeraire de Neferirkare-Kakai (Les Papyrus d'Abousir) Traduction et Commentaire I et II* (BdÉ 65. Cairo: IFAO, 1976), pp. 611–612; P. Posener-Kriéger –M. Verner – H. Vymazalova, *Abusir X. The Pyramid Complex of Raneferef: The Papyrus Archive* (Prague: Czech Institute of Egyptology, 2007), pp. 383–384; H. Vymazalová, "The Abusir Papyrus Archives and the Fifth Dynasty Royal Funerary Cults," in M. Dolinska – H. Beinlich (eds.), *8. Ägyptologische Tempeltagung: Interconnections between Temples* (Königtum, Staat und Gesellschaft früher Hochkulturen 3/3. Wiesbaden, 2010), pp. 200–203; H. Vymazalová, "The Economic Connection between the Royal Cult in the Pyramid Temples and the Sun Temples in Abusir," in H. Strudwick – N. Strudwick (eds.), *Old Kingdom: New Perspectives on Egyptian Art and Archaeology, 2750–2150 B.C.* (Oxford, 2011), pp. 296–297.

132 P. Posener-Kriéger, *Les Archives du Temple Funeraire de Neferirkare-Kakai (Les Papyrus d'Abousir) Traduction et Commentaire I et II* (BdÉ 65. Cairo: IFAO, 1976), pp. 631–634; H. Vymazalová, "The Economic Connection between the Royal Cult in the Pyramid Temples and the Sun Temples in Abusir," in H. Strudwick – N. Strudwick (eds.), *Old Kingdom: New Perspectives on Egyptian Art and Archaeology, 2750–2150 B.C.* (Oxford, 2011), pp. 302–303.

133 K. Sethe, *Urk.* I 1–7; H. Goedicke, *Die privaten Rechtsinschriften aus dem Alten Reich* (Beihefte zur WZKM 5. Wien: 1970), pp. 5–20; N. Strudwick, *Texts from the Pyramid Age* (SBL Writings from the Ancient World. Atlanta: SBL, 2005), pp. 192–194 (Text 108).

134 H. Goedicke, *Die privaten Rechtsinschriften aus dem Alten Reich* (Beihefte zur WZKM 5. Wien: 1970), pp. 68–74; N. Strudwick, *Texts from the Pyramid Age* (SBL Writings from the Ancient World. Atlanta: SBL, 2005), pp. 200–201 (Text 112).

135 K. Sethe, *Urk.* I 163–165; H. Goedicke, *Die privaten Rechtsinschriften aus dem Alten Reich* (Beihefte zur WZKM 5. Wien: 1970), pp. 122–130; N. Strudwick, *Texts from the Pyramid Age* (SBL Writings from the Ancient World. Atlanta: SBL, 2005), pp. 202–203 (Text 115).

136 H.K. Jacquet-Gordon, *Les noms des domaines funéraires sous l'Ancien Empire Égyptien* (BdÉ 34. Cairo: IFAO, 1962), pp. 201–455.

137 A.M. Roth, *Egyptian Phyles in the Old Kingdom, the Evolution of a System of Social Organization* (SAOC 48. Chicago: Oriental Institute, 1991), pp. 91–118.

138 K. Sethe, *Urk.* I 1–7; N. Strudwick, *Texts from the Pyramid Age* (SBL Writings from the Ancient World. Atlanta: SBL, 2005), pp. 192–194 (Text 108).

139 H. Goedicke, *Die privaten Rechtsinschriften aus dem Alten Reich* (Beihefte zur WZKM 5. Wien: 1970), pp. 174–177.

140 B. Menu – I. Harari, "La notion de propriété privé dans l'ancien Empire Egyptien," *CRIPEL* 2 (1974), pp. 125–154.

141 A. Monson, "Communal Agriculture in the Ptolemaic and Roman Fayyum," pp. 173–186 in S. Lippert – M. Schentuleit (eds.), *Graeco-Roman Fayum – Texts and Archaeology* (Wiesbaden: Harrassowitz, 2008).

142 B. Menu, "Ventes de maisons sous l'ancient empire égyptien," in eadem, *Recherches sur l'histoire juridique, économique et sociale de l'ancienne Égypte 2* (BdÉ 122. Cairo: 1998), pp. 271–287.

143 K. Sethe, *Urk.* I 157–158; H. Goedicke, *Die privaten Rechtsinschriften aus dem Alten Reich* (Beihefte zur WZKM 5. Wien: 1970), pp. 149–173; B. Menu, "Ventes de maisons sous l'ancient empire égyptien," in eadem, *Recherches sur l'histoire juridique, économique et sociale de l'ancienne Égypte 2* (BdÉ 122. Cairo: 1998), pp. 274–278; N. Strudwick, *Texts from the Pyramid Age* (SBL Writings from the Ancient World. Atlanta: SBL, 2005), pp. 205–206 (Text 121).

144 P. Posener-Kriéger, "Le prix de étoffes," in M. Görg – E. Pusch (eds.), *Festschrift Elmar Edel* (ÄAT 1. Bamberg: 1979), pp. 318–331; P. Posener-Kriéger, *I papyri di Gebelein – scavi G. Farina 1935* (Studi del Museo Egizio di Torino 1. Torino: 2004); N. Strudwick, *Texts from the Pyramid Age* (SBL Writings from the Ancient World. Atlanta: SBL, 2005), pp. 185–186 (text 102).

145 H. Goedicke, *Die privaten Rechtsinschriften aus dem Alten Reich* (Beihefte zur WZKM 5. Wien: 1970), pp. 174–177.

146 H. Goedicke, *Die privaten Rechtsinschriften aus dem Alten Reich* (Beihefte zur WZKM 5. Wien: 1970), pp. 178–181; N. Strudwick, *Texts from the Pyramid Age* (SBL Writings from the Ancient World. Atlanta: SBL, 2005), pp. 191–192 (Text 107).

147 H. Goedicke, *Die privaten Rechtsinschriften aus dem Alten Reich* (Beihefte zur WZKM 5. Wien: 1970), pp. 31–43; N. Strudwick, *Texts from the Pyramid Age* (SBL Writings from the Ancient World. Atlanta: SBL, 2005), p. 203 (Text 116).

148 K. Sethe, *Urk.* I 24–32, 161–162; H. Goedicke, *Die privaten Rechtsinschriften aus dem Alten Reich* (Beihefte zur WZKM 5. Wien: 1970), pp. 131–148; N. Strudwick, *Texts from the Pyramid Age* (SBL Writings from the Ancient World. Atlanta: SBL, 2005), pp. 195–199 (Text 110).

149 S. Hassan, "Excavations at Saqqara, 1937–1938," *ASAE* 38 (1938), p. 520 and pl. 96; S. Hassan, "The causeway of *Wnis* at Sakkara," *ZÄS* 80 (1955), p. 139, Taf. 13, Abb. 2; and A. Labrousse – A. Moussa, *La chaussée du complexe funéraire du roi Ounas* (BdÉ 134. Cairo: IFAO, 2002), pp. 33–34, figs. 36–40 (Docs. 22–26).

150 G. Steindorff, *Das Grab des Ti* (Veröffentlichungen der Ernst von Sieglin Expedition in Ägypten 2. Leipzig: J.C. Hinrichs'sche Buchhandlung, 1913), taf. 133.
151 A.M. Moussa – H. Altenmüller, *Das Grab des Nianchchnum und Chnumhotep* (Archäologische Veröffentlichungen 21, Deutsches Archäologisches Institut, Abteilung Kairo. Mainz: Philipp Von Zabern, 1977), pp. 81–86, Taf. 24–25, Abb. 10; Y. Harpur – P. Scremin, *The Chapel of Niankhkhnum & Khnumhotep: Scene Details* (Egypt in Miniature 3. Oxford: Expedition to Egypt, 2010), pp. 146–157 (pls. 153–167), and p. 624 (fig. 71).
152 S.I. Hodjash – O.D. Berlev. "A Market-Scene in the Mastaba of *D3d3-m-'nḫ (Tp-m-'nḫ)*," *Altorientalische Forschungen* 7 (1980), pp. 31–49.
153 Y. Harpur – P. Scremin, *The Chapel of Kagemni: Scene Details* (Egypt in Miniature 1. Oxford: Expedition to Egypt, 2006), pp. 182–184 (pls. 292–294), and p. 500 (fig. 17).
154 A. Badawy, *The Tomb of Nyhetep-Ptah at Giza and 'Ankhm'ahor at Saqqara* (Berkeley: University of California Press, 1978), pp. 19–21, figs. 29–31, pls. 32–34.
155 S.I. Hodjash – O.D. Berlev. "A Market-Scene in the Mastaba of *D3d3-m-'nḫ (Tp-m-'nḫ)*," *Altorientalische Forschungen* 7 (1980), pp. 46–47.
156 K. Sethe, *Urk.* I 98–110; M. Lichtheim, *Ancient Egyptian Literature, Volume I: The Old and Middle Kingdoms* (Berkeley: University of California Press, 1973), pp. 18–23; N. Strudwick, *Texts from the Pyramid Age* (SBL Writings from the Ancient World. Atlanta: SBL, 2005), pp. 352–357 (Text 256).
157 E. Eichler, *Untersuchungen zum Expeditionswesen des ägyptischen Alten Reiches* (Göttinger Orientforschungen. IV. Ägypten, 26. Wiesbaden: Harrassowitz, 1993).
158 T.A. Wilkinson, *Royal Annals of Ancient Egypt. Palermo Stone and Its Associated Fragments* (London: Kegan Paul International, 2000), pp. 141–143.
159 K. Sethe, *Urk.* I 131–135; N. Strudwick, *Texts from the Pyramid Age* (SBL Writings from the Ancient World. Atlanta: SBL, 2005), pp. 333–335 (Text 242).
160 N. Strudwick, *Texts from the Pyramid Age* (SBL Writings from the Ancient World. Atlanta: SBL, 2005), pp. 339–340 (Text 244).
161 K. Sethe, *Urk.* I 120–131; M. Lichtheim, *Ancient Egyptian Literature, Volume I: The Old and Middle Kingdoms* (Berkeley: University of California Press, 1973), pp. 23–27; N. Strudwick, *Texts from the Pyramid Age* (SBL Writings from the Ancient World. Atlanta: SBL, 2005), pp. 328–333 (Text 241).
162 K. Sethe, *Urk.* I 140–141; N. Strudwick, *Texts from the Pyramid Age* (SBL Writings from the Ancient World. Atlanta: SBL, 2005), p. 340 (Text 245).
163 K. N. Sowada, *Egypt in the Eastern Mediterranean during the Old Kingdom: An Archaeological Perspective* (Orbis Biblicus et Orientalis 237. Fribourg – Göttingen: Academic Press – Vandenhoeck & Ruprecht. 2009), pp. 5–15.
164 K. Sethe, *Urk.* I 98–110; M. Lichtheim, *Ancient Egyptian Literature, Volume I: The Old and Middle Kingdoms* (Berkeley: University of California Press, 1973), pp. 18–23; N. Strudwick, *Texts from the Pyramid Age* (SBL Writings from the Ancient World. Atlanta: SBL, 2005), pp. 352–357 (Text 256).
165 I. Shaw, *Hatnub: Quarrying Travertine in Ancient Egypt* (EES Excavation Memoir 88. London: EES, 2010).
166 K. Sethe, *Urk.* I 98–110; M. Lichtheim, *Ancient Egyptian Literature, Volume I: The Old and Middle Kingdoms* (Berkeley: University of California Press, 1973), pp. 18–23; N. Strudwick, *Texts from the Pyramid Age* (SBL Writings from the Ancient World. Atlanta: SBL, 2005), pp. 352–357 (Text 256).
167 J. Couyat – P. Montet, *Les inscriptions hiéroglyphiques et hiératiques du Ouâdi Hammâmât* (MIFAO 34. Cairo: IFAO, 1912); G. Goyon, *Nouvelles inscriptions rupestres du Wadi Hammamat* (Paris: Imprimerie Nationale, 1957).
168 P. Tallet – G. Marouard, "An Early Pharaonic Harbour on the Red Sea Coast," *Egyptian Archaeology* 40 (2012), pp. 2–5; P. Tallet – G. Marouard – D. Laisney, "Un port de la IVe dynastie au Ouadi al-Jarf (mer Rouge)," *BIFAO* 112 (2012), pp. 399–446.
169 T.A. Wilkinson, *Royal Annals of Ancient Egypt. Palermo Stone and Its Associated Fragments* (London: Kegan Paul International, 2000), pp. 141–144.
170 M. Abd el-Raziq – G. Castel – P. Tallet – G. Marouard, "The Pharaonic Site of Ayn Soukhna in the Gulf of Suez, 2001–2009, Progress Report," pp. 3–20 in P. Tallet – El-Sayed Mahfouz (eds.), *The Red Sea in Pharaonic times: Recent Discoveries along the Red Sea Coast. Proceedings of the Colloquium held in Cairo / Ayn Soukhna 11th – 12th*

January 2009 (BdÉ 155. Cairo: IFAO, 2012), esp. p. 6; and P. Tallet, "New Inscriptions from Ayn Soukhna 2002–2009," pp. 105–115 in P. Tallet – El-Sayed Mahfouz (eds.), *The Red Sea in Pharaonic times: Recent Discoveries along the Red Sea Coast. Proceedings of the Colloquium held in Cairo / Ayn Soukhna 11th – 12th January 2009* (BdÉ 155. Cairo: IFAO, 2012).

171 G.D. Mumford – S. Parcak, "Pharaonic Ventures into South Sinai: El-Markha Plain Site 346," *JEA* 89 (2003), pp. 83–116; G. Mumford, "Tell Ras Budran (Site 345): Defining Egypt's Eastern Frontier and Mining Operations in South Sinai during the Late Old Kingdom (Early EB IV/MB I)," *BASOR* 342 (May 2006), pp. 13–67; P. Tallet – G. Marouard – D. Laisney, "Un port de la IVe dynastie au Ouadi al-Jarf (mer Rouge)," *BIFAO* 112 (2012), pp. 399–446, esp. p. 425.

172 T.A. Wilkinson, *Royal Annals of Ancient Egypt. Palermo Stone and Its Associated Fragments* (London: Kegan Paul International, 2000), pp. 168–171.

173 T. El-Awady, *Abusir XVI. Sahure – The Pyramid Causeway: History and Decoration Program in the Old Kingdom* (Prague: Charles University, 2009), pp. 155–186.

174 T.A. Wilkinson, *Royal Annals of Ancient Egypt. Palermo Stone and Its Associated Fragments* (London: Kegan Paul International, 2000), pp. 235–236.

175 R. Kuper, "The Abu Ballas Trail: Pharaonic Advances into the Libyan Desert," pp. 372–376 in Z. Hawass – L. Pinch Brock (eds.), *Egypt at the Dawn of the Twenty-First Century, Proceedings of the Eighth International Congress of Egyptologists, Cairo 2000*, vol. 2 (Cairo, 2003); F. Förster, "With Donkeys, Jars and Water Bags into the Libyan Desert: The Abu Ballas Trail in the Late Old Kingdom/ First Intermediate Period," *British Museum Studies in Ancient Egypt and Sudan* 7 (2007), pp. 1–39.

176 S. Kröpelin – R. Kuper, "More Corridors to Africa," *CRIPEL* 26 (2006–2007), pp. 219–229.

177 W. Schenkel, *Memphis · Herakleopolis · Theben: die epigraphischen Zeugnisse der 7.-11. Dynastie Ägyptens* (ÄA 12. Wiesbaden: Harrassowitz, 1965), pp. 25–28.

178 I. Shaw, *Hatnub: Quarrying Travertine in Ancient Egypt* (EES Excavation Memoir 88. London: EES, 2010).

179 D. Franke, "Zwischen Herakleopolis und Theben: Neues zu den Gräbern von Assiut." *SAK* 14 (1987), pp. 49–60.

180 J. Vandier, *Mo'alla: la tombe d'Ankhtifi et la tombe de Sébekhotep* (BdÉ 18. Cairo: IFAO, 1950).

181 J.C. Darnell, *Theban Desert Road Survey in the Egyptian Western Desert, I: Gebel Tjauti Rock Inscriptions 1–45 and Wadi el-Hol Rock Inscriptions 1–45* (OIP 119. Chicago: Oriental Institute, 2002).

182 M. Lehner, *The Complete Pyramids* (London-New York: Thames and Hudson, 1997), pp. 84–94.

183 M. Lehner, *The Complete Pyramids* (London-New York: Thames and Hudson, 1997), pp. 97–139.

184 M. Lehner, *The Complete Pyramids* (London-New York: Thames and Hudson, 1997), pp. 140–155.

185 M. Lehner, *The Complete Pyramids* (London-New York: Thames and Hudson, 1997), pp. 156–163.

186 M. Nuzzolo, "The Sun Temples of the Vth Dynasty," *SAK* 36 (2007), pp. 217–247.

187 H. Papazian, "Perspectives on the Cult of Pharaoh during the Third Millennium B.C.: A Chronological Overview," in H. Vymazalová – M. Barta (eds.), *Chronology and Archaeology in Ancient Egypt (The Third Millennium B.C.)* (Prague: Czech Institute of Egyptology, Faculty of Arts, Charles University in Prague, 2008), pp. 74–79.

188 M. Lehner, *The Complete Pyramids* (London-New York: Thames and Hudson, 1997), p. 164.

189 M. Lehner, *The Complete Pyramids* (London-New York: Thames and Hudson, 1997), pp. 165–167; L. Postel, *Protocole des souverains égyptiens et dogme monarchique au début du Moyen Empire* (Monographies Reine Élisabeth 10. Turnhout: Brepols, 2004).

3. THE MIDDLE KINGDOM AND THE SECOND INTERMEDIATE PERIOD (c. 2025–1550 BCE)

1 K.S.B. Ryholt, *The Political Situation in Egypt during the Second Intermediate Period c. 1800–1550 BC.* (CNI 20. Copenhagen: Museum Tusculanum Press, 1997), pp. 69–93.

2 M. Bietak, "Zum Königreich des aA-zH-Ra Neḥesi," *SAK* 11 (1984), pp. 59–75; K.S.B. Ryholt, *The Political Situation in Egypt during*

the Second Intermediate Period c. *1800–1550 BC*. (CNI 20. Copenhagen: Museum Tusculanum Press, 1997), pp. 94–117.

3 K.S.B. Ryholt, *The Political Situation in Egypt during the Second Intermediate Period* c. *1800–1550 BC*. (CNI 20. Copenhagen: Museum Tusculanum Press, 1997), pp. 118–150.

4 K.S.B. Ryholt, *The Political Situation in Egypt during the Second Intermediate Period* c. *1800–1550 BC*. (CNI 20. Copenhagen: Museum Tusculanum Press, 1997), pp. 151–183.

5 J. Baines, *Visual and Written Culture in Ancient Egypt* (Oxford: University Press, 2007), pp. 33–62 (chapter 2. Literacy and ancient Egyptian society), especially p. 59.

6 W.C. Hayes, *A Papyrus of the Late Middle Kingdom* (New York: The Brooklyn Museum, 1955), pp. 71–72.

7 A. Philip-Stéphan, *Dire le droit en Égypte pharaonique* (Connaissance de l'Égypte Ancienne 9. Bruxelles, Éditions Safran, 2008), pp. 155–160.

8 For lines 8–11, see S. Quirke, *The Administration of Egypt in the Late Middle Kingdom, The Hieratic Documents* (New Malden: Sia Publishing, 1990), pp. 142–143.

9 For lines 5–6, see S. Quirke, *The Administration of Egypt in the Late Middle Kingdom, The Hieratic Documents* (New Malden: Sia Publishing, 1990), pp. 142–143 and 145.

10 A. Philip-Stéphan, *Dire le droit en Égypte pharaonique* (Connaissance de l'Égypte Ancienne 9. Bruxelles: Éditions Safran, 2008), pp. 150–154.

11 W. Grajetzki, "Setting a State Anew: The Central Administration from the End of the Old Kingdom to the End of the Middle Kingdom," in J.C. Moreno García (ed.), *Ancient Egyptian Administration* (HdO 104. Leiden: Brill, 2013), pp. 217–225.

12 J.J. Shirley, "Crisis and Restructuring of the State: From the Second Intermediate Period to the Advent of the Ramesses," in J.C. Moreno García (ed.), *Ancient Egyptian Administration* (HdO 104. Leiden: Brill, 2013), pp. 521–570.

13 S. Quirke, *Titles and Bureaux of Egypt 1850–1700 BC* (Egyptology 1. London: Golden House Publications, 2004), p. 25, pp. 85–96; W. Grajetzki, "Setting a State Anew: The Central Administration from the End of the Old Kingdom to the End of the Middle Kingdom," in J.C. Moreno García (ed.), *Ancient Egyptian Administration* (HdO 104. Leiden: Brill, 2013), pp. 225–237.

14 S. Quirke, *Titles and Bureaux of Egypt 1850–1700 BC* (Egyptology 1. London: Golden House Publications, 2004), pp. 17–23.

15 A. Philip-Stéphan, *Dire le droit en Égypte pharaonique* (Connaissance de l'Égypte Ancienne 9. Bruxelles: Éditions Safran, 2008), pp. 81–84, 241–243.

16 A. Philip-Stéphan, *Dire le droit en Égypte pharaonique* (Connaissance de l'Égypte Ancienne 9. Bruxelles: Éditions Safran, 2008), pp. 78–81, 93–99.

17 G.P.F. van den Boorn, *The Duties of the Vizier, Civil Administration in the Early New Kingdom* (London: Kegan Paul International, 1988), pp. 276–281; S. Quirke, *Titles and Bureaux of Egypt 1850–1700 BC* (Egyptology 1. London: Golden House Publications, 2004), p. 22.

18 S. Quirke, *The Administration of Egypt in the Late Middle Kingdom, The Hieratic Documents* (New Malden: Sia Publishing, 1990), pp. 130–140; A. Philip-Stéphan, *Dire le droit en Égypte pharaonique* (Connaissance de l'Égypte Ancienne 9. Bruxelles: Éditions Safran, 2008), p. 98.

19 P. Lacau, *Une stèle juridique de Karnak* (Supplément aux ASAE 13. Cairo: IFAO, 1949).

20 cf. B. Kelly, *Petitions, Litigation, and Social Control in Roman Egypt* (Oxford: University Press, 2011), pp. 6–18.

21 H.K. Jacquet-Gordon, *Les noms des domaines funéraires sous l'Ancien Empire Égyptien* (BdÉ 34. Cairo: IFAO, 1962), pp. 3–25; M. Atzler, "Einige Bemerkungen zu *ḥw.t* und *niw.t* im Alten Reich," *CdÉ* 47 (1972), pp. 17–44; W. Helck, *Wirtschaftsgeschichte des Alten Ägypten im 3. und 2. Jahrtausend vor Chr.* (HdO 1, Abschnitte 5. Leiden-Köln: Brill, 1975), pp. 34–44; J.C. Moreno Garcia, *Ḥwt et le milieu rural égyptien du IIIe millénaire. Économie, administration et organisation territoriale* (Bibliothèque de l'école des hautes études sciences historiques et philologiques 337. Paris: Librairie Honoré Champion, 1999), pp. 266–269.

22 J.C. Moreno Garcia, *Ḥwt et le milieu rural égyptien du IIIe millénaire. Économie, administration et organisation territoriale* (Bibliothèque de l'école des hautes études sciences historiques et philologiques 337. Paris: Librairie Honoré Champion, 1999), pp. 179–182.

23 S. Quirke, *Titles and Bureaux of Egypt 1850–1700 BC* (Egyptology 1. London: Golden House Publications, 2004), p. 112.

24 J.C. Moreno Garcia, *Ḥwt et le milieu rural égyptien du IIIe millénaire. Économie, administration et organisation territoriale* (Bibliothèque de l'école des hautes études sciences historiques et philologiques 337. Paris: Librairie Honoré Champion, 1999), pp. 188–190.

25 C.J. Eyre, "The Village Economy in Pharaonic Egypt," in A.K. Bowman – E. Rogan (eds.), *Agriculture in Egypt, from Pharaonic to Modern Times* (Proceedings of the British Academy 96. Oxford: University Press, 1999), p. 42; J.C. Moreno Garcia, *Ḥwt et le milieu rural égyptien du IIIe millénaire. Économie, administration et organisation territoriale* (Bibliothèque de l'école des hautes études sciences historiques et philologiques 337. Paris: Librairie Honoré Champion, 1999), pp. 190–193.

26 S. Quirke, *Titles and Bureaux of Egypt 1850–1700 BC* (Egyptology 1. London: Golden House Publications, 2004), pp. 18–24.

27 C.J. Eyre, "The Village Economy in Pharaonic Egypt," in A.K. Bowman – E. Rogan (eds.), *Agriculture in Egypt, from Pharaonic to Modern Times* (Proceedings of the British Academy 96. Oxford: University Press, 1999), p. 43.

28 S. Quirke, *Titles and Bureaux of Egypt 1850–1700 BC* (Egyptology 1. London: Golden House Publications, 2004), pp. 111–112.

29 G.P.F. van den Boorn, *The Duties of the Vizier, Civil Administration in the Early New Kingdom* (London: Kegan Paul International, 1988), pp. 146–171; S. Quirke, *Titles and Bureaux of Egypt 1850–1700 BC* (Egyptology 1. London: Golden House Publications, 2004), p. 20.

30 G.P.F. van den Boorn, *The Duties of the Vizier, Civil Administration in the Early New Kingdom* (London: Kegan Paul International, 1988), pp. 185–192; S. Quirke, *Titles and Bureaux of Egypt 1850–1700 BC* (Egyptology 1. London: Golden House Publications, 2004), p. 21.

31 G.P.F. van den Boorn, *The Duties of the Vizier, Civil Administration in the Early New Kingdom* (London: Kegan Paul International, 1988), pp. 265–275; S. Quirke, *Titles and Bureaux of Egypt 1850–1700 BC* (Egyptology 1. London: Golden House Publications, 2004), p. 22.

32 P.C. Smither, "A Tax-assessor's Journal of the Middle Kingdom," *JEA* 27 (1941), pp. 74–76.

33 S. Berger, "A Note on Some Scenes of Land-Measurement," *JEA* 20 (1934), pp. 54–56: Tombs of Menna (TT 69), Khaemhat (TT 57), Karasonb (TT 38), Amenhotepsasi (TT 75), and Menkheperresonb (TT 86).

34 W. Grajetzki, "Setting a State Anew: The Central Administration from the End of the Old Kingdom to the End of the Middle Kingdom," in J.C. Moreno García (ed.), *Ancient Egyptian Administration* (HdO 104. Leiden: Brill, 2013), pp. 247–250.

35 S. Quirke, *Titles and Bureaux of Egypt 1850–1700 BC* (Egyptology 1. London: Golden House Publications, 2004), pp. 113–114.

36 G.P.F. van den Boorn, *The Duties of the Vizier, Civil Administration in the Early New Kingdom* (London: Kegan Paul International, 1988), pp. 120–132; S. Quirke, *Titles and Bureaux of Egypt 1850–1700 BC* (Egyptology 1. London: Golden House Publications, 2004), p. 20.

37 R.J. Demarée – Dominique Valbelle, *Les registres de recensement du village de Deir el-Medineh (Le Stato Civile)* (Leuven: Peeters, 2011), pp. 88–91.

38 D. Valbelle, "Eléments sur la démographie et le paysage urabains, d'après les papyrus documentaires d'époque pharaonique," in Sociétés urbaines en Egypte et au Soudan: *CRIPEL* 7 (1985), pp. 75–78.

39 Papyri UC 32163–32165 (*Kahun* I 3–5).

40 Papyrus UC 32163 (*Kahun* I 3), line 2.

41 K.A. Kóthay, "Houses and Households at Kahun: Bureaucratic and Domestic Aspects of Social Organization during the Middle Kingdom," in H. Győry (ed.), *"le lotus qui sort de terre": Mélanges offerts à Edith Varga* (Bulletin du Musée Hongrois des Beaux-Arts – Supplément 2001. Budapest: Musée Hongrois des Beaux-Art, 2002), pp. 359–362.

42 Papyrus UC 32164 (*Kahun* I 4) verso, line 1; and Papyrus UC 32163 (*Kahun* I 3), line 9.

43 F.Ll. Griffith, *Hieratic Papyri from Kahun and Gurob* (London: Bernard Quaritch, 1898), p. 25, pl. 10, and 11, lines 1–9; M. Collier – S. Quirke, *The UCL Lahun Papyri: Religious, Literary, Legal, Mathematical and Medical* (BAR International Series 1209, Oxford, 2004), pp. 116–117.

44 F.Ll. Griffith, *Hieratic Papyri from Kahun and Gurob* (London: Bernard Quaritch, 1898), pp. 19–23, pl. 9; M. Collier – S. Quirke, *The UCL Lahun Papyri: Religious, Literary, Legal, Mathematical and Medical* (BAR International Series 1209, Oxford, 2004), pp. 110–115.

45 F.Ll. Griffith, *Hieratic Papyri from Kahun and Gurob* (London: Bernard Quaritch, 1898), p. 23, pl. 9, lines 22–32; M. Collier – S. Quirke, *The UCL Lahun Papyri: Religious, Literary, Legal,*

Mathematical and Medical (BAR International Series 1209, Oxford, 2004), pp. 112–113.

46 F.Ll. Griffith, *Hieratic Papyri from Kahun and Gurob* (London: Bernard Quaritch, 1898), pp. 22–23, pl. 9, lines 16–21; M. Collier – S. Quirke, *The UCL Lahun Papyri: Religious, Literary, Legal, Mathematical and Medical* (BAR International Series 1209, Oxford, 2004), pp. 114–115.

47 F.Ll. Griffith, *Hieratic Papyri from Kahun and Gurob* (London: Bernard Quaritch, 1898), pp. 19–22, pl. 9, lines 1–15; M. Collier – S. Quirke, *The UCL Lahun Papyri: Religious, Literary, Legal, Mathematical and Medical* (BAR International Series 1209. Oxford, 2004), pp. 110–111.

48 S. Quirke, *The Administration of Egypt in the Late Middle Kingdom, the Hieratic Documents* (New Malden: Sia Publishing, 1990), pp. 130–140.

49 A. Philip-Stéphan, *Dire le droit en Égypte pharaonique* (Connaissance de l'Égypte Ancienne 9. Bruxelles: Éditions Safran, 2008), p. 98.

50 F.Ll. Griffith, *Hieratic Papyri from Kahun and Gurob* (London: Bernard Quaritch, 1898), pp. 36–38, pl. 13, lines 19–38; M. Collier – S. Quirke, *The UCL Lahun Papyri: Religious, Literary, Legal, Mathematical and Medical* (BAR International Series 1209, Oxford, 2004), pp. 102–103.

51 F.Ll. Griffith, *Hieratic Papyri from Kahun and Gurob* (London: Bernard Quaritch, 1898), pp. 29–31, pl. 11, lines 10–26; M. Collier – S. Quirke, *The UCL Lahun Papyri: Religious, Literary, Legal, Mathematical and Medical* (BAR International Series 1209. Oxford: 2004), pp. 100–101.

52 F.Ll. Griffith, *Hieratic Papyri from Kahun and Gurob* (London: Bernard Quaritch, 1898), pp. 31–35, pl. 12, lines 1–14, and pl. 13, lines 1–8; M. Collier – S. Quirke, *The UCL Lahun Papyri: Religious, Literary, Legal, Mathematical and Medical* (BAR International Series 1209. Oxford: 2004), pp. 104–106, pl. 6.

53 K.A. Kóthay, "Houses and Households at Kahun: Bureaucratic and Domestic Aspects of Social Organization during the Middle Kingdom," in H. Győry (ed.), *"le lotus qui sort de terre": Mélanges offerts à Edith Varga* (Bulletin du Musée Hongrois des Beaux-Arts – Supplément 2001. Budapest: Musée Hongrois des Beaux-Art, 2002), pp. 363–365.

54 J.H. Johnson, "Speculations on Middle Kingdom Marriage," in A. Leahy – J. Tait (eds.), *Studies on Ancient Egypt in Honour of H.S. Smith* (EES Occasional Publications 13. London: EES, 1999), pp. 169–172.

55 F.Ll. Griffith, *Hieratic Papyri from Kahun and Gurob* (London: Bernard Quaritch, 1898), pp. 35–36, pl. 13, lines 9–18; M. Collier – S. Quirke, *The UCL Lahun Papyri: Religious, Literary, Legal, Mathematical and Medical* (BAR International Series 1209. Oxford: 2004), pp. 118–119.

56 S. Quirke, *Titles and Bureaux of Egypt 1850–1700 BC* (Egyptology 1. London: Golden House Publications, 2004), pp. 113–114.

57 G.P.F. van den Boorn, *The Duties of the Vizier, Civil Administration in the Early New Kingdom* (London: Kegan Paul International, 1988), pp. 172–184; S. Quirke, *Titles and Bureaux of Egypt 1850–1700 BC* (Egyptology 1. London: Golden House Publications, 2004), P. 20.

58 P.C. Smither, "The Report Concerning the Slave-Girl Senbet," *JEA* 34 (1948), pp. 31–34; S. Quirke, *The Administration of Egypt in the Late Middle Kingdom, The Hieratic Documents* (New Malden: Sia Publishing, 1990), pp. 203–207; and G. Vittmann, "The Hieratic Texts" in B. Porten – J.J. Farber (eds.), *The Elephantine Papyri in English: Three Millennia of Cross-Cultural Continuity and Change* (Leiden: Brill, 1996), pp. 35–40.

59 P. Lacau, *Une stèle juridique de Karnak* (Supplément aux ASAE 13. Le Caire: IFAO, 1949), pp. 24–26.

60 C.J. Eyre, "The Performance of the Peasant," in A.M. Gnirs (ed.), *Reading the Eloquent Peasant* (Lingua Aegyptia 8. Göttingen 2000), p. 19, sees a reference to a form of shatis in the Middle Kingdom literary text "The Eloquent Peasant," but E.F. Wente, "A Note on 'The Eloquent Peasant,' B I, 13–15," *JNES* 24 (1965), pp. 105–109, has shown that it must mean price in this context, as in the Hekanakht papyri.

61 T.E. Peet, *The Rhind Mathematical Papyrus, British Museum 10057 and 10058* (London: Hodder & Stoughton Ltd., 1923; reprinted Nendeln Liechtenstein: Kraus, 1970), pp. 104–107 and pl. R.

62 T.E. Peet, *The Rhind Mathematical Papyrus, British Museum 10057 and 10058* (London: Hodder & Stoughton Ltd., 1923; reprinted Nendeln Liechtenstein: Kraus, 1970), p. 33 and pl. A.

63 H.G. Fischer, "Notes on the Mo'alla Inscriptions and Some Contemporaneous Texts," *WZKM*

57 (1961), pp. 60–64 (2. "Copper" as an expression for one's "means").

64 E.W. Castle, "Shipping and Trade in Ramesside Egypt," *JESHO* 35 (1992): pp. 256–273, contra T.E. Peet, "The Unit of Value *šʿty* in Papyrus Boulaq 11," in *Mélanges Maspero* I (MIFAO 66/1. Cairo: IFAO, 1935–38), pp. 185–199, who argues for pieces not rings.

65 T.E. Peet, *The Rhind Mathematical Papyrus, British Museum 10057 and 10058* (London: Hodder & Stoughton Ltd., 1923; reprinted Nendeln Liechtenstein: Kraus, 1970), pp. 104–107 and pl. R.

66 J. Černý, "Prices and Wages in Egypt in the Ramesside Period," *Cahiers d' histoire mondiale* 1 (1954), p. 904.

67 T.G.H. James, *The Hekanakhte Papers and Other Early Middle Kingdom Documents* (Publications of the Metropolitan Museum of Art Egyptian Expedition 19. New York: 1962), Documents I-VIII, pp. 1–70 and pls. 1–15; K. Baer, "An Eleventh Dynasty Farmer's Letters to his Family," *JAOS* 83 (1963), p. 16; T.G.H. James, "An Early Middle Kingdom Account," *JEA* 54 (1968), pp. 51–56 (P. Purches); and J.P. Allen, *The Heqanakht Papyri* (Publications of the Metropolitan Museum of Art Egyptian Expedition 27. New York: Metropolitan Museum of Art, 2002).

68 K. Baer, "An Eleventh Dynasty Farmer's Letters to his Family," *JAOS* 83 (1963), p. 16.

69 J.J. Janssen, "Debts and Credit in the New Kingdom," *JEA* 80 (1994), pp. 129–136.

70 W. Grajetzki, "Setting a State Anew: The Central Administration from the End of the Old Kingdom to the End of the Middle Kingdom," in J.C. Moreno García (ed.), *Ancient Egyptian Administration* (HdO 104. Leiden: Brill, 2013), pp. 237–247.

71 G. Goyon, *Nouvelles inscriptions rupestres du Wadi Hammamat* (Paris: Imprimerie Nationale, 1957), pp. 17–20, 81–85 and pls. 23–24 (No. 61); D. Mueller, "Some Remarks on Wage Rates in the Middle Kingdom," *JNES* 34, no. 4 (1975), pp. 256–257, 261–262; D. Farout, "La carrière du wHmw Ameny et l'organisation des expéditions au ouadi Hammamat au Moyen Empire," *BIFAO* 94 (1994), pp. 145–147, 170 and pl. 2 (Text T2).

72 Cf. S. Quirke, "The Residence in Relations between Places of Knowledge, Production and Power: Middle Kingdom Evidence," pp. 111–130 in R. Gundlach and J.H. Taylor (eds.), *Egyptian Royal Residences, 4. Symposium zur ägyptischen Königsideologie / 4th Symposium on Egyptian Royal Ideology* (Königtum, Staat und Gesellschaft früher Hochkulturen 4,1. Wiesbaden: Harrassowitz, 2009). Quirke argues that the Twelfth and Thirteenth Dynasty Residence was "unilocal" and located in Itjtawy, but not associated with any specific building or structure.

73 A. Scharff, "Ein Rechnungbuch des Koniglichen Hofes aus der 13. Dynastie," *ZÄS* 57 (1922), pp. 51–58 and pls. 1–24; and S. Quirke, *The Administration of Egypt in the Late Middle Kingdom: The Hieratic Documents* (New Malden Surrey: SIA Publishing 1990), pp. 10–121 and 196–197. The translations of the titles used here are those of S. Quirke, "The Regular Titles of the Late Middle Kingdom," *RdÉ* 37 (1986), pp. 107–130.

74 G. Miniaci – S. Quirke, "Reconceiving the Tomb in the Late Middle Kingdom. The Burial of the Accountant of the Main Enclosure Nerferhotep at Dra Abu al-Naga," *BIFAO* 109 (2009), pp. 338–383.

75 S. Quirke, *Titles and Bureaux of Egypt 1850–1700 BC* (Egyptology 1. London: Golden House Publications, 2004), pp. 111–112.

76 D. Franke, "The Career of Khnumhotep III. of Beni Hasan and the so-called 'Decline of the Nomarchs,'" in S. Quirke (ed.), *Middle Kingdom Studies* (New Malden: SIA Publishing, 1991), pp. 52–53.

77 Hapidjefa Contracts 3 (lines 284 and 288), 5 (line 301), 6 (line 303), 9 (line 313), 10 (line 321).

78 Hapidjefa Contracts 2 (line 279) and 8 (line 309).

79 Hapidjefa Contracts 1 (line 275) and 4 (line 292).

80 Hapidjefa Contract 4 (line 293).

81 W.K. Simpson, *Papyrus Reisner I: The Records of a Building Project in the Reign of Sesostris I* (Boston: Museum of Fine Arts, 1963), pp. 17–18.

82 W.K. Simpson, *Papyrus Reisner II: Accounts of the Dockyard Workshop at This in the Reign of Sesostris I* (Boston: Museum of Fine Arts, 1965), pp. 16–17.

83 W.K. Simpson, *Papyrus Reisner II: Accounts of the Dockyard Workshop at This in the Reign of Sesostris I* (Boston: Museum of Fine Arts, 1965), pp. 20–23.

84 W.K. Simpson, *Papyrus Reisner II: Accounts of the Dockyard Workshop at This in the Reign of Sesostris I* (Boston: Museum of Fine Arts, 1965), pp. 24–35.

85 W.K. Simpson, *Papyrus Reisner III: The Records of a Building Project in the Early Twelfth Dynasty* (Boston: Museum of Fine Arts, 1969), pp. 10–11.

86 W.K. Simpson, *Papyrus Reisner III: The Records of a Building Project in the Early Twelfth Dynasty* (Boston: Museum of Fine Arts, 1969), pp. 18–21.

87 W.K. Simpson, *Papyrus Reisner III: The Records of a Building Project in the Early Twelfth Dynasty* (Boston: Museum of Fine Arts, 1969), pp. 22–36.

88 W.K. Simpson, *Papyrus Reisner I: The Records of a Building Project in the Reign of Sesostris I* (Boston: Museum of Fine Arts, 1963), pp. 19–21.

89 W.K. Simpson, *Papyrus Reisner I: The Records of a Building Project in the Reign of Sesostris I* (Boston: Museum of Fine Arts, 1963), pp. 24–36.

90 W.K. Simpson, *Papyrus Reisner I: The Records of a Building Project in the Reign of Sesostris I* (Boston: Museum of Fine Arts, 1963), pp. 37–47.

91 W.K. Simpson, *Papyrus Reisner I: The Records of a Building Project in the Reign of Sesostris I* (Boston: Museum of Fine Arts, 1963), pp. 48–51.

92 W.K. Simpson, *Papyrus Reisner I: The Records of a Building Project in the Reign of Sesostris I* (Boston: Museum of Fine Arts, 1963), pp. 52–85.

93 W.K. Simpson, *Papyrus Reisner IV: Personnel Accounts in the Early Twelfth Dynasty* (Boston: Museum of Fine Arts, 1986).

94 A.H. Sayed, "Discovery of the Site of the 12th Dynasty Port at Wadi Gawasis on the Red Sea Shore," *RdÉ* 29 (1977), p. 170 and pl. 16b; D. Farout, "La carrière du wHmw Ameny et l'organisation des expéditions au ouadi Hammamat au Moyen Empire," *BIFAO* 94 (1994), pp. 144, 169, and pl. 1 (Text T1).

95 J Baines, "The Stela of Khusobek: Private and Royal Military Narrative and Values," in J. Osing – G. Dreyer (eds.), *Form und Mass, Beiträge zur Literatur, Sprache und Kunst des alten Ägypten. Festschrift für Gerhard Fecht* (ÄAT 12. Wiesbaden: Otto Harrassowitz, 1987), pp. 43–61.

96 A.H. Sayed, "Discovery of the Site of the 12th Dynasty Port at Wadi Gawasis on the Red Sea Shore," *RdÉ* 29 (1977), p. 170 and pl. 16b; D. Farout, "La carrière du wHmw Ameny et l'organisation des expéditions au ouadi Hammamat au Moyen Empire," *BIFAO* 94 (1994), pp. 144, 169, and pl. 1 (Text T1).

97 G. Goyon, *Nouvelles inscriptions rupestres du Wadi Hammamat* (Paris: Imprimerie Nationale, 1957), pp. 17–20, 81–85 and pls. 23–24 (No. 61); D. Mueller, "Some Remarks on Wage Rates in the Middle Kingdom," *JNES* 34, no. 4 (1975), pp. 256–257, 261–262; Dominique Farout, "La carrière du wHmw Ameny et l'organisation des expéditions au ouadi Hammamat au Moyen Empire," *BIFAO* 94 (1994), pp. 145–147, 170, and pl. 2 (Text T2).

98 P. Smither, "The Semneh Despatches," *JEA* 31 (1945), pp. 3–10 and pls. 2–7.

99 C. Vogel, *Ägyptische Festungen und Garnisonen bis zum Ende des Mittleren Reiches* (HÄB 46. Hildesheim: Gerstenberg Verlag, 2004), pp. 104–105; D. Stefanovic, *The Holders of Regular Military Titles in the Period of the Middle Kingdom: Dossiers* (Egyptology 4. London: Golden House Publications, 2006), pp. 95–144 (*šmsw*, 304 examples), pp. 145–147 (*šmsw ꜥryt*, 16 examples), pp. 148–151 (*šmsw n rmn tp*, 21 examples), pp. 152–155 (*šmsw n ḥḳꜣ*, 18 examples), and pp. 156–169 (*sḥḏ šmsw*, 63 examples); and D. Stefanovic, "*šmsw* – Soldiers of the Middle Kingdom," *WZKM* 98 (2008), pp. 233–248.

100 D. Stefanovic, *The Holders of Regular Military Titles in the Period of the Middle Kingdom: Dossiers* (Egyptology 4. London: Golden House Publications, 2006), pp. 49–57 (*ꜣṯw ꜥꜣ n niwt*, 40 examples), pp. 58–60 (*ꜣṯw n niwt*, 13 examples), and pp. 72–94 (*ꜣṯw n ṯt ḥḳꜣ*, 83 examples).

101 C. Vogel, *Ägyptische Festungen und Garnisonen bis zum Ende des Mittleren Reiches* (HÄB 46. Hildesheim: Gerstenberg Verlag, 2004), pp. 105–107; D. Stefanovic, *The Holders of Regular Military Titles in the Period of the Middle Kingdom: Dossiers* (Egyptology 4. London: Golden House Publications, 2006), pp. 1–48 (*ꜥnḫw n niwt*, 275 examples), and pp. 61–71 (*ꜥnḫw n ṯt ḥḳꜣ*, 69 examples).

102 O. Berlev, "Les prétendus 'citadins' au moyen empire," *RdÉ* 23 (1971), pp. 27–31 (*ꜥnḫw*), pp. 31–37 (*ꜣṯw*), and pp. 37–41 (organization).

103 R.J. Leprohan, "Les forces du maintein de l'ordre dans la Nubie au Moyen Empire," in C. Berger – G. Clerc – N. Grimal (eds.), *Hommages à Jean Leclant, 2. Nubie, Soudan, Ethiopie* (BdÉ 106/2. Cairo: IFAO, 1993),

p. 287; C. Vogel, *Ägyptische Festungen und Garnisonen bis zum Ende des Mittleren Reiches* (HÄB 46. Hildesheim: Gerstenberg Verlag, 2004), pp. 107–108.

104 O. Berlev, "Les prétendus 'citadins' au moyen empire," *RdÉ* 23 (1971), p. 38.

105 O. Berlev, "Les prétendus 'citadins' au moyen empire," *RdÉ* 23 (1971), pp. 28, 31, 37; followed by R.J. Leprohan, "Les forces du maintein de l'ordre dans la Nubie au Moyen Empire," in C. Berger – G. Clerc – N. Grimal (eds.), *Hommages à Jean Leclant, 2. Nubie, Soudan, Ethiopie* (BdÉ 106/2. Cairo: IFAO, 1993), pp. 285–291; A. Spalinger, "The Organisation of the Pharaonic Army (Old to New Kingdom)," in J.C. Moreno García (ed.), *Ancient Egyptian Administration* (HdO 104. Leiden: Brill, 2013), pp. 424–425.

106 D. Franke, "Die Stele Inv. Nr. 4403 im Landesmuseum in Oldenburg. Zur Lebensmittelproduktion in der 13. Dynastie," *SAK* 10 (1983), pp. 167–168 (*ꜥnḫw n niwt*), and pp. 172–173 (*ꜥnḫw n ṯt ḥḳꜣ*); followed by C. Vogel, *Ägyptische Festungen und Garnisonen bis zum Ende des Mittleren Reiches* (HÄB 46. Hildesheim: Gerstenberg Verlag, 2004), pp. 105–107.

107 S.L.D. Katary, "Land-Tenure in the New Kingdom: the Role of Women Smallholders and the Military," in A.K. Bowman – E. Rogan (eds.), *Agriculture in Egypt from Pharaonic to Modern Times* (Proceedings of the British Academy 96, Oxford: University Press, 1999), pp. 70–78.

108 S. Quirke, *Lahun: A Town in Egypt 1800 BC, and the History of Its Landscape* (London: Golden House Publications, 2005), pp. 30–39.

109 A. Scharff, "Brief aus Illahun," *ZÄS* 59 (1924), pp. 20–51 and pl. 1–12 (Anhang: Autographische Texte); U. Luft, *Das Archiv von Illahun: Briefe.* 1 (Hieratische Papyri aus den Staatlichen Museen zu Berlin Preussischer Kulturbesitz, Lieferung 1. Berlin: Akademie Verlag, 1992).

110 S. Quirke, "A Preliminary Study of Technical Terms in Accounts of the Illahun Temple Archive," *Ägypten und Levante* 7 (1998), pp. 9–16; A. Spalinger, "Praise God and Pay the Priests," *Ägypten und Levante* 7 (1998), pp. 43–57.

111 L. Borchardt, "Besolderingsverhältnisse von Priestern im mittleren Reich," *ZÄS* 40 (1902/3), pp. 113–117; A.H. Gardiner, "The Daily Income of Sesostris II's Funerary Temple," *JEA* 42 (1956), p. 119.

112 L. Borchardt, "Der zweite Papyrusfund von Kahun und die zeitliche Festlegung des mittleren Reiches der ägyptischen Geschichte," *ZÄS* 37 (1899), p. 94.

113 L. Borchardt, "Der zweite Papyrusfund von Kahun und die zeitliche Festlegung des mittleren Reiches der ägyptischen Geschichte," *ZÄS* 37 (1899), pp. 97–98.

114 R. Bussmann, *Die Provinztempel Ägyptens von der 0. bis zur 11. Dynastie: Archäologie und Geschichte einer gesellschaftlichen Institution zwischen Residenz und Provinz, Teil. I: Text. Teil. II: Abbildungen* (Probleme der Ägyptologie 30. Leiden: Brill, 2010).

115 Contracts 1 (lines 273–276), 2 (lines 277–282) and 4 (lines 290–295), see F. Ll. Griffith, *The Inscriptions of Siût and Dêr Rîfeh* (London: Trübner & Co., 1889), pls. 6–7.

116 Contract 3 (lines 283–289), see F. Ll. Griffith, *The Inscriptions of Siût and Dêr Rîfeh* (London: Trübner & Co., 1889), pl. 7.

117 Contract 5 (lines 296–301), see F. Ll. Griffith, *The Inscriptions of Siût and Dêr Rîfeh* (London: Trübner & Co., 1889), pl. 7.

118 Contract 6 (lines 302–304), see F. Ll. Griffith, *The Inscriptions of Siût and Dêr Rîfeh* (London: Trübner & Co., 1889), pl. 7.

119 Contracts 3 (lines 285–287) and 5 (lines 300–301), see F. Ll. Griffith, *The Inscriptions of Siût and Dêr Rîfeh* (London: Trübner & Co., 1889), pl. 7.

120 Contracts 1–10 (lines 273–324), see F. Ll. Griffith, *The Inscriptions of Siût and Dêr Rîfeh* (London: Trübner & Co., 1889), pls. 6–8.

121 Lines 269–272, see F. Ll. Griffith, *The Inscriptions of Siût and Dêr Rîfeh* (London: Trübner & Co., 1889), pl. 6.

122 Contracts 7 (lines 305–306), 9 (lines 312–318) and 10 (lines 319–324), see F. Ll. Griffith, *The Inscriptions of Siût and Dêr Rîfeh* (London: Trübner & Co., 1889), pl. 8.

123 F.Ll. Griffith, *Hieratic Papyri from Kahun and Gurob* (London: Bernard Quaritch, 1898), pp. 29–31, pl. 11; M. Collier – S. Quirke, *The UCL Lahun Papyri: Religious, Literary, Legal, Mathematical and Medical* (BAR International Series 1209, Oxford, 2004), pp. 100–101.

124 F.Ll. Griffith, *Hieratic Papyri from Kahun and Gurob* (London: Bernard Quaritch, 1898), pp. 31–35, pl. 12–13; M. Collier – S. Quirke, *The UCL Lahun Papyri: Religious, Literary, Legal,*

Mathematical and Medical (BAR International Series 1209, Oxford, 2004), pp. 104–106, pl. 6.

125 T.G.H. James, *The Hekanakhte Papers and Other Early Middle Kingdom Documents* (Publications of the Metropolitan Museum of Art, Egyptian Expedition 19. New York: 1962), pp. 92–94, pls. 26–27 (Document XVII); Abd-el-Mohsen Bakir, "The Middle-Kingdom Cairo Letter, A Reconsideration (Papyrus 91061 = CGC No. 58045)," *JEA* 54 (1968), pp. 57–59.

126 F.Ll. Griffith, *Hieratic Papyri from Kahun and Gurob* (London: Bernard Quaritch, 1898), pp. 35–36, pl. 13, lines 9–18; M. Collier – S. Quirke, *The UCL Lahun Papyri: Religious, Literary, Legal, Mathematical and Medical* (BAR International Series 1209, Oxford, 2004), pp. 118–119.

127 F.Ll. Griffith, *Hieratic Papyri from Kahun and Gurob* (London: Bernard Quaritch, 1898), pp. 31–35, pl. 12–13; M. Collier – S. Quirke, *The UCL Lahun Papyri: Religious, Literary, Legal, Mathematical and Medical* (BAR International Series 1209, Oxford, 2004), pp. 104–106, pl. 6.

128 Contracts 3 (lines 283–289), 5 (lines 296–301) and 6 (lines 302–304), see F. Ll. Griffith, *The Inscriptions of Siût and Dêr Rîfeh* (London: Trübner & Co., 1889), pl. 7.

129 F.Ll. Griffith, *Hieratic Papyri from Kahun and Gurob* (London: Bernard Quaritch, 1898), pp. 36–38, pl. 13; M. Collier – S. Quirke, *The UCL Lahun Papyri: Religious, Literary, Legal, Mathematical and Medical* (BAR International Series 1209, Oxford, 2004), pp. 102–103.

130 P. Lacau, *Une stèle juridique de Karnak* (Supplément aux ASAE 13. Le Caire: IFAO, 1949).

131 Contracts 1 (lines 273–276), 2 (lines 277–282), 4 (lines 290–295) and 8 (lines 307–311), see F. Ll. Griffith, *The Inscriptions of Siût and Dêr Rîfeh* (London: Trübner & Co., 1889), pls. 6–8.

132 Contracts 2 (lines 277–282) and 8 (lines 307–311), see F. Ll. Griffith, *The Inscriptions of Siût and Dêr Rîfeh* (London: Trübner & Co., 1889), pls. 6, 8.

133 Contract 6 (lines 302–304), see F. Ll. Griffith, *The Inscriptions of Siût and Dêr Rîfeh* (London: Trübner & Co., 1889), pl. 7.

134 A.P. Zingarelli, *Trade and Market in New Kingdom Egypt* (BAR International Series 2063. Oxford, Archaeopress, 2010), p. 37.

135 G. Meurer, *Nubier in Ägypten bis zum Beginn des Neuen Reiches: Zur Bedeutung der Stele Berlin 14753* (Abhandlungen des Deutschen Archäologischen Instituts Kairo, Ägyptologische Reihe 13. Berlin: 1996), pp. 10–27.

136 M. de J. Ellis, "Taxation in Ancient Mesopotamia: The History of the Term *miksu*," *Journal of Cuneiform Studies* 26 (1974), pp. 225–233; Betina I. Faist, *Der Fernhandel des assyrischen Reiches zwischen dem 14. und 11. Jh. v. Chr.* (Alter Orient und Altes Testament 265. Münster: Ugarit-Verlag, 2001), pp. 184–194; Nicholas Postgate, *Bronze Age Bureaucracy: Writing and the Practice of Government in Assyria* (Cambridge: University Press, 2013), pp. 267, 341.

137 J.M.A. Janssen, "The Stela (Khartoum Museum No. 3) from Uronarti," *JNES* 12 (1953), pp. 51–55.

138 S. Farag, "Une Inscription Memphite de la XIIe Dynastie," *RdÉ* 32 (1980), pp. 75–82; H. Altenmüller – A.H. Moussa, "Die Inschrift Amenemhets II. Aus den Ptah-Tempel von Memphis. ein Vorbericht," *SAK* 18 (1991), pp. 1–48; J. Malek – S. Quirke, "Memphis, 1991: Epigraphy," *JEA* 78 (1992), pp. 13–18; E.S. Marcus, "Amenemhet II and the Sea: Maritime Aspects of the Mit Rahina (Memphis) Inscription," *Ägypten und Levante* 17 (2007), pp. 137–190.

139 J.P. Allen, "The Historical Inscription of Khnumhotep at Dahshur: Preliminary Report," *BASOR* 352 (Nov., 352), pp. 29–39.

140 R. Flammini, "Elite Emulation and Patronage Relationships in the Middle Bronze: the Egyptianized Dynasty of Byblos," *Tel Aviv* 37, no. 2 (2010), pp. 154–168.

141 J. Couyat – P. Montet, *Les inscriptions hiéroglyphiques et hiératiques du Ouâdi Hammâmât* (MIFAO 34. Cairo: IFAO, 1912); G. Goyon, *Nouvelles inscriptions rupestres du Wadi Hammamat* (Paris: Imprimerie Nationale, 1957); K.-J. Seyfried, *Beiträge zu den Expeditionen des Mittleren Reiches in die Ost-Wüste* (HÄB 15. Hildesheim: Gerstenberg Verlag, 1981), pp. 241–285.

142 J. Couyat – P. Montet, *Les inscriptions hiéroglyphiques et hiératiques du Ouâdi Hammâmât* (MIFAO 34. Cairo: IFAO, 1912), pp. 77–81 and pl. 29 (nos. 110, 113), and pp. 97–100 and pls. 36–37 (nos. 191–192); D. Sweeney, "The Vizir Amenemhat at Wadi Hammamat – a Macbeth Moment?," *GM* 238 (2013), pp. 107–124.

143 G. Goyon, *Nouvelles inscriptions rupestres du Wadi Hammamat* (Paris: Imprimerie Nationale, 1957), pp. 17–20, 81–85 and pls. 23–24 (No. 61); D. Farout, "La carrière du wHmw Ameny et l'organisation des expéditions au ouadi Hammamat au Moyen Empire," *BIFAO* 94 (1994), pp. 145–147, 170 and pl. 2 (Text T2).

144 I. Shaw, *Hatnub: Quarrying Travertine in Ancient Egypt* (EES Excavation Memoir 88. London: EES, 2010).

145 A.I. Sadek, *The Amethyst Mining Inscriptions of Wadi el-Hudi*, 2 vols. (Warminster: 1980–1985); K.-J. Seyfried, *Beiträge zu den Expeditionen des Mittleren Reiches in die Ost-Wüste* (HÄB 15. Hildesheim: Gerstenberg Verlag, 1981), pp. 5–151.

146 A. Gasse, "Wadi Hammamat and the Sea from the Origins to the End of the New Kingdom," in P. Tallet – El-Sayed Mahfouz (eds.), *The Red Sea in Pharaonic Times: Recent Discoveries along the Red Sea Coast. Proceedings of the Colloquium held in Cairo / Ayn Soukhna 11th – 12th January 2009* (BdÉ 155. Cairo: IFAO, 2012), pp. 133–143.

147 A.M. A-H. Sayed, "Discovery of the Site of the 12th Dynasty Port at Wadi Gawasis on the Red Sea Shore," *RdÉ* 29 (1977), pp. 138–178; A.M.A-H. Sayed, "New Light on the Recently Discovered Port on the Red Sea Shore," *CdÉ* 58 (1983), pp. 23–37; D. Farout, "La carrière du wHmw Ameny et l'organisation des expéditions au ouadi Hammamat au Moyen Empire," *BIFAO* 94 (1994), pp. 144, 169, and pl. 1 (Text T1); R. Fattovich – K.A. Bard (eds.), *Harbour of the Pharaohs to the Land of Punt, Archaeological Investigations at Mersa/Wadi Gawasis, Egypt, 2001–2005* (Naples: Universita degli Studi di Napoli "L'Orientale," 2007); R. Pirelli, "Two New Stelae from Mersa Gawasis," *RdÉ* 58 (2007), pp. 87–109; E-S. Mahfouz, "Les ostraca hiératiques du ouadi Gaouasis," *RdÉ* 59 (2008), pp. 267–286 and pls. 34–57; E-S. Mahfouz, "Amenemhat III au ouadi Gaouasis," *BIFAO* 108 (2008), pp. 253–279; E-S. Mahfouz, "Amenemhat IV au ouadi Gaouasis," *BIFAO* 110 (2010), pp. 165–173; E-S. Mahfouz, "New Epigraphic Material from Wadi Gawasis," in P. Tallet – E-S. Mahfouz (eds.), *The Red Sea in Pharaonic Times: Recent Discoveries along the Red Sea Coast. Proceedings of the Colloquium held in Cairo / Ayn Soukhna 11th – 12th January 2009* (BdÉ 155. Cairo: IFAO, 2012), pp. 117–143.

148 M. Abd el-Raziq – G. Castel – P. Tallet – V. Ghica, *Les inscriptions d'Ayn Soukhna*, vol. I (MIFAO 122. Cairo: IFAO, 2002); M. Abd el-Raziq – G. Castel – P. Tallet – G. Marouard, "The Pharaonic Site of Ayn Soukhna in the Gulf of Suez, 2001–2009, Progress Report," in P. Tallet – E-S. Mahfouz (eds.), *The Red Sea in Pharaonic Times: Recent Discoveries along the Red Sea Coast. Proceedings of the Colloquium held in Cairo / Ayn Soukhna 11th – 12th January 2009* (BdÉ 155. Cairo: IFAO, 2012), pp. 3–20.

149 D. Valbelle – C. Bonnet, *Le sanctuaire d'Hathor, maîtresse de la turquoise* (Paris: Picard Editeur, 1996); P. Tallet, "Amenemhat II et la chapelle des rois à propos d'une stèle rupestre redécouverte à Sérabit al-Khadim," *BIFAO* 109 (2009), pp. 473–493.

150 A. Gardiner, "The Defeat of the Hyksos by Kamose: The Carnarvon Tablet, No. 1," *JEA* 3 (1916), pp. 95–110; P. Lacau, "Une stèle du roi 'Kamosis'," *ASAE* 39 (1939), pp. 245–271; L. Habachi, *The Second Stela of Kamose and His Struggle against the Hyksos Ruler and His Capital* (Abhandlungen des Deutschen Archäologischen Instituts Kairo, Ägyptologische Reihe 8. Glückstadt: Augustin, 1972), pp. 45–47.

151 L. Habachi, *The Second Stela of Kamose and His Struggle against the Hyksos Ruler and His Capital* (Abhandlungen des Deutschen Archäologischen Instituts Kairo, Ägyptologische Reihe 8. Glückstadt: Augustin, 1972), pp. 16–44.

152 C. Van Siclen III, "The Third Stela of Kamose," in M. Marée (ed.), *The Second Intermediate Period (Thirteenth-Seventeenth Dynasties): Current Research, Future Prospects* (OLA 192. Leuven: Peeters, 2010), pp. 355–358.

153 M. Lehner, *The Complete Pyramids* (London-New York: Thames and Hudson, 1997), pp. 166–183.

154 S. Quirke, *Lahun: A Town in Egypt 1800 BC, and the History of Its Landscape* (London: Golden House Publications, 2005).

155 J. Wegner, *The Mortuary Temple of Senwosret III at Abydos* (Publications of the Pennsylvania-Yale expedition to Egypt 8. New Haven: Peabody Museum of Natural History of Yale University, 2007).

156 D. O'Connor, "The Dendereh Chapel of Nebhepetre Mentuhotep: A New Perspective," in A. Leahy – J. Tait (eds.), *Studies on Ancient Egypt*

in Honour of H. S. Smith (London: EES, 1999), pp. 215–220; R. Bussmann, *Die Provinztempel Ägyptens von der 0. bis zur 11. Dynastie: Archäologie und Geschichte einer gesellschaftlichen Institution zwischen Residenz und Provinz, Teil. I: Text. Teil. II: Abbildungen* (Probleme der Ägyptologie 30. Leiden: Brill, 2010).

157 B.J. Kemp, "Large Middle Kingdom Granary Buildings (and the Archaeology of Administration)," *ZÄS* 113 (1986), pp. 134–136 (Appendix: Temporary Campaign Palaces in Nubia).

158 J.M.A. Janssen, "The Stela (Khartoum Museum No. 3) from Uronarti," *JNES* 12 (1953), pp. 51–55.

159 B.J. Kemp, "Large Middle Kingdom Granary Buildings (and the Archaeology of Administration)," *ZÄS* 113 (1986), pp. 123–136; and S.T. Smith, *Askut in Nubia: The Economics and Ideology of Egyptian Imperialism in the Second Millennium B.C.* (Studies in Egyptology. London: Kegan Paul International, 1995), pp. 39–50.

160 G. Meurer, *Nubier in Ägypten bis zum Beginn des Neuen Reiches: Zur Bedeutung der Stele Berlin 14753* (Abhandlungen des Deutschen Archäologischen Instituts Kairo, Ägyptologische Reihe 13. Berlin: 1996), pp. 10–27.

161 M. Lehner, *The Complete Pyramids* (London-New York: Thames and Hudson, 1997), pp. 184–187.

162 K. Baer, "An Eleventh Dynasty Farmer's Letters to His Family," *JAOS* 83 (1963), p. 16; J.P. Allen, *The Heqanakht Papyri* (Publications of the Metropolitan Museum of Art Egyptian Expedition 27. New York: Metropolitan Museum of Art, 2002), pp. 160–171.

163 J.P. Allen, *The Heqanakht Papyri* (Publications of the Metropolitan Museum of Art Egyptian Expedition 27. New York: Metropolitan Museum of Art, 2002), pp. 107–117.

164 J.P. Allen, *The Heqanakht Papyri* (Publications of the Metropolitan Museum of Art Egyptian Expedition 27. New York: Metropolitan Museum of Art, 2002), pp. 120–126.

165 J.P. Allen, *The Heqanakht Papyri* (Publications of the Metropolitan Museum of Art Egyptian Expedition 27. New York: Metropolitan Museum of Art, 2002), pp. 172–178.

166 J.P. Allen, *The Heqanakht Papyri* (Publications of the Metropolitan Museum of Art Egyptian Expedition 27. New York: Metropolitan Museum of Art, 2002), pp. 172–178.

4. THE NEW KINGDOM (c. 1550–1069 BCE)

1 A.G. McDowell, *Jurisdiction in the Workmen's Community of Deir el-Medîna* (EU 5. Leiden: NINO, 1990), pp. 235–244.

2 A.G. McDowell, *Jurisdiction in the Workmen's Community of Deir el-Medîna* (EU 5. Leiden: NINO, 1990), p. 237; E.F. Wente, *Letters from Ancient Egypt* (SBL Writings from the Ancient World. 1. Atlanta: Scholars Press, 1990), p. 146 (Text 196).

3 J. Černý, *Late Ramesside Letters* (Bibliotheca Aegyptiaca 9. Bruxelles: Édition de la fondation égyptologique Reine Élisabeth, 1939), pp. 57–60 (no. 37); E.F. Wente, *Late Ramesside Letters* (SAOC 33. Chicago: University of Chicago Press, 1967), pp. 71–74 (no. 37); E.F. Wente, *Letters from Ancient Egypt* (SBL Writings from the Ancient World 1. Atlanta: Scholars Press, 1990), pp. 174–175 (No. 290. LRL No. 37); A.G. McDowell, *Jurisdiction in the Workmen's Community of Deir el-Medîna* (EU 5. Leiden: NINO, 1990), pp. 237–240.

4 A. de Buck, "The Judicial Papyrus of Turin," *JEA* 23 (1937), pp. 152–164.

5 After A. de Buck, "The Judicial Papyrus of Turin," *JEA* 23 (1937), pp. 152–164.

6 F. Payraudeau, *Administration, société et pouvoir à Thebes sous la XXIIe dynastie bubastite*, 2 vols. (BdÉ 160: 1–2. Cairo: IFAO, 2014), vol. 1, p. 173.

7 J. Černý, "Papyrus Salt 124 (Brit. Mus. 10055)," *JEA* 15 (1929), pp. 243–258.

8 W. Spiegelberg, "Ein Papyrus aus der Zeit Ramses'V," *ZÄS* 29 (1891), pp. 73–84; T.E. Peet, "A Historical Document of Ramesside Age," *JEA* 10 (1924), pp. 116–127; A.H. Gardiner, "Ramesside Texts Relating to the Taxation and Transport of Corn," *JEA* 27 (1941), pp. 60–62. [Nr. 6. the Elephantine Scandal (P.Turin 1887)]; and A.H. Gardiner, *Ramesside Administrative Documents* (Oxford: Griffith Institute – London: Oxford University Press, 1948), pp. 73–82 [Text 25: The Turin Indictment Papyrus].

9 A.G. McDowell, *Jurisdiction in the Workmen's Community of Deir el-Medîna* (EU 5. Leiden: NINO, 1990), pp. 69–73, 76–80.

10 J. Černý – T.E. Peet, "A Marriage Settlement of the Twentieth Dynasty: An Unpublished Document from Turin," *JEA* 13 (1927), pp. 30–39.

11 A.G. McDowell, *Jurisdiction in the Workmen's Community of Deir el-Medîna* (EU 5. Leiden: NINO, 1990), pp. 187–234.

12 T.E. Peet, *The Great Tomb-Robberies of the Twentieth Egyptian Dynasty*, I. *Text* (Oxford: Clarendon Press, 1930), pp. 18–19, 42.

13 T.E. Peet, *The Great Tomb-Robberies of the Twentieth Egyptian Dynasty*, I. *Text* (Oxford: Clarendon Press, 1930), p. 49 (P. Amherst), p. 60 (P. BM 10054 verso).

14 T.E. Peet, *The Mayer Papyri A & B, Nos. M 11162 and M. 11186 of the Free Public Museums, Liverpool* (London: EES, 1920), p. 10 (P. Mayer A); and T.E. Peet, *The Great Tomb-Robberies of the Twentieth Egyptian Dynasty*, I. *Text* (Oxford: Clarendon Press, 1930), p. 146 (P. BM 10052).

15 A.H. Gardiner, *The Inscription of Mes. A Contribution to the Study of Egyptian Juridical Procedure* (Untersuchungen zur Geschichte und Altertumskunde Ägyptens, Band 4, Heft 3. Leipzig: J.C. Hinrichs'sche Buchhandlung, 1905), pp. 33–38.

16 J. Černý – T.E. Peet, "A Marriage Settlement of the Twentieth Dynasty: An Unpublished Document from Turin," *JEA* 13 (1927), pp. 30–39.

17 K.A. Kitchen, *RI* I, pp. 125–126 no. 67 and *RI* VII, p. 428 lines 3–7 (corrigenda); A. David, *Syntactic and Lexico-Semantic Aspects of the Legal Register in Ramesside Royal Decrees* (Göttinger Orientforschungen IV. Reihe Ägypten 38. Wiesbaden, Harrassowitz, 2006), pp. 108–111.

18 K.A. Kitchen, *RI* II, pp. 712–713 no. 261D; A. David, *Syntactic and Lexico-Semantic Aspects of the Legal Register in Ramesside Royal Decrees* (Göttinger Orientforschungen IV. Reihe Ägypten 38. Wiesbaden, Harrassowitz, 2006), pp. 133–135.

19 K.A. Kitchen, *RI* IV, pp. 263–266 no. 18; A. David, *Syntactic and Lexico-Semantic Aspects of the Legal Register in Ramesside Royal Decrees* (Göttinger Orientforschungen IV. Reihe Ägypten 38. Wiesbaden, Harrassowitz, 2006), pp. 136–140.

20 K.A. Kitchen, *RI* V, pp. 343–345 no. 138B; A. David, *Syntactic and Lexico-Semantic Aspects of the Legal Register in Ramesside Royal Decrees* (Göttinger Orientforschungen IV. Reihe Ägypten 38. Wiesbaden, Harrassowitz, 2006), pp. 141–154.

21 K.A. Kitchen, *RI* I, pp. 65–70 no. 32; S. Schott, *Kanais. Der Tempel Sethos I. im Wadi Mia* (Nachrichten der Akademie der Wissenschaften in Göttingen, I. Philologisch-historisch klasse, Nr. 6. Göttingen: Vandenhoeck & Ruprecht, 1961), pp. 123–189 and Taf. 1–19; A. David, *Syntactic and Lexico-Semantic Aspects of the Legal Register in Ramesside Royal Decrees* (Göttinger Orientforschungen IV. Reihe Ägypten 38. Wiesbaden, Harrassowitz, 2006), pp. 112–132.

22 K.A. Kitchen, *RI* I, pp. 45–58 no. 24 and p. 416 no. 180 lines 9–14 (corrigenda); F.Ll. Griffith, "The Abydos Decree of Seti I at Nauri," *JEA* 13 (1927), pp. 193–208 and pls 37–43; W.F. Edgerton, "The Nauri Decree of Seti I: A Translation and Analysis of the Legal Portion," *JNES* 6 (1947), pp. 219–230; A.H. Gardiner, "Some Reflections on the Nauri Decree," *JEA* 38 (1952), pp. 24–33; A. David, *Syntactic and Lexico-Semantic Aspects of the Legal Register in Ramesside Royal Decrees* (Göttinger Orientforschungen IV. Reihe Ägypten 38. Wiesbaden, Harrassowitz, 2006), pp. 17–107.

23 W.F. Edgerton, "The Nauri Decree of Seti I: A Translation and Analysis of the Legal Portion," *JNES* 6 (1947), pp. 219–230.

24 K. Pflüger, "The Edict of King Haremhab," *JNES* 5 (1946), pp. 260–276; W. Helck, "Das Dekret des Königs Haremheb," *ZÄS* 80 (1955), pp. 109–136, pls. 10–11; J.-M. Kruchten, *Le Décret d'Horemheb. Traduction, commentaire épigraphique, philologique et institutionnel* (Bruxelles: Editions de l'Université de Bruxelles, 1981).

25 J.-M. Kruchten, *Le Décret d'Horemheb. Traduction, commentaire épigraphique, philologique et institutionnel* (Bruxelles: Editions de l'Université de Bruxelles, 1981), pp. 28–47.

26 J.-M. Kruchten, *Le Décret d'Horemheb. Traduction, commentaire épigraphique, philologique et institutionnel* (Bruxelles: Editions de l'Université de Bruxelles, 1981), pp. 48–56.

27 J.-M. Kruchten, *Le Décret d'Horemheb. Traduction, commentaire épigraphique, philologique et institutionnel* (Bruxelles: Editions de l'Université de Bruxelles, 1981), pp. 58–79. In this context the verb *kfc*, "capture" indicates misappropriation, see W.F. Edgerton, "The Nauri Decree of Seti I: A Translation and Analysis of the Legal Portion," *JNES* 6 (1947), p. 227.

28 J.-M. Kruchten, *Le Décret d'Horemheb. Traduction, commentaire épigraphique, philologique et institutionnel* (Bruxelles: Editions de l'Université de Bruxelles, 1981), pp. 80–95.

29 J.-M. Kruchten, *Le Décret d'Horemheb. Traduction, commentaire épigraphique, philologique et institutionnel* (Bruxelles: Editions de l'Université de Bruxelles, 1981), pp. 148–161.

30 A.G. McDowell, *Jurisdiction in the Workmen's Community of Deir el-Medina* (EU 5. Leiden: NINO, 1990), pp. 70–73, 76–80, 159–165.
31 A.G. McDowell, *Jurisdiction in the Workmen's Community of Deir el-Medina* (EU 5. Leiden: NINO, 1990), pp. 143–186.
32 A.G. McDowell, *Jurisdiction in the Workmen's Community of Deir el-Medina* (EU 5. Leiden: NINO, 1990), pp. 170–186.
33 A.H. Gardiner, "Four Papyri of the 18th Dynasty from Kahun," *ZÄS* 43 (1906), pp. 38–43.
34 A.H. Gardiner, "A Lawsuit Arising from the Purchase of Two Slaves," *JEA* 21 (1935), pp. 140–146.
35 A. Erman, "Beiträge zur Kenntniss des ägyptischen Gerichtsverfahrens," *ZÄS* 17 (1879), pp. 71–76, pl. 1; K. Baer, "The Low Price of Land in Ancient Egypt," *JARCE* 1 (1962), pp. 36–39; W. Helck, "Der Papyrus Berlin P. 3047," *JARCE* 2 (1963), pp. 65–73, pls. 9–12; S.L.D. Katary, *Land Tenure in the Ramesside Period* (Studies in Egyptology. London – New York: Kegan Paul International, 1989), pp. 223–225.
36 J.-M. Kruchten, *Le Décret d'Horemheb. Traduction, commentaire épigraphique, philologique et institutionnel* (Bruxelles: Editions de l'Université de Bruxelles, 1981), pp. 148–161.
37 G.P.F. van den Boorn, *The Duties of the Vizier: Civil Administration in the Early New Kingdom* (Studies in Egyptology. London – New York: Kegan Paul International, 1988), pp. 12–13 (R2), 22–32 (n. 18).
38 N. de Garis Davies, *The Tomb of Rekh-mi-Rē at Thebes* (New York: 1973), pls. 24–25.
39 S. Quirke, *Titles and Bureaux of Egypt 1850–1700 BC* (Egyptology 1. London: Golden House Publications, 2004), pp. 20–22.
40 J.J. Janssen – P.W. Pestman, "Burial and Inheritance in the Community of the Necropolis Workman at Thebes," *JESHO* 11 (1968), pp. 137–170.
41 J. Černý – T.E. Peet, "A Marriage Settlement of the Twentieth Dynasty: An Unpublished Document from Turin," *JEA* 13 (1927), pp. 30–39.
42 J. Toivari-Viitala, "O. DeM 764: A Note Concerning Property Rights," *GM* 195 (2003), pp. 87–96.
43 A.G. McDowell, *Jurisdiction in the Workmen's Community of Deir el-Medina* (EU 5. Leiden: NINO, 1990), pp. 107–141.
44 For possible but very ambiguous earlier examples, see J. Baines, "Practical Religion and Piety," *JEA* 73 (1987), pp. 88–90; and J. Baines – R.B. Parkinson, "An Old Kingdom Record of an Oracle? Sinai Inscription 13," in J. van Dijk (ed.), *Essays on Ancient Egypt in Honour of Herman te Velde* (Egyptological Memoirs 1. Groningen, 1997), pp. 9–27.
45 J. Černy, "Egyptian Oracles," in R.A. Parker, *A Saite Oracle Papyrus from Thebes in the Brooklyn Museum [Papyrus Brooklyn 47.218.3]* (Brown Egyptological Studies 4. Providence, 1962), pp. 35–36.
46 S.P. Vleeming, "The Days on which the *Ḳnbt* used to gather," in R.J. Demarée – J.J. Janssen (eds), *Gleanings from Deir el-Medîna* (EU 1. Leiden: NINO, 1982), pp. 187–189; A.G. McDowell, *Jurisdiction in the Workmen's Community of Deir el-Medina* (EU 5. Leiden: NINO, 1990), pp. 108–114.
47 M. Römer, *Gottes- und Priester-herrschaft in Ägypten am Einde des Neuen Reiches. Ein religions-gechichtliches Phänomen und seine sozialen Grundlagen* (ÄAT 21. Wiesbaden, 1994), pp. 161–166; J. Winand, "Les décrets oraculaires pris en l'honneur d'Henouttaouy et de Maâtkarê (Xe et VIIe Pylônes)," *Cahiers de Karnak* XI, Fasicle 2 (Cairo, 2003), pp. 607–612.
48 J.J. Janssen – P.W. Pestman, "Burial and Inheritance in the Community of the Necropolis Workman at Thebes," *JESHO* 11 (1968), pp. 137–170.
49 J. Černý, "Papyrus Salt 124 (Brit. Mus. 10055)," *JEA* 15 (1929), pp. 243–258.
50 After J. Černý, "Papyrus Salt 124 (Brit. Mus. 10055)," *JEA* 15 (1929), pp. 243–258.
51 S.L.D. Katary, "The Administration of Institutional Agriculture in the New Kingdom," in J.C. Moreno García (ed.), *Ancient Egyptian Administration* (HdO 104. Leiden: Brill, 2013), pp. 744–758.
52 K.A. Kitchen, *RI* I, p. 231 no. 100; D. Kessler, "Eine Stele Sethos I. aus Kom el-Lufi (Minia)," *SAK* 10 (1989), pp. 215–220.
53 K.A. Kitchen, *RI* I, p. 45 no. 23.
54 A. David, *Syntactic and Lexico-Semantic Aspects of the Legal Register in Ramesside Royal Decrees* (Göttinger Orientforschungen IV. Reihe Ägypten 38. Wiesbaden, Harrassowitz, 2006), pp. 192–193.
55 A. Gardiner, *Late Egyptian Miscellanies* (Bibliotheca Aegyptiaca 7. Bruxelles: Fondation Egyptologique Reine Elisabeth, 1937), p. 87

(VIII. Pap. Sallier I, no. 11); R.A. Caminos, *Late Egyptian Miscellanies* (Brown Egyptological Studies 1. Oxford: University Press, 1954), pp. 325–328 (VIII. Pap. Sallier I, no. 11).

56 A.H. Gardiner, *The Inscription of Mes* (Leipzig, 1905).

57 S.L.D. Katary, *Land Tenure in the Ramesside Period* (Studies in Egyptology. London – New York: Kegan Paul International, 1989), pp. 1–18.

58 C.J. Eyre, "Feudal Tenure and Absentee Landlords," in S. Allam (ed.), *Grund und Boden in Alägypten, Akten des internationalen Symposions Tübingen 18.-20. Juni 1990* (Untersuchungen zum Rechtsleben im Alten Ägypten 2. Tübingen, 1994), pp. 107–133.

59 A. Gardiner, *The Wilbour Papyrus*, vol. 1: *Plates* (London, 1941); idem, *The Wilbour Papyrus*, vol. 2: *Commentary* (London, 1948); and idem, *The Wilbour Papyrus*, vol. 3: *Translation* (London, 1948).

60 S.L.D. Katary, "Land-Tenure in the New Kingdom: the Role of Women Smallholders and the Military," in A.K. Bowman – E. Rogan (eds.), *Agriculture in Egypt from Pharaonic to Modern Times* (Proceedings of the British Academy 96, Oxford: University Press, 1999), pp. 61–82.

61 S.L.D. Katary, "Land-Tenure in the New Kingdom: the Role of Women Smallholders and the Military," pp. 61–82 in A.K. Bowman – E. Rogan (eds.), *Agriculture in Egypt from Pharaonic to Modern Times* (Proceedings of the British Academy 96, Oxford: University Press, 1999). Herdsmen, Sherden, and scribes are also common, according to D. O'Connor, "The Geography of Settlement in Ancient Egypt," in P.J. Ucko – R. Tringham – G. W. Dimbleby (eds.), *Man, Settlement and Urbanism* (London, 1972), pp. 681–698.

62 B.J.J. Haring, *Divine Households, Administrative and Economic Aspects of the New Kingdom Royal Memorial Temples in Western Thebes* (EU 12, Leiden, NINO, 1997), pp. 156–191.

63 R.J. Demarée – D. Valbelle, *Les registres de recensement du village de Deir el-Medineh (Le Stato Civile)* (Leuven: Peeters, 2011), Texts SC 1–23; Texts SC 1 and 2 are on the same papyrus.

64 R.J. Demarée – D. Valbelle, *Les registres de recensement du village de Deir el-Medineh (Le Stato Civile)* (Leuven: Peeters, 2011), pp. 92–94.

65 D. Valbelle, "Eléments sur la démographie et le paysage urabains, d'après les papyrus documentaires d'époque pharaonique," in Sociétés urbaines en Egypte et au Soudan: *CRIPEL* 7 (1985), pp. 86–87; R.J. Demarée – D. Valbelle, *Les registres de recensement du village de Deir el-Medineh (Le Stato Civile)* (Leuven: Peeters, 2011), p. 88.

66 T.E. Peet, *The Great Tomb Robberies of the Twentieth Egyptian Dynasty* (Oxford: Clarendon, 1930), vol. 1, pp. 55–56, 64–65; vol. 2, pl. VII-VIII.

67 T.E. Peet, *The Great Tomb Robberies of the Twentieth Egyptian Dynasty* (Oxford: Clarendon, 1930), vol. 1, pp. 83–85, 93–98; vol. 2, pl. XIV-XVI.

68 J.J. Janssen, "The Water Supply of a Desert Village," *Medelhavsmuseet Bulletin* 14 (1979), pp. 9–15.

69 J. Černý, *Catalogue des ostraca hiératiques non-littéraires de Deir el-Médineh* IV (nos. 242–339) (DFIFAO 6. Cairo: IFAO, 1939), p. 5, pl. 6.

70 W.F. Edgerton, "The Nauri Decree of Seti I: A Translation and Analysis of the Legal Portion," *JNES* 6 (1947), p. 227.

71 J.-M. Kruchten, *Le Décret d'Horemheb. Traduction, commentaire épigraphique, philologique et institutionnel* (Bruxelles: Editions de l'Université de Bruxelles, 1981), pp. 58–79.

72 W.F. Edgerton, "The Nauri Decree of Seti I: A Translation and Analysis of the Legal Portion," *JNES* 6 (1947), pp. 219–230.

73 J.-M. Kruchten, *Le Décret d'Horemheb. Traduction, commentaire épigraphique, philologique et institutionnel* (Bruxelles: Editions de l'Université de Bruxelles, 1981), pp. 80–95.

74 A.-el-M. Bakir, *Egyptian Epistolography from the Eighteenth to the Twenty-first Dynasty* (BdÉ 48. Cairo: IFAO, 1970), pls. 6 and VIII; S. Allam, "Trois lettres d'affaires (P. Cairo CG 58056, 58058, 58060)," in P. Posener-Kriéger (ed.), *Mélanges Gamal eddin Mokhtar*, vol. 1 (BdÉ 97/1. Cairo: IFAO, 1985), pp. 24–28 and pls. 3–4; E.F. Wente, *Letters from Ancient Egypt* (SBL Writings from the Ancient World 1. Atlanta: Scholars Press, 1990), p. 113 (Text 131).

75 A.J. Spalinger, "Some Revisions of Temple Endowments in the New Kingdom," *JARCE* 28 (1991), pp. 21–39; B. Haring, "Ramesside Temples and the Economic Interests of the State: Crossroads of the Sacred and the Profane," in M. Fitzenreiter (ed.), *Das Heilige und die Ware: Zum Spannungsfeld von Religion und Ökonomie* (IBAES 7. London: Golden House Publications, 2007), p. 165.

76 W. Helck, *Urk.* IV, 2025–2032.

77 A.A.M.A. Amer, "Tutankhamun's Decree for the Chief Treasurer Maya," *RdÉ* 36 (1985), pp. 17–20; A.J. Spalinger, "Some Revisions of Temple Endowments in the New Kingdom," *JARCE* 28 (1991), pp. 27–28.

78 K.A. Kitchen, *RI* IV, p. 26 no. 9A/B and no. 10; A.J. Spalinger, "Some Revisions of Temple Endowments in the New Kingdom," *JARCE* 28 (1991), pp. 26–27; A. David, *Syntactic and Lexico-Semantic Aspects of the Legal Register in Ramesside Royal Decrees* (Göttinger Orientforschungen IV. Reihe Ägypten 38. Wiesbaden, Harrassowitz, 2006), pp. 207–208.

79 P. Barguet, "Tôd. Rapport de fouilles de la saison février-avril 1950," *BIFAO* 51 (1952), pp. 99–101; A.J. Spalinger, "Some Revisions of Temple Endowments in the New Kingdom," *JARCE* 28 (1991), pp. 22–24; P. Grandet, *Le Papyrus Harris* I (BdÉ 109. Cairo: IFAO, 1994), vol. 1, pp. 95–98; A. David, *Syntactic and Lexico-Semantic Aspects of the Legal Register in Ramesside Royal Decrees* (Göttinger Orientforschungen IV. Reihe Ägypten 38. Wiesbaden, Harrassowitz, 2006), pp. 209–214.

80 K.A. Kitchen, *RI* V, p. 232 no. 65.

81 K.A. Kitchen, *RI* V, p. 233 no. 66.

82 P. Grandet, "Un texte historique de Ramsès III à El-Kâb (et autres textes ramessides)," *RdÉ* 41 (1990), pp. 95–99.

83 K.A. Kitchen, *RI* V, p. 233 no. 67.

84 K.A. Kitchen, *RI* V, p. 233 no. 68.

85 H. Ricke, "Eine Inventartafel aus Heliopolis im Turiner Museum," *ZÄS* 71 (1935), pp. 111–133, pls. 2–3.

86 P. Grandet, *Le Papyrus Harris* I (BdÉ 109. Cairo: IFAO, 1994), vol. 1, pp. 98–100.

87 A. David, *Syntactic and Lexico-Semantic Aspects of the Legal Register in Ramesside Royal Decrees* (Göttinger Orientforschungen IV. Reihe Ägypten 38. Wiesbaden, Harrassowitz, 2006), p. 215.

88 K.A. Kitchen, *RI* V, pp. 237–247 no. 71; P. Grandet, *Le Papyrus Harris* I (BdÉ 109. Cairo: IFAO, 1994), vol. 1, pp. 86, 97.

89 P. Grandet, *Le Papyrus Harris* I (BdÉ 109. Cairo: IFAO, 1994), vol. 1, pp. 85–101.

90 P. Grandet, *Le Papyrus Harris* I (BdÉ 109. Cairo: IFAO, 1994), vol. 1, pp. 225–255.

91 P. Grandet, *Le Papyrus Harris* I (BdÉ 109. Cairo: IFAO, 1994), vol. 1, pp. 257–281.

92 P. Grandet, *Le Papyrus Harris* I (BdÉ 109. Cairo: IFAO, 1994), vol. 1, pp. 283–302.

93 P. Grandet, *Le Papyrus Harris* I (BdÉ 109. Cairo: IFAO, 1994), vol. 1, pp. 303–321.

94 P. Grandet, *Le Papyrus Harris* I (BdÉ 109. Cairo: IFAO, 1994), vol. 1, pp. 323–332.

95 Contra S. Allam, "Sind die nichtliterarischen Schriftostraka Brouillons?," *JEA* 54 (1968), pp. 121–128; K. Donker van Heel – B.J.J. Haring, *Writing in a Workmen's Village. Scribal Practice in Ramesside Deir el-Medina* (EU 16. Leiden: NINO, 2003), p. 18, pp. 27–30.

96 H. Goedicke, "Hieratische Ostraka in Wien," *WZKM* 59/60 (1963/1964), p. 2, pl. 2.

97 A.H. Gardiner, "Four Papyri of the 18th Dynasty from Kahun," *ZÄS* 43 (1906), pp. 28–35.

98 J. Černý, "The Will of Naunakhte and the Related Documents," *JEA* 31 (1945), pp. 29–53.

99 A.H. Gardiner, *The Inscription of Mes. A Contribution to the Study of Egyptian Juridical Procedure* (Untersuchungen zur Geschichte und Altertumskunde Ägyptens, Band 4, Heft 3. Leipzig: J.C. Hinrichs'sche Buchhandlung, 1905).

100 A.H. Gardiner, *The Inscription of Mes. A Contribution to the Study of Egyptian Juridical Procedure* (Untersuchungen zur Geschichte und Altertumskunde Ägyptens, Band 4, Heft 3. Leipzig: J.C. Hinrichs'sche Buchhandlung, 1905).

101 J. Černý – T.E. Peet, "A Marriage Settlement of the Twentieth Dynasty: An Unpublished Document from Turin," *JEA* 13 (1927), pp. 30–39.

102 D. Meeks, "Les donations aux temples dans l'Égypte du Ier millénaire avant J.-C.," in E. Lipiński (ed.), *State and Temple Economy in the Ancient Near East* II (OLA 6. Leuven, 1979), pp. 661–665.

103 D. Meeks, "Les donations aux temples dans l'Égypte du Ier millénaire avant J.-C.," in E. Lipiński (ed.), *State and Temple Economy in the Ancient Near East* II (OLA 6. Leuven, 1979), pp. 608–610.

104 W.J. Murnane – C.C. Van Siclen III, *The Boundary Stelae of Akhenaten* (London: Kegan Paul International, 1993), pp. 147–148.

105 Stela Cairo JdE 65830 of Year 45 of Thutmosis III, see W. Helck, *Urk.* IV, 1372–73; Stela Cairo JE 28019 = CG 34187 of Year 3 of Ay, see C. Zivie, *Giza au deuxième millénaire* (BdÉ 70. Cairo: IFAO, 1976), pp. 177–182 (NE 47), pp. 273–274, and pl.13; and Stela Cairo JdE 66612, of Year 6 of Ramesses III, see G.A. Gaballa, "Three

Documents from the Reign of Ramesses III," *JEA* 59 (1973), pp. 109–113 and pl. 38, and K.A. Kitchen, *RIV*, p. 229 no. 60.

106 J. Černý, "Prices and Wages in Egypt in the Ramesside Period," *Cahiers d' histoire mondiale* 1 (1954), pp. 904–906.

107 J. Černý, "Prices and Wages in Egypt in the Ramesside Period," *Cahiers d' histoire mondiale* 1 (1954), pp. 914–916.

108 J. Černý, "Fluctuations in Grain Prices during the Twentieth Egyptian Dynasty," *Archiv Orientální* 6 (1934), pp. 173–178.

109 J. Černý, "Fluctuations in Grain Prices during the Twentieth Egyptian Dynasty," *Archiv Orientální* 6 (1934), pp. 173–178.

110 J. Černý, "Prices and Wages in Egypt in the Ramesside Period," *Cahiers d' histoire mondiale* 1 (1954), pp. 906–907; B. Kemp, *Ancient Egypt, Anatomy of a Civilization* (London: Routledge, 1989), pp. 248–250.

111 B. Kemp, *Ancient Egypt, Anatomy of a Civilization* (London: Routledge, 1989), pp. 242–246.

112 E.W. Castle, "Shipping and Trade in Ramesside Egypt," *JESHO* 35 (1992), pp. 263–270.

113 B. Kemp, *Ancient Egypt, Anatomy of a Civilization* (London: Routledge, 1989), pp. 244–246.

114 C. Lilyquist, "Treasures from Tell Basta: Goddesses, Officials, and Artists in an International Age," *Metropolitan Museum Journal* 47 (2012), pp. 9–72.

115 J.J. Janssen, "Debts and Credit in the New Kingdom," *JEA* 80 (1994), pp. 129–136.

116 A. Gardiner, *Late Egyptian Miscellanies* (Bibliotheca Aegyptiaca 7. Bruxelles: Fondation Egyptologique Reine Elisabeth, 1937), pp. 80–82 (VIII. Pap. Sallier I, no. 4); R.A. Caminos, *Late Egyptian Miscellanies* (Brown Egyptological Studies 1. Oxford: University Press, 1954), pp. 306–312 (VIII. Pap. Sallier I, no. 4).

117 A.H. Gardiner, "Ramesside Texts Relating to the Taxation and Transport of Corn," *JEA* 27 (1941), pp. 56–58; S.L.D. Katary, *Land Tenure in the Ramesside Period* (Studies in Egyptology. London – New York: Kegan Paul International, 1989), pp. 193–196.

118 M. Megally, *Considérations sur les variations et la transformation des forms des signes hiératiques du papyrus E. 3226 du Louvre* (BdÉ 49. Cairo: IFAO, 1971); M. Megally, *Le papyrus hiératique compatable E. 3226 du Louvre* (BdÉ 53. Cairo: IFAO, 1971); M. Megally, *Recherches sur l'économie, l'administration et la comptabilité égyptiennes à la XVIIIe dynastie, d'après le papyrus E. 3226 du Louvre* (BdÉ 71. Cairo: IFAO, 1977); M. Megally, *Notions de comptabilité à propos du papyrus E. 3226 du Musée du Louvre* (BdÉ 72. Cairo: IFAO, 1977).

119 A.H. Gardiner, "Ramesside Texts Relating to the Taxation and Transport of Corn," *JEA* 27 (1941), pp. 22–37; A.H. Gardiner, *Ramesside Administrative Documents* (Oxford: Griffith Institute – London: Oxford University Press, 1948); S.L.D. Katary, *Land Tenure in the Ramesside Period* (Studies in Egyptology. London – New York: Kegan Paul International, 1989), pp. 169–182.

120 W. Pleyte, *Les Papyrus Rollin de la Bibliothèque Impériale de Paris* (Leiden: E.J. Brill, 1868); W. Spiegelberg, *Rechnungen aus der Zeit Setis I* (Strasbourg: Karl J. Trübner, 1896); P.E. Newberry, *The Amherst Papyri* (London, 1899); K.A. Kitchen, *RI* I, pp. 243–281 no. 112.

121 F.Ll. Griffith, *Hieratic Papyri from Kahun and Gurob* (London: 1898), *Text*, pp. 94–98, *Plates*, pls. 39–40; A.H. Gardiner, *Ramesside Administrative Documents* (London: Oxford University Press, 1948), pp. ix–xiii and 14–35.

122 S. Pasquali, "La date du Papyrus BM 10056: Tuthmosis II ou Amenhotep II?," *RdÉ* 58 (2007), pp. 76–77.

123 S.R.K. Glanville, "Records of a Royal Dockyard in the Time of Tuthmosis III: Papyrus British Museum 10056. Part I," *ZÄS* 66 (1931), pp. 105–121; S.R.K. Glanville, "Records of a Royal Dockyard in the Time of Tuthmosis III: Papyrus British Museum 10056. Part II," *ZÄS* 68 (1932), pp. 7–41.

124 M. Bietak, "The Thutmoside Stronghold of Perunefer," *Egyptian Archaeology* 26 (2005), pp. 13–17; D. Jeffreys, "Perunefer: at Memphis or Avaris?," *Egyptian Archaeology* 28 (2006), pp. 36–37; M. Bietak, "Perunefer: The Principal New Kingdom Naval Base," *Egyptian Archaeology* 34 (2009), pp. 15–17; M. Bietak, "Perunefer: An Update," *Egyptian Archaeology* 35 (2009), pp. 16–17.

125 S. Pasquali, "La date du Papyrus BM 10056: Tuthmosis II ou Amenhotep II?," *RdÉ* 58 (2007), pp. 81–82.

126 W. Golenischeff, *Les Papyrus No 1115, 1116A et 1116B de l'Ermitage Imperial a St-Petersbourg* (St-Petersbourg: L'Ermitage Imperial, 1913), p. 8, pls. 26–28.

127 W. Golenischeff, *Les Papyrus No 1115, 1116A et 1116B de l'Ermitage Imperial a St-Petersbourg*

(St-Petersbourg: L'Ermitage Imperial, 1913), pp. 4–6, pls. 15–22.

128 Decree of Horemheb, lines 8 right – 10 right; J.-M. Kruchten, *Le Décret d'Horemheb. Traduction, commentaire épigraphique, philologique et institutionnel* (Bruxelles: Editions de l'Université de Bruxelles, 1981), pp. 162–177; A.M. Gnirs, "Coping with the Army: The Military and the State in the New Kingdom," in J.C. Moreno García (ed.), *Ancient Egyptian Administration* (HdO 104. Leiden: Brill, 2013), pp. 660–661, 664.

129 A.M. Gnirs, "Coping with the Army: The Military and the State in the New Kingdom," in J.C. Moreno García (ed.), *Ancient Egyptian Administration* (HdO 104. Leiden: Brill, 2013), pp. 700–708.

130 K.A. Kitchen, *RI* I, pp. 65–70 no. 32; S. Schott, *Kanais. Der Tempel Sethos I. im Wadi Mia* (Nachrichten der Akademie der Wissenschaften in Göttingen, I. Philologisch-historisch klasse, Nr. 6. Göttingen: Vandenhoeck & Ruprecht, 1961), pp. 123–189 and Taf. 1–19; A. David, *Syntactic and Lexico-Semantic Aspects of the Legal Register in Ramesside Royal Decrees* (Göttinger Orientforschungen IV. Reihe Ägypten 38. Wiesbaden, Harrassowitz, 2006), pp. 112–132. K.A. Kitchen, *RI* I, pp. 45–58 no. 24 and p. 416 no. 180 lines 9–14 (corrigenda); F. Ll. Griffith, "The Abydos Decree of Seti I at Nauri," *JEA* 13 (1927), pp. 193–208 and pls 37–43; W.F. Edgerton, "The Nauri Decree of Seti I: A Translation and Analysis of the Legal Portion," *JNES* 6 (1947), pp. 219–230; A.H. Gardiner, "Some Reflections on the Nauri Decree," *JEA* 38 (1952), pp. 24–33; A. David, *Syntactic and Lexico-Semantic Aspects of the Legal Register in Ramesside Royal Decrees* (Göttinger Orientforschungen IV. Reihe Ägypten 38. Wiesbaden, Harrassowitz, 2006), pp. 17–107.

131 Decree of Horemheb, lines 23–27; J.-M. Kruchten, *Le Décret d'Horemheb. Traduction, commentaire épigraphique, philologique et institutionnel* (Bruxelles: Editions de l'Université de Bruxelles, 1981), pp. 80–95.

132 A. Spalinger, "The Organisation of the Pharaonic Army (Old to New Kingdom)," in J.C. Moreno García (ed.), *Ancient Egyptian Administration* (HdO 104. Leiden: Brill, 2013), pp. 415–416.

133 A.M. Gnirs, "Coping with the Army: The Military and the State in the New Kingdom," in J.C. Moreno García (ed.), *Ancient Egyptian Administration* (HdO 104. Leiden: Brill, 2013), pp. 650–651.

134 S.L.D. Katary, *Land Tenure in the Ramesside Period* (Studies in Egyptology. London – New York: Kegan Paul International, 1989), pp. 299–301; SL.D. Katary, "Land-Tenure in the New Kingdom: The Role of Women Smallholders and the Military," in A.K. Bowman – E. Rogan (eds.), *Agriculture in Egypt from Pharaonic to Modern Times* (Proceedings of the British Academy 96, Oxford: University Press, 1999), p. 69.

135 S.L.D. Katary, *Land Tenure in the Ramesside Period* (Studies in Egyptology. London – New York: Kegan Paul International, 1989), pp. 133–135; S.L.D. Katary, "Land-Tenure in the New Kingdom: the Role of Women Smallholders and the Military," in A.K. Bowman – E. Rogan (eds.), *Agriculture in Egypt from Pharaonic to Modern Times* (Proceedings of the British Academy 96, Oxford: University Press, 1999), pp. 75–78.

136 A. Gardiner, *The Wilbour Papyrus*, vol. 1: *Plates* (London, 1941); idem, *The Wilbour Papyrus*, vol. 2: *Commentary* (London, 1948); and idem, *The Wilbour Papyrus*, vol. 3: *Translation* (London, 1948).

137 S.L.D. Katary, "Land-Tenure in the New Kingdom: the Role of Women Smallholders and the Military," in A.K. Bowman – E. Rogan (eds.), *Agriculture in Egypt from Pharaonic to Modern Times* (Proceedings of the British Academy 96, Oxford: University Press, 1999), pp. 70–78.

138 J.J. Janssen, *Two Ancient Egyptian Ship's Logs, Papyrus Leiden I 350 verso and Papyrus Turin 2008 + 2016* (Oudheidkundige Mededelingen uit het Rijksmuseum van Oudheden te Leiden 42. Leiden: E.J. Brill, 1961), pp. 1–52.

139 B.J. Kemp, *The City of Akhenaten and Nefertiti: Amarna and Its People* (New Aspects of Antiquity. London: Thames and Hudson, 2012), p. 191; M. Müller, "Deir el-Medina in the Dark – the Amarna Period in the History of the Village," in J. Toivari-Viitala – T. Vartiainen – S. Uvanto (eds.), *Deir el-Medina Studies, Helsinki June 24–26, 2009 Proceedings* (The Finnish Egyptological Society – Occasional Publications 2. Helsinki: in press).

140 S. Häggman, *Directing Deir el-Medina. The External Administration of the Necropolis* (Uppsala Studies in Egyptology 4. Uppsala:

Akademitryck AB, 2002), pp. 193–288 for the late Twentieth Dynasty.

141 D. Valbelle, *«Les ouvriers de la tombe» Deir el-Médineh à l'époque Ramesside* (BdÉ 96. Cairo: IFAO, 1985), pp. 99–113 (2. L'équipe); J. Černý, *A Community of Workmen at Thebes in the Ramesside Period, 2e édition* (BdÉ 50. Chicago: IFAO, 2001), pp. 99–110 (10. The "Gang" of Workmen).

142 J. Černý, *A Community of Workmen at Thebes in the Ramesside Period, 2e édition* (BdÉ 50. Chicago: IFAO, 2001), pp. 121–132 (11. The Chief Workmen).

143 J. Černý, *A Community of Workmen at Thebes in the Ramesside Period, 2e édition* (BdÉ 50. Chicago: IFAO, 2001), pp. 133–147 (12. The "Deputy of the Gang").

144 J. Černý, *A Community of Workmen at Thebes in the Ramesside Period, 2e édition* (BdÉ 50. Chicago: IFAO, 2001), pp. 190–231 (17. The Scribes of the Tomb).

145 J. Černý, *A Community of Workmen at Thebes in the Ramesside Period, 2e édition* (BdÉ 50. Chicago: IFAO, 2001), pp. 110–120 (10. The "Gang" of Workmen).

146 D. Valbelle, *«Les ouvriers de la tombe» Deir el-Médineh à l'époque Ramesside* (BdÉ 96. Cairo: IFAO, 1985), pp. 148–157 (6. Les salaires); J.J. Janssen, *Village Varia. Ten Studies on the History and Administration of Deir el-Medina* (EU 11. Leiden: NINO, 1997), pp. 1–11 (1. The Sources of the Workmen's Provisions), especially p. 1; and S. Häggman, *Directing Deir el-Medina. The External Administration of the Necropolis* (Uppsala Studies in Egyptology 4. Uppsala: Akademitryck AB, 2002), pp. 79–86.

147 J.J. Janssen, *Village Varia. Ten Studies on the History and Administration of Deir el-Medina* (EU 11. Leiden: NINO, 1997), pp. 1–11 (1. The Sources of the Workmen's Provisions), especially pp. 4–8; and S. Häggman, *Directing Deir el-Medina. The External Administration of the Necropolis* (Uppsala Studies in Egyptology 4. Uppsala: Akademitryck AB, 2002), pp. 86–94.

148 J.J. Janssen, *Village Varia. Ten Studies on the History and Administration of Deir el-Medina* (EU 11. Leiden: NINO, 1997), pp. 13–35 (2. Rations and Ranks), especially pp. 13–21.

149 A.H. Gardiner, *Ramesside Administrative Documents* (Oxford: 1948), pp. 45–58 (Text 18); W.F. Edgerton, "The Strikes in Ramses III's Twenty-Ninth Year," *JNES* 10 (1951), pp. 137–145; P.J. Frandsen, "Editing Reality: The Turin Strike Papyrus," in S. Israelit-Groll (ed.), *Studies in Egyptology Presented to Miriam Lichtheim* I (Jerusalem: 1990), pp. 166–199; M. Müller, "Der Turiner Streikpapyrus (pTurin 1880)," in B. Janowski – G. Wilhelm (eds.), *Texte zum Rechts- und Wirtschaftsleben* (Texte aus der Umwelt des Alten Testaments, Neue Folge 1. Gütersloh, 2004), pp. 165–184.

150 D. Valbelle, *«Les ouvriers de la tombe» Deir el-Médineh à l'époque Ramesside* (BdÉ 96. Cairo: IFAO, 1985), pp. 129–133; J. Černý, *A Community of Workmen at Thebes in the Ramesside Period, 2e édition* (BdÉ 50. Chicago: IFAO, 2001), pp. 183–190 (16. Serfs of the Tomb); J.J. Janssen, *Village Varia. Ten Studies on the History and Administration of Deir el-Medina* (EU 11. Leiden: NINO, 1997), pp. 1–11 (1. The Sources of the Workmen's Provisions), especially p. 2, and pp. 13–35 (2. Rations and Ranks), especially pp. 33–34; and S. Häggman, *Directing Deir el-Medina. The External Administration of the Necropolis* (Uppsala Studies in Egyptology 4. Uppsala: Akademitryck AB, 2002), pp. 94–106.

151 L.-A. Christophe, "Les porteurs d'eau de Deir el-Médineh pendent la règne de Ramsès III," *BIE* 36 (1953–54), pp. 381–408; S. Eichler, "Untersuchungen zu den Wasserträgern von Deir el-Medineh I," *SÄK* 17 (1990), pp. 135–175; S. Eichler, "Untersuchungen zu den Wasserträgern von Deir el-Medineh II," *SÄK* 18 (1991), pp. 173–205; S. Allam, "À propos de l'approvisionnement en eau de la colonie ouvrière de Deir el-Médîneh," in B. Menu (ed.), *Les problèmes institutionnels de l'eau en Égypte ancienne et dans l'Antiquité méditerranéenne, Colloque AIDEA vogüé 1992* (BdÉ 110. Cairo: IFAO, 1994), pp. 1–14; D. Gentet – N. Sweydan, "À propos de la comptabilité de l'eau en khar au Nouvel Empire," in B. Menu (ed.), *Les problèmes institutionnels de l'eau en Égypte ancienne et dans l'Antiquité méditerranéenne, Colloque AIDEA vogüé 1992* (BdÉ 110. Cairo: IFAO, 1994), pp. 177–185.

152 J.J. Janssen, "The Woodcutters," in J.J. Janssen – E. Frood – M. Goecke-Bauer (eds.), *Woodcutters, Potters and Doorkeepers: Service Personnel of the Deir el-Medina Workemen* (EU 17. Leiden: NINO, 2003), pp. 1–28.

153 L.-A. Christophe, "Le ravitaillement en poissons des artisans de la nécropole thébaine à la fin du règne de Ramsès III," *BIFAO* 65 (1967),

pp. 177–199; J. J. Janssen, "Fish and Fishermen," in J.J. Janssen, *Village Varia. Ten Studies on the History and Administration of Deir el-Medina* (EU 11. Leiden: NINO, 1997), pp. 37–54.

154 E. Frood, "The Potters: Organization, Delivery, and Product of work," in J.J. Janssen – E. Frood – M. Goecke-Bauer (eds.), *Woodcutters, Potters and Doorkeepers: Service Personnel of the Deir el-Medina Workemen* (EU 17. Leiden: NINO, 2003), pp. 29–62.

155 J.J. Janssen – R.J. Janssen, "The Laundrymen of the Theban Necropolis," *Archiv Orientální* 70 (2002), pp. 1–12.

156 S. Häggman, *Directing Deir el-Medina. The External Administration of the Necropolis* (Uppsala Studies in Egyptology 4. Uppsala: Akademitryck AB, 2002), pp. 135–146.

157 J.J. Janssen, *Village Varia. Ten Studies on the History and Administration of Deir el-Medina* (EU 11. Leiden: NINO, 1997), pp. 1–11 (1. The Sources of the Workmen's Provisions), especially p. 1; and S. Häggman, *Directing Deir el-Medina. The External Administration of the Necropolis* (Uppsala Studies in Egyptology 4. Uppsala: Akademitryck AB, 2002), p. 86, pp. 129–130.

158 B.J.J. Haring, *Divine Households: Administrative and Economic Aspects of the New Kingdom Royal Memorial Temples in Western Thebes* (EU 12. Leiden: NINO, 1997), pp. 1–12.

159 B.J.J. Haring, *Divine Households: Administrative and Economic Aspects of the New Kingdom Royal Memorial Temples in Western Thebes* (EU 12. Leiden: NINO, 1997), p. 19.

160 B. Haring, "The Rising Power of the House of Amun in the New Kingdom," in J.C. Moreno García (ed.), *Ancient Egyptian Administration* (HdO 104. Leiden: Brill, 2013), pp. 617–635.

161 B.J.J. Haring, *Divine Households: Administrative and Economic Aspects of the New Kingdom Royal Memorial Temples in Western Thebes* (EU 12. Leiden: NINO, 1997), pp. 20–34.

162 S.L.D. Katary, "The Administration of Institutional Agriculture in the New Kingdom," in J.C. Moreno García (ed.), *Ancient Egyptian Administration* (HdO 104. Leiden: Brill, 2013), pp. 765–783.

163 B. Haring, "The Rising Power of the House of Amun in the New Kingdom," in J.C. Moreno García (ed.), *Ancient Egyptian Administration* (HdO 104. Leiden: Brill, 2013), pp. 613–617.

164 S.S. Eichler, *Die Verwaltung des "Hauses des Amun" in der 18. Dynastie* (SAK Beiheft 7. Hamburg: Helmut Buske Verlag, 2000), pp. 9–24.

165 B. Haring, "The Rising Power of the House of Amun in the New Kingdom," in J.C. Moreno García (ed.), *Ancient Egyptian Administration* (HdO 104. Leiden: Brill, 2013), pp. 610–613.

166 S.S. Eichler, *Die Verwaltung des "Hauses des Amun" in der 18. Dynastie* (SAK Beiheft 7. Hamburg: Helmut Buske Verlag, 2000), pp. 25–48 (granary), 49–72 (fields), 73–96 (cattle), 97–113 (production centers), 115–139 (treasury), and 141–161 (craftsmen).

167 A.H. Gardiner, "Ramesside Texts Relating to the Taxation and Transport of Corn," *JEA* 27 (1941), pp. 37–56; S.L.D. Katary, *Land Tenure in the Ramesside Period* (Studies in Egyptology. London – New York: Kegan Paul International, 1989), pp. 184–192; J.J. Janssen, *Grain Transport in the Ramesside Period, Papyrus Baldwin (BM EA 10061) and Papyrus Amiens* (Hieratic Papyri in the British Museum 8. London: The British Museum Press, 2004).

168 B. Haring, "Ramesside Temples and the Economic Interests of the State: Crossroads of the Sacred and the Profane," in M. Fitzenreiter (ed.), *Das Heilige und die Ware: Zum Spannungsfeld von Religion und Ökonomie* (IBAES 7. London: Golden House Publications, 2007), pp. 165–166.

169 J.J. Janssen, "Requisitions from Upper-Egyptian Temples," *JEA* 77 (1991), pp. 79–94, and pl. 4.

170 W. Helck, "Eine Briefsammlung aus der Verwaltung des Amun-tempels," *JARCE* 6 (1967), pp. 137–140 (Text B), and pp. 144–145 (Text E).

171 W. Helck, "Die Inschrift über die Belohnung des Hohenpriesters *Imn-ḥtp*," *Mitteilungen des Instituts für Orientforschung* 4 (1956), pp. 161–178.

172 A.H. Gardiner, "Ramesside Texts Relating to the Taxation and Transport of Corn," *JEA* 27 (1941), pp. 22–37; A.H. Gardiner, *Ramesside Administrative Documents* (Oxford: Griffith Institute – London: Oxford University Press, 1948).

173 B.J.J. Haring, *Divine Households: Administrative and Economic Aspects of the New Kingdom Royal Memorial Temples in Western Thebes* (EU 12. Leiden: NINO, 1997), pp. 142–155; S.L.D. Katary, "The Administration of Institutional

Agriculture in the New Kingdom," in J.C. Moreno García (ed.), *Ancient Egyptian Administration* (HdO 104. Leiden: Brill, 2013), pp. 758–765.

174 W. Helck, *Urk.* IV, 1611 (no. 532); P. Lacau, *Stèles du Nouvel Empire* (Catalogue général des antiquités égyptiennes du Musée du Caire, nos. 34001–34189. Cairo: IFAO, 1909–1957), pp. 41–42, & pl. 12.

175 W. Helck, *Urk.* IV, 2078 (no. 798); P. Lacau, *Stèles du Nouvel Empire* (Catalogue général des antiquités égyptiennes du Musée du Caire, nos. 34001–34189. Cairo: IFAO, 1909–1957), pp. 232–233.

176 K.A. Kitchen, *RI* III, p. 75, no. 38; H. Gauthier, "Une fondation pieuse en Nubie," *ASAE* 36 (1936), pp. 49–71 and pl. 3; D. Meeks, "Les donations aux temples dans l'Égypte du Ier millénaire avant J.-C.," in E. Lipiński (ed.), *State and Temple Economy in the Ancient Near East* II (OLA 6. Leuven, 1979), p. 609 n.12. A *khet* was a linear measurement, an aroura being one square *khet*.

177 D. Kessler, "Eine Landschenkung Ramses' III. zugunsten eines 'Grossen der Thrw' aus Mr-mšᶜ.f," *SAK* 2 (1975), pp. 103–134 and pl. 2; W. Helck, "Einige Bemerkungen zu Artikeln im *SAK* 2," *SAK* 4 (1976), pp. 115–116.

178 K.A. Kitchen, *RI* I, pp. 3–4, no. 5; W. Spiegelberg, "Neue Schenkungsstelen über Landstiftungen an Tempel," *ZÄS* 56 (1920), pp. 55–56 & pl. 4.

179 J.A. Wilson, "The Theban Tomb (No. 409) of Si-Mut, called Kiki," *JNES* 29 (1970), pp. 191–192; M. Negm, *The Tomb of Simut called Kyky: Theban Tomb 409 at Qurneh* (Warminster: 1997), pp. 43–46; C.J. Eyre, *The Use of Documents in Pharaonic Egypt* (Oxford: University Press, 2013), p. 76.

180 W. Helck, *Urk.* IV, 1793–1801 (no. 642), especially 1796, lines 9–16; R.G. Morkot, "*Nb-mꜣᶜt-Rᶜ*–United-with-Ptah," *JNES* 49 (1990), pp. 323–337; C.J. Eyre, *The Use of Documents in Pharaonic Egypt* (Oxford: University Press, 2013), p. 125.

181 K.A. Kitchen, *RI* I, pp. 3–4, no. 5; W. Spiegelberg, "Neue Schenkungsstelen über Landstiftungen an Tempel," *ZÄS* 56 (1920), pp. 55–56 and pl. 4.

182 J.A. Wilson, "The Theban Tomb (No. 409) of Si-Mut, called Kiki," *JNES* 29 (1970), pp. 191–192; M. Negm, *The Tomb of Simut Called Kyky: Theban Tomb 409 at Qurneh* (Warminster: 1997), pp. 43–46; C.J. Eyre, *The Use of Documents in Pharaonic Egypt* (Oxford: University Press, 2013), p. 76.

183 W. Helck, *Urk.* IV, 1793–1801 (no. 642), especially 1796, lines 9–16; R.G. Morkot, "*Nb-mꜣᶜt-Rᶜ*–United-with-Ptah," *JNES* 49 (1990), pp. 323–337; C.J. Eyre, *The Use of Documents in Pharaonic Egypt* (Oxford: University Press, 2013), p. 125.

184 K.A. Kitchen, *RI* III, p. 75, no. 38; H. Gauthier, "Une fondation pieuse en Nubie," *ASAE* 36 (1936), pp. 49–71 and pl. 3; D. Meeks, "Les donations aux temples dans l'Égypte du Ier millénaire avant J.-C.," in E. Lipiński (ed.), *State and Temple Economy in the Ancient Near East* II (OLA 6. Leuven, 1979), p. 609 n.12.

185 D. Kessler, "Eine Landschenkung Ramses' III. zugunsten eines 'Grossen der Thrw' aus Mr-mšᶜ.f," *SAK* 2 (1975), pp. 103–134 and pl. 2; W. Helck, "Einige Bemerkungen zu Artikeln im *SAK* 2," *SAK* 4 (1976), pp. 115–116.

186 W. Helck, "Die Opferstiftung des Śn-mwt," *ZÄS* 85 (1960), pp. 23–34; P. Dorman, *The Monuments of Senenmut: Problems in Historical Methodology* (London: Kegan Paul International Ltd., 1988), pp. 29–31; and B.J.J. Haring, *Divine Households: Administrative and Economic Aspects of the New Kingdom Royal Memorial Temples in Western Thebes* (EU 12. Leiden: NINO, 1997), pp. 143–145.

187 A.H. Gardiner, "Four Papyri of the 18th Dynasty from Kahun," *ZÄS* 43 (1906), pp. 27–47.

188 A.H. Gardiner, "Four Papyri of the 18th Dynasty from Kahun," *ZÄS* 43 (1906), pp. 28–35.

189 K. Baer, "The Low Price of Land in Ancient Egypt," *JARCE* 1 (1962), pp. 25–45.

190 A.G. McDowell, *Jurisdiction in the Workmen's Community of Deir el-Medîna* (EU 5. Leiden: NINO, 1990), pp. 122–123.

191 J.J. Janssen – P.W. Pestman, "Burial and Inheritance in the Community of the Necropolis Workman at Thebes," *JESHO* 11 (1968), pp. 147–152 and 158–164.

192 J. Černý – A.H. Gardiner, *Hieratic Ostraca, Vol.* 1 (Oxford: Griffith Institute, 1957), pl. 23 no. 4; E.F. Wente, *Letters From Ancient Egypt* (SBL Writings from the Ancient World 1. Atlanta: Scholars Press, 1990), p. 147 (no. 199).

193 J. Toivari-Viitala, *Women at Deir el-Medina. A Study of the Status and Roles of the Female Inhabitants in the Workmen's Community during the Ramesside Period* (EU 15. Leiden: NINO, 2001), pp. 90–91.

194 J. Toivari-Viitala, *Women at Deir el-Medina. A Study of the Status and Roles of the Female Inhabitants in the Workmen's Community during the Ramesside Period* (EU 15. Leiden: NINO, 2001), p. 212.

195 A.G. McDowell, *Jurisdiction in the Workmen's Community of Deir el-Medîna* (EU 5. Leiden: NINO, 1990), pp. 123–124.

196 A.H. Gardiner, "A Lawsuit Arising from the Purchase of Two Slaves," *JEA* 21 (1935), pp. 140–146.

197 A.H. Gardiner, "Four Papyri of the 18th Dynasty from Kahun," *ZÄS* 43 (1906), pp. 38–43.

198 A.H. Gardiner, "Four Papyri of the 18th Dynasty from Kahun," *ZÄS* 43 (1906), pp. 28–35.

199 A.H. Gardiner, "Four Papyri of the 18th Dynasty from Kahun," *ZÄS* 43 (1906), pp. 35–38.

200 J.J. Janssen, *Commodity Prices from the Ramessid Period. An Economic Study of the Village of Necropolis Workmen at. Thebes* (Leiden: Brill, 1975), pp. 167–172; J.J. Janssen, *Donkeys at Deir el-Medîna* (EU 19. Leiden: NINO, 2005), pp. 87–89.

201 J.J. Janssen, *Donkeys at Deir el-Medîna* (EU 19. Leiden: NINO, 2005), pp. 81–86.

202 J.J. Janssen, *Donkeys at Deir el-Medîna* (EU 19. Leiden: NINO, 2005), pp. 96–110.

203 K. Sethe, *Urk.* IV, 1019–1021 (no. 304); B.J.J. Haring, *Divine Households: Administrative and Economic Aspects of the New Kingdom Royal Memorial Temples in Western Thebes* (EU 12. Leiden: NINO, 1997), pp. 145–147.

204 A.H. Gardiner, "Four Papyri of the 18th Dynasty from Kahun," *ZÄS* 43 (1906), pp. 28–35.

205 A.H. Gardiner, "Four Papyri of the 18th Dynasty from Kahun," *ZÄS* 43 (1906), pp. 38–43.

206 Jac. J. Janssen, *Commodity Prices from the Ramessid Period. An Economic Study of the Village of Necropolis Workmen at. Thebes* (Leiden: Brill, 1975), pp. 172–177.

207 Jac. J. Janssen, *Commodity Prices from the Ramessid Period. An Economic Study of the Village of Necropolis Workmen at. Thebes* (Leiden: Brill, 1975), pp. 165–167.

208 Jac. J. Janssen, *Commodity Prices from the Ramessid Period. An Economic Study of the Village of Necropolis Workmen at. Thebes* (Leiden: Brill, 1975), pp. 177–178.

209 Jac. J. Janssen, *Commodity Prices from the Ramessid Period. An Economic Study of the Village of Necropolis Workmen at. Thebes* (Leiden: Brill, 1975), pp. 178–179.

210 C. Pino, "The Market Scene in the Tomb of Khaemhat (TT57)," *JEA* 91 (2005), pp. 95–96; A.P. Zingarelli, *Trade and Market in New Kingdom Egypt* (BAR International Series 2063. Oxford: Archaeopress, 2010), pp. 37–44. Huy dates to Tuthmosis IV, but the market scene dates to Kenro's usurpation of the tomb in the early Nineteenth Dynasty.

211 cf. P. Leiden I 350 verso, and P. Turin 2008 + 2016: J.J. Janssen, *Two Ancient Egyptian Ship's Logs* (Leiden: 1961); and P. Anastasi VIII: E.F. Wente, *Letters from Ancient Egypt* (SBL Writings from the Ancient World 1. Atlanta, 1990), pp. 120–122.

212 K. Sethe, *Urk.* IV, 1–11; V. Loret, *L'inscription d'Ahmès fils d'Abana* (BdÉ 3. Cairo: IFAO, 1910); C. Vandersleyen, *Les Guerres d' Amosis, fondateur de la XVIIIe dynastie* (Monographies Reine Élisabeth 1. Brussels, 1971), pp. 17–87; M. Lichtheim, *Ancient Egyptian Literature, Volume II: The New Kingdom* (Berkeley: University of California Press, 1976), pp. 12–15.

213 A.R. Schulman, "The Nubian war of Akhenaton," in Anonymous (ed.), *L'Égyptologie en 1979: axes prioritaires de recherches* 2 (Paris: Éditions du Centre national de la Recherche scientifique, 1982), pp. 299–316.

214 E.F. Wente, "The Suppression of the High Priest Amenhotep," *JNES* 25,2 (April 1966), pp. 73–87.

215 K. Jansen-Winkeln, "Das Ende des Neuen Reiches," *ZÄS* 119 (1992), pp. 22–37.

216 K. Sethe, *Urk.* IV, 1–11; V. Loret, *L'inscription d'Ahmès fils d'Abana* (BdÉ 3. Cairo: IFAO, 1910); C. Vandersleyen, *Les Guerres d' Amosis, fondateur de la XVIIIe dynastie* (Monographies Reine Élisabeth 1. Brussels, 1971), pp. 17–87; M. Lichtheim, *Ancient Egyptian Literature, Volume II: The New Kingdom* (Berkeley: University of California Press, 1976), pp. 12–15.

217 A.J. Spalinger, "A Critical Analysis of the 'annals' of Thutmose III (Stücke V-VI)," *JARCE* 14 (1977), pp. 41–54; J.P. Allen, "After Hatshepsut: The Military Campaigns of Thutmose III," in C.H. Roehrig – R.

Dreyfus – C.A. Keller (eds.), *Hatshepsut: From Queen to Pharaoh* (New York; New Haven: Metropolitan Museum of Art; Yale University Press, 2005), pp. 261–262; H. Sternberg-el Hotabi, "Aus den Annalen Thutmosis' III.: erster Feldzug gegen Megiddo," in B. Janowski – G. Wilhelm (eds), *Staatsverträge, Herrscherinschriften und andere Dokumente zur politischen Geschichte* (Gütersloh: Gütersloher Verlagshaus, 2005), pp. 212–220.

218 W. Helck, *Urk.* IV, 1287–1299, no. 374.

219 W. Helck, *Urk.* IV, 1299–1309, no. 375A (Memphis), and 1310–1316, no. 375B (Karnak); P. Der Manuelian, *Studies in the Reign of Amenophis II* (HÄB 26. Hildesheim: Gerstenberg, 1987), pp. 45–97 (chapter 2. The Military Campaigns of Amenophis II).

220 K.A. Kitchen, *RI* I, pp. 6–37 (Texts 1–17); W.F. Albright, "The Smaller Beth-Shan Stele of Sethos I (1309–1290 BC)," *BASOR* 125 (1952), pp. 24–32; A.J. Spalinger, "The Northern Wars of Seti I: An Integrative Study," *JARCE* 16 (1979), pp. 29–47; W.J. Murnane, *The Road to Kadesh. A Historical Interpretation of the Battle Reliefs of King Sety I at Karnak* (SAOC 42. Chicago: Oriental Institute, 1985); Epigraphic Survey, *Reliefs and Inscriptions at Karnak, Volume 4: The Battle Reliefs of King Sety I* (OIP 107. Chicago: Oriental Institute, 1986); C. Broadhurst, "An Artistic Interpretation of Sety I's War Reliefs," *JEA* 75 (1989), pp. 229–234; H. el-Saady, "The Wars of Sety I at Karnak: A New Chronological Structure," *SAK* 19 (1992), pp. 285–294; A. Degrève, "La campagne asiatique de l'an 1 de Séthy Ier représentée sur le mur extérieur nord de la salle hypostyle du temple d'Amon à Karnak," *RdÉ* 57 (2006), pp. 47–64.

221 K.A. Kitchen, *RI* II, pp. 1–224.

222 K.A. Kitchen, *RI* V, pp. 8–111; E. Edel, "Der Seevölkerbericht aus dem 8. Jahre Ramses' III. (MH II, pl. 46, 15–18): Übersetzung und Struktur," in P. Posener-Kriéger (ed.), *Mélanges Gamal eddin Mokhtar* 1 (Cairo: IFAO, 1985), pp. 223–237; B. Cifola, "Ramses III and the Sea Peoples: A Structural Analysis of the Medinet Habu Inscriptions," *Orientalia* 57 (1988), pp. 275–306.

223 Thomas Hikade, *Das Expeditionswesen im ägyptischen Neuen Reich: Ein Beitrag zu Rohstoffversorgung und Aussenhandel* (Studien zur Archäologie und Geschichte Altägyptens 21. Heidelberg: Heidelberger Orientverlag, 2001), pp. 33–56; Thomas Hikade, "Expeditions to the Wadi Hammamat during the New Kingdom," *JEA* 92 (2006), pp. 153–168.

224 T. Hikade, *Das Expeditionswesen im ägyptischen Neuen Reich: Ein Beitrag zu Rohstoffversorgung und Aussenhandel* (Studien zur Archäologie und Geschichte Altägyptens 21. Heidelberg: Heidelberger Orientverlag, 2001), pp. 57–64, 69–71; T. Hikade, "Expeditions to the Wadi Hammamat during the New Kingdom," *JEA* 92 (2006), pp. 153–168.

225 T. Hikade, *Das Expeditionswesen im ägyptischen Neuen Reich: Ein Beitrag zu Rohstoffversorgung und Aussenhandel* (Studien zur Archäologie und Geschichte Altägyptens 21. Heidelberg: Heidelberger Orientverlag, 2001), pp. 3–24.

226 T. Hikade, "Economic Aspects of the New Kingdom – the Expeditions to the Copper Mines of the Sinai," *Bulletin of the Australian Centre for Egyptology* 9 (1998), pp. 43–52; T. Hikade, *Das Expeditionswesen im ägyptischen Neuen Reich: Ein Beitrag zu Rohstoffversorgung und Aussenhandel* (Studien zur Archäologie und Geschichte Altägyptens 21. Heidelberg: Heidelberger Orientverlag, 2001), pp. 24–32.

227 K. Sethe, *Urk.* IV, 319–347; T. Hikade, *Das Expeditionswesen im ägyptischen Neuen Reich: Ein Beitrag zu Rohstoffversorgung und Aussenhandel* (Studien zur Archäologie und Geschichte Altägyptens 21. Heidelberg: Heidelberger Orientverlag, 2001), pp. 76–79.

228 K.A. Kitchen, *RI* IV, pp. 1–41; A. Niccacci, "La Stèle d'Israël: grammaire et stratégie de communication," in M. Sigrist (ed.), *Études égyptologiques et bibliques à la mémoire du Père B. Couroyer* (Paris: J. Gabalda et Cie Éditeurs, 1997), pp. 43–107.

229 K.A. Kitchen, *RI* V, pp. 8–111.

230 R. Morkot, "Nubia in the New Kingdom: The Limits of Egyptian Control," in W.V. Davies (ed.), *Egypt and Africa: Nubia from Prehistory to Islam* (London: British Museum Press in association with the EES, 1991), pp. 294–301; R. Morkot, "The Economy of Nubia in the New Kingdom," *Société Urbaines en Égypte et au Soudan. CRIPEL* 17:1 (1995), pp. 175–190; R. Morkot, "From Conquered to Conqueror: The Organization of Nubia in the New Kingdom and the Kushite Administration of Egypt," in J.C. Moreno García (ed.), *Ancient Egyptian Administration* (HdO 104: Leiden: Brill, 2013), pp. 911–963.

231 E.F. Morris, *The Architecture of Imperialism: Military Bases and the Evolution of Foreign*

Policy in Egypt's New Kingdom (Probleme der Ägyptologie 22. Leiden – Boston: Brill, 2005), pp. 68–113.

232 E.F. Morris, *The Architecture of Imperialism: Military Bases and the Evolution of Foreign Policy in Egypt's New Kingdom* (Probleme der Ägyptologie 22. Leiden – Boston: Brill, 2005), pp. 180–211, 310–342.

233 E.F. Morris, *The Architecture of Imperialism: Military Bases and the Evolution of Foreign Policy in Egypt's New Kingdom* (Probleme der Ägyptologie 22. Leiden – Boston: Brill, 2005), pp. 645–682, 782–799.

234 E.F. Morris, *The Architecture of Imperialism: Military Bases and the Evolution of Foreign Policy in Egypt's New Kingdom* (Probleme der Ägyptologie 22. Leiden – Boston: Brill, 2005), pp. 27–67.

235 E.F. Morris, *The Architecture of Imperialism: Military Bases and the Evolution of Foreign Policy in Egypt's New Kingdom* (Probleme der Ägyptologie 22. Leiden – Boston: Brill, 2005), pp. 116–180, 217–310.

236 E.F. Morris, *The Architecture of Imperialism: Military Bases and the Evolution of Foreign Policy in Egypt's New Kingdom* (Probleme der Ägyptologie 22. Leiden – Boston: Brill, 2005), pp. 343–611.

237 E.F. Morris, *The Architecture of Imperialism: Military Bases and the Evolution of Foreign Policy in Egypt's New Kingdom* (Probleme der Ägyptologie 22. Leiden – Boston: Brill, 2005), pp. 691–773.

238 E.F. Morris, *The Architecture of Imperialism: Military Bases and the Evolution of Foreign Policy in Egypt's New Kingdom* (Probleme der Ägyptologie 22. Leiden – Boston: Brill, 2005), pp. 645–682, 774–782.

239 B. Haring, "Ramesside Temples and the Economic Interests of the State: Crossroads of the Sacred and the Profane," in M. Fitzenreiter (ed.), *Das Heilige und die Ware: Zum Spannungsfeld von Religion und Ökonomie* (IBAES 7. London: Golden House Publications, 2007), p. 166, pp. 167–169.

240 K.A. Kitchen, *RI* I, pp. 65–70 no. 32; S. Schott, *Kanais. Der Tempel Sethos I. im Wadi Mia* (Nachrichten der Akademie der Wissenschaften in Göttingen, I. Philologisch-historisch klasse, Nr. 6. Göttingen: Vandenhoeck & Ruprecht, 1961), pp. 123–189 and Taf. 1–19; A. David, *Syntactic and Lexico-Semantic Aspects of the Legal Register in Ramesside Royal Decrees* (Göttinger Orientforschungen IV. Reihe Ägypten 38. Wiesbaden, Harrassowitz, 2006), pp. 112–132.

241 K.A. Kitchen, *RI* I, pp. 45–58 no. 24 and p. 416 no. 180 lines 9–14 (corrigenda); F. Ll. Griffith, "The Abydos Decree of Seti I at Nauri," *JEA* 13 (1927), pp. 193–208 and pls 37–43; W.F. Edgerton, "The Nauri Decree of Seti I: A Translation and Analysis of the Legal Portion," *JNES* 6 (1947), pp. 219–230; A.H. Gardiner, "Some Reflections on the Nauri Decree," *JEA* 38 (1952), pp. 24–33; A. David, *Syntactic and Lexico-Semantic Aspects of the Legal Register in Ramesside Royal Decrees* (Göttinger Orientforschungen IV. Reihe Ägypten 38. Wiesbaden, Harrassowitz, 2006), pp. 17–107.

242 P. Grandet, *Le Papyrus Harris* I (BdÉ 109. Cairo: IFAO, 1994), vol. 1, p. 238.

243 Y. Koenig, "Livraisons d'or et de galènee au trésor du temple d'Amon sous la XXe dynastie," in *Hommages à la mémoire de Serge Sauneron 1927–1976*, I. *Égypte pharaonique* (BdÉ 81. Cairo: IFAO, 1979), pp. 185–220, pls. XXX-XXXVII; Y. Koening, "Livraisons d'or et de galène au trésor du temple d'Amon sous la XXe dynastie: document A, partie inférieure," *BIFAO* 83 (1983), pp. 249–255, pls. LII-LIV.

244 W. Helck, "Eine Briefsammlung aus der Verwaltung des Amun-tempels," *JARCE* 6 (1967), pp. 135–137 (Text A), and pp. 140–144 (Texts C and D).

245 J.-M. Kruchten, *Le Décret d'Horemheb. Traduction, commentaire épigraphique, philologique et institutionnel* (Bruxelles: Editions de l'Université de Bruxelles, 1981), pp. 28–56.

246 W.F. Edgerton, "The Nauri Decree of Seti I: A Translation and Analysis of the Legal Portion," *JNES* 6 (1947), pp. 219–230.

247 J.J. Janssen, *Two Ancient Egyptian Ship's Logs, Papyrus Leiden I 350 verso and Papyrus Turin 2008 + 2016* (Oudheidkundige Mededelingen uit het Rijksmuseum van Oudheden te Leiden 42. Leiden: E.J. Brill, 1961), pp. 53–95.

248 K.M. Cooney, *The Cost of Death: The Social and Economic Value of Ancient Egyptian Funerary Art in the Ramesside Period* (EU 22. Leiden: NINO, 2007), pp. 12–16.

249 K.M. Cooney, *The Cost of Death: The Social and Economic Value of Ancient Egyptian Funerary Art in the Ramesside Period* (EU 22. Leiden: NINO, 2007), pp. 44–65.

250 K.M. Cooney, *The Cost of Death: The Social and Economic Value of Ancient Egyptian Funerary Art*

in the Ramesside Period (EU 22. Leiden: NINO, 2007), pp. 131–175.

251 K.M. Cooney, *The Cost of Death: The Social and Economic Value of Ancient Egyptian Funerary Art in the Ramesside Period* (EU 22. Leiden: NINO, 2007), pp. 72–75.

252 K.M. Cooney, *The Cost of Death: The Social and Economic Value of Ancient Egyptian Funerary Art in the Ramesside Period* (EU 22. Leiden: NINO, 2007), pp. 127–130.

253 A.H. Gardiner, "A Lawsuit Arising from the Purchase of Two Slaves," *JEA* 21 (1935), pp. 140–146.

5. THE THIRD INTERMEDIATE PERIOD (c. 1069–664 BCE)

1 K.A. Kitchen, *The Third Intermediate Period in Egypt (1100–650 BC)*, 2nd ed. rev. (Warminster: Aris & Phillips, 1996), pp. 255–312.

2 K.A. Kitchen, *The Third Intermediate Period in Egypt (1100–650 BC)*, 2nd ed. rev. (Warminster: Aris & Phillips, 1996), pp. 313–361.

3 F. Payraudeau, *Administration, société et pouvoir à Thebes sous la XXIIe dynastie bubastite*, 2 vols. (BdÉ 160: 1–2. Cairo: IFAO, 2014), vol. 1, pp. 9–25, with literature.

4 K.A. Kitchen, *The Third Intermediate Period in Egypt (1100–650 BC)*, 2nd ed. rev. (Warminster: Aris & Phillips, 1996), pp. 362–398.

5 F. Payraudeau, *Administration, société et pouvoir à Thebes sous la XXIIe dynastie bubastite*, 2 vols. (BdÉ 160: 1–2. Cairo: IFAO, 2014), vol. 1, p. 173.

6 J.-M. Kruchten, *Le grand texte oraculaire de Djehoutymose, Intendent du Domaine d'Amon dous le Pontificat de Pinedjem II* (Monographies Reine Elisabeth 5. Bruxelles, 1986), pp. 325–336.

7 J. von Beckerath, "Die «Stele der Verbannten» im Museum des Louvre," *RdÉ* 20, 1968, pp. 7–36 and pl. 1; K. Jansen-Winkeln, *Inschriften der Spätzeit, Teil I: Die 21. Dynastie* (Wiesbaden, 2007), pp. 72–74; R.K. Ritner, *The Libyan Anarchy, Inscriptions from Egypt's Third Intermediate Period* (SBL Writings from the Ancient World 21. Atlanta: SBL, 2009), pp. 124–129 (no. 28).

8 J.-M. Kruchten, *Le grand texte oraculaire de Djehoutymose, Intendent du Domaine d'Amon dous le Pontificat de Pinedjem II* (Monographies Reine Elisabeth 5. Bruxelles, 1986); and K. Jansen-Winkeln, *Inschriften der Spätzeit, Teil I: Die 21. Dynastie* (Wiesbaden, 2007), pp. 169–177.

9 F. Payraudeau, *Administration, société et pouvoir à Thebes sous la XXIIe dynastie bubastite*, 2 vols. (BdÉ 160: 1–2. Cairo: IFAO, 2014), vol. 1, pp. 175–176.

10 F. Payraudeau, *Administration, société et pouvoir à Thebes sous la XXIIe dynastie bubastite*, 2 vols. (BdÉ 160: 1–2. Cairo: IFAO, 2014), vol. 1, pp. 176–177.

11 Epigraphic Survey, *Reliefs and Inscriptions at Karnak, 3. The Bubastite Portal* (OIP 74. Chicago: University of Chicago Press, 1954), pl. 21, lines 17–20, and pl. 22, line 1; R.A. Caminos, *The Chronicle of Prince Osorkon* (Analecta Orientalia 37. Rome: Pontificium Institutum Biblicum, 1958), pp. 88–91; R.K. Ritner, *The Libyan Anarchy, Inscriptions from Egypt's Third Intermediate Period* (SBL Writings from the Ancient World 21. Atlanta: SBL, 2009), pp. 348–377 (no. 82), especially pp. 362–366.

12 P. Vernus, "Inscriptions de la Troisième Période Intermédiare (IV), Le texte oraculaire réemployé dans le passage axial du IIIe pylône dans le temple de Karnak," *Cahiers de Karnak* 6 (1980), pp. 215–233; R.K. Ritner, *The Libyan Anarchy, Inscriptions from Egypt's Third Intermediate Period* (SBL Writings from the Ancient World 21. Atlanta: SBL, 2009), pp. 380–382 (no. 85).

13 F. Payraudeau, *Administration, société et pouvoir à Thebes sous la XXIIe dynastie bubastite*, 2 vols. (BdÉ 160: 1–2. Cairo: IFAO, 2014), vol. 1, pp. 178–181.

14 S. Allam, "Egyptian Law Courts in Pharaonic and Hellenistic Times," *JEA* 77 (1991), p. 115; F. Payraudeau, *Administration, société et pouvoir à Thebes sous la XXIIe dynastie bubastite*, 2 vols. (BdÉ 160: 1–2. Cairo: IFAO, 2014), vol. 1, pp. 181–195.

15 R.A. Parker, *A Saite Oracle Papyrus from Thebes in the Brooklyn Museum [Papyrus Brooklyn 47.218.3]* (Brown Egyptological Studies 4. Providence, 1962), pp. 49–52 and pls. 17–19 (Appendix 1).

16 J. Von Beckerath, "Zur Datierung des Papyrus Brooklyn 16.205," *GM* 140 (1994), pp. 15–17.

17 W. Spiegelberg, "Eine Stele aus der Oase Dachel," *RecTrav.* 21 (1899), pp. 12–21; A.H. Gardiner, "The Dakhleh Stela," *JEA* 19 (1933), pp. 19–30 and pls. 5–7; K. Jansen-Winkeln, *Inschriften der Spätzeit, Teil II: Die 22. – 24. Dynastie* (Wiesbaden, 2007), pp. 23–26; R.K. Ritner, *The Libyan Anarchy, Inscriptions from Egypt's Third Intermediate Period* (SBL Writings

from the Ancient World 21. Atlanta: SBL, 2009), pp. 173–178 (no. 43).

18 K. Ryholt, "A Pair of Oracle Petitions Addressed to Horus-of-the-Camp," *JEA* 79 (1993), pp. 189–198; H.-W. Fischer-Elfert, "Two Oracle Petitions Addressed to Horus-khau with Some Notes on the Oracular Amuletic Decrees (P. Berlin P 8525 and P 8526)," *JEA* 82 (1996), pp. 129–144.

19 S.P. Vleeming, "The Sale of a Slave in the Time of Pharaoh *Py*," *Oudheidkundige Mededelingen uit het Rijksmuseum van Oudheden* 61 (1980), p. 15 note 53; G. Vittmann, "Zwei kursivhieratische Urkunden in Kairo," *Enchoria* 26 (2000), p. 134 note bb.

20 G. Vittmann, "Zwei kursivhieratische Urkunden in Kairo," *Enchoria* 26 (2000), p. 136.

21 B.P. Muhs, "Clear Title, Public Protests and P. Brux. dem. 4," in K. Ryholt (ed.), *Acts of the Seventh International Conference of Demotic Studies, Copenhagen, 23–27 August 1999* (CNI 27. Copenhagen, 2002), pp. 259–272.

22 M. Malinine, "Un jugement rendu à Thèbes sous la XXVe dynastie (Pap. Louvre E. 3228c)," *RdÉ* 6 (1951), pp. 159–161.

23 S. Allam, "The Agreement after Judgement," *Acta Demotica* (*EVO* 17 [1994]), pp. 19–28, argues that the agreement after judgment was traditional in Egyptian law. Note however that the earlier agreements are promises to perform with penalties for failure, but not actual transfers of title.

24 P.W. Pestman, "Réflexions à propos du soi-disant Code de Hermoupolis", *JESHO* 26 (1983), pp. 17–18.

25 S.L. Lippert, *Ein demotisches juristisches Lehrbuch. Untersuchungen zu P. Berlin 23757 rto* (ÄA 66. Wiesbaden, Harrassowitz, 2004), pp. 155–157.

26 R.K. Ritner, "Third Intermediate Period Antecedents of Demotic Legal Terminology," in Kim Ryholt (ed.), *Acts of the Seventh International Conference of Demotic Studies, Copenhagen, 23–27 August 1999* (CNI 27. Copenhagen: Museum Tusculanum Press, 2002), pp. 350–351.

27 S.P. Vleeming, *Papyrus Reinhardt* (Hieratische Papyri aus den Staatlichen Museen zu Berlin 2, Berlin, 1993).

28 A. Gasse, *Données nouvelles administratives et sacerdotales sur l'organisation du domaine d'Amon, XXe-XXIe dynasties, à la lumière des papyrus Prachov, Reinhardt et Grundbuch (avec édition princeps des papyrus Louvre AF 6345 et 6346–7)*, (BdÉ 104. Cairo: IFAO, 1988); reviewed by S.P. Vleeming, *Enchoria* 18 (1991), pp. 218–226.

29 B. Menu, "La stèle dite de l'Apanage," in B. Menu, *Recherches sur l'histoire juridique, économique et sociale de l'ancienne Égypte 2* (BdÉ 122. Cairo: IFAO, 1998), pp. 183–203; R.K. Ritner, *The Libyan Anarchy, Inscriptions from Egypt's Third Intermediate Period* (SBL Writings from the Ancient World 21. Atlanta: SBL, 2009), pp. 271–278 (no. 69).

30 For land-registers (*dny.w*), see C.J. Eyre, *The Use of Documents in Pharaonic Egypt* (Oxford: University Press, 2013), pp. 165–167.

31 R.K. Ritner, *The Libyan Anarchy, Inscriptions from Egypt's Third Intermediate Period* (SBL Writings from the Ancient World 21. Atlanta: SBL, 2009), p. 393 (no. 92).

32 S.P. Vleeming, *Papyrus Reinhardt* (Hieratische Papyri aus den Staatlichen Museen zu Berlin 2, Berlin, 1993), pp. 51–55.

33 P. Tresson, "L'Inscription de Chechanq Ier, au Musée du Caire: Un frappant exemple d'impôt progressif en matière religieuse," in *Mélanges Maspero*, vol. 1, fasc. 2 (MIFAO 66/1. Cairo: IFAO, 1938), pp. 817–840; and R.K. Ritner, *The Libyan Anarchy, Inscriptions from Egypt's Third Intermediate Period* (SBL Writings from the Ancient World 21. Atlanta: SBL, 2009), pp. 180–186 (no. 45).

34 D. Meeks, "Une fondation memphite de Taharqa," in *Hommages à la mémoire de Serge Sauneron, 1927–1976*, vol. 1 (BdÉ 81. Cairo: IFAO, 1979), pp. 221–259; R.K. Ritner, *The Libyan Anarchy, Inscriptions from Egypt's Third Intermediate Period* (SBL Writings from the Ancient World 21. Atlanta: SBL, 2009), pp. 512–516 (no. 157).

35 R.J. Demarée – D. Valbelle, *Les registres de recensement du village de Deir el-Medineh (Le Stato Civile)* (Leuven: Peeters, 2011), pp. 88–96.

36 Herodotus, Book II, 177.

37 W. Clarysse – D.J. Thompson, *Counting the People in Hellenistic Egypt, Volume 2: Historical Studies* (Cambridge Classical Studies. Cambridge: University Press, 2006), pp. 10–35: "2. The census."

38 W. Clarysse – D.J. Thompson, *Counting the People in Hellenistic Egypt, Volume 2: Historical Studies* (Cambridge Classical Studies. Cambridge: University Press, 2006), pp. 73–74.

39 R.A. Parker, *A Saite Oracle Papyrus from Thebes in the Brooklyn Museum [Papyrus Brooklyn 47.218.3]* (Brown Egyptological Studies 4. Providence,

1962), pp. 49–52 and pls. 17–19 (Appendix 1); and J. von Beckerath, "Zur Datierung des Papyrus Brooklyn 16.205," *GM* 140 (1994), pp. 15–17.

40 K. Ryholt, "A Pair of Oracle Petitions Addressed to Horus-of-the-Camp," *JEA* 79 (1993), pp. 189–198; and H.-W. Fischer-Elfert, "Two Oracle Petitions Addressed to Horus-khau with Some Notes on the Oracular Amuletic Decrees (P. Berlin P 8525 and P 8526)," *JEA* 82 (1996), pp. 129–144.

41 H. Munier, "Un Achat de Terrains au temps du Roi Si-Amon," in *Recueil d'Etudes Egyptologiques dediees a la memoire de Jean-Francois Champollion*, (Bibliothèque de l'École de Hautes Études 234. Paris, 1922), pp. 361–366; K. Jansen-Winkeln, *Inschriften der Spätzeit, Teil I: Die 21. Dynastie* (Wiesbaden, 2007), pp. 150–151; R.K. Ritner, *The Libyan Anarchy, Inscriptions from Egypt's Third Intermediate Period* (SBL Writings from the Ancient World 21. Atlanta: SBL, 2009), pp. 161–162 (no. 38).

42 J. Winand, "Les décrets oraculaires pris en l'honneur d'Henouttaouy et de Maâtkarê (Xe et VIIe Pylônes)," *Cahiers de Karnak* XI, Fasicle 2 (Cairo, 2003), p. 639.

43 J. Winand, "Les décrets oraculaires pris en l'honneur d'Henouttaouy et de Maâtkarê (Xe et VIIe Pylônes)," *Cahiers de Karnak* XI, Fasicle 2 (Cairo, 2003), pp. 668–670.

44 H. Sottas, *La préservation de la propriété funéraire dans l'ancienne Égypte avec le recueil des formules d'imprécation* (Bibliothèque de l'École des Hautes Études 205. Paris, 1913), pp. 161–165; B. Menu, "La stèle dite de l'Apanage," in B. Menu, *Recherches sur l'histoire juridique, économique et sociale de l'ancienne Égypte 2* (BdÉ 122. Cairo: IFAO, 1998), pp. 200–201.

45 K.A. Kitchen, *The Third Intermediate Period in Egypt (1100–650 BC)*, 2nd ed. rev. (Warminster: Aris & Phillips, 1996), pp. 56–57 (§46–47), p. 277 (§233); J. Winand, "Les décrets oraculaires pris en l'honneur d'Henouttaouy et de Maâtkarê (Xe et VIIe Pylônes)," pp. 603–710 in *Cahiers de Karnak XI* (2003), Fasicle 2, pp. 630–633.

46 K.A. Kitchen, *The Third Intermediate Period in Egypt (1100–650 BC)*, 2nd ed. rev. (Warminster, 1996), pp. 60–61 (§49), p. 306 (§265); J. Winand, "Les décrets oraculaires pris en l'honneur d'Henouttaouy et de Maâtkarê (Xe et VIIe Pylônes)," pp. 603–710 in *Cahiers de Karnak* XI (2003), Fasicle 2, pp. 676–680.

47 K.A. Kitchen, *The Third Intermediate Period in Egypt (1100–650 BC)*, 2nd ed. rev. (Warminster, 1996), p. 121 (§96), p. 195 (§157), p. 306 (§265).

48 Epigraphic Survey, *The Temple of Khonsu 2: Scenes and Inscriptions in the Court and First Hypostyle Hall* (OIP 103. Chicago: Oriental Institute, 1981), pp. 17–20, pl. 133; and R.K. Ritner, *The Libyan Anarchy, Inscriptions from Egypt's Third Intermediate Period* (SBL Writings from the Ancient World 21. Atlanta: SBL, 2009), pp. 130–135 (no. 30).

49 A.H. Gardiner, "The Gods of Thebes as Guarantors of Personal Property," *JEA* 48 (1962), pp. 57–64 (I. The Property of the Lady Hentowe); J. Winand, "Les décrets oraculaires pris en l'honneur d'Henouttaouy et de Maâtkarê (Xe et VIIe Pylônes)," in *Cahiers de Karnak* XI (2003), Fasicle 2, pp. 614–672; K. Jansen-Winkeln, *Inschriften der Spätzeit, Teil I: Die 21. Dynastie* (2007), pp. 177–182; and R.K. Ritner, *The Libyan Anarchy, Inscriptions from Egypt's Third Intermediate Period* (SBL Writings from the Ancient World 21. Atlanta: SBL, 2009), pp. 138–143 (no. 33).

50 A.H. Gardiner, "The Gods of Thebes as Guarantors of Personal Property," *JEA* 48 (1962), pp. 64–69 (II. The Property of the Lady Makare); J. Winand, "Les décrets oraculaires pris en l'honneur d'Henouttaouy et de Maâtkarê (Xe et VIIe Pylônes)," in *Cahiers de Karnak* XI (2003), Fasicle 2, pp. 672–690; K. Jansen-Winkeln, *Inschriften der Spätzeit, Teil I: Die 21. Dynastie* (Wiesbaden: Harrassowitz, 2007), pp. 182–183; and R.K. Ritner, *The Libyan Anarchy, Inscriptions from Egypt's Third Intermediate Period* (SBL Writings from the Ancient World 21. Atlanta: SBL, 2009), pp. 163–166 (no. 40).

51 G. Legrain, "Deux steles trouvees a Karnak en fevrier 1897, I. Stele de l'apanage," *ZÄS* 35 (1897), pp. 13–16; A. Erman, "Zu den Legrain'schen Inschriften, I. Das Testament eines Hohenpriesters," *ZÄS* 35 (1897), pp. 19–24; B. Menu, "La stèle dite de l'Apanage," in B. Menu, *Recherches sur l'histoire juridique, économique et sociale de l'ancienne Égypte 2* (BdÉ 122. Cairo: IFAO, 1998), pp. 193–203; K. *Jansen-Winkeln, Inschriften der Spätzeit, Teil II: Die 22. – 24. Dynastie* (Wiesbaden, 2007), pp. 77–80; and R.K. Ritner, *The Libyan Anarchy, Inscriptions from Egypt's Third Intermediate Period* (SBL Writings from the Ancient World 21. Atlanta: SBL, 2009), pp. 271–278 (no. 69).

52 D. Meeks, "Les donations aux temples dans l'Égypte du Ier millénaire avant J.-C.," in E. Lipiński (ed.), *State and Temple Economy in the Ancient Near East* II (OLA 6. Leuven, 1979), pp. 605–687.

53 A.M. Blackman, "The Stela of Shoshenk, Great Chief of the Meshwesh," *JEA* 27 (1941), pp. 83–95, pls. 10–12; K. Jansen-Winkeln, *Inschriften der Spätzeit, Teil I: Die 21. Dynastie* (Wiesbaden, 2007), pp. 159–162; and R.K. Ritner, *The Libyan Anarchy, Inscriptions from Egypt's Third Intermediate Period* (SBL Writings from the Ancient World 21. Atlanta: SBL, 2009), pp. 166–172 (no. 41).

54 G. Daressy, "Trois stèles de la période Bubastite," *ASAE* 15 (1915), pp. 140–143; E. Iversen, *Two Inscriptions Concerning Private Donations to Temples* (Det Kgl. Danske Videnskabernes Selskab. Historisk-filologiske Meddeleelser. 27, 5. Copenhagen, 1941), pp. 3–18; K. Jansen-Winkeln, *Inschriften der Spätzeit, Teil II: Die 22. – 24. Dynastie* (Wiesbaden, 2007), pp. 131–133; and R.K. Ritner, *The Libyan Anarchy, Inscriptions from Egypt's Third Intermediate Period* (SBL Writings from the Ancient World 21. Atlanta: SBL, 2009), pp. 344–347 (no. 80).

55 H. Sottas, *La préservation de la propriété funéraire dans l'ancienne Égypte avec le recueil des formules d'imprécation* (Bibliothèque de l'École des Hautes Études 205. Paris, 1913), pp. 145–154.

56 D. Meeks, "Les donations aux temples dans l'Égypte du Ier millénaire avant J.-C.," in E. Lipiński (ed.), *State and Temple Economy in the Ancient Near East* II (OLA 6. Leuven, 1979), pp. 665–673, lists fifty-six donation stelae from the Twenty-second through the Twenty-fifth Dynasties, of which thirty are said to be Hieroglyphic and twenty-two Hieratic; the others are not identified.

57 Stela Cairo JdE 36159, see R.K. Ritner, *The Libyan Anarchy, Inscriptions from Egypt's Third Intermediate Period* (SBL Writings from the Ancient World 21. Atlanta: SBL, 2009), pp. 379–380 (no. 84).

58 B. Muhs, "Partisan Royal Epithets in the Late Third Intermediate Period and the Dynastic Affiliation of Pedubast I and Iuput II," *JEA* 84 (1998), pp. 220–223.

59 F. Payraudeau, "Le règne de Takélot II et les débuts de la domination koushite à Thèbes," *GM* 198 (2004), pp. 82–85.

60 K. Donker van Heel, "The Scribbling-Pad of Djedmontefankh son of Aafenmut, Priest of Amonrasonter and Overseer of the King's Treasury (P. Berlin 3048 verso)," in K. Ryholt (ed.), *Acts of the Seventh International Conference of Demotic Studies, Copenhagen 23–27 August 1999* (CNI 27. Copenhagen, 2002), pp. 139–147.

61 G. Möller, *Zwei ägyptische Eheverträge aus vorsaitischer Zeit* (Abhandlungen der preussischen Akademie der Wissenschaften, phil.-hist. Klasse, Nr. 3. Berlin, 1918), pp. 1–31; E. Lüddeckens, *Ägyptische Eheverträge* (ÄA 1. Wiesbaden, 1960), pp. 10–11.

62 G. Möller, "Ein ägyptischer Schuldschein der zweiundzwanzigsten Dynastie," *Sitzungsberichte der preussischen Akademie der Wissenschaften, philosophisch-historischen Klasse* 15 (1921), pp. 298–304.

63 P.W. Pestman, *L'archivo di Amenothes figlio di Horos (P. Tor. Amenothes)*, (Milano, 1981), p. 161; P.W. Pestman, *Les papyrus démotiques de Tsenhor (P. Tsenhor)*, I. *Textes* (Studia Demotica 4. Leuven, 1994), pp. 26–27, 30–31.

64 M. Depauw, "Autograph Confirmation in Demotic Contracts", *CdÉ* 78 (2003), pp. 66–88.

65 P.W. Pestman, *L'archivo di Amenothes figlio di Horos (P. Tor. Amenothes)*, (Milano, 1981), pp. 161–162; P.W. Pestman, *Les papyrus démotiques de Tsenhor (P. Tsenhor)*, I. *Textes* (Studia Demotica 4. Leuven, 1994), pp. 21–22.

66 S.P. Vleeming, "The Sale of a Slave in the Time of Pharaoh *Py*," *Oudheidkundige Mededelingen uit het Rijksmuseum van Oudheden* 61 (1980), p. 10.

67 P. Cairo CG 30907 + 30909 (*Eheverträge* 2), dated to Year 13 of Taharka, see E. Lüddeckens, *Ägyptische Eheverträge* (ÄA 1. Wiesbaden, 1960).

68 P. Cairo CG 30859 + 30880–30883 + 30887 + 30910 + 31181–31184, dated to Taharka, see G. Vittmann, "Zwei kursivhieratische Urkunden in Kairo," *Enchoria* 26 (2000), pp. 126–127.

69 P. Leiden F 1942/5.15, dated to Year 21 of Piye (slave sale), see S.P. Vleeming, "The Sale of a Slave in the Time of Pharaoh Py," *Oudheidkundige Mededelingen uit het Rijksmuseum van Oudheden* 61 (1980), p. 10; P. Vatican 2038c, dated to Year 22 of Piye (slave sale), see M. Malinine, "Une vente d'esclave à l'époque de Psammétique Ier (Papyrus du Vatican 10574, en hiératique "anormale")," *RdÉ* 5 (1946), pp. 119–131, corrected in R.A. Parker, "King *Py*, a Historical Problem," *ZÄS* 93 (1966), p. 112; P. Louvre E 3228e (*Choix* I 6), dated to Year 10 of Shabaka (slave sale), see M. Malinine, *Choix de Textes Juridiques en Hieratique 'Anormal' et en Demotique, Premiere*

Partie (Bibliotheque de l'Ecole des Hautes Etudes 300. Paris: Librairie Ancienne Honore Champion, 1953), pp. 35–42 (Texte VI); and P. Louvre E 3228d (*Choix* I 7), dated to Year 3 of Taharka (slave sale), see M. Malinine, *Choix de Textes Juridiques en Hieratique 'Anormal' et en Demotique, Premiere Partie* (Bibliotheque de l'Ecole des Hautes Etudes 300. Paris: Librairie Ancienne Honore Champion, 1953), pp. 43–49 (Texte VII).

70 P. Louvre E 3228b (*Choix* I 1), dated to Year 13 of Shabaka (money loan), see M. Malinine, *Choix de Textes Juridiques en Hieratique 'Anormal' et en Demotique, Premiere Partie* (Bibliotheque de l'Ecole des Hautes Etudes 300. Paris: Librairie Ancienne Honore Champion, 1953), pp. 3–14 (Texte I); and T. MMA 35.3.318 ro + vo, dated to Years 3 and 5 of Taharka (grain and money loans), see J. Černý – R.A. Parker, "An Abnormal Hieratic Tablet," *JEA* 57 (1971), pp. 127–128.

71 P. Louvre E 7851 ro + vo, dated to Taharka, see K. Donker van Heel, "Papyrus Louvre E 7851 Recto and Verso: Two More Land Leases from the Reign of Taharka," *RdÉ* 50 (1999), pp. 138, 143.

72 P. Louvre E 3228c, dated to Year 6 of Taharka, see Michel Malinine, "Un jugement rendu à Thèbes sous la XXVe dynastie (Pap. Louvre E. 3228 c)," *RdÉ* 6 (1951), pp. 159–161.

73 P. Cairo CG 30884 + 30864 + 31182, dated to Year 5 of Taharka, see G. Vittmann, "Zwei kursivhieratische Urkunden in Kairo," *Enchoria* 26 (2000), p. 136.

74 K. Donker van Heel, "The Scribbling-Pad of Djedmontefankh son of Aafenmut, Priest of Amonrasonter and Overseer of the King's Treasury (P. Berlin 3048 verso)," in K. Ryholt (ed.), *Acts of the Seventh International Conference of Demotic Studies, Copenhagen 23–27 August 1999* (CNI 27. Copenhagen, 2002), pp. 139–147.

75 cf. R.K. Ritner, *The Libyan Anarchy, Inscriptions from Egypt's Third Intermediate Period* (SBL Writings from the Ancient World 21. Atlanta: SBL, 2009), p. 104.

76 Epigraphic Survey, *The Temple of Khonsu 2: Scenes and Inscriptions in the Court and First Hypostyle Hall* (OIP 103. Chicago: Oriental Institute, 1981), pp. 17–20, pl. 133; and R.K. Ritner, *The Libyan Anarchy, Inscriptions from Egypt's Third Intermediate Period* (SBL Writings from the Ancient World 21. Atlanta: Society of Biblical Literature, 2009), pp. 130–135 (no. 30).

77 R.A. Parker, *A Saite Oracle Papyrus from Thebes in the Brooklyn Museum [Papyrus Brooklyn 47.218.3]* (Brown Egyptological Studies 4. Providence, 1962), pp. 49–52 and pls. 17–19 (Appendix 1).

78 J. Von Beckerath, "Zur Datierung des Papyrus Brooklyn 16.205," *GM* 140 (1994), pp. 15–17.

79 H. Munier, "Un Achat de Terrains au temps du Roi Si-Amon," in *Recueil d'Etudes Egyptologiques dediees a la memoire de Jean-Francois Champollion*, (Bibliothèque de l'École de Hautes Études 234. Paris, 1922), pp. 361–366; K. Jansen-Winkeln, *Inschriften der Spätzeit, Teil I: Die 21. Dynastie* (Wiesbaden, 2007), pp. 150–151; R.K. Ritner, *The Libyan Anarchy, Inscriptions from Egypt's Third Intermediate Period* (SBL Writings from the Ancient World 21. Atlanta: SBL, 2009), pp. 161–162 (no. 38).

80 A.M. Blackman, "The Stela of Shoshenk, Great Chief of the Meshwesh," *JEA* 27 (1941), pp. 83–95, pls. 10–12; K. Jansen-Winkeln, *Inschriften der Spätzeit, Teil I: Die 21. Dynastie* (Wiesbaden, 2007), pp. 159–162; and R.K. Ritner, *The Libyan Anarchy, Inscriptions from Egypt's Third Intermediate Period* (SBL Writings from the Ancient World 21. Atlanta: SBL, 2009), pp. 166–172 (no. 41).

81 G. Legrain, "Deux steles trouvees a Karnak en fevrier 1897, I. Stele de l'apanage," *ZÄS* 35 (1897), pp. 13–16; A. Erman, "Zu den Legrain'schen Inschriften, I. Das Testament eines Hohenpriesters," *ZÄS* 35 (1897), pp. 19–24; B. Menu, "La stèle dite de l'Apanage," in B. Menu, *Recherches sur l'histoire juridique, économique et sociale de l'ancienne Égypte 2* (BdÉ 122. Cairo: IFAO, 1998), pp. 193–203; K. Jansen-Winkeln, *Inschriften der Spätzeit, Teil II: Die 22. – 24. Dynastie* (Wiesbaden, 2007), pp. 77–80; and R.K. Ritner, *The Libyan Anarchy, Inscriptions from Egypt's Third Intermediate Period* (SBL Writings from the Ancient World 21. Atlanta: SBL, 2009), pp. 271–278 (no. 69).

82 G. Legrain, "Deux stèles inédites," *ASAE* 7 (1906), pp. 226–227; R.K. Ritner, *The Libyan Anarchy, Inscriptions from Egypt's Third Intermediate Period* (SBL Writings from the Ancient World 21. Atlanta: SBL, 2009), pp. 573–574 (no. 170).

83 G. Möller, "Ein ägyptischer Schuldschein der zweiundzwanzigsten Dynastie," *Sitzungsberichte der preussischen Akademie der Wissenschaften, philosophisch-historischen Klasse* 15 (1921), pp. 298–304; the unpublished abstract of a house sale contract is called Urkunden C.

84 F.Ll. Griffith, *Catalogue of Demotic Papyri in the John Rylands Library, Manchester* (Manchester: University Press, 1909), vol. 3, p. 76.

85 R. Müller-Wollermann, "Ägypten auf dem Weg zur Geldwirtschaft," in J-C. Goyon and C. Cardin (eds.), *Proceedings of the Ninth International Congress of Egyptologists/Actes du Neuvième Congrès International des Égyptologues, Grenoble, 6–12 septembre 2004* (OLA 150. Leuven, 2007), vol. II, pp. 1351–1359; idem., "Die ökonomische Bedeutung von Tempelschatzhäusern," in M. Fitzenreiter (ed.), *Das Heilige und die Ware, Zum Spannungsfeld von Religion und Ökonomie, Workshop vom 26.05 bis 28.05.2006* (IBAES 7. London: Golden House Publications, 2007), pp. 176–178.

86 S.P.Vleeming, *The Gooseherds of Hou (Pap. Hou)*, (Studia Demotica 3. Leuven: Peeters, 1991), pp. 87–89 n. uu.

87 H.-C. Noeske, "Ein Hacksilberfund aus Elephantine", in H.-C. Noeske – H. Schubert (eds.), *Die Münze: Bild, Botschaft, Bedeutung: Festschrift für Maria R.–Alföldi* (Frankfurt–New York: 1991), pp. 342–351; and H.-C. Noeske, "Prämonetäre Wertmesser und Münzfunde aus Elephantine," *MDAIK* 49 (1993), pp. 204–205.

88 M. Malinine, *Choix de Textes Juridiques en Hieratique 'Anormal' et en Demotique, Premiere Partie* (Bibliotheque de l'Ecole des Hautes Etudes 300. Paris: Librairie Ancienne Honore Champion, 1953), pp. 3–14 (Texte I).

89 J. Černý – R.A. Parker, "An Abnormal Hieratic Tablet," *JEA* 57 (1971), pp. 127–128.

90 G. Möller, "Ein ägyptischer Schuldschein der zweiundzwanzigsten Dynastie," *Sitzungsberichte der preussischen Akademie der Wissenschaften, philosophisch-historischen Klasse* 15 (1921), pp. 298–304.

91 J. Černý – R.A. Parker, "An Abnormal Hieratic Tablet," *JEA* 57 (1971), p. 128.

92 R.K. Ritner, "The End of the Libyan Anarchy in Egypt: P. Rylands IX cols. 11–12," *Enchoria* 17 (1998), pp. 101–108; R.K. Ritner, "Fragmentation and Re-Integration in the Third Intermediate Period," in G.P.F. Broekman – R.J. Demarée – O.E. Kaper (eds.), *The Libyan Period in Egypt, Historical and Cultural Studies into the 21st – 24th Dynasties: Proceedings of a Conference at Leiden University, 25–27 October 2007* (EU 23. Leiden – Leuven: NINO – Peeters, 2009), pp. 327–340.

93 S. Häggman, *Directing Deir el-Medina. The External Administration of the Necropolis* (Uppsala Studies in Egyptology 4. Uppsala: Akademitryck AB, 2002), pp. 193–288 for the late Twentieth Dynasty, and pp. 309–375 for the Twenty-first Dynasty.

94 W. Spiegelberg, "Der Titel λεσῶνις," *Recueil de Travaux* 24 (1902), p. 188; F. de Cenival, *Les associations religieuses en Égypte, d'après les documents démotiques* (BdÉ 46. Cairo: IFAO, 1972), p. 154; H. de Meulenaere, "Une princesse libyenne ignorée," *CdÉ* 57 (1982), pp. 218–222; R.K. Ritner, *The Libyan Anarchy, Inscriptions from Egypt's Third Intermediate Period* (SBL Writings from the Ancient World 21. Atlanta: SBL, 2009), pp. 25–31; F. Payraudeau, *Administration, société et pouvoir à Thebes sous la XXIIe dynastie bubastite*, 2 vols. (BdÉ 160: 1–2. Cairo: IFAO, 2014), vol. 1, p. 258, and vol. 2, p. 478 (no. 118), pp. 496–497 (no. 135-G), p. 503 (no. 139), pp. 570–571 (no. 218-A, B), p. 584 (no. 245), pp. 588–589 (no. 251), p. 597 (no. 263-K), p. 615 (no. 287).

95 G.R. Hughes, "The So-called Pherendates Correspondence," in H.-J. Thissen – K.-T. Zauzich (eds.), *Grammata Demotica, Festschrift fur Erich Luddeckens zum 15. Juni 1983* (Wurzburg: Gisela Zauzich Verlag, 1984), pp. 75–88.

96 W. Clarysse, "The Archive of the Praktor Milon", in K. Vandorpe – W. Clarysse (eds.), *Edfu, An Egyptian Provincial Capital in the Ptolemaic Period. Brussels, 3 September 2001* (Brussels: Koninklijke Vlaamse Academie van België voor Wetenschappen en Kunsten, 2003), pp. 17–27.

97 A.M. Blackman, "The Stela of Shoshenk, Great Chief of the Meshwesh," *JEA* 27 (1941), pp. 83–95, pls. 10–12; K. Jansen-Winkeln, *Inschriften der Spätzeit, Teil I: Die 21. Dynastie* (Wiesbaden 2007), pp. 159–162; R.K. Ritner, *The Libyan Anarchy, Inscriptions from Egypt's Third Intermediate Period* (SBL Writings from the Ancient World 21. Atlanta: SBL, 2009), pp. 166–172 (no. 41).

98 Published by K. Donker van Heel, "Papyrus Louvre E 7852, A Land Lease from the Reign of Taharka," *RdÉ* 48 (1997), pp. 81–93; K. Donker van Heel, "Papyrus Louvre E 7856 Verso and Recto: Leasing Land in the Reign of Taharka," *RdÉ* 49 (1998), pp. 91–102; and K. Donker van Heel, "Papyrus Louvre E 7851 Recto and Verso: Two More Land Leases from the Reign of Taharka," *RdÉ* 50 (1999), pp. 135–144.

99 K. Donker van Heel, "Papyrus Louvre E 7851 Recto and Verso: Two More Land Leases from the Reign of Taharka," *RdÉ* 50 (1999), p. 141, note IV.

100 D. Meeks, "Les donations aux temples dans l'Égypte du Ier millénaire avant J.-C.," in E. Lipiński (ed.), *State and Temple Economy in the Ancient Near East* II (OLA 6. Leuven, 1979), pp. 651–652.

101 K. Baer, "The Low Price of Land in Ancient Egypt", *JARCE* 1 (1962), pp. 25–45.

102 Epigraphic Survey, *The Temple of Khonsu 2: Scenes and Inscriptions in the Court and First Hypostyle Hall* (OIP 103. Chicago: Oriental Institute, 1981), pp. 17–20, pl. 133; and R.K. Ritner, *The Libyan Anarchy, Inscriptions from Egypt's Third Intermediate Period* (SBL Writings from the Ancient World 21. Atlanta: SBL, 2009), pp. 130–135 (no. 30).

103 J. Von Beckerath (1994), "Zur Datierung des Papyrus Brooklyn 16.205," *GM* 140 (1994), pp. 15–17.

104 R.A. Parker, *A Saite Oracle Papyrus from Thebes in the Brooklyn Museum [Papyrus Brooklyn 47.218.3]* (Brown Egyptological Studies 4. Providence, 1962), pp. 49–52.

105 H. Munier, "Un Achat de Terrains au temps du Roi Si-Amon," in *Recueil d'Etudes Egyptologiques dediees a la memoire de Jean-Francois Champollion*, (Bibliothèque de l'École de Hautes Études 234. Paris, 1922), pp. 361–366; K. Jansen-Winkeln, *Inschriften der Spätzeit, Teil I: Die 21. Dynastie* (Wiesbaden, 2007), pp. 150–151; R.K. Ritner, *The Libyan Anarchy, Inscriptions from Egypt's Third Intermediate Period* (SBL Writings from the Ancient World 21. Atlanta: SBL, 2009), pp. 161–162 (no. 38).

106 A.H. Gardiner, "The Gods of Thebes as Guarantors of Personal Property," *JEA* 48 (1962), pp. 57–64 (I. The Property of the Lady Hentowe); Jean Winand, "Les décrets oraculaires pris en l'honneur d'Henouttaouy et de Maâtkarê (Xe et VIIe Pylônes)," pp. 603–710 in *Cahiers de Karnak* XI (2003), Fasicle 2, pp. 614–672; K. Jansen-Winkeln, *Inschriften der Spätzeit, Teil I: Die 21. Dynastie* (2007), pp. 177–182; and R.K. Ritner, *The Libyan Anarchy, Inscriptions from Egypt's Third Intermediate Period* (SBL Writings from the Ancient World 21. Atlanta: SBL, 2009), pp. 138–143 (no. 33).

107 A.H. Gardiner, "The Gods of Thebes as Guarantors of Personal Property," *JEA* 48 (1962), pp. 64–69 (II. The Property of the Lady Makare); J. Winand, "Les décrets oraculaires pris en l'honneur d'Henouttaouy et de Maâtkarê (Xe et VIIe Pylônes)," in *Cahiers de Karnak* XI (2003), Fasicle 2, pp. 672–690; K. Jansen-Winkeln, *Inschriften der Spätzeit, Teil I: Die 21. Dynastie* (Wiesbaden: Harrassowitz, 2007), pp. 182–183; and R.K. Ritner, *The Libyan Anarchy, Inscriptions from Egypt's Third Intermediate Period* (SBL Writings from the Ancient World 21. Atlanta: SBL, 2009), pp. 163–166 (no. 40).

108 A.M. Blackman, "The Stela of Shoshenk, Great Chief of the Meshwesh," *JEA* 27 (1941), pp. 83–95, pls. 10–12; K. Jansen-Winkeln, *Inschriften der Spätzeit, Teil I: Die 21. Dynastie* (Wiesbaden, 2007), pp. 159–162; and R.K. Ritner, *The Libyan Anarchy, Inscriptions from Egypt's Third Intermediate Period* (SBL Writings from the Ancient World 21. Atlanta: SBL, 2009), pp. 166–172 (no. 41).

109 G. Legrain, "Deux steles trouvees a Karnak en fevrier 1897, I. Stele de l'apanage," *ZÄS* 35 (1897), pp. 13–16; A. Erman, "Zu den Legrain'schen Inschriften, I. Das Testament eines Hohenpriesters," *ZÄS* 35 (1897), pp. 19–24; B. Menu, "La stèle dite de l'Apanage," in B. Menu, *Recherches sur l'histoire juridique, économique et sociale de l'ancienne Égypte 2* (BdÉ 122. Cairo: IFAO, 1998), pp. 193–203; K. Jansen-Winkeln, *Inschriften der Spätzeit, Teil II: Die 22. – 24. Dynastie* (Wiesbaden, 2007), pp. 77–80; and R.K. Ritner, *The Libyan Anarchy, Inscriptions from Egypt's Third Intermediate Period* (SBL Writings from the Ancient World 21. Atlanta: SBL, 2009), pp. 271–278 (no. 69).

110 Urkunden C mentioned in G. Möller, "Ein ägyptischer Schuldschein der zweiundzwanzigsten Dynastie," *Sitzungsberichte der preussischen Akademie der Wissenschaften, philosophisch-historischen Klasse* 15 (1921), pp. 298–304.

111 A.M. Blackman, "The Stela of Shoshenk, Great Chief of the Meshwesh," *JEA* 27 (1941), pp. 83–95, pls. 10–12; K. Jansen-Winkeln, *Inschriften der Spätzeit, Teil I: Die 21. Dynastie* (Wiesbaden, 2007), pp. 159–162; and R.K. Ritner, *The Libyan Anarchy, Inscriptions from Egypt's Third Intermediate Period* (SBL Writings from the Ancient World 21. Atlanta: SBL, 2009), pp. 166–172 (no. 41).

112 G. Legrain, "Deux steles trouvees a Karnak en fevrier 1897, I. Stele de l'apanage," *ZÄS* 35 (1897), pp. 13–16; A. Erman, "Zu den Legrain'schen Inschriften, I. Das Testament eines Hohenpriesters," *ZÄS* 35 (1897), pp. 19–24; B. Menu, "La stèle dite de l'Apanage," in B. Menu, *Recherches sur l'histoire juridique, économique et sociale de l'ancienne Égypte 2* (BdÉ 122. Cairo: IFAO, 1998), pp. 193–203; K. Jansen-Winkeln, *Inschriften der Spätzeit, Teil II: Die 22. – 24. Dynastie* (Wiesbaden, 2007), pp. 77–80; and R.K. Ritner, *The Libyan Anarchy, Inscriptions from Egypt's Third Intermediate Period* (SBL Writings from the Ancient World 21. Atlanta: SBL, 2009), pp. 271–278 (no. 69).

113 S.P.Vleeming, "The Sale of a Slave in the Time of Pharaoh *Py*," *Oudheidkundige Mededelingen uit het Rijksmuseum van Oudheden* 61 (1980), pp. 1–17.

114 M. Malinine, "Une vente d'esclave à l'époque de Psammétique Ier (Papyrus du Vatican 10574, en hiératique 'anormale')," *RdÉ* 5 (1946), pp. 119–131, corrected in R.A. Parker, "King *Py*, a Historical Problem," *ZÄS* 93 (1966), p. 112.

115 M. Malinine, *Choix de Textes Juridiques en Hieratique 'Anormal' et en Demotique, Premiere Partie* (Bibliotheque de l'Ecole des Hautes Etudes 300. Paris: Librairie Ancienne Honore Champion, 1953), pp. 35–42 (Texte VI), and pp. 43–49 (Texte VII).

116 M. Malinine, "Transcriptions hiéroglyphiques de quatre textes du Musée du Louvre écrits en hiératique anormale," *RdÉ* 34 (1982–1983), pp. 94–95, pl. 4.

117 M. Malinine, "Un judgement rendu à Thèbes sous la XXVe dynastie (Pap. Louvre E. 3228c)," *RdÉ* 6 (1951), pp. 157–178, pls. 4–6.

118 1 Kings 14:25, and 2 Chronicles 12:1–12.

119 Epigraphic Survey, *Reliefs and Inscriptions at Karnak, Volume 3. The Bubastite Portal* (OIP 74. Chicago: University of Chicago Press, 1954); R.K. Ritner, *The Libyan Anarchy, Inscriptions from Egypt's Third Intermediate Period* (SBL Writings from the Ancient World 21. Atlanta: SBL, 2009), pp. 193–213 (no. 48).

120 R.K. Ritner, *The Libyan Anarchy, Inscriptions from Egypt's Third Intermediate Period* (SBL Writings from the Ancient World 21. Atlanta: SBL, 2009), pp. 218–219 (no. 51).

121 N. Grimal, *Études sur la propagande royale égyptienne, 1, La stèle triomphale de Pi-ânkh-y au musée du Caire, JE 48862 et 47086–47089* (MIFAO 105. Cairo: IFAO, 1981); R.K. Ritner, *The Libyan Anarchy, Inscriptions from Egypt's Third Intermediate Period* (SBL Writings from the Ancient World 21. Atlanta: SBL, 2009), pp. 465–492 (no. 145).

122 2 Kings 19:9, and Isaiah 37:9.

123 Published by K. Donker van Heel, "Papyrus Louvre E 7852, A Land Lease from the Reign of Taharka," *RdÉ* 48 (1997), pp. 81–93; K. Donker van Heel, "Papyrus Louvre E 7856 Verso and Recto: Leasing Land in the Reign of Taharka," *RdÉ* 49 (1998), pp. 91–102; and K. Donker van Heel, "Papyrus Louvre E 7851 Recto and Verso: Two More Land Leases from the Reign of Taharka," *RdÉ* 50 (1999), pp. 135–144.

6. THE SAITE AND PERSIAN PERIODS (664–332 BCE)

1 P. Rylands 9, col. 11, lines 17–19, see G. Vittmann, *Der demotische Papyrus Rylands 9. Teil I. Text und Übersetzung* (ÄAT 38, 1. Wiesbaden: Harrassowitz, 1998), pp. 152–153.

2 P. Rylands 9, col. 15, lines 8–9, see G. Vittmann, *Der demotische Papyrus Rylands 9. Teil I. Text und Übersetzung* (ÄAT 38, 1. Wiesbaden: Harrassowitz, 1998), pp. 166–167; and G. Vittmann, *Der demotische Papyrus Rylands 9. Teil II. Kommentare und Indizes* (ÄAT 38, 2. Wiesbaden: Harrassowitz, 1998), pp. 510–511.

3 G. Vittmann, "Rupture and Continuity. On Priests and Officials in Egypt during the Persian Period," in P. Briant – Michel Chauveau (eds.), *Organisation des pouvoirs et contacts culturels dans les pays de l'empire achéménide: Actes du colloque organisé au Collège de France, 9–10 novembre 2007* (Persika 14. Paris: De Boccard, 2009), p. 100.

4 Abydos Tombs D57 and D13 respectively, see A. Leahy, "Nespamedu, 'King' of Thinis," *GM* 35 (1979), pp. 31–38.

5 Theban Tomb 312, see G. Vittmann, "Rupture and Continuity. On Priests and Officials in Egypt during the Persian Period," in P. Briant – Michel Chauveau (eds.), *Organisation des pouvoirs et contacts culturels dans les pays de l'empire achéménide: Actes du colloque organisé au Collège de France, 9–10 novembre 2007* (Persika 14. Paris: De Boccard, 2009). p. 94.

6 P. Louvre E. 3228c, line 5, see Michel Malinine, "Un jugement rendu à Thèbes sous la XXVe dynastie (Pap. Louvre E. 3228 c)," *RdÉ* 6 (1951), pp. 157–179 and pls. 4–6.

7 G. Vittmann, "Rupture and Continuity. On Priests and Officials in Egypt during the Persian Period," in P. Briant – Michel Chauveau (eds.), *Organisation des pouvoirs et contacts culturels dans les pays de l'empire achéménide: Actes du colloque organisé au Collège de France, 9–10 novembre 2007* (Persika 14. Paris: De Boccard, 2009). pp. 95–96.

8 P. Rylands dem. 1 and 2, lines 6–7, see F. Ll. Griffith, *Catalogue of Demotic Papyri in the John Rylands Library, Manchester*, 3 vols. (Manchester: University Press, 1909), vol. 3, pp. 44–48, 207–209; and G. Vittmann, *Der demotische Papyrus Rylands 9. Teil II. Kommentare und Indizes* (ÄAT 38, 2. Wiesbaden: Harrassowitz, 1998), pp. 510–511.

9 P. Rylands dem. 9, col. 15, lines 9 and 15, see G. Vittmann, *Der demotische Papyrus Rylands 9. Teil I. Text und Übersetzung* (ÄAT 38, 1. Wiesbaden: Harrassowitz, 1998), pp. 166–167; and G. Vittmann, *Der demotische Papyrus Rylands 9. Teil II. Kommentare und Indizes* (ÄAT 38, 2. Wiesbaden: Harrassowitz, 1998), pp. 510–511.

10 D. Agut-Labordère, "The Saite Period: The Emergence of a Mediterranean Power," in J.C. Moreno García (ed.), *Ancient Egyptian Administration* (HdO 104. Leiden: Brill, 2013), pp. 975–984.

11 P. Rylands 9, col. 11, lines 11–15; and col. 12, lines 2–3, 9–21, see G. Vittmann, *Der demotische Papyrus Rylands 9. Teil I. Text und Übersetzung* (ÄAT 38, 1. Wiesbaden: Harrassowitz, 1998), pp. 150–157.

12 P. Rylands 9, col. 11, lines 17–18, see G. Vittmann, *Der demotische Papyrus Rylands 9. Teil I. Text und Übersetzung* (ÄAT 38, 1. Wiesbaden: Harrassowitz, 1998), pp. 152–153.

13 P. Rylands 9, col. 15, lines 3–4, see G. Vittmann, *Der demotische Papyrus Rylands 9. Teil I. Text und Übersetzung* (ÄAT 38, 1. Wiesbaden: Harrassowitz, 1998), pp. 164–165.

14 G. Vittmann, *Der demotische Papyrus Rylands 9. Teil II. Kommentare und Indizes* (ÄAT 38, 2. Wiesbaden: Harrassowitz, 1998), pp. 507–508.

15 P. Rylands 9, col. 19, lines 8–21; col. 20, lines 1–20; and col. 21, line 2, see G. Vittmann, *Der demotische Papyrus Rylands 9. Teil I. Text und Übersetzung* (ÄAT 38, 1. Wiesbaden: Harrassowitz, 1998), pp. 180–189.

16 S. Allam, "Egyptian Law Courts in Pharaonic and Hellenistic Times," *JEA* 77 (1991), pp. 116–119.

17 F.Ll. Griffith, *Catalogue of Demotic Papyri in the John Rylands Library, Manchester*, 3 vols. (Manchester: University Press, 1909), vol. 3, pp. 52–53, 210–211.

18 A.F. Shore, "Swapping Property at Asyut in the Persian Period," in J. Baines (ed.), *Pyramid Studies and Other Essays presented to I.E.S. Edwards* (London: 1988): pp. 200–206 and pls. 41–42; and J.H. Johnson, "'Annuity Contracts' and Marriage," in D.P. Silverman (ed.), *For His Ka, Essays Offered in Memory of Klaus Baer* (SAOC 55. Chicago: The Oriental Institute, 1994), pp. 113–132.

19 P.W. Pestman, *Les papyrus démotiques de Tsenhor (P. Tsenhor). Les archives privées d'une femme égyptienne du temps de Darius Ier. I. Textes* (Studia Demotica 4. Leuven: 1994), pp. 85–87 (Text 15).

20 S.P. Vleeming, *The Gooseherds of Hou* (Pap. Hou), (Studia Demotica 3. Leuven: Peeters, 1991), pp. 127–141 (Text 8).

21 E. Cruz-Uribe, "A 30th Dynasty Document of Renunciation from Edfu," *Enchoria* 13 (1985), pp. 41–49.

22 F. de Cenival, "Un document démotique relatif au partage d'une maison (P. Louvre N. 2430)," *RdÉ* 18 (1966), pp. 7–30.

23 F. de Cenival, "Une vente d'esclaves de l'époque d'Artaxerxès III (P. Inv. Sorbonne nos. 1276 et 1277)," *RdÉ* 24 (1972), pp. 31–39.

24 S.L. Lippert, *Ein demotisches juristisches Lehrbuch. Untersuchungen zu P. Berlin 23757 rto* (ÄA 66. Wiesbaden, Harrassowitz, 2004), pp. 155–157.

25 S.L. Lippert, "Die sogennante Zivilprozessordnung, weitere fragmente der ägyptischen Gesetzessammlung," *JJP* 33 (2003), pp. 134–135.

26 B. Porten, *Archives from Elephantine, The Life of an Ancient Jewish Military Colony* (Berkeley - Los Angeles: University of California Press, 1968), pp. 47–50.

27 B. Porten, *Archives from Elephantine, The Life of an Ancient Jewish Military Colony* (Berkeley - Los Angeles: University of California Press, 1968), pp. 151–158.

28 P. Rylands 9, col. 8, lines 1–3, see G. Vittmann, *Der demotische Papyrus Rylands 9. Teil I. Text und Übersetzung* (ÄAT 38, 1. Wiesbaden: Harrassowitz, 1998), pp. 138–139.

29 P. Rylands 9, col. 11, lines 16–18, see G. Vittmann, *Der demotische Papyrus Rylands 9. Teil I. Text und Übersetzung* (ÄAT 38, 1. Wiesbaden: Harrassowitz, 1998), pp. 152–153.

30 P. Rylands 9, col. 14, line 17 – col. 15, line 7, see G. Vittmann, *Der demotische Papyrus Rylands 9. Teil I. Text und Übersetzung* (ÄAT 38, 1. Wiesbaden: Harrassowitz, 1998), pp. 162–167.

31 P. Rylands 9, col. 15, lines 8–11, see G. Vittmann, *Der demotische Papyrus Rylands 9. Teil I. Text und Übersetzung* (ÄAT 38, 1. Wiesbaden: Harrassowitz, 1998), pp. 166–167.

32 P. Rylands 9, col. 15, lines 12–17, see G. Vittmann, *Der demotische Papyrus Rylands 9. Teil I. Text und Übersetzung* (ÄAT 38, 1. Wiesbaden: Harrassowitz, 1998), pp. 166–169.

33 P. Rylands 9, col. 15, lines 17–19, see G. Vittmann, *Der demotische Papyrus Rylands 9. Teil I. Text und Übersetzung* (ÄAT 38, 1. Wiesbaden: Harrassowitz, 1998), pp. 168–169.

34 F. De Cenival, "Comptes d'une association religieuse thébaine datant des années 29 à 33 du roi Amasis," *RdÉ* 37 (1986), pp. 13–29.

35 F. De Cenival, "Papyrus Seymour de Ricci: le plus ancien des règlements d'association religieuse (4ème siècle av. J.-C.) (Pap. Bibl. Nationale E 241)," *RdÉ* 39 (1988), pp. 37–46.

36 B.P. Muhs, "Membership in Private Associations in Ptolemaic Tebtunis," *JESHO* 44 (2001), pp. 1–21.

37 J.J. McLaughlin, *The Marzēaḥ in the Prophetic Literature. References and Allusions in Light of the Extra-Biblical Evidence* (Supplements to Vetus Testamentum 86, Leiden, 2001).

38 M. Kowaleski, *Local Markets and Regional Trade in Medieval Exeter* (Cambridge, 1995), pp. 179–221.

39 G. Vittmann, *Der demotische Papyrus Rylands 9. Teil II. Kommentare und Indizes* (ÄAT 38, 2. Wiesbaden: Harrassowitz, 1998), pp. 382–385.

40 P. Rylands 9, col. 16, lines 1–14, see G. Vittmann, *Der demotische Papyrus Rylands 9. Teil I. Text und Übersetzung* (ÄAT 38, 1. Wiesbaden: Harrassowitz, 1998), pp. 168–171.

41 P. Rylands 9, col. 16, line 14 – col. 17, line 1, see G. Vittmann, *Der demotische Papyrus Rylands 9. Teil I. Text und Übersetzung* (ÄAT 38, 1. Wiesbaden: Harrassowitz, 1998), pp. 170–173.

42 P. Rylands 9, col. 17, lines 1–9, see G. Vittmann, *Der demotische Papyrus Rylands 9. Teil I. Text und Übersetzung* (ÄAT 38, 1. Wiesbaden: Harrassowitz, 1998), pp. 172–175.

43 P. Rylands 9, col. 17, line 9 – col. 18, line 4, see G. Vittmann, *Der demotische Papyrus Rylands 9. Teil I. Text und Übersetzung* (ÄAT 38, 1. Wiesbaden: Harrassowitz, 1998), pp. 174–177.

44 P. Rylands 9, col. 5, lines 14–15, see G. Vittmann, *Der demotische Papyrus Rylands 9. Teil I. Text und Übersetzung* (ÄAT 38, 1. Wiesbaden: Harrassowitz, 1998), pp. 130–131.

45 P. Rylands 9, col. 9, line 20 – col. 10, line 1, see G. Vittmann, *Der demotische Papyrus Rylands 9. Teil I. Text und Übersetzung* (ÄAT 38, 1. Wiesbaden: Harrassowitz, 1998), pp. 144–145.

46 P. Rylands 9, col. 10, lines 6–7, see G. Vittmann, *Der demotische Papyrus Rylands 9. Teil I. Text und Übersetzung* (ÄAT 38, 1. Wiesbaden: Harrassowitz, 1998), pp. 146–147.

47 P. Rylands 9, col. 5, line 18, see G. Vittmann, *Der demotische Papyrus Rylands 9. Teil I. Text und Übersetzung* (ÄAT 38, 1. Wiesbaden: Harrassowitz, 1998), pp. 130–131.

48 P. Rylands 9, col. 6, line 1, see G. Vittmann, *Der demotische Papyrus Rylands 9. Teil I. Text und Übersetzung* (ÄAT 38, 1. Wiesbaden: Harrassowitz, 1998), pp. 130–131.

49 P. Rylands 9, col. 6, line 5, see G. Vittmann, *Der demotische Papyrus Rylands 9. Teil I. Text und Übersetzung* (ÄAT 38, 1. Wiesbaden: Harrassowitz, 1998), pp. 132–133.

50 J.-C. Goyon, "La statuette funéraire I.E. 84 de Lyon et le titre saïte *imy-r ḫwᶜ*; nsw," *BIFAO* 67 (1969), pp. 159–171; D. Agut-Labordère, "The Saite Period: The Emergence of a Mediterranean Power," in J.C. Moreno García (ed.), *Ancient Egyptian Administration* (HdO 104. Leiden: Brill, 2013), pp. 997–999.

51 D. Agut-Labordère, "The Saite Period: The Emergence of a Mediterranean Power," in J.C. Moreno García (ed.), *Ancient Egyptian Administration* (HdO 104. Leiden: Brill, 2013), pp. 1000–1002.

52 J. Yoyotte, "Le nom égyptien du «ministre de l'économie» - de Saïs a Méroé," *Comptes rendus, Académie des inscriptions & belles-lettres (CRAIBL)*, 1989 (Paris, Diffusion de Boccard, 1989), pp. 73–90.

53 J. Yoyotte, "Le nom égyptien du «ministre de l'économie» - de Saïs a Méroé," *Comptes rendus, Académie des inscriptions & belles-lettres (CRAIBL)*, 1989 (Paris, Diffusion de Boccard, 1989), pp. 75–76 (¶2).

54 D. Inconnu-Bocquillon, "Les titres *ḥry idb* et *ḥry wḏb* dans les inscriptions des temples greco-romains," *RdÉ* 40 (1989), pp. 65–89; and J. Quaegebeur, "*Phritob* comme titre d'un haut fonctinnaire ptolémaïque," *Ancient Society* 20 (1989), pp. 159–168.

55 P. Berlin P. 13540, line 2, see G.R. Hughes, "The So-called Pherendates Correspondence," pp. 75–88 in H.-J. Thissen – K.-T. Zauzich (eds.), *Grammata Demotica, Festschrift fur Erich Luddeckens zum 15. Juni 1983* (Wurzburg: Gisela Zauzich Verlag, 1984), corrected by M. Chauveau, "La chronologie de la correspondence dite «de Phérendatès»," *RdÉ* 50 (1999), p. 270 note 7.

56 J. Yoyotte, "Le nom égyptien du «ministre de l'économie» - de Saïs a Méroé," *Comptes rendus, Académie des inscriptions & belles-lettres (CRAIBL)*, 1989 (Paris, Diffusion de Boccard, 1989), pp. 75–76 (¶2); D. Agut-Labordère, "The Saite Period: The Emergence of a Mediterranean Power," in J.C. Moreno García (ed.), *Ancient Egyptian Administration* (HdO 104. Leiden: Brill, 2013), pp. 999–1000.

57 In P. Rylands 9, col. 17, lines 1–20, see G. Vittmann, *Der demotische Papyrus Rylands 9. Teil I. Text und Übersetzung* (ÄAT 38, 1. Wiesbaden: Harrassowitz, 1998), pp. 172–177; and G. Vittmann, *Der demotische Papyrus Rylands 9. Teil 2. Kommentare und Indizes* (ÄAT 38, Wiesbaden, Harrassowitz, 1998), pp. 516–517.

58 J. Yoyotte, "Le nom égyptien du «ministre de l'économie» - de Saïs a Méroé," *Comptes rendus, Académie des inscriptions & belles-lettres (CRAIBL)*, 1989 (Paris, Diffusion de Boccard, 1989), p. 75 (¶1); O. Perdu, "Le «directeur des scribes du conseil»," *RdÉ* 49 (1999), pp. 175–194; D. Agut-Labordère, "The Saite Period: The Emergence of a Mediterranean Power," in J.C. Moreno García (ed.), *Ancient Egyptian Administration* (HdO 104. Leiden: Brill, 2013), pp. 996–997.

59 J. Yoyotte, "Le nom égyptien du «ministre de l'économie» - de Saïs a Méroé," *Comptes rendus, Académie des inscriptions & belles-lettres (CRAIBL)*, 1989 (Paris, Diffusion de Boccard, 1989), p. 76 (¶3).

60 P.W. Pestman, "A Family of Egyptian Scribes," *BASP* 5, 2–3 (1968), p. 61; J. Quaegebeur, "À la recherche du haut clergé Thébaine à l'époque Gréco-Romaine," in S.P. Vleeming (ed.), *Hundred-Gated Thebes. Acts of a Colloquium on Thebes and the Theban Area in the Graeco-Roman Period* (PLB 27. Leiden: Brill, 1995), pp. 152–155.

61 B.P. Muhs, *Tax Receipts, Taxpayers, and Taxes in Early Ptolemaic Thebes* (OIP 126. Chicago: Oriental Institute, 2005), pp. 14–19.

62 J.G. Manning, "Demotic Egyptian Instruments of Transfer as Evidence for Private Ownership of Real Property," *Chicago-Kent Law Review* 70 (1996), pp. 101–132.

63 K. Donker van Heel, *Abnormal Hieratic and Early Demotic Texts Collected by the Theban Choachytes in the Reign of Amasis* (Leiden University PhD Thesis, 1996): P. Louvre 7845A (Text 6), dated to Year 17 of Amasis (554 BCE); P. Louvre 7836 (Text 17), dated to Year 35 of Amasis (536 BCE); P. Louvre 7833 (Text 19) and P. Louvre 7837 (Text 20), dated to Year 36 of Amasis (535 BCE); and P. Louvre 7839 (Text 21), dated to Year 37 of Amasis (534 BCE).

64 K. Donker van Heel, *Abnormal Hieratic and Early Demotic Texts Collected by the Theban Choachytes in the Reign of Amasis* (Leiden University PhD Thesis, 1996): From the Archive of Itourodj son of Djechy, there are P. Louvre 7842 (Text 12), dated to Year 31 of Amasis (540 BCE); P. Louvre 7835 (Text 14), dated to Year 34 of Amasis (537 BCE); and P. Louvre 7838 (Text 15) and P. Louvre 7834 (Text 16), both dated to Year 35 of Amasis (536 BCE).

65 S.P. Vleeming, *The Gooseherds of Hou* (Studia Demotica 3. Leuven: Peeters, 1991), pp. 77–78 n. ee, and p. 85 n. nn and oo.

66 Herodotus, Book II, 177; A.B. Lloyd, *Herodotus, Book II: Commentary 99–182* (Leiden: Brill, 1988), pp. 219–221.

67 Pseudo-Aristotle, *Oikonomika*, 2.2.

68 R.J. Demarée – D. Valbelle, *Les registres de recensement du village de Deir el-Medineh (Le Stato Civile)* (Leuven: Peeters, 2011), pp. 88–96.

69 W. Clarysse – D.J. Thompson, *Counting the People in Hellenistic Egypt, Volume 2: Historical Studies* (Cambridge Classical Studies. Cambridge: University Press, 2006), pp. 10–35: "2. The census."

70 S.P. Vleeming, "The Tithe of the Scribes (and) Representatives," in J.H. Johnson (ed.), *Life in a Multi-Cultural Society, Egypt from Cambyses to Constantine and Beyond* (SAOC 51. Chicago, 1992), pp. 343–350; M. Depauw, *The Archive of Teos and Thabis from Early Ptolemaic Thebes, P. Brux. dem. inv. E. 8252–8256* (Monographies Reine Élisabeth 8. Turnhout BE: Brepols, 2000), pp. 56–63.

71 M. Malinine, *Choix de Textes Juridiques en Hieratique "Anormal" et en Demotique, Premiere Partie* (Bibliotheque de l'Ecole des Hautes Etudes 300. Paris: 1953), pp. 56–71 (Texte IX) and 72–84 (Texte X).

72 N. Reich, *Papyri juristischen Inhalts in hieratischer und demotischer Schrift aus dem British Museum* (Denkschriften der Kaiserlichen Akademie der Wissenschaften in Wien, philosophisch–historische Klasse, 55,3. Wien: 1914), pp. 9–25.

73 M. Malinine, *Choix de Textes Juridiques en Hieratique "Anormal" et en Demotique, Premiere Partie* (Bibliotheque de l'Ecole des Hautes Etudes 300. Paris: 1953), pp. 85–88 (Texte XI); P.W. Pestman, *Les papyrus démotiques de Tsenhor (P. Tsenhor). Les archives privées d'une femme égyptienne du temps de Darius Ier.* I. Textes (Studia Demotica 4. Leuven: 1994), pp. 71–73 (Texte 10).

74 Pseudo-Aristotle, *Oikonomika*, 2.2.

75 M. Malinine, "Vente de tombes à l'Époque Saïte," *RdÉ* 27 (1975), pp. 168–174.

76 S. Bosticco, *Museo Archeologico di Firenze. Le stele egiziane di Epoca Tarda* (Cataloghi dei musei e gallerie d'Italia. Roma: 1972), pp. 38–39 (no. 28), and pl. 28.

77 M. Malinine, *Choix de Textes Juridiques en Hieratique "Anormal" et en Demotique, Premiere Partie* (Bibliotheque de l'Ecole des Hautes Etudes 300. Paris: 1953), pp. 85–88 (Texte XI); P.W. Pestman, *Les papyrus démotiques de Tsenhor (P. Tsenhor). Les archives privées d'une femme égyptienne du temps de Darius Ier.* I. Textes (Studia Demotica 4. Leuven: 1994), pp. 71–73 (Texte 10).

78 D. Devauchelle, "Notes sur l'administration funéraire égyptienne à l'époque gréco–romaine," *BIFAO* 87 (1987), pp. 154–155 and pl. 23; K. Donker van Heel, *Abnormal Hieratic and Early Demotic Texts Collected by the Theban Choachytes in the Reign of Amasis.* (Proefschrift, Leiden University: 1996), pp. 222–225 (Text 22); K. Donker van Heel, *Djekhy & Son: Doing Business in Ancient Egypt* (Cairo: 2012), pp. 149–150.

79 W. Spiegelberg, *Die Demotischen Denkmaler III – Die Demotische Inschriften und Papyri (Fortsetzung)* (Catalogue général des antiquités égyptiennes du Musée du Caire, Nos. 50023–50165. Berlin: 1932), pp. 52–53, and pls. 26–27.

80 G. Meurer, *Nubier in Ägypten bis zum Beginn des Neuen Reiches: Zur Bedeutung der Stele Berlin 14753* (Abhandlungen des Deutschen Archäologischen Instituts Kairo, Ägyptologische Reihe 13. Berlin: 1996), pp. 10–27.

81 S. Aḥituv, "Sources for the Study of the Egyptian–Canaanite Border Administration," *Israel Exploration Journal* 46 (1996), pp. 219–224.

82 M. de J. Ellis, "Taxation in Ancient Mesopotamia: The History of the Term *miksu*," *Journal of Cuneiform Studies* 26 (1974), pp. 225–233; B.I. Faist, *Der Fernhandel des assyrischen Reiches zwischen dem 14. und 11. Jh. v. Chr.* (Alter Orient und Altes Testament 265. Münster: Ugarit-Verlag, 2001), pp. 184–194; N. Postgate, *Bronze Age Bureaucracy: Writing and the Practice of Government in Assyria* (Cambridge: University Press, 2013), pp. 267, 341.

83 G.Van Driel, *Elusive Silver: In Search of a Role for a Market in an Agrarian Environment* (Publications de l'Institut historique-archeologique neerlandais de Stamboul 95. Leiden: NINO, 2002), pp. 274–282; M. Jursa, "On Aspects of Taxation in Achaemenid Babylonia: New Evidence from Borsippa," in P. Briant – M. Chauveau (eds.), *Organisation des pouvoirs et contacts culturels dans les pays de l'empire achéménide* (Paris: Boccard, 2009), p. 263.

84 Herodotus, Book II, 178; A.B. Lloyd, *Herodotus Book II: Commentary 99–182* (Leiden: Brill, 1988), pp. 222–229.

85 Herodotus, Book II, 179; A.B. Lloyd, *Herodotus Book II: Commentary 99–182* (Leiden: Brill, 1988), pp. 229–231.

86 G. Posener, "Les douanes de la Méditerranée dans l'Égypte saïte," *Revue de philologie de littérature et d''histoire anciennes* 21 (1947), pp. 117–131; S. Pfeiffer, "Naukratis, Heracleion-Thonis and Alexandria – Remarks on the Presence and Trade Activities of Greeks in the North-west Delta from the Seventh Century BC to the End of the Fourth Century BC," in D. Robinson – A. Wilson (eds.), *Alexandria and the North-Western Delta* (Oxford Centre for Maritime Archaeology: Monograph 5. Oxford: 2010), pp. 15–17; D. Agut-Labordère, "The Saite Period: The Emergence of a Mediterranean Power," in J.C. Moreno García (ed.), *Ancient Egyptian Administration* (HdO 104. Leiden: Brill, 2013), pp. 1002–1006.

87 B. Porten – A. Yardeni, *Texts and Aramaic Documents of Ancient Egypt 3: Literature, Accounts, Lists* (Jerusalem: 1993), pp. 82–193 (text C3.7); A. Yardeni, "Maritime Trade and Royal Accountancy in an Erased Customs Account from 475 B.C.E. on the Ahiqar Scroll from Elephantine," *BASOR* 293 (1994), pp. 67–78; and P. Briant – R. Descat, "Un registre douanier

de la satrapie d'Égypte à l'époque achéménide (TAD C3,7)," in N. Grimal – B. Menu (eds.), *Le commerce en Égypte ancienne* (BdÉ 121. Cairo: 1998), pp. 59–104.

88 A. Yardeni, "Maritime Trade and Royal Accountancy in an Erased Customs Account from 475 B.C.E. on the Ahiqar Scroll from Elephantine," *BASOR* 293 (1994), pp. 70–73; P. Briant – R. Descat, "Un registre douanier de la satrapie d'Égypte à l'époque achéménide (TAD C3,7)," in N. Grimal – B. Menu (eds.), *Le commerce en Égypte ancienne* (BdÉ 121. Cairo: 1998), pp. 73–79.

89 P. Briant – R. Descat, "Un registre douanier de la satrapie d'Égypte à l'époque achéménide (TAD C3,7)," in N. Grimal – B. Menu (eds.), *Le commerce en Égypte ancienne* (BdÉ 121. Cairo: 1998), pp. 91–92; S. Pfeiffer, "Naukratis, Heracleion-Thonis and Alexandria – Remarks on the Presence and Trade Activities of Greeks in the North-west Delta from the Seventh Century BC to the End of the Fourth Century BC," in D. Robinson – A. Wilson (eds.), *Alexandria and the North-Western Delta* (Oxford Centre for Maritime Archaeology: Monograph 5. Oxford: 2010), pp. 18–19.

90 J. Yoyotte, "An Extraordinary Pair of Twins: The Steles of the Pharaoh Nektanebo I," in F. Goddio – D. Fabre (eds.), *Egypt's Sunken Treasures* (Munich: 2006), pp. 232–240; S. Pfeiffer, "Naukratis, Heracleion-Thonis and Alexandria – Remarks on the Presence and Trade Activities of Greeks in the North-west Delta from the Seventh Century BC to the End of the Fourth Century BC," in D. Robinson – A. Wilson (eds.), *Alexandria and the North-Western Delta* (Oxford Centre for Maritime Archaeology: Monograph 5. Oxford: 2010), pp. 19–20; A.-S. Von Bomhard, *The Decree of Saïs, The Stelae of Thonis-Heracleion and Naukratis* (Oxford Centre for Maritime Archaeology: Monograph 7. Oxford: 2012).

91 M. Lichtheim, "The Naucratis Stela Once Again," in J.H. Johnson – E.F. Wente (eds.), *Studies in Honor of George R. Hughes* (SAOC 39. Chicago: 1976), pp. 139–147; A.-S. Von Bomhard, *The Decree of Saïs, The Stelae of Thonis-Heracleion and Naukratis* (Oxford Centre for Maritime Archaeology: Monograph 7. Oxford: 2012), pp. 93–97.

92 P.W. Pestman, *Les papyrus démotiques de Tsenhor (P. Tsenhor), I. Textes* (Studia Demotica 4. Leuven, 1994), p. 165.

93 M. Depauw, *A Companion to Demotic Studies* (Papyrologica Bruxellensia 28. Bruxelles, 1997), pp. 124–125; but see M. Depauw, *The Demotic Letter* (Demotische Studien 14. Sommerhausen, 2006), pp. 317–321.

94 F.Ll. Griffith, *Catalogue of Demotic Papyri in the John Rylands Library, Manchester* (Manchester: University Press, 1909), vol. 3, p. 11; O. El-Aguizy, *A Palaeographical Study of Demotic Papyri* (MIFAO 113. Cairo: IFAO, 1998), pp. 1–2, 219–224.

95 P.W. Pestman, *Les papyrus démotiques de Tsenhor (P. Tsenhor), I. Textes* (Studia Demotica 4. Leuven, 1994), pp. 155–163; K. Donker van Heel, "The Lost Battle of Peteamonip Son of Petehorresbe," *Acta Demotica* (*EVO* 17 [1994]), pp. 115–124.

96 B. Porten, "Aramaic-Demotic Equivalents: Who is the Borrower and Who the Lender?," in J. Johnson (ed.), *Life in a Multi-Cultural Society* (SAOC 51. Chicago: 1992), pp. 259–264.

97 R.K. Ritner, "Third Intermediate Period Antecedents of Demotic Legal Terminology," in K. Ryholt (ed.), *Acts of the Seventh International Conference of Demotic Studies, Copenhagen, 23–27 August 1999* (CNI 27. Copenhagen: Museum Tusculanum Press, 2002), pp. 343–359; A.F. Botti, *The Aramaic and Egyptian Legal Traditions at Elephantine: An Egyptological Approach* (Library of Second Temple Studies 64. London – New York: T & T Clark, 2009).

98 P. Mattha, col. ii, lines 23–27, see G. Mattha, *The Demotic Legal Code of Hermopolis West* (BdÉ 45. Cairo: IFAO, 1975), pp. 22–23, with additional notes by G. Hughes, pp. 77–81.

99 P. Mattha, col. ix, lines 26–29, see G. Mattha, *The Demotic Legal Code of Hermopolis West* (BdÉ 45. Cairo: IFAO, 1975), pp. 41–42, with additional notes by G. Hughes, pp. 122–123.

100 M. Chauveau, "La première mention du statère d'argent en Égypte," *Transeuphratène* 20 (2000), pp. 134–143.

101 B. Porten, *Archives from Elephantine, The Life of an Ancient Jewish Military Colony* (Berkeley-Los Angeles: University of California Press, 1968), p. 62.

102 B. Porten, *Archives from Elephantine, The Life of an Ancient Jewish Military Colony* (Berkeley-Los Angeles: University of California Press, 1968), pp. 66–67.

103 B. Porten, *Archives from Elephantine, The Life of an Ancient Jewish Military Colony* (Berkeley-Los

Angeles: University of California Press, 1968), p. 64 and n. 13.

104 A. Yardeni, "Maritime Trade and Royal Accountancy in an Erased Customs Account from 475 B.C.E. on the Ahiqar Scroll from Elephantine," *BASOR* 293 (1994), p. 70; P. Briant – R. Descat, "Un registre douanier de la satrapie d'Égypte à l'époque achéménide (TAD C3,7)," in N. Grimal – B. Menu (eds.), *Le commerce en Égypte ancienne* (BdÉ 121. Cairo: IFAO, 1998), pp. 75–78.

105 K. Donker van Heel, *Abnormal Hieratic and Early Demotic Texts Collected by the Theban Choachytes in the Reign of Amasis* (Leiden University PhD Thesis, 1996), pp. 222–225 (Text 22).

106 W. Spiegelberg, *Die Demotischen Denkmaler III- Die Demotische Inschriften und Papyri (Fortsetzung)* (Catalogue général des antiquités égyptiennes du Musée du Caire, Nos. 50023–50165. Berlin: Reichsdruckerei, 1932), pp. 52–53 and pls. 26–27.

107 W. Spiegelberg, *Die Demotischen Denkmaler III- Die Demotische Inschriften und Papyri (Fortsetzung)* (Catalogue général des antiquités égyptiennes du Musée du Caire, Nos. 50023–50165. Berlin: Reichsdruckerei, 1932), pp. 46–48 and pls. 21–22.

108 F.Ll. Griffith, *Catalogue of Demotic Papyri in the John Rylands Library, Manchester* (Manchester: University Press, 1909), vol. 3, p. 76.

109 R. Müller-Wollermann, "Ägypten auf dem Weg zur Geldwirtschaft," in J-C. Goyon – C. Cardin (eds.), *Proceedings of the Ninth International Congress of Egyptologists/Actes du Neuvième Congrès International des Égyptologues, Grenoble, 6–12 septembre 2004* (OLA 150. Leuven, 2007), vol. II, pp. 1351–1359; idem., "Die ökonomische Bedeutung von Tempelschatzhäusern," in M. Fitzenreiter (ed.), *Das Heilige und die Ware, Zum Spannungsfeld von Religion und Ökonomie, Workshop vom 26.05 bis 28.05.2006* (IBAES 7. London, 2007), pp. 176–178.

110 S.P. Vleeming, *The Gooseherds of Hou (Pap. Hou)*, (Studia Demotica 3. Leuven: Peeters, 1991), pp. 87–89 n. uu.

111 B. Porten, *Archives from Elephantine, The Life of an Ancient Jewish Military Colony* (Berkeley-Los Angeles: University of California Press, 1968), p. 63 and n.6.

112 B. Porten, *Archives from Elephantine, The Life of an Ancient Jewish Military Colony* (Berkeley-Los Angeles: University of California Press, 1968), p. 63 and n.7.

113 B. Porten, *Archives from Elephantine, The Life of an Ancient Jewish Military Colony* (Berkeley-Los Angeles: University of California Press, 1968), p. 63 and n.8.

114 M. Chauveau, "La première mention du statère d'argent en Égypte," *Transeuphratène* 20 (2000), pp. 134–143.

115 B. Porten, *Archives from Elephantine, The Life of an Ancient Jewish Military Colony* (Berkeley–Los Angeles: 1968), p. 64 and n. 13.

116 P.G.Van Alfen, "The 'owls' from the 1989 Syria Hoard with a Review of Pre-Macedonian Coinage in Egypt," *American Journal of Numismatics* 14 (2002), pp. 15–23; P.G. Van Alfen, "Mechanisms for the Imitations of Athenian Coinage: Dekeleia and Mercenaries Reconsidered," *Revue belge de numismatique et de sigillographie* 157 (2011), pp. 66–71.

117 A. Meadows, "Athenian Coin Dies from Egypt: The New Discovery at Heraklion," *Revue belge de numismatique et de sigillographie* 157 (2011), pp. 95–116.

118 P.G.Van Alfen, "The 'owls' from the 1989 Syria Hoard with a Review of Pre-Macedonian Coinage in Egypt," *American Journal of Numismatics* 14 (2002), pp. 23–24; P.G. Van Alfen, "Mechanisms for the Imitations of Athenian Coinage: Dekeleia and Mercenaries Reconsidered," *Revue belge de numismatique et de sigillographie* 157 (2011), p. 70; T. Faucher – W. Fischer–Bossert – S. Dhennin, "Les monnaies en or aux types hiéroglyphiques *nwb nfr*," *BIFAO* 112 (2012), pp. 147–169.

119 P.G.Van Alfen, "The 'owls' from the 1989 Syria Hoard with a Review of Pre-Macedonian Coinage in Egypt," *American Journal of Numismatics* 14 (2002), pp. 27–32; P.G. Van Alfen, "Mechanisms for the Imitations of Athenian Coinage: Dekeleia and Mercenaries Reconsidered," *Revue belge de numismatique et de sigillographie* 157 (2011), pp. 71–73.

120 P.G.Van Alfen, "The 'owls' from the 1989 Syria Hoard with a Review of Pre–Macedonian Coinage in Egypt," *American Journal of Numismatics* 14 (2002), pp. 32–48; P.G. Van Alfen, "Mechanisms for the Imitations of Athenian Coinage: Dekeleia and Mercenaries Reconsidered," *Revue belge de numismatique et de sigillographie* 157 (2011), pp. 55–57, 84–85.

121 J. Kroll, "A Small Bullion Find from Egypt," *American Journal of Numismatics* 13 (2001), pp. 3–4.

122 R. Engelbach, "The Treasure of Athribis (Benha)," *ASAE* 24 (1924), pp. 181–185.

123 C.H. Kraay – O. Mørkholm – M. Thompson, *An Inventory of Greek Coin Hoards* (New York: 1973), pp. 227–230 (nos. 1632, 1634–1643); M.J. Price, *Coin Hoards*, vol. 1 (London: 1975), no. 7; M.J. Price, *Coin Hoards*, vol. 2 (London: 1976), no. 10.

124 J. Kroll, "A Small Bullion Find from Egypt," *American Journal of Numismatics* 13 (2001), pp. 4–5; P.G. Van Alfen, "Herodotos' 'Aryandic' Silver and Bullion Use in Persian Period Egypt," *American Journal of Numismatics* 16/17 (2004/2005), p. 40 (table 4. Archaic Egypt).

125 C.H. Kraay – O. Mørkholm – M. Thompson, *An Inventory of Greek Coin Hoards* (New York: 1973), pp. 230–233 (nos. 1644–1663); T.V. Buttrey, "Pharaonic Imitations of Athenian Tetradrachms," in T. Hackens – R. Weiller (eds.), *Proceedings of the 9th International Congress of Numismatics, Berne, September 1979*, vol. 1 (Louvain-la-Neuve: 1982), pp. 137–140; M.J. Price – K. McGregor – U. Wartenberg, *Coin Hoards*, vol. 8 (London: 1994), nos. 57, 125, 151; J. Kroll, "A Small Bullion Find from Egypt," *American Journal of Numismatics* 13 (2001), pp. 1–3; P.G. Van Alfen, "Two Unpublished Hoards and Other 'owls' from Egypt," *American Journal of Numismatics* 14 (2002), pp. 62–64 (Nahman's and Endicott's Hoards); P.G. Van Alfen, "Herodotos' 'Aryandic' Silver and Bullion Use in Persian Period Egypt," *American Journal of Numismatics* 16/17 (2004/2005), pp. 8–13.

126 J. Kroll, "A Small Bullion Find from Egypt," *American Journal of Numismatics* 13 (2001), pp. 5–7; P.G. Van Alfen, "Herodotos' 'Aryandic' Silver and Bullion Use in Persian Period Egypt," *American Journal of Numismatics* 16/17 (2004/2005), pp. 41–42 (table 5. Classical Egypt).

127 J. Kroll, "A Small Bullion Find from Egypt," *American Journal of Numismatics* 13 (2001), p. 8; P.G. Van Alfen, "Herodotos' 'Aryandic' Silver and Bullion Use in Persian Period Egypt," *American Journal of Numismatics* 16/17 (2004/2005), p. 27.

128 J. Kroll, "A Small Bullion Find from Egypt," *American Journal of Numismatics* 13 (2001), pp. 11–16; P.G. Van Alfen, "Herodotos' 'Aryandic' Silver and Bullion Use in Persian Period Egypt," *American Journal of Numismatics* 16/17 (2004/2005), pp. 17–19.

129 M. Malinine, *Choix de Textes Juridiques en Hieratique 'Anormal' et en Demotique, Premiere Partie* (Bibliotheque de l'Ecole des Hautes Etudes 300. Paris: Librairie Ancienne Honore Champion, 1953), pp. 20–24 (Texte III).

130 S.P. Vleeming, *The Gooseherds of Hou (Pap. Hou)*, (Studia Demotica 3. Leuven: Peeters, 1991), pp. 178–188 (Text 13).

131 B. Porten, *Archives from Elephantine, The Life of an Ancient Jewish Military Colony* (Berkeley: University of California Press, 1968), pp. 78–79; B. Porten – A. Yardeni, *Textbook of Aramaic Documents from Ancient Egypt, 2. Contracts* (Winona Lake IN: Eisenbrauns, 1989), pp. 98–100 (B3.13).

132 M. Malinine, *Choix de Textes Juridiques en Hieratique 'Anormal' et en Demotique, Premiere Partie* (Bibliotheque de l'Ecole des Hautes Etudes 300. Paris: Librairie Ancienne Honore Champion, 1953), pp. 15–19 (Texte II).

133 S.P. Vleeming, *The Gooseherds of Hou (Pap. Hou)*, (Studia Demotica 3. Leuven: Peeters, 1991), pp. 156–177 (Text 12).

134 M. Malinine, *Choix de Textes Juridiques en Hieratique 'Anormal' et en Demotique, Premiere Partie* (Bibliotheque de l'Ecole des Hautes Etudes 300. Paris: Librairie Ancienne Honore Champion, 1953), pp. 30–34 (Texte V).

135 B. Porten, *Archives from Elephantine, The Life of an Ancient Jewish Military Colony* (Berkeley: University of California Press, 1968), pp. 77–78; B. Porten – A. Yardeni, *Textbook of Aramaic Documents from Ancient Egypt, 2. Contracts* (Winona Lake IN: Eisenbrauns, 1989), pp. 103–105 (B4.2).

136 B. Porten, *Archives from Elephantine, The Life of an Ancient Jewish Military Colony* (Berkeley: University of California Press, 1968), pp. 77–78; B. Porten – A. Yardeni, *Textbook of Aramaic Documents from Ancient Egypt, 2. Contracts* (Winona Lake IN: Eisenbrauns, 1989), pp. 54–57 (B3.1).

137 B. Porten – A. Yardeni, *Textbook of Aramaic Documents from Ancient Egypt, 2. Contracts* (Winona Lake IN: Eisenbrauns, 1989), pp. 112–113 (B4.5).

138 B. Porten – A. Yardeni, *Textbook of Aramaic Documents from Ancient Egypt, 2. Contracts* (Winona Lake IN: Eisenbrauns, 1989), pp. 114–115 (B4.6).

139 B. Porten, *Archives from Elephantine, The Life of an Ancient Jewish Military Colony* (Berkeley: University of California Press, 1968), pp. 58–61.

140 B. Porten – A. Yardeni (eds.), *Texts and Aramaic Documents of Ancient Egypt 3: Literature, Accounts, Lists* (Jerusalem, 1993), pp. 82–193 (Text C3.7); and A. Yardeni, "Maritime Trade and Royal Accountancy in an Erased Customs Account from 475 B.C.E. on the Ahiqar Scroll from Elephantine," *BASOR* 293 (1994), pp. 67–78; and P. Briant – R. Descat, "Un registre douanier de la satrapie d'Égypte à l'époque achéménide (TAD C3,7)," in N. Grimal – B. Menu (eds.), *Le commerce en Égypte ancienne* (BdÉ 121. Cairo: 1998), pp. 59–104.

141 B. Muhs, *Tax Receipts, Taxpayers, and Taxes in Early Ptolemaic Thebes* (OIP 126. Chicago: Oriental Institute, 2005), pp. 2–5.

142 Herodotus, Book III, 91.

143 P. Briant, "Table du roi, tribut et redistribution chez les Achéménides," in P. Briant – C. Herrenschmidt (eds.), *Le tribut dans l'empire Perse: Actes de la Table Ronde de Paris 12–13 Decembre 1986* (Leuven: Peeters, 1989), pp. 35–45.

144 B. Porten, *Archives from Elephantine, The Life of an Ancient Jewish Military Colony* (Berkeley: University of California Press, 1968), pp. 72–74.

145 M. Jursa, "Taxation and Service Obligations in Babylonia from Nebuchadnezzer to Darius and the Evidence for Darius' Tax Reform," in R. Rollinger – B. Truschnegg – R. Bichler (eds.), *Herodot und das Persische Weltreich* (Classica et Orientalia. Wiesbaden: Harrassowitz, 2011), pp. 431–448.

146 R.A. Caminos, "The Nitocris Adoption Stela," *JEA* 50 (1964), pp. 71–101; P. Der Manuelian, *Living in the Past. Studies in the Archaism of the Egyptian Twenty-sixth Dynasty* (Studies in Egyptology. London: Kegan Paul International, 1994), pp. 297–321.

147 G.A. Driver, *Aramaic Documents of the Fifth Century B.C.*, 2nd ed. (Oxford: Clarendon Press, 1965), pp. 27–28, 56–62 (Text 6); B. Porten – A. Yardeni, *Textbook of Aramaic Documents from Ancient Egypt*, Volume 1. *Letters* (Jerusalem, 1986), pp. 114–115 (Text A6.9).

148 G.A. Driver, *Aramaic Documents of the Fifth Century B.C.*, 2nd ed. (Oxford: Clarendon Press, 1965), pp. 28–30, 62–66 (Text 7); B. Porten – A. Yardeni, *Textbook of Aramaic Documents from Ancient Egypt*, Volume 1. *Letters* (Jerusalem, 1986), pp. 116–117 (Text A6.10).

149 G.A. Driver, *Aramaic Documents of the Fifth Century B.C.*, 2nd ed. (Oxford: Clarendon Press, 1965), pp. 25–27, 51–56 (Text 5); B. Porten – A. Yardeni, *Textbook of Aramaic Documents from Ancient Egypt*, Volume 1. *Letters* (Jerusalem, 1986), pp. 110–111 (Text A6.7).

150 G.A. Driver, *Aramaic Documents of the Fifth Century B.C.*, 2nd ed. (Oxford: Clarendon Press, 1965), p. 32, pp. 71–74 (Text 9); B. Porten – A. Yardeni, *Textbook of Aramaic Documents from Ancient Egypt*, Volume 1. *Letters* (Jerusalem, 1986), pp. 120–121 (Text A6.12).

151 A.B. Lloyd, "Trieremes and the Saite Navy," *JEA* 58 (1972), pp. 268–279; A.B. Lloyd, "The So-called Galleys of Necho," *JEA* 58 (1972), pp. 307–308; A.B. Lloyd, "Were Necho's Triremes Phoenician?," *Journal of Hellenic Studies* 95 (1975), pp. 45–61; J.C. Darnell, "The *Kbn.wt* Vessels of the Late Period," in J.H. Johnson (ed.), *Life in a Multi-Cultural Society: Egypt from Cambyses to Constantine and Beyond* (SAOC 51. Chicago: Oriental Institute, 1992), pp. 67–89.

152 Herodotus, Book II, 159; A.B. Lloyd, *Herodotus, Book II: Commentary 99–182* (Leiden: Brill, 1988), pp. 158–161.

153 Herodotus, Book II, 161; A.B. Lloyd, *Herodotus, Book II: Commentary 99–182* (Leiden: Brill, 1988), pp. 170–172.

154 Herodotus, Book II, 182; A.B. Lloyd, *Herodotus, Book II: Commentary 99–182* (Leiden: Brill, 1988), pp. 240–241.

155 Herodotus, Book VII, 89–99.

156 Diodorus, Book 15, 3.4.

157 Diodorus, Book 15, 92.2; Plutarch, *Life of Agesilaus*, 37.1.

158 A. Cowley, *Aramaic Papyri of the Fifth Century B.C.* (Oxford: Clarendon Press, 1923), pp. 88–97 (Text 26); B. Porten – A. Yardeni, *Textbook of Aramaic Documents from Ancient Egypt*, Volume 1. *Letters* (Jerusalem, 1986), pp. 96–101 (Text A6.2).

159 C. Grataloup, "12: Occupation and Trade at Heracleion-Thonis – the Evidence from the Pottery," in D. Robinson – A. Wilson (eds.), *Alexandria and the North-Western Delta* (Oxford Centre for Maritime Archaeology 5. Oxford: 2010), pp. 151–159.

160 D. Fabre, "1: The Shipwrecks of Heracleion-Thonis: A Preliminary Study," in D. Robinson – A. Wilson (eds.), *Maritime Archaeology and Ancient Trade in the Mediterranean* (Oxford Centre for Maritime Archaeology 6. Oxford: 2011), pp. 13–32.

161 Herodotus, Book II, 30; A.B. Lloyd, *Herodotus, Book II: Commentary 1–98* (Leiden: Brill, 1976), p. 130.

162 E.D. Oren, "Migdol: A New Fortress on the Edge of the Eastern Nile Delta," *BASOR* 256 (1984), pp. 7–44; D.B. Redford, "A Report on the 1993 and 1997 Seasons at Tell Qedwa," *JARCE* 35 (1998), pp. 45–60.

163 L.A. Heidorn, "The Saite and Persian Period Forts at Dorginarti," in W.V. Davies (ed.), *Egypt and Africa, Nubia from Prehistory to Islam* (London: British Museum Press, 1991), pp. 205–219; L.A. Heidorn, "Dorginarti, Fortress at the Mouth of the Rapids," in F. Jesse – C. Vogel (eds.), *The Power of Walls – Fortifications in Ancient Northeastern Africa, Proceedings of the International Workshop held at the University of Cologne 4th-7th August 2011* (Colloquium Africanum 5. Köln: Heinrich-Barth-Institut e.V., 2013), pp. 293–307.

164 Herodotus, Book II, 30; A.B. Lloyd, *Herodotus, Book II: Commentary 1–98* (Leiden: Brill, 1976), p. 130.

165 H. Schäfer, "Die Auswandering der Krieger unter Psammetich I. und den Söldner-Aufstand in Elephantine unter Apries," *Klio* 4 (1904), pp. 152–163.

166 Herodotus, Book II, 154; A.B. Lloyd, *Herodotus. Book II. Commentary 99–182* (Leiden: Brill, 1988), p. 137.

167 C. Fischer-Bovet, *Army and Society in Ptolemaic Egypt* (Cambridge, 2014), p. 31 n. 69, assumes that they received plots at least as large as the twelve arouras given to the machimoi (Herodotus 2.168), because Herodotus says the machimoi were jealous of them (Herodotus 2.161–162).

168 Herodotus, Book II, 163; A.B. Lloyd, *Herodotus. Book II. Commentary 99–182* (Leiden: Brill, 1988), p. 180; C. Fischer-Bovet, *Army and Society in Ptolemaic Egypt* (Cambridge, 2014), pp. 18–20.

169 Herodotus, Book II, 169.

170 Herodotus, Book II, 154.

171 Herodotus, Book II, 30; A.B. Lloyd, *Herodotus, Book II: Commentary 1–98* (Leiden: Brill, 1976), p. 130.

172 D. Valbelle, "Les garnisons de Migdol (Tell el-Herr) de l'époque achéménide au Bas-Empire: état de la question en 1998," *Comptes rendus des séances de l'académie des Inscriptions et Belles-Lettres*, 142, 3 (1998), pp. 799–813.

173 D.B. Redford, "A Report on the 1993 and 1997 Seasons at Tell Qedwa," *JARCE* 35 (1998), pp. 45–60, contra E.D. Oren, "Migdol: A New Fortress on the Edge of the Eastern Nile Delta," *BASOR* 256 (1984), pp. 7–44.

174 Herodotus, Book III, 91.

175 B. Porten, *Archives from Elephantine, The Life of an Ancient Jewish Military Colony* (Berkeley – Los Angeles: University of California Press, 1968), pp. 29–32.

176 B. Porten, *Archives from Elephantine, The Life of an Ancient Jewish Military Colony* (Berkeley – Los Angeles: University of California Press, 1968), p. 35.

177 B. Porten, *Archives from Elephantine, The Life of an Ancient Jewish Military Colony* (Berkeley – Los Angeles: University of California Press, 1968), pp. 72–73.

178 B. Porten, *Archives from Elephantine, The Life of an Ancient Jewish Military Colony* (Berkeley – Los Angeles: University of California Press, 1968), pp. 73–80.

179 Diodorus, Book 15, 29.1–2.

180 Diodorus, Book 15, 92.2; Plutarch, *Life of Agesilaus*, 37.1.

181 T. Faucher – W. Fischer–Bossert – S. Dhennin, "Les monnaies en or aux types hiéroglyphiques *nwb nfr*," *BIFAO* 112 (2012), pp. 147–169.

182 D. Agut–Labordère, "L'oracle et l'hoplite: les élites sacerdotales et l'effort de guerre sous les dynasties égyptiennes indigenes," *JESHO* 54 (2011), pp. 627–645.

183 Herodotus, Book II, 164–166; A.B. Lloyd, *Herodotus. Book II. Commentary 99–182* (Leiden: Brill, 1988), pp. 185–195.

184 Herodotus, Book II, 168; A.B. Lloyd, *Herodotus. Book II. Commentary 99–182* (Leiden: Brill, 1988), p. 200.

185 Herodotus, Book IX, 32.

186 J.K. Winnicki, "Die Kalasirier der spätdynastischen und der ptolemäischen Zeit. Zu einem Problem der Ägyptischen Heeresgeschichte," *Historia: Zeitschrift für Alte Geschichte* 26, 3 (1977), pp. 257–268; J.K. Winnicki, "Zwei Studien über die Kalasirier," *Orientalia Lovaniensia Periodica* 17 (1986), pp. 17–32; H.-J. Thissen, "Varia onomastica," *GM* 141 (1994), pp. 89–91 (1. 'Ερμοτὑβιες); G. Vittmann, *Der demotische Papyrus Rylands 9, Teil 2. Kommentare und Indizes* (ÄAT 38,2. Wiesbaden: Harrassowitz Verlag, 1998), p. 554; J.K Winnicki, "Zur Bedeutung der Termini Kalasiriier und Ermotybier," in W. Clarysse – A. Schoors, et al. (eds.), *Egyptian*

Religion: The Last Thousand Years. Studies Dedicated to the Memory of Jan Quaegebeur, Vol. 2 (OLA 85. Leuven: Peeters, 1998), pp. 1503–1507; C. Fischer-Bovet, "Egyptian Warriors: The Machimoi of Herodotus and the Ptolemaic Army," *Classical Quarterly* 63.1 (2013), pp. 213–214.

187 A.B. Lloyd, *Herodotus. Book II. Commentary 99–182* (Leiden, 1988), pp. 182–183; C. Fischer-Bovet, "Egyptian Warriors: The Machimoi of Herodotus and the Ptolemaic Army," *Classical Quarterly* 63.1 (2013), p. 212.

188 C. Fischer-Bovet, "Egyptian Warriors: The Machimoi of Herodotus and the Ptolemaic Army," *Classical Quarterly* 63.1 (2013), pp. 215–219.

189 A.B. Lloyd, *Herodotus. Book II. Commentary 99–182* (Leiden, 1988), p. 184; R.K. Ritner, "The End of the Libyan Anarchy in Egypt: P. Rylands IX cols. 11–12," *Enchoria* 17 (1998), p. 107 n. 27.

190 Papyrus Rylands 9, col. 11, line 9 – col. 12, line 21, see G. Vittmann, *Der demotische Papyrus Rylands 9. Teil I. Text und Übersetzung* (ÄAT 38, 1. Wiesbaden: Harrassowitz, 1998), pp. 150–157.

191 Papyrus Rylands 9, col. 19, line 13, see G. Vittmann, *Der demotische Papyrus Rylands 9. Teil I. Text und Übersetzung* (ÄAT 38, 1. Wiesbaden: Harrassowitz, 1998), pp. 182–183.

192 C. Fischer-Bovet, "Egyptian Warriors: The Machimoi of Herodotus and the Ptolemaic Army," *Classical Quarterly* 63.1 (2013), p. 213.

193 A. Leahy, "Saite Lamp Donations," *GM* 49 (1981), pp. 37–46.

194 A. Leahy, "Beer for the Gods of Memphis in the Reign of Amasis," in W. Clarysse – A. Schoors – H. Willems (eds.), *Egyptian Religion: The Last Thousand Years. Studies Dedicated to the Memory of Jan Quaegebeur*, Part 1. (OLA 84. Leuven: Peeters, 1998), pp. 377–392.

195 D. Agut-Labordère, "Le titre du «Décret de Cambyse» (P. Bn 215 verso colonne D)," *RdÉ* 56 (2005), pp. 45–54; and D. Agut-Labordère, "Le sens du *Décret de Cambyse*," *Transeuphratène* 29 (2005), pp. 9–16.

196 D. Agut–Labordère, "L'oracle et l'hoplite: les élites sacerdotales et l'effort de guerre sous les dynasties égyptiennes indigenes," *JESHO* 54 (2011), pp. 627–645.

197 Pseudo-Aristotle, *Oikonomika* 2.2.

198 J.J. Janssen, "Requisitions from Upper-Egyptian Temples," *JEA* 77 (1991), pp. 79–94, and pl. 4.

199 R.S. Simpson, *Demotic Grammar in the Ptolemaic Sacerdotal Decrees* (Oxford: Griffith Institute, 1996), pp. 264–265.

200 G.R. Hughes, "The So-called Pherendates Correspondence," in H.-J. Thissen – K.-T. Zauzich (eds.), *Grammata Demotica, Festschrift fur Erich Luddeckens zum 15. Juni 1983* (Wurzburg: Gisela Zauzich Verlag, 1984), pp. 75–88.

201 W. Clarysse, "The Archive of the Praktor Milon," in K. Vandorpe – W. Clarysse (eds.), *Edfu, An Egyptian Provincial Capital in the Ptolemaic Period. Brussels, 3 September 2001* (Brussels: Koninklijke Vlaamse Academie van België voor Wetenschappen en Kunsten, 2003), pp. 17–27.

202 P.W. Pestman, *Les papyrus démotiques de Tsenhor (P. Tsenhor), I. Textes* (Studia Demotica 4. Leuven, 1994), p. 45 note V.

203 M. Malinine, *Choix de Textes Juridiques en Hieratique "Anormal" et en Demotique, Premiere Partie* (Bibliotheque de l'Ecole des Hautes Etudes 300. Paris: Librairie Ancienne Honore Champion, 1953), Textes IX (P. Turin 2118A (246)), X (P. Turin 2120 (247)) and XVIII (P. Turin 2121 (248)); Sergio Pernigotti, "Un nuovo testo giuridico in ieratico 'anormale'," *BIFAO* 75, 1975, pp. 73–95 and pls. 11–12 (P. Turin 2118B (246)).

204 P.W. Pestman, *Les papyrus démotiques de Tsenhor (P. Tsenhor). Les archives privées d'une femme égyptienne du temps de Darius Ier*. I. Textes, II. Planches (Studia Demotica 4, Leuven, Peeters, 1994).

205 K. Donker van Heel, *Abnormal Hieratic and Early Demotic Texts Collected by the Theban Choachytes in the Reign of Amasis* (Leiden University PhD Thesis, 1996); K. Donker van Heel, *Djekhy & Son: Doing Business in Ancient Egypt* (Cairo: American Research Center in Cairo Press, 2012).

206 G.R. Hughes, *Saite Demotic Land Leases* (SAOC 28, Chicago: University of Chicago Press, 1952), pp. 45–50 (Text IV); M. Malinine, *Choix de Textes Juridiques en Hieratique 'Anormal' et en Demotique, Premiere Partie* (Bibliotheque de l'Ecole des Hautes Etudes, Fascicule 300. Paris: Librairie Ancienne Honore Champion, 1953), pp. 95–98 (Text XIII); and K. Donker van Heel, *Abnormal Hieratic and Early Demotic Texts Collected by the Theban Choachytes in the Reign of Amasis* (Leiden University PhD Thesis, 1996), pp. 192–196 (Text 17).

207 G.R. Hughes, *Saite Demotic Land Leases* (SAOC 28, Chicago: University of Chicago Press, 1952), pp. 71–73 (Text VII); M. Malinine, *Choix de Textes Juridiques en Hieratique "Anormal" et en Demotique, Premiere Partie* (Bibliotheque de l'Ecole des Hautes Etudes, Fascicule 300. Paris: Librairie Ancienne Honore Champion, 1953), pp. 98–101 (Text XIV); and K. Donker van Heel, *Abnormal Hieratic and Early Demotic Texts Collected by the Theban Choachytes in the Reign of Amasis* (Leiden University PhD Thesis, 1996), pp. 216–221 (Text 21).

208 M. Malinine, *Choix de Textes Juridiques en Hieratique "Anormal" et en Demotique, Premiere Partie* (Bibliotheque de l'Ecole des Hautes Etudes 300. Paris: Librairie Ancienne Honore Champion, 1953), Textes IX (P. Turin 2118A (246)), X (P. Turin 2120 (247)) and XVIII (P. Turin 2121 (248)); and S. Pernigotti, "Un nuovo testo giuridico in ieratico 'anormale'," *BIFAO* 75 (1975), pp. 73–95 and pls. 11–12 (P. Turin 2118B (246)).

209 P.W. Pestman, *Les papyrus démotiques de Tsenhor (P. Tsenhor). Les archives privées d'une femme égyptienne du temps de Darius Ier.* I. Textes, II. Planches (Studia Demotica 4, Leuven, Peeters, 1994).

210 M. Malinine, "Vente de tombes à l'Époque Saïte," *RdÉ* 27 (1975), pp. 168–174.

211 S. Bosticco, *Museo Archeologico di Firenze. Le stele egiziane di Epoca Tarda* (Cataloghi dei musei e gallerie d'Italia. Roma: 1972), pp. 38–39 (no. 28), and pl. 28.

212 M. Malinine, *Choix de Textes Juridiques en Hieratique "Anormal" et en Demotique, Premiere Partie* (Bibliotheque de l'Ecole des Hautes Etudes 300. Paris: 1953), pp. 85–88 (Texte XI); P.W. Pestman, *Les papyrus démotiques de Tsenhor (P. Tsenhor). Les archives privées d'une femme égyptienne du temps de Darius Ier.* I. Textes (Studia Demotica 4. Leuven: 1994), pp. 71–73 (Texte 10).

213 M. Malinine, "Vente de tombes à l'Époque Saïte," *RdÉ* 27 (1975), pp. 164–168; S. Pernigotti, "Ancora sulla stele Firenze 1639 (2507)," *EVO* 2 (1979), pp. 21–37; and S.P. Vleeming, "La phase initiale du démotique ancien," *CdÉ* 56 (1981), pp. 46–48.

214 B. Porten, *Archives from Elephantine, The Life of an Ancient Jewish Military Colony* (Berkeley: University of California Press, 1968), pp. 244–245; B. Porten – A. Yardeni, *Textbook of Aramaic Documents from Ancient Egypt, 2. Contracts* (Winona Lake IN: Eisenbrauns, 1989), pp. 34–37 (B2.7 = Cowley 13).

215 B. Porten, *Archives from Elephantine, The Life of an Ancient Jewish Military Colony* (Berkeley: University of California Press, 1968), pp. 213–219, 225–234; B. Porten – A. Yardeni, *Textbook of Aramaic Documents from Ancient Egypt, 2. Contracts* (Winona Lake IN: Eisenbrauns, 1989), pp. 64–67 (B3.4 = Kraeling 3), 68–71 (B3.5 = Kraeling 4), 74–77 (B3.7 = Kraeling 6), 86–89 (B3.10 = Kraeling 9), 90–93 (B3.11 = Kraeling 10), 94–97 (B3.12 = Kraeling 12).

216 K. Donker van Heel, *Abnormal Hieratic and Early Demotic Texts Collected by the Theban Choachytes in the Reign of Amasis* (Leiden University PhD Thesis, 1996), pp. 177–182 (Text 13); K. Donker van Heel, *Djekhy & Son: Doing Business in Ancient Egypt* (Cairo: American Research Center in Cairo Press, 2012), pp. 133–138.

217 P.W. Pestman, *Les papyrus démotiques de Tsenhor (P. Tsenhor). Les archives privées d'une femme égyptienne du temps de Darius Ier.* I. Textes, II. Planches (Studia Demotica 4, Leuven, Peeters, 1994).

218 B. Porten – A. Yardeni, *Textbook of Aramaic Documents from Ancient Egypt, 2. Contracts* (Winona Lake IN: Eisenbrauns, 1989), pp. 128–129 (B5.6).

219 E. Cruz-Uribe, *Saite and Persian Demotic Cattle Documents, A Study in Legal Forms and Principles in Ancient Egypt* (ASP 26. Chico CA: Scholars Press 1985).

220 S.P. Vleeming, *The Gooseherds of Hou (Pap. Hou)* (Studia Demotica 3. Leuven: In Aedibus Peeters, 1991).

221 F.Ll. Griffith, *Catalogue of Demotic Papyri in the John Rylands Library, Manchester,* 3 vols. (Manchester: University Press, 1909), vol. 3, pp. 44–48, 207–209; G. Vittmann, *Der demotische Papyrus Rylands 9. Teil I. Text und Übersetzung* (ÄAT 38, 1. Wiesbaden: Harrassowitz, 1998), pp. 224–226; G. Vittmann, *Der demotische Papyrus Rylands 9. Teil II. Kommentare und Indizes* (ÄAT 38, 2. Wiesbaden: Harrassowitz, 1998), pp. 674–675.

222 E. Jelínková-Reymond, "Gestion des Rentes d'Office," *CdÉ* 28 (1953), pp. 228–237; A.F. Shore, "Swapping Property at Asyut in the Persian Period," in J. Baines (ed.), *Pyramid Studies and Other Essays Presented to I.E.S. Edwards* (London: 1988), pp. 200–206 and pls.

41–42; J.H. Johnson, "'Annuity Contracts' and Marriage," in D.P. Silverman (ed.), *For His Ka, Essays Offered in Memory of Klaus Baer* (SAOC 55 (Chicago: The Oriental Institute, 1994), pp. 113–132.

223 W. Erichsen, "Eine demotische Schenkungsurkunde aus der Zeit des Darius," *Akademie d. Wiss. und Lit. in Mainz, Abh. d. geistes- und socialwiss. Kl. 1962, Nr. 6*, pp. 343–363, and taf. 1–2; E. Lüddeckens, "P. Wien D 10151, eine neue Urkunde zum agyptischen Pfrundenhandel in der Perserzeit," in S. Schott (ed.), *Gottinger Vortrage vom Agyptologischen Kolloquium der Akademie am 25. und 26. August 1964* (Nachrichten der Akademie der Wissenschaften in Gottingen, I. Philologisch-Historische Klasse 1965, Nr. 5. Gottingen: Vandenhoeck & Ruprecht, 1965), pp. 103–120; and E. Lüddeckens, "Nachtrag zum P. Wien D 10151," *Enchoria* 1 (1971), p. 73 and pls. 5–7.

224 K. Donker van Heel, *Abnormal Hieratic and Early Demotic Texts Collected by the Theban Choachytes in the Reign of Amasis*. (Proefschrift, Leiden University: 1996), pp. 197–199 (Text 18); K. Donker van Heel, *Djekhy & Son: Doing Business in Ancient Egypt* (Cairo: 2012), pp. 145–147.

225 P.W. Pestman, *Les papyrus démotiques de Tsenhor (P. Tsenhor). Les archives privées d'une femme égyptienne du temps de Darius Ier. I. Textes* (Studia Demotica 4. Leuven: 1994), pp. 88–89 (Text 16).

226 Herodotus Book II, 157; A.B. Lloyd, *Herodotus, Book II: Commentary 99–182* (Leiden: Brill, 1988), pp. 146–149.

227 H. Goedicke, "Psammetik I. und die Libyer," *MDAIK* 18 (1962), pp. 26–49; P. Der Manuelian, *Living in the Past. Studies in the Archaism of the Egyptian Twenty-sixth Dynasty* (Studies in Egyptology. London: Kegan Paul International, 1994), pp. 323–332.

228 Herodotus Book II, 159; A.B. Lloyd, *Herodotus, Book II: Commentary 99–182* (Leiden: Brill, 1988), pp. 158–163. Lloyd argues against Megiddo in favor of Migdol.

229 2 Kings 23:29–30, and 2 Chronicles 35:20–25. The latter gives the destination as Carchemish, perhaps because of the battle fought there several years later.

230 2 Kings 23:31–34.

231 Herodotus, Book II, 161; A.B. Lloyd, *Herodotus, Book II: Commentary 99–182* (Leiden: Brill, 1988), pp. 167–169.

232 H.S.K. Bakry, "Psammetichus II and His Newly-Found Stela at Shellâl," *Oriens Antiquus* 6 (1967), pp. 225–244; H. Goedicke, "The Campaign of Psammetik II against Nubia," *MDAIK* 37 (1981), pp. 187–198; P. Der Manuelian, *Living in the Past. Studies in the Archaism of the Egyptian Twenty-sixth Dynasty* (Studies in Egyptology. London: Kegan Paul International, 1994), pp. 337–350.

233 S. Sauneron – J. Yoyotte, "La campagne nubienne de Psammétique II et sa signifaction historique," *BIFAO* 50 (1952), pp. 161–172, pls. 1–2; P. Der Manuelian, *Living in the Past. Studies in the Archaism of the Egyptian Twenty-sixth Dynasty* (Studies in Egyptology. London: Kegan Paul International, 1994), pp. 351–355.

234 S. Sauneron – J. Yoyotte, "La campagne nubienne de Psammétique II et sa signifaction historique," *BIFAO* 50 (1952), pp. 173–187, pls. 3–4; P. Der Manuelian, *Living in the Past. Studies in the Archaism of the Egyptian Twenty-sixth Dynasty* (Studies in Egyptology. London: Kegan Paul International, 1994), pp. 365–371.

235 Papyrus Rylands 9, col. 3, line 16, and col. 14, line 16 – col. 15, line 2, see G. Vittmann, *Der demotische Papyrus Rylands 9. Teil I. Text und Übersetzung* (ÄAT 38, 1. Wiesbaden: Harrassowitz, 1998), pp. 124–125 and 162–165.

236 Herodotus, Book II, 161; A.B. Lloyd, *Herodotus, Book II: Commentary 99–182* (Leiden: Brill, 1988), pp. 170–172.

237 Herodotus, Book II, 161–163, 169; A.B. Lloyd, *Herodotus, Book II: Commentary 99–182* (Leiden: Brill, 1988), pp. 173–182, 201–202.

238 Herodotus, Book II, 182; A.B. Lloyd, *Herodotus, Book II: Commentary 99–182* (Leiden: Brill, 1988), pp. 240–241.

239 E. Edel, "Amasis und Nebukadrezar II," *GM* 29 (1978), pp. 13–20; A. Leahy, "The Earliest Dated Monument of Amasis and the End of the Reign of Apries," *JEA* 74 (1988), pp. 183–199.

240 G. Posener, *La première domination Perse en Égypte. Recueil d'inscriptions hiéroglyphiques* (BdÉ 11. Cairo: IFAO, 1936), pp. 88–130.

241 E. Cruz-Uribe, "On the Existence of Psammetichus IV," *Serapis* 5 (1980), pp. 35–39; P.W. Pestman, "The Diospolis Parva Documents: Chronological Problems concerning Psammetichus III and IV," in H.-J. Thissen – K.-Th. Zauzich (eds.), *Grammata Demotica, Festschrift für Erich Lüddeckens* (Würzburg: Gisela Zauzich Verlag, 1984), pp. 145–155.

242 Herodotus Book III, 12, 15, 160, and Book VII, 7; and Thucydides Book 1, 104, 109–110, 112.
243 Diodorus Book XV, 29.1–2.
244 Plutarch, *Life of Agesilaus*, 36:9.
245 Stela Cairo JdE 22182 (The Satrap Stela), see D. Schäfer, *Makedonische Pharaonen und hieroglyphische Stelen. Historische Untersuchungen zur Satrapenstele und verwandten Denkmälern* (Studia Hellenistica 50, Leuven: Peeters, 2011), pp. 34–38.
246 Herodotus, Book II, 30; A.B. Lloyd, *Herodotus, Book II: Commentary 1–98* (Leiden: Brill, 1976), p. 130.
247 Herodotus, Book II, 154; A.B. Lloyd, *Herodotus, Book II: Commentary 99–182* (Leiden: Brill, 1988), pp. 137–139.
248 Herodotus, Book II, 158; A.B. Lloyd, *Herodotus, Book II: Commentary 99–182* (Leiden: Brill, 1988), pp. 150–157.
249 Herodotus, Book IV, 42.
250 Herodotus, Book II, 178; A.B. Lloyd, *Herodotus, Book II: Commentary 99–182* (Leiden: Brill, 1988), pp. 222–229.
251 Herodotus, Book II, 179; A.B. Lloyd, *Herodotus, Book II: Commentary 99–182* (Leiden: Brill, 1988), pp. 229–231.
252 Herodotus, Book II, 30; A.B. Lloyd, *Herodotus, Book II: Commentary 1–98* (Leiden: Brill, 1976), p. 130.
253 G. Posener, *La première domination Perse en Égypte. Recueil d'inscriptions hiéroglyphiques* (BdÉ 11. Cairo: IFAO, 1936), pp. 48–87.
254 P. Rylands 9, col. 7, lines 1–6, see G. Vittmann, *Der demotische Papyrus Rylands 9. Teil I. Text und Übersetzung* (ÄAT 38, 1. Wiesbaden: Harrassowitz, 1998), pp. 134–135.
255 P. Rylands 9, col. 8, lines 1–3, see G. Vittmann, *Der demotische Papyrus Rylands 9. Teil I. Text und Übersetzung* (ÄAT 38, 1. Wiesbaden: Harrassowitz, 1998), pp. 138–139.
256 P. Rylands 9, col. 9, lines 12–13, see G. Vittmann, *Der demotische Papyrus Rylands 9. Teil I. Text und Übersetzung* (ÄAT 38, 1. Wiesbaden: Harrassowitz, 1998), pp. 144–145.
257 P. Rylands 9, col. 14, line 17 – col. 15, line 19, see G. Vittmann, *Der demotische Papyrus Rylands 9. Teil I. Text und Übersetzung* (ÄAT 38, 1. Wiesbaden: Harrassowitz, 1998), pp. 162–169.
258 K. Donker van Heel, *Abnormal Hieratic and Early Demotic Texts Collected by the Theban Choachytes in the Reign of Amasis* (Leiden University PhD Thesis, 1996); K. Donker van Heel, *Djekhy & Son: Doing Business in Ancient Egypt* (Cairo: American Research Center in Cairo Press, 2012).
259 G.R. Hughes, *Saite Demotic Land Leases* (SAOC 28, Chicago: University of Chicago Press, 1952), pp. 45–50 (Text IV); M. Malinine, *Choix de Textes Juridiques en Hieratique 'Anormal' et en Demotique, Premiere Partie* (Bibliotheque de l'Ecole des Hautes Etudes, Fascicule 300. Paris: Librairie Ancienne Honore Champion, 1953), pp. 95–98 (Text XIII); and K. Donker van Heel, *Abnormal Hieratic and Early Demotic Texts Collected by the Theban Choachytes in the Reign of Amasis* (Leiden University PhD Thesis, 1996), pp. 192–196 (Text 17).
260 G.R. Hughes, *Saite Demotic Land Leases* (SAOC 28, Chicago: University of Chicago Press, 1952), pp. 71–73 (Text VII); M. Malinine, *Choix de Textes Juridiques en Hieratique 'Anormal' et en Demotique, Premiere Partie* (Bibliotheque de l'Ecole des Hautes Etudes, Fascicule 300. Paris: Librairie Ancienne Honore Champion, 1953), pp. 98–101 (Text XIV); and K. Donker van Heel, *Abnormal Hieratic and Early Demotic Texts Collected by the Theban Choachytes in the Reign of Amasis* (Leiden University PhD Thesis, 1996), pp. 216–221 (Text 21).
261 B. Porten – A. Yardeni, *Textbook of Aramaic Documents from Ancient Egypt, 2. Contracts* (Winona Lake IN: Eisenbrauns, 1989), pp. 11–13 (B1.1).
262 G.A. Driver, *Aramaic Documents of the Fifth Century B.C.*, 2nd ed. (Oxford: Clarendon Press, 1965), pp. 33–35, 75–80 (Texts 10–11); B. Porten – A. Yardeni, *Textbook of Aramaic Documents from Ancient Egypt*, Volume 1. *Letters* (Jerusalem, 1986), pp. 122–125 (Text A6.13–14).
263 G.A. Driver, *Aramaic Documents of the Fifth Century B.C.*, 2nd ed. (Oxford: Clarendon Press, 1965), pp. 35–37, 80–84 (Text 12); B. Porten – A. Yardeni, *Textbook of Aramaic Documents from Ancient Egypt*, Volume 1. *Letters* (Jerusalem, 1986), pp. 126–127 (Text A6.15).
264 G.A. Driver, *Aramaic Documents of the Fifth Century B.C.*, 2nd ed. (Oxford: Clarendon Press, 1965), pp. 33–35, 75–80 (Texts 10–11); B. Porten – A. Yardeni, *Textbook of Aramaic Documents from Ancient Egypt*, Volume 1. *Letters* (Jerusalem, 1986), pp. 122–125 (Text A6.13–14).
265 G.A. Driver, *Aramaic Documents of the Fifth Century B.C.*, 2nd ed. (Oxford: Clarendon Press, 1965), pp. 30–31, 66–71 (Text 8); B. Porten – A. Yardeni, *Textbook of Aramaic*

Documents from Ancient Egypt, Volume 1. *Letters* (Jerusalem, 1986), pp. 118–119 (Text A6.11).

266 G.A. Driver, *Aramaic Documents of the Fifth Century B.C.*, 2nd ed. (Oxford: Clarendon Press, 1965), pp. 35–37, 80–84 (Text 12); B. Porten – A. Yardeni, *Textbook of Aramaic Documents from Ancient Egypt*, Volume 1. *Letters* (Jerusalem, 1986), pp. 126–127 (Text A6.15).

7. THE PTOLEMAIC PERIOD (332–30 BCE)

1 G. Hölbl, *A History of the Ptolemaic Empire* (London: Routledge, 2001), pp. 90–92.

2 A. Di Bitonto, "Le petizioni al re. Studia sul formulario," *Aegyptus* 47 (1967), pp. 5–57 (173 examples).

3 For two petitions personally delivered by the recluse Ptolemaios to Ptolemy and Cleopatra when they were in Saqqara, see U. Wilcken, *UPZ* I 41, lines 4–5; and 42, line 4.

4 For a petition by the recluse Ptolemaios to Ptolemy and Cleopatra that was personally subscribed by king, see U. Wilcken, *UPZ* I 14, column 1.

5 O. Guéraud, *ENTEYΞEIΣ* (Cairo, 1931); N. Lewis, *Greeks in Ptolemaic Egypt: Case Studies in the Social History of the Hellenistic World* (Oxford: Clarendon Press, 1986), pp. 56–68.

6 J. Bauschatz, *Law and Enforcement in Ptolemaic Egypt* (Cambridge: University Press, 2013), pp. 49–159.

7 C. Armoni, *Studien zur Verwaltung des Ptolemäischen Ägypten: Das Amt de Basilikos Grammeteus* (Papyrologica Coloniensia 36. Paderborn: Verlag Ferdinand Schöningh, 2012), pp. 26–32.

8 J. Yoyotte, "Le nom égyptien du «ministre de l'économie» – de Saïs a Méroé," *Comptes rendus, Académie des inscriptions & belles-lettres (CRAIBL)*, 1989 (Paris, Diffusion de Boccard, 1989), pp. 73–90.

9 A. Di Bitonto, "Le petizioni ai funzionari nel periodo tolemaico. Studio sul formulario," *Aegyptus* 48 (1968), pp. 53–107 (196 examples); M. Depauw, *The Demotic Letter* (Demotische Studien 14. Sommerhausen, 2006), pp. 323–330 (33 examples).

10 C. Preaux – M. Hombert, "Recherches sur le *prosangelma* à l'époque Ptolémaïque," *CdÉ* 34 (1942), pp. 259–286; M. Parca, "Prosangelmata ptolémaiques: une mise à jour," *CdÉ* 60 (1985), pp. 240–247.

11 A. Di Bitonto, "Le petizioni ai funzionari nel periodo tolemaico. Studio sul formulario," *Aegyptus* 48 (1968), pp. 56–62; J. Bauschatz, *Law and Enforcement in Ptolemaic Egypt* (Cambridge: University Press, 2013), pp. 160–217.

12 J. Bauschatz, *Law and Enforcement in Ptolemaic Egypt* (Cambridge: University Press, 2013), pp. 218–280.

13 J. Bauschatz, *Law and Enforcement in Ptolemaic Egypt* (Cambridge: University Press, 2013), pp. 281–327.

14 D.J. Thompson, "Policing the Ptolemaic Countryside," in B. Kramer –W. Luppe – H. Maehler – G. Poethke (eds.), *Akten des 21. Internationalen Papyrologenkongress, Berlin, 13.-19.8.1995*, vol. 2 (AfP Beiheft 3. Stuttgart-Leipzig, 1997), pp. 961–966.

15 C. Homoth-Kuhs, *Phylakes und Phylakon-steuer im Griechisch-Römischen Ägypten* (AfP Beiheft 17. München-Leipzig: K.G. Saur, 2005), pp. 7–29 (2. Phylakes in ptolemäischer Zeit).

16 J. Modrzejewski, "Chrématistes et laocrites," in J. Bingen – G. Cambier – G. Nachtergael (eds.), *Hommages à Claire Préaux* (Bruxelles, 1975), pp. 699–708; P.W. Pestman, "The Competence of Greek and Egyptian Tribunals according to the Decree of 118 B.C.," *BASP* 22 (1985), pp. 265–269.

17 H. Thompson, *A Family Archive from Siut, from Papyri in the British Museum, Including an Account of a Trial before the Laocritae in the Year B.C. 170* (Oxford: University Press, 1934); and A.F. Shore – H.S. Smith, "Two Unpublished Demotic Documents from the Asyūṭ Archive," *JEA* 45 (1959), pp. 52–60.

18 Papyrus BM 10591 recto, col. I, lines 1–7, see H. Thompson, *A Family Archive from Siut, from Papyri in the British Museum, Including an Account of a Trial before the Laocritae in the Year B.C. 170* (Oxford: University Press, 1934), p. 3, pp. 12–13.

19 G. Mattha, *The Demotic Legal Code of Hermopolis West* (BdÉ 45. Cairo, IFAO, 1975), with additional notes by G. Hughes; K. Donker van Heel, *The Legal Manual of Hermopolis [P. Mattha], Text and Translation* (Uitgaven vanwege de Stichting "Het Leids Papyrologisch Instituut" 11, Leiden, 1990).

20 W. Spiegelberg, *Aus einer ägyptischen Zivilprozeßordnung der Ptolemäerzeit (3.-2. vorchristl. Jahrh.) (Pap. demot. Berlin 13621)* (Abhandlungen der Bayerischen Akademie der Wissenschaften, Philosophisch-historische Abteilung, Neue Folge 1, München, 1929); K.

Sethe – W. Spiegelberg, *Zwei Beiträge zu dem Bruchstück einer ägyptischen Zivelprozeßordnung in demotischer Schrift* (Abhandlungen der Bayerischen Akademie der Wissenschaften, Philosophisch-historische Abteilung, Neue Folge 4, München, 1929); T. Mrsich, "Eine Zwischenbilanz zum 'zivilprozessualen' Abschnitt des demotischen Rechtsbuches 'S' (P. Berl. 13621 Rc. Col. II)," in D. Nörr – D. Simon (eds.), *Gedächtnisschrift für Wolfgang Kunkel* (Frankfurt am Main, 1984), pp. 205–282; and S.L. Lippert, "Die Sogenannte Zivilprozessordnung. Weitere Fragmente der Ägyptischen Gesetzessammlung," *JJP* 33 (2003), pp. 91–135.

21 S.L. Lippert, *Ein demotisches juristisches Lehrbuch. Untersuchungen zu P. Berlin 23757 rto* (ÄA 66. Wiesbaden, Harrassowitz, 2004).

22 E. Bresciani, "Frammenti da un 'prontuario legale' demotico da Tebtuni nell' istituto papirologico G. Vitelli di Firenze," *EVO* 4 (1981), pp. 201–215; and M. Chauveau, "P. Carlsberg 301: Le manuel juridique de Tebtynis," in P.J. Frandsen (ed.), *The Carlsberg Papyri 1. Demotic Texts from the Collection* (CNI Publications 15, Copenhagen, 1991), pp. 103–127.

23 S.L. Lippert, "Fragmente demotischer juristischer Bücher (pBerlin 23890 a-b, d-g rto und pCarlsberg 628)," in F. Hoffmann – H.-J. Thissen (eds.), *Res severa verum gaudium, Feschrift für Karl-Theodor Zauzich zum 65. Geburtstag am 8. Juni 2004* (Studa Demotica 6. Leuven, Peeters, 2004), pp. 389–405 (Texte Nr. 41–42).

24 S.L. Lippert, "Die sogennante Zivilprozessordnung, weitere fragmente der ägyptischen Gesetzessammlung," *JJP* 33 (2003), pp. 134–135; S.L. Lippert, *Ein demotisches juristisches Lehrbuch. Untersuchungen zu P. Berlin 23757 rto* (ÄA 66. Wiesbaden, Harrassowitz, 2004), pp. 155–157.

25 P.W. Pestman, "Réflexions à propos du soi-disant Code de Hermoupolis," *JESHO* 26 (1983), pp. 17–18.

26 Papyrus BM 10591 recto, col. I, lines 17–20, and col. II, lines 20–23 (incorrectly cited by Chratianch); and col. X, lines 7–9 (correctly cited by the judges), see H. Thompson, *A Family Archive from Siut, from Papyri in the British Museum, Including an Account of a Trial before the Laocritae in the Year B.C. 170* (Oxford: University Press, 1934), pp. 3, 4, 11, 13, 16, 32.

27 G. Mattha, *The Demotic Legal Code of Hermopolis West* (BdÉ 45. Cairo, IFAO, 1975), with additional notes by G. Hughes; K. Donker van Heel, *The Legal Manual of Hermopolis [P. Mattha], Text and Translation* (Uitgaven vanwege de Stichting "Het Leids Papyrologisch Instituut" 11, Leiden, 1990).

28 W. Spiegelberg, *Aus einer ägyptischen Zivilprozeßordnung der Ptolemäerzeit (3.-2. vorchristl. Jahrh.) (Pap. demot. Berlin 13621)* (Abhandlungen der Bayerischen Akademie der Wissenschaften, Philosophisch-historische Abteilung, Neue Folge 1, München, 1929); K. Sethe – W. Spiegelberg, *Zwei Beiträge zu dem Bruchstück einer ägyptischen Zivelprozeßordnung in demotischer Schrift* (Abhandlungen der Bayerischen Akademie der Wissenschaften, Philosophisch-historische Abteilung, Neue Folge 4, München, 1929); T. Mrsich, "Eine Zwischenbilanz zum 'zivilprozessualen' Abschnitt des demotischen Rechtsbuches 'S' (P. Berl. 13621 Rc. Col. II)," in D. Nörr – D. Simon (eds.), *Gedächtnisschrift für Wolfgang Kunkel* (Frankfurt am Main, 1984), pp. 205–282; and S.L. Lippert, "Die Sogenannte Zivilprozessordnung. Weitere Fragmente der Ägyptischen Gesetzessammlung," *JJP* 33 (2003), pp. 91–135.

29 H.J. Wolff, *Das Justizwesen der Ptolemäer* (Münchener Beiträge zur Papyrusforschung und antiken Rechtsgeschichte 44. München: C.H. Beck'sche Verlagsbuchhandlung, 1962), pp. 64–89, 96–112.

30 H.J. Wolff, *Das Justizwesen der Ptolemäer* (Münchener Beiträge zur Papyrusforschung und antiken Rechtsgeschichte 44. München: C.H. Beck'sche Verlagsbuchhandlung, 1962), pp. 37–56, 96–112.

31 B.P. Muhs, "Membership in Private Associations in Ptolemaic Tebtunis," *JESHO* 44, Part 1 (February 2001), pp. 1–21.

32 F. de Cenival, *Les associations religieuses en Égypte, d'après les documents démotiques* (BdÉ 46. Cairo: IFAO, 1972), pp. 73–81.

33 A. Monson, "The Ethics and Economics of Ptolemaic Religious Associations," *Ancient Society* 36 (2006), pp. 223–232.

34 A. Monson, "Religious Associations and Temples in Ptolemaic Tebtunis," Volume 2, pp. 769–779 in J. Frösén – T. Purola – E. Salmenkivi (eds.), *Proceedings of the 24th International Congress of Papyrology, Helsinki, 1st-7th of August 2004* (Commentationes Humanarum Litterarum 122: 1–2. Helsinki: Societas Scientiarum Fennica, 2007); A. Monson, "Private Associations in the

Ptolemaic Fayyum: The Evidence of Demotic Accounts," in M. Capasso – P. Davoli (eds.), *New Archaeological and Papyrological Researches on the Fayyum* (Papyrologica Lupiensia 14. Lecce: Congedo Editore, 2007), pp. 179–196.

35 A. Monson, "The Ethics and Economics of Ptolemaic Religious Associations," *Ancient Society* 36 (2006), pp. 233–238.

36 S. Von Reden, *Money in Ptolemaic Egypt, from the Macedonian Conquest to the End of the Third Century BC* (Cambridge: University Press, 2007), pp. 228–231.

37 M. Piatowska, *La Skepê dans l'Égypte ptolémaïque* (Archiwum filologiczne 32. Warsaw: 1975), pp. 9–19.

38 M. Piatowska, *La Skepê dans l'Égypte ptolémaïque* (Archiwum filologiczne 32. Warsaw: 1975), pp. 41–54.

39 M. Piatowska, *La Skepê dans l'Égypte ptolémaïque* (Archiwum filologiczne 32. Warsaw: 1975), pp. 55–62.

40 M. Piatowska, *La Skepê dans l'Égypte ptolémaïque* (Archiwum filologiczne 32. Warsaw: 1975), pp. 52–54; S. Von Reden, *Money in Ptolemaic Egypt, from the Macedonian Conquest to the End of the Third Century BC* (Cambridge: University Press, 2007), pp. 229–231.

41 C. Armoni, *Studien zur Verwaltung des Ptolemäischen Ägypten: Das Amt de Basilikos Grammeteus* (Papyrologica Coloniensia 36. Paderborn: Verlag Ferdinand Schöningh, 2012), pp. 172–228.

42 J. Yoyotte, "Le nom égyptien du «ministre de l'économie» – de Saïs à Meroe," *Comptes rendus, Académie des inscriptions & belles-lettres (CRAIBL), 1989* (Paris, Diffusion de Boccard, 1989), pp. 73–90.

43 P.W. Pestman, "A Family of Egyptian Scribes," *BASP* 5, 2–3 (1968), p. 61; J. Quaegebeur, "À la recherche du haut clergé Thébaine à l'époque Gréco-Romaine," in S.P. Vleeming (ed.), *Hundred-Gated Thebes. Acts of a Colloquium on Thebes and the Theban Area in the Graeco-Roman Period* (PLB 27. Leiden: Brill, 1995), pp. 152–155.

44 B. Muhs, *Tax Receipts, Taxpayers, and Taxes in Early Ptolemaic Thebes* (OIP 126. Chicago: Oriental Institute, 2005), pp. 14–19.

45 D.J. Crawford, *Kerkeosiris, An Egyptian Village in the Ptolemaic Period* (Cambridge: University Press, 1971), pp. 5–38; A.M.F.W. Verhoogt, *Menches, Komogrammateus of Kerkeosiris. The Doings and Dealings of a Village Scribe in the Late Ptolemaic Period (120–110 B.C.)* (PLB 29. Leiden: Brill, 1998), pp. 131–148; Andrew Monson, *Agriculture and Taxation in Early Ptolemaic Egypt, Demotic Land Surveys and Accounts (P. Agri)*, (Papyrologische Texte und Abhandlungen 46. Bonn: Dr. Rudolf Habelt, 2012), pp. 1–36.

46 K. Vandorpe, "The Ptolemaic Epigraphe or Harvest Tax (*shemu*)," *AfP* 46/2 (2000), pp. 169–232.

47 K. Vandorpe, "Agriculture, Temples and Tax Law in Ptolemaic Egypt," *CRIPEL* 25 (2007), pp. 165–168.

48 W. Clarysse – K. Vandorpe, "The Ptolemaic Apomoira," in H. Melaerts (ed.), *Le culte du souverain dans l' Égypte ptolémaïque au IIIe siècle avant notre ère. Actes du colloque international, Bruxelles 10 mai 1995* (Studia Hellenistica 34. Leuven: Peeters, 1998), pp. 5–42; K. Vandorpe, "Agriculture, Temples and Tax Law in Ptolemaic Egypt," *CRIPEL* 25 (2007), pp. 165–166.

49 R. Bagnall – P.S. Derow, *The Hellenistic Period: Historical Sources in Translation*, 2nd ed. (Oxford: Blackwell, 2004), pp. 181–195 (Text 114. "Revenue Laws" of Ptolemy Philadelphos).

50 K. Vandorpe, "Agriculture, Temples and Tax Law in Ptolemaic Egypt," *CRIPEL* 25 (2007), pp. 168–169.

51 R.S. Simpson, *Demotic Grammar in the Ptolemaic Sacerdotal Decrees* (Oxford: Griffith Institute, 1996), pp. 260–261.

52 A. Bernand, *De Thèbes à Syène* (Paris, 1989), pp. 190–260 (Text 244); G. Dietze, "Der Streit um die Insel Pso. Bemerkungen zu einem epigraphischen Dossier des Khnumtempels von Elephantine (Th. Sy. 244)," *Ancient Society* 26 (1995), pp. 157–184.

53 Most but not all have been published or republished in W. Clarysse – D.J. Thompson, *Counting the People in Hellenistic Egypt, Volume 1: Population Registers (P. Count)*, (Cambridge Classical Studies. Cambridge: University Press, 2006).

54 W. Clarysse – D.J. Thompson, *Counting the People in Hellenistic Egypt, Volume 2: Historical Studies* (Cambridge Classical Studies. Cambridge: University Press, 2006), pp. 10–35 (2. The census).

55 W. Clarysse – D.J. Thompson, *Counting the People in Hellenistic Egypt, Volume 2: Historical Studies* (Cambridge Classical Studies. Cambridge: University Press, 2006), pp. 206–225 (6. Counting the animals).

56 B.P. Muhs, *Tax Receipts, Taxpayers, and Taxes in Early Ptolemaic Thebes* (OIP 126. Chicago: Oriental Institute, 2005), pp. 16–17; W. Clarysse – D.J. Thompson, *Counting the People in Hellenistic Egypt, Volume 2: Historical Studies* (Cambridge Classical Studies. Cambridge: University Press, 2006), pp. 21–30; A. Monson, *Agriculture and Taxation in Early Ptolemaic Egypt, Demotic Land Surveys and Accounts (P. Agri)*, (Papyrologische Texte und Abhandlungen 46. Bonn: Dr. Rudolf Habelt, 2012), p. 2.

57 W. Clarysse – D.J. Thompson, *Counting the People in Hellenistic Egypt, Volume 2: Historical Studies* (Cambridge Classical Studies. Cambridge: University Press, 2006), pp. 10–35 (2. The census).

58 B.P. Muhs, *Tax Receipts, Taxpayers, and Taxes in Early Ptolemaic Thebes* (OIP 126. Chicago: Oriental Institute, 2005), p. 36 and pp. 57–60; B.P. Muhs, *Receipts, Scribes and Collectors in Early Ptolemaic Thebes (O. Taxes 2)* (Studia Demotica 8. Leuven: Peeters, 2011), pp. 127–136.

59 W. Clarysse – D.J. Thompson, *Counting the People in Hellenistic Egypt, Volume 2: Historical Studies* (Cambridge Classical Studies. Cambridge: University Press, 2006), pp. 73–74.

60 B.P. Muhs, *Tax Receipts, Taxpayers, and Taxes in Early Ptolemaic Thebes* (OIP 126. Chicago: Oriental Institute, 2005), pp. 30–36; B.P. Muhs, *Receipts, Scribes and Collectors in Early Ptolemaic Thebes (O. Taxes 2)* (Studia Demotica 8. Leuven: Peeters, 2011), pp. 7–17.

61 B.P. Muhs, *Tax Receipts, Taxpayers, and Taxes in Early Ptolemaic Thebes* (OIP 126. Chicago: Oriental Institute, 2005), pp. 37–39; B.P. Muhs, *Receipts, Scribes and Collectors in Early Ptolemaic Thebes (O. Taxes 2)* (Studia Demotica 8. Leuven: Peeters, 2011), pp. 17–19.

62 B.P. Muhs, *Tax Receipts, Taxpayers, and Taxes in Early Ptolemaic Thebes* (OIP 126. Chicago: Oriental Institute, 2005), pp. 41–51; W. Clarysse – D.J. Thompson, *Counting the People in Hellenistic Egypt, Volume 2: Historical Studies* (Cambridge Classical Studies. Cambridge: University Press, 2006), pp. 36–89 (3. The salt-tax and other taxes); B.P. Muhs, *Receipts, Scribes and Collectors in Early Ptolemaic Thebes (O. Taxes 2)* (Studia Demotica 8. Leuven: Peeters, 2011), pp. 21–86.

63 B.P. Muhs, *Tax Receipts, Taxpayers, and Taxes in Early Ptolemaic Thebes* (OIP 126. Chicago: Oriental Institute, 2005), pp. 55–56; B.P. Muhs, *Receipts, Scribes and Collectors in Early Ptolemaic Thebes (O. Taxes 2)* (Studia Demotica 8. Leuven: Peeters, 2011), pp. 91–105.

64 B.P. Muhs, *Tax Receipts, Taxpayers, and Taxes in Early Ptolemaic Thebes* (OIP 126. Chicago: Oriental Institute, 2005), pp. 51–54; B.P. Muhs, *Receipts, Scribes and Collectors in Early Ptolemaic Thebes (O. Taxes 2)* (Studia Demotica 8. Leuven: Peeters, 2011), pp. 86–90.

65 W. Clarysse – D.J. Thompson, *Counting the People in Hellenistic Egypt, Volume 2: Historical Studies* (Cambridge Classical Studies. Cambridge: University Press, 2006), pp. 350–356.

66 F.A.J. Hoogendijk, "The Practice of Taxation in Three Late Ptolemaic Papyri," in T. Gagos (ed.), *Proceedings of the Twenty-Fifth International Congress of Papyrology* (Ann Arbor: 2010), pp. 313–321; A. Monson, "Late Ptolemaic Capitation Taxes and the Poll Tax in Roman Egypt," *BASP* 51 (2014), pp. 130–136.

67 A. Monson, "Late Ptolemaic Capitation Taxes and the Poll Tax in Roman Egypt," *BASP* 51 (2014), pp. 143–152.

68 A. Monson, "Receipts for Sitonion, Syntaxis, and Epistatikon from Karanis: Evidence for Fiscal Reform in Augustan Egypt?," *ZPE* 191 (2014), pp. 207–230; A. Monson, "Late Ptolemaic Capitation Taxes and the Poll Tax in Roman Egypt," *BASP* 51 (2014), pp. 137–143.

69 S.P. Vleeming, "The Tithe of the Scribes (and) Representatives," in J.H. Johnson (ed.), *Life in a Multi-Cultural Society, Egypt from Cambyses to Constantine and Beyond* (SAOC 51. Chicago: Oriental Institute, 1992), pp. 343–350; M. Depauw, *The Archive of Teos and Thabis from Early Ptolemaic Thebes, P. Brux. dem. inv. E. 8252–8256* (Monographies Reine Élisabeth 8. Turnhout BE: Brepols, 2000), pp. 56–63; B.P. Muhs, *Tax Receipts, Taxpayers, and Taxes in Early Ptolemaic Thebes* (OIP 126. Chicago: Oriental Institute, 2005), pp. 66–71.

70 P. Hibeh gr. I 29 = Chrest. Wilck 259, see U. Wilcken, *Grundzüge und Chrestomathie der Papyruskunde 1: Historischer Teil 2* (Leipzig-Berlin, 1912), pp. 306–308; B.P. Muhs, *Tax Receipts, Taxpayers, and Taxes in Early Ptolemaic Thebes* (OIP 126. Chicago: Oriental Institute, 2005), pp. 19–21.

71 B.P. Muhs, *Tax Receipts, Taxpayers, and Taxes in Early Ptolemaic Thebes* (OIP 126. Chicago: Oriental Institute, 2005), pp. 71–72.

72 Brian Muhs, *Tax Receipts, Taxpayers and Taxes in Early Ptolemaic Thebes* (OIP 126, Chicago: Oriental Institute, 2005), pp. 88–95.

73 Brian Muhs, *Tax Receipts, Taxpayers and Taxes in Early Ptolemaic Thebes* (OIP 126, Chicago: Oriental Institute, 2005), pp. 95–98.

74 M. Depauw, *The Archive of Teos and Thabis from Early Ptolemaic Thebes, P. Brux. dem. inv. E. 8252–8256* (Monographies Reine Élisabeth 8. Turnhout BE: Brepols, 2000), pp. 65–70.

75 B.P. Muhs, "Demotic Ostraca from Ptolemaic Edfu and the Ptolemaic Tax System," in K. Vandorpe – W. Clarysse (eds.), *Edfu, an Egyptian Provincial Capital in the Ptolemaic Period, Brussels, 3 September 2001* (Brussels: Koninklijke Vlaamse Academie van Belgie voor Wetenschappen en Kunsten, 2003), pp. 102–105.

76 M. Depauw, *The Archive of Teos and Thabis from Early Ptolemaic Thebes, P. Brux. dem. inv. E. 8252–8256* (Monographies Reine Élisabeth 8. Turnhout BE: Brepols, 2000), pp. 70–73.

77 B.P. Muhs, "Demotic Ostraca from Ptolemaic Edfu and the Ptolemaic Tax System," in K. Vandorpe – W. Clarysse (eds.), *Edfu, an Egyptian Provincial Capital in the Ptolemaic Period, Brussels, 3 September 2001* (Brussels: Koninklijke Vlaamse Academie van Belgie voor Wetenschappen en Kunsten, 2003), pp. 82–91.

78 B.P. Grenfell – A.S. Hunt – J.G. Smyly, *The Tebtunis Papyri, Part I* (University of California Publications, Graeco-Roman Archaeology 1. London: Henry Frowde, 1902), pp. 17–58 (Text 5); R. Bagnall – P. Derow, *The Hellenistic Period: Historical Sources in Translation*, 2nd ed. (Oxford: Blackwell, 2004), pp. 95–100 (Text 54. Decree of Amnesty and Regulation).

79 C.C. Edgar, *Zenon Papyri I* (Catalogue général des antiquités égyptiennes du Musée du Caire 79, nos. 59001–59139. Cairo: IFAO, 1925), pp. 21–27.

80 C.C. Edgar, *Zenon Papyri I* (Catalogue général des antiquités égyptiennes du Musée du Caire 79, nos. 59001–59139. Cairo: IFAO, 1925), pp. 27–30; W. Clarysse – C. Galazzi – N. Kruit, "Three Joins from the Zenon Archive," *Ancient Society* 30 (2000), pp. 15–27 (P.Cair.Zen. 59014).

81 Alain Bresson, "Wine, Oil and Delicacies at the Pelousion Customs," in L.-M. Günther – V. Grieb (eds.), *Das imperiale Rom und der hellenistische Osten. Festschrift für Jürgen Deininger zum 75. Geburtstag* (Wiesbaden: Steiner, 2012), pp. 69–70.

82 R. Bagnall – P. Derow, *The Hellenistic Period: Historical Sources in Translation*, 2nd ed. (Oxford: Blackwell, 2004), pp. 181–195 (Text 114. "Revenue Laws" of Ptolemy Philadelphos).

83 P. J. Sijpesteijn, *Customs Duties in Graeco-Roman Egypt* (Studia Amstelodamensia ad epigraphicam, ius antiquum et papyrologicam pertinentia 17. Zutphen, 1987), pp. 1–4; D.J. Thompson, *Memphis under the Ptolemies* (Princeton: University Press, 1988), pp. 61–65.

84 M. Depauw, *A Companion to Demotic Studies* (Papyrologica Bruxellensia 28. Bruxelles, 1997), pp. 123–124; but see M. Depauw, *The Demotic Letter* (Demotische Studien 14. Sommerhausen, 2006), pp. 317–321.

85 M. Depauw, *A Companion to Demotic Studies* (Papyrologica Bruxellensia 28. Bruxelles, 1997), pp. 124–125; but see M. Depauw, *The Demotic Letter* (Demotische Studien 14. Sommerhausen, 2006), pp. 317–321.

86 P.W. Pestman, *Textes et études de papyrologie grecque, démotique et copte* (PLB 23. Leiden: Brill, 1985), pp. 174–175 note a; and P.W. Pestman, *The Archive of the Theban Choachytes (Second Century B.C.)* (Studia Demotica 2. Leuven: Peeters, 1993), pp. 116–117 note c; but see M. Depauw, *A Companion to Demotic Studies* (Papyrologica Bruxellensia 28. Bruxelles, 1997), p. 125.

87 U. Yiftach-Firanko, "Who Killed the Double Document in Ptolemaic Egypt?," *AfP* 54, 2 (2008), pp. 203–218.

88 P.W. Pestman, "Agoranomoi et actes agoranomiques: Krokodilopolis et Pathyris, 145–88 av. J.-C.," in P.W. Pestman (ed.), *Textes et études de papyrologie grecque, démotique et copte* (PLB 23. Leiden: Brill, 1985), pp. 33–44; U. Yiftach-Firanko, "Who Killed the Double Document in Ptolemaic Egypt?," *AfP* 54, 2 (2008), pp. 212–214.

89 S.P. Vleeming, "The Tithe of the Scribes (and) Representatives," in J.H. Johnson (ed.), *Life in a Multi-Cultural Society, Egypt from Cambyses to Constantine and Beyond* (SAOC 51. Chicago: Oriental Institute, 1992), pp. 343–350; M. Depauw, *The Archive of Teos and Thabis from Early Ptolemaic Thebes, P. Brux. dem. inv. E. 8252–8256* (Monographies Reine Élisabeth 8. Turnhout BE: Brepols, 2000), pp. 56–63; B.P. Muhs, *Tax Receipts, Taxpayers, and Taxes in Early Ptolemaic Thebes* (OIP 126. Chicago: Oriental Institute, 2005), pp. 66–70.

90 P. Hibeh gr. I 29 = Chrest. Wilck 259, see U. Wilcken, *Grundzüge und Chrestomathie der Papyruskunde 1: Historischer Teil 2* (Leipzig-Berlin, 1912), pp. 306–308; B.P. Muhs, *Tax Receipts, Taxpayers, and Taxes in Early Ptolemaic Thebes* (OIP 126. Chicago: Oriental Institute, 2005), p. 21.

91 B. Kramer, *Griechische Texte 13. Das Vertragsregister von Theogonis (P. Vindob. G 40618)* (Corpus Papyrorum Ranieri 18.Vienna, 1991), pp. 16–34.

92 N.J. Reich, "The Greek Deposit-Notes of the Record-Office on the Demotic Contracts of the Papyrus-Archive in the University Museum," *Mizraim* 9 (1938), pp. 19–32; B.P. Muhs, *Tax Receipts, Taxpayers, and Taxes in Early Ptolemaic Thebes* (OIP 126. Chicago: Oriental Institute, 2005), pp. 19–20.

93 Fr. de Cenival, "Répetoire journalier d'un bureau de notaire de l'époque ptolémaïque en démotique (P. dém. Lille 120)," *Enchoria* 15 (1987), pp. 1–9.

94 B. Kramer, *Griechische Texte 13. Das Vertragsregister von Theogonis (P. Vindob. G 40618)* (Corpus Papyrorum Ranieri 18.Vienna, 1991), pp. 26–27.

95 P.W. Pestman, "Registration of Demotic Contracts in Egypt, P. Par. 65; 2nd Cent. B.C." in J.A Ankum – J.E. Spruit – F.B.J. Wubbe (eds.), *Satura Roberto Feenstra, sexagesimum quintum annum aetatis complenti ab alumnis collegis amicis oblata* (Fribourg, 1985), pp. 17–25; U. Yiftach-Firanko, "Who Killed the Double Document in Ptolemaic Egypt?," *AfP* 54, 2 (2008), p. 214.

96 B.P. Muhs, "The Berkeley Tebtunis Grapheion Archive," in G. Widmer – D. Devauchelle (eds.), *Actes du IXe Congrès International des Études Démotiques, Paris, 31 août – 3 septembre 2005* (BdÉ 147. Cairo: IFAO, 2009), pp. 243–251; B.P. Muhs, "A Late Ptolemaic Grapheion Archive in Berkeley," in T. Gagos (ed.), *Proceedings of the 25th International Congress of Papyrology, Ann Arbor, July 29 – August 4, 2007* (ASP Special Edition. Ann Arbor: Scholarly Publishing Office, the University of Michigan Library, 2010), pp. 581–588.

97 U. Yiftach-Firanko, "Who Killed the Double Document in Ptolemaic Egypt?," *AfP* 54, 2 (2008), pp. 214–216.

98 K. Vandorpe, "A Greek Register from Pathyris' Notarial Office: Loans and Sales from the Pathyrite and Latopolite Nomes," *ZPE* 150 (2004), pp. 161–186.

99 B.P. Muhs, *Tax Receipts, Taxpayers, and Taxes in Early Ptolemaic Thebes* (OIP 126. Chicago, 2005), pp. 23–27.

100 J. Černý, "Prices and Wages in Egypt in the Ramesside Period," *Cahiers d' histoire mondiale* 1 (1954), pp. 904–906.

101 B.P. Muhs, *Taxes, Taxpayers, and Tax Receipts in Early Ptolemaic Thebes. Demotic and Greek Ostraca from the Oriental Institute Museum, Chicago* (OIP 126. Chicago: Oriental Institute, 2005), p. 11.

102 C.H. Kraay – O. Mørkholm – M. Thompson, *An Inventory of Greek Coin Hoards* (New York, 1973), pp. 234–236 (nos. 1664–1679).

103 C.H. Kraay – O. Mørkholm – M. Thompson, *An Inventory of Greek Coin Hoards* (New York, 1973), pp. 236–239 (nos. 1680–1685, and 1687–1700). To these, add the hoard of 456 bronze coins from Saqqara described by M. Jessop Price, "The Coins," in D.G. Jeffreys – H.S. Smith (eds.), *The Anubieion at Saqqara 1: The Settlement and the Temple Precinct* (EES Excavation Memoir 54, London, 1988), pp. 66–70; and the hoard of 679 bronze coins of Ptolemy II and III from Elephantine described by H.-C. Noeske, "Prämonetäre Wertmesser und Münzfunde aus Elephantine," *MDAIK* 49 (1993), pp. 206–208.

104 C.H. Kraay – O. Mørkholm – M. Thompson, *An Inventory of Greek Coin Hoards* (New York, 1973), pp. 239–240 (nos. 1702–1703, and 1705–1709).

105 C.H. Kraay – O. Mørkholm – M. Thompson, *An Inventory of Greek Coin Hoards* (New York, 1973), pp. 240–242 (nos. 1710–1725).

106 M.I. Finley, *The Ancient Economy*, 2nd updated ed. (Berkeley: University of California Press, 1999), pp. 141–144.

107 S. Von Reden, *Money in Ptolemaic Egypt, from the Macedonian Conquest to the End of the Third Century BC* (Cambridge: University Press, 2007), pp. 151–152.

108 S. Von Reden, *Money in Ptolemaic Egypt, from the Macedonian Conquest to the End of the Third Century BC* (Cambridge: University Press, 2007), pp. 153–155.

109 P.W. Pestman, "Loans Bearing No Interest?," *JJP* 16–17 (1971), pp. 8–9.

110 P. Berlin 3048 verso, see G. Möller, "Ein ägyptischer Schuldschein der zweiundzwanzigsten Dynastie," *Sitzungsberichte der preussischen Akademie der Wissenschaften, philosophisch-historischen Klasse* 15 (1921), pp. 298–304.

111 P. Loeb 48 (P. Hou 12), see S.P. Vleeming, *The Gooseherds of Hou* (Pap. Hou), (Studia Demotica 3. Leuven: Peeters, 1991), pp. 156–177 (Text 12).

112 S. Von Reden, *Money in Ptolemaic Egypt, from the Macedonian Conquest to the End of the Third Century BC* (Cambridge: University Press, 2007), pp. 155–174.

113 S. Von Reden, *Money in Ptolemaic Egypt, from the Macedonian Conquest to the End of the Third Century BC* (Cambridge: University Press, 2007), pp. 181–198.

114 S. Von Reden, *Money in Ptolemaic Egypt, from the Macedonian Conquest to the End of the Third Century BC* (Cambridge: University Press, 2007), pp. 198–203.

115 S. Von Reden, *Money in Ptolemaic Egypt, from the Macedonian Conquest to the End of the Third Century BC* (Cambridge: University Press, 2007), pp. 205–226.

116 S. Von Reden, *Money in Ptolemaic Egypt, from the Macedonian Conquest to the End of the Third Century BC* (Cambridge: University Press, 2007), pp. 227–252.

117 S. Von Reden, *Money in Ptolemaic Egypt, from the Macedonian Conquest to the End of the Third Century BC* (Cambridge: University Press, 2007), pp. 257–279.

118 S. Von Reden, *Money in Ptolemaic Egypt, from the Macedonian Conquest to the End of the Third Century BC* (Cambridge: University Press, 2007), pp. 280–295.

119 J.G. Manning, *The Last Pharaohs, Egypt under the Ptolemies, 305–30 BC* (Princeton: University Press, 2010), pp. 120–130.

120 B.P. Muhs, *Receipts, Scribes, and Collectors in Early Ptolemaic Thebes* (Studia Demotica 8. Leuven: Peeters, 2011), pp. 237, 264.

121 R. Duttenhöfer, "Die Funktion und Stellung des *ergasterion* in der Getreideverwaltung der Ptolemäerzeit," *ZPE* 98 (1993), pp. 253–262.

122 T. Reekmans – E. Van 't Dack, "A Bodleian Archive on Corn Transport," *CdÉ* 27 (1952), pp. 149–195; K. Vandorpe, "Paying Taxes to the Thesauroi of the Pathyrites in a Century of Rebellion (186–88 BC)," in L. Mooren (ed.) *Politics, Administration and Society in the Hellenistic and Roman world. Proceedings of the International Colloquium, Bertinoro 19–24 July 1997* (Studia Hellenistica 36 Leuven: Peeters, 2000), pp. 406–408.

123 Z.M. Packman, *The Taxes in Grain in Ptolemaic Egypt: Granary Receipts from Diospolis Magna, 164–88 BC* (ASP 4. New Haven-Toronto, 1968); K. Vandorpe, "Paying Taxes to the Thesauroi of the Pathyrites in a Century of Rebellion (186–88 BC)," in L. Mooren (ed.) *Politics, Administration and Society in the Hellenistic and Roman world. Proceedings of the International Colloquium, Bertinoro 19–24 July 1997* (Studia Hellenistica 36 Leuven: Peeters, 2000), pp. 405–436; K. Vandorpe, "The Epigraphe or Harvest Tax in the Apollonopolite Nome," in K. Vandorpe – W. Clarysse (eds.), *Edfu, An Egyptian Provincial Capital in the Ptolemaic Period. Brussels, 3 September 2001* (Brussels: Koninklijke Vlaamse Academie van België voor Wetenschappen en Kunsten, 2003), pp. 107–122.

124 C. Armoni, *Studien zur Verwaltung des Ptolemäischen Ägypten: Das Amt de Basilikos Grammeteus* (Papyrologica Coloniensia 36. Paderborn:Verlag Ferdinand Schöningh, 2012), pp. 33–102.

125 P.A. Verdult, P. *Erasmianae II. Parts of the Archive of an Arsinoite Sitologos from the Middle of the Second Century BC* (Studia Amstelodamensia 32. Amsterdam: Gieben, 1991), pp. 10–12.

126 T. Reekmans – E. Van 't Dack, "A Bodleian Archive on Corn Transport," *CdE* 27 (1952), pp. 149–195.

127 B.P. Muhs, *Tax Receipts, Taxpayers, and Taxes in Early Ptolemaic Thebes* (OIP 126. Chicago: Oriental Institute, 2005), p. 10; C. Fischer-Bovet, *Army and Society in Ptolemaic Egypt* (Cambridge: University Press, 2014), pp. 67–68.

128 Jerome, *Commentariorum in Danielem*, 11, 5.

129 Aurelius Victor, *Epitome de Caesaribus* I, 6.

130 Justinian, *Edict* XIII, 8.

131 B.P. Muhs, *Tax Receipts, Taxpayers, and Taxes in Early Ptolemaic Thebes* (OIP 126. Chicago: Oriental Institute, 2005), pp. 6–10.

132 S. von Reden, *Money in Ptolemaic Egypt, from the Macedonian Conquest to the End of the Third Century BC* (Cambridge: University Press, 2007), pp. 268–273.

133 S. von Reden, *Money in Ptolemaic Egypt, from the Macedonian Conquest to the End of the Third Century BC* (Cambridge: University Press, 2007), pp. 280–295.

134 C. Préaux, "De la Grèce classique à l'Égypte hellénistique: la banque-témoin," *CdÉ* 33 (1958), pp. 243–255; J. Bingen, *Le papyrus Revenue Laws: tradition grecque et adaptation hellénistique* (Rheinische-Westfälische Akademie der Wissenschaften, Vorträge G 231. Opladen: 1978); translated in J. Bingen, *Hellenistic Egypt: Monarchy, Society, Economy, Culture* (Berkeley-Los Angeles: University of California Press, 2007), pp. 157–188: "Chapter 13. The Revenue Laws Papyrus: Greek tradition and Hellenistic adaptation," especially pp. 183–184.

135 R. Bogaert, "Les modèles des banques ptolémaiques," in *Egypt and the Hellenistic World, Proceedings of the International Colloquium, Leuven, 24–26 May 1982* (Studia Hellenistica 27. Leuven, 1983), pp. 13–14; reprinted in R. Bogaert, *Trapezitica Aegyptica* (Papyrologica Florentina 25. Florence, 1994), pp. 33–34.

136 F. Preisigke, *Girowesen im griechischen Ägypten* (Strassburg, 1910).

137 R. Bogaert, "Liste géographique des banques et des banquiers de l'Égypte ptolémaïque," *ZPE* 120 (1998), pp. 166–168; S. von Reden, *Money in Ptolemaic Egypt, from the Macedonian Conquest to the End of the Third Century BC* (Cambridge: University Press, 2007), pp. 257–268; K. Geens, "Financial Archives of Graeco-Roman Egypt," in K. Verboven – K. Vandorpe – V. Chankowski (eds.), *Pistoi dia tèn technèn. Bankers, Loans and Archives in the Ancient World. Studies in Honour of Raymond Bogaert* (Studia Hellenistica 44. Leuven: Peeters, 2008), pp. 133–134, 138–140.

138 R. Bogaert, "Liste géographique des banques et des banquiers de l'Égypte ptolémaïque," *ZPE* 120 (1998), pp. 169–170.

139 B.P. Muhs, *Receipts, Scribes, and Collectors in Early Ptolemaic Thebes* (Studia Demotica 8. Leuven: Peeters, 2011), pp. 213–214, 252–253.

140 B.P. Muhs, *Receipts, Scribes, and Collectors in Early Ptolemaic Thebes* (Studia Demotica 8. Leuven: Peeters, 2011), pp. 254–255.

141 B.P. Muhs, *Receipts, Scribes, and Collectors in Early Ptolemaic Thebes* (Studia Demotica 8. Leuven: Peeters, 2011), pp. 219–220, 232–233, 258.

142 S. von Reden, *Money in Ptolemaic Egypt, from the Macedonian Conquest to the End of the Third Century BC* (Cambridge: University Press, 2007), pp. 130–144, 219–226, 268–279.

143 K. Geens, "Financial Archives of Graeco-Roman Egypt," in K. Verboven – K. Vandorpe – V. Chankowski (eds.), *Pistoi dia tèn technèn. Bankers, Loans and Archives in the Ancient World. Studies in Honour of Raymond Bogaert* (Studia Hellenistica 44. Leuven: Peeters, 2008), pp. 144–145.

144 K. Geens, "Financial Archives of Graeco-Roman Egypt," in K. Verboven – K. Vandorpe – V. Chankowski (eds.), *Pistoi dia tèn technèn. Bankers, Loans and Archives in the Ancient World. Studies in Honour of Raymond Bogaert* (Studia Hellenistica 44. Leuven: Peeters, 2008), pp. 140–142, p. 146.

145 C. Armoni, *Studien zur Verwaltung des Ptolemäischen Ägypten: Das Amt de Basilikos Grammeteus* (Papyrologica Coloniensia 36. Paderborn: Verlag Ferdinand Schöningh, 2012), pp. 70–84.

146 K. Geens, "Financial Archives of Graeco-Roman Egypt," in K. Verboven – K. Vandorpe – V. Chankowski (eds.), *Pistoi dia tèn technèn. Bankers, Loans and Archives in the Ancient World. Studies in Honour of Raymond Bogaert* (Studia Hellenistica 44. Leuven: Peeters, 2008), pp. 144–145.

147 B.P. Muhs, *Tax Receipts, Taxpayers, and Taxes in Early Ptolemaic Thebes* (OIP 126. Chicago: Oriental Institute, 2005), p. 10; C. Fischer-Bovet, *Army and Society in Ptolemaic Egypt* (Cambridge: University Press, 2014), pp. 67–68.

148 Jerome, *Commentariorum in Danielem*, 11, 5.

149 Diodorus Siculus, 17.52.6.

150 Strabo, 17.1.13.

151 C. Fischer-Bovet, *Army and Society in Ptolemaic Egypt* (Cambridge: University Press, 2014), p. 68.

152 J. Bingen, *Le papyrus Revenue Laws: tradition grecque et adaptation hellénistique* (Rheinische-Westfälische Akademie der Wissenschaften, Vorträge G 231. Opladen: 1978); translated in J. Bingen, *Hellenistic Egypt: Monarchy, Society, Economy, Culture* (Berkeley-Los Angeles: University of California Press, 2007), pp. 157–188: "Chapter 13. The Revenue Laws Papyrus: Greek tradition and Hellenistic adaptation," especially pp. 183–184.

153 R. Bagnall – P. Derow, *The Hellenistic Period: Historical Sources in Translation*, 2nd ed. (Oxford: Blackwell, 2004), pp. 181–195 (Text 114. "Revenue Laws" of Ptolemy Philadelphos).

154 K. Sethe – J. Partsch, *Demotisch Urkunden zum ägyptischen Bürgschaftsrechte vorzüglich der Ptolemäerzeit* (ASAW 32. Leipzig, 1920), p. 607 n. 2 (P. Cairo dem. II 31219) and n. 3 (P. Cairo dem. II 31225); for the dates see B. Muhs – A. Grünewald – G. van den Berg, "The Papyri of Phanesis son of Nechthuris, Oil-Merchant of Tebtunis, and the Ptolemaic Cloth Monopoly," *Enchoria* 28 (2002 / 2003), pp. 64–65.

155 F. de Cenival, *Cautionnnements démotiques du début de l'Époque Ptolémaïque: P. dém. Lille 34 à 96* (Paris: Klincksieck, 1974), pp. 48–53.

156 B.P. Muhs, *Tax Receipts, Taxpayers and Taxes in Early Ptolemaic Thebes* (OIP 126, Chicago: Oriental Institute, 2005), pp. 73–78; B.P. Muhs, *Receipts, Scribes and Collectors in Early*

Ptolemaic Thebes (O. Taxes 2) (Studia Demotica 8. Leuven: Peeters, 2011), pp. 107–123.

157 B. Grenfell – A.S. Hunt, *The Hibeh Papyri, Part 1* (Egypt Exploration Fund, Graeco-Roman Memoirs 7. London: 1906), pp. 214–218.

158 A.S. Hunt – J. G. Smyly, *The Tebtunis Papyri, Volume III, Part I* (Egypt Exploration Fund, Graeco-Roman Memoirs 23. London: Humphrey Milford, 1933), pp. 66–102; R. Bagnall – P. Derow, *The Hellenistic Period: Historical Sources in Translation*, 2nd ed. (Oxford: Blackwell, 2004), pp. 165–169 (Text 103. Instructions of the *Dioketes* to an *Oikonomos*).

159 B. Muhs – A. Grünewald – G. van den Berg, "The Papyri of Phanesis son of Nechthuris, Oil-Merchant of Tebtunis, and the Ptolemaic Cloth Monopoly," *Enchoria* 28 (2002 / 2003), pp. 62–81; B.P. Muhs, "Nachtrag zu 'The Papyri of Phanesis son of Nechthuris, Oil-Merchant of Tebtunis, and the Ptolemaic Cloth Monopoly,'" *Enchoria* 28 (2002/2003)," *Enchoria* 29 (2004/2005), pp. 53–54 and pls. 3–5.

160 Athenaeus, *Deipnosophistai*, 5.203d; W.M. Murray, *The Age of Titans: The Rise and Fall of the Great Hellenistic Navies* (Oxford: University Press, 2011), pp. 188–189.

161 C. Fischer-Bovet, *Army and Society in Ptolemaic Egypt* (Cambridge: University Press, 2014), pp. 71–72.

162 C. Fischer-Bovet, *Army and Society in Ptolemaic Egypt* (Cambridge: University Press, 2014), pp. 75–78.

163 W.M. Murray, *The Age of Titans: The Rise and Fall of the Great Hellenistic Navies* (Oxford: University Press, 2011), pp. 188–200.

164 C. Fischer-Bovet, *Army and Society in Ptolemaic Egypt* (Cambridge: University Press, 2014), pp. 148–153.

165 C. Fischer-Bovet, *Army and Society in Ptolemaic Egypt* (Cambridge: University Press, 2014), pp. 261–279.

166 C. Fischer-Bovet, *Army and Society in Ptolemaic Egypt* (Cambridge: University Press, 2014), pp. 118–123.

167 C. Fischer-Bovet, *Army and Society in Ptolemaic Egypt* (Cambridge: University Press, 2014), pp. 212–221.

168 Polybius, *Histories*, 5.65; C. Fischer-Bovet, *Army and Society in Ptolemaic Egypt* (Cambridge: University Press, 2014), pp. 78–82.

169 C. Fischer-Bovet, *Army and Society in Ptolemaic Egypt* (Cambridge: University Press, 2014), pp. 73–75.

170 S. von Reden, *Money in Ptolemaic Egypt, from the Macedonian Conquest to the End of the Third Century BC* (Cambridge: University Press, 2007), pp. 130–144.

171 S. von Reden, *Money in Ptolemaic Egypt, from the Macedonian Conquest to the End of the Third Century BC* (Cambridge: University Press, 2007), pp. 219–226; C. Armoni, *Studien zur Verwaltung des Ptolemäischen Ägypten: Das Amt de Basilikos Grammeteus* (Papyrologica Coloniensia 36. Paderborn: Verlag Ferdinand Schöningh, 2012), pp. 20–23.

172 A.M.F.W. Verhoogt, *Regaling Officials in Ptolemaic Egypt: A Dramatic Reading of Official Accounts from the Menches Papers* (PLB 32. Leiden: Brill, 2005), pp. 5–68.

173 S. von Reden, *Money in Ptolemaic Egypt, from the Macedonian Conquest to the End of the Third Century BC* (Cambridge: University Press, 2007), pp. 217–219.

174 A.M.F.W. Verhoogt, *Menches, Komogrammateus of Kerkeosiris. The Doings and Dealings of a Village Scribe in the Late Ptolemaic Period (120–110 B.C.)* (PLB 29. Leiden: Brill, 1998), pp. 53–69; C. Armoni, *Studien zur Verwaltung des Ptolemäischen Ägypten: Das Amt de Basilikos Grammeteus* (Papyrologica Coloniensia 36. Paderborn: Verlag Ferdinand Schöningh, 2012), pp. 20–23.

175 M. Rostovtzeff, *A Large Estate in Egypt in the Third Century B.C.* (University of Wisconsin studies in the social sciences and history 6. Madison: University of Wisconsin, 1922; reprinted New York: Arno Press, 1979), pp. 42–55.

176 L. Criscuolo, "I miriaruri nell'Egitto tolemaico: note sull'amministrazione dell'Arsinoite nell III secolo a.c.," *Aegyptus* 57 (1977), pp. 109–122; L. Criscuolo, "Miriaruri: nuove riflessioni," *Aegyptus* 61 (1981), pp. 116–118.

177 M. Rostovtzeff, *A Large Estate in Egypt in the Third Century B.C.* (University of Wisconsin studies in the social sciences and history 6. Madison: University of Wisconsin, 1922; reprinted New York: Arno Press, 1979), pp. 56–125; S. Von Reden, *Money in Ptolemaic Egypt, from the Macedonian Conquest to the End of the Third Century BC* (Cambridge: University Press, 2007), pp. 144–150.

178 T. Reekmans, *La sitométrie dans les archives de Zénon* (Papyrologica Bruxellensia 3. Bruxelles: Fondation égyptologique Reine Elisabeth, 1966).

179 S. Héral, "Archives bilingues de nomarques dans les papyrus de Ghôran," in J.H. Johnson (ed.), *Life in a Multi-Cultural Society: Egypt from Cambyses to Constantine and Beyond* (SAOC 51. Chicago: Oriental Institute, 1992), p. 152.

180 R. Bagnall – P. Derow, *The Hellenistic Period: Historical Sources in Translation*, 2nd ed. (Oxford: Blackwell, 2004), pp. 181–195 (Text 114. "Revenue Laws" of Ptolemy Philadelphos).

181 U. Kaplony-Heckel, "Rund um die thebanischen Tempel (Demotische Ostraka zur Pfründen-Wirtschaft)," in F. Hoffmann – H.J. Thissen (eds.), *Res severa verum gaudium. Festschrift für Karl-Theodor Zauzich zum 65. Geburtstag am 8. Juni 2004* (Studia Demotica 6. Leuven: Peeters, 2004), pp. 283–337; B.P. Muhs, "Demotic Ostraca in Amsterdam," *Enchoria* 30 (2006/2007), pp. 63–67 (V. Transfers of Revenues).

182 R.S. Simpson, *Demotic Grammar in the Ptolemaic Sacerdotal Decrees* (Oxford: Griffith Institute, 1996), pp. 264–265.

183 R.S. Simpson, *Demotic Grammar in the Ptolemaic Sacerdotal Decrees* (Oxford: Griffith Institute, 1996), pp. 264–265.

184 W. Clarysse, "The Archive of the Praktor Milon," in K. Vandorpe – W. Clarysse (eds.), *Edfu, An Egyptian Provincial Capital in the Ptolemaic Period. Brussels, 3 September 2001* (Brussels: Koninklijke Vlaamse Academie van België voor Wetenschappen en Kunsten, 2003), pp. 17–27.

185 C.A.R. Andrews, *Catalogue of Demotic Papyri in the British Museum, IV. Ptolemaic Legal Texts from the Theban Area* (London: British Museum Publications, 1990), pp. 48–50.

186 B.P. Muhs, *Receipts, Scribes, and Collectors in Early Ptolemaic Thebes* (Studia Demotica 8. Leuven: Peeters, 2011), pp. 208–209.

187 N. Reich, *Papyri juristischen Inhalts in hieratischer und demotischer Schrift aus dem British Museum* (Denkschriften der Kaiserlichen Akademie der Wissenschaften in Wien, philosophisch–historische Klasse, 55,3. Wien: 1914), pp. 56–59.

188 C.A.R. Andrews, *Catalogue of Demotic Papyri in the British Museum, IV. Ptolemaic Legal Texts from the Theban Area* (London: British Museum Publications, 1990), pp. 46–47.

189 M. el-Amir, *A Family Archive from Thebes, Demotic Papyri in the Philadelphia and Cairo Museums from the Ptolemaic Period* (Cairo: 1959), pp. 110–114.

190 K.-T. Zauzich, *Die ägyptische Schreibertradition in Aufbau, Sprache und Schrift der demotischen Kaufverträge aus Ptolemäischer Zeit, I. Text* (ÄA 19. Wiesbaden: Harrassowitz, 1968), pp. 14–15.

191 K.-T. Zauzich, *Die ägyptische Schreibertradition in Aufbau, Sprache und Schrift der demotischen Kaufverträge aus Ptolemäischer Zeit, I. Text* (ÄA 19. Wiesbaden: Harrassowitz, 1968), pp. 79–81.

192 C.A.R. Andrews, *Catalogue of Demotic Papyri in the British Museum, IV. Ptolemaic Legal Texts from the Theban Area* (London: British Museum Publications, 1990), pp. 22–24.

193 J.G. Manning, *The Last Pharaohs, Egypt under the Ptolemies, 305–30 BC* (Princeton: University Press, 2010), pp. 11–13, 45–49.

194 J.G. Manning, *Land and Power in Ptolemaic Egypt, The Structure of Land Tenure* (Cambridge: University Press, 2003), pp. 65–125.

195 S. Vinson, *The Nile Boatman at Work* (Münchner Ägyptologische Studien 48. Mainz: Philipp von Zabern, 1998), pp. 120–122.

196 S. Vinson, *The Nile Boatman at Work* (Münchner Ägyptologische Studien 48. Mainz: Philipp von Zabern, 1998), p. 73.

197 S. Vinson, *The Nile Boatman at Work* (Münchner Ägyptologische Studien 48. Mainz: Philipp von Zabern, 1998), p. 128.

198 S. Vinson, *The Nile Boatman at Work* (Münchner Ägyptologische Studien 48. Mainz: Philipp von Zabern, 1998), pp. 68–71.

199 J.G. Manning, "The Auction of Pharaoh," in E. Teeter – J.A. Larson (eds.), *Gold of Praise. Studies on Ancient Egypt in Honor of Edward F. Wente* (SAOC 58. Chicago: Oriental Institute, 1999), pp. 277–284.

200 M. Rostovtzeff, *A Large Estate in Egypt in the Third Century BC. A Study in Economic History* (Madison: University of Wisconsin, 1922).

201 C. Preaux, *L'Économie royale des Lagides* (Brussels: Fondation égyptologique Reine Élisabeth, 1939); M. Rostovtzeff, *The Social and Economic History of the Hellenistic World*, 3 vols. (Oxford: Oxford University Press, 1941).

202 J.G. Manning, "The Land-Tenure Regime in Ptolemaic Upper Egypt," in A.K. Bowman – E. Rogan (eds.), *Agriculture in Egypt from Pharaonic to Modern Times* (Proceedings of the British Academy 96, Oxford: University Press, 1999), pp. 83–105; J.G. Manning, *Land and Power in Ptolemaic Egypt* (Cambridge: University Press, 2003), pp. 65–125.

203 A. Monson, "Royal Land in Ptolemaic Egypt: A Demographic Model," *JESHO* 50/4 (2007), p. 384 n. 30–31.
204 A. Monson, "Royal Land in Ptolemaic Egypt: A Demographic Model," *JESHOS* 50/4 (2007), pp. 363–397.
205 B.P. Muhs, "The Girls Next Door. Marriage Patterns among the Mortuary Priests in Early Ptolemaic Thebes," *JJP* 35 (2005), pp. 169–194; B.P. Muhs, "Fractions of Houses in Ptolemaic Hawara," in S. Lippert – M. Schentuleit (eds.), *Graeco-Roman Fayum – Texts and Archaeology, Proceedings of the Third International Fayum Symposium, Freudenstadt, May 29 – June 1 2007* (Wiesbaden, Harrassowitz, 2008), pp. 187–197.
206 M. Depauw, *The Archive of Teos and Thabis from Early Ptolemaic Thebes, P. Brux. dem. inv. E. 8252–8256* (Monographies Reine Élisabeth 8. Turnhout BE: Brepols, 2000), pp. 56–63.
207 G. Botti, *L'archivo demotico da Deir el-Medineh* (Catalogo del museo Egizio di Torino 1. Florence: Felice Le Monnier, 1967).
208 M. Schentuleit – G. Vittmann, *"Du hast mein Herz zufriedengestellt …," Ptolemäerzeitliche Demotische Urkunden aus Soknopaiu Nesos* (Corpus Papyrorum Raineri 29. Berlin – New York: Walter de Gruyter, 2009), pp. 2–3.
209 cf. M. Schentuleit, "Tempel zu verkaufen? P. Wien D 6846," in F. Hoffmann – H.-J. Thissen (eds.), *Res severa verum gaudium. Festschrift für Karl-Theodor Zauzich zum 65. Geburtstag am 8. Juni 2004* (Studia Demotica 6. Leuven: Peeters, 2004), p. 549.
210 P.W. Pestman, *Recueil de textes démotiques et bilingues* (Leiden: Brill, 1977), vol. 2, *Traductions*, pp. 73–80: "Archives privées d'Amenôthes ~ *Sjlws*, fils d'Hôros, pastophore du lieu de repos de l'ibis et pastophore du *ml* du scribe royal Amenôthês."
211 U. Wilcken, *Urkunden der Ptolemäerzeit (Ältere Funde)*, Band I-II (Berlin-Leipzig: Walter de Gruyter, 1927–1934), vol. 2, pp. 6–12, texts 153–155; and A. Pelletier – M. Malinine, "Planchette gréco-égyptienne du Cabinet de Médailles," *Revue des études grecques* 58 (1945), pp. 184–195.
212 U. Kaplony-Heckel, "Rund um die thebanischen Tempel (Demotische Ostraka zur Pfründen-Wirtschaft)," in F. Hoffmann – H.J. Thissen (eds.), *Res severa verum gaudium. Festschrift für Karl-Theodor Zauzich zum 65. Geburtstag am 8. Juni 2004* (Studia Demotica 6. Leuven: Peeters, 2004), pp. 283–337; B.P. Muhs, "Demotic Ostraca in Amsterdam," *Enchoria* 30 (2006/2007), pp. 63–67 (V. Transfers of Revenues).
213 M. Schentuleit, "Tempel zu verkaufen? P. Wien D 6846," in F. Hoffmann – H.-J. Thissen (eds.), *Res severa verum gaudium. Festschrift für Karl-Theodor Zauzich zum 65. Geburtstag am 8. Juni 2004* (Studia Demotica 6. Leuven: Peeters, 2004), p. 549; B. Muhs, "A Demotic Donation Contract from Early Ptolemaic Thebes (P. Louvre N. 3263)," in Z. Hawass – J. Houser Wegner (eds.), *Millions of Jubilees: Studies in Honor of David P. Silverman* (Supplément aux ASAE, Cahier No. 39. Cairo: Conseil suprême des antiquités de l'Égypte, 2010), p. 444.
214 C. Fischer-Bovet, *Army and Society in Ptolemaic Egypt* (Cambridge: University Press, 2014), pp. 73–75.
215 C. Fischer-Bovet, *Army and Society in Ptolemaic Egypt* (Cambridge: University Press, 2014), pp. 71–72.
216 C. Fischer-Bovet, *Army and Society in Ptolemaic Egypt* (Cambridge: University Press, 2014), pp. 67–70.
217 L. Casson, "Ptolemy II and the Hunting of African Elephants," *Transactions of the American Philological Association* 123 (1993), pp. 247–260; S.M. Burstein, "Elephants for Ptolemy II: Ptolemaic Policy in Nubia in the Third Century BC," in P. McKechnie – P. Guillaume (eds.), *Ptolemy II Philadelphus and His World* (Mnemosyne Supplements 300. Leiden: Brill, 2008), pp. 135–147; S.E. Sidebotham, *Berenike and the Ancient Maritime Spice Route* (Berkeley: University of California Press, 2011), pp. 39–53.
218 J.S. McKenzie, "Glimpsing Alexandria from Archaeological Evidence," *Journal of Roman Archaeology* 16 (2003), pp. 35–61.
219 S. Héral, "Archives bilingues de nomarques dans les papyrus de Ghôran," in J.H. Johnson (ed.), *Life in a Multi-Cultural Society. Egypt from Cambyses to Constantine and Beyond* (SAOC 51. Chicago: Oriental Institute, 1992), pp. 149–157.
220 K. Mueller, *Settlements of the Ptolemies. City Foundations and New Settlement in the Hellenistic World* (Studia Hellenistica 43. Leuven: Peeters, 2006), pp. 149–151.
221 K. Mueller, *Settlements of the Ptolemies. City Foundations and New Settlement in the Hellenistic World* (Studia Hellenistica 43. Leuven: Peeters, 2006), pp. 146–149.

222 B. Kramer, "Der κτίστης Boethos und die Einrichtung einer neuen Stadt I," *AfP* 43 (1997), pp. 315–339; H. Heinen, "Der κτίστης Boethos und die Einrichtung einer neuen Stadt II," *AfP* 43 (1997), pp. 340–363; and K. Mueller, *Settlements of the Ptolemies. City Foundations and New Settlement in the Hellenistic World* (Studia Hellenistica 43. Leuven: Peeters, 2006), pp. 161–164.

223 L. Török, *The Kingdom of Kush. Handbook of the Napatan-Meroitic Civilization* (HdO 31; Leiden, 1997), pp. 393–396 and 427–431; J. Locher, *Topographie und Geschichte der Region am ersten Nilkatarakt in Griechisch-Römischer Zeit* (AfP Beiheft 5. Stuttgart-Leipzig, 1999), pp. 235–238; S.M. Burstein, "Elephants for Ptolemy II: Ptolemaic Policy in Nubia in the Third Century BC," in P. McKechnie – P. Guillaume (eds.) *Ptolemy II Philadelphus and His World* (Mnemosyne Supplements 300. Leiden, 2008), pp. 135–147; L. Török, *Between Two Worlds. The Frontier Region between Ancient Nubia and Egypt 3700 BC – AD 500* (Probleme der Ägyptologie 29. Leiden, 2009), pp. 384–389, 391–395, and 400–410.

224 W.Y. Adams, "Primis and the 'Aethiopian' Frontier," *JARCE* 20 (1983), pp. 93–104.

225 A. Bernand, *De Thèbes à Syène* (Paris, 1989), Inscription 302; K. Mueller, *Settlements of the Ptolemies. City Foundations and New Settlement in the Hellenistic World* (Studia Hellenistica 43. Leuven: Peeters, 2006), pp. 161–164.

226 L. Casson, "Ptolemy II and the Hunting of African Elephants," *Transactions of the American Philological Association* 123 (1993), pp. 247–260; K. Mueller, *Settlements of the Ptolemies. City Foundations and New Settlement in the Hellenistic World* (Studia Hellenistica 43. Leuven: Peeters, 2006), pp. 151–157; S.M. Burstein, "Elephants for Ptolemy II: Ptolemaic Policy in Nubia in the Third Century BC," in P. McKechnie – P. Guillaume (eds.), *Ptolemy II Philadelphus and His World* (Mnemosyne Supplements 300. Leiden: Brill, 2008), pp. 135–147; S.E. Sidebotham, *Berenike and the Ancient Maritime Spice Route* (Berkeley: University of California Press, 2011), pp. 28–53.

227 W. Clarysse, "The Archive of the Praktor Milon," in K. Vandorpe – W. Clarysse (eds.), *Edfu, An Egyptian Provincial Capital in the Ptolemaic Period. Brussels, 3 September 2001* (Brussels: Koninklijke Vlaamse Academie van België voor Wetenschappen en Kunsten, 2003), pp. 17–27.

228 B.P. Muhs, *Receipts, Scribes, and Collectors in Early Ptolemaic Thebes* (Studia Demotica 8. Leuven: Peeters, 2011), p. 220.

229 U. Kaplony-Heckel, "Rund um die thebanischen Tempel (Demotische Ostraka zur Pfründen-Wirtschaft)," in F. Hoffmann – H.J. Thissen (eds.), *Res severa verum gaudium. Festschrift für Karl-Theodor Zauzich zum 65. Geburtstag am 8. Juni 2004* (Studia Demotica 6. Leuven: Peeters, 2004), pp. 283–337.

CONCLUSION

1 C.J. Eyre, *The Use of Documents in Pharaonic Egypt* (Oxford: University Press, 2013), pp. 1–5, 122–124, 351.

2 Ma. de J. Ellis, "Taxation in Ancient Mesopotamia: The History of the Term *miksu*," *Journal of Cuneiform Studies* 26 (1974), pp. 225–233; B.I. Faist, *Der Fernhandel des assyrischen Reiches zwischen dem 14. und 11. Jh. v. Chr.* (Alter Orient und Altes Testament 265. Münster: Ugarit-Verlag, 2001), pp. 184–194; N. Postgate, *Bronze Age Bureaucracy: Writing and the Practice of Government in Assyria* (Cambridge: University Press, 2013), pp. 267, 341.

3 G. Van Driel, *Elusive Silver: In Search of a Role for a Market in an Agrarian Environment* (Publications de l'Institut historique-archeologique neerlandais de Stamboul 95. Leiden: NINO, 2002), pp. 274–282; M. Jursa, "On Aspects of Taxation in Achaemenid Babylonia: New Evidence from Borsippa," in P. Briant – M. Chauveau (eds.), *Organisation des pouvoirs et contacts culturels dans les pays de l'empire achéménide* (Persika 14. Paris: Boccard, 2009), p. 263.

4 K. Radner, "Money in the Neo-Assyrian empire," in J.G. Dercksen (ed.), *Trade and Finance in Ancient Mesopotamia (MOS Studies 1): Proceedings of the First MOS Symposium, Leiden 1997* (Publications de l'Institut historique-archeologique neerlandais de Stamboul 84. Istanbul: Nederlands historisch-archaeologisch Instituut, 1999), pp. 128–129; R.J. Van der Spek, "The 'Silverization' of the Economy of the Achaemenid and Seleukid Empires and Early Modern China," in Z.H. Archibald – J.K. Davies – V. Gabrielsen (eds.), *The Economies of Hellenistic Societies, Third to First Centuries BC* (Oxford: University Press, 2011), pp. 402–420.

5 D.M. Schaps, *The Invention of Coinage and the Monetization of Ancient Greece* (Ann Arbor: University of Michigan Press, 2003), pp. 111–193.

6 J.J. Janssen, *Commodity Prices from The Ramessid Period. An Economic Study of the Village of Necropolis Workmen at Thebes* (Leiden: E. J. Brill, 1975), pp. 539–562.

7 B. Menu, "Le système économique de l'Égypte pharaonique," in B. Menu, *Égypte pharaonique. Nouvelles recherches sur l'histoire juridique, économique et sociale de l'ancienne Égypte* (Paris: L'Harmattan, 2004), pp. 210–212; and B. Menu, "Deir el-Médîna au crible de l'économie politique," in B. Menu, *Égypte pharaonique. Nouvelles recherches sur l'histoire juridique, économique et sociale de l'ancienne Égypte* (Paris: L'Harmattan, 2004), pp. 217–220.

8 B. Kelly, *Petitions, Litigation, and Social Control in Roman Egypt* (Oxford: University Press, 2011), pp. 18–34.

9 B.P. Muhs, "The Grapheion and the Disappearance of Demotic Contracts in Early Roman Tebtynis and Soknopaiou Nesos," in S. Lippert – M. Schentuleit (eds.), *Tebtynis und Soknopaiou Nesos – Leben im römerzeitlichen Fajum. Akten des Internationalen Symposions vom 11. bis 13. Dezember 2003 in Sommerhausen bei Würzburg* (Wiesbaden: Harrassowitz Verlag, 2005), pp. 93–104.

10 A. Monson, *From the Ptolemies to the Romans. Political and Economic Change in Egypt* (Cambridge: University Press, 2012), pp. 209–246.

11 A. Monson, *From the Ptolemies to the Romans. Political and Economic Change in Egypt* (Cambridge: University Press, 2012), pp. 159–208.

12 A. Monson, *From the Ptolemies to the Romans. Political and Economic Change in Egypt* (Cambridge: University Press, 2012), pp. 236–245.

13 D. Rathbone, *Economic Rationalism and Rural Society in Third-Century A.D. Egypt: The Heroninos Archive and the Appianus Estate* (Cambridge: University Press, 1991), pp. 188–200, 278–306.

14 D.P. Kehoe, *Management and Investment on Estates in Roman Egypt during the Early Empire* (Papyrologische Texte und Abhandlungen 40. Bonn: R. Habelt, 1992).

15 T.M. Hickey, "An Inconvenient Truth? P.Oxy. 18.2196 verso, the Apion Estate, and *fiscqlité* in the Late Antique Oxyrhynchite," *BASP* 45 (2008), pp. 96–100; T.M. Hickey, *Wine, Wealth, and the State in Late Antique Egypt: The House of Apion at Oxyrhynchus* (Ann Arbor: The University of Michigan Press, 2012), pp. 1–8, 22–27, 156–160.

16 T.M. Hickey, *Wine, Wealth, and the State in Late Antique Egypt: The House of Apion at Oxyrhynchus* (Ann Arbor: The University of Michigan Press, 2012), pp. 52–58.

BIBLIOGRAPHY

Mahmoud Abd el-Raziq, Georges Castel, Pierre Tallet, and Victor Ghica, *Les inscriptions d'Ayn Soukhna*, vol. I (MIFAO 122. Cairo: IFAO, 2002).

Mahmout Abd el-Raziq, Georges Castel, Pierre Tallet, and Grégory Marouard, "The Pharaonic Site of Ayn Soukhna in the Gulf of Suez, 2001–2009, Progress Report," pp. 3–20 in Pierre Tallet and El-Sayed Mahfouz (eds.), *The Red Sea in Pharaonic Times: Recent Discoveries along the Red Sea Coast*. Proceedings of the Colloquium Held in Cairo/Ayn Soukhna, January 11–12, 2009 (BdÉ 155. Cairo: IFAO, 2012).

William Y. Adams, "Primis and the 'Aethiopian' Frontier," *JARCE* 20 (1983), pp. 93–104.

Damien Agut-Labordère, "Le titre du «Décret de Cambyse» (P. Bn 215 verso colonne D)," *RdÉ* 56 (2005), pp. 45–54.

Damien Agut-Labordère, "Le sens du Décret de Cambyse," *Transeuphratène* 29 (2005), pp. 9–16.

Damien Agut-Labordère, "L'oracle et l'hoplite: les élites sacerdotales et l'effort de guerre sous les dynasties égyptiennes indigenes," *JESHO* 54 (2011), pp. 627–645.

Damien Agut-Labordère, "The Saite Period: The Emergence of a Mediterranean Power," pp. 965–1027 in Juan Carlos Moreno García (ed.), *Ancient Egyptian Administration* (HdO 104. Leiden: Brill, 2013).

Shmuel Aḥituv, "Sources for the Study of the Egyptian–Canaanite Border Administration," *Israel Exploration Journal* 46 (1996), pp. 219–224.

William F. Albright, "The Smaller Beth-Shan Stele of Sethos I (1309–1290 BC)," *BASOR* 125 (1952), pp. 24–32.

Schafik Allam, "Sind die nichtliterarischen Schriftostraka Brouillons?," *JEA* 54 (1968), pp. 121–128.

Schafik Allam, "Trois lettres d'affaires (P. Cairo CG 58056, 58058, 58060)," pp. 19–30, pls. 1–6 in P. Posener-Kriéger (ed.), *Mélanges Gamal eddin Mokhtar*, vol. 1 (BdÉ 97/1. Cairo: IFAO, 1985).

Schafik Allam, "Egyptian Law Courts in Pharaonic and Hellenistic Times," *JEA* 77 (1991), pp. 109–127.

Schafik Allam, "The Agreement after Judgement," *Acta Demotica* (*EVO* 17 [1994]), pp. 19–28.

Schafik Allam, "À propos de l'approvisionnement en eau de la colonie ouvrière de Deir el-Médîneh," pp. 1–14 in Bernadette Menu (ed.), *Les problèmes institutionnels de l'eau en Égypte ancienne et dans l'Antiquité méditerranéenne, Colloque AIDEA vogüé 1992* (BdÉ 110. Cairo: IFAO, 1994).

James P. Allen, *The Heqanakht Papyri* (Publications of the Metropolitan Museum of Art Egyptian Expedition 27. New York: Metropolitan Museum of Art, 2002).

James P. Allen, "After Hatshepsut: the military campaigns of Thutmose III," pp. 261–262 in Catharine H. Roehrig – Renée Dreyfus – Cathleen A. Keller (eds.), *Hatshepsut: From Queen to Pharaoh* (New York – New Haven: Metropolitan Museum of Art – Yale University Press, 2005).

James P. Allen, "The Historical Inscription of Khnumhotep at Dahshur: Preliminary Report," *BASOR* 352 (Nov., 2008), pp. 29–39.

Hartwig Altenmüller – Ahmed M. Moussa, "Die Inschrift Amenemhets II. Aus den Ptah-Tempel von Memphis. ein Vorbericht," *SAK* 18 (1991), pp. 1–48.

Amin A.M.A. Amer, "Tutankhamun's Decree for the Chief Treasurer Maya," *RdÉ* 36 (1985), pp. 17–20.

Mustafa el-Amir, *A Family Archive from Thebes, Demotic Papyri in the Philadelphia and Cairo Museums from the Ptolemaic Period* (Cairo: 1959).

Petra Andrássy, *Untersuchungen zum ägyptischen Staat des Alten Reiches und seinen Institutionen* (IBAES 11. London, Golden House Publications, 2008).

Carol A.R. Andrews, *Catalogue of Demotic Papyri in the British Museum, IV. Ptolemaic Legal Texts from the Theban Area* (London: British Museum Publications, 1990).

Charikleia Armoni, *Studien zur Verwaltung des Ptolemäischen Ägypten: Das Amt de Basilikos Grammeteus* (Papyrologica Coloniensia 36. Paderborn: Verlag Ferdinand Schöningh, 2012).

Michael Atzler, "Einige Bemerkungen zu ḥw.t und niw.t im Alten Reich," *CdÉ* 47 (1972), pp. 17–44.

Tarek El-Awady, *Abusir XVI. Sahure – The Pyramid Causeway: History and Decoration Program in the Old Kingdom* (Prague: Charles University, 2009).

Alexander Badawy, *The Tomb of Nyhetep-Ptah at Giza and 'Ankhm'ahor at Saqqara* (Berkeley: University of California Press, 1978).

Klaus Baer, *Rank and Title in the Old Kingdom, the Structure of the Egyptian Administration in the Fifth and Sixth Dynasties* (Chicago: University of Chicago Press, 1960).

Klaus Baer, "The Low Price of Land in Ancient Egypt," *JARCE* 1 (1962), pp. 25–45.

Klaus Baer, "An Eleventh Dynasty Farmer's Letters to His Family," *JAOS* 83 (1963), pp. 1–19.

Klaus Baer, "A Deed of Endowment in a Letter of the Time of Ppjj I?," *ZÄS* 93 (1966), pp. 1–9.

Roger Bagnall – Peter Derow, *The Hellenistic Period: Historical Sources in Translation*, 2nd ed. (Oxford: Blackwell, 2004).

John Baines, "The Stela of Khusobek: Private and Royal Military Narrative and Values," pp. 43–61 in Jürgen Osing – Günter Dreyer (eds.), *Form und Mass, Beiträge zur Literatur, Sprache und Kunst des alten Ägypten. Festschrift für Gerhard Fecht* (ÄAT 12. Wiesbaden: Otto Harrassowitz, 1987).

John Baines, "Practical Religion and Piety," *JEA* 73 (1987), pp. 79–98.

John Baines, *Visual and Written Culture in Ancient Egypt* (Oxford: University Press, 2007).

John Baines – Richard B. Parkinson, "An Old Kingdom Record of an Oracle? Sinai Inscription 13," pp. 9–27 in Jaap van Dijk (ed.), *Essays on Ancient Egypt in Honour of Herman te Velde* (Egyptological Memoirs 1. Groningen, 1997).

Abd-el-Mohsen Bakir, "The Middle-Kingdom Cairo Letter, a Reconsideration (Papyrus 91061 = CGC No. 58045)," *JEA* 54 (1968), pp. 57–59.

Abd-el-Mohsen Bakir, *Egyptian Epistolography from the Eighteenth to the Twenty-first Dynasty* (BdÉ 48. Cairo: IFAO, 1970).

H.S.K. Bakry, "Psammetichus II and His Newly-Found Stela at Shellâl," *Oriens Antiquus* 6 (1967), pp. 225–244.

Paul Barguet, "Tôd. Rapport de fouilles de la saison février-avril 1950," *BIFAO* 51 (1952), pp. 80–110.

Michel Baud – Vassil Dobrev, "De nouvelles annales de l'ancien émpire égyptien: une 'Pierre de Palerme' pour la VIe dynastie," *BIFAO* 95 (1995), pp. 23–92.

Michel Baud, "Le verso des annales de la VIe dynastie, Pierre de Saqqara-Sud," *BIFAO* 97 (1997), pp. 35–42.

John Bauschatz, *Law and Enforcement in Ptolemaic Egypt* (Cambridge: University Press, 2013).

Suzanne Berger, "A Note on Some Scenes of Land-Measurement," *JEA* 20 (1934), pp. 54–56.

Oleg D. Berlev, "Les prétendus 'citadins' au moyen empire," *RdÉ* 23 (1971), pp. 23–48.

A. Bernand, *De Thèbes à Syène* (Paris, 1989).

Suzanne Bickel, "Commerçants et bateliers au Nouvel Empire. Mode de vie et statut d'un groupe sociale," in Nicolas Grimal – Bernadette Menu (eds.), *Le commerce en Égypte ancienne* (BdÉ 121. Cairo: IFAO, 1998), pp. 157–172.

Manfred Bietak, "Zum Königreich des aA-zH-Ra Neḥesi," *SAK* 11 (1984), pp. 59–75.

Manfred Bietak, "The Thutmoside Stronghold of Perunefer," *Egyptian Archaeology* 26 (2005), pp. 13–17.

Manfred Bietak, "Perunefer: The Principal New Kingdom Naval Base," *Egyptian Archaeology* 34 (2009), pp. 15–17.

Manfred Bietak, "Perunefer: An Update," *Egyptian Archaeology* 35 (2009), pp. 16–17.

Jean Bingen, *Le papyrus Revenue Laws: tradition grecque et adaptation hellénistique* (Rheinische-Westfälische Akademie der Wissenschaften,Vorträge G 231. Opladen: 1978); translated in Jean Bingen, *Hellenistic Egypt: Monarchy, Society, Economy, Culture* (Berkeley-Los Angeles: University of California Press, 2007), pp. 157–188: "Chapter 13. The Revenue Laws Papyrus: Greek tradition and Hellenistic adaptation."

Jean Bingen, *Hellenistic Egypt: Monarchy, Society, Economy, Culture* (Berkeley-Los Angeles: University of California Press, 2007).

Aylward M. Blackman, "The Stela of Shoshenk, Great Chief of the Meshwesh," *JEA* 27 (1941), pp. 83–95, pls. 10–12.

Edward Bleiberg, "The King's Privy Purse During the New Kingdom: An Examination of *INW*," *JARCE* 21 (1984), pp. 155–167.

Edward Bleiberg, "The Redistributive Economy in New Kingdom Egypt: An Examination of *B3kw(t)*," *JARCE* 25 (1988), pp. 157–168.

Edward Bleiberg, *The Official Gift in Ancient Egypt (Inw)*, (Norman, 1996).

Raymond Bogaert, "Liste géographique des banques et des banquiers de l'Égypte ptolémaïque," *ZPE* 120 (1998), pp. 165–202.

Raymond Bogaert, "Les modèles des banques ptolémaiques," pp. 13–29 in *Egypt and the Hellenistic World, Proceedings of the International Colloquium, Leuven, 24–26 May 1982* (Studia Hellenistica 27. Leuven, 1983); reprinted pp. 33–45 in Raymond Bogaert, *Trapezitica Aegyptica* (Papyrologica Florentina 25. Florence, 1994).

A.C.V.M. Bongenaar, "Money in the Neo-Babylonian Institutions," pp. 159–174 in Jan G. Dercksen (ed.), *Trade and Finance in Ancient Mesopotamia (MOS Studies 1): Proceedings of the First MOS Symposium, Leiden 1997* (Publications de l'Institut historique-archeologique neerlandais de Stamboul 84. Istanbul: Nederlands historisch-archaeologisch Instituut, 1999).

Ludwig Borchardt, "Der zweite Papyrusfund von Kahun und die zeitliche Festlegung des mittleren Reiches der ägyptischen Geschichte," *ZÄS* 37 (1899), pp. 89–103.

Ludwig Borchardt, "Besolderingsverhältnisse von Priestern im mittleren Reich," *ZÄS* 40 (1902/3), pp. 113–117.

Ester Boserup, *The Conditions of Agricultural Growth: The Economics of Agrarian Change under Population Pressure* (Chicago: Aldine, 1965).

Sergio Bosticco, *Museo Archeologico di Firenze. Le stele egiziane di Epoca Tarda* (Cataloghi dei musei e gallerie d'Italia. Roma: 1972).

Alejandro F. Botti, *The Aramaic and Egyptian Legal Traditions at Elephantine: An Egyptological Approach* (Library of Second Temple Studies 64. London- New York: T & T Clark, 2009).

Giuseppe Botti, *L'archivo demotico da Deir el-Medineh* (Catalogo del museo Egizio di Torino 1. Florence: Felice Le Monnier, 1967).

James H. Breasted, *A History of Egypt from the Earliest Times to the Persian Conquest* (New York, 1905, 1912).

Edda Bresciani, "Frammenti da un 'prontuario legale' demotico da Tebtuni nell' istituto papirologico G. Vitelli di Firenze," *EVO* 4 (1981), pp. 201–215.

Alain Bresson, *L'économie de la Grèce des cités (fin VIe – Ier siècle a.C.)*, 2 vols. (Paris: Armand Colin, 2007).

Alain Bresson, "Wine, Oil and Delicacies at the Pelousion Customs," pp. 69–88 in Linda-Marie Günther – Volker Grieb (eds.), *Das imperiale Rom und der hellenistische Osten. Festschrift für Jürgen Deininger zum 75. Geburtstag* (Wiesbaden: Steiner, 2012).

Pierre Briant, "Table du roi, tribut et redistribution chez les Achéménides," pp. 35–45 in Pierre Briant – Clarisse Herrenschmidt (eds.), *Le tribut dans l'empire Perse: Actes de la Table Ronde de Paris 12–13 Decembre 1986* (Leuven: Peeters, 1989).

Pierre Briant – Raymond Descat, "Un registre douanier de la satrapie d'Égypte à l'époque achéménide (TAD C3,7)," pp. 59–104 in Nicolas Grimal – Bernadette Menu (eds.), *Le commerce en Égypte ancienne* (BdÉ 121. Cairo: IFAO, 1998).

Clive Broadhurst, "An Artistic Interpretation of Sety I's War Reliefs," *JEA* 75 (1989), pp. 229–234.

Karl Bücher, *Die Entstehung der Volkswirtschaft* (1893), pp. 98–99; reprinted in Moses I.

Finley (ed.), *The Bücher-Meyer Controversy* (New York: Arno Press, 1979).

Stanley M. Burstein, "Elephants for Ptolemy II: Ptolemaic Policy in Nubia in the Third Century BC," pp. 135–147 in Paul McKechnie – Philippe Guillaume (eds.), *Ptolemy II Philadelphus and His World* (Mnemosyne Supplements 300. Leiden: Brill, 2008).

Richard Bussmann, *Die Provinztempel Ägyptens von der 0. bis zur 11. Dynastie: Archäologie und Geschichte einer gesellschaftlichen Institution zwischen Residenz und Provinz, Teil. I: Text. Teil. II: Abbildungen* (Probleme der Ägyptologie 30. Leiden: Brill, 2010).

Theodore V. Buttrey, "Pharaonic Imitations of Athenian Tetradrachms," pp. 137–140 in Tony Hackens – Raymond Weiller (eds.), *Proceedings of the 9th International Congress of Numismatics, Berne, September 1979*, vol. 1 (Louvain-la-Neuve: 1982).

Karl W. Butzer, *Early Hydraulic Civilization in Egypt* (Chicago: University Press, 1976).

Ricardo A. Caminos, *Late Egyptian Miscellanies* (Brown Egyptological Studies 1. Oxford: University Press, 1954).

Ricardo A. Caminos, *The Chronicle of Prince Osorkon* (Analecta Orientalia 37. Rome: Pontificium Institutum Biblicum, 1958).

Ricardo A. Caminos, "The Nitocris Adoption Stela," *JEA* 50 (1964), pp. 71–101.

Lionel Casson, "Ptolemy II and the Hunting of African Elephants," *Transactions of the American Philological Association* 123 (1993), pp. 247–260.

Edward W. Castle, "Shipping and Trade in Ramesside Egypt," *JESHO* 35 (1992), pp. 239–277.

Jaroslav Černý, "Papyrus Salt 124 (Brit. Mus. 10055)," *JEA* 15 (1929), pp. 243–258.

Jaroslav Černý, "Fluctuations in Grain Prices during the Twentieth Egyptian Dynasty," *Archiv Orientální* 6 (1934), pp. 173–178.

Jaroslav Černý, *Late Ramesside Letters* (Bibliotheca Aegyptiaca 9. Bruxelles: Édition de la fondation égyptologique Reine Élisabeth, 1939).

Jaroslav Černý, *Catalogue des ostraca hiératiques non-littéraires de Deir el-Médineh* IV (nos. 242–339) (DFIFAO 6. Cairo: IFAO, 1939).

Jaroslav Černý, "The Will of Naunakhte and the Related Documents," *JEA* 31 (1945), pp. 29–53.

Jaroslav Černý, "Prices and Wages in Egypt in the Ramesside Period," *Cahiers d' histoire mondiale* 1 (1954), pp. 903–21.

Jaroslav Černý, "Egyptian Oracles," pp. 35–48 in Richard A. Parker, *A Saite Oracle Papyrus from Thebes in the Brooklyn Museum [Papyrus Brooklyn 47.218.3]* (Brown Egyptological Studies 4. Providence, 1962).

Jaroslav Černý, *A Community of Workmen at Thebes in the Ramesside Period, 2e édition* (BdÉ 50. Chicago: IFAO, 2001).

Jaroslav Černý – Alan H. Gardiner, *Hieratic Ostraca*, Vol. 1 (Oxford: Griffith Institute, 1957).

Jaroslav Černý – Richard A. Parker, "An Abnormal Hieratic Tablet," *JEA* 57 (1971), pp. 127–131.

Jaroslav Černý – T. Eric Peet, "A Marriage Settlement of the Twentieth Dynasty: An Unpublished Document from Turin," *JEA* 13 (1927), pp. 30–39.

Dominique Charpin (translated by Jane Marie Todd), *Reading and Writing in Babylonia* (Harvard, 2010).

Michel Chauveau, "P. Carlsberg 301: Le manuel juridique de Tebtynis," pp. 103–127 in Paul J. Frandsen (ed.), *The Carlsberg Papyri 1. Demotic Texts from the Collection* (CNI 15, Copenhagen: Museum Tusculanum Press, 1991).

Michel Chauveau, "La chronologie de la correspondence dite «de Phérendatès»," *RdÉ* 50 (1999), pp. 269–271.

Michel Chauveau, "La première mention du statère d'argent en Égypte," *Transeuphratène* 20 (2000), pp. 134–143.

Louis-A. Christophe, "Les porteurs d'eau de Deir el-Médineh pendent la règne de Ramsès III," *BIE* 36 (1953–54), pp. 381–408.

Louis-A. Christophe, "Le ravitaillement en poissons des artisans de la nécropole thébaine à la fin du règne de Ramsès III," *BIFAO* 65 (1967), pp. 177–199.

Barbara Cifola, "Ramses III and the Sea Peoples: A Structural Analysis of the Medinet Habu Inscriptions," *Orientalia* 57 (1988), pp. 275–306.

Willy Clarysse, "The Archive of the Praktor Milon," pp. 17–27 in Katelijn Vandorpe – Willy

Clarysse (eds.), *Edfu, An Egyptian Provincial Capital in the Ptolemaic Period. Brussels, 3 September 2001* (Brussels: Koninklijke Vlaamse Academie van België voor Wetenschappen en Kunsten, 2003).

Willy Clarysse – Claudio Galazzi – Nico Kruit, "Three Joins from the Zenon Archive," *Ancient Society* 30 (2000), pp. 5–27.

Willy Clarysse – Dorothy J. Thompson, *Counting the People in Hellenistic Egypt, Volume 1: Population Registers (P. Count)*, (Cambridge Classical Studies. Cambridge: University Press, 2006).

Willy Clarysse, *Counting the People in Hellenistic Egypt, Volume 2: Historical Studies* (Cambridge Classical Studies. Cambridge: University Press, 2006).

Willy Clarysse – Katelijn Vandorpe, "The Ptolemaic Apomoira," pp. 5–42 in Henri Melaerts (ed.), *Le culte du souverain dans l'Égypte ptolémaïque au IIIe siècle avant notre ère. Actes du colloque international, Bruxelles 10 mai 1995* (Studia Hellenistica 34. Leuven: Peeters, 1998).

Ronald Coase, "The Nature of the Firm," *Economica* 4, no. 16 (1937), pp. 386–405.

Mark Collier – Stephen Quirke, *The UCL Lahun Papyri: Religious, Literary, Legal, Mathematical and Medical* (BAR International Series 1209. Oxford, 2004).

Virginia Condon, "Two Account Papyri of the Late Eighteenth Dynasty (Brooklyn 35.1453 A and B)," *RdÉ* 35 (1984), pp. 57–82.

Virginia Condon, "'Two Variant Accounts?' by Janssen? (VA 1,3, 109–112)," *Varia Aegyptiaca* 2 (1986), pp. 23–29.

Kathlyn M. Cooney, *The Cost of Death: The Social and Economic Value of Ancient Egyptian Funerary Art in the Ramesside Period* (EU 22. Leiden: NINO, 2007).

Jules Couyat – Pierre Montet, *Les inscriptions hiéroglyphiques et hiératiques du Ouâdi Hammâmât* (MIFAO 34. Cairo: IFAO, 1912).

Arthur E. Cowley, *Aramaic Papyri of the Fifth Century B.C.* (Oxford: Clarendon Press, 1923).

Dorothy J. Crawford, *Kerkeosiris, An Egyptian Village in the Ptolemaic Period* (Cambridge: University Press, 1971).

Lucia Criscuolo, "I miriaruri nell' Egitto tolemaico: note sull'amministrazione dell'Arsinoite nell III secolo a.c.," *Aegyptus* 57 (1977), pp. 109–122.

Lucia Criscuolo, "Miriaruri: nuove riflessioni," *Aegyptus* 61 (1981), pp. 116–118.

Eugene Cruz-Uribe, "On the Existence of Psammetichus IV," *Serapis* 5 (1980), pp. 35–39.

Eugene Cruz-Uribe, *Saite and Persian Demotic Cattle Documents, A Study in Legal Forms and Principles in Ancient Egypt* (ASP 26. Chico CA: Scholars Press1985).

Eugene Cruz-Uribe, "A 30th Dynasty Document of Renunciation from Edfu," *Enchoria* 13 (1985), pp. 41–49.

George Dalton (ed.), *Primitive, Archaic and Modern Economies, Essays of Karl Polanyi* (Boston, 1968).

Georges Daressy, "Trois stèles de la période Bubastite," *ASAE* 15 (1915), pp. 140–147.

John Coleman Darnell, "The *Kbn.wt* Vessels of the Late Period," pp. 67–89 in Janet H. Johnson (ed.), *Life in a Multi-Cultural Society: Egypt from Cambyses to Constantine and Beyond* (SAOC 51. Chicago: Oriental Institute, 1992).

John Coleman Darnell, *Theban Desert Road Survey in the Egyptian Western Desert, I: Gebel Tjauti Rock Inscription 1–45 and Wadi el-Hol Rock Inscriptions 1–45* (OIP 119. Chicago: Oriental Institute, 2002).

Arlette David, *Syntactic and Lexico-Semantic Aspects of the Legal Register in Ramesside Royal Decrees* (Göttinger Orientforschungen IV. Reihe Ägypten 38. Wiesbaden, Harrassowitz, 2006).

Adriaan de Buck, "The Judicial Papyrus of Turin," *JEA* 23 (1937), pp. 152–164.

Françoise de Cenival, "Un document démotique relatif au partage d'une maison (P. Louvre N. 2430)," *RdÉ* 18 (1966), pp. 7–30.

Françoise de Cenival, "Une vente d'esclaves de l'époque d'Artaxerxès III (P. Inv. Sorbonne nos. 1276 et 1277)," *RdÉ* 24 (1972), pp. 31–39.

Françoise de Cenival, *Les associations religieuses en Égypte, d'après les documents démotiques* (BdÉ 46. Cairo: IFAO, 1972).

Françoise de Cenival, *Cautionnnements démotiques du début de l'Époque Ptolémaïque: P. dém. Lille 34 à 96* (Paris: Klincksieck, 1974).

Françoise de Cenival, "Répetoire journalier d'un bureau de notaire de l'époque ptolémaïque en démotique (P. dém. Lille 120)," *Enchoria* 15 (1987), pp. 1–9.

Françoise de Cenival, "Comptes d'une association religieuse thébaine datant des années 29 à 33 du roi Amasis," *RdÉ* 37 (1986), pp. 13–29.

Françoise de Cenival, "Papyrus Seymour de Ricci: le plus ancien des règlements d'association religieuse (4ème siècle av. J.-C.) (Pap. Bibl. Nationale E 241)," *RdÉ* 39 (1988), pp. 37–46.

N. de Garis Davies, *The Tomb of Rekh-mi-Rē at Thebes* (New York: Arno Press, 1973).

Agnès Degrève, "La campagne asiatique de l'an 1 de Séthy Ier représentée sur le mur extérieur nord de la salle hypostyle du temple d'Amon à Karnak," *RdÉ* 57 (2006), pp. 47–64.

Robert J. Demaree – Dominique Valbelle, *Les registres de recensement du village de Deir el-Medineh (Le Stato Civile)* (Leuven: Peeters, 2011).

Herman de Meulenaere, "Une princesse libyenne ignorée," *CdÉ* 57 (1982), pp. 218–222.

Harold Demsetz, "Toward a Theory of Property Rights," *The American Economic Review* 57, No. 2 (May 1967), pp. 347–359.

Mark Depauw, *A Companion to Demotic Studies* (Papyrologica Bruxellensia 28. Bruxelles, 1997).

Mark Depauw, *The Archive of Teos and Thabis from Early Ptolemaic Thebes, P. Brux. dem. inv. E. 8252–8256* (Monographies Reine Élisabeth 8. Turnhout BE: Brepols, 2000).

Mark Depauw, "Autograph Confirmation in Demotic Contracts," *CdÉ* 78 (2003), pp. 66–88.

Mark Depauw, *The Demotic Letter* (Demotische Studien 14. Sommerhausen, 2006).

Peter Der Manuelian, *Studies in the reign of Amenophis II* (HÄB 26. Hildesheim: Gerstenberg, 1987).

Peter Der Manuelian, *Living in the Past. Studies in the Archaism of the Egyptian Twenty-sixth Dynasty* (Studies in Egyptology. London: Kegan Paul International, 1994).

Didier Devauchelle, "Notes sur l'administration funéraire égyptienne à l'époque gréco–romaine," *BIFAO* 87 (1987), pp. 141–160.

Anna Di Bitonto, "Le petizioni al re. Studia sul formulario," *Aegyptus* 47 (1967), pp. 5–57.

Anna Di Bitonto, "Le petizioni ai funzionari nel periodo tolemaico. Studio sul formulario," *Aegyptus* 48 (1968), pp. 53–107.

Gertrud Dietze, "Der Streit um die Insel Pso. Bemerkungen zu einem epigraphischen Dossier des Khnumtempels von Elephantine (Th. Sy. 244)," *Ancient Society* 26 (1995), pp. 157–184.

Koenraad Donker van Heel, *The Legal Manual of Hermopolis [P. Mattha], Text and Translation* (Uitgaven vanwege de Stichting "Het Leids Papyrologisch Instituut" 11, Leiden, 1990).

Koenraad Donker van Heel, "The Lost Battle of Peteamonip Son of Petehorresbe," *Acta Demotica* (*EVO* 17 [1994]), pp. 115–124.

Koenraad Donker van Heel, *Abnormal Hieratic and Early Demotic Texts collected by the Theban Choachytes in the Reign of Amasis* (Leiden University PhD Thesis, 1996).

Koenraad Donker van Heel, "Papyrus Louvre E 7852, A Land Lease from the Reign of Taharka," *RdÉ* 48 (1997), pp. 81–93.

Koenraad Donker van Heel, "Papyrus Louvre E 7856 Verso and Recto: Leasing Land in the Reign of Taharka," *RdÉ* 49 (1998), pp. 91–102.

Koenraad Donker van Heel, "Papyrus Louvre E 7851 Recto and Verso: Two More Land Leases from the Reign of Taharka," *RdÉ* 50 (1999), pp. 135–144.

Koenraad Donker van Heel, "The Scribbling-Pad of Djedmontefankh Son of Aafenmut, Priest of Amonrasonter and Overseer of the King's Treasury (P. Berlin 3048 verso)," pp. 139–147 in Kim Ryholt (ed.), *Acts of the Seventh International Conference of Demotic Studies, Copenhagen 23–27 August 1999* (CNI 27. Copenhagen: Museum Tusculanum Press, 2002).

Koenraad Donker van Heel, *Djekhy & Son: Doing Business in Ancient Egypt* (Cairo: American University in Cairo Press, 2012).

Koen Donker van Heel – Ben J.J. Haring, *Writing in a Workmen's Village. Scribal Practice in Ramesside Deir el-Medina* (EU 16. Leiden: NINO, 2003).

Peter Dorman, *The Monuments of Senenmut: Problems in Historical Methodology* (London: Kegan Paul International Ltd., 1988).

Günter Dreyer – Ulrich Hartung – Frauke Pumpenmeier, *Umm el-Qaab I: das prädynastische Königsgrab U-j und seine frühen Schriftzeugnisse* (Archäologische Veröffentlichungen 86. Mainz: Philipp von Zabern, 1998).

Godfrey R. Driver, *Aramaic Documents of the Fifth Century B.C.*, 2nd ed. (Oxford: Clarendon Press, 1965).

Ruth Duttenhöfer, "Die Funktion und Stellung des ergasterion in der Getreideverwaltung der Ptolemäerzeit," *ZPE* 98 (1993), pp. 253–262.

Elmar Edel, "Amasis und Nebukadrezar II," *GM* 29 (1978), pp. 13–20.

Elmar Edel, "Der Seevölkerbericht aus dem 8. Jahre Ramses' III. (MH II, pl. 46, 15–18): Übersetzung und Struktur," pp. 223–237 in Paule Posener-Kriéger (ed.), *Mélanges Gamal eddin Mokhtar* 1 (Cairo: IFAO, 1985).

Campbell Cowan Edgar, *Zenon Papyri I* (Catalogue général des antiquités égyptiennes du Musée du Caire 79, nos. 59001–59139. Cairo: IFAO, 1925).

William F. Edgerton, "The Nauri Decree of Seti I: A Translation and Analysis of the Legal Portion," *JNES* 6 (1947), pp. 219–230.

William F. Edgerton, "The Strikes in Ramses III's Twenty-Ninth Year," *JNES* 10 (1951), pp. 137–145.

Eckhard Eichler, *Untersuchungen zum Expeditionswesen des ägyptischen Alten Reiches* (Göttinger Orientforschungen. IV. Ägypten, 26. Wiesbaden: Harrassowitz, 1993).

Selke Susan Eichler, "Untersuchungen zu den Wasserträgern von Deir el-Medineh I," *SAK* 17 (1990), pp. 135–175.

Selke Susan Eichler, "Untersuchungen zu den Wasserträgern von Deir el-Medineh II," *SAK* 18 (1991), pp. 173–205.

Selke Susan Eichler, *Die Verwaltung des "Hauses des Amun" in der 18. Dynastie* (SAK Beiheft 7. Hamburg: Helmut Buske Verlag, 2000).

Ola El-Aguizy, *A Palaeographical Study of Demotic Papyri* (MIFAO 113. Cairo: IFAO, 1998).

Maria de J. Ellis, "Taxation in Ancient Mesopotamia: The History of the Term *miksu*," *Journal of Cuneiform Studies* 26 (1974), pp. 211–250.

Erika Endesfelder, "Zu einigen Aspekten der ökonomischen Entwicklung in der Frühdynastischen Zeit Ägyptens," *Altorientalische Forschungen* 7 (1980), pp. 5–29.

Eva-Maria Engel, "The Organisation of a Nascent State: Egypt until the Beginning of the 4th Dynasty," pp. 19–40 in Juan Carlos Moreno García (ed.), *Ancient Egyptian Administration* (HdO 104. Leiden: Brill, 2013).

Reginald Engelbach, "The Treasure of Athribis (Benha)," *ASAE* 24 (1924), pp. 178–185.

Epigraphic Survey, *Reliefs and Inscriptions at Karnak, 3. The Bubastite Portal* (OIP 74. Chicago: University of Chicago Press, 1954).

Epigraphic Survey, *The Temple of Khonsu 2: Scenes and Inscriptions in the Court and First Hypostyle Hall* (OIP 103. Chicago: Oriental Institute, 1981).

Epigraphic Survey, *Reliefs and inscriptions at Karnak, Volume 4: The Battle Reliefs of King Sety I* (OIP 107. Chicago: Oriental Institute, 1986).

Wolja Erichsen, "Eine demotische Schenkungsurkunde aus der Zeit des Darius," *Akademie d. Wiss. und Lit. in Mainz, Abh. d. geistes- und socialwiss. Kl.* 1962, Nr. 6, pp. 343–363, and taf. 1–2.

Adolf Erman, "Beiträge zur Kenntniss des ägyptischen Gerichtsverfahrens," *ZÄS* 17 (1879), pp. 71–76, pl. 1.

Adolf Erman, "Zu den Legrain'schen Inschriften, I. Das Testament eines Hohenpriesters," *ZÄS* 35 (1897), pp. 19–24.

Christopher J. Eyre, "Work and the Organization of Work in the Old Kingdom," pp. 5–47 in Marvin A. Powell (ed.), *Labor in the Ancient Near East* (American Oriental Series 68. New Haven: American Oriental Society, 1987).

Christopher J. Eyre, "Feudal Tenure and Absentee Landlords," pp. 107–133 in Schafik Allam (ed.), *Grund und Boden in Alägypten, Akten des internationalen Symposions Tübingen 18.-20. Juni 1990* (Untersuchungen zum Rechtsleben im Alten Ägypten 2. Tübingen, 1994).

Christopher J. Eyre, "Peasants and 'Modern' Leasing Strategies in Ancient Egypt," *JESHO* 40, 4 (1997), pp. 367–390.

Christopher J. Eyre, "The Market Women of Pharaonic Egypt," pp. 173–191 in Nicolas Grimal – Bernadette Menu (eds.), *Le commerce en Égypte ancienne* (BdÉ 121. Cairo: IFAO, 1998).

Christopher J. Eyre, "The Village Economy in Pharaonic Egypt," pp. 33–60 in Alan K. Bowman – Eugene Rogan (eds.), *Agriculture in Egypt, from Pharaonic to Modern Times* (Proceedings of the British Academy 96. Oxford: University Press, 1999).

Christopher J. Eyre, "The Performance of the Peasant," pp. 9–25 in Andrea M. Gnirs (ed.), *Reading the Eloquent Peasant* (Lingua Aegyptia 8. Göttingen 2000).

Christopher J. Eyre, *The Use of Documents in Pharaonic Egypt* (Oxford: University Press, 2013).

David Fabre, "1: The Shipwrecks of Heracleion-Thonis: A Preliminary Study," pp. 13–32 in Damian Robinson – Andrew Wilson (eds.), *Maritime Archaeology and Ancient Trade in the Mediterranean* (Oxford Centre for Maritime Archaeology 6. Oxford: 2011).

Betina I. Faist, *Der Fernhandel des assyrischen Reiches zwischen dem 14. und 11. Jh. v. Chr.* (Alter Orient und Altes Testament 265. Münster: Ugarit-Verlag, 2001).

Sami Farag, "Une Inscription Memphite de la XIIe Dynastie," *RdÉ* 32 (1980), pp. 75–82.

Dominique Farout, "La carrière du wHmw Ameny et l'organisation des expéditions au ouadi Hammamat au Moyen Empire," *BIFAO* 94 (1994), pp. 143–172.

Rudolfo Fattovich – Kathryn A. Bard (eds.), *Harbour of the Pharaohs to the Land of Punt, Archaeological Investigations at Mersa/Wadi Gawasis, Egypt, 2001–2005* (Naples: Universita degli Studi di Napoli "L'Orientale," 2007).

Thomas Faucher – Wolfgang Fischer–Bossert – Sylvain Dhennin, "Les monnaies en or aux types hiéroglyphiques nwb nfr," *BIFAO* 112 (2012), pp. 147–169.

Moses I. Finley, *The Ancient Economy*, 2nd ed. (Berkeley: University of California Press, 1985).

Henry G. Fischer, "Notes on the Mo'alla Inscriptions and Some Contemporaneous Texts," *WZKM* 57 (1961), pp. 59–77.

Christelle Fischer-Bovet, "Egyptian Warriors: The Machimoi of Herodotus and the Ptolemaic Army," *Classical Quarterly* 63.1 (2013), pp. 209–236.

Christelle Fischer-Bovet, *Army and Society in Ptolemaic Egypt* (Cambridge: University Press, 2014).

Hans-Werner Fischer-Elfert, "Two Oracle Petitions Addressed to Horus-khau with Some Notes on the Oracular Amuletic Decrees (P. Berlin P 8525 and P 8526)," *JEA* 82 (1996), pp. 129–144.

Roxana Flammini, "Elite Emulation and Patronage Relationships in the Middle Bronze: The Egyptianized Dynasty of Byblos," *Tel Aviv* 37, no. 2 (2010), pp. 154–168.

Frank Förster, "With Donkeys, Jars and Water Bags into the Libyan Desert: The Abu Ballas Trail in the Late Old Kingdom/First Intermediate Period," *British Museum Studies in Ancient Egypt and Sudan* 7 (2007), pp. 1–39.

Paul J. Frandsen, "Editing Reality: The Turin Strike Papyrus," pp. 166–199 in Sarah Israelit-Groll (ed.), *Studies in Egyptology Presented to Miriam Lichtheim* I (Jerusalem: 1990).

Detlef Franke, "Die Stele Inv. Nr. 4403 im Landesmuseum in Oldenburg. Zur Lebensmittelproduktion in der 13. Dynastie," *SAK* 10 (1983), pp. 157–178.

Detlef Franke, "Zwischen Herakleopolis und Theben: Neues zu den Gräbern von Assiut." *SAK* 14 (1987), pp. 49–60.

Detlef Franke, "The Career of Khnumhotep III. of Beni Hasan and the so-called 'Decline of the Nomarchs,'" pp. 51–67 in Stephen Quirke (ed.), *Middle Kingdom Studies* (New Malden: SIA Publishing, 1991).

Elizabeth Frood, "The Potters: Organization, Delivery, and Product of Work," pp. 29–62 in Jac. J. Janssen – Elizabeth Frood – Maren Goecke-Bauer (eds.), *Woodcutters, Potters and Doorkeepers: Service Personnel of the Deir el-Medina Workemen* (EU 17. Leiden: NINO, 2003).

Gaballa Aly Gaballa, "Three Documents from the Reign of Ramesses III," *JEA* 59 (1973), pp. 109–113 and pl. 38.

Alan H. Gardiner, *The Inscription of Mes. A Contribution to the Study of Egyptian Juridical Procedure* (Untersuchungen zur Geschichte und Altertumskunde Ägyptens,

Band 4, Heft 3. Leipzig: J.C. Hinrichs'sche Buchhandlung, 1905).

Alan H. Gardiner, "Four Papyri of the 18th Dynasty from Kahun," *ZÄS* 43 (1906), pp. 27–47.

Alan H. Gardiner, "The Defeat of the Hyksos by Kamose: The Carnarvon Tablet, No. 1," *JEA* 3 (1916), pp. 95–110.

Alan H. Gardiner, "The Dakhleh Stela," *JEA* 19 (1933), pp. 19–30 & pls. 5–7.

Alan H. Gardiner, "A Lawsuit Arising from the Purchase of Two Slaves," *JEA* 21 (1935), pp. 140–146.

Alan H. Gardiner, *Late Egyptian Miscellanies* (Bibliotheca Aegyptiaca 7. Bruxelles: Fondation Egyptologique Reine Elisabeth, 1937).

Alan H. Gardiner, "Ramesside Texts Relating to the Taxation and Transport of Corn," *JEA* 27 (1941), pp. 19–73.

Alan H. Gardiner, *The Wilbour Papyrus, Volume 1: Plates* (London, 1941).

Alan H. Gardiner, "Regnal Years and Civil Calender in Pharaonic Egypt," *JEA* 31 (1945), pp. 11–28.

Alan H. Gardiner, *The Wilbour Papyrus, volume 2: Commentary* (London, 1948).

Alan H. Gardiner, *The Wilbour Papyrus, Volume 3: Translation* (London, 1948).

Alan H. Gardiner, *Ramesside Administrative Documents* (Oxford: Griffith Institute – London: Oxford University Press, 1948).

Alan H. Gardiner, "Some Reflections on the Nauri Decree," *JEA* 38 (1952), pp. 24–33.

Alan H. Gardiner, "The Daily Income of Sesostris II's Funerary Temple," *JEA* 42 (1956), pp. 119.

Alan H. Gardiner, "The Gods of Thebes as Guarantors of Personal Property," *JEA* 48 (1962), pp. 57–69.

Steven J. Garfinkle, "Was the Ur III State Bureaucratic? Patrimonialism and Bureaucracy in the Ur III Period," pp. 55–61 in Steven J. Garfinkle – J. Cale Johnson (eds.), *The Growth of an Early State in Mesopotamia: Studies in Ur III Administration* (Biblioteca del Próximo Oriente Antiguo 5. Madrid: Consejo Superior de Investigaciones Cientificas, 2008).

Anne Gasse, *Données nouvelles administratives et sacerdotales sur l'organisation du domaine d'Amon, XXe-XXIe dynasties, à la lumière des papyrus Prachov, Reinhardt et Grundbuch (avec édition princeps des papyrus Louvre AF 6345 et 6346–7),* (BdÉ 104. Cairo: IFAO, 1988).

Anne Gasse, "Wadi Hammamat and the Sea from the Origins to the End of the New Kingdom," pp. 133–143 in Pierre Tallet – El-Sayed Mahfouz (eds.), *The Red Sea in Pharaonic Times: Recent Discoveries along the Red Sea Coast. Proceedings of the Colloquium held in Cairo / Ayn Soukhna 11th – 12th January 2009* (BdÉ 155. Cairo: IFAO, 2012).

Henri Gauthier, "Une fondation pieuse en Nubie," *ASAE* 36 (1936), pp. 49–71 and pl. 3.

Karolien Geens, "Financial Archives of Graeco-roman Egypt," pp. 133–151 in Koenraad Verboven – Katelijn Vandorpe – Véronique Chankowski (eds.), *Pistoi dia tèn technèn. Bankers, Loans and Archives in the Ancient World. Studies in Honour of Raymond Bogaert* (Studia Hellenistica 44. Leuven: Peeters, 2008).

Generalverwaltung, *Hieratische Papyrus aus den Koniglichen museen zu Berlin, Dritter Band: Schriftstucke der VI Dynastie aus Elephantine, Zauberspruche fur Mutter und Kind, Ostraka* (Leipzig: J. C. Hinrichs'sche Buchhandlung, 1911).

Didier Gentet – Nabil Sweydan, "À propos de la comptabilité de l'eau en khar au Nouvel Empire," pp. 177–185 in Bernadette Menu (ed.), *Les problèmes institutionnels de l'eau en Égypte ancienne et dans l'Antiquité méditerranéenne, Colloque AIDEA vogüé 1992* (BdÉ 110. Cairo: IFAO, 1994).

Stephen R.K. Glanville, "Records of a Royal Dockyard in the Time of Tuthmosis III: Papyrus British Museum 10056. Part I," *ZÄS* 66 (1931), pp. 105–121.

Stephen R.K. Glanville, "Records of a Royal Dockyard in the Time of Tuthmosis III: Papyrus British Museum 10056. Part II," *ZÄS* 68 (1932), pp. 7–41.

Andrea M. Gnirs, "Coping with the Army: The Military and the State in the New Kingdom," pp. 639–717 in Juan Carlos Moreno García (ed.), *Ancient Egyptian Administration* (HdO 104. Leiden: Brill, 2013).

Hans Goedicke, "Psammetik I. und die Libyer," *MDAIK* 18 (1962), pp. 26–49.

Hans Goedicke, "Hieratische Ostraka in Wien," *WZKM* 59/60 (1963/1964), pp. 1–8, pls. 1–22.

Hans Goedicke, "Ein Brief aus dem Alten Reich (Pap. Boulaq 8)," *MDAIK* 22 (1967), pp. 1–8 & pl. I.

Hans Goedicke, *Die privaten Rechtsinschriften aus dem Alten Reich* (Beihefte zur WZKM 5. Wien: 1970).

Hans Goedicke, "The Campaign of Psammetik II against Nubia," *MDAIK* 37 (1981), pp. 187–198.

Wladimir Golenischeff, *Les Papyrus No 1115, 1116A et 1116B de l'Ermitage Imperial a St-Petersbourg* (St-Petersbourg: L'Ermitage Imperial, 1913).

Georges Goyon, *Nouvelles inscriptions rupestres du Wadi Hammamat* (Paris: Imprimerie Nationale, 1957).

Jean-Claude Goyon, "La statuette funéraire I.E. 84 de Lyon et le titre saïte *imy-r ḥwᶜ*; nsw," *BIFAO* 67 (1969), pp. 159–171.

Wolfram Grajetzki, "Setting a State Anew: The Central Administration from the End of the Old Kingdom to the End of the Middle Kingdom," pp. 215–258 in Juan Carlos Moreno García (ed.), *Ancient Egyptian Administration* (HdO 104. Leiden: Brill, 2013).

Pierre Grandet, "Un texte historique de Ramsès III à El-Kâb (et autres textes ramessides)," *RdÉ* 41 (1990), pp. 95–99.

Pierre Grandet, *Le Papyrus Harris* I (BdÉ 109. Cairo: IFAO, 1994).

Mark Granovetter, "The Strength of Weak Ties," *The American Journal of Sociology* 78, Issue 6 (May, 1973), pp. 1360–1380.

Mark Granovetter, "Economic Action and Social Structure: The Problem of Embeddedness," *The American Journal of Sociology* 91, No. 3 (November, 1985), pp. 481–510.

Mark Granovetter, "Comment on Liverani and Bedford," pp. 84–88 in Joseph G. Manning – Ian Morris (eds.), *The Ancient Economy: Evidence and Models* (Stanford: University Press, 2005).

Catharine Grataloup, "12: Occupation and Trade at Heracleion-Thonis – the Evidence from the Pottery," pp. 151–159 in Damian Robinson – Andrew Wilson (eds.), *Alexandria and the North-Western Delta* (Oxford Centre for Maritime Archaeology 5. Oxford: 2010).

Michael Green, "A Means of Discouraging Perjury," *GM* 39 (1980), pp. 33–39.

Avner Greif, "Reputation and Coalitions in Medieval Trade: Evidence on the Maghrebi Traders," *Journal of Economic History* 49, no. 4 (Dec. 1989), pp. 857–882.

Avner Greif, "Contract Enforceability and Economic Institutions in Early Trade: Lessons from the Commercial Revolution," *American Economic Review* 82 No. 2 (May 1992), pp. 128–133.

Avner Greif, "Contract Enforceability and Economic Institutions in Early Trade: The Maghribi Traders' Coalition," *American Economic Review* 83, No. 3 (June 1993), pp. 525–548.

Avner Greif, "Cultural Beliefs and the Organization of Society: A Historical and Theoretical Reflection on Collectivist and Individualist Societies," *The Journal of Political Economy* 102, No. 5, (Oct. 1994), pp. 912–950.

Avner Greif, *Institutions and the Path to the Modern Economy: Lessons from Medieval Trade* (Cambridge: University Press, 2006).

Avner Greif – Paul Milgrom – Barry R. Weingast, "Coordination, Commitment and Enforcement: The Case of the Merchant Gild," *Journal of Political Economy* 102, No. 4, (Aug. 1994), pp. 745–776.

Bernard Grenfell – Arthur S. Hunt, *The Hibeh Papyri, Part 1* (Egypt Exploration Fund, Graeco-Roman Memoirs 7. London: 1906).

Francis Llewellyn Griffith, *The Inscriptions of Siût and Dêr Rîfeh* (London: Trübner & Co., 1889).

Francis Llewellyn Griffith, *Hieratic Papyri from Kahun and Gurob* (London: Bernard Quaritch, 1898).

Francis Llewellyn Griffith, *Catalogue of Demotic Papyri in the John Rylands Library, Manchester*, 3 vols. (Manchester: University Press, 1909).

Francis Llewellyn Griffith, "The Abydos Decree of Seti I at Nauri," *JEA* 13 (1927), pp. 193–208 and pls 37–43.

Nicolas Grimal, *Études sur la propagande royale égyptienne, 1, La stèle triomphale de Pi-ânkh-y au musée du Caire, JE 48862 et 47086–47089* (MIFAO 105. Cairo: IFAO, 1981).

Octave Guéraud, *ENTEYΞΕΙΣ, Requêtes et plaintes adressées au Roi d'Égypte au IIIe siècle avant J.C.* (Publications de la société royale égyptienne de papyrologie, textes et documents 1. Cairo: IFAO, 1931).

Labib Habachi, *Tell Basta* (Supplément aux ASAE 22. Cairo: IFAO, 1957).

Labib Habachi, *The Second Stela of Kamose and His Struggle against the Hyksos Ruler and His Capital* (Abhandlungen des Deutschen Archäologischen Instituts Kairo, Ägyptologische Reihe 8. Glückstadt: Augustin, 1972).

Sofia Häggman, *Directing Deir el-Medina. The External Administration of the Necropolis* (Uppsala Studies in Egyptology 4. Uppsala: Akademitryck AB, 2002).

Ben J.J. Haring, *Divine Households, Administrative and Economic Aspects of the New Kingdom Royal Memorial Temples in Western Thebes* (EU 12, Leiden, NINO, 1997).

Ben J.J. Haring, "Ramesside Temples and the Economic Interests of the State: Crossroads of the Sacred and the Profane," pp. 165–170 in Martin Fitzenreiter (ed.), *Das Heilige und die Ware: Zum Spannungsfeld von Religion und Ökonomie* (IBAES 7. London: Golden House Publications, 2007).

Ben J.J. Haring, "The Rising Power of the House of Amun in the New Kingdom," pp. 607–637 in Juan Carlos Moreno García (ed.), *Ancient Egyptian Administration* (HdO 104. Leiden: Brill, 2013).

Yvonne Harpur – Paolo Scremin, *The Chapel of Kagemni: Scene Details* (Egypt in Minature 1. Oxford: Expedition to Egypt, 2006).

Yvonne Harpur, *The Chapel of Niankhkhnum & Khnumhotep: Scene Details* (Egypt in Minature 3. Oxford: Expedition to Egypt, 2010).

Selim Hassan, "Excavations at Saqqara, 1937–1938," *ASAE* 38 (1938), pp. 503–521.

Selim Hassan, "The Causeway of *Wnis* at Sakkara," *ZÄS* 80 (1955), pp. 136–139.

William C. Hayes, "Royal Decrees from the Temple of Min at Coptus," *JEA* 32 (1946), pp. 3–23.

William C. Hayes, *A Papyrus of the Late Middle Kingdom* (New York: The Brooklyn Museum, 1955).

Lisa A. Heidorn, "The Saite and Persian Period Forts at Dorginarti," pp. 205–219 in W. Vivian Davies (ed.), *Egypt and Africa, Nubia from Prehistory to Islam* (London: British Museum Press, 1991).

Lisa A. Heidorn, "Dorginarti, Fortress at the Mouth of the Rapids," pp. 293–307 in Friederike Jesse – Carola Vogel (eds.), *The Power of Walls – Fortifications in Ancient Northeastern Africa, Proceedings of the International Workshop held at the University of Cologne 4th-7th August 2011* (Colloquium Africanum 5. Köln: Heinrich-Barth-Institut e.V., 2013).

Heinz Heinen, "Der κτίστης Boethos und die Einrichtung einer neuen Stadt II," *AfP* 43 (1997), pp. 340–363.

Wolfgang Helck, "Das Dekret des Königs Haremheb," *ZÄS* 80 (1955), pp. 109–136, pls. 10–11.

Wolfgang Helck, "Die Inschrift über die Belohnung des Hohenpriesters *Imn-ḥtp*," *Mitteilungen des Instituts für Orientforschung* 4 (1956), pp. 161–178.

Wolfgang Helck, *Urkunden der 18. Dynastie*, Abteilung IV, Heft 17–22 (Urkunden des ägyptischen Altertums. Berlin: Akademie-Verlag, 1956–58) = Urk. IV, 1227–2179.

Wolfgang Helck, "Die Opferstiftung des *Śn-mwt*," *ZÄS* 85 (1960), pp. 23–34.

Wolfgang Helck, "Der Papyrus Berlin P. 3047," *JARCE* 2 (1963), pp. 65–73, pls. 9–12.

Wolfgang Helck, "Eine Briefsammlung aus der Verwaltung des Amun-tempels," *JARCE* 6 (1967), pp. 134–151.

Wolfgang Helck, *Wirtschaftsgeschichte des Alten Ägypten im 3. und 2. Jahrtausend vor Chr.* (HdO 1, Abschnitte 5. Leiden-Köln: Brill, 1975).

Wolfgang Helck, "Einige Bemerkungen zu Artikeln im *SAK* 2," *SAK* 4 (1976), pp. 115–124.

Wolfgang Helck, "Wege zum Eigentum an Grund und Boden im Alten Reich," pp. 9–13 in Schafik Allam (ed.), *Grund und Boden in Altägypten, Akten des internationalen Symposions Tübingen 18.-20. Juni 1990* (Untersuchungen zum Rechtsleben im Alten Ägypten 2. Tübingen, 1994).

Suzanne Héral, "Archives bilingues de nomarques dans les papyrus de Ghôran," pp. 149–157 in Janet H. Johnson (ed.), *Life in a Multi-Cultural Society. Egypt from Cambyses to Constantine and Beyond* (SAOC 51. Chicago: Oriental Institute, 1992).

Todd M. Hickey, "An Inconvenient Truth? P.Oxy. 18.2196 verso, the Apion Estate, and *fiscalité* in the Late Antique Oxyrhynchite," *BASP* 45 (2008), pp. 87–100.

Todd M. Hickey, *Wine, Wealth, and the State in Late Antique Egypt: The House of Apion at Oxyrhynchus* (Ann Arbor: The University of Michigan Press, 2012).

Thomas Hikade, "Economic Aspects of the New Kingdom – the Expeditions to the Copper Mines of the Sinai," *Bulletin of the Australian Centre for Egyptology* 9 (1998), pp. 43–52.

Thomas Hikade, *Das Expeditionswesen im ägyptischen Neuen Reich: Ein Beitrag zu Rohstoffversorgung und Aussenhandel* (Studien zur Archäologie und Geschichte Altägyptens 21. Heidelberg: Heidelberger Orientverlag, 2001).

Thomas Hikade, "Expeditions to the Wadi Hammamat during the New Kingdom," *JEA* 92 (2006), pp. 153–168.

Svetlana I. Hodjash – Oleg D. Berlev. "A Market-Scene in the Mastaba of *Ḏ3ḏ3-m-ꜥnḫ* (*Tp-m-ꜥnḫ*)," *Altorientalische Forschungen* 7 (1980), pp. 31–49.

Günther Hölbl, *A History of the Ptolemaic Empire* (London: Routledge, 2001).

Clemens Homoth-Kuhs, *Phylakes und Phylakonsteuer im Griechisch-Römischen Ägypten* (AfP, Beiheft 17. München-Leipzig: K.G. Saur, 2005).

Francisca A.J. Hoogendijk, "The Practice of Taxation in Three Late Ptolemaic Papyri," pp. 313–321 in Trianos Gagos (ed.), *Proceedings of the Twenty-Fifth International Congress of Papyrology* (Ann Arbor: 2010).

George Robert Hughes, *Saite Demotic Land Leases* (SAOC 28, Chicago: University of Chicago Press, 1952).

George Robert Hughes, "The So-called Pherendates Correspondence," pp. 75–88 in Heinz-Josef Thissen – Karl-Theodor Zauzich (eds.), *Grammata Demotica, Festschrift fur Erich Luddeckens zum 15. Juni 1983* (Wurzburg: Gisela Zauzich Verlag, 1984).

Arthur S. Hunt – J. Gilbart Smyly, *The Tebtunis Papyri, Volume III, Part I* (Egypt Exploration Fund, Graeco-Roman Memoirs 23. London: Humphrey Milford, 1933).

Danielle Inconnu-Bocquillon, "Les titres ḥry idb et ḥry wḏb dans les inscriptions des temples greco-romains," *RdÉ* 40 (1989), pp. 65–89.

Erik Iversen, *Two Inscriptions Concerning Private Donations to Temples* (Det Kgl. Danske Videnskabernes Selskab. Historisk-filologiske Meddeleelser. 27, 5. Copenhagen, 1941), pp. 3–18.

Helen K. Jacquet-Gordon, *Les noms des domaines funéraires sous l'Ancien Empire Égyptien* (BdÉ 34. Cairo: IFAO, 1962).

Thomas G.H. James, *The Hekanakhte Papers and Other Early Middle Kingdom Documents* (Publications of the Metropolitan Museum of Art Egyptian Expedition 19. New York: 1962).

Thomas G.H. James, "An Early Middle Kingdom Account," *JEA* 54 (1968), pp. 51–56.

Thomas G.H. James – Michael R. Apted, *The Mastaba of Khentika Called Ikhekhi* (London: EES, 1953).

Karl Jansen-Winkeln, "Das Ende des Neuen Reiches," *ZÄS* 119 (1992), pp. 22–37.

Karl Jansen-Winkeln, *Inschriften der Spätzeit, Teil I: Die 21. Dynastie* (Wiesbaden, 2007).

Karl Jansen-Winkeln, *Inschriften der Spätzeit, Teil II: Die 22. – 24. Dynastie* (Wiesbaden, 2007).

Jac J. Janssen, *Two Ancient Egyptian Ship's Logs, Papyrus Leiden I 350 verso and Papyrus Turin 2008 + 2016* (Oudheidkundige Mededelingen uit het Rijksmuseum van Oudheden te Leiden 42. Leiden: E.J. Brill, 1961).

Jac J. Janssen, *Commodity Prices from the Ramessid Period. An Economic Study of the Village of Necropolis Workmen at. Thebes* (Leiden: Brill, 1975).

Jac J. Janssen, "Prolegomena to the Study of Egypt's Economic History during the New Kingdom," *SAK* 3 (1975), pp. 127–185.

Jac J. Janssen, "The Water Supply of a Desert Village," *Medelhavsmuseet Bulletin 14* (1979), pp. 9–15.

Jac J. Janssen, *De Markt op de Oever* (Inaugural Professorial Lecture. Leiden, 1980).

Jac J. Janssen, "Gift-Giving in Ancient Egypt as an Economic Feature," *JEA* 68 (1982), pp. 253–258.

Jac J. Janssen, "Two Variant Accounts?," *Varia Aegyptiaca* 1 (1985), pp. 109–112.

Jac J. Janssen, "Requisitions from Upper-Egyptian Temples," *JEA* 77 (1991), pp. 79–94, and pl. 4.

Jac J. Janssen, "Debts and Credit in the New Kingdom," *JEA* 80 (1994), pp. 129–136.

Jac J. Janssen, *Village Varia. Ten Studies on the History and Administration of Deir el-Medina* (EU 11. Leiden: NINO, 1997).

Jac J. Janssen, "The Woodcutters," pp. 1–28 in Jac. J. Janssen – Elizabeth Frood – Maren Goecke-Bauer (eds.), *Woodcutters, Potters and Doorkeepers: Service Personnel of the Deir el-Medina Workemen* (EU 17. Leiden: NINO, 2003).

Jac J. Janssen, *Grain Transport in the Ramesside Period, Papyrus Baldwin (BM EA 10061) and Papyrus Amiens* (Hieratic Papyri in the British Museum 8. London: The British Museum Press, 2004).

Jac J. Janssen, *Donkeys at Deir el-Medîna* (EU 19. Leiden: NINO, 2005).

Jac. J. Janssen – Rosalind J. Janssen, "The Laundrymen of the Theban Necropolis," *Archiv Orientální* 70 (2002), pp. 1–12.

Jac J. Janssen – Pieter W. Pestman, "Burial and Inheritance in the Community of the Necropolis Workman at Thebes," *JESHO* 11 (1968), pp. 137–170.

Jozef M.A. Janssen, "The Stela (Khartoum Museum No. 3) from Uronarti," *JNES* 12 (1953), pp. 51–55.

David Jeffreys, "Perunefer: At Memphis or Avaris?," *Egyptian Archaeology* 28 (2006), pp. 36–37.

Eva Jelínková-Reymond, "Gestion des Rentes d'Office," *CdÉ* 28 (1953), pp. 228–237.

Janet H. Johnson, "'Annuity Contracts' and Marriage," pp. 113–132 in David P. Silverman (ed.), *For His Ka, Essays Offered in Memory of Klaus Baer* (SAOC 55. Chicago: The Oriental Institute, 1994).

Janet H. Johnson, "Speculations on Middle Kingdom Marriage," pp. 169–172, in Anthony Leahy – John Tait (eds.), *Studies on Ancient Egypt in Honour of H.S. Smith* (EES Occasional Publications 13. London: EES, 1999).

Michael Jursa, "Accounting in Neo-Babylonian Institutional Archives: Structure, Usage, and Implications," pp. 145–198 in Michael Hudson – Cornelia Wunsch (eds.), *Creating Economic Order. Record-Keeping, Standardization, and the Development of Accounting in the Ancient Near East* (International Scholars Conference on Ancient Near Eastern Economies 4. Bethesda MD: CDL Press, 2004).

Michael Jursa, "Agricultural Management, Tax Farming and Banking: Aspects of Entrepreneurial Activity in Babylonia in the Late Achaemenid and Hellenistic Periods," pp. 137–222 in Pierre Briant – Francis Joannès (eds.), *La transition entre l'empire achéménide et les royaumes hellénistiques (vers 350–300 av. J.-C.)* (Persika 9. Paris: De Boccard, 2006), pp. 157–169.

Michael Jursa, "On Aspects of Taxation in Achaemenid Babylonia: New Evidence from Borsippa," pp. 237–269 in Pierre Briant – Michel Chauveau (eds.), *Organisation des pouvoirs et contacts culturels dans les pays de l'empire achéménide* (Persika 14. Paris: Boccard, 2009).

Michael Jursa, *Aspects of the Economic History of Babylonia in the First Millennium BC* (Alter Orient und Altes Testament: Veröffentlichungen zur Kultur und Geschichte des Alten Orients und des Alten Testaments 377. Münster: Ugarit-Verlag, 2010), pp. 282–315.

Michael Jursa, "Taxation and Service Obligations in Babylonia from Nebuchadnezzer to Darius and the Evidence for Darius' Tax Reform," pp. 431–448 in Robert Rollinger – Brigitte Truschnegg – Robert Bichler (eds.), *Herodot und das Persische Weltreich* (Classica et Orientalia. Wiesbaden: Harrassowitz, 2011).

Jochem Kahl, "Zur Problematik der sogenannten Steuervermerke im Ägypten der

0.-1. Dynastie," pp. 168–176 in Cäcilia Fluck – Lucia Langener – Siegfried Richter (eds.), *Divitiae Aegypti: Koptologie und verwandte Studien zu Ehren von Martin Krause* (Wiesbaden: L. Reichert Verlag, 1995).

Ursula Kaplony-Heckel, "Rund um die thebanischen Tempel (Demotische Ostraka zur Pfründen-Wirtschaft)," pp. 283–337 in Friedhelm Hoffmann – Heinz-Josef Thissen (eds.), *Res severa verum gaudium. Festschrift für Karl-Theodor Zauzich zum 65. Geburtstag am 8. Juni 2004* (Studia Demotica 6. Leuven: Peeters, 2004).

Sally L.D. Katary, *Land Tenure in the Ramesside Period* (Studies in Egyptology. London – New York: Kegan Paul International, 1989).

Sally L.D. Katary, "Land-Tenure in the New Kingdom: the Role of Women Smallholders and the Military," pp. 61–82 in Alan K. Bowman – Eugene Rogan (eds.), *Agriculture in Egypt from Pharaonic to Modern Times* (Proceedings of the British Academy 96, Oxford: University Press, 1999).

Sally L.D. Katary, "The Administration of Institutional Agriculture in the New Kingdom," pp. 719–783 in Juan Carlos Moreno García (ed.), *Ancient Egyptian Administration* (HdO 104. Leiden: Brill, 2013).

Dennis P. Kehoe, *Management and Investment on Estates in Roman Egypt during the Early Empire* (Papyrologische Texte und Abhandlungen 40. Bonn: R. Habelt, 1992).

Benjamin Kelly, *Petitions, Litigation, and Social Control in Roman Egypt* (Oxford: University Press, 2011).

Barry J. Kemp, "Large Middle Kingdom Granary Buildings (and the archaeology of administration)," *ZÄS* 113 (1986), pp. 120–136.

Barry J. Kemp, *Ancient Egypt, Anatomy of a Civilization* (London: Routledge, 1989).

Barry J. Kemp, *The City of Akhenaten and Nefertiti: Amarna and its People* (New Aspects of Antiquity. London: Thames and Hudson, 2012).

Dieter Kessler, "Eine Landschenkung Ramses' III. zugunsten eines 'Grossen der Thrw' aus Mr-mš^{c}.f," *SAK* 2 (1975), pp. 103–134 and pl. 2.

Dieter Kessler, "Eine Stele Sethos I. aus Kom el-Lufi (Minia)," *SAK* 10 (1989), pp. 215–220.

Kenneth A. Kitchen, *Ramesside Inscriptions: Historical and Biographical*, Vol. 1 (Oxford: Blackwell, 1975) = *RI* I.

Kenneth A. Kitchen, *Ramesside Inscriptions: Historical and Biographical*, Vol. 2 (Oxford: Blackwell, 1979) = *RI* II.

Kenneth A. Kitchen, *Ramesside Inscriptions: Historical and Biographical*, Vol. 3 (Oxford: Blackwell, 1980) = *RI* III.

Kenneth A. Kitchen, *Ramesside Inscriptions: Historical and Biographical*, Vol. 4 (Oxford: Blackwell, 1982) = *RI* IV.

Kenneth A. Kitchen, *Ramesside Inscriptions: Historical and Biographical*, Vol. 5 (Oxford: Blackwell, 1983) = *RI* V.

Kenneth A. Kitchen, *Ramesside Inscriptions: Historical and Biographical*, vol. 7 (Oxford: Blackwell, 1989) = *RI* VII.

Kenneth A. Kitchen, *The Third Intermediate Period in Egypt (1100–650 BC)*, 2nd ed. rev. (Warminster: Aris & Phillips, 1996).

Yvan Koenig, "Livraisons d'or et de galènee au trésor du temple d'Amon sous la XXe dynastie," pp. 185–220, pls. XXX-XXXVII in *Hommages à la mémoire de Serge Sauneron 1927–1976, I. Égypte pharaonique* (BdÉ 81. Cairo: IFAO, 1979).

Yvan Koenig, "Livraisons d'or et de galène au trésor du temple d'Amon sous la XXe dynastie: document A, partie inférieure," *BIFAO* 83 (1983), pp. 249–255, pls. LII-LIV.

Katalin Anna Kóthay, "Houses and Households at Kahun: Bureaucratic and Domestic Aspects of Social Organization during the Middle Kingdom," pp. 349–368 in Hedvig Győry (ed.), *"le lotus qui sort de terre": Mélanges offerts à Edith Varga* (Bulletin du Musée Hongrois des Beaux-Arts – Supplément 2001. Budapest: Musée Hongrois des Beaux-Art, 2002).

Maryanne Kowaleski, *Local Markets and Regional Trade in Medieval Exeter* (Cambridge, 1995).

Colin M. Kraay – Otto Mørkholm – Margaret Thompson, *An Inventory of Greek Coin Hoards* (New York: 1973).

Bärbel Kramer, *Griechische Texte 13. Das Vertragsregister von Theogonis* (P. Vindob. G

40618) (Corpus Papyrorum Ranieri 18. Vienna, 1991).

Bärbel Kramer, "Der κτίστης Boethos und die Einrichtung einer neuen Stadt I," *AfP* 43 (1997), pp. 315–339.

John H. Kroll, "A Small Find of Silver Bullion from Egypt," *American Journal of Numismatics* 13 (2001), pp. 1–20.

John H. Kroll, "Weighed Bullion in Archaic Greece," pp. 12–37 in William V. Harris (ed.), *The Monetary Systems of the Greeks and Romans* (Oxford: University Press, 2008).

Stefan Kröpelin – Rudolph Kuper, "More Corridors to Africa," *CRIPEL* 26 (2006–2007), pp. 219–229.

Jean-Marie Kruchten, *Le Décret d'Horemheb. Traduction, commentaire épigraphique, philologique et institutionnel* (Bruxelles: Editions de l'Université de Bruxelles, 1981).

Jean-Marie Kruchten, *Le grand texte oraculaire de Djehoutymose, Intendent du Domaine d'Amon dous le Pontificat de Pinedjem II* (Monographies Reine Elisabeth 5. Bruxelles, 1986).

Rudolph Kuper, "The Abu Ballas Trail: Pharaonic Advances into the Libyan Desert," pp. 372–376 in Zahi Hawass – Lyla Pinch Brock (eds.), *Egypt at the Dawn of the Twenty-First Century, Proceedings of the Eighth International Congress of Egyptologists, Cairo 2000, vol.* 2 (Cairo, 2003).

Audran Labrousse – Ahmed Moussa, *La chaussée du complexe funéraire du roi Ounas* (BdÉ 134. Cairo: IFAO, 2002).

Pierre Lacau, *Stèles du Nouvel Empire* (Catalogue général des antiquités égyptiennes du Musée du Caire, nos. 34001–34189. Cairo: IFAO, 1909–1957).

Pierre Lacau, "Une stèle du roi 'Kamosis'," *ASAE* 39 (1939), pp. 245–271.

Pierre Lacau, *Une stèle juridique de Karnak* (Supplément aux ASAE 13. Cairo: IFAO, 1949).

Anthony Leahy, "Nespamedu, 'King' of Thinis," *GM* 35 (1979), pp. 31–38.

Anthony Leahy, "Saite Lamp Donations," *GM* 49 (1981), pp. 37–46.

Anthony Leahy, "The Libyan Period in Egypt: An Essay in Interpretation," *Libyan Studies* 16 (1985), pp. 51–65.

Anthony Leahy, "The Earliest Dated Monument of Amasis and the End of the Reign of Apries," *JEA* 74 (1988), pp. 183–199.

Anthony Leahy, "Beer for the gods of Memphis in the reign of Amasis," pp. 377–392 in Willy Clarysse – Antoon Schoors – Harco Willems (eds.), *Egyptian Religion: The Last Thousand Years. Studies Dedicated to the Memory of Jan Quaegebeur, Part 1.* (OLA 84. Leuven: Peeters, 1998).

Georges Legrain, "Deux steles trouvees a Karnak en fevrier 1897, I. Stele de l'apanage," *ZÄS* 35 (1897), pp. 13–16.

Georges Legrain, "Deux stèles inédites," *ASAE* 7 (1906), pp. 226–227.

Mark Lehner, *The Complete Pyramids* (London-New York: Thames and Hudson, 1997).

Mark Lehner, "Fractal House of Pharaoh: Ancient Egypt as a Complex Adaptive System, a Trial Formation," pp. 275–353 in Timothy A. Kohler – George J. Gumerman (eds.), *Dynamics in Human and Primate Societies: Agent-Based Modeling of Social and Spatial Processes* (Oxford: University Press, 2000).

Ron J. Leprohan, "Les forces du maintein de l'ordre dans la Nubie au Moyen Empire," pp. 285–291 in Catherine Berger – Gisèle Clerc – Nicolas Grimal (eds.), *Hommages à Jean Leclant, 2. Nubie, Soudan, Ethiopie* (BdE 106/2. Cairo: IFAO, 1993).

Naphtali Lewis, *Greeks in Ptolemaic Egypt: Case Studies in the Social History of the Hellenistic World* (Oxford: Clarendon Press, 1986).

Miriam Lichtheim, *Ancient Egyptian Literature, Volume I: The Old and Middle Kingdoms* (Berkeley: University of California Press, 1973).

Miriam Lichtheim, *Ancient Egyptian Literature, Volume II: The New Kingdom* (Berkeley: University of California Press, 1976).

Miriam Lichtheim, "The Naucratis Stela Once Again," pp. 139–147 in Janet H. Johnson – Edward F. Wente (eds.), *Studies in Honor of George R. Hughes* (SAOC 39. Chicago: 1976).

Christine Lilyquist, "Treasures from Tell Basta: Goddesses, Officials, and Artists in an International Age," *Metropolitan Museum Journal* 47 (2012), pp. 9–72.

Sandra Luisa Lippert, "Die sogennante Zivilprozessordnung, weitere fragmente der ägyptischen Gesetzessammlung," *JJP* 33 (2003), pp. 91–135.

Sandra Luisa Lippert, *Ein demotisches juristisches Lehrbuch. Untersuchungen zu P. Berlin 23757 rto* (ÄA 66. Wiesbaden, Harrassowitz, 2004).

Sandra Luisa Lippert, "Fragmente demotischer juristischer Bücher (pBerlin 23890 a-b, d-g rto und pCarlsberg 628)," pp. 389–405 (Texte Nr. 41–42) in Friedhelm Hoffmann – Heinz-Josef Thissen (eds.), *Res severa verum gaudium, Feschrift für Karl-Theodor Zauzich zum 65. Geburtstag am 8. Juni 2004* (Studa Demotica 6. Leuven, Peeters, 2004).

Alan B. Lloyd, "Trieremes and the Saite Navy," *JEA* 58 (1972), pp. 268–279.

Alan B. Lloyd, "The So-called Galleys of Necho," *JEA* 58 (1972), pp. 307–308.

Alan B. Lloyd, "Were Necho's Triremes Phoenician?," *Journal of Hellenic Studies* 95 (1975), pp. 45–61.

Alan B. Lloyd, *Herodotus, Book II: Commentary 1–98* (Leiden: Brill, 1976).

Alan B. Lloyd, *Herodotus Book II: Commentary 99–182* (Leiden: Brill, 1988).

Josef Locher, *Topographie und Geschichte der Region am ersten Nilkatarakt in Griechisch-Römischer Zeit* (AfP Beiheft 5. Stuttgart-Leipzig, 1999).

Victor Loret, *L'inscription d'Ahmès fils d'Abana* (BdÉ 3. Cairo: IFAO, 1910).

Erich Lüddeckens, *Ägyptische Eheverträge* (ÄA 1. Wiesbaden, 1960).

Erich Lüddeckens, "P. Wien D 10151, eine neue Urkunde zum agyptischen Pfrundenhandel in der Perserzeit," pp. 103–120 in Siegfried Schott (ed.), *Gottinger Vortrage vom Agyptologischen Kolloquium der Akademie am 25. und 26. August 1964* (Nachrichten der Akademie der Wissenschaften in Gottingen, I. Philologisch-Historische Klasse 1965, Nr. 5. Gottingen: Vandenhoeck & Ruprecht, 1965).

Erich Lüddeckens, "Nachtrag zum P. Wien D 10151," *Enchoria* 1 (1971), pp. 73 and pls. 5–7.

Ulrich Luft, *Das Archiv von Illahun: Briefe.* 1 (Hieratische Papyri aus den Staatlichen Museen zu Berlin Preussischer Kulturbesitz, Lieferung 1. Berlin: Akademie Verlag, 1992).

El-Sayed Mahfouz, "Les ostraca hiératiques du ouadi Gaouasis," *RdÉ* 59 (2008), pp. 267–286 and pls. 34–57.

El-Sayed Mahfouz, "Amenemhat III au ouadi Gaouasis," *BIFAO* 108 (2008), pp. 253–279.

El-Sayed Mahfouz, "Amenemhat IV au ouadi Gaouasis," *BIFAO* 110 (2010), pp. 165–173.

El-Sayed Mahfouz, "New Epigraphic Material from Wadi Gawasis," pp. 117–143 in Pierre Tallet –El-Sayed Mahfouz (eds.), *The Red Sea in Pharaonic times: Recent Discoveries along the Red Sea Coast. Proceedings of the Colloquium held in Cairo / Ayn Soukhna 11th – 12th January 2009* (BdÉ 155. Cairo: IFAO, 2012).

Jaromir Malek – Stephen Quirke, "Memphis, 1991: Epigraphy," *JEA* 78 (1992), pp. 13–18.

Michel Malinine, "Une vente d'esclave à l'époque de Psammétique Ier (Papyrus du Vatican 10574, en hiératique "anormale")," *RdÉ* 5 (1946), pp. 119–131.

Michel Malinine, "Un jugement rendu à Thèbes sous la XXVe dynastie (Pap. Louvre E. 3228 c)," *RdÉ* 6 (1951), pp. 157–179 and pls. 4–6.

Michel Malinine, *Choix de Textes Juridiques en Hieratique "Anormal" et en Demotique, Premiere Partie* (Bibliotheque de l'Ecole des Hautes Etudes 300. Paris: Librairie Ancienne Honore Champion, 1953).

Michel Malinine, "Vente de tombes à l'Époque Saïte," *RdÉ* 27 (1975), pp. 164–174.

Michel Malinine, "Transcriptions hiéroglyphiques de quatre textes du Musée du Louvre écrits en hiératique anormale," *RdÉ* 34 (1982–1983), pp. 93–100, pls 4–7.

Joeseph G. Manning, "Demotic Egyptian Instruments ofTransfer as Evidence for Private Ownership of Real Property," *Chicago-Kent Law Review* 70 (1996), pp. 101–132.

Joeseph G. Manning, "The Auction of Pharaoh," pp. 277–284 in Emily Teeter – John A. Larson (eds.), *Gold of Praise. Studies on Ancient Egypt in Honor of Edward F. Wente* (SAOC 58. Chicago: Oriental Institute, 1999).

Joeseph G. Manning, "The Land-Tenure Regime in Ptolemaic Upper Egypt," pp. 83–105 in Alan K. Bowman – Eugene Rogan (eds.), *Agriculture in Egypt from Pharaonic to Modern Times* (Proceedings of the British Academy 96, Oxford: University Press, 1999).

Joeseph G. Manning, *Land and Power in Ptolemaic Egypt, The Structure of Land Tenure* (Cambridge: University Press, 2003).

Joeseph G. Manning, *The Last Pharaohs, Egypt under the Ptolemies, 305–30 BC* (Princeton: University Press, 2010).

Ezra S. Marcus, "Amenemhet II and the Sea: Maritime Aspects of the Mit Rahina (Memphis) Inscription," *Ägypten und Levante* 17 (2007), pp. 137–190.

Auguste Mariette, *Les Papyrus Egyptiennes du Musee de Boulaq, Tome Premier, Papyrus Nos 1–9* (Paris: Librairie A. Franck, 1871).

Émilie Martinet, *Le Nomarque sous l'Ancien Empire* (Paris: Presses de l'Université Paris-Sorbonne, 2011).

Eva Martin-Pardey, *Untersuchungen zur ägyptischen Provinzialverwaltung bis zum Ende des Alten Reiches* (HÄB 1. Hildesheim: Gebrüder Gerstenberg, 1976).

Girgis Mattha, *The Demotic Legal Code of Hermopolis West* (BdÉ 45. Cairo: IFAO, 1975), with additional notes by George Hughes.

Andrea G. McDowell, *Jurisdiction in the Workmen's Community of Deir el-Medîna* (EU 5. Leiden: NINO, 1990).

Judith S. McKenzie, "Glimpsing Alexandria from Archaeological Evidence," *Journal of Roman Archaeology* 16 (2003), pp. 35–61.

John L. McLaughlin, *The Marzēaḥ in the Prophetic Literature. References and Allusions in Light of the Extra-Biblical Evidence* (Supplements to Vetus Testamentum 86, Leiden, 2001).

Andrew Meadows, "Athenian Coin Dies from Egypt: The New Discovery at Heraklion," *Revue belge de numismatique et de sigillographie* 157 (2011), pp. 95–116.

Dimitri Meeks, "Une fondation memphite de Taharqa," pp. 221–259 in *Hommages à la mémoire de Serge Sauneron, 1927–1976*, vol. 1 (BdÉ 81. Cairo: IFAO, 1979).

Dimitri Meeks, "Les donations aux temples dans l'Égypte du Ier millénaire avant J.-C.," pp. 605–687 in E. Lipiński (ed.), *State and Temple Economy in the Ancient Near East* II (OLA 6. Leuven, 1979).

Mounir Megally, *Considérations sur les variations et la transformation des forms des signes hiératiques du papyrus E. 3226 du Louvre* (BdÉ 49. Cairo: IFAO, 1971).

Mounir Megally, *Le papyrus hiératique compatable E. 3226 du Louvre* (BdÉ 53. Cairo: IFAO, 1971).

Mounir Megally, *Recherches sur l'économie, l'administration et la comptabilité égyptiennes à la XVIIIe dynastie, d'après le papyrus E. 3226 du Louvre* (BdÉ 71. Cairo: IFAO, 1977).

Mounir Megally, *Notions de comptabilité à propos du papyrus E. 3226 du Musée du Louvre* (BdÉ 72. Cairo: IFAO, 1977).

Bernadette Menu, "Ventes de maisons sous l'ancient empire égyptien," pp. 249–262 in Francis Geus – Florence Thill (eds.), *Mélanges offerts à Jean Vercoutter* (Paris: Éditions Recherche sur les Civilizations, 1985), reprinted pp. 271–287 in Bernadette Menu, *Recherches sur l'histoire juridique, économique et sociale de l'ancienne Égypte* 2 (BdÉ 122. Cairo: IFAO, 1998).

Bernadette Menu, "La stèle dite de l'Apanage," pp. 337–357 in Marie-Madeleine Mactoux – Évelyne Geny (eds.), *Mélanges Pierre Lévêque 2. Anthropologie et société* (Centre de Recherches d'Histoire Ancienne 82; Annales Littéraires de l'Université de Besançon 377. Besançon 1989); reprinted pp. 183–203 in Bernadette Menu, *Recherches sur l'histoire juridique, économique et sociale de l'ancienne Égypte* 2 (BdÉ 122. Cairo: IFAO, 1998).

Bernadette Menu, "Le système économique de l'Égypte pharaonique," *Mediterranées* 17 (1998), pp. 71–97, reprinted pp. 189–213 in Bernadette Menu, *Égypte pharaonique. Nouvelles recherches sur l'histoire juridique, économique et sociale de l'ancienne Égypte* (Paris: L'Harmattan, 2004).

Bernadette Menu, "Deir el-Médîna au crible de l'économie politique," pp. 251–257 in Robert J. Demarée – Arno Egberts (eds.), *Deir el-Medina in the Third Millenium AD. A Tribute to Jac. J. Janssen* (Leiden: 2000), reprinted pp. 215–222 in Bernadette Menu, *Égypte pharaonique. Nouvelles recherches sur l'histoire juridique, économique et sociale de l'ancienne Égypte* (Paris: L'Harmattan, 2004).

Bernadette Menu – Ibram Harari, "La notion de propriété privé dans l'ancien Empire Egyptien," *CRIPEL* 2 (1974), pp. 125–154.

Georg Meurer, *Nubier in Ägypten bis zum Beginn des Neuen Reiches: Zur Bedeutung der Stele Berlin 14753* (Abhandlungen des Deutschen Archäologischen Instituts Kairo, Ägyptologische Reihe 13. Berlin: 1996).

Eduard Meyer, "Die wirtschaftliche Entwickelung des Altertums," *Jahrbücher für Nationalökonomie und Statistik*, 3. Folge, Bd. 9 (1895), pp. 696–750; reprinted in Moses I. Finley (ed.), *The Bücher-Meyer Controversy* (New York: Arno Press, 1979).

Paul R. Milgrom – Douglass C. North – Barry R. Weingast, "The Role of Institutions in the Revival of Trade: The Medieval Law Merchant, Private Judges, and the Champagne Fairs," *Economics and Politics* 2, Issue 1 (March 1990), pp. 1–23.

Gianluca Miniaci – Stephen Quirke, "Reconceiving the Tomb in the Late Middle Kingdom. The Burial of the Accountant of the Main Enclosure Nerferhotep at Dra Abu al-Naga," *BIFAO* 109 (2009), pp. 338–383.

Joseph Modrzejewski, "Chrématistes et laocrites," pp. 699–708 in Jean Bingen – Guy Cambier – Georges Nachtergael (eds.), *Hommages à Claire Préaux* (Bruxelles, 1975).

Georg Möller, *Zwei ägyptische Eheverträge aus vorsaitischer Zeit* (Abhandlungen der preussischen Akademie der Wissenschaften, phil.-hist. Klasse, Nr. 3. Berlin, 1918), pp. 1–31.

Georg Möller, "Ein ägyptischer Schuldschein der zweiundzwanzigsten Dynastie," *Sitzungsberichte der preussischen Akademie der Wissenschaften, philosophisch-historischen Klasse* 15 (1921), pp. 298–304.

Andrew Monson, "The Ethics and Economics of Ptolemaic Religious Associations," *Ancient Society* 36 (2006), pp. 221–238.

Andrew Monson, "Religious Associations and Temples in Ptolemaic Tebtunis," vol. 2, pp. 769–779 in Jaakko Frösén – Tiina Purola – Erja Salmenkivi (eds.), *Proceedings of the 24th International Congress of Papyrology, Helsinki, 1st-7th of August 2004* (Commentationes Humanarum Litterarum 122: 1–2. Helsinki: Societas Scientiarum Fennica, 2007).

Andrew Monson, "Private Associations in the Ptolemaic Fayyum: The Evidence of Demotic Accounts," pp. 179–196 in Mario Capasso – Paola Davoli (eds.), *New Archaeological and Papyrological Researches on the Fayyum* (Papyrologica Lupiensia 14. Lecce: Congedo Editore, 2007).

Andrew Monson, "Royal Land in Ptolemaic Egypt: A Demographic Model," *JESHO* 50/4 (2007), pp. 363–397.

Andrew Monson, "Communal Agriculture in the Ptolemaic and Roman Fayyum," pp. 173–186 in Sandra Lippert – Maren Schentuleit (eds.), *Graeco-Roman Fayum – Texts and Archaeology* (Wiesbaden: Harrassowitz, 2008).

Andrew Monson, *From the Ptolemies to the Romans. Political and Economic Change in Egypt* (Cambridge: University Press, 2012).

Andrew Monson, *Agriculture and Taxation in Early Ptolemaic Egypt, Demotic Land Surveys and Accounts (P. Agri)*, (Papyrologische Texte und Abhandlungen 46. Bonn: Dr. Rudolf Habelt, 2012).

Andrew Monson, "Receipts for Sitonion, Syntaxis, and Epistatikon from Karanis: Evidence for Fiscal Reform in Augustan Egypt?," *ZPE* 191 (2014), pp. 207–230.

Andrew Monson, "Late Ptolemaic Capitation Taxes and the Poll Tax in Roman Egypt," *BASP* 51 (2014), pp. 127–160.

Juan Carlos Moreno García, *Ḥwt et le milieu rural égyptien du IIIe millénaire. Économie, administration et organisation territoriale* (Bibliothèque de l'école des hautes études sciences historiques et philologiques 337. Paris: Librairie Honoré Champion, 1999).

Juan Carlos Moreno García, "Introduction. Élites et états tributaires: le cas de l'Égypte pharaonique," pp. 11–50 in Juan Carlos Moreno García (ed.), *Élites et pouvoir en Égypte ancienne. Actes du colloque Université Charles-de-Gaulle-Lille 3, 7 et 8 juillet 2006* (CRIPEL 28, 2009–2010. Lille: Université Charles-de-Gaulle-Lille 3, 2009).

Juan Carlos Moreno García, "The Territorial Administration of the Kingdom in the Third

Millenium," pp. 85–151 in Juan Carlos Moreno García (ed.), *Ancient Egyptian Administration* (HdO 104. Leiden: Brill, 2013).

Robert Morkot, "*Nb-mꜢꜥt-Rꜥ*–United-with-Ptah," *JNES* 49 (1990), pp. 323–337.

Robert Morkot, "Nubia in the New Kingdom: The Limits of Egyptian Control," pp. 294–301 in W. Vivian Davies (ed.), *Egypt and Africa: Nubia from Prehistory to Islam* (London: British Museum Press in association with the EES, 1991).

Robert Morkot, "The Economy of Nubia in the New Kingdom," *Société Urbaines en Égypte et au Soudan. CRIPEL* 17:1 (1995), pp. 175–190.

Robert Morkot, "From Conquered to Conqueror: The Organization of Nubia in the New Kingdom and the Kushite Administration of Egypt," pp. 911–963 in Juan Carlos Moreno García (ed.), *Ancient Egyptian Administration* (HdO 104: Leiden: Brill, 2013).

Ellen Fowles Morris, *The Architecture of Imperialism: Military Bases and the Evolution of Foreign Policy in Egypt's New Kingdom* (Probleme der Ägyptologie 22. Leiden – Boston: Brill, 2005).

Ian Morris – Joseph G. Manning, "Introduction," pp. 1–44 in Joseph G. Manning – Ian Morris (eds.), *The Ancient Economy: Evidence and Models* (Stanford: University Press, 2005).

Ahmed M. Moussa – Hartwig Altenmüller, *Das Grab des Nianchchnum und Chnumhotep* (Archäologische Veröffentlichungen 21, Deutsches Archäologisches Institut, Abteilung Kairo. Mainz: Philipp Von Zabern, 1977).

Tycho Mrsich, "Eine Zwischenbilanz zum 'zivilprozessualen' Abschnitt des demotischen Rechtsbuches 'S' (P. Berl. 13621 Rc. Col. II)," pp. 205–288 in Dieter Nörr – Dieter Simon (eds.), *Gedächtnisschrift für Wolfgang Kunkel* (Frankfurt am Main: Vittorio Klostermann, 1984).

Dieter Mueller, "Some Remarks on Wage Rates in the Middle Kingdom," *JNES* 34, no. 4 (1975), pp. 249–263.

Katja Mueller, *Settlements of the Ptolemies. City Foundations and New Settlement in the Hellenistic World* (Studia Hellenistica 43. Leuven: Peeters, 2006).

Brian P. Muhs, "Partisan Royal Epithets in the Late Third Intermediate Period and the Dynastic Affiliation of Pedubast I and Iuput II," *JEA* 84 (1998), pp. 220–223.

Brian P. Muhs, "Membership in Private Associations in Ptolemaic Tebtunis," *JESHO* 44, Part 1 (February 2001), pp. 1–21.

Brian P. Muhs, "Clear Title, Public Protests and P. Brux. dem. 4," pp. 259–272 in Kim Ryholt (ed.), *Acts of the Seventh International Conference of Demotic Studies, Copenhagen, 23–27 August 1999* (CNI 27. Copenhagen: Museum Tusculanum Press, 2002).

Brian P. Muhs, "Nachtrag zu 'The Papyri of Phanesis son of Nechthuris, Oil-Merchant of Tebtunis, and the Ptolemaic Cloth Monopoly,'" *Enchoria* 28 (2002/2003)," *Enchoria* 29 (2004/2005), pp. 53–54 and pls. 3–5.

Brian P. Muhs, "Demotic Ostraca from Ptolemaic Edfu and the Ptolemaic Tax System," pp. 75–105 in Katelijn Vandorpe – Willy Clarysse (eds.), *Edfu, an Egyptian Provincial Capital in the Ptolemaic Period, Brussels, 3 September 2001* (Brussels: Koninklijke Vlaamse Academie van Belgie voor Wetenschappen en Kunsten, 2003).

Brian P. Muhs, *Tax Receipts, Taxpayers, and Taxes in Early Ptolemaic Thebes* (OIP 126. Chicago: Oriental Institute, 2005).

Brian P. Muhs, "The Grapheion and the Disappearance of Demotic Contracts in Early Roman Tebtynis and Soknopaiou Nesos," pp. 93–104 in Sandra Lippert – Maren Schentuleit (eds.), *Tebtynis und Soknopaiou Nesos – Leben im römerzeitlichen Fajum. Akten des Internationalen Symposions vom 11. bis 13. Dezember 2003 in Sommerhausen bei Würzburg* (Wiesbaden: Harrassowitz Verlag, 2005).

Brian P. Muhs, "The Girls Next Door. Marriage Patterns among the Mortuary Priests in Early Ptolemaic Thebes," *JJP* 35 (2005), pp. 169–194.

Brian P. Muhs, "Demotic Ostraca in Amsterdam," *Enchoria* 30 (2006/2007), pp. 53–70 and pls. 29–32.

Brian P. Muhs, "Fractions of Houses in Ptolemaic Hawara," pp. 187–197 in Sandra Lippert – Maren Schentuleit (eds.), *Graeco-Roman Fayum – Texts and Archaeology, Proceedings of the Third International Fayum Symposium,*

Freudenstadt, May 29 – June 1 2007 (Wiesbaden, Harrassowitz, 2008).

Brian P. Muhs, "The Berkeley Tebtunis Grapheion Archive," pp. 243–251 in Ghislaine Widmer – Didier Devauchelle (eds.), *Actes du IXe Congrès International des Études Démotiques, Paris, 31 août – 3 septembre 2005* (BdÉ 147. Cairo: IFAO, 2009).

Brian P. Muhs, "A Late Ptolemaic Grapheion Archive in Berkeley," pp. 581–588 in Trianos Gagos (ed.), *Proceedings of the 25th International Congress of Papyrology, Ann Arbor, July 29 – August 4, 2007* (ASP Special Edition. Ann Arbor: Scholarly Publishing Office, The University of Michigan Library, 2010).

Brian P. Muhs, "A Demotic Donation Contract from Early Ptolemaic Thebes (P. Louvre N. 3263)," pp. 439–455 in Zahi Hawass – Jennifer Houser Wegner (eds.), *Millions of Jubilees: Studies in Honor of David P. Silverman* (Supplément aux ASAE, Cahier No. 39. Cairo: Conseil suprême des antiquités de l'Égypte, 2010).

Brian P. Muhs, *Receipts, Scribes, and Collectors in Early Ptolemaic Thebes* (Studia Demotica 8. Leuven: Peeters, 2011).

Brian P. Muhs, "Property Title, Domestic Architecture, and Household Lifecycles in Egypt," pp. 321–347 in Miriam Muller (ed.), *Household Studies in Complex Societies, (Micro) Archaeological and Textual Approaches* (Oriental Institute Seminars 10. Chicago: Oriental Institute, 2015).

Brian Muhs – Arno Grünewald – Gonnie van den Berg, "The Papyri of Phanesis Son of Nechthuris, Oil-Merchant of Tebtunis, and the Ptolemaic Cloth Monopoly," *Enchoria* 28 (2002 / 2003), pp. 62–81.

Matthias Müller, "Der Turiner Streikpapyrus (pTurin 1880)," pp. 165–184 in Bernd Janowski – Gernot Wilhelm (eds.), *Texte zum Rechts- und Wirtschaftsleben* (Texte aus der Umwelt des Alten Testaments, Neue Folge 1. Gütersloh, 2004).

Miriam Müller, "Deir el-Medina in the Dark – the Amarna Period in the History of the Village," in Jaana Toivari-Viitala – Turo Vartiainen – Saara Uvanto (eds.), *Deir el-Medina Studies, Helsinki June 24–26, 2009 Proceedings* (The Finnish Egyptological Society – Occasional Publications 2. Helsinki: in press).

Renate Müller-Wollermann, "Ägypten auf dem Weg zur Geldwirtschaft," vol. II, pp. 1351–1359 in Jean-Claude Goyon – Christine Cardin (eds.), *Proceedings of the Ninth International Congress of Egyptologists/Actes du Neuvième Congrès International des Égyptologues, Grenoble, 6–12 septembre 2004* (OLA 150. Leuven, 2007).

Renate Müller-Wollermann, "Die ökonomische Bedeutung von Tempelschatzhäusern," pp. 171–178 in Martin Fitzenreiter (ed.), *Das Heilige und die Ware, Zum Spannungsfeld von Religion und Ökonomie, Workshop vom 26.05 bis 28.05.2006* (IBAES 7. London: Golden House Publications, 2007).

Gregory Mumford, "Tell Ras Budran (Site 345): Defining Egypt's Eastern Frontier and Mining Operations in South Sinai during the Late Old Kingdom (Early EB IV/MB I)," *BASOR* 342 (May 2006), pp. 13–67.

Gregory D. Mumford – Sarah Parcak, "Pharaonic Ventures into South Sinai: El-Markha Plain Site 346," *JEA* 89 (2003), pp. 83–116.

Henri Munier, "Un Achat de Terrains au temps du Roi Si-Amon," pp. 361–366 in *Recueil d'Etudes Egyptologiques dediees a la memoire de Jean-Francois Champollion,* (Bibliothèque de l'École de Hautes Études 234. Paris, 1922).

William J. Murnane, *The Road to Kadesh. A Historical Interpretation of the Battle Reliefs of King Sety I at Karnak* (SAOC 42. Chicago: Oriental Institute, 1985).

William J. Murnane – Charles C. Van Siclen III, *The Boundary Stelae of Akhenaten* (London: Kegan Paul International, 1993).

William M. Murray, *The Age of Titans: The Rise and Fall of the Great Hellenistic Navies* (Oxford: University Press, 2011).

Maged Negm, *The Tomb of Simut Called Kyky: Theban Tomb 409 at Qurneh* (Warminister: Aris & Phillips, 1997).

Percy E. Newberry, *The Amherst Papyri* (London: Bernard Quaritch, 1899).

Alviero Niccacci, "La Stèle d'Israël: grammaire et stratégie de communication," pp. 43–107 in Marcel Sigrist (ed.), *Études égyptologiques et bibliques à la mémoire du Père B. Couroyer* (Paris: J. Gabalda et Cie Éditeurs, 1997).

Hans-Christoph Noeske, "Ein Hacksilberfund aus Elephantine," pp. 342–351 in Hans-Christoph Noeske – Helmut Schubert (eds.), *Die Münze: Bild, Botschaft, Bedeutung: Festschrift für Maria R.–Alföldi* (Frankfurt–New York: 1991).

Hans-Christoph Noeske, "Prämonetäre Wertmesser und Münzfunde aus Elephantine," *MDAIK* 49 (1993), pp. 203–209.

John S. Nolan, "The Original Lunar Calendar and Cattle Counts in Old Kingdom Egypt," pp. 75–97 in Suzanne Bickel – Antonio Loprieno (eds.), *Basel Egyptology Prize 1: Junior Research in Egyptian History, Archaeology, and Philology* (Aegyptiaca Helvetica 17. Basel: Schwabe & Co. AG, 2003).

Douglass C. North, "Markets and Other Allocation Systems in History: The Challenge of Karl Polanyi," *Journal of European Economic History* 6 (1977), pp. 703–716.

Douglass C. North, *Structure and Change in Economic History* (New York, 1981), pp. 36–37.

Douglass C. North, "Government and the Cost of Exchange in History," *Journal of Economic History* 44, 2 (1984), pp. 255–264.

Douglass C. North, "Transaction Costs in History," *Journal of European Economic History* 14 (1985), pp. 557–576.

Douglass C. North – Robert Paul Thomas, *The Rise of the Western World: A New Economic History* (Cambridge, 1973), pp. 93, 135–136.

Massimiliano Nuzzolo, "The Sun Temples of the Vth Dynasty," *SAK* 36 (2007), pp. 217–247.

David O'Connor, "The Geography of Settlement in Ancient Egypt," pp. 681–698 in Peter J. Ucko – Ruth Tringham – G.W. Dimbleby (eds.), *Man, Settlement and Urbanism* (London: Duckworth, 1972).

David O'Connor, "The Dendereh Chapel of Nebhepetre Mentuhotep: A New Perspective," pp. 215–220 in Anthony Leahy – John Tait (eds.), *Studies on Ancient Egypt in Honour of H. S. Smith* (London: EES, 1999).

Eliazer D. Oren, "Migdol: A New Fortress on the Edge of the Eastern Nile Delta," *BASOR* 256 (1984), pp. 7–44.

Xiaoli Ouyang, *Monetary Role of Silver and Its Administration in Mesopotamia during the Ur III Period (c. 2112–2004 BCE): A Case Study of the Umma Province* (Biblioteca del Próximo Oriente Antiguo 11. Madrid: Consejo Superior de Investigaciones Científicas, 2013).

Zola M. Packman, *The Taxes in Grain in Ptolemaic Egypt: Granary Receipts from Diospolis Magna, 164–88 BC* (ASP 4. New Haven-Toronto, 1968).

Laure Pantalacci, "Un décret de Pépi II en faveur des gouverneurs de l'oasis de Dakhla," *BIFAO* 85 (1985), pp. 245–254.

Laure Pantalacci, "Balat, a Frontier Town and Its Archive," pp. 197–214 in Juan Carlos Moreno García (ed.), *Ancient Egyptian Administration* (HdO 104. Leiden: Brill, 2013).

Hratch Papazian, "Perspectives on the Cult of Pharaoh during the Third Millennium B.C.: A Chronological Overview," pp. 61–80 in Hana Vymazalová – Miroslav Barta (eds.), *Chronology and Archaeology in Ancient Egypt* (The Third Millennium B.C.) (Prague: Czech Institute of Egyptology, Faculty of Arts, Charles University in Prague, 2008).

Hratch Papazian, *Domain of Pharaoh. The Structure and Components of the Economy of Old Kingdom Egypt* (HÄB 52. Hildesheim, Gebrüder Gerstenberg, 2012).

Hratch Papazian, "The Central Administration of Resources in the Old Kingdom: Departments, Treasuries, Granaries and Work Centers," pp. 41–83 in Juan Carlos Moreno García (ed.), *Ancient Egyptian Administration* (HdO 104. Leiden: Brill, 2013).

Maryline Parca, "Prosangelmata ptolémaiques: une mise à jour," *CdÉ* 60 (1985), pp. 240–247.

Richard A. Parker, *A Saite Oracle Papyrus from Thebes in the Brooklyn Museum [Papyrus Brooklyn 47.218.3]* (Brown Egyptological Studies 4. Providence, 1962).

Stéphane Pasquali, "La date du Papyrus BM 10056: Tuthmosis II ou Amenhotep II?," *RdÉ* 58 (2007), pp. 71–86.

Frédéric Payraudeau, "Le règne de Takélot II et les débuts de la domination koushite à Thèbes," *GM* 198 (2004), pp. 82–85.

Frédéric Payraudeau, *Administration, société et pouvoir à Thebes sous la XXIIe dynastie bubastite*, 2 vols. (BdÉ 160: 1–2. Cairo: IFAO, 2014).

T. Eric Peet, *The Mayer Papyri A & B, Nos. M 11162 and M. 11186 of the Free Public Museums, Liverpool* (London: EES, 1920).

T. Eric Peet, *The Rhind Mathematical Papyrus, British Museum 10057 and 10058* (London: Hodder & Stoughton Ltd., 1923; reprinted Nendeln Liechtenstein: Kraus, 1970).

T. Eric Peet, "A Historical Document of Ramesside Age," *JEA* 10 (1924), pp. 116–127.

T. Eric Peet, *The Great Tomb-Robberies of the Twentieth Egyptian Dynasty, I. Text* (Oxford: Clarendon Press, 1930).

T. Eric Peet, "The Unit of Value *šꜥty* in Papyrus Boulaq 11," in *Mélanges Maspero I* (MIFAO 66/1. Cairo: IFAO, 1935–38), pp. 185–199.

André Pelletier – Michel Malinine, "Planchette gréco-égyptienne du Cabinet de Médailles," *Revue des études grecques* 58 (1945), pp. 184–195.

Olivier Perdu, "Le «directeur des scribes du conseil»," *RdÉ* 49 (1999), pp. 175–194.

Sergio Pernigotti, "Un nuovo testo giuridico in ieratico 'anormale'," *BIFAO* 75 (1975), pp. 73–95 and pls. 11–12.

Sergio Pernigotti, "Ancora sulla stele Firenze 1639 (2507)," *EVO* 2 (1979), pp. 21–37.

Pieter Willem Pestman, "A Family of Egyptian Scribes," *BASP* 5, 2–3 (1968), pp. 61.

Pieter Willem Pestman, "The Law of Succession in Ancient Egypt," pp. 58–77 in J. Brugman – M. David – F.R. Kraus – P.W. Pestman – M.H. van den Valk (eds.), *Essays on Oriental Laws of Succession* (Studia et Documenta ad Iura Orientis Antiqui Pertinentia 9. Leiden: E.J. Brill, 1969).

Pieter Willem Pestman, "Loans Bearing No Interest?," *JJP* 16–17 (1971), pp. 7–29.

Pieter Willem Pestman, *Recueil de textes démotiques et bilingues*, 3 vols. (Leiden: Brill, 1977).

Pieter Willem Pestman, *L'archivo di Amenothes figlio di Horos* (P. Tor. Amenothes), (Milano: Istituto Editoriale Cisalpino-La Goliardica, 1981).

Pieter Willem Pestman, "Réflexions à propos du soi-disant Code de Hermoupolis," *JESHO* 26 (1983), pp. 14–21.

Pieter Willem Pestman, "The Diospolis Parva Documents: Chronological Problems concerning Psammetichus III and IV," pp. 145–155 in Heinz-Josef Thissen – Karl-Theodor Zauzich (eds.), *Grammata Demotica, Festschrift für Erich Lüddeckens* (Würzburg: Gisela Zauzich Verlag, 1984).

Pieter Willem Pestman, "The Competence of Greek and Egyptian Tribunals According to the Decree of 118 B.C.," *BASP* 22 (1985), pp. 265–269.

Pieter Willem Pestman, "Registration of Demotic Contracts in Egypt, P. Par. 65; 2nd Cent. B.C." pp. 17–25 in Johan A. Ankum – Johannes E. Spruit – Felix B.J. Wubbe (eds.), *Satura Roberto Feenstra, sexagesimum quintum annum aetatis complenti ab alumnis collegis amicis oblata* (Fribourg, 1985).

Pieter Willem Pestman, *Textes et études de papyrologie grecque, démotique et copte* (PLB 23. Leiden: Brill, 1985).

Pieter Willem Pestman, "Agoranomoi et actes agoranomiques: Krokodilopolis et Pathyris, 145–88 av. J.-C.," pp. 9–44 in Pieter W. Pestman (ed.), *Textes et études de papyrologie grecque, démotique et copte* (PLB 23. Leiden: Brill, 1985).

Pieter Willem Pestman, *The Archive of the Theban Choachytes (Second Century B.C.)* (Studia Demotica 2. Leuven: Peeters, 1993).

Pieter Willem Pestman, *Les papyrus démotiques de Tsenhor (P. Tsenhor). Les archives privées d'une femme égyptienne du temps de Darius Ier. I. Textes* (Studia Demotica 4. Leuven: 1994).

Stefan Pfeiffer, "Naukratis, Heracleion-Thonis and Alexandria – Remarks on the Presence and Trade Activities of Greeks in the North-west Delta from the Seventh Century BC to the End of the Fourth Century BC," pp. 15–24 in Damian Robinson – Andrew Wilson (eds.), *Alexandria and the North-Western Delta* (Oxford Centre for Maritime Archaeology: Monograph 5. Oxford: 2010).

Kurt Pflüger, "The Edict of King Haremhab," *JNES* 5 (1946), pp. 260–276.

Alexandra Philip-Stéphan, *Dire le droit en Égypte pharaonique* (Connaissance de l'Égypte Ancienne 9. Bruxelles: Éditions Safran, 2008).

Patrizia Piacentini, "On the Titles of the *ḥqꜣw ḥwt*," pp. 235–249 in Schafik Allam (ed.), *Grund und Boden in Altägypten, Akten des internationalen Symposions Tübingen 18.-20. Juni 1990* (Untersuchungen zum Rechtsleben im Alten Ägypten 2. Tübingen, 1994).

M. Piatowska, *La Skepê dans l'Égypte ptolémaïque* (Archiwum filologiczne 32. Warsaw: 1975).

Christina Pino, "The Market Scene in the Tomb of Khaemhat (TT57)," *JEA* 91 (2005), pp. 95–105.

Rosanna Pirelli, "Two New Stelae from Mersa Gawasis," *RdÉ* 58 (2007), pp. 87–109.

Willem Pleyte, *Les Papyrus Rollin de la Bibliothèque Impériale de Paris* (Leiden: E.J. Brill, 1868).

Karl Polanyi, *The Great Transformation* (New York: Farrar and Rinehart, 1944).

Karl Polanyi – Conrad M. Arensberg – Harry W. Pearson (eds.), *Trade and Markets in the Early Empires* (Glencoe IL: Free Press, 1957).

Bezalel Porten, *Archives from Elephantine, the Life of an Ancient Jewish Military Colony* (Berkeley – Los Angeles: University of California Press, 1968).

Bezalel Porten, "Aramaic-Demotic Equivalents: Who is the Borrower and Who the Lender?," pp. 259–264 in J. Johnson (ed.), *Life in a Multi-Cultural Society* (SAOC 51. Chicago: 1992).

Bezalel Porten – Ada Yardeni, *Textbook of Aramaic Documents from Ancient Egypt, Volume 1. Letters* (Jerusalem, 1986).

Bezalel Porten, *Textbook of Aramaic Documents from Ancient Egypt, 2. Contracts* (Winona Lake IN: Eisenbrauns, 1989).

Bezalel Porten, *Texts and Aramaic Documents of Ancient Egypt 3: Literature, Accounts, Lists* (Jerusalem: 1993).

Georges Posener, *La première domination Perse en Égypte. Recueil d'inscriptions hiéroglyphiques* (BdÉ 11. Cairo: IFAO, 1936).

Georges Posener, "Les douanes de la Méditerranée dans l'Égypte saïte," *Revue de philologie de littérature et d'histoire anciennes* 21 (1947), pp. 117–131.

Paule Posener-Kriéger, *Les Archives du Temple Funeraire de Neferirkare-Kakai (Les Papyrus d'Abousir) Traduction et Commentaire I et II* (BdÉ 65. Cairo: IFAO, 1976).

Paule Posener-Kriéger, "Le prix de étoffes," pp. 318–331 in Manfred Görg – Edgar Pusch (eds.), *Festschrift Elmar Edel* (ÄAT 1. Bamberg: 1979).

Paule Posener-Kriéger, "Les papyrus d'Abousir et l'économie des temples funéraires de l'ancien empire," pp. 133–151 in Edward Lipiński (ed.), *State and Temple Economy in the Ancient Near East, Vol.* 1 (OLA 5. Leuven: Department Oriëntalistiek, 1979).

Paule Posener-Kriéger, *I papyri di Gebelein – scavi G. Farina 1935* (Studi del Museo Egizio di Torino 1. Torino: 2004).

Paule Posener-Kriéger – Miroslav Verner – Hana Vymazalová, *Abusir X. The Pyramid Complex of Raneferef: The Papyrus Archive* (Prague: Czech Institute of Egyptology, 2007).

Lilian Postel, *Protocole des souverains égyptiens et dogme monarchique au début du Moyen Empire* (Monographies Reine Élisabeth 10. Turnhout: Brepols, 2004).

Nicholas Postgate, *Bronze Age Bureaucracy: Writing and the Practice of Government in Assyria* (Cambridge: University Press, 2013).

Claire Préaux, *L'Économie royale des Lagides* (Brussels: Fondation égyptologique Reine Élisabeth, 1939).

Claire Préaux, "De la Grèce classique à l'Égypte hellénistique: la banque-témoin," *CdÉ* 33 (1958), pp. 243–255.

Claire Préaux – Marcel Hombert, "Recherches sur le prosangelma à l'époque Ptolémaïque," *CdÉ* 34 (1942), pp. 259–286.

Friedrich Preisigke, *Girowesen im griechischen Ägypten* (Strassburg: Verlag Von Schlesier & Schweikhardt, 1910).

Martin Jessop Price, *Coin Hoards*, vol. 1 (London: Royal Numismatic Society, 1975).

Martin Jessop Price, *Coin Hoards*, vol. 2 (London: Royal Numismatic Society, 1976).

Martin Jessop Price, "The Coins," pp. 66–70 in David G. Jeffreys – Harry Sidney Smith (eds.), *The Anubieion at Saqqara 1: The Settlement and the Temple Precinct* (EES Excavation Memoir 54, London, 1988).

Martin Jessop Price – Kaelyn McGregor – Ute Wartenberg, *Coin Hoards*, vol. 8 (London: Royal Numismatic Society, 1994).

Jan Quaegebeur, "Phritob comme titre d'un haut fonctinnaire ptolémaïque," *Ancient Society* 20 (1989), pp. 159–168.

Jan Quaegebeur, "À la recherche du haut clergé Thébaine à l'époque Gréco-Romaine," pp. 139–161 in Sven P. Vleeming (ed.), *Hundred-Gated Thebes. Acts of a Colloquium on Thebes and the Theban Area in the Graeco-Roman Period* (PLB 27. Leiden: Brill, 1995).

Stephen Quirke, "The Regular Titles of the Late Middle Kingdom," *RdÉ* 37 (1986), pp. 107–130.

Stephen Quirke, *The Administration of Egypt in the Late Middle Kingdom, The Hieratic Documents* (New Malden: Sia Publishing, 1990).

Stephen Quirke, "A Preliminary Study of Technical Terms in Accounts of the Illahun Temple Archive," *Ägypten und Levante* 7 (1998), pp. 9–16.

Stephen Quirke, *Titles and Bureaux of Egypt 1850–1700 BC* (Egyptology 1. London: Golden House Publications, 2004).

Stephen Quirke, *Lahun: A Town in Egypt 1800 BC, and the History of its Landscape* (London: Golden House Publications, 2005).

Stephen Quirke, "The Residence in Relations between Places of Knowledge, Production and Power: Middle Kingdom Evidence," pp. 111–130 in Rolf Gundlach – John H. Taylor (eds.), *Egyptian Royal Residences, 4. Symposium zur ägyptischen Königsideologie / 4th Symposium on Egyptian Royal Ideology* (Königtum, Staat und Gesellschaft früher Hochkulturen 4,1. Wiesbaden: Harrassowitz, 2009).

Karen Radner, "Money in the Neo-Assyrian empire," pp. 127–157 in Jan G. Dercksen (ed.), *Trade and Finance in Ancient Mesopotamia (MOS Studies 1): Proceedings of the First MOS Symposium, Leiden 1997* (PIHANS 84. Istanbul: Nederlands historisch-archaeologisch Instituut, 1999).

Dominic Rathbone, *Economic Rationalism and Rural Society in Third-Century A.D. Egypt: The Heroninos Archive and the Appianus Estate* (Cambridge: University Press, 1991).

Donald B. Redford, "A Report on the 1993 and 1997 Seasons at Tell Qedwa," *JARCE* 35 (1998), pp. 45–60.

Tony Reekmans, *La sitométrie dans les archives de Zénon* (Papyrologica Bruxellensia 3. Bruxelles: Fondation égyptologique Reine Elisabeth, 1966).

Tony Reekmans – Edmond Van 't Dack, "A Bodleian Archive on Corn Transport," *CdE* 27 (1952), pp. 149–195.

Nathaniel J. Reich, *Papyri juristischen Inhalts in hieratischer und demotischer Schrift aus dem British Museum* (Denkschriften der Kaiserlichen Akademie der Wissenschaften in Wien, philosophisch–historische Klasse, 55,3. Wien: 1914).

Nathaniel J. Reich, "The Greek Deposit-Notes of the Record-Office on the Demotic Contracts of the Papyrus-Archive in the University Museum," *Mizraim* 9 (1938), pp. 19–32.

Herbert Ricke, "Eine Inventartafel aus Heliopolis im Turiner Museum," *ZÄS* 71 (1935), pp. 111–133, pls. 2–3.

Robert K. Ritner, "The End of the Libyan Anarchy in Egypt: P. Rylands IX cols. 11–12," *Enchoria* 17 (1998), pp. 101–108.

Robert K. Ritner, "Third Intermediate Period Antecedents of Demotic Legal Terminology," pp. 343–359 in Kim Ryholt (ed.), *Acts of the Seventh International Conference of Demotic Studies, Copenhagen, 23–27 August 1999* (CNI 27. Copenhagen: Museum Tusculanum Press, 2002).

Robert K. Ritner, *The Libyan Anarchy, Inscriptions from Egypt's Third Intermediate Period* (SBL Writings from the Ancient World 21. Atlanta: SBL, 2009).

Robert K. Ritner, "Fragmentation and Re-Integration in the Third Intermediate Period," pp. 327–340 in Gerard P.F. Broekman – Robert J. Demarée – Olaf E. Kaper (eds.), *The Libyan Period in Egypt, Historical and Cultural Studies into the 21st – 24th Dynasties: Proceedings of a Conference at Leiden University, 25–27 October 2007* (EU 23. Leiden – Leuven: NINO – Peeters, 2009).

Malte Römer, "Der Handel und die Kaufleute im Alten Ägypten," *SAK* 19 (1992), pp. 257–284.

Malte Römer, *Gottes- und Priester-herrschaft in Ägypten am Einde des Neuen Reiches. Ein religions-gechichtliches Phänomen und seine sozialen Grundlagen* (ÄAT 21. Wiesbaden, 1994).

Michael Rostovtzeff, *A Large Estate in Egypt in the Third Century B.C.* (University of Wisconsin studies in the social sciences and history 6. Madison: University of Wisconsin, 1922; reprinted New York: Arno Press, 1979).

Michael Rostovtzeff, *The Social and Economic History of the Hellenistic World*, 3 vols. (1st ed. 1941, 2nd ed. Oxford, 1953).

Michael Rostovtzeff, *The Social and Economic History of the Roman Empire*, 2 vols. (1st ed. 1926, 2nd ed. Oxford, 1957).

Ann Macy Roth, *Egyptian Phyles in the Old Kingdom, The Evolution of a System of Social Organization* (SAOC 48. Chicago: Oriental Institute, 1991).

Kim S.B. Ryholt, "A Pair of Oracle Petitions addressed to Horus-of-the-Camp," *JEA* 79 (1993), pp. 189–198.

Kim S.B. Ryholt, *The Political Situation in Egypt during the Second Intermediate Period c. 1800–1550 BC.* (CNI 20. Copenhagen: Museum Tusculanum Press, 1997).

Hassan El-Saady, "The Wars of Sety I at Karnak: A New Chronological Structure," *SAK* 19 (1992), pp. 285–294.

A.I. Sadek, *The Amethyst Mining Inscriptions of Wadi el-Hudi*, 2 vols. (Warminster: Aris & Phillips, 1980–1985).

Serge Sauneron – Jean Yoyotte, "La campagne nubienne de Psammétique II et sa signifaction historique," *BIFAO* 50 (1952), pp. 157–207.

Ahmad El-Sawi, *Excavations at Tell Basta: Report of Seasons 1967–1971 and Catalogue of Finds* (Prague: Charles University, 1979).

Abdel Moneim Al-Hakim Sayed, "Discovery of the Site of the 12th Dynasty Port at Wadi Gawasis on the Red Sea Shore," *RdÉ* 29 (1977), pp. 138–178 and pls. 8–16.

Abdel Moneim Al-Hakim Sayed, "New Light on the Recently Discovered Port on the Red Sea Shore," *CdÉ* 58 (1983), pp. 23–37.

Donata Schäfer, *Makedonische Pharaonen und hieroglyphische Stelen. Historische Untersuchungen zur Satrapenstele und verwandten Denkmälern* (Studia Hellenistica 50. Leuven: Peeters, 2011).

Heinrich Schäfer, "Die Auswandering der Krieger unter Psammetich I. und den Söldner-Aufstand in Elephantine unter Apries," *Klio* 4 (1904), pp. 152–163.

David M. Schaps, *The Invention of Coinage and the Monetization of Ancient Greece* (Ann Arbor: University of Michigan Press, 2003).

Alexander Scharff, "Ein Rechnungbuch des Koniglichen Hofes aus der 13. Dynastie," *ZÄS* 57 (1922), pp. 51–58 and pls. 1–24.

Alexander Scharff, "Brief aus Illahun," *ZÄS* 59 (1924), pp. 20–51 and pl. 1–12 (Anhang: Autographische Texte).

Walter Scheidel – Sitta von Reden (eds.), *The Ancient Economy* (Edinburgh: University Press, 2002).

Wolfgang Schenkel, *Memphis · Herakleopolis · Theben: die epigraphischen Zeugnisse der 7.-11. Dynastie Ägyptens* (ÄA 12. Wiesbaden: Harrassowitz, 1965).

Maren Schentuleit, "Tempel zu verkaufen? P. Wien D 6846," pp. 535–549 in Friedhelm Hoffmann – Heinz-Josef Thissen (eds.), *Res severa verum gaudium. Festschrift für Karl-Theodor Zauzich zum 65. Geburtstag am 8. Juni 2004* (Studia Demotica 6. Leuven: Peeters, 2004).

Maren Schentuleit – Günter Vittmann, *"Du hast mein Herz zufriedengestellt .," Ptolemäerzeitliche Demotische Urkunden aus Soknopaiu Nesos* (Corpus Papyrorum Raineri 29. Berlin – New York: Walter de Gruyter, 2009).

David Schloen, *The House of the Father as Fact and Symbol: Patrimonialism in Ugarit and the Ancient Near East* (Studies in the Archaeology and History of the Levant 2. Winona Lake: Eisenbrauns, 2001).

Siegfried Schott, *Kanais. Der Tempel Sethos I. im Wadi Mia* (Nachrichten der Akademie der Wissenschaften in Göttingen, I. Philologisch-historisch klasse, Nr. 6. Göttingen: Vandenhoeck & Ruprecht, 1961), pp. 123–189 and Taf. 1–19.

Alan R. Schulman, "The Nubian War of Akhenaton," pp. 299–316 in Anonymous (ed.), *L'Égyptologie en 1979: axes prioritaires de recherches* 2 (Paris: Éditions du Centre national de la Recherche scientifique, 1982).

Kurt Sethe, *Urkunden des Alten Reichs*, Abteilung I, Band I, Heft 1–4 (Urkunden des ägyptischen

Altertums. Leipzig: J.C. Hinrichs'sche Buchhandlung, 1st ed. 1903–06, 2nd ed. 1932–33) = Urk. I.

Kurt Sethe, *Urkunden der 18. Dynastie*, Abteilung IV, Band I-IV, Heft 1–16 (Urkunden des ägyptischen Altertums. Leipzig: J.C. Hinrichs'sche Buchhandlung, 1906–09) = Urk. IV, 1–1226.

Kurt Sethe, "Ein Prozessteil aus dem alten Reich," *ZAS* 61 (1926), pp. 67–79.

Kurt Sethe – Josef Partsch, *Demotisch Urkunden zum ägyptischen Bürgschaftsrechte vorzüglich der Ptolemäerzeit* (ASAW 32. Leipzig, 1920).

Kurt Sethe – Wilhelm Spiegelberg, *Zwei Beiträge zu dem Bruchstück einer ägyptischen Zivilprozeßordnung in demotischer Schrift* (Abhandlungen der Bayerischen Akademie der Wissenschaften, Philosophisch-historische Abteilung, Neue Folge 4, München, 1929).

Karl-Joachim Seyfried, *Beiträge zu den Expeditionen des Mittleren Reiches in die Ost-Wüste* (HÄB 15. Hildesheim: Gerstenberg Verlag, 1981).

Ian Shaw, *Hatnub: Quarrying Travertine in Ancient Egypt* (EES Excavation Memoir 88. London: EES, 2010).

J.J. Shirley, "Crisis and Restructuring of the State: From the Second Intermediate Period to the Advent of the Ramesses," pp. 521–606 in Juan Carlos Moreno García (ed.), *Ancient Egyptian Administration* (HdO 104. Leiden: Brill, 2013).

Arthur F. Shore, "Swapping Property at Asyut in the Persian Period," pp. 200–206, and pls. 41–42 in John Baines (ed.), *Pyramid Studies and Other Essays presented to I.E.S. Edwards* (London: 1988).

Arthur F. Shore – Harry S. Smith, "Two Unpublished Demotic Documents from the Asyūṭ Archive," *JEA* 45 (1959), pp. 52–60.

Steven E. Sidebotham, *Berenike and the Ancient Maritime Spice Route* (Berkeley: University of California Press, 2011).

Pieter J. Sijpesteijn, *Customs duties in Graeco-Roman Egypt* (Studia Amstelodamensia ad epigraphicam, ius antiquum et papyrologicam pertinentia 17. Zutphen, 1987).

R.S. Simpson, *Demotic Grammar in the Ptolemaic Sacerdotal Decrees* (Oxford: Griffith Institute, 1996).

William Kelly Simpson, *Papyrus Reisner I: The Records of a Building Project in the Reign of Sesostris* I (Boston: Museum of Fine Arts, 1963).

William Kelly Simpson, *Papyrus Reisner II: Accounts of the Dockyard Workshop at This in the Reign of Sesostris* I (Boston: Museum of Fine Arts, 1965).

William Kelly Simpson, *Papyrus Reisner III: The Records of a Building Project in the Early Twelfth Dynasty* (Boston: Museum of Fine Arts, 1969).

William Kelly Simpson, *Papyrus Reisner IV: Personnel Accounts in the Early Twelfth Dynasty* (Boston: Museum of Fine Arts, 1986).

Adam Smith, *An Inquiry into the Nature and Causes of the Wealth of Nations* (1776).

Stuart Tyson Smith, *Askut in Nubia: The Economics and Ideology of Egyptian Imperialism in the Second Millenium B.C.* (Studies in Egyptology. London: Kegan Paul International, 1995).

Paul C. Smither, "A Tax-assessor's Journal of the Middle Kingdom," *JEA* 27 (1941), pp. 74–76.

Paul C. Smither, "The Semnah Despatches," *JEA* 31 (1945), pp. 3–10 and pls. 2–7.

Paul C. Smither, "The Report Concerning the Slave-Girl Senbet," *JEA* 34 (1948), pp. 31–34.

Henri Sottas, *La préservation de la propriété funéraire dans l'ancienne Égypte avec le recueil des formules d'imprécation* (Bibliothèque de l'École des Hautes Études 205. Paris, 1913).

Karin N. Sowada, *Egypt in the Eastern Mediterranean during the Old Kingdom: An Archaeological Perspective* (Orbis Biblicus et Orientalis 237. Fribourg – Göttingen: Academic Press – Vandenhoeck & Ruprecht. 2009).

Anthony J. Spalinger, "A Critical Analysis of the 'annals' of Thutmose III (Stücke V-VI)," *JARCE* 14 (1977), pp. 41–54.

Anthony J. Spalinger, "The Northern Wars of Seti I: An Integrative Study," *JARCE* 16 (1979), pp. 29–47.

Anthony J. Spalinger, "Some Revisions of Temple Endowments in the New Kingdom," *JARCE* 28 (1991), pp. 21–39.

Anthony J. Spalinger, "Dated Texts of the Old Kingdom," *SAK* 21 (1994), pp. 275–319.

Anthony J. Spalinger, "Praise God and Pay the Priests," *Ägypten und Levante* 7 (1998), pp. 43–57.

Anthony J. Spalinger, "The Organisation of the Pharaonic Army (Old to New Kingdom)," pp. 393–478 in Juan Carlos Moreno García (ed.), *Ancient Egyptian Administration* (HdO 104. Leiden: Brill, 2013).

Wilhelm Spiegelberg, "Ein Papyrus aus der Zeit Ramses'V," *ZÄS* 29 (1891), pp. 73–84.

Wilhelm Spiegelberg, *Rechnungen aus der Zeit Setis I* (Strasbourg: Karl J. Trübner, 1896).

Wilhelm Spiegelberg, "Eine Stele aus der Oase Dachel," *Recueil de Travaux* 21 (1899), pp. 12–21.

Wilhelm Spiegelberg, "Der Titel λεσῶνις," *Recueil de Travaux* 24 (1902), pp. 187–189.

Wilhelm Spiegelberg, "Neue Schenkungsstelen über Landstiftungen an Tempel," *ZÄS* 56 (1920), pp. 55–60 and pls. 4–6.

Wilhelm Spiegelberg, *Aus einer ägyptischen Zivilprozeßordnung der Ptolemäerzeit (3.-2. vorchristl. Jahrh.) (Pap. demot. Berlin 13621)* (Abhandlungen der Bayerischen Akademie der Wissenschaften, Philosophisch-historische Abteilung, Neue Folge 1, München, 1929).

Wilhelm Spiegelberg, *Die Demotischen Denkmaler III – Die Demotische Inschriften und Papyri (Fortsetzung)* (Catalogue général des antiquités égyptiennes du Musée du Caire, Nos. 50023–50165. Berlin: 1932).

Danijela Stefanovic, *The Holders of Regular Military Titles in the Period of the Middle Kingdom: Dossiers* (Egyptology 4. London: Golden House Publications, 2006).

Danijela Stefanovic, "šmsw – Soldiers of the Middle Kingdom," *WZKM* 98 (2008), pp. 233–248.

Georg Steindorff, *Das Grab des Ti* (Veröffentlichungen der Ernst von Sieglin Expedition in Ägypten 2. Leipzig: J.C. Hinrichs'sche Buchhandlung, 1913).

Piotr Steinkeller, "The Function of Written Documentation in the Administration Praxis of Early Babylonia," pp. 65–88 in Michael Hudson – Cornelia Wunsch (eds.), *Creating Economic Order. Record-Keeping, Standardization, and the Development of Accounting in the Ancient Near East* (International Scholars Conference on Ancient Near Eastern Economies 4. Bethesda MD: CDL Press, 2004).

Heike Sternberg-el Hotabi, "Aus den Annalen Thutmosis' III.: erster Feldzug gegen Megiddo," pp. 212–220 in Bernd Janowski – Gernot Wilhelm (eds.), *Staatsverträge, Herrscherinschriften und andere Dokumente zur politischen Geschichte* (Gütersloh: Gütersloher Verlagshaus, 2005).

Nigel Strudwick, *The Administration of Egypt in the Old Kingdom: The Highest Titles and their Holders* (Studies in Egyptology. London: Kegan Paul International, 1985).

Nigel Strudwick, *Texts from the Pyramid Age* (SBL Writings from the Ancient World 16. Atlanta: SBL, 2005).

Deborah Sweeney, "The Vizir Amenemhat at Wadi Hammamat – a Macbeth Moment?," *GM* 238 (2013), pp. 107–124.

Pierre Tallet, "Amenemhat II et la chapelle des rois à propos d'une stèle rupestre redécouverte à Sérabit al-Khadim," *BIFAO* 109 (2009), pp. 473–493.

Pierre Tallet, "New Inscriptions from Ayn Soukhna 2002–2009," pp. 105–115 in Pierre Tallet – El-Sayed Mahfouz (eds.), *The Red Sea in Pharaonic Times: Recent Discoveries along the Red Sea Coast. Proceedings of the Colloquium held in Cairo / Ayn Soukhna 11th – 12th January 2009* (BdÉ 155. Cairo: IFAO, 2012).

Pierre Tallet – Grégory Marouard, "An Early Pharaonic Harbour on the Red Sea Coast," *Egyptian Archaeology* 40 (2012), pp. 2–5.

Pierre Tallet – Grégory Marouard – Damien Laisney, "Un port de la IVe dynastie au Ouadi al-Jarf (mer Rouge)," *BIFAO* 112 (2012), pp. 399–446.

Heinz-Josef Thissen, "Varia onomastica," *GM* 141 (1994), pp. 89–95.

Christine M. Thompson, "Sealed Silver in Iron Cisjordan and the 'Invention' of Coinage." *Oxford Journal of Archaeology* 22 (2003), pp. 67–107.

Dorothy J. Thompson, *Memphis under the Ptolemies* (Princeton: University Press, 1988).

Dorothy J. Thompson, "Policing the Ptolemaic Countryside," pp. 961–966 in Barbel Kramer –Wolfgang Luppe – Herwig Maehler – Gunter Poethke (eds.), *Akten des 21. Internationalen Papyrologenkongress, Berlin, 13.-19.8.1995*, vol. 2 (AfP Beiheft 3. Stuttgart-Leipzig, 1997).

Herbert Thompson, *A Family Archive from Siut, from Papyri in the British Museum, including an Account of a Trial before the Laocritae in the Year B.C. 170* (Oxford: University Press, 1934).

Jaana Toivari-Viitala, *Women at Deir el-Medina. A Study of the Status and Roles of the Female Inhabitants in the Workmen's Community during the Ramesside Period* (EU 15. Leiden: NINO, 2001).

Jaana Toivari-Viitala, "O. DeM 764: A Note Concerning Property Rights," *GM* 195 (2003), pp. 87–96.

László Török, *The Kingdom of Kush. Handbook of the Napatan-Meroitic Civilization* (HdO 31. Leiden: 1997).

László Török, *Between Two Worlds. The Frontier Region between Ancient Nubia and Egypt 3700 BC – AD 500* (Probleme der Ägyptologie 29. Leiden: 2009).

Paul Tresson, "L'Inscription de Chechanq Ier, au Musée du Caire: Un frappant exemple d'impôt progressif en matière religieuse," pp. 817–840 in *Mélanges Maspero*, vol. 1, fasc. 2 (MIFAO 66/1. Cairo: IFAO, 1938).

Dominique Valbelle, *«Les ouvriers de la tombe» Deir el-Médineh à l'époque Ramesside* (BdÉ 96. Cairo: IFAO, 1985).

Dominique Valbelle, "Eléments sur la démographie et le paysage urbains, d'après les papyrus documentaires d'époque pharaonique," in *Sociétés urbaines en Egypte et au Soudan: CRIPEL* 7 (1985), pp. 75–87.

Dominique Valbelle, "Les garnisons de Migdol (Tell el-Herr) de l'époque achéménide au Bas-Empire: état de la question en 1998," *Comptes rendus des séances de l'académie des Inscriptions et Belles-Lettres*, 142, 3 (1998), pp. 799–813.

Dominique Valbelle – Charles Bonnet, *Le sanctuaire d'Hathor, maîtresse de la turquoise* (Paris: Picard Editeur, 1996).

Peter G. Van Alfen, "The 'owls' from the 1989 Syria Hoard with a Review of Pre-Macedonian coinage in Egypt," *American Journal of Numismatics* 14 (2002), pp. 1–57.

Peter G. Van Alfen, "Two Unpublished Hoards and Other 'owls' from Egypt," *American Journal of Numismatics* 14 (2002), pp. 59–71.

Peter G. Van Alfen, "Herodotos' 'Aryandic' Silver and Bullion Use in Persian period Egypt," *American Journal of Numismatics* 16/17 (2004/2005), pp. 7–46.

Peter G. Van Alfen, "Mechanisms for the Imitations of Athenian Coinage: Dekeleia and Mercenaries Reconsidered," *Revue belge de numismatique et de sigillographie* 157 (2011), pp. 55–93.

Marc Van de Mieroop, "Why Did they Write on Clay?," *Klio* 79, 1 (1997), pp. 7–18.

G.P.F. van den Boorn, *The Duties of the Vizier: Civil Administration in the Early New Kingdom* (Studies in Egyptology. London – New York: Kegan Paul International, 1988).

Claude Vandersleyen, *Les Guerres d' Amosis, fondateur de la XVIIIe dynastie* (Monographies Reine Élisabeth 1. Brussels, 1971).

Robartus J. Van der Spek, "The 'Silverization' of the Economy of the Achaemenid and Seleukid Empires and Early Modern China," pp. 402–420 in Zosia H. Archibald – John K. Davies – Vincent Gabrielsen (eds.), *The Economies of Hellenistic Societies, Third to First Centuries BC* (Oxford: University Press, 2011).

Jacques Vandier, *Mo'alla: la tombe d'Ankhtifi et la tombe de Sébekhotep* (BdÉ 18. Cairo: IFAO, 1950).

Katelijn Vandorpe, "The Ptolemaic Epigraphe or Harvest Tax (Shemu)," *AfP* 46/2 (2000), pp. 169–232.

Katelijn Vandorpe, "Paying Taxes to the Thesauroi of the Pathyrites in a Century of Rebellion (186–88 BC)," pp. 405–436 in L. Mooren (ed.) *Politics, Administration and Society in the Hellenistic and Roman World. Proceedings of the International Colloquium, Bertinoro 19–24 July 1997* (Studia Hellenistica 36 Leuven: Peeters, 2000).

Katelijn Vandorpe, "The Epigraphe or Harvest Tax in the Apollonopolite Nome," pp. 107–122 in

Katelijn Vandorpe – Willy Clarysse (eds.), *Edfu, an Egyptian Provincial Capital in the Ptolemaic Period. Brussels, 3 September 2001* (Brussels: Koninklijke Vlaamse Academie van België voor Wetenschappen en Kunsten, 2003).

Katelijn Vandorpe, "A Greek Register from Pathyris' Notarial Office: Loans and Sales from the Pathyrite and Latopolite Nomes," *ZPE* 150 (2004), pp. 161–186.

Katelijn Vandorpe, "Agriculture, Temples and Tax Law in Ptolemaic Egypt," *CRIPEL* 25 (2007), pp. 165–171.

Govert Van Driel, *Elusive Silver: In Search of a Role for a Market in an Agrarian Environment* (Publications de l'Institut historique-archeologique neerlandais de Stamboul 95. Leiden: NINO, 2002).

Charles Van Siclen III, "The Third Stela of Kamose," pp. 355–358 in Marcel Marée (ed.), *The Second Intermediate Period (Thirteenth-Seventeenth Dynasties): Current Research, Future Prospects* (OLA 192. Leuven: Peeters, 2010).

Philip A. Verdult, *P. Erasmianae II. Parts of the Archive of an Arsinoite Sitologos from the Middle of the Second Century BC* (Studia Amstelodamensia 32. Amsterdam: Gieben, 1991).

Arthur M.F.W. Verhoogt, *Menches, Komogrammateus of Kerkeosiris. The Doings and Dealings of a Village Scribe in the Late Ptolemaic Period (120–110 B.C.)* (PLB 29. Leiden: Brill, 1998).

Arthur M.F.W. Verhoogt, *Regaling Officials in Ptolemaic Egypt: A Dramatic Reading of Official Accounts from the Menches Papers* (PLB 32. Leiden: Brill, 2005).

Miroslav Verner, "The System of Dating in the Old Kingdom," pp. 23–43 in Hana Vymazalová – Miroslav Barta (eds.), *Chronology and Archaeology in Ancient Egypt* (The Third Millennium B.C.) (Prague: Czech Institute of Egyptology, Faculty of Arts, Charles University in Prague, 2008).

Pascal Vernus, "Inscriptions de la Troisième Période Intermédiare (IV), Le texte oraculaire réemployé dans le passage axial du IIIe pylône dans le temple de Karnak," *Cahiers de Karnak* 6 (1980), pp. 215–233.

Steve Vinson, *The Nile Boatman at Work* (Münchner Ägyptologische Studien 48. Mainz: Philipp von Zabern, 1998).

Günter Vittmann, "The Hieratic Texts," pp. 30–73 in Bezalel Porten – J. Joel Farber (eds.), *The Elephantine Papyri in English: Three Millennia of Cross-Cultural Continuity and Change* (Leiden: Brill, 1996).

Günter Vittmann, *Der demotische Papyrus Rylands 9. Teil I. Text und Übersetzung* (ÄAT 38, 1. Wiesbaden: Harrassowitz, 1998).

Günter Vittmann, *Der demotische Papyrus Rylands 9. Teil II. Kommentare und Indizes* (ÄAT 38, 2. Wiesbaden: Harrassowitz, 1998).

Günter Vittmann, "Zwei kursivhieratische Urkunden in Kairo," *Enchoria* 26 (2000), pp. 125–150.

Günter Vittmann, "Rupture and Continuity. On Priests and Officials in Egypt during the Persian Period," pp. 89–121 in Pierre Briant – Michel Chauveau (eds.), *Organisation des pouvoirs et contacts culturels dans les pays de l'empire achéménide: Actes du colloque organisé au Collège de France, 9–10 novembre 2007* (Persika 14. Paris: De Boccard, 2009).

Sven P. Vleeming, "The Sale of a Slave in the Time of Pharaoh Py," *Oudheidkundige Mededelingen uit het Rijksmuseum van Oudheden* 61 (1980), pp. 1–17.

Sven P. Vleeming, "La phase initiale du démotique ancien," *CdÉ* 56 (1981), pp. 31–48.

Sven P. Vleeming, "The Days on Which the Ḳnbt Used to Gather," pp. 183–192, in Robert J. Demarée – Jac. J. Janssen (eds.), *Gleanings from Deir el-Medîna* (EU 1. Leiden: NINO, 1982).

Sven P. Vleeming, "Review of A. Gasse, *Données nouvelles administratives et sacerdotales sur l'organisation du domaine d'Amon, XXe-XXIe dynasties, à la lumière des papyrus Prachov, Reinhardt et Grundbuch (avec édition princeps des papyrus Louvre AF 6345 et 6346–7)*, (BdÉ 104. Cairo, 1988)," *Enchoria* 18 (1991), pp. 218–226.

Sven P. Vleeming, *The Gooseherds of Hou* (Pap. Hou), (Studia Demotica 3. Leuven: Peeters, 1991).

Sven P. Vleeming, "The Tithe of the Scribes (and) Representatives," pp. 343–350 in Janet H.

Johnson (ed.), *Life in a Multi-Cultural Society, Egypt from Cambyses to Constantine and Beyond* (SAOC 51. Chicago: Oriental Institute, 1992).

Sven P. Vleeming, *Papyrus Reinhardt* (Hieratische Papyri aus den Staatlichen Museen zu Berlin 2, Berlin, 1993).

Carola Vogel, *Ägyptische Festungen und Garnisonen bis zum Ende des Mittleren Reiches* (HÄB 46. Hildesheim: Gerstenberg Verlag, 2004).

Jürgen von Beckerath, "Die «Stele der Verbannten» im Museum des Louvre," *RdÉ* 20 (1968), pp. 7–36 and pl. 1.

Jürgen von Beckerath, "Zur Datierung des Papyrus Brooklyn 16.205," *GM* 140 (1994), pp. 15–17.

Anne-Sophie Von Bomhard, *The Decree of Saïs, The Stelae of Thonis-Heracleion and Naukratis* (Oxford Centre for Maritime Archaeology: Monograph 7. Oxford: 2012).

Sitta Von Reden, *Money in Ptolemaic Egypt, from the Macedonian Conquest to the End of the Third Century BC* (Cambridge: University Press, 2007).

Hana Vymazalová, "The Abusir Papyrus Archives and the Fifth Dynasty Royal Funerary Cults," pp. 197–203 in Monika Dolinska – Horst Beinlich (eds.), *8. Ägyptologische Tempeltagung: Interconnections between Temples* (Königtum, Staat und Gesellschaft früher Hochkulturen 3/3. Wiesbaden, 2010).

Hana Vymazalová, "The Economic Connection between the Royal Cult in the Pyramid Temples and the Sun Temples in Abusir," pp. 295–303 in Helen Strudwick – Nigel Strudwick (eds.), *Old Kingdom: New Perspectives on Egyptian Art and Archaeology, 2750–2150 B.C.* (Oxford, 2011).

Hana Vymazalová, "The Administration of Royal Funerary Complexes," pp. 177–195 in Juan Carlos Moreno García (ed.), *Ancient Egyptian Administration* (HdO 104. Leiden: Brill, 2013).

David Warburton, "Keynes'sche Überlegungen zur altägyptischen Wirtschaft," *ZÄS* 118 (1991), pp. 76–85.

David Warburton, "The Economy of Ancient Egypt Revisited yet Again," *GM* 146 (1995), pp. 103–111.

David Warburton, *State and Economy in Ancient Egypt: Fiscal Vocabulary of the New Kingdom* (Orbis Biblicus et Orientalis 151. Freiburg & Göttingen: 1997).

David Warburton, "Before the IMF: The Economic Implications of Unintentional Structural Adjustment in Ancient Egypt," *JESHO* 43 (2000), pp. 65–131.

David Warburton, *Macroeconomics from the Beginning.* (Civilisations du Proche-Orient. Série IV. Histoire — Essais 2. Neuchâtel: 2003).

David Warburton, "Economics, Anthropological Models and the Ancient Near East," *Anthropology of the Middle East* 4 (2009), pp. 65–90.

Leslie Anne Warden, *Pottery and Economy in Old Kingdom Egypt* (Culture and History of the Ancient Near East 65. Leiden: Brill, 2014).

Max Weber (translated by R.I. Frank), *The Agrarian Sociology of Ancient Civilizations* (London: 1976).

Max Weber (translated by Guenther Roth – Claus Wittich), *Economy and Society: An Outline of Interpretive Sociology* (Berkeley: University of California Press, 1978).

Josef Wegner, *The Mortuary Temple of Senwosret III at Abydos* (Publications of the Pennsylvania-Yale expedition to Egypt 8. New Haven: Peabody Museum of Natural History of Yale University, 2007).

Edward F. Wente, "A Note on 'The Eloquent Peasant,' B I, 13–15," *JNES* 24 (1965), pp. 105–109.

Edward F. Wente, "The Suppression of the High Priest Amenhotep," *JNES* 25,2 (April 1966), pp. 73–87.

Edward F. Wente, *Late Ramesside Letters* (SAOC 33. Chicago: University of Chicago Press, 1967).

Edward F. Wente, *Letters From Ancient Egypt* (SBL Writings from the Ancient World 1. Atlanta: Scholars Press, 1990).

Ulrich Wilcken, *Grundzüge und Chrestomathie der Papyruskunde 1: Historischer Teil 2* (Leipzig-Berlin, 1912).

Ulrich Wilcken, *Urkunden der Ptolemäerzeit (Ältere Funde)*, Band I-II (Berlin-Leipzig: Walter de Gruyter, 1927–1934) = UPZ I-II.

Henri Wild, *Le tombeau de Ti, fascicule 3. La chapelle (deuxième partie)* (MIFAO 65. Cairo: IFAO, 1966).

Toby A.H. Wilkinson, *Early Dynastic Egypt* (London – New York: Routledge, 1999).

Toby A.H. Wilkinson, *Royal Annals of Ancient Egypt. Palermo Stone and its Associated Fragments* (London: Kegan Paul International, 2000).

Oliver E. Williamson, "Transaction Cost Economics: The Governance of Contractual Relations," *Journal of Law and Economics* 22, 2 (Oct. 1979), pp. 233–261.

John A. Wilson, "The Theban Tomb (No. 409) of Si-Mut, called Kiki," *JNES* 29 (1970), pp. 187–192.

Jean Winand, "Les décrets oraculaires pris en l'honneur d'Henouttaouy et de Maâtkarê (Xe et VIIe Pylônes)," pp. 603–710 in *Cahiers de Karnak XI, Fasicle 2* (Cairo: 2003).

Jan Krzysztof Winnicki, "Zwei Studien über die Kalasirier," *Orientalia Lovaniensia Periodica* 17 (1986), pp. 17–32.

Jan Krzysztof Winnicki, "Zur Bedeutung der Termini Kalasiriier und Ermotybier," pp. 1503–1507 in Willy Clarysse – Antoon Schoors – Harco Willems (eds.), *Egyptian Religion: The Last Thousand Years. Studies Dedicated to the Memory of Jan Quaegebeur*, vol. 2 (OLA 85. Leuven: Peeters, 1998).

Karl A. Wittfogel, *Oriental Despotism: A Comparative Study of Total Power* (New Haven: Yale University Press, 1957).

Hans Julius Wolff, *Das Justizwesen der Ptolemäer* (Münchener Beiträge zur Papyrusforschung und antiken Rechtsgeschichte 44. München: C.H. Beck'sche Verlagsbuchhandlung, 1962).

Ada Yardeni, "Maritime Trade and Royal Accountancy in an Erased Customs Account from 475 B.C.E. on the Ahiqar Scroll from Elephantine," *BASOR* 293 (1994), pp. 67–78.

Uri Yiftach-Firanko, "Who Killed the Double Document in Ptolemaic Egypt?," *AfP* 54, 2 (2008), pp. 203–218.

Jean Yoyotte, "Le nom égyptien du «ministre de l'économie» – de Saïs a Méroé," *Comptes rendus, Académie des inscriptions & belles-lettres (CRAIBL), 1989* (Paris: Diffusion de Boccard, 1989), pp. 73–90.

Jean Yoyotte, "An Extraordinary Pair of Twins: The Steles of the Pharaoh Nektanebo I," pp. 232–240 in Franck Goddio and David Fabre (eds.), *Egypt's Sunken Treasures* (Munich: 2006).

Karl-Theodor Zauzich, *Die ägyptische Schreibertradition in Aufbau, Sprache und Schrift der demotischen Kaufverträge aus Ptolemäischer Zeit*, 2 vols. (ÄA 19. Wiesbaden: Harrassowitz, 1968)

Andrea Paula Zingarelli, *Trade and Market in New Kingdom Egypt, Internal Socio-economic Processes and Transformations* (BAR International Series 2063. Oxford: Archaeopress, 2010).

Christiane Zivie, *Giza au deuxième millénaire* (BdÉ 70. Cairo: IFAO, 1976).

SOURCE INDEX

Note: An *n* following a page number indicates a note.

SUBJECT INDEX

Note: A *t* following a page number indicates a table.